Preface

Information is paramount to the healthcare sector, entailing intense data, medical epidemiologic sets, Internet browsing records, surveys, complex engineering models, and so on via the Cloud. This quest for knowledge prompts data dimensionality, which calls for more sophisticated and efficient information strategies. Health science and biology are very complex fields fully embedded in information technology, but the associated processes are much too intricate to be faithfully modeled. It is not easy to extract knowledge starting from raw data, and it is also expensive.

Artificial intelligence (AI) in healthcare (AIH) has been the primary concern to develop expert systems aimed at diagnostic and decision-making in knowledge acquisition, representation, reasoning, and explanation. Many healthcare facilities (HFs) have data acquisition, monitoring, and storage systems integrated into larger-scale information systems. This vast amount of information and databases stemming from medical applications cause hindrances to analysis and decision making. Hence, there is a need to develop better tools for accessing/storing/analyzing knowledge while effectively using multimodal data. These necessities become essential in the healthcare realm as decision-making relies on knowledge from multidisciplinary areas. This book intends to provide computational methods for intelligent health data analysis to narrow the gap between data gathering and data comprehension with applications in medicine, health care, biology, pharmacology, and related areas. Intelligent Data Analysis (IDA) expedites healthcare analyses and applications. IDA employs specialized statistical, pattern recognition, machine learning (ML), data abstraction, and visualization tools for the analysis of data and discovery of mechanisms that created them. Healthcare data typically involve many records/variables, subtle interactions between entities, or a combination of all factors. Engineering, computing science, and ML empower data analysis tasks. The IDA extracts knowledge from vast data, with a huge quantity of variables, data that represents very complex, nonlinear, real-life problems. IDA can help with raw data analysis, coping with prediction tasks without knowing the theoretical description of the underlying process, classification tasks of new events, or modeling unknown processes. Classification, prediction, and modeling are the cornerstones brought in by IDA. This book focuses on AIH methods and tools to bridge data gathering and data comprehension. Emphasis will also be given to problem-solving within HFs to handle patient records, data warehousing, intelligent alarming, competent monitoring, and more. In medicine, overcoming this gap is particularly crucial since medical decision-making needs comprehension of healthcare data regularities and trends. This book tackles different IDA approaches.

This book has three parts and a total of 18 chapters as follows:

1. Introduction to Intelligent Healthcare in a Post-Pandemic World
2. The Building Blocks of Health 4.0 – Internet of Things, Big Data with Cloud and Fog Computing
3. Internet of Medical Things (IoMT) Layers for Medical Cyber-Physical Systems
4. Ad Hoc Networks in Healthcare Intelligent Transportation Systems – MANETs, VANETs, and FANETs
5. Scale and Resolution Issues regarding Medical Images: Challenges Ahead
6. Some Issues regarding Content-Based Image Retrieval (CBIR) for Remote Healthcare Thera diagnosis
7. Blockchain Technology Enabling Better Services in the Healthcare Domain
8. 6G in Healthcare – Anticipating Needs and Requirements
9. Remote Sensing Applications in Disease Mapping and Public Health Analysis
10. On DICOM, HEVC and 3D Medical Image Compression for Volumetric Theragnostics
11. Deep Learning as a Drive Force for Better Drug Development
12. In-Body Devices and Sensors Communication - How Implantables, Ingestibles, and Injectables Interact with the Internet
13. Nanotechnology, Internet of Nano things and Nanorobotics in Healthcare – Nano for All
14. Digital Twin Framework for Intelligent Healthcare Facilities through ISO/IEEE 11073
15. Medical Visual Theragnostic Systems Using Artificial Intelligence (AI) - Principles and Perspectives
16. Metaheuristics Applied to Pathology Image Analysis
17. Super-resolution Image Processing for Hemoglobin Quantification: A Case Study
18. BrATCat: Data Augmentation of MRI Scans via Image-to-Image Translation using CycleGAN Followed by Pre-Trained Model Categorization

Prospective readers will experience several facets of intelligence in terms of AI and assorted smart designs besides observing the target subjects' evolving nature. This book offers different alternatives and methods to expand existing implementations with effective results in several realms, for instance, graduate course classrooms, research facilities, healthcare services, non-destructive investigations, ambient intelligence, medical education, and healthcare facilities' plants. This book also made it possible to gather an interesting group of invited international authors, who put forward a different understanding within their respective chosen research fields with experimental outcomes.

Vania V. Estrela
Duque de Caxias, Rio de Janeiro, Brazil

Contents

Part II: Infrastructural Medical Applications

Part III: Advanced Applications Using AI

Part I
Intelligence Meanings and Roles in Healthcare: Introductory Aspects

Introduction to Intelligent Healthcare in a Post-Pandemic World

V.V. Estrela[1] [0000-0002-4465-7691], A.A. Laghari[2] [0000-0001-5831- 5943],
R.T. Lopes[3] [0000-0001-7250-824X], A.A. Khan[4] [0000-0003-2838-7641], S. Yin[5]
[0000-0002-5367-1372], A. Deshpande[6] [0000-0002-1500-0981], J.J.P.C. Rodrigues[7]
[0000-0001-8657-3800]

[1] Telecommunications Department, Fluminense Federal University (UFF), RJ, Brazil,
vania.estrela.phd@ieee.org
[2] Department of Electronics and Power Engineering, National University of Sciences
and Technology (NUST), Pakistan, asif.laghari@smiu.edu.pk
[3] University Federal of Rio de Janeiro (COPPE/UFRJ), Rio de Janeiro, RJ, Brazil,
rlopes@coppe.ufrj.br
[4] Research Lab of Artificial Intelligence and Information Security, Faculty of Computing
Science and Information Technology, Benazir Bhutto Shaheed University, Lyari, Karachi
(75660), Sindh, Pakistan, abdullah.khan0076@gmail.com
[5] Shenyang Normal University, Shenyang, Liaoning Province, 110034, China,
yslin@hit.edu.cn
[6] Electronics and Communication Engineering, Angadi Institute of Technology and
Management, Belagavi, India, deshpande.anandb@gmail.com
[7] Federal University of Piaui (UFPI), Electrical Engineering, Fortaleza, CE, Brazil,
joeljr@ieee.org

1. Introduction

Several countries work on engendering smart medical outlines for their population. However, given the consequences of the COVID-19 pandemic, new inexpensive, scalable, and easy-to-deploy structures are called for generating a final smart planet with a sound world economy including politics for the future. Therefore, Smart Healthcare Facilities (SHFs) are vital to developing intelligent healthcare management. Utilizing the Cyber-Physical System (CPS) paradigm is paramount for better future healthcare [1-4].

1.1. Meaning of Intelligence in Healthcare

Smart healthcare (SH) uses technology to dynamically access data, connect individuals, materials, and institutions related to wellbeing, and then actively manages and responds to healthcare ecosystem necessities intelligently. SH can promote interaction between all healthcare stakeholders, ensuringeverybody gets the services they need, helps parties make informed decisions, and simplifies the rational allocation of resources. In short, SH is a higher stage of medical information construction.

Intelligence in this book refers to (i) Artificial Intelligence (AI), (ii) smart designs of medical gadgets, apps, health facilities, medical CPSs (MCPSs), and logistics, to name areas that need to look carefully into a human being's body, and (iii) a combination of both.

1.2. Artificial Intelligence in Medicine

Recently, AI has sent enormous waves across healthcare, even stimulating active discussions. AI can assist physicians in making better clinical resolutions or even replacing human judgment in specific functional healthcare areas (e.g., radiology). The snowballing disposal of healthcare data and the fast development of big data analytic methods have made the recent positive applications of AI in welfare [8, 11-16, 19, 66, 92]. Guided by pertinent clinical questions, robust AI methodologies can unlock clinically significant information concealed in the massive amount of data, assisting clinical decision-making. The current AI status in healthcare entails four relevant aspects [27-49, 50-70]:

  (i)   Motivation to apply AI in healthcare,
  (ii) Data types analyzed by AI systems,
  (iii) Mechanisms enabling AI systems to produce clinically meaningful outcomes, and
  (iv) Disease types tackled by AI communities.

Motivation: Literature extensively discusses AI advantages: (i) sophisticated algorithms to learn features from a large volume of healthcare data; (ii) to obtain insights to assist clinical practice; and (iii) to implement learning and self-correcting skills to ameliorate diagnoses accuracy using feedback. Such a system can help healthcare staff, caretakers, and patients by providing up-to-date information from social networks, journals, blogs, textbooks, and ongoing clinical practices to promote proper care. Moreover, an AI system can lessen inevitable therapeutic and diagnostic errors occurring in human clinical practices. Likewise, an AI system extracts valuable information from a large population to make real-time inferences for health risk alerts and outcome predictions.

Healthcare data: Before deploying AI systems in healthcare applications, they need training with clinically generated data like screening, diagnosis, treatment choices, learning similar groups of subjects, relations between subject features, and outcomes of interest. Such clinical data often exists in but are not limited to medical notes, demographics, electronic records from health devices, physical checkups, and laboratory exams. Specifically, a substantial proportion of the AI literature analyzes diagnosis imaging [50, 60, 76-82, 85-91], genetic testing, and electrodiagnosis. For instance, radiologists can adopt AI to explore diagnostic imageries containing vast data, study abnormal gene expression in long non-coding RNAs to detect gastric cancer, and develop support systems for localizing neural injuries. Additionally, physical inspection notes and clinical laboratory fallouts are the other two primary data sources. One distinguishes them with imageries, genetic and electrophysiological (EP) data. This situation stems from the fact that they contain significant visual clues, vital signs recorded at different times, chemical components from exams, unstructured descriptive texts, clinical notes, and prescriptions, which are not simply analyzable. Hence, similar AI applications focus on first transforming unstructured texts to machine-understandable electronic medical records (EMR).

AI devices: The previous discussion suggests that AI devices are mainly twofold. The first category comprises machine learning (ML), deep learning (DL), and metaheuristic techniques [27-49, 50-70] that analyze structured data like imageries, genetic info, and EP [50, 60, 76-82, 85-91]. In medical applications, soft computing procedures cluster patient traits or deduce the probability of disease outcomes. The second category includes Natural Language Processing (NLP) methods that extract unstructured information such as clinical notes/medical periodicals to supplement and enhance structured medical data. NLP procedures target turning texts into machine-readable structured records, which ML techniques can then analyze. The use of powerful AI techniques can be motivated by clinical difficulties and finally be applied to support clinical practices.

Disease focus: Despite the progressively richer AI literature tackling healthcare, the research mainly concentrates on a few disease types: cancer, nervous system disease, and cardiovascular disease [27-49, 50-70]. The IBM Watson for oncology assisted cancer diagnosis through double-blinded validation studies, and clinical images [76-82] helped identify skin cancer subtypes. In neurology, an AI system restored movement control in patients with quadriplegia. Other frameworks scrutinized the power of offline man/machine interfaces relying on discharge timings of spinal motor neuron medical notes for upper-limb prostheses' control [99, 100]. Cardiology can employ an AI system to diagnose heart disease through cardiac images and provide automated, editable ventricle segmentations based on conventional cardiac MRI images [85-91]. The concentration around these three diseases is not entirely unexpected. All three conditions are leading causes of death. Therefore, early diagnoses are crucial to preventing patients' health status deterioration. Still, early diagnoses can potentially happen through improved analysis procedures for imaging [50, 60, 76-82, 85-91], genetics, EP, or EMR, which is the strength of the AI system. AI can also perform other tasks like (i) diagnosing congenital cataracts using ocular image data and (ii) detecting referable diabetic retinopathy with retinal fundus pictures.

1.3. Intelligent Medical Devices and Facilities Design

Giving a progressive framework to smart medical outreach is a helpful program according to various situations throughout the world. Several components within the SHF framework need investigation and improvements. Each chapter of this book includes a specific SHF definition.

SH has another benefit for advancing information and communication technology (ICT) that has helpedpeople improve the quality of health care with better treatment for patients, superior interaction between caregivers and healthcare staff, better diagnostic tools, and devices that ameliorate everybody the quality of individual life . The main SH concepts include electronic record management, health services, smart home services, ingenious medical devices, and connections. Some focal SH elements follow:

- Cloud computing (CC) and Fog computing (FC) have recently entered the field of medicine [88-96, 99, 100]. CC's unlimited resources and its inherent flexibility have led to this technology being used for the development and delivery of health services. In addition, CC fosters advances in medical studies such as genetics/molecular medicine, telemedicine, holding video conferences, and management of a patient's medical information. In clinical research, CC makes it feasible to receive and store patient information regularly, and enabling researchers to conduct their research by accessing data stored from different places in the cloud [88-96, 99, 100].
- Local and global (remote) patient information storage, whether in the form of old physical archives or electronic records on internal servers, is costly and brings special complexities to medical centers. For this reason, hospitals and medical centers are reverting to cloud storage of patient information, which allows doctors and patients to gather and examine the information they need at any time without going to medical centers.
- Traditionally, teamwork simplification entails coordinating medical team meetings and sharing patient information among team members, which is time-consuming. In healthcare CPSs, when a patient's condition calls for a critical decision, CC and the Internet of Medical Things (IoMT) permits easy patient information sharing without the need for face-to-face meetings [52, 53, 78].
- Creating interaction between Information and Communication Technology (ICT) and medical science to make use of ICT services such as collecting, storing and retrieving, sending, processing, and representing information in the field of health and medicine [5].
- Healthcare Management Information Systems (HMIS).
- Clinical information systems that work harmonically with medical care. These systems have databases to process assorted patient information in multimedia, including vital parameters of individuals, medical images, and thereby expanding the physician's diagnosis and treatment abilities with powerful tools [50, 60, 76-82, 85-91].
- Health Information Systems (HISs) are interconnected components in collecting evidence, analyzing data, and understanding phenomena.
- Virtual Augmented Reality (VAR) can simulate much of the interaction of the material and virtual worlds associated with healthcare stakeholders. VAR has a wide range of applications in medicine. For example, simulating the anatomy and physiology of the human body as a laboratory sample facilitates performing experiments and medical research [6].

1.4. Outline

Section 2 looks at values and practices within SHFs. Requirements for evidence gathering and analyses in them emerge in Section 3. Developing a SHF promotion framework is the scope of Section 4. Section 5 examines SH prospects, and conclusions appear in Section 6.

2. Values and Practices within Smart Healthcare Facilities (SHFs)

This section briefly introduces the book SH content and briefly analyzes the guiding values within the Smart Healthcare Facilities (SHFs) rationale and the real-life situations.

2.1. Real-life SHFs

The SHFs require network information technology [52, 53, 78], like sensors, which are implanted and prepared in different objects such as SHFs, health care staff, and patient equipment to connect them [7] to computer services and CC. Japan has allocated a big budget for ICT and formulated the iJapan Strategy 2015 [8], focusing on hospitals, three schools, and significant public-sector management. Apple introduced a medical app based on iOS, namely HealthKit, for managing fitness and health. This App analyzes people's health status by reading the phone sensors' information for giving a valuable data source to better health [9]. As far as China and Brazil are concerned, smart medical care is still in its preliminary stages. Recently, the Chinese health system has tended to progress from metropolitan to rural zones, and many cities have put together some SH accomplishments.

2.2. Human Values in the Smart Healthcare (SH) Realm

By considering practice environments, SH gives sufficient peace to the people from several viewpoints with notable achievements. For instance, network technology has been employed by the US MEREK Corporation to figure medical assistance to reduce hospitalization costs. Another example is the German pharmaceutical companies that adopt UHF tags for drug tracking and dropping losses [7, 10]. Another example is the medical reform service in China. Many cities converse via telephone registration services and the official network booking system. By developing the application of cellphone devices in daily life, they are turned into one of the fastest outpatient appointment channels for patients and their families, inquire about the outpatient treatment process, control outpatient personal details, and attain expert healthcare information [11]. Furthermore, the service self-help, which converses smoothly with IoT-friendly intelligent devices [52, 53, 78], is utilized in hospitals.

3. Requirements for Evidence Gathering and Analyses in SHFs

Requirements for evidence gathering and analyses in SHFs involve exploring what individuals are already utilizing, collecting evidence, making definite requirements, and examining the critical operations to promote an intelligent healthcare framework. So, practical evidence from all healthcare parties aids in solving some urgent problems.

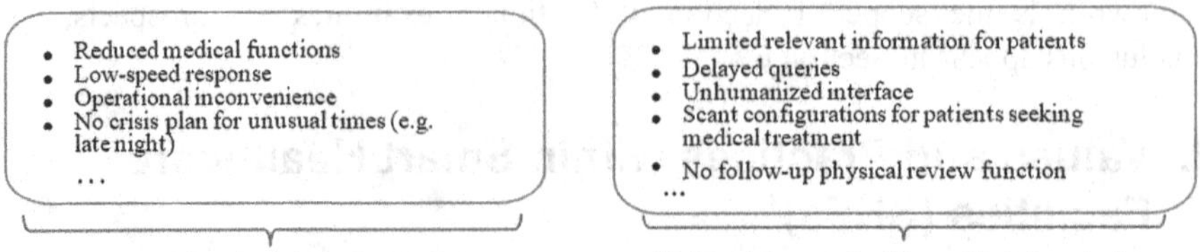

(a) Mobile device software   (b) Healthcare facility official website

Figure 1. Application problems under the SHF frameworks

3.1. Evidence Congregation

Figure 1 depicts problems identified during the recent health crisis.

For SH smartphone software, one can say that existing systems have:

- Slower response speed: With the progress of the centralized service software, the volume of data in these systems has exponentially increased. This exerts high pressure on the software and consequent low response speeds.
- Unsatisfactory performance of medicine: Due to focusing most cities on construction services from all smart city aspects on the mobile device software, contribution has been made by each part.
- Lack of proper emergency strategy for sensitive situations: This type of planning does not exist in most smart health care services. This is due to the online scheduling of medical care services and online bookings in the system, which creates time constraints, especially for patients and caregivers at certain times such as midnight, which prevents them from utilizing the smart healthcare system.
- Dissatisfaction with the system: According to the survey, most smart healthcare services include software and hardware essentials of the intelligent outlines of the city. The interface for smart healthcare services/devices may be simple. However, when facing distress, users and caretakers may not feel at ease.

For official SHF websites, one finds

- Delays in requests: Most medical centers have counselling and patient services on their website. If one cannot diagnose the symptoms or is taking medication without a doctor's diagnosis, one can consult a specialist online. This is a very sensitive bottleneck.
- Inadequate material for patients and caretakers: Currently, mainstream healthcare facilities have limited information on their certified websites. Most of the healthcare facilities websites offer insufficient information or induce stress.
- Absence of follow-up physical review: Some official websites only provide necessary healthcare staff data and online reservation services [12]. Nevertheless, they lack subsequent examination services. The development of this function can significantly assist the patient's recovery after treatment, saving energy, time, and funds for many people.
- Inhuman user interface: This happens especially when one interacts with elderly or digitally illiterate patients. Therefore, using the inhuman interface in

patient's hospitals in such cases will be impossible for these patients for online bookings.

- A lack of caregivers and patients for treatment occurs when monitoring large population databases. The resulting disproportion between the number of healthcare professionals and the number of patients complicates the rational usage of healthcare logistics. One can develop better online appointment services/software and elect a location for treatment after identifying patients and priorities to allocate a healthcare professional.

The advancement of network infrastructure has taken all health-related fields to a new stage. Currently, people's needs have soared, which in turn requires advanced technologies. Smart healthcare implies that an ICT support system works with big data and hefty network traffic [8, 11-16, 19, 66, 92], which requires high-speed data storage capacity. These characteristics make the healthcare sector smarter. However, they should also rely on more humane approaches relying on innovative designs that learn and change somehow [10, 13]. This book examines the above problems in today's society while merging network resources and other innovations, e.g., servers and routing based on CC and IoMT technologies [52, 53, 78]. The Section underneath elucidates the implementation process.

4. Developing a SHF promotion framework

4.1. Analysis of SHF Needs

New methods and design practices entailing intelligent systems for healthcare stem from the cases described in the previous sections. For example, if the patient's condition worsens, it is first checked whether he should immediately go to a health center. If the symptoms are bearable, the patient can use video conferencing technology on various digital devices to contact healthcare personnel to seek help, report their conditions, and receive the necessary advice. This method is especially suitable when the healthcare unit is closed on holidays or late at night and is inaccessible. One of the advantages of this method is the direct communication between health care workers, caregivers, and patients. In addition to solving the patient's minor problems, this also helps caregivers and patients' time and energy. In the next case, if the doctor cannot meet the needs of patients remotely, medical services should be provided directly in the patient's home as outdoor services. To be exact, if the patient cannot go to the healthcare facility, physicians have to arrange for door-to-door services. An emergency hotline can be supplied as a mobile service but with better interfaces and humane treatment. This service lets physicians reach patients fast. This technique reduces the problem of having patients/caretakers going to a healthcare facility, register, queue up, and buy medicine, especially when sick. This method saves nearly half the time and energy based on statistical information. It also maximizes the usage of hospital resources while satisfying patient needs and medical resources.

Some patients can be tested, diagnosed, and treated over the counter. Hence, building a 24-hour clinic to offer medical resources like drug supplies to patients at any time and place can be an online function. These functions can also play an essential role in simplifying treatment and alleviating the tension between healthcare staff and patients. Further enhancement of the processes involves the dual management of public funds and technical personnel. Table 1 enlists some instances and possible specific solutions.

Assessments of and for a healthcare institution's official networks are analogous to mobile software solutions, and this text will not refer to them.

Table 1. Framework relying on smartphones

Problems	Framework (New functions)
Few medical functions, e.g., information search, online booking	Further features, including reservation, online consultation, seeing a doctor on video, and more.
Low response speed	Via a heterogeneous database and DDS [15] technology to ameliorate the response speed.
Inconveniences regarding operation	Designing specialized and convenient smart medical software.
No emergency strategy for a particular situation (e.g., late-night)	Building a 24-hour healthcare facility.

4.2. SHF Promotion Strategies and Approaches

4.2.1. Data Aggregation (DA)

A Data Aggregation (DA) unit integrates received data from heterogeneous infrastructures (Figure 2) with different types of networks containing sensors and actuators [14]. The nodes may include sensing technologies such as Radio-Frequency Identification (RFID), body sensors, Geographic Information System (GIS), and Global Positioning System (GPS), to name a few. Examples of actuators are drugs inside implanted nanorobots and self-regulating stents.

4.2.2. DA Description

An illustration of a heterogeneous database utilizing a Web Service depicts the simple data aggregation process in smart healthcare appears in Figures 3 and 4. The data from patients or source nodes comes from prompting or in the event of an emergency. The adapter gets records, places the data into a queue, dispatches the information according to its priority, and stores the files accordingly. On reaching a certain information level, the data aggregation process comes about. Usually, the module is a Web Service that works according to the system diagram underneath [15]. The fundamental rationale for merging data in a scenario with heterogeneous databases is as follows.

At present, heterogeneous databases are the leading aggregation media. Taking SHSs as an example, many specialists' information and observations are generated, e.g., about the departments visited, visiting time, appointment contacts, and so on, into the background database [16]. When a patient requests an appointment through an App or queries about the healthcare facility online, SQL, NoSQL, or other search tools/technologies/paradigms contribute to exploring the databases.

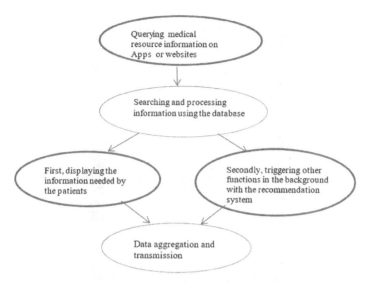

Figure 2. The framework of data aggregation

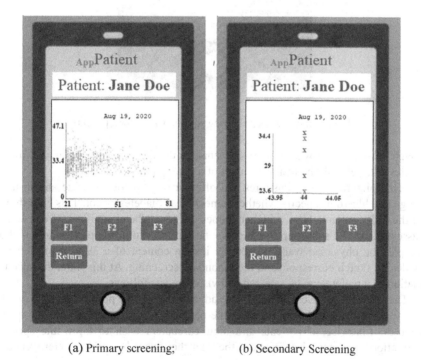

(a) Primary screening; (b) Secondary Screening

Figure 3. Screening of medical data [17]

4.2.3. Triage Approaches

Source information can be aggregated in heterogeneous databases so that AI helps select and display the data necessary for screening. AI procedures can boost triage

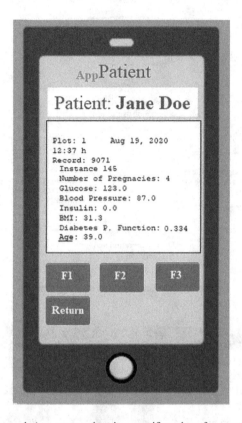

Figure 4. App screen showing specific values for a patient

through clustering software to correctly analyze the desired data. Figure 2 shows a diabetes data set with the insulin content of a given diabetic patient.

This picture clearly illustrates and offers a way to compare age and insulin. Orange and blue dots specify whether someone has diabetes or not. This case shows that the older patients have a higher propensity for diabetes mellitus. If one wants to assess a specific subgroup of patients, one can refer to it in a particular way. For example, the physician wants to see the insulin content of a 39-year-old female. The design sketch corresponds to the secondary screening. At this time, the specific situation of a patient can be selected and visualized as follows.

The above examples illustrate the advantages of the promotion framework. Healthcare professionals can discover the patient's records according to the query attributes. Likewise, if patients and their caretakers wish to know the specific information, they can also filter out the data they want by mining heterogeneous databases.

4.2.4. Data Distribution

The specific healthcare information comes from data screening processes. In such cases, healthcare personnel, patients, or caretakers can search for the looked-for information through keywords. Still, displaying this material, together with online consultation, recommended information, remote medical treatment, and other functions, requires data distribution support. Issues like security and privacy must be guaranteed to all healthcare stakeholders [84-87].

4.2.5. Data Distribution Structure

Data distribution denotes the process in which data creators, e.g., source nodes, transmit information to users in various ways [18]. Next, the Distributed Healthcare System (DHS) appears.

Almost every source node in the DHS is autonomous. Hence, every patient is registered as a backup of published data. Middleware performs data distribution once the patient's tasks (e.g., login, registration, search, and other operations) and the heterogeneous data integration happen at the source node. The source node needs to handle essential healthcare software. Then, the source node converses with various applications via the distribution service platform. This communication occurs according to the heterogeneous information about the healthcare stakeholders involved. Figure 5 displays the structure of a general distributed healthcare system.

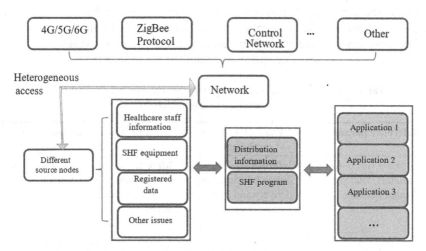

Figure 5. The framework of the Distributed Healthcare System (DHS)

4.2.6. SHF Strategies and Approaches

The Data Distribution Service (DDS) [15] for real-time systems stands for an Object Management Group (OMG) Machine-to-Machine (M2M) standard [9, 15-20]. DDS is sometimes termed middleware or connectivity framework, which enables high-performance, reliable, real-time, interoperable, scalable data exchanges utilizing a publish-subscribe pattern.

DDS addresses the necessities of applications like aerospace security, air-traffic control, robotics, operation of autonomous vehicles, medical devices, power generation, simulations, component testing, smart grid management, transportation structures, and others that entail real-time data exchange. Since, DDS itself has the characteristics of persistence, priority, and good coordination, consequently, one will develop DDS strategies and approaches. DDS is the most mainstream DHS for most SHFs.

The healthcare field yields patient data every day that is voluminous and assorted (multimodal). Through research and development, one can realize that some smart medical Apps on the market pose some problems. These shortcomings can help multidisciplinary groups propose new IoMT scenarios about smart healthcare consistent with the schemes discussed in this book's chapters. The specific data can be compared as follows.

Table 2 shows the slow response speed of many functions that may result from the Manufacturing Message Specification (MMS) protocol by many smart healthcare Apps. MMS is an international standard (ISO 9506) widely employed in some smart healthcare apps. Under this protocol, data packet transmission delay is more than DDS transmission of the same data packet sizes in real-time [19, 20]. However, under a new scenario for smart healthcare relying on DDS, nearly 95% of the data packets sent and received within 1 s reached 3900-4500 packets, and the data delay reached the standard. These figures amount to a 90% margin real-time requirement, and they can impact patient health outcomes. DDS distribution technology is more critical in the implementation of new smart healthcare schemes because of its small delay in the process of data aggregation and distribution, real-time communication, and trustworthiness in patient registration, data search, queries, consultation, online booking, remote diagnosis, treatment, and simultaneous theragnostics.

Table 2. A hypothetical scenario for comparisons of parameters related to healthcare stakeholders

Reference parameters	Examples of Apps' on the market	Smart healthcare scenario
Healthcare functions, parameters, vital signs, and other quantities	Information search, online booking, drug delivery and therapies	More features, including telephone reservation, online consultation, healthcare person visitation, video accompaniment
Response speed	0.5s-2s	Below 0.1s
Maximum task capacity	Maximum number of packets/s (peak value)	4500 packets/s
......	......	......

5. SH Prospects

From the feasible developmental perspectives and current situation of smart healthcare, intelligent healthcare generally evolves from paper to paperless, wired to wireless, artificially to intelligently controlled, and single to diversified. The aspects below sum up specific development trends [21-26]:

- *More extensive population coverage*: The current network information technology has dramatically broken through regional constraints after the efficient use and availability of satellites, Ad Hoc technology, and cables.
- *More sensitive data perception*: The vertiginous growth of smart healthcare results mainly from the rapid development of multimodal sensors, actuators, and other hardware pieces. At present, hardware advances fast concerning miniaturization, sensitization, high efficiency, and automation. However, its cost gradually decreases, affecting healthcare at several levels, even in urban and rural systems.
- *Deeper intelligence*: The so-called big data (BD) denotes large amounts of information access and processing points [8, 11-16, 19, 66, 92]. Applications like intelligent medicine delivery and dispensing, for instance, need to process records reasonably fast and transmit them cleverly by digitizing, representing, integrating, and storing data from patients, caretakers, health staff, and health organizations. Deep learning (DL) has seen significant success in several fields of Artificial Intelligence (AI) research during the last decade [50-68]. This practice, which arose from prior research on artificial neural networks, has outperformed conventional machine learning algorithms in image and speech recognition [50, 60, 76-82, 85-91], natural language processing, and others. The initial deep learning applications in pharmaceutical research appeared in recent years. Its value has expanded beyond bioactivity forecasts to addressing a wide range of drug development challenges. Bioactivity prediction, new types of molecule design, synthesis prediction, and biological image breakdowns are extremely vital and must be addressed.

Metaheuristics: The growing usage of digital image processing practices focused on health is explicit, aiding in the solution, improving diagnosis, and creating new diagnostic schemes [50, 60, 76-82, 85-91]. Histopathological assessments are the first and most common inspections made to catch the general patient clinical picture. Still, their cost cannot be met by populations of less favored nations. Digital Image Processing allows the analysis of several image regions besides extracting quantitative information from them, performing measurements impossible to make manually, and permitting multiple data types. Metaheuristic techniques are great tools for the digital image segmentation of tissues. This text will handle the separation and calculation of blood cells as a case study where each imagery has red blood cells, leukocytes, and platelets. Metaheuristics will enhance the computational blood image analysis, but this analysis still faces shortcomings as cyber-physical systems advance and more effective big data methodologies arrive [8, 11-16, 19, 66, 92].

Nanotechnology and the Internet of Nano Things (IoNT): Healthcare, as a major human right, needs to devise and assimilate new-fangled technology towards high-quality, on-time, acceptable, and cheap welfare. Nanotechnology and the IoNT have been unfailingly ameliorating health and meaningfully impacting its evolution, occasioning better aftermaths. Nanotechnology shows up in the form of nanomaterials working with nanodevices and supports manifold treatments by providing many paybacks such as sickness prevention, all types of diagnoses/analyses, and therapies.

Appending nanodevices enroute to the Internet engenders new challenges to the IoNT paradigm. In biomedical applications, IoNT models have led to more personalized, timely, and proper health surveillance, remote medicine distribution, and therapy. As an end result, nanotechnology and the IoNT are entirely altering the health sector, simplifying early sickness detection and diagnoses, followed by exact, on-time, and fruitful treatments to a great extent lowering health price tags. The roles of nanotechnology and IoNT in welfare help acquire an understanding of nanoscale hopes, solutions, and techniques, highlighting advantages while also noting potential hazards and concerns. Despite the privacy, safety, and nanotoxicity concerns, the snowballing usage and new developments regarding nanotechnology and IoNT will make evident their full potential in healthcare in future.

Blockchain: In recent times, there has been an intensification in the need for Healthcare Organizations (HOs) to empower individuals to control their health records. However, security concerns regarding how various HOs communicate healthcare data have hindered the implementation of such systems. The capacity to safely transmit data allows for the growth of integrated healthcare services to patients. Blockchain technology (BT) is a good driver for transitioning towards integrated healthcare due to its decentralized character, addressing new insights and the critical issues of many healthcare domains [83-87, 97, 98]. BT enables HOs to record and monitor peer-to-peer transactions across a network that lacks a centralized authority.

Theragnostics: Disease theragnostics approaches and handles health issues an individual may have, and this undertaking can sometimes be very stress releiving, while in other circumstances may be a bit awkward. Large data sets can limit tool accuracy to determine the patterns and make predictions. The traditional methods used to diagnose/treat diseases are manual and error-prone. AI predictive techniques enable auto diagnosis and lessen detection errors compared to exclusive human expertise. This chapter overviews and classifies the most used AI techniques for medical diagnostic systems. Various diseases and corresponding AI tatics are further discussed.

Digital Twins (DTs): These structures have become progressively more popular in contemporary years and may continue to get escalating acceptance. The terminology Personal Health Devices (PHDs) means the set of healthcare gadgets comprising on-body and in-body devices, i.e., wearables, injectables, implantables, ingestibles, and other non-mainstream possibilities [10, 83-87, 97]. The options for its use have increased because of the DT reframing as a living or nonliving entity rather than an exact digital duplication of something tangible. In smart cities, the DT disrupts industrial processes while simultaneously extending health and well-being to drive the development of new healthcare services. A standardized DT design for health follows rules according to the ISO/IEEE 11073 framework operating in a loop cycle, collecting data from personal health devices, analyzing it, and delivering feedback to the stakeholder. It is possible to integrate not only X73-compliant PHDs but also non-compliant PHDs into the framework by attaching them to aX73 wrapper subsystem. It also reports that a corresponding customizable mobile application has been built for any compatible device. Possible ecosystems and the X73 mobile applications must be experimented with to demonstrate DT viability in the well-being of smart societies. In order to get insights into someone's well-being and provide feedback to health specialists, individuals, and caregivers, promising outcomes and the prospective advantages of the proposed framework are given.

6. Conclusion

SH treatment is essential and urgent in people's lives. Its promotion framework points towards cleverly introducing, improving, and perfecting healthcare innovation for people to interact with healthcare workers effortlessly. At the same time, the innovations discussed still call for standards, protocols, and other features. There is room for a lot of future exploration and debates in SH development and promotion methodologies. Typically speaking, SH has taken a significant step towards building smart local and global communities. It has made life more convenient, accessible, organized, and coordinated. Because of the existence of more vulnerable people and the risk of future depletion of resources, a comprehensive analysis of urban/rural IoMT designs is of considerable worth to smart healthcare and the concepts of smart cities, communities, and collectives.

References

1. Marinho, C.E.V., Estrela, V.V., Loschi, H.J., Razmjooy, N., Herrmann, A.E. et al. (2019). A model for medical staff idleness minimization. *In:* Iano, Y. et al. (eds). Proceedings of the 4th Brazilian Technology Symposium (BTSym'18). BTSym 2018. Smart Innovation, Systems and Technologies, vol 140. Springer, Cham.
2. Khelassi, A. and Estrela, V.V. (2020). Advances in multidisciplinary medical technologies — Engineering, modeling and findings. Proc. Int'l Workshop on Medical Technologies 2019 (ICHSMT 2019), Springer Nature, Zurich, Switzerland.
3. Kanna, K., Estrela, V.V. and Rodrigues, J.J.P.C. (2021). Cyber security and digital forensics. Proc. ICCSDF 2021, Springer Nature, Zurich, Switzerland.
4. Ibrahim, M., Adams, C. and El-Zaart, A. (2015). Paving the way to smart sustainable cities: Transformation models and challenges. J. Inf. Syst. Technol. Manag. (JISTEM), 12(3), 559-576.
5. Mammadova, M. and Jabrayilova, Z. (2017). Development of a multi-scenario approach to intelligent management of human resources in the field of medicine. Eastern-European Journal of Enterprise Technologies, 2, 4-14.
6. Reeves, J.J., Hollandsworth, H.M., Torriani, F., Taplitz, R., Abeles, S.R. (2020). Rapid response to COVID-19: Health informatics support for outbreak management in an academic health system. J. American Medical Informatics Association (JAMIA), 27, 853-859.
7. Zhang, A. and Pan, M. (2020). "Smart Process" of medical innovation: The synergism based on network and physical space. Int'l J. Environmental Research and Public Health, 17.
8. Wang, N. and Mao, B. (2019). The research on the problems of smart old-age care in the background of smart city construction. 2019 International Conference on Intelligent Transportation, Big Data & Smart City (ICITBS), 151-154.

9. Mukudu, N., Ventura, N., Mwangama, J.B., Elmangoush, A., Steinke, R. et al. (2016). Prototyping smart city applications over large scale M2M testbed. 2016 IST-Africa Week Conference, 1-11.

10. Tsoutsouras, V., Xydis, S. and Soudris, D. (2014). A HW/SW framework emulating wearable devices for remote wound monitoring and management. Proc. 4th Int'l Conf. Wireless Mobile Communication and Healthcare – Transforming Healthcare Through Innovations in Mobile and Wireless Technologies (MOBIHEALTH), 369-372.

11. Wang, D., Liu, J. and Yao, D. (2020). An energy-efficient distributed adaptive cooperative routing based on reinforcement learning in wireless multimedia sensor networks. Comput. Networks, 178, 107313.

12. Chusheng, G. (2015). On semantic web and semantic web management. Journal of Nanhua University: Social Science Edition, 2015(3), 107-110.

13. Quanyou, Z. (2017). Intelligent convergence of intelligent city information based on semantic Web. D.Sc. Dissertation, Xuchang College. 2017(16).

14. Jing, X. and Jia, B. (2017). Research on the application of vehicle network in optimization of automobile supply chain. IOP Conference Series: Materials Science and Engineering, 242. doi: 10.1088/1757-899X/242/1/012067

15. Corsaro, A., Pardo-Castellote, G. and Tucker, C. (2009). DDS Interoperability Demo. Object Management Group. Retrieved December 8, 2019.

16. Sebaa, A., Chikh, F., Nouicer, A. and Tari, A. (2018). Medical big data warehouse: Architecture and system design, a case study: Improving healthcare resources distribution. Journal of Medical Systems, 42, 1-16.

17. Feng, B., He, P., Li, P., Yao, H., Ji, Y. et al. (2019). Developing a smart healthcare framework with an "Aboriginal lens". ITQM, 162, 347-354.

18. Yuan, C., Yang, H. and Pan, Y. (2019). Research on data link ontology mapping algorithm based on Bayesian network model. IEEE Access, 7, 185698-185709.

19. Sahoo, P.K. and Dehury, C.K. (2018). Efficient data and CPU-intensive job scheduling algorithms for healthcare cloud. Comput. Electr. Eng., 68, 119-139.

20. Morais, R., Silva, N., Mendes, J., Adão, T., Pádua, L. et al. (2019). mySense: A comprehensive data management environment to improve precision agriculture practices. Comput. Electron. Agric., 162, 882-894.

21. Chen, X., Jiang, J., Zhou, H., Xie, H., Zhou, L. et al. (2020). Rapid layout and development strategy of sospital artificial intelligence during the COVID-19 pandemic. Chinese Journal of Engineering Science, 22, 130-137.

22. Estrela, V.V., Saotome, O., Loschi, H.J., Hemanth, D.J., Farfan, W.S. et al. (2018). Emergency response cyber-physical framework for landslide avoidance with sustainable electronics. Technologies, 6, 42. doi:10.3390/technologies6020042.

23. Sun, L., Jiang, X., Ren, H. and Guo, Y. (2020). Edge-cloud computing and artificial intelligence in Internet of Medical Things: Architecture, technology and application. IEEE Access, 8, 101079-101092.

24. Alabdulatif, A., Khalil, I., Yi, X. and Guizani, M. (2019). Secure edge of things for smart healthcare surveillance framework. IEEE Access, 7, 31010-31021.

25. Engineer, M., Tusha, R., Shah, A.K. and Adhvaryu, D.K. (2019). Insight into the importance of fog computing in Internet of Medical Things (IoMT). 2019 International Conference on Recent Advances in Energy-efficient Computing and Communication (ICRAECC), 1-7.

26. Pustokhina, I., Pustokhin, D.A., Gupta, D., Khanna, A., Shankar, K. et al. (2020). An effective training scheme for deep neural network in edge computing enabled Internet of Medical Things (IoMT) systems. IEEE Access, 8, 107112-107123.

27. Gopal, N.N. and Karnan, M. (2010). Diagnose brain tumor through MRI using

image processing clustering algorithms such as fuzzy c means along with intelligent optimization techniques. 2010 IEEE International Conference on Computational Intelligence and Computing Research. IEEE, pp. 1–4.

28. Chen, H.-L., Huang, C.-C., Yu, X.-G., Xu, X., Sun, X. et al. (2013). An efficient diagnosis system for detection of Parkinson's disease using fuzzy k-nearest neighbor approach. Expert Systems with Applications, 40(1), 263-271.

29. Patra, S. and Thakur, G. (2013). A proposed neuro-fuzzy model for adult asthma disease diagnosis. Comput. Sci. Informa. Technol., 3, 191-205.

30. Miranda, G.H.B. and Felipe, J.C. (2015). Computer-aided diagnosis system based on fuzzy logic for breast cancer categorization. Comp. Biology and Med., 64, 334-346.

31. Nilashi, M., Ibrahim, O., Ahmadi, H. and Shahmoradi, L. (2017). A knowledge-based system for breast cancer classification using fuzzy logic method. Telematics and Informatics, 34(4), 133-144.

32. Satarkar, S. and Ali, M. (2015). Fuzzy expert system for the diagnosis of common liver disease. Int'l Engineering J. Research & Development, 1(1), 2-7.

33. Allahverdi, N. and Akcan, T. (2011). A fuzzy expert system design for diagnosis of periodontal dental disease. Proc. 2011 5th Int'l Conf. Application of Inf. and Comm. Technologies (AICT). IEEE, pp. 1-5.

34. Son, L.H., Tuan, T.M., Fujita, H., Dey, N. and Ashour, A.S. (2018). Dental diagnosis from X-ray images: An expert system based on fuzzy computing. Biom. Signal Proc. Control, 39, 64-73.

35. Godil, S.S., Shamim, M.S., Enam, S.A. and Qidwai, U. (2011). Fuzzy logic: "A simple" solution for complexities in neurosciences. Surgical Neurology International, 2.

36. Brust-Renck, P.G., Reyna, V.F., Wilhelms, E.A. and Lazar, A.N. (2016). A fuzzy-trace theory of judgment and decision-making in health care: Explanation, prediction, and application. *In:* Handbook of Health Decision Science. Springer, pp. 71-86.

37. Roveri, M.I., Manoel, E., Onodera, A.N., Ortega, N.R. and Tessutti, V.D. (2017). Assessing experience in the deliberate practice of running using a fuzzy decision-support system. PloS One, 12(8), e0183389.

38. Zhang, G. (2009). A modified SVM classifier based on RS in medical disease prediction. *In:* Proc. 2009 2nd Int'l Symp. Comp. Intell. and Design, vol. 1, pp. 144-147. IEEE.

39. Sinha, P. and Sinha, P. (2015). Comparative study of chronic kidney disease prediction using KNN and SVM. Int'l J. Eng. Research and Technology, 4(12), 608-612.

40. Charleonnan, A., Fufaung, T., Niyomwong, T., Chokchueypattanakit, W., Suwannawach, S. et al. (2016). Predictive analytics for chronic kidney disease using machine learning techniques. *In:* Proc. 2016 Manag. and Inn. Techn. Int'l Conf. (MITicon). IEEE, pp. MIT–80.

41. Zheng, B., Yoon, S.W. and Lam, S.S. (2014). Breast cancer diagnosis based on feature extraction using a hybrid of k-means and support vector machine algorithms. Expert Systems with Applications, 41(4), 1476-1482.

42. Fernandes, S.R., de Assis, J.T., Estrela, V.V., Razmjooy, N. and Deshpande, A. et al. (2021). Nondestructive diagnosis and analysis of computed microtomography images via texture descriptors. *In:* Khelassi, A. and Estrela, V.V. (eds). Advances in Multidisciplinary Medical Technologies — Engineering, Modeling and Findings. Springer, Cham.

43. Asri, H., Mousannif, H., Al Moatassime, H. and Noel, T. (2016). Using machine learning algorithms for breast cancer risk prediction and diagnosis. Procedia Computer Science, 83, 1064-1069.

44. Bhargava, N., Purohit, R., Sharma, S. and Kumar, A. (2017). Prediction of arthritis using classification and regression tree algorithm. *In:* Proc. 2017 2nd Int'l Conf. Comm. and Electronics Systems (ICCES), pp. 606-610. IEEE.

45. Sriram, T.V., Rao, M.V., Narayana, G.S., Kaladhar, D. and Vital, T.P.R. (2013). Intelligent Parkinson disease prediction using machine learning algorithms. Int'l J. Eng. and Innovative Techn. (IJEIT), 3(3), 1568-1572.

46. Salvatore, C., Cerasa, A., Castiglioni, I., Gallivanone, F., Augimeri, A. et al. (2014). Machine learning on brain MRI data for differential diagnosis of Parkinson's disease and progressive supranuclear palsy. J. Neurosc. Meth., 222, 230-237.

47. Pineda, A.L., Ye, Y., Visweswaran, S., Cooper, G.F., Wagner, M.M. et al. (2015). Comparison of machine learning classifiers for influenza detection from emergency department free-text reports. J. Biomed. Inform., 58, 60–69.

48. Dwivedi, S.A., Borse, R. and Yametkar, A.M. (2014). Lung cancer detection and classification by using machine learning & multinomial Bayesian. IOSR J. Electronics and Communication Engineering (IOSR-JECE), 9(1), 69-75.

49. Kononenko, I., Bratko, I. and Kukar, M. (1997). Application of machine learning to medical diagnosis. Machine Learning and Data Mining: Methods and Applications, 389, 408.

50. Suzuki, K. (2017). Overview of deep learning in medical imaging. Radiological Physics and Technology, 10(3), 257-273.

51. LeCun, Y., Bengio, Y. and Hinton, G. (2015). Deep learning. Nature, 521(7553), 436-444.

52. Suzuki, H., Ohsaki, H. and Sawai, H. (2010). A network-based computational model with learning. *In:* Proc. Int'l Conf. Unconventional Computation. Springer, pp. 193-193.

53. Miotto, R., Wang, F., Wang, S., Jiang, X. and Dudley, J.T. (2018). Deep learning for healthcare: Review, opportunities and challenges. Briefings in Bioinf., 19(6), 1236-1246.

54. Anderson, R., Biong, A. and Gómez-Gualdrón, D.A. (2020). Adsorption isotherm predictions for multiple molecules in MOFs using the same deep learning model. J. Chem. Th. and Comp., 16, 2, doi: 10.26434/chemrxiv.9894224.v1

55. Deshpande, A., Estrela, V.V. and Patavardhan, P. (2021). The DCT-CNN-ResNet50 architecture to classify brain tumours with super-resolution, convolutional neural network, and the ResNet50. Neuroscience Informatics, 1, 4, 100013.

56. Shoieb, D.A., Youssef, S.M. and Aly, W.M. (2016). Computer-aided model for skin diagnosis using deep learning. Journal of Image and Graphics, 4(2), 122-129.

57. Abdel-Zaher, A.M. and Eldeib, A.M. (2016). Breast cancer classification using deep belief networks. Expert Systems with Applications, 46, 139-144.

58. Charan, S., Khan, M.J. and Khurshid, K. (2018). Breast cancer detection in mammograms using convolutional neural network. *In:* Int'l Conf. Computing, Math. and Eng. Technologies (iCoMET). pp. 1-5. IEEE.

59. Miao, K.H. and Miao, J.H. (2018). Coronary heart disease diagnosis using deep neural networks. Int. J. Adv. Comput. Sci. Appl., 9(10), 1-8.

60. Sun, W., Zheng, B. and Qian, W. (2016). Computer aided lung cancer diagnosis with deep learning algorithms. *In:* Medical imaging 2016: Computer-Aided Diagnosis, vol. 9785. International Society for Optics and Photonics, p. 97850Z.

61. Jain, G., Mittal, D., Thakur, D. and Mittal, M.K. (2020). A deep learning approach to detect Covid-19 coronavirus with x-ray images. Biocybernetics and Biomedical Engineering, 40(4), 1391-1405.

62. El-Rashidy, N., El-Sappagh, S., Islam, S., El-Bakry, H.M., Abdelrazek, S. et al. (2020). End-to-end deep learning framework for coronavirus (Covid-19) detection and monitoring. Electronics, 9(9), 1439.

63. Toraman, S., Alakus, T.B. and Turkoglu, I. (2020). Convolutional CAPSNET: A novel artificial neural network approach to detect Covid-19 disease from X-ray images using capsule networks. Chaos, Solitons & Fractals, 140, 110122.

64. Jaiswal, A., Gianchandani, N., Singh, D., Kumar, V., Kaur, M. et al. (2020). Classification of the Covid-19 infected patients using densenet201 based deep transfer learning. J. Biomolecular Structure and Dynamics, 1-8.

65. Ginat, D.T. (2020). Analysis of head CT scans flagged by deep learning software for acute intracranial hemorrhage. Neuroradiology, 62(3), 335-340.

66. Lewick, T., Kumar, M., Hong, R. and Wu, W. (2020). Intracranial hemorrhage detection in CT scans using deep learning. *In:* Proc. 2020 IEEE 6th Int'l Conf. Big Data Computing Service and Applications (BigDataService). pp. 169-172. IEEE.

67. Chen, F.-C. and Jahanshahi, M.R. (2017). NB-CNN: Deep learning-based crack detection using convolutional neural network and naïve Bayes data fusion. IEEE Trans. Ind. Electronics, 65(5), 4392-4400.

68. Elasnaoui, K. and Chawki, Y. (2020). Using X-ray images and deep learning for automated detection of coronavirus disease. J. Biomol. Struct. and Dynamics (no. just-accepted), 1-22.

69. Holzinger, A., Langs, G., Denk, H., Zatloukal, K. and Müller, H. et al. (2019). Causability and explainability of artificial intelligence in medicine. Wiley Interdisciplinary Reviews: Data Mining and Knowledge Discovery, 9(4), e1312.

70. Elazab, N., Soliman, H., El-Sappagh, S., Islam, S. and Elmogy, M. et al. (2020). Objective diagnosis for histopathological images based on machine learning techniques: Classical approaches and new trends. Mathematics, 8(11), 1863.

71. Tellez, D., Litjens, G.J., Bandi, P., Bulten, W., Bokhorst, J.M. et al. (2019). Quantifying the effects of data augmentation and stain color normalization in convolutional neural networks for computational pathology. Med. Image Analysis, 58, 101544.

72. Saha, S.K., Islam, S.R., Kwak, K.-S., Rahman, M.S., Cho, S.-G. et al. (2020). Prom1 and prom2 expression differentially modulates clinical prognosis of cancer: A multiomics analysis. Cancer Gene Therapy, 27(3), 147-167.

73. El-Sappagh, S., Abuhmed, T., Islam, S.R. and Kwak, K.S. (2020). Multimodal multitask deep learning model for Alzheimer's disease progression detection based on time series data. Neurocomputing, 412, 197-215.

74. Yaya, X. and Bi-Geng, Z. (2020). Research on medical image storage and retrieval system based on Hadoop. Journal of Physics: Conf. Series, 1544(1). IOP Publishing, 012119.

75. Estrela, V.V., Andreopoulos, N., Sroufer, R., Jesus, M.A., Mamani, W.D. et al. (2021). Transmedia Ecosystems, Quality of Experience and Quality of Service in Fog Computing for Comfortable Learning. 2021 IEEE Global Engineering Education Conference (EDUCON), 1003-1009.

76. Estrela, V.V., Hemanth, J.D., Saotome, O., Nikolakopoulos, G. and Sabatini, R. (2020). Introduction to·advances in UAV avionics for imaging and sensing. (Control, Robotics and Sensors, 2020), Imaging and Sensing for Unmanned Aircraft Systems. Vol. 1: Control and Performance, Chap. 1, pp. 1-21, IET, London, UK.

77. Zielke, T. (2020). Is artificial intelligence ready for standardization? *In:* Proc. European Conference on Software Process Improvement. Springer, pp. 259-274.

78. Hussain, F., Hussain, R., Hassan, S.A. and Hossain, E. (2020). Machine learning in IoT security: Current solutions and future challenges. IEEE Communications Surveys & Tutorials, 2020.

79. Monteiro, A.C.B., França, R.P., Estrela, V.V., Razmjooy, N., Iano Y. et al. (2021). Metaheuristics applied to blood image analysis. *In:* Razmjooy, N. et al. (eds).

Metaheuristics and Optimization in Computer and Electrical Engineering. Lecture Notes in Electrical Engineering, vol. 696. Springer, Cham.

80. Deshpande, A., Razmjooy, N. and Estrela V.V. (2021). Introduction to computational intelligence and super-resolution. *In:* Deshpande, A. et al. (eds). Computational Intelligence Methods for Super-Resolution in Image Processing Applications. Springer, Cham, Switzerland.

81. Chaabane, L., Khelassi, A., Terziev, A., Andreopoulos, N., Jesus, M.A. et al. (2021). Particle swarm optimization with tabu search algorithm (PSO-TS) applied to multiple sequence alignment problem. *In:* Khelassi, A. and Estrela, V.V. (eds). Advances in Multidisciplinary Medical Technologies – Engineering, Modeling and Findings. Springer, Cham, Switzerland.

82. Kalantari, S., Ramezani, M., Madadi, A. and Estrela, V.V. (2021). Reduction AWGN from digital images using a new local optimal low-rank approximation method. *In:* Iano, Y. et al. (eds). Proc. 5th Brazilian Technology Symposium (BTSym 2019). Smart Innovation, Systems and Technologies, vol 201. Springer, Cham.

83. Jiang, S., Cao, J., Wu, H., Yang, Y., Ma, M. et al. (2018). Blochie: A blockchain-based platform for healthcare information exchange. *In:* Proc. SMARTCOMP 2018: The 4th IEEE Int'l Conf. Smart Computing, Sicily, Italy, 18-20 June 2018, pp. 49-56.

84. Cichosz, S.L., Stausholm, M.N., Kronborg, T., Vestergaard, P., Hejlesen, O. et al. (2018). How to use blockchain for diabetes health care data and access management: An operational concept. J. Diabetes Sci. Technol., 13, 248-253.

85. Zhang, P., White, J., Schmidt, D.C., Lenz, G., Rosenbloom, S.T et al. (2018). FHIRChain: Applying Blockchain to Securely and Scalably Share Clinical Data. Comput. Struct. Biotechnol. J., 16, 267-278.

86. Guo, R., Shi, H., Zhao, Q. and Zheng, D. (2018). Secure attribute-based signature scheme with multiple authorities for blockchain in electronic health records systems. IEEE Access, 6, 11676-11686.

87. Yue, X., Wang, H., Jin, D., Li, M., Jiang, W. et al. (2016). Healthcare data gateways: Found healthcare intelligence on blockchain with novel privacy risk control. J. Med. Syst., 40, 218.

88. El-Rashidy, N., El-Sappagh, S., Islam, S., El-Bakry, H.M., Abdelrazek, S. et al. (2020). End-to-end deep learning framework for coronavirus (Covid-19) detection and monitoring. Electronics, 9(9), 1439.

89. Nur-A.-Alam, Ahsan, M., Based, M.A., Haider, J. and Kowalski, M. (2021). COVID-19 detection from chest X-ray images using feature fusion and deep learning. Sensors (Basel, Switzerland), 21.

90. Balaha, H.M., El-Gendy, E.M. and Saafan, M.M. (2022). A complete framework for accurate recognition and prognosis of COVID-19 patients based on deep transfer learning and feature classification approach. Artificial Intelligence Review, 55, 5063-5108.

91. Ginat, D.T. (2020). Analysis of head CT scans flagged by deep learning software for acute intracranial hemorrhage. Neuroradiology, 62(3), 335-340.

92. Lewick, T., Kumar, M., Hong, R. and Wu, W. (2020). Intracranial hemorrhage detection in CT scans using deep learning. *In:* Proc. 2020 IEEE 6th Int'l Conf. Big Data Computing Service and Applications (BigDataService), pp. 169-172. IEEE.

93. Chen, F.-C. and Jahanshahi, M.R. (2017). NB-CNN: Deep learning-based crack detection using convolutional neural network and naïve Bayes data fusion. IEEE Trans. Ind. Electronics, 65(5), 4392-4400.

94. Albahli, S. and Albattah, W. (2020). Detection of coronavirus disease from X-ray images using deep learning and transfer learning algorithms. Journal of X-Ray Science and Technology, 28, 841-850.

95. Holzinger, A., Langs, G., Denk, H., Zatloukal, K., Müller, H. et al. (2019). Causability and explainability of artificial intelligence in medicine. Wiley Interdisciplinary Reviews: Data Mining and Knowledge Discovery, 9(4), e1312.

96. Sakallaris, B.R., Miller, W.L., Saper, R.B., Kreitzer, M.J., Jonas, W.B. et al. (2016). Meeting the challenge of a more person-centered future for US Healthcare. Global Advances in Health and Medicine, 5, 51-60.

97. Khan, A.A., Laghari, A., Shaikh, A.A., Dootio, M.A., Estrela et al. (2021). A Blockchain Security Module for Brain-Computer Interface (BCI) with Multimedia Life Cycle Framework (MLCF). Neuroscience Informatics, 2(1), 100030.

98. Bahri, L. and Girdzijauskas, S. (2018). When Trust Saves Energy: A Reference Framework for Proof of Trust (PoT) Blockchains. Companion Proceedings of The Web Conference 2018.

99. Guo, S., Guo, X., Zhang, X. and Vogel, D.R. (2018). Doctor-patient relationship strength's impact in an online healthcare community. Information Technology for Development, 24, 279-300.

100. Chang, Y., Hsu, P., Wang, Y. and Chang, P. (2019). Integration of online and offline health services: The role of doctor-patient online interaction. Patient Education and Counseling, 102(10), 1905-1910.

The Building Blocks of Health 4.0 – Internet of Things, Big Data with Cloud and Fog Computing

Vania V. Estrela[1] [0000-0002-4465-7691], Anand Deshpande[2] [0000-0002-1500-0981],
Ricardo T. Lopes[3] [0000-0001-7250-824X], Hugo H.P. da Silva[4] [0000-0001-6764-8432],
Aline C. Intorne[5,6] [0000-0001-8015-6926], Dalmo Stutz[7] [0000-0003-1408-1756],
J.J.P.C. Rodrigues[8] [0000-0001-8657-3800], Luciana P. Oliveira[9] [0000-0002-3375-3346]

[1] Telecommunications Department, Fluminense Federal University (UFF), RJ, Brazil,
vania.estrela.phd@ieee.org
[2] Electronics and Communication Engineering, Angadi Institute of Technology and
Management, Belagavi, India, deshpande.anandb@gmail.com
[3] University Federal of Rio de Janeiro (COPPE/UFRJ), Rio de Janeiro, RJ, Brazil,
rlopes@coppe.ufrj.br
[4] Instituto de Telecomunicacoes, Instituto Superior Tecnico, Torre Norte - Piso 10, Av.
Rovisco Pais, 1, 1049-001, Lisboa, Lisboa, Portugal, hsilva@lx.it.pt
[5] Laboratory of Physiology and Biochemistry of Microorganisms, Universidade Estadual
do Norte Fluminense Darcy Ribeiro, Campos dos Goytacazes, RJ, 28013-602, Brazil
[6] Laboratory of Chemistry and Biology, Instituto Federal de Educação, Ciência e Tecnologia
do Rio de Janeiro, Volta Redonda, RJ, 27213-100, Brazil, aline.intorne@ifrj.edu.br
[7] Instituto Politecnico do Rio de Janeiro, Nova Friburgo, RJ, Brazil, stutz@iprj.uerj.br
[8] Federal University of Piaui (UFPI), Electrical Engineering, Fortaleza, CE, Brazil,
joeljr@ieee.org
[9] IFPB Campus Joao Pessoa, Av. Primeiro de Maio, 720, Jaguaribe, Joao Pessoa, PB, Brazil,
oliveira.ifpb@gmail.com

1. Introduction

Healthcare poses challenges worldwide, requiring advanced solutions. Information and Communication Technologies (ICTs) have influenced the access, productivity, and quality of virtually all healthcare processes positively. The term eHealth signifies ICTs providing a pathway towards superior healthcare and has attracted significant public and private interest with increased investment [1, 2].

eHealth evolves based on Industry 4.0 standard (I4S) that can be viewed as an explicit governmental commitment to foster a collection of technologies while laying the cultural and legal foundations to achieve the full potential to ICT benefits in healthcare. In addition to the technologies involved, there are also development plans, including enterprise management and labor organization, protocols, dissemination, and training. Healthcare 4.0 or Health 4.0 (H4.0) relies mainly on the conception of Cyber-Physical Systems (CPSs), which integrate communication, computing, and control [3, 4]. CPSs rely heavily on three technological paradigms:

(a) Internet of Things (IoT): It has the pervasive presence of a diversity of distinctively addressable cooperating items such as mobile gadgets, sensors, and actuators;
(b) Cloud Computing (CC)/Fog Computing (FC): They provide virtually boundless storage, computing, and communication means as conveniences, i.e., on-demand as well as pay-per-use; and
(c) Big Data (BD) Analytics: It refers to extract worth from perplexing, massive amounts of data.

The healthcare sector experiences the I4.0 impact, moving eHealth towards H4.0. Smart health refers to embracing ICT-based healthcare solutions, but the H4.0 paradigm has its peculiarities. H4.0 employs three main paradigms: the IoT, BD, and CC. The H4.0 multidisciplinary nature prevents stakeholders in this arena from following technological progress. This chapter introduces the technical I4S elements appropriate for healthcare to improve H4.0's understanding, while it overviews the cross-disciplinary interactions underneath H4.0.

The H4.0 contributions are fivefold [5-11]: (i) introduction of the I4S pillars' relevant properties; (ii) review state-of-art applications; (iii) discuss main benefits and challenges; and (iv) draw lessons learned.

Section 2 describes each pillar's impact on H4.0. Then, Section 3 reviews all the foremost application scenarios advantageous to H4.0. The leading ICT benefits and challenges for H4.0 appear in Section 4, bearing in mind patients', caretakers', and healthcare specialists' points of view. Section 5 extracts the lessons learned and concludes this chapter.

2. ICT Fundamentals of Health 4.0

Wireless and mobile technologies excel regarding connectivity with affordable services, and inexpensive wireless sensors/actuators, e.g.,

(i) Large-scale Data Centers (DCs) with virtualization technologies enable new services or quality levels with good cost-efficiency;
(ii) The escalating availability and quality of medical apps linking mobile devices and clinical practice; and
(iii) Support for obesity, chronic diseases, or the aging population, among other needs, through large-scale analysis of massive data.

The P4 Medicine concept results from this radical change [24], i.e., preventive, predictive, personalized, and participatory. P4 relies on a broad comprehension of each patient's biology instead of seeking treatment groups. P4 expressively shrinks health budgets by minimizing hospitalization, unnecessary drug use, and other procedures [24, 26] by focusing on three major H4.0 enablers (pillars): IoT, CC, and BD. Other technological and nontechnological aspects related to H4.0 can be considered either secondary or addressable by less mature technologies, e.g., 5G and 6G [27] undoubtedly play significant roles with near-zero latency, cutting-edge Quality of Service (QoS) capabilities, and higher data rates that bring multiple benefits to health solutions [28].

2.1. Internet of Medical Things (IoMT) in H4.0

IoT objects have many understandings and undertones, including Radio Frequency Identification (RFID) [29] and Wireless Sensor Networks (WSNs) [30], and all share strict requirements regarding size, power consumption, processing capabilities among others. Specifically, Wireless Body Area Networks (Wireless BANs or WBANs) contain wireless devices like sensors and actuators attached to or implanted in the human body [31]. This complex and heterogeneous IoT scenario often addresses these different logical layers from bottom to top [1, 2]:

   (i) Perception Layer (PL), which contains sensors and actuators;
  (ii) Transmission Layer (TL) that conveys sensed data to the upper layers;
 (iii) Computation Layer (CL) in charge of processing information and making decisions; and
  (iv) Application Layer (AL) built on the IoT infrastructure for high-level intentions such as healthcare, home automation, transport, manufacturing and more.

Most IoT research has handled TL and its communication protocols. IoT still appears fuzzy for some aspects, although designing and implementing low-power, highly-reliable, and Internet-enabled communication are common requirements. [33] discusses standards, related challenges, and opportunities.

The most recent IoT advances overlap with I4.0 but upgrade IoT. They either add reference architectures with logistic and business specifics [35] or add IoT to already automated processes, with some new opportunities and challenges as a consequence [36]. The H4.0 paradigm is restyling healthcare with high-tech, financial benefits, in addition to social prospects. IoT is the primary expediter for distributed applications, expressively decreasing costs while increasing health outcomes. However, behavioral stakeholders' changes are necessary since wireless communication progress heavily supports real-time physiological parameter monitoring, persistent chronic disease care, early diagnosis and medical emergency management [14, 38].

Hence, H4.0 devices depend strongly on IoT while also functioning with general-purpose smart devices [14]. For instance, IoT empowers interactions among intelligent machines to learn about users and their environment for decision-making [43]. Some IoT paradigm variations follow:

   (i) Wearable Internet of Things (WIoT): It implements telehealth to create an ecosystem for automated interventions. Body sensors with WIoT can observe valuable data pieces to enrich individuals' everyday life quality (e.g., tracking behaviors, wellness levels, habits and more and connect patients/caretakers to medical infrastructures [44].
  (ii) Internet of Health Things (IoHT): It combines mobile apps, wearable devices, and other connected apparatuses and leverages continuous context-aware sensor equipment.

(iii) Internet of Medical Things (IoMT): It covers implantable, injectable, ingestible, wearable, and personal mobile items connected to the Internet thus acting as a personal hub.

(iv) Internet of Nano Things (IoNT): It refers to nanomedicine applications of IoT to implement more personalized monitoring, diagnostics, and treatment to implement proactive checking, preventive health, chronic illness management, and follow-up care [2].

(v) Internet of Mobile Health Things (m-IoT): Its connectivity model concerns low-power personal-area networks and growing 5G/6G networks, accentuating the existing features intrinsic to contributing entities' global mobility [46].

2.2. Cloud and Fog Computing in H4.0

The CC paradigm permits utility computing, i.e., leasing computing resources (i.e., computational power, data warehousing, and networking assets) in real-time, with minimal provider interaction. Hence, CC simplifies operations. It does not require a cautious dimensioning and forecast of mandatory resources, permitting pay-per-use billing. Moreover, cloud customers profit from seemingly infinite resources on-demand and can either leverage or dispense Everything-as-a-Service (XaaS). The most typical are Infrastructure-as-a-Service (IaaS), Platform-as-a-Service (PaaS), or Software-as-a-Service (SaaS) [47], with further variations as these are cases of Function-as-a-Service (FaaS, aka, serverless computing). Notably, CC satisfies many IoT needs even to the IoT upper layers [49, 32]. Migration to Cloud services is a growing trend whose main drives are [1, 2]

1. Responsiveness,
2. Storage scalability,
3. Processing scalability,
4. Easy data sharing/acquisition/integration,
5. Better service performance,
6. Superior security,
7. Improved reliability, and
8. Economic gains.

CC shortcomings initiate primarily in the communication process amid the end-device and the DC hosting Cloud services like bandwidth, latency, cost, and connection readiness limiting CC uses. The burst of pervasive gadgets leads to service degradation. It significantly challenges the CC model making it incompatible to meet all healthcare requirements from different architectures, concepts, terms, and expressions [31].

FC transfers some CC services to the edge network, handy to stakeholder devices also relying on user resources. In consequence, distributing the burden among end devices and cloud DCs brings local-term security, low-latency rates, faster responsiveness, and better system performance scalability, among other advantages. FC heightens on-time service delivery and mitigates several Cloud caveats, like delay, cost overheads, and jitter while transferring information [31].

FC also supports stakeholder mobility, resources, heterogeneity of interfaces, and distributed data analytics for applications' requiring low latency. Likewise, it simplifies managing computing, storage, and networking services between DCs and end-devices. Therefore, FC is a powerful tool supporting decentralized, intelligent processing of BD to integrate physical and CPSs, thus helping the IoT reach its huge potential.

When clients correspond to mobile nodes, and the processing capabilities drift to radio networks, this concept becomes Mobile Edge Computing (MEC). The term Mobile Cloud connotes that mobile devices (i) are remote servers' clients running applications (resources-rich); (ii) are CC resource providers in a mobile peer-to-peer network; (iii) transfer assignments to a (local) edge cloud.

The cloudlet idea refers to a middle-tier in the mobile device and the CC context. The cloudlet is a self-managed DC in a box, a mini cloud with enough resources to host workloads for a few mobile consumers concurrently. Other H4.0 elements are indirectly embedded by CC, namely Big Data (BD) and IoT, Visual/Virtual Computing, and other medical applications.

Characteristic CC benefits include integrating costs and resource optimization specifically significant for the healthcare scenario. CC can simplify health processes [9, 10, 33], promote better practices, inspire and prompt more innovations.

Healthcare-as-a-Service (HaaS) consists of CC adoption in healthcare [59, 47]. HaaS applications benefit from on-demand, scalable, and virtually inestimable computation power, storage, and networking resources compared with the expected drivers to espouse CC in more wide-ranging applications and the IoT paradigm. Additional aspects are necessary, such as easy information sharing, uncomplicated data collection, and integration with boosted performance, convenience, reliability, and security [35-37]. Moreover, mobile and personal device technologies benefit from CC and FC for managing data growth and anywhere-and-anytime call for medical services [9]. Specific healthcare contributions concern the overall QoS improvement: when many intelligent devices grow into an increasing portion of the patients' (besides caretakers', and physicians') daily lives, availability and communication latency can affect predictability, delaying decisions, and potentially disrupt healthcare service delivery [38]. Mobile CC alleviates or solves these issues, provides contextual information systems, improves user-friendliness and personalized services with quality adaptive service management.

2.3. Big Data in Health 4.0

Existing technologies entail datasets inadequate for all-purpose computers. Over time, the expression BD has moved from dataset features concerning current technologies to others that aim at economically extracting value from massive volumes of heterogeneous data with high-velocity capture, discovery, or analysis [39]. The 5-V methodology captures the most significant standard BD properties:

  (i)   Volume accounts for data scale increases;
 (ii)   Velocity entails collection and analysis subject to time bounds;
(iii)   Variety means that data may contain various types, i.e., structured, unstructured, and semi-structured elements;
(iv)   Veracity implies changeable trustworthiness degrees in data, according to provenance, management, and processing; and

(v) Value measures the whole architecture, and it targets economic value extraction.

This 5-V classification shows the strong context-dependent BD nature. These requirements challenge the available BD technologies.

BD and other H4.0 concepts derive from I4.0 directly and massively [39]. Awareness about the wide-ranging variety of data sources is paramount to reach BD's effectiveness in H4.0 fully. The most traditional BD source is Social Media (SM). I4.0 uses data more directly to tune the value chain in an automated manner. From this point of view, the whole I4.0 emerges as an effort to foster timely feedback between raw data collection and the design-production-delivery cycle. Additionally, SMs are reshaping health-related interactions, altering how healthcare stakeholders view and share health records. As web resources access affords more valuable information, SM and correlated technologies dramatically change medical practices.

Another important BD source is enterprise data. Enterprises already yield and manage BD by the same token as healthcare institutions ranging from internal accounting, employee data, internal communications, scheduling to data custody requirements from regulations. Even if not strictly related to health, this data enriches the list of potential sources with implementations encompassing biological, medical, and other aspects. The extensive stream data exploitation, enriched with more data sources and metadata, will increase I4.0 demands. This will add to external data (i.e., from outside the enterprise) from all stakeholders calling for growing application and evolution of BD technologies.

Progress prompts further data increase with real-time systems monitoring people well-being, generating structured and unstructured streamed BD. Furthermore, medical tests, imageries, and descriptions from clinicians yield patient clinical records under several forms and denominations [39-43] like

(a) Electronic Health Records (EHRs) that report episodes of medicinal care across manifold care delivery organizations;

(b) Electronic Medical Records (EMRs) emblematize real-time patient health records (HRs) with access to evidence-based decision support tools, possibly aiding clinicians in decision-making; and

(c) Personal Health Records (PHR) are a layperson's permanent tools, typically operated by patients/caretakers, to handle relevant information, promote health preservation, and chronic disease controlling.

Finally, the creation of large amounts of biological data from transcriptomics, microbiomics, proteomics, genomics, metabolomics, epigenomics, etc. occurring at a colossal speed and scale [26] is organized in the fourfold levels [44]: (i) molecular, (ii) tissue, (iii) patient, and (iv) population.

3. Health 4.0 Application Scenarios

H4.0's trust on IoT brings about all remote monitoring facets to enable implementation in different settings, stretching from long-term elderly care and home-produced surveillance to acute rehabilitation structures. They produce escalating heterogeneous data volumes thanks to the high-velocity acquisition, discovery, and analysis requiring new-generation BD designs to mine their value [45]. Then, cloud architectures arise to securely and reliably meet processing and storage requirements to explore BD [45].

Combining IoT, CC/FC, and BD allows ways out towards efficiently renewing consolidated practices or even providing groundbreaking results to mitigate long-lasting healthcare issues. The main health-related scenarios utilizing these ICT pillars and their convergence follow (refer to Figure 1).

Figure 1. Main H4.0 application scenarios

3.1. Monitoring Physiological and Pathological Signals

The IoT paradigm supported by mobile communication technologies, wearables [16-27, 66-72], and sensing devices often requires WSNs, WBANs, on-demand CC/FC resources, and BD technologies as a valuable framework for pervasive monitoring. The resulting framework supports the collection of HRs, potentially generating statistical information related to health conditions [2, 12, 43, 76], and the delivery of novel cloud services [47], able to replace or complement hospital information systems in effect. This automated approach lowers dramatically the possibility of introducing errors compared to methods requiring manual intervention [47]. Patients' remote data monitoring consists of three main components:

(i) Data sensing to gather physiological and activity data;
(ii) Communication hardware and software to convey data to a remote center; and
(iii) Analysis systems to extract clinically-relevant information.

Applications can be either in-body or on-body, depending on the types of sensors [35]. Advanced sensors [31] often appear in mobile devices, e.g., accelerometers, gyroscopes, and sensors for temperature, humidity, ECG, glucose, blood pressure, and gas. These devices monitor patient conditions continuously. IoT devices can transmit data to remote DCs for data grouping, leveraging apparently infinite data warehousing, scalable processing aptitude, and the high service availability provided by CC [43]. This scheme requires reliable networks for storing, processing, and retrieving medical records remotely in the Cloud and imposes many challenges for network connectivity and traffic [38]. Indeed, ultra-reliable monitoring is a necessity among the scenarios driving the 5G evolution [27]. Other options take advantage of FC at intelligent gateways with information mining, distributed storage, and warning services at the network's edge to alleviate remote cloud services challenges. FC also helps in augmented-reality latency-sensitive applications, ubiquitous brain monitoring via EEG-based brain-computer interfaces, cognitive support systems, and implantable/wearable medical devices to improve/restore body functions [1, 2, 53].

3.2. Self-Management, Monitoring, and Prevention

H4.0 significantly supports self-management. Indeed, BD technologies allow a shift from illness cure to its prevention [45], which agrees with P4 medicine [24]. Researchers envision intelligent services beyond simple functions, e.g., indicating measured data and storing records temporarily, while providing effective feedback to individuals. These solutions can implement algorithms to prevent diseases by finding modifiable risk factors and designing health behavior change interventions. Chronic disease management is another vital self-management feature. For instance, systems for managing and preventing diabetes and obesity can promote good habits [48, 49] and fitness programs [38, 14]).

3.3. Medication Intake Monitoring and Smart Pharmaceuticals

Mature and chronically ill subjects tend toward medication noncompliance intensified by cognitive impairments. Medication intake monitoring systems are valuable to address these concerns as they assess treatment efficacy [82] quantitatively. Early prototypes designed for the elderly leveraged the combined use of WSNs and RFID [93]. According to the extreme relevance of drug delivery timing for attaining optimal effectiveness and minimizing adverse effects, several mobile apps are available to remind scheduling, prescription details, and medication intake tracking [94]. Advanced wearable or ingestible sensors or Smart Pharmaceuticals (SFs) also appear [95]. SFs are contingent to intelligent electronic packages, delivery systems, or pills [53, 54] using IoT connections to communicate with remote systems to compile, store, and analyze data. Future SFs will collect micro and macro-level metadata to obtain different disease insights, aid service, theragnostics, and Personalized Healthcare (PH).

3.4. Personalized Healthcare

PH intends to be user-centric, i.e., decisions are patient-specific rather than related to patient treatment groups [14, 44]. Data analyses from multiple sources like implantable, wearable, or extra therapy delivery devices facilitate health/social care decision-making and delivery. This work calls bodily sources as wearables in short [16-27, 66-72]. Highly personalized services follow H4.0 properties as user-centrality and data integration from heterogeneous sources, emphasizing the P4 paradigm [24, 55], heavily relying on each individual's genetic information. Personalized omics broadly understand each individual's biology, impacting inclinations, screening, diagnosis, prospects, pharmacogenomics, and surveillance [26]. Accordingly, BD analytics is fundamental for customized healthcare, both at the individual and population level [55, 56].

3.5. Cloud-Based Health Systems

CC architectures have mainly strengthened and simplified the design, improvement, and deployment of systems for collecting, processing, and sharing clinical records [57, 58], administrative information [60], or medicinal images [5, 61, 62]. These architectures enhance the data collection. For example, entities often have mobile user interfaces with CC services for gathering and managing information. Furthermore, information sharing across different medical structures [61] or between hospitals and patients [59, 103] improves as these systems also integrate dissimilar data formats [60, 63]. However, focusing on security and privacy often disregards system performance.

3.6. Telepathology, Telemedicine, and Disease Monitoring

The initial telepathology attempts included remote acquisition, transmission, and inspection of pathology specimens. The mixing of robotics, microscopy, video imaging, databases, and broadband telecommunications promised an infrastructure for telepathology services. Nowadays, ICTs support telemedicine, telepathology, and disease watching [31, 63]. Available applications belong to two classes: (i) generic frameworks for most use cases and (ii) platforms for particular diseases, e.g., cancer, cardiovascular problems, Parkinson, diabetes, and Alzheimer [35]. In turn, these monitoring systems can feed large-scale studies and inform treatments tailored to the specific individual outcomes (like in P4 medicine).

Indeed, cameras coupled with operating room lights capture open surgery for a potentially unrestricted total of spectators. These tools enable teleconsultation, avoiding the consultant's physical presence. Using movable cameras in surgery may help telepresence and enable telesurgery [53].

Best-effort Internet connections do not support several application classes (e.g., recreate a microscope's effect locally) that become viable with constrained virtual paths to Fog services without higher CC access delays.

3.7. Ambient-Assisted Living (AAL)

Better nutrition and healthcare improve people getting old help handle the rising costs including the elderly and those with chronic conditions [38], i.e., Enhanced Living Environments (ELEs) avoid hospitalization. Several ICTs enable homecare relying on:

(1) Remote patient monitoring entailing safety and easy implementation of clinical interventions [82]; and

(2) Robotics which can connect the elderly with others (e.g., distant relatives, caretakers, or physicians) without moving/traveling and learning new technologies [7].

Vital signs such as blood pressure, heartbeat rate, and accelerometer data can help estimate elderly and disabled people's overall health. Wearables and WBANs are paramount to Ambient-Assisted Living (AAL). WBANs can mingle with ambient sensors to combine the enormous amount of monitoring parameters and efficiently handle AAL patients. Artificial Intelligence (AI) can aid AAL healthcare systems with automated learning, decision-making, and planning to alert a healthcare facility automatically when deviations from the usual activities and parameters appear or arrange for medical or lifestyle changes. CC and FC can provide on-demand AAL infrastructure capabilities to collect patients' data in real-time while processing information [62].

Table 1. Main benefits and challenges from the adoption of I4S pillars in healthcare

Technology	Benefits	Challenges
IoMT	• Improved medical devices (with closed-loop design such as new service lines and predictive maintenance) [73] • Open communication standards promote interoperability, and evolvability [74]	• Power restrictions [73] • Security [76, 47]. • Scalability [47, 76, 77]
Cloud/Fog Computing	• Infrastructure aimed at high-level functions (such as data breakdown and information systems) • Paradigmatic framework affording services to patients, caretakers, or healthcare staff [29]	• Performance monitoring • Infrastructure opacity • Data secrecy [10] • Infrastructure readiness [9, 10]
Big Data	• New perceptions and actionable info from fresh data sources [82] • Usual descriptive research transformation into predictive besides prescriptive parts [83]	• Greater heterogeneity [84] • Analytical opacity [86]

3.8. Rehabilitation

Home-Based Rehabilitation (HBR) will significantly save costs and improve quality for the patient and care taker AAL systems. WBANs are the primary tools for detecting and tracking human actions in rehabilitation. Unlike generic AAL, HBR contains several specific constraints, requirements, and solutions [63-72], integrating multi-sensor data, real-time patient feedback, and virtual reality. Biofeedback is a key WBAN feature in HBR to measure physiological activity and other parameters while providing stakeholder feedback. Hence, patients and caretakers can control, modify and accomplish physiological activities effectively [63-72].

4. Discussion

The I4S converging paradigms change and trigger a progressive evolution towards e-health to expand further and accelerate the H4.0 usage with new prospects, obstacles, and risks in MCPSs regarding a conscious and effective integration of novel methods and technologies and tools.

4.1. Benefits

Several IoT aspects apply to healthcare almost entirely as [73-81] below:

(a) Closed-loop design: Feedback from all stakeholders helps designers understand product usability and effectiveness to improve projects by analyzing real-world usage data, despite eventual design delays.
(b) Predictive maintenance: IoT permits fault forecasting and maintenance before failures occur thanks to continuous data flow, allowing for timely servicing or substitution or avoiding machine downtime altogether. The impact on the economy and management of life-critical services can hardly be overstated.
(c) New service lines: Manufacturers can offer better or more convenient remote monitoring and maintenance services through devices that can be continuously improved or fixed.

Electro-medical communication systems require robustness and reliability and are often tightly bound with latency and jitter. Additionally, the robustness of mutual radio interference allows the multiple WSNs to coexist, with different radio technologies, in small volumes (the human body's surroundings). The adoption of open standard protocols like IEEE 802.15.6 and IEEE 802.15.4 [74] foster various non-mutually exclusive solutions, improving interoperability among different retailer devices and components, with cost reductions and improved system evolvability. Along these lines, the TCP/IP communication ubiquity and interoperability have already provided real-world testing, wide Wi-Fi adoption, and Internet access [73-81]. H4.0 benefits from technologies, merging WBANs, Personal Area Networks (PANs), Local Area Networks, and other Internet know-hows globally.

The overall CC emerging picture is a fundamental H4.0enabler. First of all, it is a potent, cost-effective infrastructure for high-level functions (data analysis, high-end information systems) and models. To start with Cloud technologies need characterization (refer to Section 2). Then CC inspires and supports the HaaS mindset by (i) offering services to patients and (ii) analyses, diagnostic, and communication services to staff. HaaS can deliver less costly services highly impacting time, transportation, comfort, and coverage. The result is better life quality for patients and some operators with competitive business advantages.

Similarly, healthcare operators can benefit from best-of-breed, physical-location independent, fully outsourced, and cost-effective Internet services backed by CC, e.g., as Software-as-a-Service. FC can provide the technical means to enjoy the previous benefits even though it uses ubiquitous as well as personal mobile terminals familiar to a large population. Pharmaceutical Cloud technologies are essential to achieve (logical) decentralization of execution and planning systems with the seamless introduction of humans where and when needed (e.g., crowdsourcing complex tasks [84-103]). Hence, the future of H4.0 will be even more tightly bound to CC research and evolution.

BD techniques can extract value (actionable information) from amounts of data previously unmanageable. Healthcare operators can now explore their processes looking for new possibilities of continuous and massive data collection, knowing that BD techniques can extract new meaning and valuable information from it. Adopting a BD approach, the medical researcher can naturally transform descriptive research questions (what happened?) into predictive ones (what could happen?) to reach the prescriptive ones (what to do, to get one specific achievable outcome?) [83]. By discovering new data sources or applying the derived data-driven results, the healthcare stakeholders can effectively use BD analytics to reduce concerns and uncertainty, and ultimately cause the improvement of the healthcare system [82] in one of its many aspects. Indeed, BD analytics can back up evidence-based medicine, genomic analysis, patient-profile studies, or pre-adjudicate fraud analysis.

4.2. Challenges

IoT in healthcare is in its infancy [14]. Most design matters relate to either smart-objects or communication technologies. Energy is a major technical challenge. Research is needed on energy harvesting, energy conservation, energy, and usage to design and develop zero-entropy systems harvesting energy from the environment and not wasting any under operation [24, 73]. Scalability is another important IoT challenge since interconnected objects will substantially outnumber average Internet, and well-being devices/ services with high demand. Therefore, architecture scalability is a main concern due to drastic escalation of the connected devices [81] that can benefit from hierarchical subdomains [47, 76, 77] and specific BANs design issues [21-23, 35, 46, 63, 64, 68, 71-74]. Moreover, further investigation will help develop and design appropriate IoMT security solutions, e.g., primitives resilient to run-time attacks as well as scalable security protocols. Today's IoT systems cannot fulfill the desired functional requirements and bear security/privacy risks [76], principally when also addressing scalability requirements [77]. Existing security solutions fail to scale to large heterogeneous networks and CPSs with constrained resources and real-time requirements.

Moreover, since sensors continuously monitoring health signals generate enormous data (often feeding critical applications), secure and effective architectures are needed for BD. The literature shows that protecting IoT requires a holistic cybersecurity framework covering all abstraction layers of heterogeneous systems and across platform boundaries [76]. Wearables generate additional security implications involving hacking that need secure, unique management and authentication [23, 24, 53, 55, 81]. Therefore, due to the resource-limited devices usually espoused, it is indispensable to design lightweight algorithms in the protected data administration system [18, 35-37, 47, 50, 76, 78, 92, 93, 101, 102]. The Cloud provides them as-a-service facility with attractive prices by masking the actual infrastructure, sparing the customer from the operation details, and offering economies-of-scale prices [9, 10, 14, 31, 33, 38, 88, 105].

Infrastructure opacity can limit CC when performance is required. Indeed, computations, communication protocols, and network performances still pose obstacles [18, 104, 107, 108]. Moreover, although cloud technologies are scalable, the literature reports scalability concerns [29, 47, 76, 77, 80-84]. The work in [29] examines issues and techniques in Cloud status and performance monitoring. Recently, research has also focused on public-cloud network performances [29-38]. Hence, when dealing with data-intensive applications, co-design approaches involving different stakeholders must be taken into account to keep control and troubleshoot service performance [57, 97-102].

The FC paradigm brings other open issues to be a viable healthcare reality. FC exacerbates scalability issues as it potentially deals with extremely high amounts of small devices possibly integrated with BANs. Scalability and decentralization need proper tests in these massive systems. Computing nodes and applications being executed on top of the Fog also need correct configuration, safety, reliability, availability, flexibility, maintainability, and power efficiency [29, 33, 46, 73].

Since CC and FC allow for processing user information in third-party hardware and software, they introduce strong concerns about privacy and loss of control over data due to distrust in the provider storing sensitive information. A recent solution introduces an identity management architecture enabling patient-controlled EHR partial disclosure to selected recipients [31, 32, 38-43, 47, 49, 53, 63]. Such solutions need research on validation, standardization, greater adoption, and complexity costs.

However, solutions increasingly leverage external services while keeping advanced security settings [57-63]. Moreover, these services offer increased availability, providing uninterrupted delivery with minimum downtimes [16]. Critical applications entail availability, especially if they involve access technologies prone to outages. 5G requires high-reliability technologies, according to the extent of their geographic and population coverage. It is worth noting that a temporally or spatially uneven 5G deployment may create or worsen the digital divide's unprecedented levels instead of relieving it.

Multi-cloud solutions have also appeared to improve critical services' availability [100-104]. CC promises can result from intelligent dynamic resource allocation depending on the service (e.g., SaaS, PaaS, or IaaS) that are computationally severe, requiring cloud resources themselves. The currently open issue of complexity tends to grow dramatically, requiring future research [31, 32, 38, 47, 49, 53, 63].

The remarkable amount of health data fulfills the BD necessities of volume and velocity, besides variety. Significant H4.0 challenges within the BD paradigm are the heterogeneity of sources, formats, and data attributes (an extreme illustration of BD Variety) [1, 42-48, 53-57, 82-86] that require semantic heterogeneity and interoperability frameworks. Moreover, due to constant real-time monitoring, the mounting data velocity has increased concerning traditional data. Indeed, its volume is growing exponentially, requiring proper solutions to stock progressively increasing information quantities, making healthcare data challenging. Finally, since BD analytics and outcomes must be error-free and trustworthy, BD practices, due to machine-learning algorithms on unparalleled and previously unknown amounts of data, present an opacity issue that is most significant when dealing with health, life-related decisions, and high-impact and socially relevant matters, such as H4.0 [5-11]. The lack of BD transparency has risen, mainly regarding AI and robotics regulation and innovation [82-86].

4.3. Patients and Professionals

Staff and patient viewpoints are necessary to investigate the H4.0 reception and extrapolating sensible hopes about their evolution to account for non-ICT actors.

The studies [91-108] have investigated staff experiences with patients accessing their EHRs and sought differences in experiences and attitudes according to hospitals, staff, psychiatry and physical care. Results revealed positive experiences with patients highlighting their EHR mistakes, omissions, and better information about their healthcare. Minor differences in experiences and attitudes emerged at the different hospitals and among staff members, while significant experience and attitude differences appeared between psychiatric and somatic care. Psychiatry professionals questioned the service's suitability for the most vulnerable patients, suggesting adaptations and training for EHR access by patients and caretakers. EHR represents an indispensable evolution component from e-health to H4.0, especially in self-management, so that H4.0 expected positive outcomes and caveats (e.g., the skepticism from fields such as psychiatry). There are two scenarios regarding expectations on patient experiences [106-108]:

- Self-management, wellness monitoring, and prevention; and
- Medication intake monitoring and smart pharmaceuticals.

Both utilized a smartphone app to monitor adjuvant endocrine therapy and its side-effects with a diary, peer support forum, and prescription reminder. The objective was to counter the low adherence to the treatment over the prescription years, resulting in a two to three-fold augmented mortality risk while exploring the acceptability, the perceived expediency of the App services, and its usability. Most patients appreciated the App and its services. This outcome supports the higher adherence hope to therapy, and therefore lowered risks are expected in the future. Single cases did not value the App more than the information provided by health professionals. Moreover, the disadvantage is the access deficiency concerning e-health platforms for low-income people, from rural communities, and the elderly.

H4.0 needs a continuous, straightforward, and bidirectional data exchange among stakeholders with better and accurate monitoring of health conditions and medicine intake. These new services will demand special care in preferring technologies that partake the broadest accessibility. Conversely, H4.0 is already extending the population served by high-quality healthcare in PH, telepathology, telemedicine, disease monitoring, and AAL scenarios. Economics restrict traditional versions heavily, and expanding service availability to the population is urgent. Users' technology acceptance and usage also require comprehensible education campaigns.

4.4. Lessons Learned

The evolution of ICTs heavily impacts the healthcare sector. First, H4.0 entails the ubiquitous and continuous PH services with wearables and IoMT for assorted medical equipment, WBANs, and nanodevices. The impact on well-being and the overall quality of people's lives will improve by promoting good habits and timely treatments while lessening hospitalization and healthcare costs. BD analysis tools and platforms, including AI, can extract knowledge from massive fast-flowing wearables data. Caveats include unprecedented data sizes and richness, while benefits encompass previously unnoticeable data patterns/correlations for assessment and further advancement of prevention, diagnostics, and cure.

CC/FC and the 5G infrastructure are less apparent in H4.0. Albeit supporting medical services' ubiquity with high performance affordably, some future drawbacks follow: (i) security of gadgets, communications, as well as processes; (ii) the extensive watching, selectiveness, and gigantic automation raise privacy and ethical issues; (iii) complexity of new systems limiting or hampering their complete understanding and control; (iv) the trouble catching up with novelty and regulation, in addition to civic vigilance; and (v) the multidisciplinary H4.0 nature involving non-technicalities.

Security and secrecy are the most prominent and well-studied multidisciplinary issues. Nonetheless, integrating different technologies into novel scenarios calls for ongoing studies and new solution assessments. The implicit tradeoff between some solutions besides other problems worsens things. For instance, security enhancements often complicate complexity, transparency, system understanding, vigilance, and regulation, obstructing potentially rapid innovation.

5. Conclusion

This work addresses the healthcare sector's needs and those in health information systems with automation to cost-effectively face the new IT field's previously unknown issues toward the envisioned H4.0 evolution. This text presents the main technological groups from the I4.0, namely the IoT, CC and FC, and BD Analytics, focusing on their application in healthcare. The healthcare sector is already moving towards ICT-backed e-health. Further transformations in H4.0 embrace CC-based health ICT, innovative monitoring of physiological and pathological signals, prescription intake, and activities. New methods, processes, and equipment will improve AAL, home-based rehabilitation, and PH, benefiting from closed-loop design, predictive maintenance, advanced service lines, and open standards development. Some caveats are infrastructure opacity, the necessity for monitoring, and heterogeneity of formats/standards.

References

1. Aceto, G., Persico, V. and Pescapé, A. (2020). Industry 4.0 and health: Internet of things, big data, and cloud computing for healthcare 4.0. J. Ind. Inf. Integr., 18, 100129.
2. Aceto, G., Persico, V. and Pescapé, A. (2018). The role of information and communication technologies in healthcare: Taxonomies, perspectives, and challenges. J. Network and Computer Applications, 107.
3. Estrela, V.V., Saotome, O., Loschi, H.J., Hemanth, J., Farfan, W.S. et al. (2018). Emergency response cyber-physical framework for landslide avoidance with sustainable electronics. Technologies, 6(2), 42.
4. Zhou, K., Liu, T. and Zhou, L. (2015). Industry 4.0: Towards future industrial opportunities and challenges. *In:* Proc. 2015 12th Int'l Conf. Fuzzy Syst. and Knowledge Disc. (FSKD). IEEE.

5. Aceto, G., Persico, V. and Pescapé, A. (2019). A survey on information and communication technologies for industry 4.0: State of the art, taxonomies, perspectives, and challenges. IEEE Communications Surveys & Tutorials.

6. Islam, S.M.R., Kwak, D., Kabir, M.H., Hossain, M., Kwak, K.S. et al. (2015). The Internet of things for health care: A comprehensive survey, IEEE Access, 3.

7. Khelassi, A. and Estrela, V.V. (2021) Advances in multidisciplinary medical technologies – Engineering, modeling and findings. Proceedings of the International Workshop on Medical Technologies 2019 (ICHSMT 2019), Springer Nature, Zurich, Switzerland.

8. Estrela, V.V., Tavares, J.M.R.S., Wang, L. and Shi, F. (2018). Special Issue: Soft computing techniques for image analysis in the medical industry – Current trends, challenges and solutions. Editorial, IEEE Access.

9. Ahuja, S.P., Mani, S. and Zambrano, J. (2012). A survey of the state of cloud computing in healthcare. Network and Communication Technologies, 1(2).

10. Ermakova, T., J. Huenges, Erek, K. and Zarnekow, R. (2013). Cloud computing in healthcare – A literature review on current state of research. Proc. AMCIS 2013, 17.

11. Archenaa, J. and Anita, E.M. (2015). A survey of big data analytics in healthcare and government. Procedia Comp. Sc., 50.

12. Zou, Q. and Li, X.-B. (2013). Survey of map reduce frame operation in bioinformatics. Briefings in Bioinformatics, 15(4).

13. Michel, J. and Ecarnot, F. (2021). Healthy ageing and vaccines: Application of the P4 medicine concept to immunizations. Gerontology, 1-7.

14. Popa, M., Albulescu, R., Neagu, M., Hinescu, M.E., Tanase, C. et al. (2019). Multiplex assay for multiomics advances in personalized-precision medicine. Journal of Immunoassay and Immunochemistry, 40, 25-33.

15. Annunziato, A. (2015). 5G vision: NGMN – 5G initiative. *In:* Proc. 2015 IEEE 81st Veh. Techn. Conf. (VTC Spring), May.

16. de Mattos, W.D. and Gondim, P.R.L. (2016). M-health solutions using 5G networks and M2M communications. IT Professional, 18(3).

17. Tajin, M.A., Jacovic, M., Dion, G., Mongan, W.M., Dandekar, K.R. et al. (2021). UHF RFID channel emulation testbed for wireless IoT systems. IEEE Access, 9, 68523-68534.

18. Ayub Khan, Abdullah, Laghari, A.A, Shaikh, A., Dootio, M., Estrela, V.V. et al. (2021). A blockchain security module for brain-computer interface (BCI) with multimedia life cycle framework (MLCF). Neuroscience Informatics, 100030. 10.1016/j. neuri.2021.100030.

19. Estrela, V.V. and Hemanth, J. (2015). Special Issue Preface. International Journal of Information and Communication Technology, Tamil Nadu.

20. Kanna, K., Estrela, V.V. and Rodrigues J.J.P.C. (2021). Cyber Security and Digital Forensics – Proc. ICCSDF 2021, Springer Nature, Zurich, Switzerland. doi: 10.1007/978-981-16-3961-6.

21. Wang, H., Wen, Y. and Zhao, D. (2018). Location verification algorithm of wearable sensors for wireless body area networks. Technology and Health Care, 26, 3-18.

22. Palattella, M.R., Accettura, N., Vilajosana, X., Watteyne, T., Grieco, L.A. et al. (2013). Standardized protocol stack for the Internet of (important) things. IEEE Communications Surveys & Tutorials, 15(3).

23. Weyrich, M. and Ebert, C. (2016). Reference architectures for the Internet of things. IEEE Software, 33(1).

24. Shrouf, F., Ordieres, J. and Miragliotta, G. (2014). Smart factories in industry 4.0: A review of the concept and of energy management approached in production based on the Internet of things paradigm. Proc. 2014 IEEE Int'l Conf. Industrial Eng. and Eng. Management (IEEM). IEEE.

25. Elsts, A., Fafoutis, X., Woznowski, P., Tonkin, E.L., Oikonomou, G.C. et al. (2018). Enabling healthcare in smart homes: The SPHERE IoT network infrastructure. IEEE Communications Magazine, 56, 164-170.

26. Santos, J., Rodrigues, J.J., Silva, B.M., Casal, J., Saleem, K. et al. (2016). An IoT-based mobile gateway for intelligent personal assistants on mobile health environments. J. Network and Computer Applications, 71.

27. Hiremath, S., Yang, G. and Mankodiya, K. (2014). Wearable internet of things: Concept, architectural components and promises for person-centered healthcare. Proc. 2014 EAI 4th Int'l Conf. Wireless Mob. Comm. and Healthcare (Mobihealth). IEEE.

28. Loschi, H.J., Estrela, V.V., Hemanth, D.J., Fernandes, S.R., Iano, Y. et al. (2020) Communications requirements, video streaming, communications links and networked UAVs. *In:* Estrela, V.V., Hemanth, J., Saotome, O., Nikolakopoulos, G., Sabatini R. (eds). Imaging and Sensing for Unmanned Aircraft Systems, Vol. 2(6), 113-132. IET, London, UK, doi: 10.1049/PBCE120G_ch6

29. Kaur, P.D. and Chana, I. (2014). Cloud based intelligent system for delivering health care as a service. Computer methods and programs in biomedicine, 113(1).

30. Atzori, L., Iera, A. and Morabito, G. (2017). Understanding the Internet of things: Definition, potentials, and societal role of a fast evolving paradigm. Ad Hoc Networks, 56.

31. Kumari, A., Tanwar, S., Tyagi, S. and Kumar, N. (2018). Fog computing for healthcare 4.0 environment: Opportunities and challenges. Computers & Electrical Engineering, 72.

32. Satyanarayanan, M., Bahl, P., Caceres, R. and Davies, N. (2009). The case for VM-based cloudlets in mobile computing. IEEE Pervasive Computing, 8(4).

33. Calabrese, B. and Cannataro, M. (2015). Cloud computing in healthcare and biomedicine. Scalable Computing: Practice and Experience, 16(1).

34. John, N. and Shenoy, S. (2014). Health cloud – Healthcare as a service (HaaS). *In:* Proc. 2014 Int'l Conf. Adv. in Computing, Communications and Informatics (ICACCI). Sept 2014.

35. Chen, M. (2014). NDNC-BAN: Supporting rich media healthcare services via named data networking in cloud-assisted wireless body area networks. Information Sciences, 284.

36. Deng, M., Petkovic, M., Nalin, M. and Baroni, I. (2011). A home healthcare system in the Cloud-addressing security and privacy challenges. *In:* Proc. 2011 IEEE Int'l Conf. Cloud Comp. (CLOUD). IEEE.

37. Ekonomou, E., Fan, L., Buchanan, W. and Thuemmler, C. (2011). An integrated Cloud based healthcare infrastructure. *In:* Proc. 2011 IEEE 3rd Int'l Conf. Cloud Comp. Techn. and Science (CloudCom), IEEE.

38. Andriopoulou, F., Dagiuklas, T. and Orphanoudakis, T. (2017). Integrating IoT and fog computing for healthcare service delivery. Comp. and Services for IoT Platforms. Springer.

39. Estrela, V.V., Hemanth, J., Loschi, H.J., Nascimento, D.A., Iano, Y. et al. (2020) Computer vision and data storage in UAVs. *In:* Estrela, V.V., Hemanth, J., Saotome, O., Nikolakopoulos, G., Sabatini R. (eds). Imaging and Sensing for Unmanned Aircraft Systems, Vol. 1(2), 23-46. IET, London, UK, doi: 10.1049/PBCE120F_ch2

40. Deshpande, A., Estrela, V.V. and Razmjooy, N. (2021). Computational Intelligence Methods for Super-Resolution in Image Processing Applications. Springer Nature, Zurich, Switzerland. doi: 10.1007/978-3-030-67921-7

41. Garets, D. and Davis, M. (2006). Electronic medical records vs. electronic health records: Yes, there is a difference. Policy White Paper. Chicago, HIMSS Analytics.

42. Smolij, K. and Dun, K. (2006). Patient health information management: Searching for the right model. Perspectives in Health Information Management, 3, 10.
43. Martin-Sanchez, F. and Verspoor, K. (2014). Big data in medicine is driving big changes. Yearb Med. Inform., 9(1), Aug 2014.
44. Herland, M., Khoshgoftaar, T.M. and Wald, R. (Jun 2014). A review of data mining using big data in health informatics. Journal of Big Data, 1(1).
45. Costa, F.F. (2014). Big data in biomedicine. Drug Discovery Today, 19(4).
46. Habib, C., Makhoul, A., Darazi, R. and Salim, C. (2016). Self-adaptive data collection and fusion for health monitoring based on body sensor networks. IEEE Trans. Ind. Informatics, 12, 6.
47. Darshan, K. and Anandakumar, K. (2015). A comprehensive review on usage of Internet of things (IoT) in healthcare system. *In:* Proc. 2015 Int'l Conf. Emerging Research in Electronics, Computer Science and Technology (ICERECT). IEEE.
48. Vicini, S., Bellini, S., Rosi, A. and Sanna, A. (2012). An internet of things enabled interactive totem for children in a living lab setting. *In:* 2012 18th International ICE Conference on Engineering, Technology and Innovation, June 2012.
49. Vazquez-Briseno, M., Navarro-Cota, C., Nieto-Hipolito, J.I., Jimenez-Garcia, E. et al. (2012). A proposal for using the Internet of things concept to increase children's health awareness. Proc. 22nd Int'l Conf. Electrical Communications and Computers (CONIELECOMP 2012), Feb. 2012.
50. Moh, M., Ho, L., Walker, Z. and Moh, T.-S. (2008). A prototype on RFID and sensor networks for elder health care. RFID Handbook: Applications, Technology, Security, and Privacy, 17.
51. Silva, B.M.., Rodrigues, J.J., de la Torre Dez, I., Lpez-Coronado, M., Saleem, K. et al. (2015). Mobile-health: A review of current state in 2015. Journal of Biomedical Informatics, 56.
52. Yang, G., Xie, L., Mantysalo, M., Zhou, X., Pang, Z. et al. (2014). A health-IoT platform based on the integration of intelligent packaging, unobtrusive bio-sensor, and intelligent medicine box. IEEE Transactions on Industrial Informatics, 10(4).
53. Thuemmler, C. and Bai, C. (2018). Health 4.0: How Virtualization and Big Data are Revolutionizing Healthcare. Springer Publishing Company, Incorporated, 1st edition, 2018.
54. Holzinger, A. (2015). From Smart Health to Smart Hospitals. Springer, Cham.
55. Issa, N.T. (2014). Big data: The next frontier for innovation in therapeutics and healthcare. Expert Review of Clinical Pharmacology, 7(3).
56. Chawla, N.V. (2013). Bringing big data to personalized healthcare: A patient-centered framework. J. Gen. Internal Med., 28(3).
57. Chen, D. and Chen, Y. (2017). Real-time or near real-time persisting daily healthcare data into HDFS and elastic search index inside a big data platform. IEEE Transactions on Industrial Informatics, 13(2).
58 Sultan, N. (2014). Making use of cloud computing for healthcare provision: Opportunities and challenges. International Journal of Information Management, 34(2).
59. Li, Z.-R. (2011). A secure electronic medical record sharing mechanism in the cloud computing platform. 2011 Proc. IEEE Int'l Symp. Consumer Electronics (ISCE), 98-103.
60. Rodriguez-Martinez, M., Valdivia, J., Rivera, J., Sequel and Geer (2012). Medbook: A Cloud-based Healthcare Billing and Record Management System. 2012 Proc. IEEE 5th Int'l Conf. Cloud Comp.
61. He, C. and Jin, X. (2010). A cloud computing solution for hospital information system. IEEE.

62. Kanagaraj, G. and Sumathi. A. (2011). Proposal of an open-source cloud computing system for exchanging medical images of a hospital information system. *In:* 3rd Int'l Conf. Trends in Information Sciences & Computing (TISC 2011). IEEE.

63. Negra, R., Jemili, I. and Belghith, A. (2016). Wireless body area networks: Applications and technologies. Procedia Computer Science, 83.

64. Chakraborty, C., Gupta, B. and Ghosh, S.K. (2013). A review on telemedicine-based WBAN framework for patient monitoring. Telemedicine and e-Health, 19(8).

65. Dahl, T.S. and Boulos, M.N.K. (2014). Robots in health and social care: A complementary technology to home care and telehealth care. Robotics, 3(1).

66. Acampora, G., Cook, D.J., Rashidi, P. and Vasilakos, A.V. (2013). A survey on ambient intelligence in healthcare. Proceedings of the IEEE, 101(12).

67. Xia, H., Asif, I. and Zhao, X. (2013). Cloud-ECG for real-time ECG monitoring and analysis. Computer Methods and Programs in Biomedicine, 110(3).

68. Chen, M. (2013). Rochas: Robotics and Cloud assisted healthcare system for empty nester. Proc. 8th Int'l Conf. Body Area Net. ICST (Institute for Computer Sciences, Social Informatics and Telecommunications Engineering).

69. Gachet, D. (2012). Integrating Internet of' things and cloud computing for health services provisioning: The virtual cloud carer project. Proc. 2012 Sixth Int. Conf. Innovative Mobile and Internet Services in Ubiquitous Computing (IMIS). IEEE.

70. Zhou, H. and Hu, H. (2008). Human motion tracking for rehabilitation: A survey. Biomedical Signal Proc. and Control, 3(1).

71. Pereira, O., Caldeira, J.M.L.P. and Rodrigues, J.J.P.C. (2011). Body sensor network mobile solutions for biofeedback monitoring. Mobile Networks and Applications, 16(6).

72. Rodrigues, J.J., Pereira, O.R. and Neves, P.A. (2011). Biofeedback data visualization for body sensor networks. Journal of Network and Computer Applications, 34(1).

73. McKnight, M. (2017). IoT, industry 4.0, industrial IoT why connected devices are the future of design. KnE Engineering, 2(2).

74. Movassaghi, S., Abolhasan, M., Lipman, J., Smith, D., Jamalipour, A. et al. (2014). Wireless body area networks: A survey. IEEE Communications Surveys & Tutorials, 16(3).

75. van Kranenburg, R. and Bassi, A. (Nov 2012). Iot challenges. Communications in Mobile Computing, 1(1).

76. Sadeghi, A.-R., Wachsmann, C. and Waidner, M. (2015). Security and privacy challenges in industrial internet of things. Proc. 2015 52nd ACM/EDAC/IEEE Design Aut. Conf. (DAC). IEEE.

77. Huang, H., Gong, T., Ye, N., Wang, R. and Dou, Y. et al. (2017). Private and secured medical data transmission and analysis for wireless sensing healthcare system. IEEE Transactions on Industrial Informatics, 13(3).

78. Alaba, F.A., Othman, M., Hashem, I.A.T. and Alotaibi, F. (2017). Internet of things security: A survey. Journal of Network and Computer Applications, 88.

79. Liu, S., Hu, S., Weng, J., Zhu, S., Chen, Z. et al. (2016). A novel asymmetric three-party based authentication scheme in wearable devices environment. J. Net. and Comp. Appl., 60.

80. Yang, Y., Zheng, X. and Tang, C. (2017). Lightweight distributed secure data management system for health internet of things. Journal of Network and Computer Applications, 89. Emerging Services for Internet of Things (IoT).

81. Kulkarni, A. and Sathe, S. (2014). Healthcare applications of the Internet of things: A review. International Journal of Computer Science and Information Technologies, 5(5).

82. Jee, K. and Kim, G.-H. (2013). Potentiality of big data in the medical sector: Focus on how to reshape the healthcare system. Healthcare Informatics Research, 19(2).

83. Chang, H. and Choi, M. (2016). Big data and healthcare: Building an augmented world. Healthcare Informatics Research, 22(3).
84. Jirkovsky, V., Obitko, M. and Marik, V. (2016). Understanding data heterogeneity in the context of cyber-physical systems integration. IEEE Trans. Ind. Informatics, 99.
85. Nilashi, M., Ibrahim, O., Ahmadi, H. and Shahmoradi, L. (2017). A knowledge-based system for breast cancer classification using fuzzy logic method. Telematics and Informatics, 34(4), 133-144.
86. O'Neil, C. (2017). Weapons of Math Destruction: How Big Data Increases Inequality and Threatens Democracy. Broadway Books.
87. Higberg, R. and Larsson, G. (2016). Realization of industry 4.0 through RFID. M.Sc. in Eng. Technology, Ind. Design Engineering. Lulea University of Technology, Department of Business Administration, Technology and Social Sciences.
88. Lasi, H., Fettke, P. and Kemper, H.-G. (2014). Industry 4.0. Business & Information Systems Engineering, 6(4).
89. Li, X. and Li, D. (2015). A review of industrial wireless networks in the context of industry 4.0. Wireless Networks, 23, 23-41.
90. Almada-Lobo, F. (2016). The industry 4.0 revolution and the future of manufacturing execution systems (MES). Journal of Innovation Management, 3(4).
91. Kehoe, B., Patil, S., Abbeel, P. and Goldberg, K. (2015). A survey of research on cloud robotics and automation. IEEE Trans. Automation Science and Engineering, 12(2).
92. Manogaran, G. and Thota, C. (2017). Big Data Security Intelligence for Healthcare Industry 4.0. Springer 2017.
93. Tong, Y., Sun, J., Chow, S.S. and Li, P. (2014). Cloud-assisted mobile-access of health data with privacy and auditability. IEEE J. Biom. and Health Informatics, 18(2).
94. Thuemmler, C., Mueller, J. and Covaci, S. (2013). Applying the software-to-data paradigm in next generation e-health hybrid clouds. Proc. 2013 Tenth Int'l Conf. Information Technology: New Generations (ITNG), IEEE.
95. Fabian, B. (2015). Collaborative and secure sharing of healthcare data in multi-clouds. Information Systems, 48.
96. Biswas, J. and Maniyeri, J. (2010). Processing of wearable sensor data on the Cloud a step towards scaling of continuous monitoring of health and well-being. Proc. 2010 Annual Int'l Conf. of the IEEE Engineering in Medicine and Biology. IEEE.
97. Aceto, G., Botta, A., de Donato, W. and Pescape, A. (2012). Cloud monitoring: Definitions, issues and future directions. Proc. 1st IEEE Int'l Conf. Cloud Netw. (CLOUDNET 2012), Paris, France, November 28-30, 2012.
98. Persico, V., Botta, A. and Marchetta, P. (2017). On the performance of the wide-area networks interconnecting public-cloud datacenters around the globe. Computer Networks, 112.
99. Antequera, R.B. et al. (2017). Socio-technical approach to engineer gigabit app performance for physical therapy-as-a-service. Proc. IEEE 19th Int'l Conf. e-Health Networking, Applications and Services (IEEE Healthcom 2017).
100. Zhang, X.M. and Zhang, N. (May 2011). An open, secure and flexible platform based on Internet of things and cloud computing for ambient aiding living and telemedicine. Proc. 2011 Int'l Conf. Computer and Management (CAMAN).
101. Sanchez-Guerrero, R., Mendoza, F.A., Dıaz-Sanchez, D., Cabarcos, P.A. et al. (2017). Collaborative ehealth meets security: Privacy-enhancing patient profile management. IEEE J. Biomed. Health Informatics, 21(6).
102. Schadt, E.E. (2012). The changing privacy landscape in the era of big data. Molecular Systems Biology, 8(1).

103. Wu, H., Wang, Q. and Wolter, K. (2013). Mobile healthcare systems with multicloud offloading. Proc. 2013 IEEE 14th Int'l Conf. Mobile Data Management, volume 2. IEEE.

104. Zhan, Z.-H., Liu, X.-F., Gong, Y.-J., Zhang, J., Chung, H.S.-H. et al. (2015). Cloud computing resource scheduling and a survey of its evolutionary approaches. ACM Computing Surveys (CSUR), 47(4).

105. Wachter, S. and Mittelstadt, B. (May 2017). Transparent, explainable, and accountable AI for robotics. Science Robotics, 2(6).

106. Johansen, M.A., Kummervold, P.E., Sørensen, T. and Zanaboni, P. (2019). Health professionals' experience with patients accessing their electronic health records: Results from an online survey.

107. Baloch, J.A., Jumani, A.K., Laghari, A.A., Estrela, V.V., Lopes, R.T. et al. (2021). A preliminary study on quality of experience assessment of compressed audio file format. 2021 IEEE URUCON, 161-165, doi: 10.1109/URUCON53396.2021.9647114.

108. Brett, J., Boulton, M. and Watson, E. (2018). Development of an e-health app to support women prescribed adjuvant endocrine therapy after treatment for breast cancer. Patient Pref. and Adherence, 12.

Internet of Medical Things (IoMT) Layers for Medical Cyber-Physical Systems

Vania V. Estrela[1] [0000-0002-4465-7691], Awais Khan Jumani[2] [0000-0001-9468-0446], Asif A. Laghari[3] [0000-0001-5831-5943], Rashid Ali Laghari[4] [0000-0002-9710-7538], Abdullah Ayub Khan[5] [0000-0003-2838-7641], Maria A. de Jesus[1] [0000-0001-6428-9438], Robert Sroufer[6] [0000-0002-7903-9180], Ricardo T. Lopes[7] [0000-0001-7250-824X]

[1] Department of Telecommunications, Federal Fluminense University (UFF), RJ, Brazil, vania.estrela.phd@ieee.org, majesus1977br@gmail.com
[2] Department of Computer Science, Sindh Madressa-tul-Islam University, Karachi, Sindh, Pakistan, awaisjumani@yahoo.com
[3] Faculty of Computer Science, Sindh Madressa-tul-Islam University, Karachi, Sindh, Pakistan, asif.laghari@smiu.edu.pk
[4] Department of Computer Science, ILMA University Karachi, Sindh, Pakistan, rashidali@nuaa.edu.cn
[5] College of Mechanical and Electrical Engineering, Nanjing University of Aeronautics and Astronautics, Nanjing 210016, China, abdullah.khan00763@gmail.com
[6] Management Department, Duquesne University, Pittsburg, PA, USA, sroufer@duq.edu
[7] Federal University of Rio de Janeiro (COPPE/UFRJ), Nuclear Engineering Laboratory (LIN), Rio de Janeiro, RJ, Brazil, ricardo@lin.ufrj.br

1. Introduction

The healthcare scenario changes drastically as the life expectancy upsurges and several diseases are increasingly pressuring healthcare systems worldwide due to the lack of resources. Significant challenges arise as healthcare systems handle various illnesses and treatments and an increasing number of patients. Telemedicine systems can be efficient solutions to avoid healthcare infrastructure overloads and reduce healthcare costs. Despite having high heterogeneity, they generally cater to limited therapeutic goals, like remote cardiac checking and stroke healing. This feature calls for efficient ways to reduce costs and healthcare infrastructure overload. The Internet of Medical Things (IoMT) can better address the need for better generality and scalability [1-3].

The IoMT combines the reliability and safety of usual medical devices with the Internet of Things (IoT). Hence, it provides dynamicity, generality, and scalability capabilities. The IoMT can support, for instance, remote management of aging and chronic diseases by managing numerous devices and patients but must be generic enough for various ailments, calling for very heterogeneous monitoring, sensor types, and actuation necessities. Moreover, IoMT helps when it comes to patient mobility since pervasive daily monitoring can relieve part of the homecare effort.

New technological solutions for demanding healthcare systems are changing healthcare delivery. The proliferation of personal computing devices with increasing computational power enables the IoMT development and addresses aging populations and other patients. The IoMT interconnects numerous devices with caretakers, patients, insurance companies, laboratories, government agencies, healthcare providers such as hospitals, medical researchers, or other private companies. The advent of the IoMT stems from an increase in the use and advancement of connected and distributed medical devices, producing promising potential applications and numerous challenges [4-8]. Personal medical devices can be mobile, implantable, or wearable devices requiring IoMT integration with the following characteristics:

- Reliability: A reliable system accomplishes its functional objectives at all times, without unexpected failure under typical operating situations. The diagnostic and therapeutic nature of IoMT means that every system component must be reliable to guarantee the acquired information accuracy.
- Safety: A safe system protects its operating environment, particularly with medical actuators, to avoid causing any harm to patients.
- Security: A medical system must bear external threats and attacks due to sensitive and private information.
- Robustness: The system must have fault-tolerant mechanisms and redundancy to guarantee alternative healthcare management if some component fails.

The IoMT interconnects healthcare devices with broader healthcare infrastructures and handles requirements from lower layers (i.e., connected medical devices). These lower layers' data must go to the higher IoMT layers (e.g., the communication and application layers). Other medical devices' interconnectivity requirements are adequate data gathering/processing, information security, file access strategies, and data lifecycle management. IoMT devices have highly heterogeneous computing capabilities, communication protocols, and application arenas. IoMT devices being abundant,IoMT systems must appropriately manage a huge number of devices. Thus, IoMT and all-purpose IoT share requirements, especially regarding a colossal number of devices with reliable communication and heterogeneity/interoperability.

A set of methods and design tools for Cyber-Physical Systems (CPSs) can achieve all these IoMT requirements to handle computing systems' growing complexity. CPSs connect computational entities, e.g., Wireless Sensor Networks (WSNs), Cloud Computing (CC), IoT, virtualization, and remote control, to name a few, to physical processes. This paradigm allows the efficient construction of large-scale systems for various medical applications such as highly reliable biomedical devices, assisted living, or telemedicine [4, 6, 7].

Medical CPSs (MCPSs) provide comprehensive modeling and design frameworks to produce reliable and safe medical devices. MCPSs, thus, afford complete solutions to the IoMT. Indeed, the device layer of the IoMT needs physical modeling to ease the constant interaction of IoMT devices with the physical world. The communication and application layers of the IoMT can use discrete models to ensure deterministic behavior under diverse operating conditions as networked MCPSs rely on hybrid models for cross-layer reliability and safety guarantees.

Physiological regulation and help pose critical aspects to IoMT devices since sensors and actuators correspondingly handle patient measurements and control inputs. Insulin pumps and chemotherapy devices are typical medical actuators modifying drug levels in the body. A comprehensive understanding of the core physiological processes is necessary to control such apparatuses optimally. MCPSs can offer an excellent theoretical and modeling framework for such devices, as hybrid models represent the physiological process and the numerical control command. Besides, discrete networking models can facilitate integration of devices into wider-scale IoMT systems.

This text has several sections as follows. Section 2 discusses the challenges of IoMT design and how MCPSs can address these matters. Section 3, then, analyzes the IoMT under a MCPS approach by adopting a layered strategy: the IoMT apparatuses, the networking of devices, and the eventual use of a Service-Oriented Approach (SOA) to building IoMT systems. Finally, section 5 identifies key research directions to attain cross-layer safety, reliability, and security simultaneously.

2. IoMT Overview

The IoMT concept is complex, and it presents various challenges requiring adequate design solutions, even if it contains partial solutions to improve its safety, dependability, and security. Eventually, the CPS approach in an IoMT context helps to organize and deploy solutions.

2.1. IoMT Challenges

Embedded systems can realize various heterogeneous applications (e.g., telemedicine, traffic control, assisted living, or smart cities among others) that require MCPSs control of physical (real-life) objects, resulting in constant dealings between the virtual and physical world [8]. The critical aspects of MCPSs fall into three groups [9]:

- Reliability, robustness, and security compliance requirements are essential. Since the physical and physiological worlds are unstable, IoMT-centered systems must sustain acceptable performance under variations and react correctly when necessary. IoMT structures' security concerns are related to system failures from life-threatening and criminal occurrences [10].
- The IoMT must rely on accurate hybrid systems models, i.e., at the intersection of the digital and physical world, both accurate physical models and precise computing abstractions. Additionally, relying on a model-based design enables the improvement of the testing procedures through simulation.
- There must be specific verification and validation mechanisms: most of the IoMT contains widely distributed structures. To pass certifications, they must have verification and validation protocols on different granularity levels.

These challenges gather experts from multidisciplinary fields to develop hybrid system models with virtual and physical components represented with their interactions. In conclusion, verification and validation methods must handle different scales (scalability) to ease the certification process and enhance reliability: from the lowest IoMT device-level networks to the top-level scale.

An Internet-operated surgical robot exemplifies a virtual IoMT-based system, where surgeons perform teleoperations from remote sites. For evident reasons, reliability, robustness, and security questions arise immediately for such applications. Likewise, accurate human body and robot characteristics models can advance and guarantee the surgery's safety. These models enable speedy detection and precise correction of unexpected behaviors. In creating an IoMT-connected surgical robot, verification and validation will significantly assist strict certification procedures for developing and commercializing medical appliances.

Albeit these problems are still active research directions and partially unsolved, there are design schemes and methodologies for IoMT ecosystems that partly satisfy safety, reliability, and security requirements.

Design methods have been described in the literature to efficiently solve the modeling, reliability, robustness, security, verification, and validation challenges of IoMT [4].

2.2. Model-Based Development of the IoMT

The most explored IoMT-related challenge is the problem raised by CPS modeling [29] since the IoMT consists of the interconnection of MCPSs. Moreover, CPS community tools can model the physical and digital characteristics of MCPSs [14]. Comprehensive systems offer better reliability and safety, including contributions from all aspects of MCPSs, mainly physiological modeling. Indeed, networking digital models to integrate IoMT devices can extend physiological modeling in a MCPS context easily.

There is abundant literature on the subject and an extensive range of potential uses for the developed models. Hybrid systems modeling starts with a good understanding of basic continuous systems modeling [11], where differential equations describe an evolving system's dynamics. Then, discrete-time systems using state machines expand the modeling framework [11]. This rationale is the basis of all further improved models of continuous-time, discrete-time, or hybrid systems.

2.2.1. Continuous-time models

Biological processes entail randomness and intrinsic physiological properties, which rely on physics, biochemistry, and other fields. Continuous systems can model (a) glucose dynamics management, (b) implantable pacemakers, (c) node-based, geometrical heart models for cardiac apparatuses; (d) complete multi-parametric patient monitoring of biomedical data (e.g., blood pressure, temperature), and (e) fluid-filled catheters to measure internal organ pressures (i.e., using continuous-time differential equations) [4]. These models are intricate, with their parameters determined through clinical experimentation.

2.2.2. Discrete Systems

The deep integration of IoMT computation resources mandates accuracy, robustness, and predictability. State machines can model discrete-time processes [11]. Several modeling philosophies complement state-machine models. Signal-processing-oriented applications can use synchronous data flow to describe targeted applications' computing processes [12]. This model uses directed graphs where nodes represent computing functions, and edges symbolize signal paths [12]. A stochastic rendezvous network model has potential delays in server-client architectures [13]. Discrete-event models can typify discrete interactions among a set of actors [14]. These models represent each interaction as an event, and actors react to events in a temporal order [14]. Other modeling tools representing computer systems exist.

2.2.3. Hybrid Systems

Still, the real strength of MCPS-based approaches to building the IoMT comes from using hybrid models, facilitating the accurate modeling of the virtual and the physical worlds. The strong relationship between the IoMT virtual and physical worlds demands hybrid models to represent these worlds accurately for efficient designs. These models generalize finite-state machines with continuous inputs and outputs as modal representations [11, 15] (Figure 1).

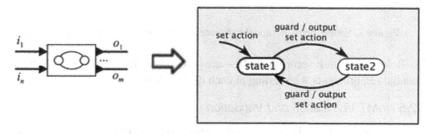

Figure 1. Graphical representation of modal representations

Usually, these systems represent the plant in continuous-state space, while the controller is a discrete symbolic domain [17]. The complementary modeling philosophy belongs to CPSs' foundations but entails understanding continuous-time and computer system modeling [16].

2.2.4. Robustness and security design concerns

Because of the robustness, resilience, and security requirements of connected healthcare devices, such consideration must occur as early as possible in the design process. The literature offers several methods to guarantee IoMT robustness. One of these methods includes some control strategy during the system design process [20], where a stochastic model considers both deterministic uncertainties and unexpected events. Game-theoretical methods or Markov processes [18, 20] also improve the system's global robustness. A more traditional controller switching appears in [19], where system metrics indicate its functional status. Lack of verification of obligatory properties results in a more robust but less precise controller.

The vast literature dealing with IoMT security on MCPS security covers several aspects: data privacy and aggregation [21], intrusion detection [22], alarm generation allowing non-interoperability detection [23], or integrity and authenticity [24] (Figure 2). Different mechanisms have controlled all security attributes successfully. E.g., (i) simple symmetric [21] or more evolved cryptography key systems using physiological human body parameters [24], (ii) a rule-based behavior model, which can allow detecting intrusions when systems deviate from their expected behavior [22], (iii) or the formulation of a set of requirements allowing the detection of interoperability problems [23, 25].

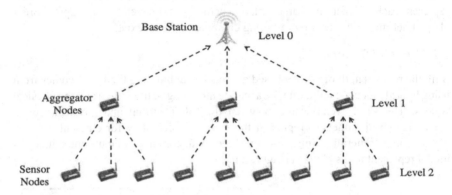

Figure 2. Simple network model to secure data transmission using cryptography.

Robustness and security studies are necessary during design to guarantee essential requirements with testing at each design step.

2.2.5. IoMT Verification and Validation

The last identified challenge when designing IoMT-based systems is integrating a verification and validation process into the product development. Figure 3 describes the emblematic verification workflow for model checking methodologies. System properties are checked against a formal system model to warrant spot-on global system performance. The generic idea behind the IoMT verification is the reachability analysis of the different states from the hybrid model [26]. Several works addressed IoMT hybrid, state-machine models [26], or Petri Net models [27]. However, literature about procedure validation is scarcer, although the verification process can be generalized to a wide range of IoMT-based systems aiming at very different application fields and particular validation requirements. An example of validation protocols and platforms concerning cardiac implantable devices appears in [28]. Rigorous design methodologies permit developing safe, secure, and robust MCPSs compatible with other medical subsystem designs.

2.2.6. MCPS as a Comprehensive Solution for IoMT Requirements

Designing medical systems is critical from both the medical and engineering viewpoints. Medical frameworks and IoMTs mainly have problems with data privacy and security [30] (Figure 3). This concern becomes more critical for implantable devices because they usually assure vital functions, and any tampering could have disastrous consequences [44]. IoMT device connectivity is also an issue, as exposure to the external world is a source of uncertainty. Robustness and reliability are uppermost concerns since medical device behaviors are deterministic despite hardware and software conditions [30, 32]. Figure 4 shows the acceptability degree of potential device malfunction graphically.

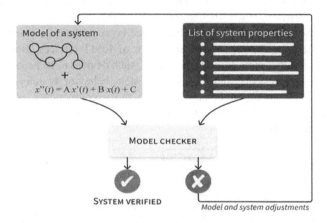

Figure 3. Model-checking based verification workflow

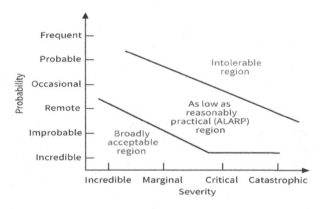

Figure 4. Risk management policy graphical representation, from [32].

Moreover, medical devices also entail other requirements, such as performing real-time data collection, improving networked infrastructures, or accurately estimating the computing load required to analyze the collected data. The extensive certification process associated with medical devices, such as the FDA, requires robust verification and validation procedures. It is also necessary to accurately capture a medical system's user requirements to ensure its adoption and correct use [30-33] through a careful validation process.

Following the CPS design approach prudently fulfills these complex requirements. This methodology allows addressing each medical system concern, from security to validation and verification, using careful system modeling and elaborate design techniques. The following section details some MCPS examples.

3. MCPSs Working with IoMT

A layer-by-layer approach better addresses the challenges and prospects of MCPSs in the context of IoMT. It was indeed noticed that the focus could be on either the device layer, the framework layer, or the service layer (Figure 5). The device layer includes all the concerns regarding the design of IoMT devices. Because of the intense hardware constraints of medical devices, such devices must be interconnected using low-energy protocols, and the global system behavior is delegated to other components. The integration layer represents those components, which specify the global behavior of interconnected medical devices. Finally, another level of abstraction is an SOA.

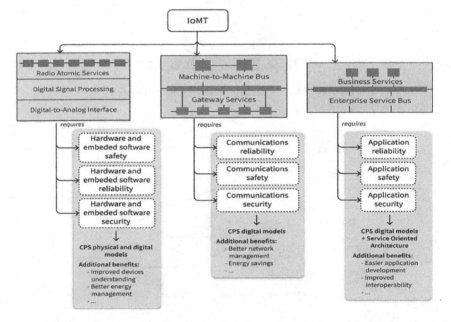

Figure 5. Layer representation of constraints and advantages of the IoMT

3.1. A CPS Approach for IoMT Devices

Wearables are non-invasive and straightforward, differing from invasive implantable devices. Both categories of medical gadgets can work according to the MCPS concept and with the IoMT.

Many sensors and actuators rely on the CPS approach, whose key aspects are safety, security, robustness, accurate models for physiological functions and computing systems, and the existence of verification and validation procedures.

The early literature works deal mainly with the MCPS development models for IoMT devices/systems. Some examples of continuous-time models describing physiological processes follow cardiac activity, the heart's electrical behavior, blood glucose/oxygen levels for artificial organs, and the human body's absorption rate of a given medication. Finite-state automata can model the heart's electrical behavior and detect cardiac faults in implantable pacemakers [4].

These models' particularity focuses on a specific physiological process while keeping their practical implementation in consideration. More generic models exist like a multi-parametric fall detection model using electroencephalography and electromyography [36], an electromyography-based model of user intention for artificial legs [37], a general human body 3D model [38], or even structured human interaction models to reach better CPS reliability [39].

Models using the human body as a whole system have also been used to validate MCPSs [40], i.e., to potentially detect sensor error by employing human physiology models. Some works use physiological modeling for computing-related purposes, such as electrocardiogram compression [41]. CPSs inspired the development of network on-chips [42]. Models of computing module temperature can ensure safety of devices in contact with the skin [43, 24]. Software architecture models in CPSs, where tasks implement hardware abstractions exist [44]. Potential attack analysis models have also been described [45] and model-based false alarm detection [46]. There are verification and validation schemes through modeling for various targets: implantables [28], the CPS verification using digital equivalents [47], and the generation of a model-based code and verification architecture [48]. Finally, in a networked architecture, MCPSs model packet loss to rehabilitate post-stroke gait [49] within IoMT-based systems [48].

The robustness and security challenges have been described independently from the modeling perspective only once using clever algorithm selection for bio signal acquisition robustness improvement [51]. Verification and validation have been considered separately from any modeling aspects in the particular situation where an implementation already existed, with the real-life testing of CPS devices such as an ECG sensor [52] or a general CPS hardware node [53].

The modeling part is the most frequently discussed device-level challenge in MCPSs [4], followed by modeling, verification, and validation as the most cumbersome processes. Finally, robustness and security come. This state of affairs leaves potential research improvements concentrating on integrating the device level's MCPS security requirements.

Techniques to design safer, more reliable, and more secure healthcare devices emerge so that they can work as IoMT building blocks. IoMT applications are highly critical. Hence, device properties and trustworthiness matter a lot. The predominant approach to improving device characteristics is model-driven development that tests implemented devices' behavior against theoretical functional models. No clear modeling framework trend exists because of the diversity and heterogeneity of devices and biological processes. Methodologies to develop reliable, safe, and secure medical devices are crucial, and they require a prerequisite before any higher-level considerations.

3.2. IoMT Integration Frameworks for Wearable Devices

Previously, contributions focused on the IoMT-device modeling strategies, while the robustness and validation concerns were less developed. However, when integrating IoMT devices, all the identified IoMT key caveats are studied more homogeneously.

The security and robustness of networked IoMT often appear independently of the two other challenges. The sensitive nature of IoMT-based devices and systems makes CPSs safety-critical. Since healthcare involves data confidentiality over the network, one must guarantee information protection measures, e.g., data encryption, user authentication, or resistance to denial-of-service attacks [24, 25, 30]. Networked IoMT structures need detailed attack prevention/security, system response studies under these attacks [54], and attack detection methods [55]. The robustness of networks using several heterogeneous sensors has also been studied by implementing an interoperability analysis framework for IoMT [56]. Models have also been used for security purposes, allowing intrusion detection based on deriving the expected behavior [22].

Then, verification and validation of IoMT-based systems was also an independently considered subject. Most literature handled real-life testing of networked IoMT devices, such as (i) the field verification of a sensor network using the 6LoWPAN protocol and aimed at the remote elderly monitoring [57], (ii) the experimental evaluation of the synchronization of two IoMT nodes [58], or (iii) the testing of Zigbee-based sensor networking to integrate a broader health structure for post-stroke rehabilitation [59].

Finally, modeling networked IoMT devices entail the following contexts: the development of a Web of Things (WoT) architecture for CPSs using widely used RESTful protocols [60], the study of a scenario, and Internet-based CPSs for assisted living with response-time minimization [61], and finally the development of an event-based model for networked IoMT devices [62]. Figure 6 illustrates how [60] networked CPSs can be architecturally modeled using a block-diagram syntax. This web-of-things approach uses popular Internet-based technologies, enabling better system interoperability.

The verification and validation of networked IoMT devices is the primary literature focus for the IoMT. The verification and validation processes relate to a modeling problem: models pose reference behaviors, and these models become references to real-life experimentations. Such approaches have been used to analyze cloud-based IoMT systems: it was explored for remote patient monitoring [63], quality of data evaluation [64], or even large-scale health data collection [65]. This model verification approach helped build a test platform for Body Area Networks (BAN) [66] and a more general network topology. Indeed, fault models for binary sensor-based networked IoMT were studied [67]. Special-need adult targeted IoMT-based systems [68] or pregnancy monitoring platforms [69] were also developed. Such methods have also been used to successfully operate computer-intensive tasks on resource-limited networked nodes [70].

Many studies addressed verification, validation, robustness, and security concerns. Numerous applications have explored the robustness of IoMT systems, such as power optimization and packet scheduling mechanisms for BANs [71],

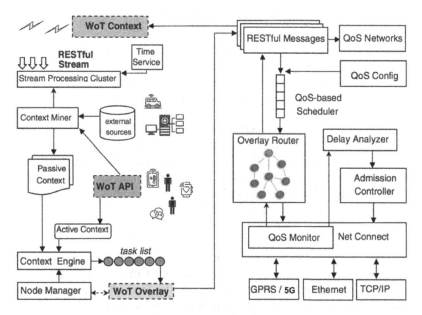

Figure 6. The architecture of networked cyber-physical systems relying on a web-of-things approach, from [60].

the development of an analysis framework allowing the improvement of IoMT interoperability [23], and analysis of the robustness of a MAC protocol for networked devices [72]. Some global reliability and safety frameworks have also been developed [43]. Finally, a verification of a physiological parameter-based key generation for encryption and data protection purposes has been discussed [73].

In summary, the integration of devices is studied mainly from a networking perspective. Since the IoMT consists of networked connected medical devices, the reliability, safety, and security of networked connected devices must be carefully studied at design time and run-time. This is achieved once again through the wide use of model-driven design and formal validation and verification tools. Providing a reliable networking framework is necessary for connected medical devices, as network failure or malicious intrusions could cause severe consequences. If considering remote surveillance, network failure could imply missing critical health events and cause severe problems for the monitored patient. However, the reliability of the target networks can be estimated using models and formal verification tools. Developing reliable and resilient networks is still an active research direction and enables a more trustworthy IoMT.

3.3. Unexplored IoMT Service Layer

The last layer is the service layer, where the IoMT employs an SOA as in previous case studies. The SOA using a CPS perspective has been less studied.

The literature's main concern using the SOA to design the IoMT is the Quality of Service (QoS) requirements, techniques, and models for such systems. The appropriate network controllers can guarantee the expected QoS in a wide-scale

IoMT, integrating patient and clinician services [74]. For general cases, the QoS requirements of MCPSs were well-developed from a different perspective: network QoS requirement for CPS [75]; QoS management architectures for MCPSs [76]; UML (unified modeling language) based QoS modeling for CPS [77]. Still, middleware can ameliorate QoS by considering resource managers and network properties [78]; a framework to guarantee appropriate QoS through radio resource management has been built [79].

Another critical aspect of the SOA is composition, which resulted in the Service-Oriented (SO) IoMT (SO-IoMT). Some solutions are (i) a framework derived from the OWL-S (web ontology language for web services) ontology model was adapted to the IoMT, allowing efficient IoMT services composition [80]; (ii) CPS adapted traditional Java-based composition techniques [81]; and finally, (iii) a framework enabling the self-architectures of SO-IoMT [82].

Some contributions have proposed a model-based design process to execute SO MCPSs successfully: architecture analysis and design languages modeled architectures [83], along with an extension of the OWL-S allowing the enhancement of service-based CPS models [84]. A three-step SO CPS design process was also defined, along with the proposed design method [85]. Figure 7 introduces this design scheme and illustrates six methodological steps to enable SO CPS.

Adequate middleware deployment also impacts SO-IoMT, adding an abstraction level to the control of devices via a generic interface for the connected objects. SO middleware architectures exist using low-level C structures [86] or higher-level XML descriptions targeted at integration of objects to large-scale IPv6 networks [87].

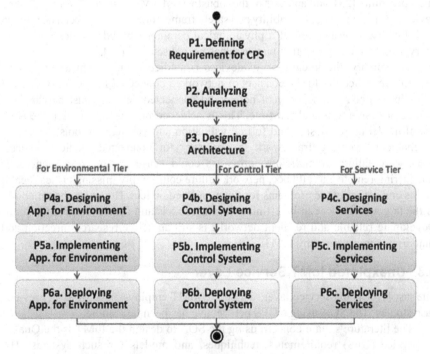

Figure 7. Service-oriented design method for cyber-physical systems, from [85].

There are fewer general aspects of SO computing, with a more application-targeted approach, e.g., the implementation of real-time data collection services for networked sensors (with security and robustness) [88], or employing the IEEE 802.15.4 protocol in MCPS, and its impact on the systems' QoS [89].

Finally, in an IoMT context, cloud computing entails developing Cloud and big-data services for telehealth scenarios [90, 65]. Data collection services can blend in a cloud-based CPS [91].

There is a lack of SO-IoMT designs. However, the concepts defined in SO architectures, where modular, self-contained software components are combined to build larger systems, are similar to the IoMT concerns. Indeed, in the IoMT, heterogeneous and self-contained medical devices must collaborate to achieve health-oriented functional goals. The similarities between the SO computing characteristics and the IoMT architectural implementations make the study of SO medical devices an exciting research direction. One of the main challenges of this direction is integrating strong hardware constraints to SO architectures where contributions exclusively consider research problems from a pure software perspective.

4. New Directions and Perspectives

AMCPS covers a wide variety of fields of expertise, gathering researchers from various backgrounds.

First, extending SO computing within IoMT-based frameworks could foster interesting medical-oriented applications. Third parties' benefit from these service paradigms that allow great modularity, interoperability, and ease of use. Mechanisms combining services to form new composite services provide the paradigm modularity results. The interoperability stems from the use of service ontologies and specifications, which describe services extensively. Improving the high-level abstraction for IoMT devices/systems could (i) enhance the reliability of device integration and (ii) deliver comprehensive and personalized healthcare solutions via service compositions.

As described in the previous section, networked architectures involve machine-to-machine (M2M) communication and standardization. The communication among these devices requires careful studies for seamless communications amid MCPS devices. Communication entails standard protocols such as IEEE 802.15.4, MAC, 6LoWPAN [57, 72, 89], others solely devoted to IoMT contexts, or more all-purpose CPS contexts. Nevertheless, M2M communication is broader than simple protocol matters. Indeed, M2M communications need to investigate heterogeneity, network architectures, QoS, energy management, and resources administration [92]. This approach can enrich IoMT by better understanding networked system properties, behavior, and management.

Moreover, standardizing M2M communications over organizations is an emerging necessity. The use of the developed IoMT standards might improve the interoperability and simplicity of use of healthcare systems. Standardization initiatives can handle interoperability globally with an Application Programming Interface (API) with bindings to standard Internet protocols such as HTTP, MQTT, and CoAP. This tactic only emphasizes interoperability at the application level, unlike generic middleware for usual device representations and access mechanisms [4].

Other initiatives provide a programing or the Medical Device Coordination Framework (MDCF). Such approaches target the interoperability of medical systems and work as potential IoMT building blocks with full medical interoperability via standardized, open-source software for various stakeholders [92, 93]. This software delivers bindings for healthcare gadgets employing the Data Distribution Service (DDS) middleware and different clinical cases to simplify real-life deployment. The interoperability of devices can rely on ad hoc methodologies with devices integrated manually into the framework utilizing software bindings. Another MDCF complementary model-driven approach uses models of healthcare equipment as communicating components. This structure employs software- orientation heavily and can verify particular medical communication scenarios using a publish/subscribe scheme. The Java Messaging Service (JMS) protocol can handle interoperability for all system communications. Unfortunately, both initiatives have restricted scalability, hindering IoMT in contexts with multiple application-specific limits and coexistent protocols due to hardware constraints. A typical physical limitation is the existence of energy-saving protocols to extend the battery life of critical devices. Hence, IoMT interoperability is still an ongoing research area, and IoMT system designers must balance specific and system-wide protocols with the heterogeneity of healthcare hardware constraints.

Finally, several systems perform tasks ranging from multi-parametric gait surveillance to multi-purpose BANs. CPS design techniques can considerably benefit reliability, testing, privacy, and safety of such systems [94, 95]. Their early use in system development ensures the quality, completeness, and security of the gathered data, a paramount requirement in healthcare devices.

It is worth noticing that holistic full-stack approaches are lacking. Contributions often consider only one layer of the architecture. If a transversal approach simultaneously handles all the layers, then it will enable better cross-layer reliability. The IoMT goal is to promote better healthcare via device interconnectivity and Internet-based technologies. It is paramount to preserve robustness, safety, and security requirements when looking at the system globally for each IoMT layer.

The IoMT epitomizes incredible opportunities ranging from the early diagnoses [95] to remotely monitor patients at risk for an urgent response if necessary. However, researchers must investigate some challenges to deploy IoMT healthcare adequately. One stimulating research direction is SO architectures to enhance IoMT modularity and interoperability.

Pervasive healthcare has numerous advantages for patients such as: (i) patient comfort thanks to remote monitoring and smaller devices, (ii) better self-awareness of health status thanks to real-time feedback, and (iii) personalized health recommendations using patient history. The self-health awareness expansion can improve IoMT disease management even with chronic and environmentally influenced conditions.

IoMT healthcare devices and infrastructures ~~validated~~ validation using good Quality of Experience (QoE) metrics is another promising research direction. IoMT technologies need to probe the systems to guarantee data reliability and long-term stability. There is an evident lack of wide-scale multidisciplinary studies for the ongoing verification and validation of healthcare devices. Popular wearables for heart or physical activity measurements [96] have poor accuracy and call for further consumer-oriented investigations. IoMT components must consider the overall resulting accuracy perspective with wide-scale and real-life data collection and experiments to be clinically accepted.

Previous IoMT efforts focused mainly on developing reliable IoMT devices, while recent efforts concentrated on IoMT integration frameworks. These are highly active areas as innovative protocols and architectures emerge. Concluding, SO-IoMT initiatives are new but offer encouraging insights into interoperability, scalability, and IoMT system development simplicity.

5. Conclusion

This text examined IoMT-based systems and devices from a multi-layer perspective. MCPSs improve a healthcare system's control, robustness, security, reliability, verification, and validation. The MCPS model is appropriate for designing, realizing, testing, and deploying these structures. This text comprehensively discusses MCPS approaches relying on the IoMT and potential research directions.

While IoMT-based applications are still developing, better device interconnection can considerably improve healthcare provision. Perhaps the most significant advantage would be enhanced operational efficiency through the growing use of networked devices. Transparent data flow from lower-level physical devices to the Cloud (and associated data analytics) could enable real-time response from remote locations, saving more lives than ever before.

Data-driven decision-making can accurately empower caregivers to monitor a patient's ample health status, take preventive actions, and instantaneously respond to emergencies. Interconnected systems can lessen the price burden on patients, intensify patient compliance, and leverage intelligent device boons to deliver instantaneous, responsive healthcare.

Automation in healthcare checking increases operational effectiveness, albeit with severe risks during implementation, e.g., data theft, unreliable data transmissions, and uneven network connections. Combined with regulatory hurdles, these challenges may drive growth in IoMT-hosted networking and data solutions.

Administrative initiatives like the Patient Protection and Affordable Care Act, which uses authenticated Electronic Health Records (EHRs), may expand the quality and efficiency of medical care by promoting consistency in caregiving. Healthcare devices and international data standards still need improvements to enable better data handling. IoMT promises solutions to improve healthcare monitoring and treatment despite its benefits and related challenges.

References

1. Hiam, L., Minton, J. and Mckee, M. (2021). What can lifespan variation reveal that life expectancy hides? Comparison of five high-income countries. Journal of the Royal Society of Medicine, 114, 389-399.
2. Jha, A.V., Mishra, S., Appasani, B. and Ghazali, A.N. (2021). Communication networks for metropolitan e-health applications. IEEE Potentials, 40, 34-42.
3. Arshaghi, A., Razmjooy, N., Estrela, V.V., Burdziakowski, P., Nascimento, D.A. et al. (2020). Image transmission in UAV MIMO UWB-OSTBC system over Rayleigh channel using multiple description coding (MDC). *In:* Estrela, V.V., Hemanth, J., Saotome, O., Nikolakopoulos, G., Sabatini, R. (eds). Imaging and Sensing for Unmanned Aircraft Systems, Vol. 2(4), 67-90, IET, London, UK.
4. Gatouillat, A., Badr, Y., Massot, B. and Sejdić, E. (2018). Internet of medical things: A review of recent contributions dealing with cyber-physical systems in medicine. IEEE Internet of Things Journal, 5, 3810-3822.
5. Han, S.M., Greenfield, G., Majeed, A. and Hayhoe, B. (2020). Impact of remote consultations on antibiotic prescribing in primary health care: Systematic review. Journal of Medical Internet Research, 22.
6. Wang, Z., Ma, P., Zou, X. and Yang, T. (2020). Security of medical cyber-physical systems: An empirical study on imaging devices. *In:* Proc. IEEE INFOCOM 2020 – IEEE Conference on Computer Communications Workshops (INFOCOM WKSHPS), 997-1002.
7. Estrela, V.V., Saotome, O., Loschi, H.J., Hemanth, J., Farfan, W.S. et al. (2018). Emergency response cyber-physical framework for landslide avoidance with sustainable electronics. Technologies, 6(2), 42.
8. Lee, E.A. (2010). CPS foundations. *In:* Proc. 47th Design Automation Conference, ACM, pp. 737-742.
9. Monteiro, A.C.B., Franca, R.P., Estrela, V.V., Fernandes, S.R., Khelassi, A. et al. (2020). UAV-CPSs as a test bed for new technologies and a primer to Industry 5.0. *In:* Estrela, V.V., Hemanth, J., Saotome, O., Nikolakopoulos, G., Sabatini, R. (eds). Imaging and Sensing for Unmanned Aircraft Systems, Vol. 2, 1, 1-22, IET, London, UK.
10. Kumar, A. (2016). Cyber physical systems (CPSs) – Opportunities and challenges for improving cyber security. International Journal of Computer Applications, 137, 19-27.
11. Yaacoub, J.A., Salman, O., Noura, H.N., Kaaniche, N., Chehab, A. et al. (2020). Cyber-physical systems security: Limitations, issues and future trends. Microprocessors and Microsystems, 77, 103201-103201.
12. Lee, E. and Messerschmitt, D.G. (1987). Synchronous data flow. Proc. IEEE, vol. 75(9), 1235-1245,.
13. Padilha, R., Iano, Y., Monteiro, A.C.B., Arthur, R., Estrela, V.V. et al. (2019). Betterment proposal to multipath fading channels potential to MIMO systems. *In:* Proc. 4th Brazilian Technology Symposium (BTSym'18): Emerging Trends and Challenges in Technology, vol. 1, p. 115. Springer.
14. França, R.P., Monteiro, A.C.B., Estrela, V.V. and Razmjooy, N. (2021). Using metaheuristics in discrete-event simulation. *In:* Razmjooy, N., Ashourian, M., Foroozandeh, Z. (eds). Metaheuristics and Optimization in Computer and Electrical Engineering. Lecture Notes in Electrical Engineering, vol. 696. Springer, Cham.
15. Lee, E.A. and Zheng, H. (2005). Operational semantics of hybrid systems. *In:* Hybrid Systems: Computation and Control. pp. 25-53. Springer.
16. Van der Schaft, J. and Schumacher, J.M. (1998). Complementarity modeling of hybrid systems. IEEE Transactions on Automatic Control, 43(4), 483-490.

17. Antsaklis, P.J., Stiver, J.A. and Lemmon, M. (1993). Hybrid system modeling and autonomous control systems. *In:* Hybrid Systems. pp. 366-392. Springer.
18. Bujorianu, M.L. and Piterman, N. (2015). A modelling framework for cyber-physical system resilience. *In:* Cyber Physical Systems: Design, Modeling, and Evaluation. pp. 67-82. Springer.
19. Kottenstette, N., Karsai, G. and Sztipanovits, J. (2009). A passivity-based framework for resilient cyber physical systems. Proc. 2nd International Symp. Resilient Control Systems. pp. 43-50. IEEE.
20. Razmjooy, N., Razmjooy, S., Vahedi, Z., Estrela, V.V., de Oliveira, G.G. et al. (2021). A new design for robust control of power system stabilizer based on moth search algorithm. *In:* Razmjooy, N., Ashourian, M., Foroozandeh, Z. (eds). Metaheuristics and Optimization in Computer and Electrical Engineering. Lecture Notes in Electrical Engineering, vol 696. Springer, Cham.
21. Parmar and Jinwala, D.C. (2015). Hybrid secure data aggregation in wireless sensor networks. *In:* Cyber Physical Systems: Design, Modeling, and Evaluation. pp. 116-131. Springer.
22. Mitchell, R. and Chen, I.-R. (2015). Behavior rule specification-based intrusion detection for safety critical medical cyber physical systems. IEEE Transactions on Dependable and Secure Computing, 12(1), 16-30.
23. Venkatasubramanian, K., Vasserman, E.Y., Sfyrla, V., Sokolsky, O., Lee, I. et al. (2015). Requirement engineering for functional alarm system for interoperable medical devices. *In:* Computer Safety, Reliability, and Security. pp. 252-266. Springer.
24. Estrela, V.V., Hemanth, J., Loschi, H.J., Nascimento, D.A., Iano, Y. et al. (2020). Computer vision and data storage in UAVs. *In:* Estrela, V.V. et al. (eds). Imaging and Sensing for Unmanned Aircraft Systems, Vol. 1(2), 23-46, IET, London, UK.
25. Dong, P., Han, Y., Guo, X. and Xie, F. (2014). A security and safety framework for cyber physical system. Proc. 7th Conf. Control and Automation. pp. 49-51. IEEE.
26. Schupp, S., Abraham, E., Chen, X., Makhlouf, I.B., Frehse, G. et al. (2015). Current challenges in the verification of hybrid systems. *In:* Cyber Physical Systems: Design, Modeling, and Evaluation. pp. 8-24. Springer.
27. Thacker, R.A., Jones, K.R., Myers, C.J. and Zheng, H. (2010). Automatic abstraction for verification of cyber-physical systems. Proc. 1st ACM/IEEE Int'l Conf. Cyber-Physical Systems. pp. 12-21. ACM.
28. Arrieta, A., Mendieta, G.S. and Elorza, L.E. (2015). Test control algorithms for the validation of cyber-physical systems product lines. Proceedings of the 19th International Conference on Software Product Line. pp. 273-282. ACM.
29. Jensen, J.C., Chang, D.H. and Lee, E.A. (2011). A model-based design methodology for cyber-physical systems. Proc. 7th International Wireless Communications and Mobile Computing Conference. pp. 1666-1671. IEEE.
30. Sawand, A., Djahel, S., Zhang, Z. and Nait-Abdesselam, F. (2014). Multidisciplinary approaches to achieving efficient and trustworthy eHealth monitoring systems. Proc. IEEE/CIC Int'l Conf. Communications in China. pp. 187-192. IEEE.
31. Paul, P.C., Loane, J., Regan, G. and McCaffery, F. (2019). Analysis of attacks and security requirements for wireless body area networks – A systematic literature review. Proc. EuroSPI, vol. 1060, pp. 439-452, Springer.
32. Rakitin, S.R. (2006). Coping with defective software in medical devices. Computer, 39(4), 40-45.
33. Martin, J.L., Murphy, E., Crowe, J.A. and Norris, B.J. (2006). Capturing user requirements in medical device development: The role of ergonomics. Physiological Measurement, 27(8), R49.

34. Banerjee, A., Gupta, S.K., Fainekos, G. and Varsamopoulos, G. (2011). Towards modeling and analysis of cyber-physical medical systems. Proc. 4th Int'l Symp. Applied Sciences in Biomedical and Communication Technologies. pp. 1-5. ACM.

35. Banerjee, A. and Gupta, S.K. (2013). Spatio-temporal hybrid automata for safe cyber-physical systems: A medical case study. Proc. ACM/IEEE Int'l Conf. Cyber-Physical Systems. pp. 71-80. IEEE.

36. Annese, V. and De Venuto, D. (2015). FPGA based architecture for fall-risk assessment during gait monitoring by synchronous EEG/EMG. Proc. 6th IEEE Int'l Work. Adv. Sensors and Interfaces. pp. 116-121. IEEE.

37. Huang, H., Sun, Y.L., Yang, Q., Zhang, F., Zhang, X. et al. (2010). Integrating neuromuscular and cyber systems for neural control of artificial legs. Proc. 1st ACM/IEEE Int'l Conf. Cyber-Physical Systems. pp. 129-138. ACM.

38. Asare, P., Dickerson, R.F., Wu, X., Lach, J. and Stankovic, J.A. et al. (2013). Bodysim: A multi-domain modeling and simulation framework for body sensor networks research and design. Proc. 8th Int'l Conf. Body Area Net. pp. 177-180. ICST.

39. Wang, H., Gao, Y., Hu, S., Wang, S., Mancuso et al. (2017). On exploiting structured human interactions to enhance sensing accuracy in cyber-physical systems. ACM Transactions on Cyber-Physical Systems, 1, 1-19.

40. Silva, C., Almeida, H.O., Perkusich, A. and Perkusich, M. (2015). A model based approach to support validation of medical cyber-physical systems. Sensors, 15(11), 27625-27670.

41. Nabar, S., Banerjee, A., Gupta, S.K. and Poovendran, R. (2011). GeM-REM: Generative model-driven resource efficient ECG monitoring in body sensor networks. Proc. Int'l Conf. Body Sensor Networks. pp. 1-6. IEEE.

42. Bogdan P. (2015). A cyber-physical systems approach to personalized medicine: Challenges and opportunities for NOC-based multicore platforms. Proc. 2015 Design, Aut. and Test in Europe Conf. and Exhibition. pp. 253-258. EDA Consortium.

43. Banerjee, A., Kandula, S., Mukherjee, T. and Gupta S.K. (2012). BAND-AiDe: A tool for cyber-physical oriented analysis and design of body area networks and devices. ACM Transactions on Embedded Comp. Systems, 11(S2), 49.

44. Troger, P., Werner, M. and Richling, J. (2015). Cyber-physical operating systems— What are the right abstractions? Proc. 4th Mediterranean Conference on Embedded Computing. pp. 13-16. IEEE.

45. Hahn, A., Thomas, R.K., Lozano, I. and Cardenas, A. (2015). A multi-layered and kill-chain based security analysis framework for cyber-physical systems. Int'l J. Critical Infrastructure Protection, 11, 39-50.

46. Haque, S.A. and Aziz, S.M. (2013). False alarm detection in cyber-physical systems for healthcare applications. AASRI Procedia, 5, 54-61.

47. Miller, F., Vahid and Givargis, T. (2012). MEDS: Mockup electronic data sheets for automated testing of cyber-physical systems using digital mockups. Proc. Design, Automation and Test in Europe Conf. and Exhibition. pp. 1417-1420. IEEE.

48. Banerjee, A. and Gupta, S.K. (2014). Model based code generation for medical cyber physical systems. Proceedings of the 1st Workshop on Mobile Medical Applications. pp. 22-27. ACM.

49. Zhang, W., Wei, Y.-H., Leng, Q. and Han, S. (2014). A high-speed, real-time mobile gait rehabilitation system. XRDS: Crossroads, The ACM Magazine for Students, 20(3), 46-51.

50. Li, T., Cao, J., Liang, J. and Zheng, J. (2014). Towards context-aware medical cyber-physical systems: Design methodology and a case study, Cyber Physical Systems, no. ahead-of-print, pp. 1-19.

51. Pawlak, K., Horoba, J., Jezewski, J., Wrobel and A. Matonia et al. (2015). Telemonitoring of pregnant women at home—Biosignals acquisition and measurement. Proc. 22nd Int'l Conf. Mixed Design of Integrated Circ. and Syst. pp. 83-87. IEEE.

52. Tobola, C., Espig, F.J., Streit, O., Korpok, B. Schmitz, C. et al. (2015). Scalable ECG hardware and algorithms for extended run-time of wearable sensors. IEEE International Symposium on Medical Measurements and Applications. pp. 255-260. IEEE.

53. Kane, D., Zhu, M., Hirose, X., Dong, B., Winter, M. et al. (2014). Development of an extensible dual-core wireless sensing node for cyber-physical systems *In:* SPIE Smart Structures and Materials+ Nondestructive Evaluation and Health Monitoring. Int'l Society for Optics and Photonics, pp. 90611U-90611U.

54. Ray and Cleaveland, R. (2015). Security assurance cases for medical cyber-physical systems. IEEE Design and Test, 32(5), 56-65.

55. Estrela, V.V., Hemanth, J., Saotome, O., Nikolakopoulos, G., Sabatini, R. et al. (2020). Introduction to advances in UAV avionics for imaging and sensing. *In:* Estrela, V.V. et al. (eds). Imaging and Sensing for Unmanned Aircraft Systems, 1(1), 1-22, IET, London, UK.

56. Larson, R., Zhang, Y., Barrett, S.C., Hatcliff, J., Jones, P.L. et al. (2015). Enabling safe interoperation by medical device virtual integration. IEEE Design and Test, 32(5), 74-88.

57. Dagale, H., Anand, S., Hegde, M., Purohit, N., Supreeth, M. et al. (2015). CyPhyS+: A reliable and managed cyber-physical system for old-age home healthcare over a 6LoWPAN using wearable motes. IEEE International Conf. Services Computing. pp. 309-316. IEEE.

58. Ghoshdastider, U., Viga, R. and Kraft, M. (2015). Experimental evaluation of a pairwise broadcast synchronization in a low-power cyber-physical system. Proc. IEEE Topical Conference on Wireless Sensors and Sensor Networks. pp. 50-52. IEEE.

59. Ma, X., Tu, X., Huang, J. and He, J. (2011). A cyber-physical system based framework for motor rehabilitation after stroke. Proc. 1st International Conf. Wireless Technologies for Humanitarian Relief. pp. 285-290. ACM.

60. Dillon, T.S., Zhuge, H., Wu, C., Singh, J., Chang, E. et al. (2011). Web-of-things framework for cyber-physical systems. Concurrency and Computation: Practice and Experience, 23(9), 905-923.

61. de Jesus, M.A., Estrela, V.V., Huacasi, W.D., Razmjooy, N., Plaza, P. et al. (2020). Using Transmedia Approaches in STEM. 2020 IEEE Global Engineering Education Conference (EDUCON), pp. 1013-1016.

62. Farfan, W.S., Saotome, O., Estrela, V.V. and Navid Razmjooy N. (2020). Integrated optical flow for situation awareness, detection and avoidance systems in UAV systems. *In:* Estrela, V.V., Hemanth, J., Saotome, O., Nikolakopoulos, G., Sabatini, R. (eds). Imaging and Sensing for Unmanned Aircraft Systems, 1(3), 4774, IET, London, UK.

63. Hossain, S. (2015). Cloud-supported cyber-physical localization framework for patients monitoring. IEEE Syst. Journal, 11, 118-127.

64. Phuong, L.T.T., Hieu, N.T., Wang, J., Lee, S., Lee, Y.-K. et al. (2011). Energy efficiency based on quality of data for cyber physical systems. Proc. Int'l Conf. Internet of Things/4th Int'l Conf. Cyber, Physical and Social Comp. pp. 232-241. IEEE

65. Zhang, Y., Qiu, M., Tsai, C.-W., Hassan, M.M. and Alamri, A. et al. (2015). HealthCPS: Healthcare cyber-physical system assisted by cloud and big data. IEEE Systems Journal, 1-8.

66. He, J., Geng, Y., Wan, Y., Li, S., Pahlavan, K. et al. (2013). A cyber physical test-bed for virtualization of RF access environment for body sensor network. IEEE Sensors Journal, 13(10), 3826-3836.

67. Gunes, V., Peter, S. and Givargis, T. (2013). Modeling and mitigation of faults in cyber-physical systems with binary sensors. Proc. IEEE 16th International Conference on Computational Science and Engineering. pp. 515-522. IEEE.
68. de Jesus, M.A. et al. (2021). Building bridges and remediating illiteracy: How intergenerational cooperation foster better engineering professionals. *In:* Khelassi, A., Estrela, V.V. (eds). Advances in Multidisciplinary Medical Technologies—Engineering, Modeling and Findings. Springer, Cham.
69. Jezewski, J., Pawlak, A., Wrobel, J., Horoba, K., Penkala, P. et al. (2015). Towards a medical cyber-physical system for home telecare of high-risk pregnancy. IFAC-PapersOnLine, 48(4), 466-473.
70. Shih, C.-S., Wang, Y.-H., Yang, C.-M. and Chao, S.-H. (2015). Elastic computation middleware for interactive wearable devices in systems. Proc. IEEE 3rd Int'l Conf. on Cyber Physical Systems, Networks, and App. pp. 1-6. IEEE.
71. Fernandes, A. Ferreira, Mendes, J. and Cabral, J. (2015). A wireless body sensor network based on dynamic power control and opportunistic packet scheduling mechanisms. Proc. IEEE Int'l Conf. Industrial Technology. pp. 2160-2165. IEEE.
72. Xia, F., Wang, L., Zhang, D., He, D. and Kong, X. (2015). An adaptive MAC protocol for real-time and reliable communications in medical cyber physical systems. Telecommunication Systems, 58(2), 125-138.
73. Banerjee, A., Venkatasubramanian, K. and Gupta, S.K. (2009). Challenges of implementing cyber-physical security solutions in body area networks. Proc. Fourth Int'l Conf. Body Area Networks. ICST (Institute for Computer Sciences, Social-Informatics and Telecommunications Engineering). p. 18.
74. Hatcliff, J., King, A., Lee, I., Macdonald, A., Fernando, A. et al. (2012,). Rationale and architecture principles for medical application platforms. IEEE/ACM Third International Conference on Cyber-Physical Systems. pp. 3-12. IEEE.
75. Xia, F., Ma, L., Dong, J. and Sun, Y. (2008). Network QoS management in cyber-physical systems. International Conference on Embedded Software and Systems Symposia. pp. 302-307. IEEE.
76. Laghari, A.A., Khan, A., He, H., Estrela, V.V., Razmjooy, N. et al. (2020). Quality of experience (QoE) and quality of service (QoS) in UAV systems. *In:* Estrela, V.V., Hemanth, J., Saotome, O., Nikolakopoulos, G., Sabatini, R. (eds). Imaging and Sensing for Unmanned Aircraft Systems, 2(10), 213-242, IET, London, UK.
77. Liu, J. and Zhang, L. (2011). QoS modeling for cyber-physical systems using aspect-oriented approach. Proc. Second International Conference on Networking and Distributed Computing. pp. 154-158. IEEE.
78. Bertoli, G.C., Saotome, O. and Estrela, V.V. (2020). Computer vision in UAV using ROS. *In:* Estrela, V.V. et al. (eds), Imaging and Sensing for Unmanned Aircraft Systems, 1(9), 217-260, IET, London, UK.
79. Lien, S.-Y., Cheng, S.-M., Shih, S.-Y. and Chen, K.-C. (2012). Radio resource management for QoS guarantees in cyber-physical systems. IEEE Transactions on Parallel and Distributed Systems, 23(9), 1752-1761.
80. Huang, J., Bastani, F.B., Yen, I. and Zhang, W. (2010). A framework for efficient service composition in cyber-physical systems. Proc. Fifth IEEE International Symposium on Service Oriented System Engineering, 291-298.
81. Wan, K., Hughes, D., Man, K.L. and Krilavicius, T. (2010). Composition challenges and approaches for cyber physical systems. Proc. 2010 IEEE International Conference on Networked Embedded Systems for Enterprise Applications. pp. 1-7. IEEE.
82. Menasce, D.A., Gomaa, H., Malek, S. and Sousa J.P. (2011). SASSY: A framework for self-architecting service-oriented systems. IEEE Software, 28(6), 78-85.

83. Zhang, W. and Zhang, L. (2015). Designing and modeling cyber physical systems by a service-based approach. Proc. 6th IEEE International Conference on Software Engineering and Service Science (ICSESS). pp. 668-671. IEEE.

84. Zhu, W., Zhou, G., Yen, I.-L. and Bastani, F. (2015). A PT-SOA model for CPS/IoT services. Proc. IEEE Int'l Conference on Web Services. pp. 647-654. IEEE.

85. La, H.J. and Kim, S.D. (2010). A service-based approach to designing cyber physical systems. IEEE/ACIS 9th International Conference on Computer and Information Science. pp. 895-900. IEEE.

86. Mechitov, K. and Agha, G. (2012). Building portable middleware services for heterogeneous cyber-physical systems. Proc. Third International Workshop on Software Engineering for Sensor Network Applications. pp. 31-36. IEEE Press.

87. Park, S.O., Do, T.H., Jeong, Y.-S. and Kim, S.J. (2013). A dynamic control middleware for cyber physical systems on an IPv6-based global network. International Journal of Communication Systems, 26(6), 690-704.

88. Estrela, V.V., Hemanth, J., Saotome, O., Grata, E.G.H., Izario, D.R.F. et al. (2019). Emergency response cyber-physical system for flood prevention with sustainable electronics. *In:* Iano Y. et al. (eds). Proc. of the 3rd Brazilian Technology Symposium. BTSym 2017, Campinas, SP, Brazil. Springer, Zurich, Switzerland.

89. Xia, F., Vinel, A.V., Gao, R., Wang, L., Qiu, T. et al. (2011). Evaluating IEEE 802.15.4 for Cyber-Physical Systems. EURASIP Journal on Wireless Communications and Networking, 1-14.

90. Dubey, H., Yang, J., Constant, N., Amiri, A.M., Yang, Q. et al. (2015). Fog data: Enhancing telehealth big data through fog computing. Proc. ASE Big Data and Social Informatics 2015. pp. 1-6. ACM.

91. Ullrich, J., Cropper, J., Fruhwirt, P. and Weippl, E.R. (2016). The role and security of firewalls in cyber-physical cloud computing. EURASIP Journal on Information Security, 2016, 18, pp. 1-20, doi: 10.1186/s13635-016-0042-3.

92. Chen, K.-C. and Lien, S.-Y. (2014). Machine-to-machine communications: Technologies and challenges. Ad Hoc Networks, 18, 3-23.

93. King, A.L., Procter, S., Andresen, D., Hatcliff, J., Warren et al. (2009). An open test bed for medical device integration and coordination. Proc. 31st International Conference on Software Engineering – Companion Volume, 141-151.

94. Gyselinckx, C., Van Hoof, J., Ryckaert, R.F., Yazicioglu, P., Fiorini et al. (2005). Human++: Autonomous wireless sensors for body area networks. Proc. IEEE 2005 Custom Integrated Circuits Conference. pp. 13-19. IEEE.

95. Montero-Odasso, M.M., Sarquis-Adamson, Y., Speechley, M., Borrie, M.J., Hachinski, V.C. et al. (2017). Association of dual-task gait with incident dementia in mild cognitive impairment: Results from the gait and brain study. JAMA Neurology, 74, 857-865.

96. Wang, R., Blackburn, G., Desai, M., Phelan, D., Gillinov, L. et al. (Jan. 2017). Accuracy of wrist-worn heart rate monitors. J. American Medical Association Cardiology, 2, 104-106.

Ad Hoc Networks in Healthcare Intelligent Transportation Systems Humanitary Relief – MANETs, VANETs, and FANETs

V.V. Estrela[1] **[0000-0002-4465-7691], A. Deshpande**[2] **[0000-0002-1500-0981], D. Stutz**[3] **[0000-0003-1408-1756], J.T. de Assis**[3] **[0000-0002-2802-1298], Awais K. Jumani**[4] **[0000-0001-9468-0446], H.H.P. da Silva**[5] **[0000-0001-6764-8432], Abdullah A. Khan**[6] **[0000-0003-2838-7641], Fuqian Shi**[7] **[0000-0003-4245-5727], Shoulin Yin**[8] **[0000-0002-5367-1372], Yu-Da Lin**[9] **[0000-0001-5100-6072], J.M.R.S. Tavares**[10] **[0000-0001-7603-6526]**

[1] Telecommunications Department, Fluminense Federal University (UFF), RJ, Brazil
vania.estrela.phd@ieee.org
[2] Electronics and Communication Engineering, Angadi Institute of Technology and
Management, Belagavi, India, deshpande.anandb@gmail.com
[3] Instituto Politecnico do Rio de Janeiro, Nova Friburgo, RJ, Brazil,
stutz@iprj.uerj.br, joaquim@iprj.br
[4] Department of Computer Science, Ilma University, Karachi, Sindh, Pakistan,
awaiskhan@yahoo.com
[5] Instituto de Telecomunicoes, Instituto Superior Tecnico, Torre Norte - Piso 10, Av.
Rovisco Pais, 1, 1049-001, Lisboa, Lisboa, Portugal, hsilva@lx.it.pt
[6] Faculty of Computer Science, Sindh Madressatul Islam University, Karachi (74000),
Sindh, Pakistan, abdullah.khan0076@gmail.com
[7] Rutgers Cancer Institute of New Jersey, United States, shifuqian@gmail.com
[8] Shenyang Normal University, Shenyang, Liaoning Province, 110034, China,
yslin@hit.edu.cn
[9] National Penghu University of Science and Technology, Magong, TW,
yudalinemail@gmail.com
[10] Departamento de Engenharia Mecanica (DEMec), Faculdade de Engenharia da
Universidade do Porto (FEUP)/Instituto de Engenharia Mecanica e Gestao Industrial
(INEGI), Porto, Portugal, tavares@fe.up.pt

1. Introduction

Presently, there is a cumulative interest in improving public safety and health services in emergency/disastrous conditions. A movable health unit relying on web service displays poses challenges. Maps can display the stakeholder dynamics and needs using different data sources (such as GPS and infrared imagery). Remote access and the development of new, unique, intelligent, and convenient computing devices impact Wireless Sensor Networks (WSNs), allowing consumers to access healthcare services at any time, notwithstanding their geographic location. WSNs are twofold: infrastructure-based and infrastructure-less (alias Ad Hoc Networks or AHNs or ANETs). An infrastructure network mobile nodes communicate through the nearest base station (BS) inside the communication range. A mobile node is comparable to a mobile terminal/workstation without routing functions, but only mobile switches perform routing and switching roles. Office wireless LANs, cellular wireless frameworks, and so forth illustrate this type of network.

The second type comprises an autonomous, wireless multi-hop mobile network without permanent infrastructure or fixed routers, where all the nodes are itinerant and can dynamically interact with other nodes in any manner. In this environment, due to the restricted wireless terminal coverage, user terminals that cannot converse straightforwardly can forward packets with the support of other nodes. Hence, each node can work as a router, discovering and keeping routes to other nodes.

AHNs can bring healthcare to distant places (Figure 1). Expansion of Smart healthcare systems is a current tendency, and wireless communications behave as their backbones. All healthcare units must possess advanced technologies to offer patient diagnoses, treatments, and numerous services within health facilities and remotely. Speedy response units can also handle patient needs and queries created during disasters/emergencies. This chapter goes over healthcare communication challenges and potential early awareness with rapid response in disastrous/emergency situations under the human-centric vision of 6G wireless technologies.

This chapter organization follows. Section 2 Overviews AHNs. Vehicular network challenges appear in Section 3. Section 4 discusses the AHNs' architectures. MANETs vs. Vehicular Ad Hoc Networks (VANETs) vs. Flying Ad Hoc Networks (FANETs)are compared in Section 5. MAC protocols for AHNs appear in Section 6. Section 7 discourses about routing protocol analysis in AHNs. Discussions and a conclusion appear in Sections 8 and 9 in that order.

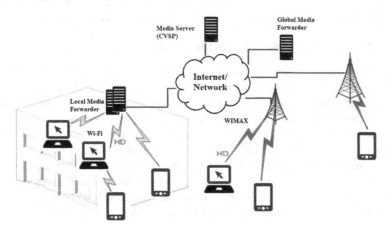

Figure 1. Mixed mobile ad hoc network (MANET)

2. Ad Hoc Networks

2.1. Mobile Ad Hoc Networks (MANETs)

The networking components (like routers and gateways) and nodes linked within the network range to the adjacent BS that comes into its communication range making up an infrastructure-reliant network. When that base station's coverage area exceeds a node's coverage area, it executes the hand-off operation to fall within the new BS scope. A well-known example of infrastructure-based WSNs is cellular communication. The infrastructure-less network, also known as an AHN, is a peer-to-peer (P2P) network that is self-forming and self-restorative.

While in motion, mobile AHNs (MANETs) can create a mobile node network, which can then be merged or segmented into separate networks. The MANET nodes rely on networking requirements and continuously manage the departure and arrival of network nodes. A MANET's primary goals are dependability, availability, and scalability. The network's nodes are self-governing processing units with limited capacity to travel around freely. The network's topology changes quickly, unpredictably, and regularly as a consequence of this feature. Each node can host or route data. The success of communication relies heavily on cooperation among nodes. Nodes are in charge of searching for and locating other nodes in the wireless range to communicate. MANET nodes regularly relocate, resulting in a break-in connection and the need to restore capacity. Furthermore, traditional computer routing methods are unsuitable for MANET because the maximum node number in a network has little battery life and computation capability.

Handheld devices such as smartphones, laptops, wearables, and other wireless mobile devices work as MANET devices. These gadgets are usually small and portable, and they come with batteries. Figure 1 depicts a heterogeneous mobile AHN and how it communicates with various devices.

For example, collected blood cell characteristics can feed a classification step that automatically categorizes cells consistent with hematological models. The classification module should identify the blood cells using features taken from real pictures. When dealing with noisy imageries, this might make categorization difficult.

2.2. Vehicular Ad Hoc Networks (VANETs)

VANETs (or vehicular AHNs) arose from the necessity to accommodate the growing variety of wireless items that may now be utilized in automobiles (Figure 2) [1, 2]. Wireless goods include keyless entry devices, tablets, computers, and cellphones. The need for Vehicle-to-Vehicle (V2V), as well as Vehicle-to-Infrastructure (V2I) broadcasting, will grow day by day as portable wireless devices and networks assume more importance [2]. VANETs can cope with a wide variety of protected and unprotected applications. For example, automatic toll payment, transportation management, better navigation, vehicle protection, location-reliant services, and pursuit for the nearest service/entertainment (such as a gas station or restaurant) [3], as well as internet-based information applications. VANETs are briefly summarized as follows:

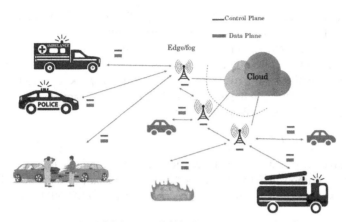

Figure 2. Vehicle-to-Vehicle (V2V) communication.

Vehicle-to-Vehicle (V2V): This technology uses a Wireless Area Network (WAN) to allow cars to communicate about their activities. This information includes their speed, position, direction, braking, and lack of stability, among other things. V2V exchanges entail Dedicated Short-Range Communication (DSRC) technology, a standard defined by the FCC and ISO. Although the frequency utilized in this connection is 5.9 GHz (the same as Wi-Fi), it is improper to refer to it as a Wi-Fi network. This network's vehicles have a range of up to 300 meters. This network's topology is mesh, which implies that each node may transmit, receive, and record signals. V2V networks enable vehicles to interact with one another without ongoing infrastructure maintenance and primarily aid safety, security, and information transmission.

Vehicle-to-Infrastructure (V2I) or On-Board Unit (OBU): It is paramount for vehicle coordination. The Road Side Unit (RSU) is a radio transceiver that allows a vehicle and a roadside transceiver to interact for protection, security, and traffic control. These networks gather data on local signals and road conditions, then apply regulations to the group of cars linked to the network for various reasons.

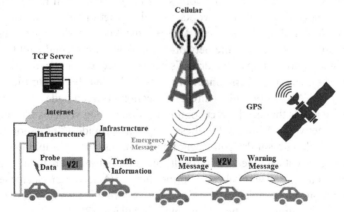

Figure 3. Vehicle-to-Infrastructure (V2I) communication

Vehicle-to-Vehicle-to-Infrastructure (V2V2I): This hybrid architecture combines vehicle-to-vehicle and vehicle-to-infrastructure communication. In this sort of communication, a vehicle can communicate with roadside infrastructure in a single hop or multi-hop fashion contingent on the distance, i.e., if it cannot directly exchange information with a road unit. It allows cars to speak with each other over long distances or connect to the internet. V2V2I is distinct from the other two forms of communication mentioned previously.

2.2.1. VANET Features

VANETs have become an essential study topic for developing nations by expanding their traffic conditions day by day. VANETs, which are part of the MANET family, have various distinguishing characteristics as compared to MANETs, including the following:

1. **High Computational Capability:** Vehicles with adequate sensors/actuators and assets for processing, such as Global Positioning Systems (GPSs), CPUs, and substantial memory capacity, are called nodes in VANETs. These assets are the most critical components in enhancing the node capabilities, which aid in achieving reliable communication by obtaining accurate information about the vehicle's direction, speed, and current location [4-5].
2. **Expected Mobility:** VANET mobility is far more predictable than that of MANETs. The final kind of vehicular network node travels at random. Still, in VANETs, the cars (nodes) generally follow the topology defined by the road, obeying the traffic lights and road signs, resulting in predictable movement [6-9].
3. **No Energy Glitches:** In comparison to MANETs, energy is not a significant concern in VANETs because automobiles continually deliver enough power to OBUs through the use of long-life batteries [5, 7, 10].
4. **Variable Network Density:** This component is solely dependent on traffic density, which might be minimal (as in domiciliary traffic) or very high (as in traffic congestion) [9, 10].
5. **Hefty Networks:** VANET network sizes range from small to big and include rural, urban, and highway networks, as well as metropolitan towns [9, 10].
6. **Network Topology Immediate Alterations:** Vehicles driving at high speeds on highways can modify the network's topology in a second, and the received information might impair the driver's performance as a result [8-10].
7. **Harmless Driving Assurance:** This is only feasible if traffic efficiency upsurges. VANETs provide a direct connection between nodes, allowing a slew of applications that need direct communication among vehicles to communicate via the network. Additionally, these programs provide information to visitors traveling along a similar path regarding the importance of rapid hard breaking or potential catastrophes. As a result, the motorist must create a larger image of the roadway layout ahead. Furthermore, VANETs can increase traveler satisfaction and efficiency by displaying information from retail malls, gas stations, restaurants and hotels, among other places [7].

8. **Time Criticality:** The VANET network data must be provided to the nodes at a specific time to make an informed choice and take quick action.

2.3. Flying Ad Hoc Networks

The utilization of Flying Ad Hoc Networks (FANETs), a subset of VANETs, is a major use case for UAVs [32, 33]. Coordination and teamwork between nodes are critical for efficient data transmission in the FANET [34-36]. The relationship between nodes is contingent upon node behavior, which may be quantified using the idea of trust [37-39]. Trust enables isolating uncooperative and malicious network nodes, and it also increases the dependability of the node-to-node data flow [40-42].

Routing protocols are inefficient in networks with too many mobile devices or do not deliver sufficient throughput in VANETs. The FANET topology, on the other hand, alternates more frequently than the topology of the VANETs or MANETs [43, 44]. Now, the primary network technologies to construct FANETs are the IEEE 802.11a, as well as 802.11s for mesh Ad Hoc Network (ANET) extension. A jet engine is used to power a FANET or a reciprocating engine that is remotely flown using pre-programmed flight plans [45, 46, 84]. This airborne aircraft operates independently of human assistance and does not take individuals onboard, unlike an autopilot.

FANET communication can be regarded as UAV–UAV (U2U) and UAV–Infrastructure (U2I) interactions. In FANETs, nodes interact via multi-hop communication, with one node connecting to the infrastructure and the others communicating via multi-hop communication [47, 48, 85]. As a result, not all UAV missions require contact with a satellite or Ground-Based System (GBS) [49-53].

2.3.1. UAV Communications Challenges

• Ecological and geographical constraints,
• Node mobility,
• Sufficient bandwidth ease of use in addition to low latency,
• Synchronization between UAV swarms.

2.3.2. Benefits of Multi-UAV Structures over a Single UAV

The most important follow:

• **Cost:** Numerous respondents stated that while collecting data using drones is not difficult, the actual issue and complexity demarcate how to use the vast volumes of data acquired. At the moment, the market is saturated with firms focused on front-end data gathering, and the pure data collection cost continues to decline. Nonetheless, few organizations can back-end data processing for cross-disciplinary applications, which leaves the front and back ends at odds. This forces end-users to verify that the quantity and quality of collected data meets business requirements and consider multi-party collaboration, thus raising expenses and communication hurdles.

• **Speed up:** Several kinds of drones can perform in diverse settings depending on their qualities. For example, fixed-wing UAVs have a long battery life, high cruising speeds, and a high payload capacity, making them ideal for high-speed, heavy-payload, large-scale, and long-distance missions such as aerial surveying and mapping. Rotary-wing UAVs are highly maneuverable and capable of vertical take-offs, landings as well as hovering. They are primarily designed for missions requiring low altitudes, slow speeds, vertical take-offs and landings, and hoverings, e.g., post-disaster search and rescue.

*   **Small radar:** A multi-UAV system's radar cross-section is relatively small, as opposed to a larger cross-section, which is critical for many applications.
*   **Mission accomplishment time:** Rapid surveillance, reconnaissance, and search missions are possible with more drones. If a single drone cannot accomplish the task, the mission fails. However, with a multi-drone system, if one of the drones takes off, the operation can continue with the assistance of other drones.

While multiple unmanned aircraft systems offer various benefits over single ones, communication between two distant nodes is unique and hard due to the changing network structure.

2.3.3. FANETs' Characteristics

One of the characteristics of FANETs is their lightness and compactness; this implies that the drone fuselage is gradually disappearing and becoming smaller. Developing new materials aerial-specific applications will significantly improve the drone's flexibility and comfort.

The second is synthesis. Drones are advancing toward system integration and extensive sensing to intensify their adaptability. The UAV interactions and integration with other platforms like manned aircraft and monitoring GBSs have been strengthened throughout the development of multi-mission aircraft.

Customization is the third. UAVs can adapt more to the unique requirements of healthcare stakeholders while being agile. Developing an impressive, customized UAV is quite possible.

Intelligence is the fourth. Drones will not only serve as transport platforms and passively accomplish numerous flying duties in the future; they will also aid as intelligent partners with a variety of capabilities like effective governance, data recording, extra analysis, and joint operations. As their intelligence grows, drones will also attain autonomous data collecting and smart learning. Simultaneously, merging Augmented Reality (AR) and Virtual Reality (VR) gadgets with UAVs will significantly enhance drone flying and control modes. In summary, UAV users should be proactive in learning about and adhering to pertinent legislation and regulations, regulating the drone industry's growth status, successfully adopting new technology, and considering how drones might help their business.

The market for unmanned aircraft has progressively shrunk, and development has slowed, which is a critical chance for all stakeholders to rethink how unmanned aircraft will be used in the future. People and companies urge users to have a long-term perspective based on a thorough grasp of the UAV properties, analyze circumstances, learn from experience, and make logical business decisions. Simultaneously, one anticipates that UAV medical applications will mature and stabilize. An increasing number of businesses exploit drone wings to get their undertakings off the ground. The FANET from Figure 6 exemplifies different traits of ad hoc networks:

- Node Mobility: FANET mobility degree is more extensive than that of VANET and MANET. The UAV node speeds vary between 30-460 km/h, triggering UAV node communication problems.
- Low node density combined with a large distance amid UAVs.
- The network topology varies habitually.
- Power ingestion and network lifespan.
- The radio propagation paradigm.
- GPS provides geospatial localization.
- Access to Line-of-Sight (LoS).

2.3.4. FANET Network Routing Protocols

A broad categorization of routing protocols exists. Still, a Jamming-Resilient Multipath Routing Protocol for FANETs has been suggested [32, 86] to minimize network interruptions, jamming assaults, and localized failures. The central concept of the Stochastic Packet Algorithm (SPA) [54] consists of randomly choosing a drone for rerouting based on a real-time combination of numerous network characteristics. The Fountain-code-based Greedy Queue and Position Assisted (FGQPA) modus operandi [55] decides the next transmission based on information about the queue and node geography to provide reliable end-to-end communication in networks of randomly and swiftly flying vehicles. The effort in [56] exhibited a Location-Aided Delay Tolerant Routing (LADTR) protocol merging geographic displacement and store relay procedures to increase the path availability of search methods used by drones during post-disaster activities. The Link-quality with Traffic-load-Aware Optimized Link-State Routing (LTA-OLSR) protocol [57] established the connection quality by analyzing the received signal strength information. The Mobility and Load-aware OLSR (ML-OLSR) [58] assigns a stabilization degree to connections based on statistical distance information.

The Predictive OLSR (P-OLSR) scrutinizes the drone's direction and relative speed, relying on onboard GPS data [59]. The controller constructs relay nodes to increase the availability of links and creates a routing table for each node based on the link length. Routing protocols are classified broadly [59-61]. A central geometric arrangement and a Software Defined Network (SDN)-based Topology Management for FANET (STFANET) techniques show up in [60]. The controller constructs relay nodes to increase the availability of links and creates a routing table for each node based on the link length [61], offering a FANET routing protocol that utilizes Particle Swarm Optimization (PSO) to enhance Greedy Forwarding Routing (GFR), aka PSO-GLFR. A Robust and Reliable Predictive Routing Protocol (RARP) appears in [62], utilizing speed, 3D coordinates, and other information to anticipate the average node position using linear extrapolation and estimates the expected contact time appropriately. A compression table for many popular routing methods in terms of land balance, routing category, computation cost, and communication overhead in a UAV network can be found in [63]. However, as science and technology advance while people continue to study and research, routing protocols for wireless ANETs have advanced significantly. As a result, we should recognize that research into routing protocols for wireless ad hoc networks is somewhat complicated. One must continue investigating and studying to propose suitable routing protocols and methods genuinely.

3. Vehicular Network Challenges

3.1. Mobility

Each ANET node can move from one locality inside the coverage region. Although mobility is still limited, VANET nodes have a high movement degree. Cars link with other vehicles they have never met before in this sort of network. This link may not last as long as these cars continue their courses, and they may never meet again. As a result, securing the mobility challenge is a serious issue [11, 87].

3.2. Volatility

The communication link amid vehicles might be highly faulty. As the nodes traverse around their coverage area and establish connections with additional nodes, this communication may not occur again. Due to rapid vehicular mobility, these links/ connections will be misplaced and may travel in the other direction [11, 12]. Since these networks lack a reasonably long-life context, the private interaction among customer devices and the hot spot require long-life passwords, which appear to be impractical for virtual connection security [13].

3.3. Privacy Verification

The node verification procedure is critical to inhibit various network assaults. A unique or distinctive identity may be assigned to each vehicle to solve this caveat, albeit not the best alternative for most stakeholders who want to keep their information secure [11, 12].

3.4. Privacy Responsibility

Responsibility will be an excellent choice for proper investigation. Any user cannot refute this information [11] if a collision or an accident happens. Furthermore, it is critical to protect the user privacy from others, and this information (e.g. ID, toll number, route and others) can be withheld from other drivers [13].

3.5. Scalability

These networks are large enough, and their scalability grows every day as the number of cars increases. Another issue is that this network lacks standards that any individual, or a company governs. Each country's DSRC requirements differ from one another and from car to vehicle [13].

3.6. Routing Protocol

Developing a new protocol capable of ensuring packet delivery in a short time frame with minimal packet losses will be regarded as a severe challenge to VANETs [14-17].

3.7. Trifling Operative Diameter

During communication, the tiny width causes a weak connection among nodes. As a result, preserving the global network topology for each node is impossible [18].

3.8. Fading of Signals

The barriers among nodes sharing information cause fading. Constructions and moving vehicles can function as barriers that fade the signal and block it from reaching its target destination [15].

3.9. Bandwidth Restrictions

This sort of network does not partake a centralized coordinator in charge of controlling bandwidth and congestion. When it comes to high-density locations, the channel congestion likelihood is significant due to the limited frequency range.

3.10. Connectivity

The primary cause of frequent network disconnections is high mobility and the reduced time for sharing information. The transmission power must be increased to attain this aim. Nonetheless, it will deteriorate throughput.

4. Architecture of VANETs

The number of vehicles on the road is also quickly rising, increasing the driving complexity, danger, and daily demand. Roads are congested, speed and safety distance restrictions are rarely respected, and motorists lack focus when traveling on the road. The key items in the VANET architecture are listed below.

4.1. Onboard Unit (OBU)

The Onboard Unit (OBU) generally is on the node board, the first component that comes with VANET architecture. For exchanging information with other Roadside Units (RSUs), this gadget employs the Wireless Access in Vehicular Environment (WAVE) framework for RSUs. Saving and recovering messages from memory demand a user interface in every OBU with all the CPU functions and a network interface for connecting to other OBUs. Finally, it is a short-range wireless device that uses the 802.11p protocol from the VANETs' MAC standard. Communication between the various OBUs/RSUs may require a wireless channel too, and this relies on the IEEE 802.11p standard for message exchange between OBUs/RSUs. Information security, IP mobility, geographic routing, message transfer with dependability, and network congestion control are OBU's primary responsibilities [19].

4.2. Application Unit (AU)

Application Units (AUs) are gadgets within the vehicle utilizing the administration mechanisms from the supplier and overuse OBU capabilities. An AU can be any mobile gadget associated with the Web or devoted to security applications. The

AU and the OBU can be wired or remotely associated and kept together in one physical unit.

4.3. Roadside Unit (RSU)

The Roadside Units (RSUs) are WAVE-enabled devices found in parking lots, signals, road segments, and intersections. The RSU has a specialized module for short-range radio transmission within the network infrastructure. RSUs can be mounted on a variety of network devices. The following are the major RSU activities connected with the congestion control communication consortium:

1. The network's range may be increased by redistributing messages to distinct OBUs as well as relaying messages to RSUs to be sent to different OBUs.
2. It uses V2I communication as a source of information for safety-related applications such as warnings for accidents, natural disasters, and work zones.
3. These units are responsible for providing internet access to OBUs.

5. MANETs vs. VANETs vs. FANETs

The link between AHNs is that nodes are autonomous and can manage data without any infrastructural support. VANETs are a subtype of MANETs with specific distinguishing characteristics. Table 1 compares these Ad Hoc networks.

5.1. Quickly Variable Topology

Topology changes quickly for all network kinds because nodes are mobilized and cannot remain in a network for long. Still, because the node speed in VANETs is comparably high compared to MANETs, the topology in VANETs changes frequently and rapidly. The topology of VANETs is predictable since the cars follow the road course, but MANETs' topology is unpredictable as nodes can relocate.

5.2. Repeated Interruptions

Networks face frequent disruption as topologies change fast. Since the link between vehicles might detach exceptionally fast due to the high vehicle speeds, the chance of disconnections in VANETs is much more elevated than in MANETs. If the node densities vary, then interruptions become less of a concern.

5.3. Energy Constraint

In contrast to MANETs, VANET nodes do not partake any energy constraints.

5.4. Production Cost

When it comes to the cost, a MANET is much cheaper than a VANET. However, both networks hold dissimilar nodes, and their manufacturing costs vary.

5.5. Reliability

When it comes to dependability, a VANET outperforms a MANET since the security factor in a MANET is significantly smaller than in a VANET. Some more ways the two networks differ from one another appear beneath.

Table 1. Difference between MANETs, VANETs, and FANETs

S. No	Parameters	MANETs	VANETs	FANETs
1	Production	Medium cost	High cost	Medium cost
2	Topology	Static	Highly variable	Highly variable
3	Mobility	Slow	Fast	Medium, Fast
4	Node density	Low	High	High
5	Bandwidth	Low rate	High rate	High rate
6	Range	Up to 100 m	Up to 500 m	Depends on the nodes. >500 m
7	Network active time	Depends on node energy	Depends on the vehicle's condition	Depends on the vehicle condition and autonomy of the batteries
8	Multi-tier routing	Available	Somewhat available	Somewhat available
9	Reliability	Medium	High	Medium, High
10	Moving pattern of nodes	Random	Regular	3D, regular, or as needed.
11	Addressing scheme	Attribute-based	Location-based	Location-based
12	Position acquisition	Using ultrasonic	Using GPS & RADAR	Using GPS, RADAR, etc.
13	Energy	Medium	Low	Medium, High
14	Node speed	Low	Medium, High	Medium, High

6. MAC Protocols in AHNs

VANETs offer safety and non-safety services to cars for the betterment of transportation networks. Vehicles must communicate when there is no collision and access the communication channel quickly to achieve this goal. For vehicular AHNs, many protocols have been suggested, each of which defines how nodes access the channel differently. Several challenges emerged during this protocol development, including high vehicle mobility, fast changes in network architecture, multi-channel separation, nearby channel interference, besides hidden node concerns. There are three major MAC protocols: Contention-based, unrestricted contention (or contention-free), in addition to hybrid MAC protocols.

6.1. VANETs' Routing Protocols

Topology-based, Cluster-based, Position-, Broadcast- and Geo-cast based routing protocols are the five types of routing protocols used in VANETs. These protocols are classified according to the services and applications that suit them best.

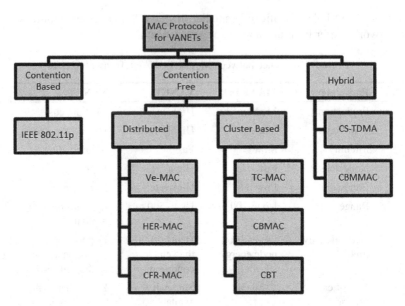

Figure 4. Types of MAC protocols

6.1.1. Topology Routing Protocol

The packets go to the nodes using information from the network's connections. They are also broken down into reactive and proactive procedures.

Reactive routing: The route toward the node opens only when a node must interact in this sort of protocol. It only keeps routes currently taken during routing, reducing the network's load. This protocol finds a route by sending a route discovery packet to all network nodes and pathways. When the source to destination path is discovered, this phase concludes. Some celebrated reactive routing protocols are the Ad-Hoc On-Demand Distance Vector (AODV), TORA, DSR, as well as PGB.

Proactive routing: Regardless of communication demands, this routing protocol retains the routing information for the next step in the background. This protocol has the advantage of not having a route discovery stage for the subsequent hop or destination, which is kept in the background. However, this pro comes with a shortcoming: this protocol has a low latency for real-time applications. In the node, the routing table is constructed and maintained. As a result, the next hop is already determined when the packet arrives at the node. However, the protocol supports the idle routes active during the conversation, limiting the network's available capacity. DSDV, LSR, OLSR, and BATMAN are examples of well-known proactive procedures.

Cluster-based routing protocol: A cluster connects a group of nodes in this sort of routing. One of these nodes becomes the cluster's head, broadcasting packets to the other cluster heads besides the gateway. This protocol may be used for extensive networks to improve scalability. However, it has a significant mobile network overhead and latency. This protocol requires the formation of virtual infrastructure to enable network scalability. AWCP, CBLR, RLSMP, CBVANET, in addition to COIN are well-known protocols.

Position-based routing: This routing algorithm group uses geographical location features to choose the next-hop to send the packet without consulting the neighborhood map beforehand. A neighbor is one hop distant from the destination node by definition. These routing protocols partake gains because there is no need to build and maintain a communication channel between the source and destination nodes. There are two types of delay-tolerant V2V protocols: position-based greedy V2V protocols and delay-tolerant V2V protocols. GPCR, CAR, DIR, MOVE, VADD, and SADV are examples of such protocols.

Broadcast routing protocol: These protocols are widely used in this network to communicate traffic, meteorological conditions, sharing, road settings, emergency information between cars, broadcasts and advertising. Recognized protocols are DV-CAST, BROADCOM, V-TRADE, and UMB.

Geo-cast routing protocol: It is a location-based multicast routing system. It distributes a given source's packets to nodes within the network's geographical range, also known as the relevance zone. Vehicles within ZOR's range cannot receive alerts, allowing them to avoid a quick unwelcome reaction. A source zone forwards the overflow of packets in this route. This flooding method reduces network congestion and message overheads generated by flooding packets throughout the whole network. Unicast routing is used in the destination zone to forward packets. The network apportioning and unfriendly neighbors obstruct packet dispatch, also being disadvantages. Examples of this kind of routing are DRG, ROVER, IVG, Cached Geo-cast, abiding Geo-cast, in addition to DG-CastoR.

7. ANET Routing Protocol Analysis

This part explains the basic AODV. VANETs diverge from MANETs and their corresponding route protocols as far as node mobility goes [32-34]. Nonetheless, due to peculiarities in both networks, these protocols underperform when applied directly to VANETs [35]. Since topologies in VANET networks vary constantly and bandwidth resources are limited, it is not necessary to maintain each node's route. This frequent topology change has an impact on routing effectiveness and decreases routing rate information. Thus, on-demand routing protocols are deemed suitable for VANETs.

Route discovery and maintenance are two procedures requiring protocols that fall under the on-demand umbrella. When the source node does not have any routing data in its table, then it creates a route to the destination. This routing establishment requests packets flooded by the source node throughout the whole network by broadcasting so that the route discovery startup process begins. The destination node transmits a route reaction packet to the source after receiving a route request packet, which creates a reverse path between the two nodes. The route maintenance procedure kicks in when the active path's definite link breaks or the node changes. When applied to VANETs, AODV is [36-38, 87], a very important MANET routing protocol, that also needs improvement.

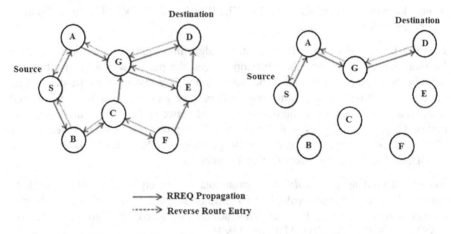

Figure 5.** Basic AODV routing protocol mechanism: (a) RREQ, (b) Source
to destination route.

7.1. VANET Basic AODV

AODV is the most common, reactive routing protocol among ANET possibilities. All of the routes are not always maintained in AODV. When a requirement for transmission route discovery arises, the procedure begins by lowering the overhead. The sequence number ensures fresh routes, and it is a loop-free topology as well, which distinguishes this protocol. Route discovery, data transfer, and route management are the three aspects of this protocol.

7.1.1. Data Transmission

Following the course revelation step, the information transmission stage begins, with packages transmitting from the source hub to the destination along the same path as before. Since, hubs are active and continue to move, a few of them may pull away from the radio extension, causing a break in the connection for transmission to halt.

7.1.2. Route Maintenance

The path support preparation seeks to fix the same interface or create a new path to the objective hub. The hub whose interface fails in this handling makes a Course Blunder (RERR), packs things, and sends it back to the source. After accepting this package, the source hub searches the old path to the destination in its directing table. If there is a course, the source selects it, and the transfer of information resumes. The source reestablishes the other goal hub path and starts transmitting it just in case it does not work.

7.1.3. Basic AODV Drawback

Route Request (RREQ) packets go to nodes near the source during route discovery. The whole network gets inundated with RREQ packets due to this operation, which raises the network's routing overhead and increases bandwidth usage. Furthermore, the source node finds several routes to the destination. The source node opts for the path with the most recent sequence number or the smallest amount of hops to complete the transmission, even if the route is not long-lasting, especially in high-dynamic VANETs.

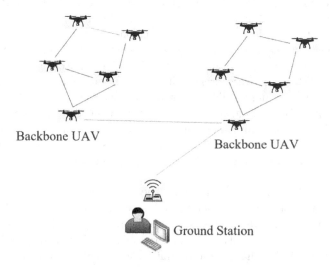

Backbone UAV

Backbone UAV

Ground Station

Figure 6. Multi-Layer, Multi-Group FANET.

7.2. FANET Basic Routing

There exist two types of communication architecture designs for multi-UAV systems in the literature: ad hoc networking and infrastructure-based networking [72-81]. According to this technique, each drone connects to either a GBS or a satellite. So, inter-UAV communications may be carried out through either of them, functioning as a relay. As a result, each drone needs significant transmission power and a steerable antenna to communicate with the infrastructure. Nonetheless, this scheme may be unrealistic due to small UAV sizes and payload limitations. Additional problems connected with this network model include dependability issues caused by drone mobility and changing environmental circumstances, high latency caused by the lack of direct connections between UAVs, and a constraint on the transmission range between drones and infrastructure.

The ad hoc UAV groupings circumvent the range constraint and handle the other problems associated with an infrastructure-based communications architecture. In a FANET, all UAVs are ANET nodes. Only a drone subset connects to the infrastructure; the remaining UAVs interact with the ground controller via intermediary drones in a multi-hop manner. A FANET happens to be a subset of VANETs and MANETs.

Although FANETs possess many characteristics, MANETs have several advantages, such as self-organizing, communicating, and establishing in-between nodes collaboration without needing a centralized controller. They not only have their infrastructure, but they also have their particular traits. The following are some of the distinctive characteristics of FANETs:

(i) There are significant differences in drone mobility in a FANET and other entities in a MANET or a VANET. The usual UAV speed is 30-460 km/h, i.e., meaningfully faster mobility and speed variation than MANET and VANET nodes. Furthermore, UAVs travel in a 3D air space, whereas the nodes in MANET and VANET move in a 2D area. So, there are several complex communication design challenges to solve. Because of the fast changes in the locations of the UAVs and the variations in the distance between UAVs, connections may emerge and disappear, and topological changes may come to be more recurrent as a result of the rapid UAV position changes and variations in the distance between drones. Still, UAV insertion and failure (because of loss of power, malfunction, or other reasons) would impact the network's topology. These can also result in a loss of connection between UAVs when sending critical information, such as control and command traffic, between them. As a result of the dynamic nature of UAVs, the network would rearrange and reorganize often. FANETs must meet specific communication and routing criteria thanks to these factors.

(ii) Due to the considerable distance between UAVs, which can be several kilometers or more, the number of nodes in FANETs is smaller than in MANETs or VANETs. This is due to the requirement for a more extended transmission range in FANETs compared to MANETs and VANETs and the fact that FANETs have a shorter transmission range. The radio connections, antenna construction, and physical layer behavior are all impacted by these changes.

(iii) Real-time FANET applications, such as collision avoidance between drones, demand packet transmissions within a specific time frame.

(iv) The existing mobility methods for VANETs and MANETs are inapplicable to FANETs since they are not designed for them. When flying in FANETs, UAVs travel in three dimensions. Although the movement of the UAVs is generally predefined, it can be modified in response to mission updates or environmental circumstances.

Contrarily, in FANETs with fully autonomous UAVs, the course taken by the UAVs is not predetermined. This means that the FANET mobility models would be affected by changes in flight plans, quick and abrupt drone movements, and various UAV formations, among other things.

- The lack of line of sight (LoS) in MANETs and VANETs stems primarily from flying nodes moving very close to the ground, and as a consequence, the obstacles are most likely to be located close to the nodes. LoS, on the other hand, is more likely to be found in FANET settings.

- The UAVs in FANETs usually partake sufficient energy and computing power compared to the nodes in MANETs because the energy required to operate a UAV is significantly more than the energy needed for data processing. However, it might continue to be a significant concern for micro and small UAVs with low cargo capacity.

- Because UAVs in the majority of FANET applications have a high and dynamic mobility degree, it is difficult to establish the precise location of the UAVs. As a result, the localization data requires updating at regular intervals rather than daily.

A FANET's main necessities are high mobility, intermittent links, frequent topology changes, limited resources, low-node density, and periodic network partitioning. These unique individualities present complex challenges when developing a reliable communication architecture solution, particularly routing areas and protocols. Correspondingly, the Quality of Service (QoS) musts for FANET wellbeing applications vary depending on the particular application. For example, real-time traffic is required for applications like surveillance besides Search and Rescue (SAR). Still, applications such as information collecting and mapping may tolerate delays. The bandwidth needs for diverse health applications are quite varied from one another. So, the fluctuating QoS prerequisites and increasing routing complexity/ flexibility exacerbate FANETs.

8. Discussion

The proper management of personal healthcare-related data is critical in the healthcare industry [78-80]. The most significant difficulty for all parties is managing health records accessible to all parties, including healthcare professionals is due to the necessity to observe/follow patients and dangerous surroundings in real-time. Deploying healthcare-oriented VANETs collaborating with wireless sensor networks is a major topic.

Because of the mounting number of vehicles on the road, implementing the Intelligent Transportation System (ITS) [62] is a top priority across the world. The population expands briskly in emerging nations, and resources are meager. Continuously congested highways are common nowadays, causing vehicle travel times to grow from minutes to hours. Highway fatalities caused by pollution or a lack of warning are no longer a rare occurrence. Vehicular Ad-Hoc Networks (VANETs) deployment becomes necessary in such a traffic situation.

This study focuses on WAVE's VANET protocol [63], based on the IEEE WLAN protocol standard 802.11p. To improve the performance characteristics and Quality of Service (QoS) [74] of a VANET [65], a sort of cooperative communication with changed functionalities is utilized on the planned network flow of the 802.11p protocol. As mobile communication between vehicle nodes of a Vehicular Ad-Hoc Network becomes more dependable [50], this scientific contribution to society may help make Intelligent Transportation Systems (ITS) [66] even safer, better, and quicker.

Multimodality imaging performed on each vehicle should receive greater attention in the future [67-69]. Different data sources must be combined when mapping an environment along with its constituents. Furthermore, AR and the ability to increase the resolution of regions of interest via super-resolution, for example, will burden moving network nodes [70, 71, 88]. Aside from the difficulties raised in this paper, fleets with many cars subjected to a rigorous schedule must provide dependability, quick processing, and smart node assignment in the event of node malfunction and concurrent high-performance computing activities [72, 73]. It's worth noting that healthcare and catastrophe recovery require a lot of computing power. Because of the high computational load, lighter systems based on metaheuristics or deep learning may become a prerequisite [73, 74, 81-83, 89-94].

UAVs can also be used as ambulance drones, allowing them to reach disaster-stricken areas faster than traditional rescue vehicles. This method saves time and effort in dealing with the various health factors and circumstances that fluctuate. Despite their differences, FANETs are similar to MANETs and VANETs. Organized UAVs become disaster relief/medical mission-based FANETs. The mission's objective and task nature influence their mobility models frequently. As a result, FANET routing protocols should consider the sorts of health applications and services, as well as the necessary mobility models. Despite this, FANET routing protocols are challenging to develop due to the extremely dynamic topologies and flying limitations they face [75-77, 90].

9. Conclusion

In the healthcare business, appropriate handling of personal health-related data is important. The most challenging challenge for all parties is keeping health records available to all stakeholders, including healthcare providers. Because of the need to monitor/follow patients and hazardous surroundings in real-time. Implementing healthcare-oriented Vehicular Ad Hoc Networks that converse with wireless sensor networks is an important topic. This study focuses on MANETs, VANETs, and FANETs based on the IEEE WLAN protocol standard 802.11p. It may help make Intelligent Transportation Systems (ITS) even better, safer, and quicker. Multimodality imaging performed on each vehicle should receive greater attention in the future. Unmanned Aerial Vehicles (UAVs) can also work as ambulance drones to reach disaster-stricken areas faster. Lighter systems based on metaheuristics may be required for FANET routing protocols.

References

1. Raya, M. and Hubaux, J. (2005). The security of vehicular ad hoc networks. Proc. 3rd ACM Workshop on Security of Ad Hoc and Sensor Networks (SASN 2005), pp. 1-11. Alexandria, VA.
2. Harsch, C., Festag, A. and Papadimitratos, P. (2007). Secure position-based routing for VANETs. Proc. IEEE 66th Vehicular Technology Conference (VTC-2007), pp. 26-30.
3. Gerlach, M. (2006). Full paper: Assessing and improving privacy in VANETs. www.network-on-wheels.de/downloads/ escar2006gerlach.pdf (accessed: May 29, 2021).
4. Olariu, S. and Weigle, M.C. (2009). Vehicular Networks: From Theory to Practice, First Edition. Chapman & Hall/CRC.
5. Nekovee, M. (2005). Sensor networks on the road: The promises and challenges of vehicular ad hoc networks and grids. Proc. Workshop on Ubiquitous Computing and e-Research.
6. Blum, J., Eskandarian, A. and Hoffman, L. (2004). Challenges of intervehicle ad hoc networks. IEEE Trans. on Intelligent Transportation Systems, 5(4), 347-351.

7. Jakubiak, J. and Koucheryavy, Y. (2008). State of the art and research challenges for VANETs. Proc. 5th IEEE Consumer Communications and Networking Conference. CCNC 2008.

8. Li, F. and Wang, Y. (2007). Routing in vehicular ad hoc networks: A survey. IEEE Vehicular Technology Magazine, pp. 12-22.

9. Toor, Y., Muhlethaler, P. and Laouiti, A. (2008). Vehicle ad hoc networks: Applications and related technical issues. IEEE Communications Surveys Tutorials, 10(3), 77-88.

10. Yousef, S., Mousavi, M.S. and Fathy, M. (2006). Vehicular ad hoc networks (VANETs): Challenges and perspectives. Proc. 6th International Conference on ITS Telecommunications.

11. Offor, P.I. (2012). Vehicle Ad Hoc Network (VANET): Safety Benefits and Security Challenges. Nova Southeastern University.

12. Singh, S. and Agrawal, S. (2014). VANET routing protocols: Issues and challenges. Proc. 2014 RAECS UIET Panjab University Chandigarh.

13. Ghassan, S., Al-Salihy, W.A.H. and Sures, R. (2010). Security Issues and Challenges of Vehicular Ad Hoc Networks (VANET). National Advanced IPv6 Center, Universiti Sains Malaysia Penang, Malaysia.

14. Chen, W., Guha, R.K., Kwon, T.T., Lee, J. and Hsu, Y. (2011). A survey and challenges in routing and data dissemination in vehicular ad hoc networks. Wireless Communications and Mobile Computing, 11(7), 787-795.

15. Hartenstein, H. and Laberteaux, K. (2008). A tutorial survey on vehicular ad hoc networks. IEEE Communications Magazine, 46(6), 164-171.

16. Lin, Y., Chen, Y. and Lee, S. (2010). Routing protocols in vehicular ad hoc networks: A survey and future perspectives. J. Information Science and Engineering, 26(3), 913-932.

17. Zhang, M. and Wolff, R. (2008). Routing Protocols in vehicular ad hoc networks in rural areas. Communication Magazine, IEEE, 46(11), 126-131.

18. Hartenstein, H. (2009). VANET Vehicular Applications and Inter-Networking Technologies. Wiley Online Library.

19. Kanna, K., Estrela, V.V. and Rodrigues J.J.P.C. (2021). Cyber Security and Digital Forensics – Proc. ICCSDF 2021, Springer Nature, Zurich, Switzerland.

20. IEEE WG, IEEE 802.11pD2.01, Draft Amendment to Part 11: Wireless Medium Access Control (MAC) and Physical Layer (PHY) Specifications: Wireless Access in Vehicular Environments, March 2007.

21. Zhang, L., Liu, Z., Zou, R., Guo, J. et al. (2014). A scalable CSMA and self-organizing TDMA MAC for IEEE 802.11 p/1609. x in VANETs. Wireless Personal Communications, 74(4), 1197-1212.

22. Khaimar, V.D. and Pradhan, S.N. (2013). Simulation based evaluation of highway road scenario between DSRC/802.11 p MAC protocol and STDMA for vehicle-to-vehicle communication. J. Transportation Technologies, 3, 88-104.

23. Omar, H.A., Zhuang, W. and Li, L. (2011). VeMAC: A novel multichannel MAC protocol for vehicular ad hoc networks. 2011 IEEE Conference on Computer Communications Workshops (INFOCOM WKSHPS), pp. 413-418. IEEE.

24. Lai, Y.-C., Lin, P., Liao, W. and Chen C.-M. (2011). A region-based clustering mechanism for channel access in vehicular ad hoc networks. IEEE J. Selected Areas in Communications, 29(I), 83-93.

25. Dang, D.N.M., Dang, H.N., Nguyen, V.D., Htike, Z., Hong, C.S. et al. (2014). HER-MAC: A hybrid efficient and reliable MAC for vehicular ad hoc networks. 2014 IEEE 28th Int'l Conf. Adv. Information Networking and Applications (AINA), pp. 186-193. IEEE.

26. Hadded, M., Muhlethaler, P., Laouiti, A., Zagrouba, R., Saidane, L.A. et al. (2015).

TDMA-Based MAC protocols for vehicular ad hoc networks: A survey, qualitative analysis, and open research issues. Communications Surveys & Tutorials, 17(4), 2461-2492. IEEE.

27. Sheu, T.L. and Lin, Y.-H. (2014). A cluster-based TDMA system for inter-vehicle communications. J. Sci. Eng., 30(1), 213-231.

28. Zhang, L., Liu, Z., Zou, R., Guo, J., Liu, Y. et al. (2014). A scalable CSMA and self-organizing TDMA MAC for IEEE 802.11 p/1609. x in VANETs. Wireless Personal Communications, 74(4), 1197-1212.

29. Su, H. and Zhang, X. (2007). Clustering-based multichannel MAC protocols for QoS provisioning over vehicular ad hoc networks. IEEE Trans. Vehicular Technology, 56(6), 3309-3323.

30. Ahmad, A., Doughan, M., Gauthier, V., Mougharbel, I. and Marot M. (2010). Hybrid Multi-Channel Multi-hop MAC in VANETs. Proc. 8th International Conf. Advances in Mobile Computing and Multimedia (MoMM 2010), November 2010, pp. 353-357.

31. Almalag, M.S., Olariu, S. and Weigle, M.C. (2012). TDMA cluster-based MAC for VANETs (TC-MAC). 2012 IEEE International Symposium on World of Wireless, Mobile and Multimedia Networks (WoWMoM), 1-6.

32. Johnson, D.B., Hu, Y. and Maltz, D.A. (2007). The Dynamic Source Routing Protocol (DSR) for Mobile Ad Hoc Networks for IPv4. RFC, 4728, pp. 1-107. doi 10.17487/RFC4728

33. Jaap, S., Bechler, M. and Wolf, L. (2005). Evaluation of routing protocols for vehicular ad hoc networks in city traffic scenarios. 11th EUNICE Open European Summer School on Networked Applications, Spain.

34. Belding-Royer, E.M. and Toh, C.K. (1999). A review of current routing protocols for ad hoc mobile wireless networks. IEEE Personal Communication.

35. Sun, X. and Li, X. (2008). Application of VANET to city road traffic management. Journal of Shanxi University of Science & Technology (Natural Science Edition), 26, 107-109.

36. Perkins, C.E. and Royer, E.M. (1999). Ad-hoc on-demand distance vector routing. Proc. 2nd IEEE Workshop on Mobile Computing Systems and Applications. pp. 90-100.

37. Perkins, C. (1997). Ad hoc on demand distance vector (AODV) routing. Internet-Draft, draft-ietf-MANET-aodv-00.

38. Perkins, C., Royer, E. and Das, S. (2001). Ad hoc on-demand distance vector (AODV) routing. Internet Draft, Internet Engineering Task Force.

39. Li, B., Liu, Y. and Chu, G.X. (2010). Optimized AODV routing protocol for vehicular ad hoc networks. 2010 Mobile Congress (GMC), 1-4.

40. Namboodiri, V., Agarwal, M. and Gao, L. (2004). A study on the feasibility of mobile gateways for vehicular ad-hoc networks. Proc. ACM VANET.

41. Kai, Z., Neng, W. and Ai-Fang, L. (2005). A new AODV based clustering routing protocol. 2005 IEEE Int'l Conf. Wireless Communications, Networking and Mobile Computing.

42. http://omnet-tutorial.com/omnet-aodv-code/ Accessed on May 12, 2020.

43. Chakrabarti, A., Sabharwal, A. and Aazhang, B. (2006). Cooperative communications. Coop. Wirel. Networks Princ. Appl., pp. 29-62.

44. Shan, H. and Zhuang, W. (2011). Multi-hop cooperative communication for vehicular ad hoc networks. 2011 6th Int. ICST Conf. Commun. Netw. China, pp. 614-619.

45. Indra, A. and Murali, R. (2014). Routing protocols for vehicular adhoc networks (VANETs): A review. J. Emerg. Trends Comput. Inf. Sci., 5(1), 56.

46. Marfia, G., Roccetti, M., Amoroso, A., Gerla, M., Pau, G. et al. (2011). Cognitive cars: Constructing a cognitive playground for VANET research testbeds. Proc. 4th Int. Conf. Cogn. Radio Adv. Spectr. Manag.

47. Amoroso, A., Marfia, G., Roccetti, M. and Pau, G. (2012). Creative testbeds for VANET research: A new methodology. 2012 IEEE Consum. Commun. Netw. Conf. CCNC'2012, pp. 477-481.

48. Tomandl, A., Herrmann, D., Fuchs, K.P., Federrath, H. et al. (2014). VANETsim: An open source simulator for security and privacy concepts in VANETs. Proc. 2014 Int. Conf. High Perform. Comput. Simulation, HPCS 2014, pp. 543-550.

49. Khairnar, P.V.D. and Pradhan, D.S.N. (2010). Comparative study of simulation for vehicular ad-hoc network. Int. J. Comput. Appl., 4(10), 15-18.

50. Dhawan, H. and Waraich, S.S. (2014). A comparative study on LEACH routing protocol and its variants in wireless sensor networks: A survey. International Journal of Computer Applications, 95, 21-27.

51. Abbas, A.H., Audah, L.M. and Alduais, N.A. (2018). An efficient load balance algorithm for vehicular ad-hoc network. 2018 Electrical Power, Electronics, Communications, Controls and Informatics Seminar (EECCIS), pp. 207-212.

52. Kurkowski, S., Navidi, W. and Camp, T. (2007). Discovering variables that affect MANET protocol performance. GLOBECOM - IEEE Glob. Telecommun. Conf., pp. 1237-1242.

53. Wahid, H., Ahmad, S., Nor, M.A.M. and Rashid, M.A. (2017). Wireless networking: Fundamentals and applications. J. Ekon. Malaysia, 51(2), 39-54.

54. Wang, Z., Chen, H., Xie, L. and Wang, K. (2009). Retransmission strategies of the generation-based network coding in packet networks. 2009 15th Asia-Pacific Conf. Commun. APCC 2009, no. APCC, pp. 745-748.

55. Azfar Yaqub, M., Hassan Ahmed, S. and Kim, D. (2018). Asking neighbors a favor: Cooperative video retrieval using cellular networks in VANETs. Veh. Commun., 12, 39-49.

56. Fawaz, W. (2018). Effect of non-cooperative vehicles on path connectivity in vehicular networks: A theoretical analysis and UAV-based remedy. Veh. Commun., 11, 12-19.

57. Ostovari, P., Wu, J. and Khreishah, A. (2015). Network coding techniques for wireless and sensor networks. Art Wirel. Sens. Networks, Vol. 1 Fundam., no. January 2015, pp. 129-162.

58. Santamaria, A.F. and Sottile, C. (2014). Smart traffic management protocol based on VANET architecture. Adv. Electr. Electron. Eng., 12(4), 279-288.

59. Ho, P.H., Peng, L., Jiang, X. and Haque, A. (2018). Special issue on secure and privacy-preserving autonomous vehicle networks (AVNs). Veh. Commun., 11, 32.

60. Mohammed, F., Mohamed, O., Abedelhalim, H. and Abdellah, E. (2014). Efficiency evaluation of routing protocols for VANET. Proc. Third IEEE International Colloquium in Information Science and Technology (CIST), 410-414.

61. Miao, M., Zheng, Q., Zheng, K. and Zeng, Z. (2014). Implementation and demonstration of WAVE networking services for intelligent transportation systems. IOV.

62. Rahem, A.A.-R.T., Ismail, M., Idris, A. and Dheyaa, A. (2014). A comparative and analysis study of VANET routing protocols. J. Theor. Appl. Inf. Technol., 66(3), 691-698.

63. Mahajan, A. and Dadhich, D.R. (2013). Comparative analysis of VANET routing protocols using VANET. RBC and IEEE 802.11p, 3(4), 531-538.

64. Teng, H., Liu, W., Wang, T., Kui, X., Zhang, S. et al. (2019). A collaborative code dissemination schemes through two-way vehicle to everything (V2X) communications for urban computing. IEEE Access, 7, 145546-145566.

65. Tripp-Barba, C., Urquiza-Aguiar, L., Zaldívar-Colado, A., Estrada-Jiménez, J., Aguilar-Calderón, J.A. et al. (2018). Comparison of propagation and packet error models in vehicular networks performance. Veh. Commun., 12, 1-13.

66. Husain, A., Raw, R.S., Kumar, B. and Doegar, A. (2011). Performance comparison of topology and position based routing protocols in vehicular network environments. Int. J. Wirel. Mob. Networks, 3(4), 289-303.

67. Arshaghi, A., Razmjooy, N., Estrela, V.V., Burdziakowski, P., Nascimento, D.A. et al. (2020). Image transmission in UAV MIMO UWB-OSTBC system over Rayleigh channel using multiple description coding (MDC) with QPSK modulation. *In:* Estrela, V.V., Hemanth, J., Saotome, O., Nikolakopoulos, G., Sabatini, R. (eds). Imaging and Sensing for Unmanned Aircraft Systems, Vol. 2, IET, London, UK.

68. Estrela, V.V., Monteiro, A.C.B., França, R.P., Iano, Y., Khelassi, A. et al. (2019). Health 4.0: Applications, management, technologies and review. Med. Tech. J., 2(4), 262-276, doi: 10.26415/2572-004X-vol2iss1p262-276. 262.

69. Estrela, V.V., Saotome, O., Loschi, H.J., Hemanth, D.J., Farfan, W.S. et al. (2018). Emergency response cyber-physical framework for landslide avoidance with sustainable electronics. Technologies, 6, 42. doi:10.3390/technologies6020042.

70. Deshpande, A., Patavardhan, P. and Rao, D.H. (2015). Super resolution based low cost vision system. 2015 IEEE International Conference on Computational Intelligence and Computing Research (ICCIC), 1-6.

71. Deshpande, A. and Patavardhan, P. (2017). Super resolution and recognition of long range captured multi-frame iris images. IET Biom., 6, 360-368.

72. Loschi, H.J., Estrela, V.V., Hemanth, D.J., Fernandes, S.R., Iano, Y. et al. (2020). Communications requirements, video streaming, communications links and networked UAVs. *In:* Estrela, V.V. et al. (eds). Imaging and Sensing for Unmanned Aircraft Systems, Vol. 2, IET, London, UK.

73. Razmjooy, N. and Estrela, V.V. (2019). Applications of Image Processing and Soft Computing Systems in Agriculture. 1-300, 2019, IGI Global, Hershey, PA, USA. doi: 10.4018/978-1-5225-8027-0

74. Razmjooy, N., Estrela, V.V., Loschi, H.J. and Farfan, W.S. (2019). A Comprehensive Survey of New Metaheuristic Algorithms. Wiley.

75. Valsan, A., Parvathy, B., Vismaya Dev, G.H., Unnikrishnan, R.S., Reddy, P.K. and Vivek A. (2020). Unmanned aerial vehicle for search and rescue mission. 4th Int'l Conference on Trends in Electronics and Informatics (ICOEI)(48184), 684-687.

76. Khan, A.A., Laghari, A., Gadekallu, T.R., Shaikh, Z.A., Javed, A.R. et al. (2022). A drone-based data management and optimization using metaheuristic algorithms and blockchain smart contracts in a secure fog environment. Computers and Electrical Engineering, 102, 108234.

77. Oubbati, O.S., Lakas, A., Zhou, F., Günes, M., Yagoubi, M.B. et al. (2017). A survey on position-based routing protocols for Flying Ad Hoc Networks (FANETs). Veh. Commun., 10, 29-56.

78. Dhivya, A.J. and Premkumar, J. (2017). Quadcopter based technology for an emergency healthcare. 2017 Third Int'l Conf. Biosignals, Images and Instr. (ICBSII), pp. 1-3.

79. Al-Absi, M.A., Al-Absi, A.A., Sain, M. and Lee, H. (2021). Moving ad hoc networks—A comparative study. Sustainability, 13, 6187.

80. Razmjooy, N., Estrela, V.V. and Sabatini, R. (2020). Vision in micro-aerial vehicles. *In:* Estrela, V.V. et al. (eds). Imaging and Sensing for Unmanned Aircraft Systems. Volume 1, Control and Performance, Chap. 8, pp. 173-216, IET, UK, London.

81. Deshpande, A., Razmjooy, N. and Estrela, V.V. (2021). Introduction to computational intelligence and super-resolution. *In:* Deshpande, A. et al. (eds). Computational Intelligence Methods for Super-Resolution in Image Processing Applications. Springer, Cham, Switzerland.

82. Khelassi, A. and Estrela V.V. (2020). Advances in Multidisciplinary Medical Technologies — Engineering, Modeling and Findings. Proc. International Workshop on Medical Technologies 2019 (ICHSMT 2019), Springer Nature, Zurich, Switzerland.

83. Hemanth, J. and Estrela, V.V. (2017). Deep Learning for Image Processing Applications. Advances in Parallel Computing, Vol. 31, IOS Press, Amsterdam, Netherlands.

84. Khan, A.A., Laghari, A.A. and Awan, S.A. (2021). Machine Learning in Computer Vision: A Review. SIS, EAI, doi: 10.4108/eai.21-4-2021.169418

85. Khan, A.A., Shaikh, A.A., Cheikhrouhou, O., Laghari, A.A., Rashid et al. (2021). IMG-forensics: Multimedia-enabled information hiding investigation using convolutional neural network. IET Image Processing. Vol. 16(11), 2854-2862.

86. Khan, A.A., Laghari, A.A., Awan, S. and Jumani, A.K. (2021). Fourth Industrial Revolution Application: Network Forensics Cloud Security Issues. Security Issues and Privacy Concerns in Industry 4.0 Applications, pp. 15-33.

87. Khan, A.A., Uddin, M., Shaikh, A., Laghari, A.A. and Rajput, A. et al. (2021). MF-Ledger: Blockchain Hyperledger Sawtooth-enabled Novel and Secure Multimedia Chain of Custody Forensic Investigation Architecture. IEEE Access.

88. Khan, A.A., Laghari, A.A., Liu, D.-S., Shaikh, A.A., Ma, D.-A. et al. (2021). EPS-Ledger: Blockchain Hyperledger Sawtooth-enabled Distributed Power Systems Chain of Operation and Control Node Privacy and Security. Electronics, 10(19), 2395. https://doi.org/10.3390/electronics10192395

89. Laghari, A.A., Wu, K., Laghari, R.A., Ali, M. and Khan, A.A. et al. (2021). A review and state of art of Internet of Things (IoT). Archives of Computational Methods in Engineering, pp. 1-19.

90. Jumani, A.K., Laghari, A.A. and Khan, A.A. (2021). Blockchain and big data: Supportive aid for daily life. Security Issues and Privacy Concerns in Industry 4.0 Applications, pp. 141-178.

91. Radu, D., Cretu, A., Parrein, B., Yi, J., Avram, C. et al. (2018). Flying ad hoc network for emergency applications connected to a fog system. Proc. Emerging Internet, Data & Web Technologies (EIDWT) 2018, Mar 2018, pp. 675-686. Tirana, Albania.

92. Laghari, A.A., Estrela, V.V. and Yin, S. (2022). Special Issue: From Nanoscale to Hyperspectral Imaging – How to Gather and Understand Medical Images Harvested in Extremely Difficult Situations. Curr. Med. Imaging, Bentham Science, UK.

93. Khan, A.A., Laghari, A.A., Shaikh, A., Dootio, M., Estrela, V.V. et al. (2021). A blockchain security module for brain-computer interface (BCI) with multimedia life cycle framework (MLCF). Neuroscience Informatics. 100030. 10.1016/j.neuri.2021.100030.

94. Deshpande, A., Estrela, V.V. and Patavardhan, P. (2021). The DCT-CNN-ResNet50 architecture to classify brain tumours with super-resolution, convolutional neural network, and the ResNet50. Neuroscience Informatics. Vol. 1, 4, 2021, 100013, ISSN 2772-5286.

Scale and Resolution Issues regarding Medical Images: Challenges Ahead

**V.V. Estrela[1] [0000-0002-4465-7691], A. Deshpande[2] [0000-0002-1500-0981],
R.T. Lopes[3] [0000-0001-7250-824X], H.H.P. da Silva[4] [0000-0001-6764-8432],
Shoulin Yin[5] [0000-0002-5367-1372], A.A. Khan[6] [0000-0003-2838-7641],
Jenice Aroma[7] [0000-0003-4022-1898], K. Raimond[7] [0000-0001-8680-8390],
R. Sroufer[8] [0000-0002-7903-9180], Yu-Da Lin[9] [0000-0001-5100-6072],
J.M.R.S. Tavares[10] [0000-0001-7603-6526], J.J.P.C. Rodrigues[11] [0000-0001-8657-3800]**

[1] Telecommunications Department, Fluminense Federal University (UFF), RJ, Brazil,
vania.estrela.phd@ieee.org
[2] Electronics and Communication Engineering, Angadi Institute of Technology and
Management, Belagavi, India, deshpande.anandb@gmail.com
[3] University Federal of Rio de Janeiro (COPPE/UFRJ), Rio de Janeiro, RJ, Brazil,
rlopes@coppe.ufrj.br
[4] Instituto Superior de Telecomunicacoes, Instituto Superior Tecnico, 1049-001, Lisboa,
Lisboa, Portugal, hsilva@lx.it.pt
[5] Harbin Institute of Technology, China, yslin@hit.edu.cn
[6] Faculty of Computer Science, Sindh Madressatul Islam University, Karachi (74000),
Sindh, Pakistan, abdullah.khan0076@gmail.com
[7] Department of Computer Science & Engineering, Karunya Institute of Technology &
Sciences, India, jenicearoma@gmail.com, kraimond@karunya.edu
[8] Operations Management, Palumbo Donahue School of Business Management, 820
Rockwell Hall, PA, USA, sroufer@duq.edu
[9] National Penghu University of Science and Technology: Magong, TW,
yudalinemail@gmail.com
[10] Departamento de Engenharia Mecanica (DEMec), Faculdade de Engenharia da
Universidade do Porto (FEUP)/Instituto de Engenharia Mecanica e Gestao Industrial
(INEGI), Porto, Portugal, tavares@fe.up.pt
[11] Federal University of Piaui (UFPI), Electrical Engineering, Fortaleza, CE, Brazil,
joeljr@ieee.org

1. Introduction

Recent advances in biomedical signal/image processing are often driven by classification and segmentation methods used to process pixel/voxel data, e.g., image segmentation, or their uses in diagnostics, treatment planning, and follow-ups. This manuscript emphasizes large medical data volumes, with proper image representations at different parts of a Medical Cyber-Physical System (MCPS) [1, 2], besides scale/resolution challenges. Lately, data has gotten bigger mainly due to medical system improvements with expanding pixel/voxel resolution and faster reconstruction. Computed Tomography (CT) and Magnetic Resonance Imaging (MRI) systems allow scaling image resolution and reconstruction time. Whole high-resolution body scans grasp massive data. Large medical image datasets stem chiefly from (i) a huge amount from, e.g., Picture Archiving and Communication Systems (PACS), and (ii) a massive single data repository. High-dimensional (HD) medical data shows erraticism (see Figure 1). For example, X-rays are usually 2D but can be 3D or 4D, making them exceptionally large. Microscope Pathology Slides (MPSs) can have pixel/voxel ranges claiming a great deal of memory.

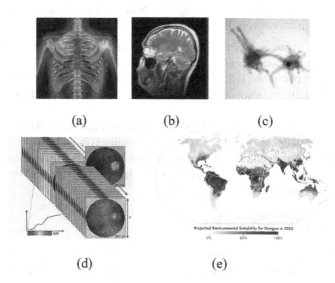

(a)   (b)   (c)

(d)   (e)

Figure 1. Examples of medical modalities and resolutions: (a) X-ray, (b) Brain MRI scan, (c) Microscope slide, (d) Super-resolution, and (e) Remote Sensing (RS) to analyze diseases (e.g., dengue).

This chapter is structured in the following manner: Section 2 outlines Multiscale/Multiresolution representations. Section 2 ponders on huge medical images and health datasets managing, the difficulty of image content-based queries, and physicians' acceptance. Section 3 examines Dimensionality Curse (DC) issues. Section 4 introduces Medical Information Fusion (MIF). Section 5 tackles systemic issues on imaging modalities, management, and storage. How to handle imageries with AI is in Section 6. Microscopy, nanoimaging, and super-resolution are debated in Section 7. Section 8 treats Virtual Reality (VR) and Augmented Reality (AR). Multispectral and Hyperspectral Imagery in healthcare appear in Section 9. Section 10 summarizes and concludes this issue.

2. Multiscale/Multiresolution Images

Objects in a scene are perceived at varying resolutions depending on their distance.

When gazing at a faraway parking lot, one initially sees buildings, automobiles, and parking. The motorist can only see potential parking places close to the automobile at the entrance. Finally, a nice spot becomes obvious when the individual approaches other cars, with resolutions comparable to observer perceived size details. Signal extrema and their first derivatives aid qualitative description. Scale and resolution affect computing majorly: when a neighborhood derivative is calculated, its size is rarely specified. Stability criteria can identify occurrences surviving large-scale changes with decompositions portraying the image as a combination of family basis signals, allowing the different representation levels to be analyzed. The ones with the most interest are picked. Multiscale (or Multiresolution) Image Decompositions (MIDs) modify images to extract distinct scale features for compression, description, segmentation, and registration. Techniques to break down an image into components so that each collects/conveys knowledge at a certain scale appear below [3-6]:

(i) Gaussian pyramids (GPs) use simple low-pass (LP) filtering and decimation to represent the same image at multiple scales.

(ii) Laplacian pyramids (LaPs) have detailed, i.e., bandpass (BP) MID components. GP and LaP are also overcomplete, with 1/3 more pixels than the original scene.

(iii) Wavelet decompositions (WDs) are multi-orientation MID approaches to expand signals organically and efficiently. Unlike GPs and LaPs, they are ample MIDs with scale and orientation breakdown employing LP and high-pass filter banks. The LP filter's regularity and vanishing-moment merits impact ordinary scene forms and representation abilities.

3. Dimensionality Issues

The health data DC is huge and rises fast. A patient's Electronic Health Records (EHRs) have biometric data from image, voice, wearables, genetic information, and other sources, producing a potentially rich patient HD health data (HDHD) portrayal [7-9]. As an example, sub-mm resolution brain MRI pixels afford voxel-rich imaging. Wearable data has tens or hundreds of samples per second. There are millions of Single Nucleotide Polymorphisms (SNPs) in humans. So, each person has a vast clinical data footprint with very detailed information. HDHD provides a huge raw input (data stream) for algorithm development. If the enormous number of features exceeds the sample size, there is a HD vs. small sample data dilemma.

These findings justify changing present clinical procedures. However, physicians lack meaningful knowledge due to raw data location information. Because AI can learn from several clinical data streams, it may solve this issue (Figure 2). Software-as-a-medical-device (SaMD) uses AI for the whole product lifecycle. Designers collect a huge training dataset with several modalities to craft a feature set and train a model. Cross-validation on a held-out test set helps pick the final model and feature sets. It is used to measure out-of-sample accuracy (after model deployment) [10, 11]. The RW model's performance may be monitored after deployment, and the model can be changed and re-deployed using Virtual Worlds (VWs).

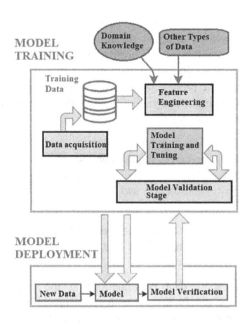

Figure 2. High-level block diagram for medical AI model development.

Short training datasets with too many features may enhance training but with poor generalizability [12, 13]. Tracking all health metrics' potential combinations can be hard. Tricky events need larger sample sizes. Dataset Blind Spots (DBSs) produce the DC, hindering model development/generalizability and causing negative effects. Too many DBSs cause catastrophic failures when dealing with unknown data. Small HD training samples are sensitive to DBSs, causing errors, e.g., massively labeled data are required to train AI models to map participants' gut signals. In models trained with tiny sample numbers, AI makes a lot of HDHD [14].

4. Medical Information Fusion

Progress in the imagery sensor field has improved robustness and enlarged the modern imaging sensors' resolutions. More notably, low-cost fabrication has popularized multiple sensors in many imaging uses. This growth vastly enlarged the data amount depicting the same scene from various sensors. Yet, the subsequent sensor information processing can be heavy since augmenting the number of sensors increases raw sensor data to be stored and processed, meaning longer execution times or increased processing units and storage devices, leading to costly solutions. Moreover, humans may face difficulties visualizing various images, leading to a major performance drop [4, 15-19]. A potential solution is to replace the whole set of sensors with a single composite depiction that unites all pertinent sensor data as in Medical Image Fusion (MIF). The idea is to mix complementary and redundant data from multiple imageries into one composite image having a better fundamental scene description than any individual source image. Hence, the fused image should help with inspection or further processing. MIF tends to be nontrivial, since: (i) acquired images may involve different dynamic range and resolution kinds of sensors; (ii) there exists complementary information (e.g., structures appearing only in some input imageries; and (iii) some common data may have reversed contrast, significantly complicating the process. Still, a fusion approach should not rely on a priori evidence about the sources and yield naturally appealing composite images to a specialist with these requirements:

(a) All relevant input image information must be preserved;
(b) No artifacts or inconsistencies should confuse an observer or subsequent processing task; and
(c) It needs reliability, robustness, and error tolerance (e.g., noise and misregistrations).

MIF may use multitemporal sensors with several focal lengths, multiple views, or captured under various exposure settings. The MIF process can occur at different data representation levels as follows:

A. *Pixel-level:* It represents data combinations at the lowest representation level since each fused pixel comes from a set of pixels in the source images. Customarily, this set has pixels within small windows like 3×3 or 5×5. Pixel-level fusion is easy, time-efficient and the resulting image contains the original information from the sources, but it is very sensitive to misregistration [15].

B. *Region-level:* It identifies all significant elements within an image for qualities such as size, shape, contrast, texture, or gray level. A region map ties each pixel to a feature based on segmentation. Thus, the extracted sections are merged. This fusion type avoids several problems such as blurring, high noise sensitivity, and misregistration [15]. The segmentation procedure quality affects the final fusion performance since mistakes might cause missing or degraded features in the fused image.

C. *Voxel-level:* Low resolution and deficient 3D scans [18-22] prevent sophisticated algorithms from matching local features on RW depth pictures. Each local volumetric patch descriptor learns a partial 3D data correspondence label. Unsupervised learning can help collect data but over-labeled RGB-D reconstruction. A descriptor can generalize fusion to diverse activities and scales. A 3D point cloud is merged with a RGB picture or other 3D modalities to compensate for the better depth, fine-grained texture, and color information. Techniques include:

  (i) Object-centric fusion applies Region of Interest (ROI)-pooling to each modality from a shared set of 3D end-to-end optimizations despite being sluggish and bulky.
  (ii) A priori mapping for each point-cloud sample permits continuous fusion to share data across all stages. Feature blurring occurs when a feature vector corresponds to many voxels in view.
  (iii) Creates a fake point cloud replica of the original image, but it is slow and needs multiple steps to create the pseudo-point cloud.

(iv) Point cloud seeding detection with semantic features taken from an image enhances accuracy but limits recall.

D. Volumetric-region: In medicine, grouping comparable voxels is difficult [20-22]. Remote sensing (RS) has the most powerful 3D merging methods. It is difficult to combine many sets of overlapping surface measurements geometrically. A discrete implicit surface representation allows immediate reconstruction of complicated objects. However, surfaces are represented at a single resolution, making big object reconstruction impossible. Surface model reconstruction is independent of object size. Multiresolution geometric fusion is done by building a hierarchical surface representation iteratively, reducing representation cost while maintaining geometric correctness.

E. Decision-level: It combines data from various sensors at the greatest degree of abstraction. A decision map is created for each source picture by classifying all input pixels. A fused map results from separate decision maps to reconcile discrepancies [20-22]. The proper level relies on the application, physical source characteristics, execution time, and accessible tools. Yet, different image fusion stages are strongly linked. Many fusion rules that determine composite picture individual pixels may also help fuse extracted features regionally. Likewise, decision-level fusion generally utilizes a regional-level segmented map to merge visible and infrared imagery.

5. Modalities, Management, and Storage

Molecular imaging (MI) focuses on molecules of interest within living patients versus histology, which handles preserved tissue samples' molecular data [23]. The patient's body may create molecules spontaneously or receive them from a specialist. In MRI, CT, and PET, a contrast agent is injected into a patient's bloodstream to follow its path throughout the body. MI evolved from radiography to better understand and monitor organisms and metabolic processes. Currently, MI research includes (i) identifying previously unknown molecules, (ii) finding additional contrast agents, and (iii) seeking functional contrast agents to educate about healthy vs. sick cells and tissues.

5.1. Data Acquisition Protocol

Most data-rich modalities in EHRs are acquired in-clinic per procedure. Collecting RW sensor health data and creating robust models is challenging because of (i) background noise, (ii) unknown variables, and (ii) intrinsic DC with growing DBSs, especially when the sample size is small. Designers could explore active tasks to replace passive data collection since data describing characteristics may produce DC issues with DBS consequences. Top performance tasks reduce the relative impact of unmeasured changes to estimate clinical contrasts of interest. Viz patients' speech may be slower and less precise when tested under a top performance job [24-27]. It would never emerge in passive data collecting since most maximum performance challenges are outside normal speaking patterns.

5.2. Training Data Collection

The size and variety of the training sample should reflect the conditions envisaged after model deployment [24-27]. More sample numbers are necessary to properly train increasingly complicated HD models, even when sampling is varied (e.g., data from many geographic locations). To estimate the sample size required to train classification algorithms properly, method designers can leverage current approaches. A covariate shift is more complicated due to a mismatch between training and post-deployment data due to regional biases in clinical AI models [24]. Biased sampling causes substantial DBSs between training and post-deployment data distributions. Creating representative datasets for training involves previous knowledge of which stratification characteristics correlate with predictors. Carefully mapping these parameters and ranges can result in strong AI models [25]. Notably, this does not assure performance equivalence between layers. To quantify model performance variability across important strata, scientists need representative data.

6. Handling Imageries with AI

HD's complicated application settings and short sample numbers favor DBSs. A prospective validation study can assess the model's performance. It looks like most HD models. Small data scenarios may not be validated. While difficult, several tactics can help construct a strong model that successfully emulates and implements complicated HD models.

6.1. Feature Engineering

The most important model design considerations are which features to embrace. Researchers do not know the best feature space for fully describing a situation. To enhance a model, they integrate the knowledge of the underlying data generation process with exploratory data-driven feature selection. While deleting unnecessary characteristics from the model improves model robustness, it does not remove DBSs if the chosen features still result in HD and a tiny data regime. Theoretical models can help lessen the DC [28, 29] by picking a limited group of traits that fluctuate with the illness but stay steady every day. A priori attention on a limited number of theoretical attributes is superior when the sample size is small. Sensor data may often be obtained in bulk, but clinical labeling is costly. Transfer learning retains reusable features in clinical applications while representing data via a relevant lower-dimensional feature space [28, 29]. Labels are optional for feature learning but may be essential for other reasons. Some dimensionality reduction (DR) schemes like Principal Component Analysis (PCA) or its variations [30-32] assume interesting directions with more variation in the original feature space that are more likely to contribute to the response. Aside from improving model generalizability, PCA-based feature reduction is unlikely to provide domain-relevant features since a direction of reduced variance can likely anticipate clinical response as the one of highest variation. Feature repeatability is important yet overlooked in AI. Sensors can gather high-density daily data. Repeatability studies use statistics to quantify how much a person's measures vary from one sample to another since human behavior changes, and most can be nonclinical. Before creating an AI model, feature variability must be investigated because there is substantial diversity in often used attributes with the same equipment and settings. Repeatability studies can improve AI models by removing extreme variability.

6.2. Model Training and Tuning

After collecting a representative training set and engineering features, model training and tweaking should follow HDHD machine learning (ML) practices that are DC-sensitive [33-35]. Many studies have inserted data-driven regularization and ensemble averaging to augment HD applicability and robustness while more resistant to attacks and damages.

6.3. Model Validation

Researchers divide datasets into training and test sets. The training set learns the model while the test set validates it. It is usual to compare candidate models using a test set without accounting for the many comparisons required for sparse data [33-35]. With repeated testing on a test set, small sample sizes can lead to overfitting and overly optimistic model performance predictions, especially for HD models. Larger sample sizes provide a barrier to test data reuse. Experts should still use rigorous model assessment procedures when gathering training and test data of smaller sizes which maintains individual samples and utilizes accuracy measures to gauge model performance to reuse a test dataset while assessing better models. Hence, in practice, designers should not try to raise performance by discovering test set edge instances where the model fails in fixing them. Without accessible DBSs, the only answer is to collect more data.

6.4. Deep Learning

Deep Learning (DL) techniques can handle hierarchical feature representations [36]. Since, HD features are cached, DL algorithms presently focus on low-resolution pictures. Novel approaches must apply DL to huge medical imageries that meet the following criteria:

(a) Capability to process just relevant imagery portions in detail;
(b) Scale to a boundless number of pertinent image parts;
(c) Scale to an infinite number of input images;
(d) Experimenting with various forms of accelerating hardware; and
(e) The ability to represent the interdependence of object parts.

Less processing time, energy, and hardware resources are required to analyze the growing medical data. It is initially compressed and then supplied to a DL model, saving memory while locating relevant picture parts from a possibly fuzzy low-resolution image. Finally, calculated locations aid in patch extraction from the high-resolution image, focusing on certain scene elements. The final forecast combines patches and low-resolution picture representations from the embedding model. A DBS only matters if the model later meets data from that feature space. While one may reduce DBS volumes during training, one won't know if a consequential DBS exists until the model is deployed.

7. Microscopy, Nanoimaging, and Super-Resolution

Since, light travels through water and air, optical microscopes (OMs) can observe in vivo. So they deal with biological things and other elements in natural settings. Color photos from OMs are more detailed than monochrome images. OMs can offer intrinsic sample properties up to 0.5 μm in the visible and mid-IR light bands [37]. Since visible light cannot photograph nanomaterials, OMs suffer from light diffraction. Surface plasmons for superlensing allow faultless nano image capture with a nanoprobe. Multicolor, 3D stochastic reconstruction microscopy can now see cellular structures with molecular-scale detail. When paired with many fluorescent probes and biochemically specific labeling procedures, multicolor fluorescence microscopy directly visualizes molecular interactions and processes in living organisms. Yet, as fluorescence microscopy has a diffraction-limited resolution, many detailed, tiny biological structures are not examined. Super-resolution (SR) schemes have boosted systems and overcome the optical SR diffraction limit, with image sensor resolutions strengthened in geometrical SR.

8. Virtual/Augmented Realities

VR is immersive, allowing users to fully engage themselves in a realistic or lifelike VW, distinct from reality. Medical AR is very effective for combining RW with VR so specialists can view things like X-rays, arm veins, shattered bones, head tumors and EHRs, before employing AR. Something floats in front of an expert in AR, with data overlaid in distinct realms. Recent developments extended VR/ AR to healthcare. While patients prefer VR, clinicians employ VR/AR in various ways. Adoption to clinical usage has been hampered by issues with QoE [23, 38, 39]. Many healthcare settings now have consumer-level VR/AR equipment accessible. Experts will determine the safety and patient benefits. Costs and integration into current procedures are other considerations. Still, experts expect additional medical AR apps. It's still uncertain which technology and apps will operate in a clinic.

8.1. Clinic-Based AR/VR

AR/VR impacts primary care, clinics, operating rooms, emergency rooms, and dental offices as it improves [40]. E.g., physicians can plan complex surgeries and use AR/ VR for various guided surgeries with software enhancing RW locations. There are several opportunities to educate people and improve procedures/care. Handheld devices can use a laser to see through skin and veins to find veins to pull blood or insert an IV. Health suppliers can lower superfluous needle poke risks and save time.

8.2. Surgery

AR/VR is only now making its way into high-risk treatment like AR surgery [41, 42]. Physicians could see through headgears, allowing them to project X-ray or CT scan pictures onto the body simultaneously. Surgeons can see X-rays if the images line up perfectly. The major advantage of freehand is speed, although it needs extensive anatomical knowledge and practice to do nearly blindly. Staff radiation exposure requires X-ray care. Its early usage in spinal surgery is due to the spine's rigidity in connecting body computer pictures. Moving the belly or chest makes keeping the VW and RW aligned more difficult. AR/VR is gradually being used in high-risk medical actions.

8.3. Medical Education

While many medical applications are not ready yet, AR is regularly used by staff in training [43, 44]. If it is not tracking correctly in the operating room, one would have errors. In teaching and learning, one does not need that level of precision. AR tools permit access to learning materials and anatomy when spinning a detailed 3D heart model around on a mobile device. They can scan a QR code in the human anatomy lab or on a corpse while studying, including surgical videos or relevant lectures.

8.4. 3D Models

Health experts no longer need to rely on their imagination to interpret radiological pictures. The issue is segmenting anatomical areas of interest, which requires human involvement. Different software platforms contain AR/VR visualization engines and DICOM images input, automated anatomical structures segmentation, and 3D mesh production of the segmented region. VR/AR visualization tools enable medical practitioners to collaborate with 3D medical representations innovatively [45].

8.5. Molecular Imaging

MI can potentially play a critical role in healthcare [23]. With increasingly high-resolution systems, multimodal imaging platforms, and large datasets generated by modern MI methods, it has become imperative to develop new approaches to store, process, and visualize information. VR/AR adaptation to visualize MI is an intuitive emerging trend that can accommodate the growing complexity and volume of multimodal molecular data. Clinical healthcare VR/AR applications highlight existing challenges for a wider adoption of these technologies before concluding with anticipated future directions.

9. Multispectral and Hyperspectral Imagery

Hyperspectral imaging (HSI) along with multispectral imaging (MSI) can evolve healthcare immensely (despite the extreme computational burden involved) by utilizing spectrometers, which were initially developed for remote sensing (RS) applications. With the benefit of acquiring 2D imageries throughout an ample electromagnetic spectrum (EM) part. Although RS can aid in the spatial mapping of illnesses and vectors, existing HSI/MSI information extraction methodologies are not standardized for disease detection. Acquisition schemes, spectral ranges, spatial/temporal resolutions, measuring mode, dispersive methods, detectors, and other techniques play a role in Medical HSI (MHSI) technology with preprocessing, feature extraction/selection, and classification processes for MHSI image analysis. MHSI predominantly takes in the electromagnetic spectrum scale parts: optical or visible (VIS), near-infrared (NIR), mid-infrared (MIR), and ultraviolet (UV). However, there exist other forthcoming options.

Hyperspectral imaging has rapidly risen as a non-destructive, quality analysis and control method in different fields, including body scans, food science, pharmaceutical research, certain types of surgery, and psychological studies, among others.

HSI merges conventional spectroscopic systems (e.g., near-infrared or Raman) with techniques combining spectral and spatial information about an item undergoing scrutiny. The ensuing hyperspectral images consist of elements identified as hypercubes or datacubes, which are three-dimensional data structures enclosing spatial dimensions (with X–Y coordinates) and spectral dimensions (i.e., results related to frequency bands). Accordingly, each pixel situated in the X–Y spatial domain holds a spectrum that reflects its chemical characteristics. Owing to its attributes, HSI benefits from both spectroscopic and imaging procedures. Alike single-point spectroscopy, HSI happens to be a non-destructive procedure with countless applications, it does not need any specimen preparation. It also presents the possibility of performing the chemical and physical mapping of the samples beneath investigation, i.e., utilizing the spatial information to discover distinctive chemical and physical components within the image setting relying on their spectral signatures.

HSI images comprehend a vast amount of data for the reason that each sample can be composed of thousands of spectra. A HSI framework with a spatial resolution of 200×200 pixels can exemplify dimensionality problems. The resultant hyperspectral imaging structure produces an image containing 40,000 spectral datacubes, with each hypercube being characterized by a high-dimensional feature vector. Depending on the selection of spectral devices, each gathered spectrum can collect more than 100 wavelengths, which means more extremely difficult to handle the data set even for such a single small image. On the one hand, this mammoth amount of data also embodies an advantage since it tolerates a detailed representation of the analyzed samples. This dilemma corresponds to the terminology curse of dimensionality (CD) that is commonly used to designate this trait. This CD conundrum stems from high-dimensional data involving concerns linked to data treatment, storage, and analysis. Thus, multivariate image analysis stands as an essential tool for analyzing hyperspectral imageries in this sense. Chemometric processes working with image processing suffer from other problems, such as data compression, visual content and meaning exploration, and classification or quantification.

A slide can be a RGB image with only 3 bands. Because of multiple EM wavelengths (aka spectral bands or channels) beyond visible light, digital HSI/MSI pathology helps diagnose/treat illnesses, handles inter-observer variability, and saves examination time [46]. The HSI/MSI spectroscopy directly measures the incoming radiance spectrum (reflection or transmission) of light and the sample's scattering and absorption. It may, yet, be used to quantify fluorescence. Each HSI/MSI pixel represents the light captured by the camera from a series of measures showing the substance's spectral signatures and permits identifying parts [47, 48]. CAD tools, as well as HSI/MSI, can tackle color, autofluorescence, as well as immunohistochemistry for stained and unstained histology samples. Refraction and reflection in non-homogeneous biological tissues are linked to light speed and direction differences, and changes in reflective/refractive indices detect illnesses. When molecules exhibit radiation absorption peaks at a certain wavelength, they show transitions amid two energy levels and serve as molecules' response fingerprints for diagnostic info. Finally, certain tissues glow when boosted by external light sources. E.g., proteins and nucleic acids produce fluorescence when stimulated by UV light. New HSI/MSI cameras, analytic schemes, and computer power can aid automatic in-vivo/ex-vivo disease detection and image-guided surgery using data about spectral and morphological samples after proper knowledge mining. There are several analytical options for HSI/MSI processing. AI can treat spectral data directly or after feature extraction. DR alters data mathematically to keep just the most vital information. Band selection ways identify major spectral bands. Recently, DL has shown promise for autonomous HSI/MSI feature extraction and categorization [48, 49]. The key DL benefit for supervised classification is determining which dataset traits better identify different materials [50].

Infrared (IR) and Raman spectrometry (aka vibrational spectroscopy) and, principally, micro-spectroscopy with micro-spectroscopic imaging techniques can help characterize developmental modifications in tissues, to observe variations in cell cultures besides detecting illnesses and drug-induced modifications. The conservative procedures for biochemical, as well as histopathological tissue description demand intricate and time-consuming sample handlings, and the outcomes are hardly ever quantifiable [52-57].

10. Discussion and Challenges

Since HIS/MSI processing involve enormous amounts of data and the curse of dimensionality can take a toll on handling such images, better ways to organize the knowledge associated with the images must be found. Hence, semantic techniques can improve imagery exploration [58, 59].

The semantic gap, or the distinction between low-level picture attributes and their high-level meanings, has grown in popularity and interest over the recent time periods. This article addresses this issue and presents a hybrid strategy for learning image semantic concepts for modeling visual characteristics during the discriminative stage of learning. It mingles the qualities of both human-in-the-loop reasoning and discriminative semantic models. The purpose of this article is to explore expert-domain knowledge and expertise as a result of expert-in-the-loop to ascertain medical-knowledge information. Semantic models are designed to discover relationships between low-level characteristics and literary keywords in order to characterize malignancy indications using semantic visual descriptors. These descriptors are created automatically from low-level picture characteristics by leveraging clinical medical expertise based on semantic concepts [60-62].

For the same Ground Truth (GT), the HSI has over a hundred bidirectional measurements referred to as bands (or simply pictures). They are acquired at disjointed frequencies. Regrettably, some bands are redundant, others are measured with excessive noise, and the large dimensionality of data results in low classification accuracy. The issue is determining which bands to use to categorize the region's points. Certain approaches make use of mutual information and thresholding in order to choose just the most pertinent photos. Others maintain control and circumvent redundancy.

Nonetheless, some designers perform dimensionality reduction, sometimes as independent selection and extraction approaches. It is worth noting here that to conduct a survey on all systems currently in operation one creates a dashboard to assist the user in examining selection and extraction aspects. To begin, one must explore and suggest a classifier stage capable of controlling and eliminating duplication by picking the band with the highest mutual information ranking. If its neighbors share a reasonable amount of mutual information with the GT, they will be judged redundant and hence deleted, which is the most inconvenient situation. As a result, some vital information might be deleted. Accepting some helpful or inevitable redundancy is a reasonable option. A band provides valuable information that may be employed to generate an estimated reference map with a greater mutual information value than the GT. To control redundancy, one might apply a complementary threshold to the most recent mutual information value. This is a filter technique, and it achieves a higher level of classification accuracy and is less costly than the wrapper strategy. Another option is that some research employs normalized forms of mutual information in medical imaging applications, such as symmetric uncertainty. As a consequence, an algorithm established on mutual knowledge may be used to choose suitable bands. The symmetric uncertainty coefficient is used to reduce redundancy and improve classification accuracy. This scheme serves as both a tool for feature selection and a wrapper technique. This is a remarkably effective way of curbing redundancy. One must achieve almost identical performance by utilizing many sources of mutual knowledge so that a strategy is successful in selecting relevant and non-redundant bands. Finally, a mutual information-based approach paired with the steepest ascent technique may be used to enhance a symmetric uncertainty coefficient-based strategy and choose appropriate bands for HSI classification. In this strategy, one needs to distinguish between the algorithm that generates the outcome and the human choice. Methods utilizing HSI can work both as a tool for selecting features and a wrapper technique in hybrid implementations. This may be considered a case study illustrating how human judgment differs from that of an intelligent system, presenting approaches constructed on or going beyond mutual information analysis that keeps just the bands with the lowest classification error probability. Additionally, one can add an alternative threshold to limit redundancy. Thus, a suitable band candidate must help reduce the likelihood of the last mistake multiplied by the threshold. This is a wrapper technique that provides excellent performance and classification accuracy but is more costly than the filter strategy [63-66].

The necessity to expedite communication among medical staff from many countries has prompted problems regarding how to express diseases and symptoms in English. It has been customary to let the corpus speak for itself when it comes to translational initiatives. Not only is a real corpus paired with logical analysis a vital tool for language education, but it is also an effective strategy for learning written/ spoken terminology. Corpora enclose enormous potential for medical vocabulary instruction. Students may be directed step by step through the analysis, imitation, learning, and application of genuine and natural corpora using corpus retrieval software, significantly improving the efficiency of medical vocabulary learning. The significance of language instruction in medical education is significantly greater than most people realize. If language organization is comparable to the skeleton of idiom linguistics, vocabulary supplies the essential components of the language. If a person does not grasp grammar, he or she may be able to communicate a small notion in words, but no meaning can be expressed without a word. To a certain degree, competency of college students is determined mostly by their vocabulary and their command on it. The primary impediment to medical students acquiring medical jargon is not grammar, but medical vocabulary, as the majority of medical language is borrowed from Greek and Latin. Numerous medical phrases are constructed using Greek and Latin morphemes such as root, stem, and affix. Due to the uniqueness and professionalism of medical terminology, our medical education places a premium on vocabulary teaching and learning. However, the overall teaching effect is not optimal, and there are still substantial prospects in terms of medical teaching and the development of new interfaces. Thus, it is critical to teach medical students how to communicate their thoughts clearly, precisely, fluently, and befittingly in a multiplicity of circumstances, places, contexts, as well as how to grow their vocabulary and develop their understanding of medical terminology [67, 68].

Another emerging problem is to retrieve or synthesize images related to several conditions from written descriptions and scattered experimental evidence [69-73]. In many instances, these images will have to undergo further processing such as (i) 2D and 3D super-resolution and (ii) normalization and rectification [36, 37, 73-77].

The advent of nanorobotics and new nanotechnological materials also poses a challenge in terms of big data amounts, a multitude of resolutions/scales, and the convenient fusion of all this knowledge. One of the most demanding objectives in pharmacological investigation and probing is to bypass the Blood-Brain Barrier (BBB) to supply drugs and/or markers to the Central Nervous System (CNS). The growing practicality of physical means like steady and alternating magnetic fields to steer nanocarriers with appropriate magnetic features may be a valuable strategy. Lots of research pieces aim to deliver an up-to-date panorama of the magnetic-driven nanotheranostic agent applications to the CNS. Even though well-consolidated work exists on the physical ground, some designs have depicted situations still under investigation. They comprise in-vitro or in-silico prototypes, while others have already joined in—or are near to—clinical validation. A concise overview of the physical principles underlying the behavior of magnetic nanoparticles (MNPs) interacting with an external magnetic field will bring more data and knowledge about nanoscale phenomena. A great challenge as far as imaging and tracing go is to grasp physiological pathways by which a substance can reach the brain from the bloodstream. Then, one must concentrate on those MNP applications that strive at a nondestructive crossing of the BBB, e.g., static magnetic fields to simplify drug transport and alternating magnetic fields to overcome the BBB permeability via magnetic heating. One needs to cite, verify and promote the most outstanding biomedical MNP applications and some pertinent observations about their safenss and possible toxicity.

11. Conclusion

Nowadays, imaging healthcare aids everything from diagnosis to surgery and follow-ups. Since, mainstream imaging modalities are digital, image processing must deal with large data volumes and ever-increasing resolution. This text's key themes are visual medical information and scalability for effective and efficient answers to various interconnected difficulties viz in personalized bioimaging, VR/AR, multispectral/hyperspectral depictions, nanoimaging, and super-resolution. Image processing and visualization solutions must fulfill new end-to-end Medical Cyber-Physical System (MCPS) prospects. Scalable, sophisticated hardware and software parallelizations can be beneficial.

List of Abbreviations

Augmented Reality – AR
Bandpass – BP
Computed Tomography – CT
Dataset Blind Spots – DBSs
Deep Learning – DL
Dimensionality Curse – DC
Electronic Health Records – EHRs
Electromagnetic Spectrum – EM
Gaussian Pyramids – Gps
High-Dimensional Health Data – HDHD
High-Dimensional – HD
Hyperspectral Imaging – HSI
Laplacian Pyramids – LaPs
Low-Pass – LP
Region of Interest – ROI
Dimensionality Reduction – DR
Machine Learning – ML
Magnetic Resonance Imaging – MRI
Medical Cyber-Physical System – MCPS
Medical Hyperspectral Imaging – MHSI
Medical Information Fusion – MIF
Microscope Pathology Slides – MPSs
Mid-Infrared – MIR
Molecular Imaging – MI
Multiscale (or Multiresolution) Image Decompositions – MIDs
Multispectral Imaging – MSI

Near-Infrared – NIR
Optical Microscopes – OMS
Picture Archiving and Communication Systems – PACS
Principal Component Analysis – PCA
Virtual World – VW
Remote Sensing – RS
Single Nucleotide Polymorphisms – SNPs
Software-as-a-Medical-Device – SaMD
Super-resolution – SR
Ultraviolet – UV
Virtual Reality – VR
Visible – VIS
Wavelet Decompositions – WDs

References

1. Nguyen, T., Nguyen, N. and Le, T. (2019). Manufacturing PACS, online medical consultation system and designing security DICOM web viewer software. Proc. of the 2019 Int'l Symp. Elect. and Electronics Eng. (ISEE), 37-42.
2. Estrela, V.V., Saotome, O., Loschi, H.J., Hemanth, D.J., Farfan, W.S. et al. (2018). Emergency response cyber-physical framework for landslide avoidance with sustainable electronics. MDPI, Technologies, 6, 42.
3. Neharkar, M., Sudhansu, S.K. and Sudhansu, P. (2012). Multiresolution mosaic images by using Laplacian of Gaussian method: A review. Int'l J. Eng. Res. Appl. (IJERA), 2(2), 20-25.
4. Su, M.S., Hwang, W.L. and Cheng, K.Y. (2004). Analysis on multiresolution mosaic images. IEEE Trans. Image Proc., 13(7), 952-959.
5. Rivera, L.A., Estrela, V.V., Carvalho, P.C.P. and Velho, L. (2004). Oriented bounding boxes based on multiresolution contours. Journal of WSCG. Proc. of the 12th Int'l Conf. Central Europe on Comp. Grap., Visualiz. and Comp. Vision (WSCG 2004), Czech Republic, February 2-6, 2004, 219-212.
6. Krishnamurthi, R. and Gopinathan, D. (2021). Wavelet transformation and machine learning techniques for digital signal analysis in IoT systems. Mach. Learn. Signal Proc., 2021.
7. Laghari, A.A., Estrela, V.V. and Yin, S. (2022). Special Issue: From Nanoscale to hyperspectral imaging – How to gather and understand medical images harvested in extremely difficult situations. Curr. Med. Imaging, Bentham Science, UK.
8. Shirly, S. and Ramesh, K. (2019). Review on 2D and 3D MRI Image Segmentation Techniques. Curr. Med. Im. Reviews, 15(2), 150-160.
9. Hashemi, S.M., Hassanpour, H., Kozegar, E. and Tan, T. (2021). Cystoscopic image classification by unsupervised feature learning and fusion of classifiers. IEEE Access, 9, 126610-126622.
10. Temel, D. and Al-Regib, G. (2016). Boosting in image quality assessment. Proc. 18th Int'l Workshop on Multimedia Signal Processing (MMSP), 1-6.
11. Estrela, V.V. and Galatsanos, N.P. (1998). Spatially-adaptive regularized pel-recursive

motion estimation based on cross-validation. Proc. IEEE ICIP 98, IEEE, Chicago, USA.

12. Berisha, V., Krantsevich, C., Hahn, P.R., Hahn, S., Dasarathy, G. et al. (2021). Digital medicine and the curse of dimensionality. NPJ Digital Medicine, 4.

13. Topol, E.J. (2019). High-performance medicine: The convergence of human and artificial intelligence. Nat. Med., 25, 44-56.

14. Verma, M., Hontecillas, R., Tubau-Juni, N., Abedi, V., Bassaganya-Riera, J. et al. (2018). Challenges in personalized nutrition and health. Front. Nutr., 5, 117.

15. Li, S., Yang, B. and Hu, J. (2011). Performance comparison of different multiresolution transforms for image fusion. Information Fusion, 12(2), 74-84.

16. Faugeras, O. (1993). Three dimensional computer vision: A geometric viewpoint. The MIT Press.

17. Parmar, K. and Kher, R.A. (2012). Comparative analysis of multimodality medical image fusion methods. Proc. of the Sixth Asia Mod. Symp., 93-97.

18. Moriya, T., Roth, H.R., Nakamura, S., Oda, H., Nagara, K. et al. (2018). Unsupervised segmentation of 3D medical images based on clustering and deep representation learning. Proc. Vol. 10578, SPIE Medical Imaging 2018: Biomedical Applications in Molecular, Structural, and Functional Imaging; 1057820, Houston, Texas, USA.

19. Mitchell, H.B. (2010). Image Fusion: Theories, Techniques and Applications. Springer-Verlag.

20. Vora, S., Lang, A.H., Helou, B. and Beijbom, O. (2020). PointPainting: Sequential fusion for 3D object detection. Proc. of the 2020 IEEE CVPR, 4603-4611.

21. Yi, R., Liu, Y. and Lai, Y.K. (2018). Content-sensitive supervoxels via uniform tessellations on video manifolds. Proc. 2018 IEEE CVPR, 646-655.

22. Berger, M., Tagliasacchi, A., Seversky, L.M., Alliez, P., Guennebaud, G. et al. (2017). A survey of surface reconstruction from point clouds. Comp. Graphics Forum, 36.

23. Mann, A., Farrell, M.B., Williams, J. and Basso, D.A. (2017). Nuclear medicine technologists' perception and current assessment of quality: A society of nuclear medicine and molecular imaging technologist section survey. J. Nucl. Med. Techn., 45, 67-74.

24. Kaushal, A., Altman, R. and Langlotz, C. (2020). Geographic distribution of US cohorts used to train deep learning algorithms. JAMA, 324(1212-1213).

25. Figueroa, R.L., Zeng-Treitler, Q., Kandula, S. and Ngo, L.H. (2012). Predicting sample size required for classification performance. BMC Med. Inform. Decis. Mak., 12, 8.

26. Charpignon, M.L., Celi, L.A. and Samuel, M.C. (2021). Who does the model learn from? Lancet Digit. Health, 3, e275-e276.

27. Maley, J.H., Wanis, K.N., Young, J.G. and Celi, L.A. (2020). Mortality prediction models, causal effects, and end-of-life decision making in the intensive care unit. BMJ Health Care Inform. 27, e100220.

28. Coveney, P.V., Dougherty, E.R. and Highfield, R.R. (2016). Big data need big theory too. Philos. Trans. R. Soc. A., 374, 20160153.

29. Raghu, M., Zhang, C., Kleinberg, J. and Bengio, S. (2019). Transfusion: Understanding transfer learning for medical imaging. Proc. of the 33rd Conf. Neural Inf. Proc. Systems.

30. Cao, L.J., Chua, K.S., Chong, W.K., Lee, H.P., Gu, Q.M. et al. (2003). A comparison of PCA, KPCA and ICA for dimensionality reduction in support vector machine. Neuro-computing, 55(321-336).

31. Jolliffe, I.T. (1982). A note on the use of principal components in regression. J. R. Stat. Soc. Ser. C. Appl. Stat., 31, 300-303.

32. Coelho, A.M., de Assis, J.T. and Estrela, V.V. (2009). Error concealment by means of clustered blockwise PCA. Proc. of the IEEE 2009 Pict. Cod. Symp. (PCS 2009), IEEE.

33. Bengio, Y., Delalleau, O. and Simard, C. (2010). Decision trees do not generalize to new variations. Comput. Intell., 26, 449-467.
34. Bühlmann, P. and Van de Geer, S. (2011). Statistics for High-Dimensional Data. Springer.
35. Li, W., Dasarathy, G. and Berisha, V. (2020). Regularization via structural label smoothing. Proc. Int'l Conf. Artificial Intell. Statistics, PMLR.
36. Deshpande, A., Estrela, V.V. and Razmjooy, N. (2021). Computational Intelligence Methods for Super-Resolution in Image Processing Applications. Springer Nature, Zurich, Switzerland.
37. Kawata, S., Inouye, Y. and Verma, P. (2009). Plasmonics for near-field nano-imaging and superlensing. Nature Photon, 3, 388-394.
38. Karim, S., He, H., Laghari, A.A., Magsi, A.H. and Laghari, R.A. (2021). Quality of service (QoS): Measurements of image formats in social cloud computing. Mult. Tools Appl., 80, 4507-4532.
39. Laghari, A.A., Khan, A., He, H., Estrela, V.V., Razmjooy, N. et al. (2020). Quality of experience (QoE) and quality of service (QoS) in UAV systems. *In:* Estrela, V.V. et al. (eds). Imaging and Sensing for Unmanned Aircraft Systems. IET, 2(10), 213-242.
40. Lebiecka, Z., Skoneczny, T., Tyburski, E., Samochowiec, J., Kucharska-Mazur, J. et al. (2021). Is virtual reality cue exposure a promising adjunctive treatment for alcohol use disorder? J. Clin. Med., 10(13), 2972.
41. Longo, U.G., De Salvatore, S., Candela, V., Zollo, G., Calabrese, G. et al. (2021). Augmented reality, virtual reality and artificial intelligence in orthopedic surgery: A systematic review. Applied Sciences, 11, 3253.
42. Lungu, A.J., Swinkels, W., Claesen, L.J., Tu, P., Egger, J. et al. (2020). A review on the applications of virtual reality, augmented reality and mixed reality in surgical simulation: An extension to different kinds of surgery. Expert Rev. Med. Dev., 18, 47-62.
43. Kaplan, A.D., Cruit, J., Endsley, M.R., Beers, S.M., Sawyer, B.D. et al. (2021). The effects of virtual reality, augmented reality, and mixed reality as training enhancement methods: A meta-analysis. Human Factors: The J. Human Factors and Ergon. Soc., 63, 706-726.
44. Uruthiralingam, U. and Rea, P.M. (2020). Augmented and virtual reality in anatomical education – A systematic review. Adv. Experim. Med. Biol., 1235, 89-101.
45. Izard, S.G., Plaza, Ó.A., Torres, R.S., Méndez, J.A., García-Peñalvo, F.J. et al. (2019). NextMed, Augmented and virtual reality platform for 3D medical imaging visualization: Explanation of the software platform developed for 3D models visualization related with medical images using augmented and virtual reality technology. Proc. 7th Int'l Conf. Techn. Ecosystems for Enhancing Multiculturality.
46. Louis, D.N., Feldman, M., Carter, A.B., Dighe, A.S., Pfeifer, J.D. et al. (2016). Computational pathology: A path ahead. Arch. Path. Lab. Med., 140(1), 41-50.
47. Tuchin, V.V. (2015). Tissue Optics: Light Scattering Methods and Instruments for Medical Diagnosis. Third Edition. SPIE.
48. Halicek, M., Fabelo, H., Ortega, S., Callico, G.M., Fei, B. et al. (2019). In-vivo and ex-vivo tissue analysis through hyperspectral imaging techniques: Revealing the invisible features of cancer. Cancers, 11(6), 756.
49. Levenson, R.M., Fornari, A. and Loda, M. (2008). Multispectral imaging and pathology: Seeing and doing more. Expert Opin. Med. Diagn., 2(9), 1067-1081.
50. Akbari, H., Uto, K., Kosugi, Y., Kojima, K. and Tanaka, N. (2011). Cancer detection using infrared hyperspectral imaging. Cancer Sci., 102(4), 852-857.
51. Lua, G. and Fei, B. (2014). Medical hyperspectral imaging: A review. J. Biom. Optics, 19(1), 010901.

52. Wolfe, W.L. (1997). Introduction to Imaging Spectrometers. SPIE Press, Bellingham, Washington.

53. Goetz, A.F.H. (2009). Three decades of hyperspectral remote sensing of the Earth: A personal view. Remote Sens. Environ., 113(Suppl. 1), S5-S16.

54. Salzer, R., Steiner, G., Mantsch, H.H., Mansfield, J.R. and Lewis, E.N. (2000). Infrared and Raman imaging of biological and biomimetic samples. Fresenius J. Anal. Chem., 366(6-7), 712-726.

55. Kurouski, D., Dazzi, A., Zenobi, R. and Centrone, A. (2020). Infrared and Raman chemical imaging and spectroscopy at the nanoscale. Chem. Soc. Rev., 49, 3315-3347.

56. Gautam, R., Samuel, A.Z., Sil, S., Chaturvedi, D., Dutta et al. (2015). Raman and mid-infrared spectroscopic imaging: Applications and advancements. Current Science, 108, 341-356.

57. Bunaciu, A.A., Hoang, V.D. and Aboul-Enein, H.Y. (2017). Vibrational micro-spectroscopy of human tissues analysis: Review. Critical Reviews in Analytical Chemistry, 47, 194-203.

58. Berisha, V., Krantsevich, C., Hahn, P.R., Hahn, S., Dasarathy, G. et al. (2021). Digital medicine and the curse of dimensionality. NPJ Digital Medicine, 4.

59. Taşkın, G., Kaya, H. and Bruzzone, L. (2017). Feature selection based on high dimensional model representation for hyperspectral images. IEEE Transactions on Image Processing, 26, 2918-2928.

60. Wei, X., Li, W., Zhang, M. and Li, Q. (2019). Medical hyperspectral image classification based on end-to-end fusion deep neural network. IEEE Transactions on Instrumentation and Measurement, 68, 4481-4492.

61. Swain, S., Banerjee, A., Bandyopadhyay, M. and Satapathy, S.C. (2021). Dimensionality reduction and classification in hyperspectral images using deep learning. Machine Learning Approaches for Urban Computing. 113-140. Springer, Zurich, Switzerland.

62. Foncubierta-Rodríguez, A., Herrera, A.G. and Müller, H. (2015). Meaningful bags of words for medical image classification and retrieval. *In:* Briassouli, A., Benois-Pineau, J., Hauptmann, A. (eds). Health Monitoring and Personalized Feedback using Multimedia Data, 73-93.

63. Ma, H., Feng, W., Cao, X. and Wang, L. (2017). Classification of hyperspectral data based on guided filtering and random forest. ISPRS – International Archives of the Photogrammetry, Remote Sensing and Spatial Information Sciences, 821-824.

64. Zhang, J., Geng, W., Zhuo, L., Tian, Q., Cao, Y. et al. (2016). Multiscale target extraction using a spectral saliency map for a hyperspectral image. Applied Optics, 55(28), 8089-8100.

65. Ren, J., Wang, R., Liu, G., Feng, R., Wang, Y. et al. (2020). Partitioned Relief-F method for dimensionality reduction of hyperspectral images. Remote. Sens., 12, 1104.

66. Liu, H., Xia, K., Li, T., Ma, J., Owoola, E.O. et al. (2020). Dimensionality reduction of hyperspectral images based on improved spatial–spectral weight manifold embedding. Sensors, 20. Basel, Switzerland.

67. Liu, C. (2019). Approach of the corpus research on medical English prepositions. Proc. 2019 International Conference on Arts, Management, Education and Innovation (ICAMEI 2019), Clasius Press.

68. Xu, X., Posadzki, P.P., Lee, G., Car, J., Smith, H.E. et al. (2019). Digital education for health professions in the field of dermatology: A systematic review by digital health education collaboration. Acta Dermato-venereologica, 99(2), 133-138.

69. Khelassi, A. and Estrela, V.V. (2021). Advances in multidisciplinary medical technologies — Engineering, modeling and findings. Proceedings of the International Workshop on Medical Technologies 2019 (ICHSMT 2019), Springer Nature, Zurich, Switzerland.

70. Sangkloy, P., Jitkrittum, W., Yang, D. and Hays, J. (2022). A Sketch is Worth a Thousand Words: Image Retrieval with Text and Sketch. ArXiv, abs/2208.03354.
71. Estrela, V.V., Hemanth, J., Saotome, O., Nikolakopoulos, G., Sabatini, R. et al. (2020). Introduction to advances in UAV avionics for imaging and sensing. *In:* Estrela, V.V., Hemanth, J., Saotome, O., Nikolakopoulos, G., Sabatini, R. (eds). Imaging and Sensing for Unmanned Aircraft Systems, 1(1), 1-22, IET, London, UK.
72. Deshpande, A., Patavardhan, P. and Estrela, V.V. (2020). Super resolution and recognition of unconstrained ear image. International Journal of Biometrics, 12, 396.
73. Abdolali, F., Zoroofi, R.A., Otake, Y. and Sato, Y. (2019). A novel image-based retrieval system for characterization of maxillofacial lesions in cone beam CT images. International Journal of Computer Assisted Radiology and Surgery, 14, 785-796.
74. Wang, D., Liu, L., Ma, W., Liu, D., Su, Q. et al. (2018). Design, fabrication, and modification protocols of functional micro-/nanoimaging probes. *In:* Liu, Z. (eds). Advances in Functional Micro-/Nanoimaging Probes. Engineering Materials, 27-36, Springer, Singapore.
75. Emeto, T.I., Alele, F.O., Smith, A.M., Smith, F.M., Dougan, T. et al. (2017). Use of nanoparticles as contrast agents for the functional and molecular imaging of abdominal aortic aneurysm. Frontiers in Cardiovascular Medicine, 4.
76. Alhibshi, A.H., Alamoudi, W. and Farooq, R.K. (2020). Applications of nanomaterials in neurological diseases. Neuronal differentiation, Neuronal protection, and Neurotoxicity. *In:* Khan, F. (eds). Applications of Nanomaterials in Human Health. Springer, Singapore.
77. D'Agata, F., Ruffinatti, F.A., Boschi, S., Stura, I., Rainero, I. et al. (2017). Magnetic nanoparticles in the central nervous system: Targeting principles, applications and safety issues. Molecules: J. Synth. Chemistry and Natural Prod, Chemistry, 23.

Some Issues Regarding Content-Based Image Retrieval (CBIR) for Remote Healthcare Theradiagnosis

Vania V. Estrela[1] [0000-0002-4465-7691], Abdullah Ayub Khan[2,3] [0000-0003-2838-7641], Aftab Ahmed Shaikh[2], Asif Ali Laghari[2] [0000-0001-5831-5943], Mazhar Ali Dootio[3] [0000-0002-6846-0439], Mudassir Hussain[4] [0000-0001-8440-8334], Awais Khan Jumani[5] [0000-0001-9468-0446], Rukhsar Ayub[6]

[1] Department of Telecommunications, Federal Fluminense University (UFF), RJ, 24220-900, Brazil, vania.estrela.phd@ieee.org

[2] Faculty of Computer Science, Sindh Madressatul Islam University, Karachi (74000), Sindh, Pakistan, abdullah.khan0076@gmail.com, aftab.shaikh@smiu.edu.pk, asif.laghari@smiu.edu.pk

[3] Research Lab of Artificial Intelligence and Information Security, Faculty of Computing Science and Information Technology, Benazir Bhutto Shaheed University, Lyari, Karachi (75660), Sindh, Pakistan, abdullah.khan0076@gmail.com, mazharaliabro@gmail.com

[4] Department of Commerce, Benazir Bhutto Shaheed University, Lyari, Karachi (75660), Sindh, Pakistan, muddasir.hussain@bbsul.edu.pk

[5] Department of Computer Science, Ilma University, Karachi, Sindh, Pakistan, awaiskhan@yahoo.com

[6] Benazir School of Business, Benazir Bhutto Shaheed University, Lyari, Karachi (75660), Sindh, Pakistan, rukhsar.ayubbba@gmail.com

1. Introduction

Medical Image Processing (MIP) hinges on quick, remote diagnosis with visual, quantitative, and analytical evaluations via a handful of computational resources [1, 2]. Nowadays, the extraction of quantitative or semi-quantitative aspects from medical pictures, aka Radiomics, plays a significant role in clinical care notably for cancer diagnosis/prognosis. There are numerous Radiomics methodologies including extracting handmade features, deep features, and hybrid schemes. Remote monitoring can detect minor therapeutic progression. Healthcare facilities (HFs) acquire multi-dimensional images, i.e., many sizes (2D, 3D, 4D, etc.) imaging, with assorted modalities from several sources [3, 4]. Alzheimer's disease, e.g., is still investigated with behavioral and cognitive tests besides full brain MRI and PET scans [5, 6]. Diverse imagery collections improve evidence-based diagnosis, administration, training, and research. Appropriate ways to survey those collections are required. Appraising data without direct patient contact can lessen statistical bias. The content can be categories, colors, texture, and forms reminiscent of the query, textures, or other relevant hints built on syntactical image properties. A Content-Based Image Retrieval (CBIR) framework locates and retrieves data resembling those itemized in a query, making use of image attributes and descriptors. A CBIR can accomplish multi-dimensional Image Retrieval (IR), Medical Data (MD) retrieval within a multimodality setting, and the recovery of unique datasets.

Narrow Domain Applications (NDAs) include Medical IR, Biometrics IR, and Remote Sensing (RS) IR. These applications might have

- (i) Small content variance,
- (ii) Specific knowledge sources as targets,
- (iii) Homogeneous semantics,
- (iv) Likely specific Ground Truth (GT),
- (v) More objective content description,
- (vi) Some way to control scenes and sensors,
- (vii) Limited interactivity,
- (viii) Quantitative and qualitative metrics,
- (ix) Tailored/data-driven architectures,
- (x) Often employed object recognition techniques, and
- (xi) Specific invariances established via model-drivel tools.

Broad Domain Applications (BDAs) stemming from collections and Internet content have

- (i) High content variance,
- (ii) Deal with generic knowledge sources,
- (iii) Heterogeneous semantics,
- (iv) Lack any ground truth,
- (v) More subjective content description,
- (vi) Pervasiveness and interactivity,
- (vii) Qualitative evaluation,
- (viii) Modular/iterative architectures,
- (ix) Sizes ranging from large to enormously bulky,
- (x) Frequent information retrieval technique exigencies, and
- (xi) Perceptual/cultural tools.

Imageries can help with real-time remote screening, consultation, therapy, drug-releasing, store-and-forward exams, home care, and overall patient surveillance. Large data sets demand web-based and other telemedicine infrastructures. The key ideas about medical CBIRSs [7, 8]:

Feature Vector (FV) is a vector whose entries represent image attributes or metrics.

Image Processing (IP) transforms images to enrich their quality or yield other developments swinging on the input images (i.e., another image or knowledge taken from image sequences).

An Image Descriptor (ID) is a model or data structure explaining an image. This piece of stored data identifies an item in a framework for data storage and retrieval. Descriptors keep appropriate content information to expedite processing in future queries exploiting essential image features for search and comparison.

Metadata comprises appearance knowledge about a large database's items, like who embedded the data and in which format. The object, its properties, associated words, attribute, aspect, and schema denote metadata in some well-being context. Utilizing only words causes inconsistencies stemming from interpretation differences triggered by the Human Visual System (HVS).

Query Image (QI) is the image entered by the user.

Relevance Feedback (RF) incorporates the user into the retrieval process by submitting the query as an image, drawing, or text. When the system fetches database photos, the user verifies their relevance.

A **Schema** (plural, schemata) describes a database's structure with corresponding data modeling conventions.

Semantic Gap (SG) is the difference between the retrieved visual data and the user's interpretation of the same data. The SG must be as little as feasible owing to visual and semantic diversity.

Similarity Metrics (SMs) assess picture quality. A CBIRS uses several SMs.

Hospital Information System (HIS) is a broad data management system addressing administrative, financial, legal, service processing needs and practices utilizing communication channels and the Internet. Integrating home care, local care, huge HFs, and global care is critical to HIS.

Picture Archiving and Communication Systems (PACSs) fuel and support low-cost storage with speedy access to medical images (viz. graphs, charts, pictures, video, streaming.). PACS automates actions, improves imagery management, besides sending reports digitally [9]. It includes (a) image capture, (b) a secure network for transmitting patient data, (c) decision-support viewing/display technology, (d) pictures suitable for interpretation, annotation, and review, and (e) acceptable file storage, trustworthiness, and retrieval (where these archives can be images, reports, or both, besides some sort of information fusion). E.g., PACS can get rid of temporal and physical barriers to accessing pictures, interpretations, and data associated with them. A full PACS should handle all digital formats with a single access point.

Radiology Information System (RIS) collects, processes, and distributes patient radiographic data and visual descriptions, often including patient following, scheduling, reporting, and associated image analysis. RIS is essential for radiology workflow efficiency and supports HIS [10, 11].

Electronic Health Records (EHRs) [12] allow well-being providers to share patient data (groups, Healthcare Staff (HS) among others). The nomenclatures MD, in addition to Medical/Health Record are equivalent, describing a patient's medical history throughout time at a single HF location. MD comprise many written notes over time by healthcare experts, noting observations, controlling remedies, monitoring therapies, test outcomes, X-rays and reports, among others. A HS must preserve MD completely and correctly as a consequence of their licensure/certification.

Computerized Physician Order Entry (CPOE) lets the HS to directly enter tests, pharmaceutical orders, and other procedures into a computational device to be directed to a pharmacy later [13].

ePrescribing involves access to prescriptions, printing for patients/caretakers, and electronic prescription diffusion to pharmacists.

Pharmaco Informatics (PI) studies medication-related data in various healthcare systems [14, 15]. Drug and prescription data are stored electronically. Patient data is evaluated, medication behavior is modeled/simulated, and their performance is controlled via tailored patient dose regimens to attain explicit treatment goals.

Telemedicine comprises remote physical and psychological diagnosis, therapy, and monitoring of patient functions.

Consumer Health Informatics is in charge of electronic well-being resources by healthy people.

Health Knowledge Management is a structure allowing an overview of the latest literature, best practice guidelines, or epidemiological trackings viz. Medscape, NIH, PubMed Central (PMC), SciELO, and MDLinx.

Virtual Healthcare Teams are composed of HS who pool resources and share patient data via digital devices and settings [13].

mHealth or m-Health entails mobile devices to amass collective and patient MDs, offering healthcare information to HS and patients, with real-time monitoring of the patient's vitals, and straight care provision.

Health Research with Grids comprises potent computing and handling data administration tools, involving large amounts of heterogeneous data [16].

Nuclear Medicine Information Management Systems (NMISs), as the term hints, cope with HF nuclear medicine concerns. Receptionists organize patient studies, record data, and write reports. Administrative staff record and print medical reports, locate patient imageries, track studies, and access statistical, billing, and resource usage data. Technologists provide guidelines, collect quality assurance data, and analyze test outcomes. These experts utilize the system to gather/record trace stocks, track preparation, manage delivery operations, and preserve records for outer criticism. HS can find past results and analyze them. Patient scheduling, film management, radio pharmacy, quality assurance, report creation, and inventory organization exemplify software for educational and commercial systems. Specifying and installing hardware is also considered.

Laboratory Information Systems (LISs) are software-based laboratories, record keeping, and information managing structures. Workflow, data processing, data sharing interfaces, and flexible design are key elements to facilitate regulations

[17]. The LIS concept was inspired by unpretentious sample tracking, incorporating an Enterprise Resource Planning (ERP) solution for managing numerous areas of laboratory data processing. LISs are dynamic, as laboratory restrictions change fast, and laboratory demands vary widely. Thus, a workable LIS definition depends on individual or group understanding. Recently, LIS capabilities have gone beyond sample management. Data management, mining, analysis, and integration are other problems that make translational medicine viable.

Clinical Decision Support delivers data electronically concerning processes and standards for healthcare specialists to apply in studying and treating patients.

These concepts are not exhaustive but show the complexity and significance of medicinal pictorial content management. Sections...

MIP fundamentals CBIRS Architectures

2. MIP Fundamentals

A 2D image is a signal holding information about the image brightness and epitomized as a function $f(x, y)$. The spatial pixel location is designated by (x, y) [18]. The value of $f(x, y)$ is also termed gray level or intensity. Images can be continuous and discrete.

A continuous imagery can be portrayed by a real function $f(x, y)$ of continuous variables x and y, comparable to a snapshot recorded on a film as $f(x, y)$.

The simplest discrete 2D imagery is a function $I(i, j)$ of integers i and j, as in a scanned, discretized 512×512 pixel matrix. Consequently, f turns out to be a 2D matrix I of size 512×512. A color image routinely partakes three discrete matrices, e.g., a 512×512 pixel color picture can be split into three 512×512 channels (or matrices): Red (R), Green (G), and Blue (B).

The subsequent struggle is how to recover relevant multimedia content, such as colors, shapes, as well as taxonomies akin to the queries, textures, or any other valid clue that can follow from consulting vast image collections via syntactical image features. The standards must impact CBIRSs minimally in practice regarding image compression, query description, and metadata. Several important CBIR aspects follow:

 (i) Network protocols, viz. TCP/IP, govern data transmission among hosts storing information and stakeholders running applications with these records;
 (ii) Image storage formats like DICOM, TIFF, or JPEG, stipulating in what way images should be encoded for storage or broadcast;
(iii) Imagery compression standards specify customary ways for compressing picture (and video) data for effective broadcast;
(iv) Database command languages offer a standard syntax to stipulate relational database queries; and
 (v) Metadata standards afford a model that includes multimedia object content and languages such as XML to describe the scope.

The Moving Picture Experts Group (MPEG) has been pursuing better scenarios as far as data definitions, representations (descriptors), and standards for CBIR [19, 20] compatible with norms similar to MPEG-7 [21] in addition to MPEG 21 [22]. Digital Imaging and Communications in Medicine (DICOM) is the most employed format [23, 24]. Non-visual data sources can be sent via PDF, JPEG 2000, or JPIP integrated into DICOM. Likewise, the IHE XDS regulation manipulates shared HF documents [25]. Teleradiology utilizes (a) JPIP streaming, (b) Health Information Exchange (HIE), (c) Electronic Medical Records (EMRs), besides (d) Personal Health Records (PHR).

XML is currently an interoperable multimedia metadata form to share across various gadgets. Many XML documents do not use all of a schema's information, so consumers download unnecessary data. The structure of XML documents is commonly specified using a XML schema, allowing programs to validate them [26]. However, a single XML document can typically relate to several, possibly huge schemata. While a schema is not inescapably required to receive an XML document, it is required to modify it [27-29]. Multiple descriptors exist for multimedia material, resulting in many XML schemata. Albums, photos, audio descriptions and movies may employ some MPEG-7 [30, 31] besides MPEG-21 descriptors [27, 28, 29, 32, 33].

Increasingly, metadata is used to help the community classify material according to standard schemata. Whether the community utilizes standard descriptors (MPEG-7) or creates its own, many XML and schema documents must be shared. Large, duplicated descriptor sets cause issues in mobile contexts. All users must participate in data growth for communities to function properly, including description changes. The MPEG community realized this issue while defining MPEG-7, leading to MPEG-7 TEM and BiM [32, 33]. However, in a collaborative environment, users must be able to access schema fragments as XML documents are parsed and processed.

An expanded RXEP protocol may rely on fragments of schemata with XML to avoid these costs [26, 32, 33]. With this information, users may design rich and huge collections of multimedia data descriptors that work in high and low bandwidth situations.

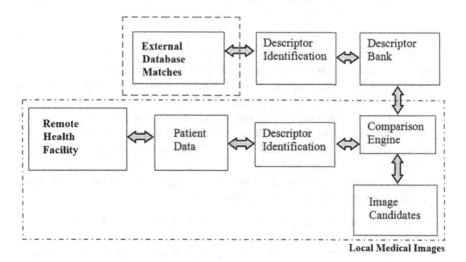

Figure 1. A characteristic CBIR system (CBIRS)

3. CBIRS Architectures

Picking up and designing features are the key underlying descriptive models. A Handcrafted Features (HC) Pipeline (HCP) entails the image acquisition/ reconstruction, preprocessing and segmentation to determine Region of Interest (ROI), feature extraction/reduction, and model building. An alternative is a Deep Learning (DL) Pipeline (DLP) using some DL architecture, differing from HCP for not needing segmentation, feature extraction, and a clear-cut model.

Visual indexing is common in computer vision. Each QI is evaluated for color, shape, and other properties. A database contains an automated image account allowing IR with the related image attributes as an index.

The CBIRS should consider the user's search needs. Questions like whether the user already recognizes the image and its relation to the application are crucial. It may be necessary to retrieve photographs that are not the intended ones. Design issues can be addressed by both manual and CBIR procedures. Figure 1 depicts a CBIRS architecture. Now, one may compare visual data by querying via selection criteria for images. A query like *retrieve all text records about poisonous food* can find CBIRS pictures containing silhouettes, colors, textures, types, or other image-related details.

CBIRS recovers similar pictures. Several illnesses look like the same wound but have different diagnoses. Recovered images should be marked as having positive or negative significance [4] to increase diagnostic performance and parameter tuning. For example, remote CBIR web services may query global picture databases, complementing text-based retrieval approaches. The system finds, collects, and displays photos visually similar to the one sought, employing a collection of characteristics unrelated to any particular investigation. Support for both novice and experienced users can increase diagnostic accuracy. The widespread adoption of HF PACs stimulate interest in emerging approaches for more efficient MD consumption [34, 35]. Several factors must be considered:

1. An effective imaging protocol for saving, analyzing, and examining pictures from multiple sources (e.g., MRI, CT, ultrasound, PET, SPECT). The categorization standards still have scalability and mis categorization concerns.
2. Quality control, data storage, delivery, and analysis are required. Even with large files, the archive access technique is critical. Data-driven systems have constraints and possible uses that may reduce IR efficiency. Existing technology can search picture-related text data, but this needs people to characterize each database image, which is difficult for large databases or when creating images in real-time.
3. Engaging patients and caretakers to create images and send them back to the imaging centers to optimize the healthcare staff use.

CBIRSs require image descriptors, feature extraction, and feature matching that can be very demanding due to resolutions, database sizes, and search strategies. Query by example compares an input image to a database. Search algorithms may differ depending on the usage, yet, the results should all share common attributes with the example. SM content comparison assists decisions during the location, recovery, and display of significant illustration cases. It is quite challenging in this domain to mine local points in specific image features and establish the similarity model. CBIR comparisons often entail a visual distance metric or SM to match images in various dimensions or categories, like form, color, texture, importance, and others [4]. The dimension refers to the number of axes representing an image (2D, 3D, 4D, and more.). Mixing specific criteria yields the best metrics, letting a full hierarchy of possible database outcomes concerning the query. A category is a concept not requiring a numerical value, like shape and color. The main planning points for a CBIRS are in Fig. 2.

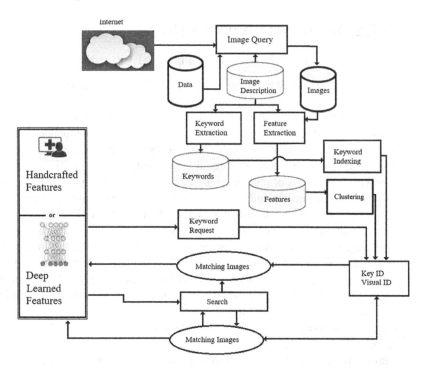

Figure 2. CBIRS from the functional viewpoint of the user and the queried system

3.1. CBIRS Development

Steps to develop a CBIRS:

1. Identify CBIRS architecture pre-requisites.
2. Study the existing IR procedures and their efficacy.
3. Maintain a real medical imagery/metadata database from various sources and classify the information acquired.
4. Identify potential visual traits to mine and select SMs.
5. Conceive a web deployable structure.
6. Limit access via authorization praxes, with patient data privacy and security.
7. Efficient web-based GUIs that handle permissions, perform visual queries, scrutinize retrieved outcomes, and so forth.

Successful CBIR deployment relies on the capacity to handle user intentions. RF can gradually refine the search outcomes by labeling images *relevant, irrelevant,* or *neutral.* Later, the scrutinized query can be searched again with the new data. Searches leaning on metadata require annotation quality and completeness. Manual registration via keywords or metadata in a bulky log can be time-intensive and fail to resolve the keywords depicting an image. The performance assessment of keywords exploration is subjective and has not been well-defined. Hence, the success of CBIRSs is difficult to measure [36]. It is also imperative to remember web-based architectures, global availability, straightforward access, and smart algorithms.

4. CBIRS Development with a HCP

The stages for Handcrafted Features within a Pipeline (HCP) follow [37-40]:

1. **Pre-processing** aims at reducing noise and artifacts from the original raw data and typically smoothens and enhances an image.
2. **Segmentation** typically extracts features from segmented parts and many tissues do not exhibit distinct borders [41, 42]. Albeit manual tumor demarcation is a standard clinical tactic, it is time-consuming and widely sensitive to inter-observer inconsistencies. It requires forward-thinking (semi) automated subdivision solutions of high accuracy that can also yield reproducible edges. Some common ones include region growing (i.e., seed-based), graph cuts, level sets, and contour-based approaches. As no methodology handles all regions and cases, the best strategy adopts a majority voting breakdown, to leverage the resultant potential outcomes from different methods to always pick up the best output according to some SM and, if possible, the ground truth. Hence, this stage can combine several methods. Since the ground truth can be nonexistent in medicine, reproducibility metrics often help the segmentation algorithm performance evaluation.
3. **Feature extraction** is the main step in the workflow and will be discussed in the next chapter subsection.
4. **Feature reduction** is also a critical step since a large number of quantitative features can be extracted from big image datasets, but most of them are irrelevant to the existing task, and/or may contribute to model overfitting.
5. **Model analysis** refers to utilizing the extracted and possibly reduced features according to some model defined by the designer.

4.1. Feature Extraction

Text-based and visual attributes can do feature extraction. In the first case, keywords and annotations can portray and index images. As for the second, one can count on and extract general qualities viz. color, texture, shape, besides other domain-specific features [43-47]. Wide-ranging features from querying other database images are extracted employing their pixel characteristics. The CBIRS stores image knowledge compactly into a feature database, aka image signature [48].

4.2 Image Description

Descriptors are the first step to depicting an image. Visual information descriptors are twofold: (a) General low-level representing color, silhouette, regions, textures and motion; and (b) Specific domain providing knowledge about scene objects and events. IDs can describe content globally or locally, for example. Next, the most widespread IDs are explained, and they can form a FV. Several descriptor types follow.

Color is a paramount visual factor. There exist different color spaces like the RGB (Red, Green, and Blue), LAB, or CIELAB (L means lightness; the color opponent dimensions A and B rely on nonlinearly compressed CIE XYZ color space coordinates), LUV, HSV (Hue, Saturation, and Value); HSL (Hue, Saturation, and Lightness), YC_BC_R (used as a part of the color video and photography pipeline) and the Hue-Min-Max-Difference (HMMD). Among these models, the HSV shows excellent perceptual nature [49]. The opponent color axes (R-G, 2B-R-G, R+G+B) model benefits from isolating the intensity data on the third axis, being invariant to intensity changes and shadows. The HSV is invariant under the object's orientation about the illumination plus camera direction. Then, one seeks clusters in a color histogram to detect which pixels belong to one uniformly tinted object. A color histogram holds each color's fraction of pixels [45]. A CBIRS computes a color histogram related to a QI to compare it to other color database histograms. Afterward, the CBIRS retrieves imageries whose color histograms match the query's histograms more closely. At the query time, an operator can either indicate a color percentage or stipulate a sample image whose color histogram serves as a reference. Histogram intersection can help feature matching. Two-color moment practices replace the color histogram and reduce the quantization effects by typifying the color distribution with its moments. Color sets work as a color histogram estimate, transforming the RGB space into a perceptually even space, viz. HSV, and next quantize the new space into M bins [36, 37, 50]. Statistical moments are invariant to image shift, rotation, and scale, representing fundamental geometric properties of a distribution of random variables.

Texture means visual patterns with homogeneous properties that cannot result from a single color or intensity, e.g., clouds, vegetation, bricks, fur, and fabric. Texture description exploiting psychology and HVS perception can approximate meaningful texture properties, i.e., contrast, coarseness, directionality, regularity, and line-resemblance [36]. However, only coarseness, contrast, and directionality strongly resemble the HVS and are widely employed, characterizing, correspondingly, the High×Low, Coarse×Fine, and Directional×Non-directional natures of image or region textures. The descriptors obtained from both the region homogeneities and their border histograms can represent Homogeneous Textures (HTs), Texture Browsing (TB), as well as Edge Histograms (EH characteristics. Co-occurrence matrices can handle the orientation and distance between pixels and it simplifies the contrast, coarseness, directionality, regularity, periodicity, directionality, and randomness estimation to help comprehend texture. A statistical methodology using the mean and variance extracted from the wavelet sub-bands can represent texture [36, 37]. A technique with the wavelet transform with Kahunen-Loeve (KL) (or

Principal Component Analysis, PCA) expansion and Kohonen maps can analyze texture [51-53]. Combining a wavelet transform with a co-occurrence matrix can handle both statistics- and transform-based texture studies [50].

Shape allows natural objects to be recognized. Some shape features are calculated for every object recognized within each warehoused imagery. Shape representations can be twofold: boundary- and region-based. The former employs only the exterior shape boundary, while the latter requires the whole shape [54]. The most effective depiction uses Fourier descriptors and moment variants. A Fourier ID uses the Fourier transformed boundary as the shape feature. Moment invariance uses region-based moments, invariant to transformations as the shape feature. CBIRS queries amount to either sample image form or sketch [50].

Motion contains important semantic evidence that requires a segmentation similar to the HVS. Still, there exist algorithms with a good approximation. These IDs portray 2D and 3D regions, contours, and shapes. The outline IDs can represent Region Shape (RS), Contour Shape (CS), besides 3D Shape (3D S) for an object's and camera's motions. This last information comes from the capture device, while image processing produces the others. The ID set can describe Motion Activity (MA), Camera Movement (CM), Motion Trajectory (MT), Warping (WM), and Parametric Motion (PM).

Element Locations in the image describe elements in the spatial and temporal realms as Region Locator (RL) and Spatial-Temporal Locator (STL).

Specific Domain Data gives information about the scene's objects and events. These IDs may not be readily extractable, even more, when the extraction is automatic. However, they can be manually processed. Face recognition exemplifies an application that automatically tries to obtain this information.

4.3. Feature Vector Creation

Once a descriptor set is found, then a FV has descriptors as its entries. With 5 features, i.e., FV is a 5-dimensional vector, e.g., Contrast (SM_1), Dissimilarity (SM_2), Homogeneity (SM_3), Angular Second Moment (SM_4), besides Entropy (SM_5) results in $FV = [SM_1, SM_2, SM_3, SM_4, SM_5]$. Next, SMs can describe the database FVs resembling the query image. E.g., the Overall SM (OSM):

$$OSM = (E_{texture} + E_{intenstiy} + E_{shape})/3. \tag{1}$$

$E_{texture}$, $E_{intenstiy}$, besides E_{shape} are partial SMs standing for texture, intensity, and shape, respectively. Thus, the OSM value can help sort similar images, i.e., past related instances are recovered. The following Subsections depict some SMs and other comparison procedures.

4.4. Comparing Images

Similarity analysis can result from the image itself viz. the difference of pixel values and results from histogram segmentation/analysis. Next, some SMs are discussed.

Pixel-Based Image Similarity

Let f and g be two gray-value image functions, $\mathbf{a}$ and $\mathbf{b}$ be two images of size $w \times h$, as well as c some image transformation assigning a numerical value to each image pixel. As an example, $c(\mathbf{a}, x, y)$ could be the gray value of the pixel at (x, y).

Differences between pixels can be characterized by distinct metrics like:

$$pd1(\mathbf{a},\mathbf{b}) = \sum_{x=1}^{w}\sum_{y=1}^{h} |\, c(\mathbf{a},x,y) - c(\mathbf{b},x,y)\,|, \text{ and} \tag{2}$$

$$pd2(\mathbf{a},\mathbf{b}) = \sum_{x=1}^{w}\sum_{y=1}^{h} (c(\mathbf{a},x,y) - c(\mathbf{b},x,y))^2. \tag{3}$$

The mean and variance can add stability to image pixel differences:

$$spd(\mathbf{a},\mathbf{b}) = \sqrt{wh}\,\frac{\overline{d(\mathbf{a},\mathbf{b})}}{s_d(\mathbf{a},\mathbf{b})}, \text{ where}$$

$$\overline{d(\mathbf{a},\mathbf{b})} = \frac{1}{wh}\sum_{x=1}^{w}\sum_{y=1}^{h} d(\mathbf{a},\mathbf{b},x,y),$$

$$(\mathbf{a},\mathbf{b}) = \frac{1}{wh-1}\sum_{x=1}^{w}\sum_{y=1}^{h} (d(\mathbf{a},\mathbf{b},x,y) - \overline{d(\mathbf{a},\mathbf{b})})^2, \text{ and}$$

$$d(\mathbf{a},\mathbf{b},x,y) = c(\mathbf{a},x,y) - c(\mathbf{b},x,y).$$

The vector $v(\mathbf{a})$ contains all $c(\mathbf{a}, x, y)$ values for all pixels in $\mathbf{a}$. Imagery SMs can be inner products of normalized vectors. A potential disparity measure producing maximum values for identical frames is

$$vd(\mathbf{a},\mathbf{b}) = 1 - \frac{v(\mathbf{a}) \bullet v(\mathbf{b})}{\|v(\mathbf{a})\| * \|v(\mathbf{b})\|}.$$

Image Histograms

An Image histogram is a vector. Assume an image $f(x, y)$ holds gray levels amid 0 and 255. Then, the corresponding histogram is $H(f)$, and $H(f)(B)$ is the quantity of pixels (i, j) with $F(i, j) = B$. Equivalent images $f(.)$ and $g(.)$ partake similar histograms. Yet, it is possible that different imageries may have extremely similar histograms:

$$d(H(f), H(g)) = (\Sigma_i [H(f)(i) - H(g)(i)]^2)^{-1/2}, i \in [0, 255].$$

Figure 3 shows some image histogram properties that can be used to assemble another FV.

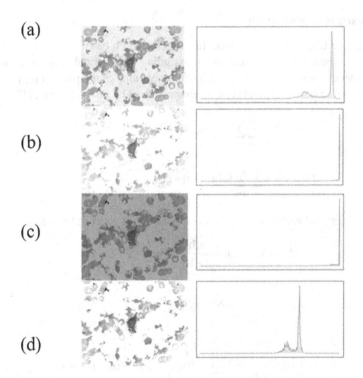

Figure 3. Image histograms of a blood smear: (a) original, (b) brighter, (c) darker, and (d) high-contrast versions

4.5. CBIR Evaluation

Humans can straightforwardly recognize the similarity among images. To test the CBIRS effectiveness, two SMs are commonly used [29, 37, 89, 92, 94]:

Precision (*P*) is the ratio concerning the number of relevant images retrieved (*NIR*), i.e., items recuperated by the system that are really significant to the query, and the total amount of recovered images (*TID*):

$$Precision = \frac{NIR}{TID}.$$

Recall (*R*) is the relative quantity arising from dividing the quantity of recovered relevant images (*NIR*) by the total amount of pertinent images in the database (*NID*):

$$Recall = \frac{NIR}{NID}.$$

High accuracy signifies that less relevant images emerge from a query or that a more pertinent image range is recovered while high *R* means few important images are abandoned.

4.6 Indexing and Retrieving

In the matching procedure, the QI image signature is compared to other image signatures stored in the database by calculating some distance measure between image signatures of the queried example and database images, subsequently ranking their images according to their distance threshold. Usually, the Euclidean distance is an important metric. Next, the system returns products visually similar to the stakeholder's query by ranking. Feature matching can compare: (i) segmented regions and, then, the distance between two regions is measured via their low-level features; and (ii) images with numerous regions. Recently, several distance measures emerged for histograms viz., the city-block- and Minkowsky distances [55].

5. CBIRS Using some DLP

A Deep Learning Pipeline (DLP) extracts deep features by specifying a pre-defined task, comprising disease diagnostics. DLP can utilize different architectures, e.g., Convolutional Neural Network (CNN), to discern the most appropriate features [56-59]. The extracted features can go through the DL net for analysis and decision-making or exit the network and enter a different analyzer like a Support Vector Machine (SVM) or a Decision Tree (DT).

DLP benefits include (i) it does not need prior knowledge, extracting features automatically, with high-level features obtained from low-level ones, (ii) DL networks can be trained in a modest end-to-end process, whose performance improves systematically with more training samples [60-62], and (iii) the deep networks can extract features from the raw image without ROI segmentation, helping the process in two ways:

(i) By-passing segmentation can significantly shrink the computational load and takes manual delineation off experts since manual annotations are extremely observer-dependent, making them unreliable information sources, and

(ii) Automatic segmentation is still highly error-prone and inaccurate in sensitive decision-making.

Furthermore, a deep network input can combine the original and segmented imageries with any other pre-processed input comparable to the gradient image (multi-channel input), everything concatenated along the third dimension [60-62]. The input type varieties can further take into account different angles such as coronal and axial. Vital DLP aspects follow.

(i) *Input Hierarchy:* A deep net can receive single slices, whole volumes, or even entire examinations' data from a specific patient. Each case necessitates its strategy, e.g., for processing the entire volume simultaneously, one should consider the inconsistent dimension size, as a different number of slices can be allotted to patients. Recurrent Neural Networks (RNNs) often handle variable size inputs (e.g., various number of slices).

(ii) *Raw and Pre-trained Models:* Pre-trained models can be fine-tuned or raw models can be trained from start, depending on the amount of the available dataset and the available time.

(iii) *DL Network Designs:* The deep network design choice is paramount to extracting meaningful and practical DLP.

This chapter will not talk about DL architectures in detail but they appear in [60-62]. Input images for DLP can belong to three main types.

Slice-level classification is the process of studying and categorizing picture slices independently of one another; nevertheless, this technique is insufficiently informative, since one makes decisions based on the labels assigned to the total Volume of Interest (VOI).

Volume-level categorization results from slice-level classification shortcomings, where either (a) a voting system fuses slice-level outputs, or (b) all image slices accompanying a scanned volume feed the classifier. Lastly, Patient-level classification refers to allocating a label to a specific patient hinging on a temporal series investigation involving several imaging modalities (e.g., CT follow-ups). CBIRSs partake in open problems and opportunities as below.

A. Handcrafted Challenges

HCP has greater limitations, as visual variety is required to distinguish, for example, malignant tumors. Hence, most people start by extracting multitudes of low-level and high-level attributes without considering the overall purpose. Simple reduction approaches (e.g., straightforward Principal Component Analysis (PCA)) can mitigate the dimensionality curse. Existing handmade characteristics are also limited in their cancer prediction discriminative capacity since they are retrieved without incorporating information from other data sources viz. gene expressions and experimental data besides requiring a segmented ROI. In healthcare, only professionals can give segmentations, both time-consuming and costly.

B. DLP Challenges

DLP advantages include generalization and independence from expert supervision. Its disadvantages comprise the necessity for large data sets, inflexibility to certain transformations, absence of optimal architectural selection techniques, and how to define the criteria for acceptable deep architectures. Sensitivity analysis is vital in explaining the link between intended options and accomplished results and establishing the factors that produce the results. e.g., picking the input image size involves choosing between the original and shrinking images. Downsizing reduces processing and makes acquired evidence invariant to translation and rotation, reducing outliers. Due to the variety of imaging modalities, DLP models and solutions must be changed or normalized before being used in medicine (e.g., MRI images). While handmade features often require less data, the number of photos necessary to train deep architectures like Convolutional Neural Networks (CNNs) depends on the model's complexity. That is, the more trainable parameters, the more training data required. The computational DL cost is reduced by cropping the input image to contain the ROI/VOI. DLP may lose information in healthcare where size is a distinguishing attribute of normal and diseased tissues. Human lives are at risk, and healthcare practice will stay constrained without adequate DLP explaining ability. The link concerning deep features vs. genetic patterns is unknown and requires more research. Numerous unresolved issues exist and require further research:

1. Adequate health depictions are challenging to gather due to strong privacy rules.
2. Finding enough data with identical clinical parameters is tough even without privacy concerns (e.g., equivalent cancer stages).
3. The only source of ground truth for analysis is clinical expertise. This necessitates the creation of domain-specific or semi-supervised solutions.
4. Contextual variances in scanner types and/or technological qualities cause large contrast and resolution variations between organizations (and datasets). To compensate for the nonexistence of health standards, new and imaginative information fusion and unifying tactics are required. Specialists may also seek different information and image landmarks, resulting in wildly divergent ground truths and annotations.
5. In unbalanced data, the classifier favors the majority class. Positive courses (disease) frequently outnumber negative classes. Working with medical data is risky. However, the topic remains unclear and requires further investigation.
6. Dealing with noise can be difficult, e.g., a patient's breathing in the CT scanning might shift lung tumor placement in successive slices, making reliable feature extraction problematic.
7. What makes new data sources problematic is that not all patients have data. Such models should handle sparse data. Modern fusion procedures demand stronger fusion requirements. Sorting/combining localized FVs from feature-level fusion viz. First hybrid aftermaths seem superior, improving multi-model solutions.

6. Solutions and Recommendations

Future CBIR development raises numerous research challenges, such as:

(i) New image annotation methodologies need to be engendered since there are no such practices available that properly handle SG.
(ii) CBIRSs for specific domain/applications must emerge from understanding their prerequisites and information-seeking behavior.
(iii) Discovering new connections, and mining patterns. Text mining might be combined with visual-based descriptions.
(iv) The process of matching queries and stored imageries can resemble HVS similarity judgments.

Probing big image databases is a demanding endeavor, largely, for meaningful content retrieval. Most search engines relate the QI and all database images and organize them according to their computed SMs, which are paramount to CBIR procedures. These processes search an image database to discover pictures analogous to some queries. Consequently, they should be capable of appraising the number of similarities amid images.

As previously stated, the SG is the discrepancy between the information that may be extracted from visual data and the interpretation that the same data has for a user in a particular context. A user seeks semantic similarity, but the database can only supply it through data processing, or the search results in a vast number of investigated items. Possible sources of errors:

(i) Incomplete query description.
(ii) Incomplete image depiction.
(iii) Color variance problems instigated by surface orientation, camera viewpoint, relative position, and illumination.
(iv) Shape perception problems like occlusion in addition to different viewpoints.
(v) Texture-related difficulties.
(vi) Object segmentation can cause hindrances.
(vii) Eventual presence of a narrow domain amid big data.

A distinction among pixels in the Color Histogram for K-Means (CHKM), Color Co-occurrence Matrix (CCM), as well as scan pattern (DBPSP) can be made as CBIRS features [63]. This modus operandi significantly lessens the FV and indexing time. Another approach for color IR selects features is based on their color, texture, besides shape [64-66], resulting in a high retrieval efficacy. Gabor Filters (GFs) as well as Zernike Moments (ZMs) support texture and form (resulting from analyses) as characteristics [67].

A fuzzy logic arrangement [68] attempted to ameliorate issues associated with classic CBIR systems handling the SG and perceptual subjectivity. Linguistic phrases helped communicate notions naturally. Membership functions mapped picture attributes into HVS concepts. Moreover, a query description language has been established for the syntax in addition to semantics to standardize the phrasing of queries in written explanations, graphic demonstrations, and RF. The query comparison component is gathered from a similarity function from user feedback while comparing the query to each database image. The user preferences have been retained to conserve their profile for the purpose of personalization. The experimental results indicated that this structure alleviated SG and perceptual subjectivity difficulties.

Numerous fuzzy tactics have recuperated comparable pictures. In [69], a quicker fuzzy CBIR SM has relied on the fuzzy sets' center of gravity. An experimental CBIRS has been built exploiting the Texture Co-occurrence Matrix [70].

Rather than employing global and local statistical features, [71] suggested a unique invariant feature set for CBIR, in which the QI and visual contents of the database are extracted using 128-dimensional FVs resulting from the Scale-Invariant Feature Transform (SIFT), as an example. Nonetheless, it would be desired to lower the size of the FVs to facilitate retrieval. This work indexes and matches FVs using a combination of the Best Bin First (BBF) KD-Tree with the Approximate Nearest Neighbor (ANN) scheme. Then, hinging on a Nearest Neighbor Distance Ratio Scoring (NNDRS) voting policy, the aggregate scores for the candidate photos in the relevant databases are computed. The top few comparable photos can be presented to viewers by sorting the database images using total scores in decreasing order.

As the SG between low-level and high-level semantics rises, the retrieval process becomes more complicated [72]. The emphasis now shifts away from developing low-level picture characteristics to lessening the SG between FVs and HVS semantics.

RF includes user knowledge in the CBIR learning process. RF techniques can dramatically improve retrieval accuracy by lowering the SG in supervised learning. Despite the fact that a CBIRS continues to receive inquiries and responses from users, the data associated with their preferences throughout query sessions are typically missing at the search conclusion. This issue results in the feedback process having to be restarted for each new inquiry. To address this matter, certain attempts have been done in the broader CBIR sector to promote long-term learning. Even so, none fulfilled the long-term similarity learning in region-based IR [73].

RF CBIRSs are debated in [74], where the authors evaluate the effect of the kind and quantity of FV components on retrieval efficiency. These authors have contrasted a CBIRS with a narrow amount of FV entries (25 for color and texture) against an MPEG-7-inspired, high-dimensional (HD) FV system.

When a large total of features lowers the ability of an image to be distinguished, the dimensionality curse occurs, resulting in dense indexing structures [75-77]. As a result, keeping the FV's dimension as small as possible is paramount. Dimensionality reduction (DR) techniques can aid in the post-processing of FVs by opting for the most noteworthy features, abolishing irrelevant ones. This required transforming the primary feature space into a more representative one via a Self-Organizing Map (SOM)-based clustering method [78]. This fact intensifies the retrieval process's speed and quality. A condensed collection of significant features simplifies the representation of visual knowledge; as a result, essential comparisons are faster and need less storage. In other words, DR reduces the dimensionality of high-dimensional data to a comprehensible representation. The new intrinsic data dimensionality refers to the fewest factors necessary to account for observable data attributes. By easing the dimensionality curse and other undesirable features of high-dimensional environments, DR enables categorization, visualization, and high-density data compression. Techniques for data recovery might be linear or nonlinear. Linear methodologies exploit the assumption that the data exists near or inside a linear HD subspace. Nonlinear DR approaches do not assume linearity, which results in more complicated data embeddings in the HD space.

Performance evaluations of medical IR tasks have been conducted using artificial and natural data, leveraging findings from MIP [79, 80], Artificial Intelligence (AI) [56-59], data mining [81-83], and multimedia [73, 84, 85]. Nonlinear approaches outperform more conventional practices viz. Principal Component Analysis (PCA) in everyday situations [73, 86].

An SVM classifier may significantly upsurge retrieval rates [87, 88]. Association rule mining is an eminent technique for knowledge extraction to disclose unusual trends, patterns, and rules present in colossal data sets. As a result, SVMs and association rules are projected to be used more frequently to accelerate IR. Additionally, innovative image classification approaches may outperform SVMs.

The process of learning with the use of captioned pictures is time-intensive. Instead, the Pseudo Labeling Method (PLM) [88] was presented, labeling pictures via fuzzy criteria. To maximize the PLM in addition to Fuzzy SVM (FSVM) benefits [89], one can develop an extended SVM unified architecture centered on the Pseudo Label FSVM (PLFSVM).

The Latent Semantic Indexing (LSI) structure [90] makes use of users' radio frequency (RF) data. The planned CBIRS makes use of region-based imageries and a Multiple Instance Learning (MIL) together with a One-Class Support Vector Machine (OSVM). MIL is capable of doing supervised learning [88] with RF as the driving force.

7. Future Research Directions

CBIRSs grounded on low-level traits may be disappointing and unexpected, as they are not equal to HVS [91, 92]. It is difficult for such algorithms to localize appropriate photos established on a stakeholder query such as "Seek photographs with cysts and lumps." Several investigators have struggled to circumvent the SG using alternate strategies [75].

Supervised Machine Learning (ML) groups may employ a set of training imageries. Then, a binary classifier is taught to pinpoint a semantic class label relying on some input metrics. Bayesian classifiers automatically assign database images to categories. A NN is an additional scheme where the user chooses the classes (concepts) to be investigated: cell, organ, tissue, pathology or others. Next, massive data feeds the neural network classifiers to create the link connecting low-level picture features and their high-level semantics [82, 92, 94].

Unsupervised ML tactics do not involve outcome metrics, they just describe the input data organization and imagery sets related to each other appearing as clusters. Each cluster has apportioned some name to maximize the possibility of attaining a similar image output from that particular cluster [82, 92].

RF can be unfeasible in some domains. Its mechanism runs when the operator enters the health query as an image, sketch, or text. When related images return from the database, the stakeholder checks the returned image's relevancy. Then, a ML algorithm gets the user feedback till the results please the user [4].

Web IR uses web information to retrieve images, such as the URL of a picture by itself, imagery name, ALT-tag, descriptive imagery text and hyperlinks among others. Nevertheless, its performance is not accurate. To ameliorate performance, research has instigated the use of visual image content with web information [92-94].

8. Conclusion

This chapter gives a comprehensive overview of CBIRSs with fundamental processing modules and supporting resources and technologies. Descriptive models describe how to pick up and design characteristics. In the first case, a Handcrafted Pipeline (HCP) includes image acquisition/reconstruction, preprocessing, image segmentation to define ROI, feature extraction, feature reduction, and model creation. A Deep Learning Pipeline (DLP) is an option that does not need segmentation, feature extraction, or a defined model. The CBIR technology covers feature extraction, picture descriptors, similarity measurements, semantic gap reduction, performance metrics, and it is still evolving. Despite much research, no general strategy for high-level semantic-based IR exists. A complete IR system requires integrating primitive feature extraction with high-level semantic extraction parameters. Open research challenges and potential directions are mentioned.

CBIR can search a vast database for a specific picture. IR does not solve the overall picture comprehension problem. Interaction, a well-designed database, and the semantic gap are other crucial challenges.

CBIR feature extraction strategies are vital. Recent algorithms recover visual components by automatically extracting and comparing image elements thought to convey appearance. Color, texture, shape, spatial layout, and multi-resolution pixel intensity changes like wavelets are common. This feature set categorization may be more precise by adding heterogeneous (viz. shape, texture) features, improved feature integration, and artificial intelligence utilization. These medical CBIR deployment characteristics highlight the necessity for collaborative tactics, common/ better standards, and convergence concerns due to increasing innovation.

References

1. Maier A., Steidl, S., Christlein, V. and Hornegger, J. (2018). Medical Imaging Systems: An Introductory Guide. Springer Nature Switzerland AG, 148-167.
2. Tadia, V.K., Gupta, S.K., Satpathy, S., Gupta, A. and Arya, S. (2021). Utilization review of imaging equipment: An insight into CT Scanning. Medico-Legal Update, 21, 1244-1252.
3. Estrela, V.V., Saotome, O., Loschi, H.J., Hemanth, J., Farfan, W.S. et al. (2018). Emergency response cyber-physical framework for landslide avoidance with sustainable electronics. Technologies, 6(2), 42.
4. Datta, R., Joshi, D., Li, J. and Wang, J.Z. (2008). Image retrieval: Ideas, influences, and trends of the new age. ACM Computing Surveys, 40, 2, 1-60.
5. Deselaers, T. (2014). Features for image retrieval: An experimental comparison. Technical Report, RWTH Aachen University.
6. Lew, M.S., Sebe, N., Djeraba, C. and Jain, R. (2006). Content-based multimedia information retrieval: State of the art and challenges. ACM Trans. Multimedia Comput. Commun. Appl., 2, 1-19.
7. Oh, H., Rizo, C., Enkin, M. and Jadad, A. (2005). What is eHealth (3): A systematic review of published definitions. Journal of Medical Internet Research, 7(1), e1.
8. Embi, P.J. and Payne, P.R. (2009). Clinical research informatics: Challenges, opportunities and definition for an emerging domain. J. Am. Med. Inform. Assoc., 16: 316-327.
9. Oosterwijk, H. (2004). PACS fundamentals. Aubrey: OTech Inc.
10. Muller, H., Michoux, N., Bandon, D. and Geissbuhler, A. (2004). A review of content-based image retrieval systems in medical applications – Clinical benefits and future directions. Int. J. Med. Informatics, 73, 1-23.
11. Constantinescu, L., Pradana, R., Kim, J., Gong, P., Fulham, M. et al. (2009). Rich internet application system for patient-centric healthcare data management using handheld devices. IEEE Proc. of the Annual Int'l Conf. Eng. in Medicine and Biology Society (EMBC 2009), Minneapolis, MN, 5167-5170.

12. Roehrs, A., da Costa, C.A., Righi, R.D., Rigo, S.J., Wichman, M.H. et al. (2019). Toward a model for personal health record interoperability. IEEE J. Biomed. and Health Informatics, 23, 867-873.

13. Lindenauer, P.K., Ling, D., Pekow, P.S., Crawford, A., Naglieri-Prescod et al. (2006). Physician characteristics, attitudes, and use of computerized order entry. J. Hosp. Med., 1(4), 221-230.

14. Holler, J. (2013). The role of information technology in advancing pharmacy practice models to improve patient safety. Pharmacy Times, 14, 1-6.

15. Goldmann, D., Montanari, F., Richter, L., Zdrazil, B., Ecker, G.F. et al. (2014). Exploiting open data: A new era in pharmacoinformatics. Future Med. Chem., 6(5), 503-514.

16. Greengard, S. (2013). A new model for healthcare. Communications of the ACM, 56(2), 1719.

17. Skobelev, D.O., Zaytseva, T.M., Kozlov, A.D., Perepelitsa, V.L., Makarova, A.S. et al. (2011). Laboratory information management systems in the work of the analytic laboratory. Measurement Techniques, 53(10), 1182-1189.

18. Gonzalez, R.C., Woods, R.E. and Eddins, S.L. (2004). Digital Image Processing using MATLAB. 3rd Edition. 94-103, Gatesmark Publishing, USA.

19. Ozer, J.L. (2013). Producing Streaming Video for Multiple Screen Delivery. Doceo Publishing, ISBN - 13: 978-0976259541

20. Estrela, V.V., de Jesus, M.A., Aroma, J., Raimond, K., Fernandes, S.R. et al. (2021). Motion estimation role in the context of 3D video. Int'l J. Multimedia Data Eng. and Manag. (IJMDEM), 12(3), 16-38. IGI, Hershey, PA, USA. http://doi.org/10.4018/IJMDEM.291556

21. Beach, A. (2008). Real World Video Compression. Peachpit Press.

22. Akramullah, S. (2014). Digital video concepts, methods, and metrics: Quality, compression, performance, and power trade-off analysis. (In press)

23. Mustra, M., Delac, K. and Grgic, M. (2008). Overview of the DICOM standard. Proceedings of the 2008 ELMAR, 50th International Symposium, pp. 39-44, Zadar, Croatia.

24. König, H. (2005). Access to persistent health information objects: Exchange of image and document data by the use of DICOM and HL7 standards. International Congress Series, 1281, 932-937.

25. Pinto dos Santos, D., Klos, G., Kloeckner, R., Oberle, R., Dueber, C. et al. (2016). Development of an IHE MRRT-compliant open-source web-based reporting platform. European Radiology, 27, 424-430.

26. Davis, S. (2006). On-demand partial schema delivery for multimedia metadata. Proc. of the Int'l Conf. Multimedia and Expo 2006 (ICME), pp. 1513-1516.

27. Gudewar, A.D. and Ragha, L. (2012). Ontology to improve CBIR system. International Journal of Computer Applications, 52, 23-30.

28. Aihkisalo, T. and Valitalo, P. (2008). A comparative analysis of the resource consumption in message oriented middleware with XML and binary encoded messages. 2008 The Fourth International Conference on Wireless and Mobile Communications, 158-166.

29. Estrela, V.V. and Herrmann, A.E. (2016). Content-based image retrieval (CBIR) in remote clinical diagnosis and healthcare. *In:* M. Cruz-Cunha, I. Miranda, R. Martinho, R. Rijo (eds). Encyclopedia of E-Health and Telemedicine. pp. 495-520. IGI Global.

30. Yakin, S., Hasanuddin, T. and Kurniati, N. (2021). Application of content based image retrieval in digital image search system. Bulletin of Electrical Engineering and Informatics, 10.

31. Pattanaik, S. and Bhalke, D.G. (2012). Efficient content based image retrieval system using MPEG-7 features. International J. Computer Applications, 53, 5.

32. Bormans, J. and Hill, K. (2002). MPEG-21 overview v.5, ISO/IEC JTC1/SC29/WG11/ N5231. International Organisation for Standardization, Shanghai.
33. Sarwar, A., Mehmood, Z., Saba, T., Qazi, K.A., Adnan, A. et al. (2019). A novel method for content-based image retrieval to improve the effectiveness of the bag-of-words model using a support vector machine. Journal of Information Science, 45, 117-135.
34. Jain, S.D. and Niranjan, U.C. (2008). Distributed framework for remote clinical diagnosis with visual query support. Proc. of the 5th IEEE Int'l Conf. on Information Technology and Application in Biomedicine, China.
35. Vuletic, T., Duffy, A.H., Hay, L., McTeague, C., Campbell, G. et al. (2019). Systematic literature review of hand gestures used in human computer interaction interfaces. Int. J. Hum. Comput. Stud., 129, 74-94.
36. Chatzichristofis, S.A. and Boutalis, Y.S. (2011). Compact composite descriptors for content based image retrieval: Basics, concepts, tools. VDM Verlag Dr. Müller.
37. Chadha, A., Mallik, S. and Johar, R. (2012). Comparative study and optimization of feature-extraction techniques for content based image retrieval. IJCA, 52, 20.
38. Afshar, P., Mohammadi, A., Plataniotis, K.N., Oikonomou, A., Benali, H. et al. (2019). From handcrafted to deep-learning-based cancer radiomics: Challenges and opportunities. IEEE Signal Processing Magazine, 36, 132-160.
39. Aerts, H.J., Velazquez, E.R., Leijenaar, R.T., Parmar, C., Grossmann, P. et al. (2014). Decoding tumour phenotype by noninvasive imaging using a quantitative radiomics approach. Nature Communications, vol. 5.
40. Zhang, Y., Oikonomou, A., Wong, A., Haider, M.A. and Khalvati, F. (2017). Radiomics-based prognosis analysis for non-small cell lung cancer. Scientific Reports, vol. 7.
41. Kumar, V., Gu, Y., Basu, S., Berglund, A.E., Eschrich, S.A. et al. (2012). Radiomics: The process and the challenges. Magnetic Resonance Imaging, 30(9), 1234-1248.
42. Gillies, R., Kinahan, P.E. and Hricak, H. (2016). Radiomics: Images are more than pictures, they are data, radiology. Radiology, 278(2), 563-577.
43. Huangyuan, Q., Song, L., Luo, Z., Wang, X., Zhao, Y. et al. (2014). Performance evaluation of H.265/MPEG-HEVC encoders for 4K video sequences. Proc. 2014 Asia-Pacific Signal and Information Processing Association Annual Summit and Conference, APSIPA 2014.
44. Grecos, C. and Wang, Q. (2011). Advances in video networking: Standards and applications. International J. Pervasive Computing and Communications, 7(1), 22-43.
45. Goel, N. and Sehgal, P. (2012). A refined hybrid image retrieval system using text and color. International J. Computer Science Issues, 9, 4.
46. Laghari, A.A., Estrela, V.V. and Yin, S. (2022). Special Issue: From nanoscale to hyperspectral imaging - How to gather and understand medical images harvested in extremely difficult situations. Curr. Med. Imaging, Bentham Science, UK.
47. Grois, D., Marpe, D., Mulayoff, A., Itzhaky, B., Hadar, O. et al. (2013). Performance comparison of H.265/MPEG-HEVC, VP9, and H.264/MPEG-AVC encoders. Proc. 2013 Picture Coding Symposium, PCS 2013, 394-397.
48. Dhobale, D.D., Patil, B.S., Patil, S.B. and Ghorpade, V.R. (2011). Semantic understanding of image content. International J. Computer Science Issues, 8(3), 2, 1694-0814.
49. Tr, A. and Varghese, A. (2017). CBIR of Brain MR Images Using Histogram of Fuzzy Oriented Gradients and Fuzzy Local Binary Patterns. IAES International Journal of Artificial Intelligence, 6, 8-17.
50. Jaworska, T. (2014). Application of fuzzy rule-based classifier to CBIR in comparison with other classifiers. 2014 11th International Conference on Fuzzy Systems and Knowledge Discovery (FSKD), 119-124.

51. Carmo, F.P., Estrela, V.V. and Teixeira de Assis, J. (2009). Estimating motion with principal component regression strategies. 2009 IEEE Int'l Work, Multim. Sig. Proc., 1-6, Brazil.

52. Coelho, A.M., de Assis, J.T. and Estrela, V.V. (2009). Error concealment by means of clustered blockwise PCA, Proc. IEEE 2009 Picture Cod. Symp. (PCS 2009), USA.

53. Jolliffe, I.T. and Cadima, J. (2016). Principal component analysis: A review and recent developments. Phil. Trans, Royal Soc. A: Math, Phys. and Eng. Sc., 374, 2065, Royal Society, UK, doi: 10.1098/rsta.2015.0202

54. Smeulders, A.W.M., Worring, M., Santini, S., Gupta, A. and Jain, R. (2000). Content-based image retrieval at the end of the early years. IEEE Trans. PAMI, 22, 12.

55. Khokher, A. and Talwar, R. (2011). Content-based image retrieval: State-of-the-art and challenges. IJAEST, 9(2), 207-211.

56. Bengio, Y. and LeCun, Y. (2007). Scaling learning algorithms towards AI. *In:* L. Bottou, O. Chapelle, D. DeCoste and J. Weston (eds). Large-Scale Kernel Machines, pp. 321-360. MIT Press.

57. Hemanth, J. and Estrela, V.V. (2017). Deep Learning for Image Processing Applications. IOS Press.

58. Deshpande, A., Estrela, V.V. and Razmjooy, N. (2021). Computational Intelligence Methods for Super-Resolution in Image Processing Applications. Springer Nature, Zurich, Switzerland. doi: 10.1007/978-3-030-67921-7

59. Estrela, V.V., Tavares, J.M.R.S., Wang, L. and Shi, F. (2018). Special Issue: Soft computing techniques for image analysis in the medical industry – Current trends. Challenges and Solutions, Editorial, IEEE Access, IEEE.

60. Ciompi, F., Chung, K., Riel, S.J., Setio, A.A., Gerke, P.K. et al. (2017). Towards automatic pulmonary nodule management in lung cancer screening with deep learning. Scientific Reports, vol. 7.

61. Cheng, J., Ni, D., Chou, Y., Qin, J., Tiu, C. et al. (2016). Computer-aided diagnosis with deep learning architecture: Applications to breast lesions in US images and pulmonary nodules in CT scans. Scientific Reports, vol. 6.

62. Kumar, D., Wong, A. and Clausi, D.A. (2015). Lung nodule classification using deep features in CT images. Proc. Int'l Conf. Comp. and R. Vis. doi: 10.1109/CRV.2015.25

63. Lin, C.-H., Chen, R.T. and Chan, Y.-K. (2009). A smart content-based image retrieval system based on color and texture feature. Image and Vision Computing, 658-665.

64. Wang, J., Zhang, Z. and Zha, H. (2005). Adaptive manifold learning. Advances in Neural Inf. Proc. Systems, 17, 1473-1480, Cambridge, MA, USA. The MIT Press.

65. Wang, C., Zhang, L. and Zhang, H.J. (2008). Learning to reduce the semantic gap in web image retrieval and annotation. Proc. SIGIR'08.

66. Wang, X.Y., Yu, Y.-J. and Yang, H.-Y. (2011). An effective image retrieval scheme using color, texture and shape features. Comp. Stand. & Interfaces, Special Issue: Secure Semantic Web, 33(1), 59-68 Elsevier.

67. Fu, X., Li, Y., Harrison, R. and Belkasim, S. (2006). Content-based image retrieval using Gabor-Zernike features. Proc. 18th ICPR 2006, vol. 2, pp. 417-420.

68. Rabe, K.E., Arboleda, E.R., Andilab, A.A. and Dellosa, R.M. (2019). Fuzzy logic based vehicular congestion estimation monitoring system using image processing and KNN classifier. Int'l J. Scientific & Techn. Res., 8, 1377-1380.

69. Li, Y., Liu, J., Li, J., Ye, W.D. and Wu, Z. (2003). The fuzzy similarity measures for content based image retrieval. Proc. IEEE 2003 Int'l Conf. on Machine Learn. and Cybernetics, vol. 5, pp. 3224-3228.

70. Saha, S.K., Das, A.K. and Chanda, B. (2004). CBIR using perception based texture and colour measure. Proc. ICPR 2004, pp. 985-988.

71. Wangming, X., Jin, W., Xinhai, L., Lei, Z., Gang, S. et al. (2008). Application of image SIFT features to the context of CBIR. Proc. IEEE 2008 Int'l Conf. on Computer Science and Software Eng., 4, 552555.

72. Murthy, V.S., Vamsidhar, E., Rao, P.S., Samuel, G., Raju, V. et al. (2010). Application of hierarchical and K-means techniques in content based image retrieval. IJEST, 2(5), 749-755.

73. Zhuo, L., Cheng, B. and Zhang, J. (2014). A comparative study of dimensionality reduction methods for large-scale image retrieval. Neurocomputing, 141, 202-210.

74. Paredes, R. (2013). Interactive image retrieval based on relevance feedback. *In:* Multimodal Interaction in Image and Video Applications. Intelligent Systems Reference Library, vol. 48. Springer, Berlin, Heidelberg.

75. Burges, C.J.C. (2005). Geometric methods for feature selection and dimensional reduction: A guided tour. Data mining and knowledge discovery handbook: A complete guide for practitioners and researchers. Kluwer Academic Publishers.

76. Chen, X., Zhang, C., Chen, S.-C. and Chen, M. (2005). A latent semantic indexing based method for solving multiple instance learning problem in region-based image retrieval. Proc. Seventh IEEE Int'l Symposium on Multimedia, pp. 37-45.

77. Cheng, B., Zhuo, L. and Zhang, J. (2013). Comparative study on dimensionality reduction in large-scale image retrieval. Proc. 15th IEEE International Symp. Multimedia – ISM 2013, pp. 445-450. Anaheim, CA, United States.

78. Guo, C. and Wilson, C. (2008). Use of self-organizing maps for texture feature selection in content-based image retrieval. Proc. 2008 IEEE World Cong. Computational Intelligence, pp. 766-771.

79. Verbeek, J. (2006). Learning nonlinear image manifolds by global alignment of local linear models. IEEE Trans. PAMI, 28(8), 1236-1250.

80. Pirolla, F.R., Felipe, J.C., Santos, M.T.P. and Ribeiro, M.X. (2012). Dimensionality reduction to improve content-based image retrieval: A clustering approach. Proc. 2012 IEEE Int'l Conf. Bioinformatics and Biomed. Workshops (BIBMW), pp. 752-753.

81. Lee, J.A. and Verleysen, M. (2005). Nonlinear dimensionality reduction of data manifolds with essential loops. Neurocomputing, 67, 29-53.

82. Veltkamp, R., Burkhardt, H. and Kriegel, H.P. (2008). State-of-the-art in content-based image and video retrieval. Kluwer Academic Publishers, New York.

83. Venkatarajan, M.S. and Braun, W. (2004). New quantitative descriptors of amino acids based on multidimensional scaling of a large number of physical chemical properties. J. Molecular Modeling, 7(12), 445-453.

84. Coelho, A.M., Estrela, V.V., Carmo, F.P. and Fernandes, S.R. (2012). Error Concealment by Means of Motion Refinement and Regularized Bregman Divergence. IDEAL.

85. Estrela, V.V., Rivera, L.A., Beggio, P.C. and Lopes, R.T. (2003). Regularized pel-recursive motion estimation using generalized cross-validation and spatial adaptation. 16th Brazilian Symposium on Computer Graphics and Image Processing (SIBGRAPI 2003), 331-338.

86. Silva, F.D., Estrela, V.V. and Matos, L.J. (2011). Hyperspectral analysis of remotely sensed images. *In:* C. Bilibio, O. Hensel and J.F. Selbach (eds). Sustainable Water Management in the Tropics and Subtropics: Case Studies in Brazil, vol. 2, pp. 398-423. University of Kassel, Germany.

87. Silva, A.C., Paiva, A.C. and Oliveira, A.C.M. (2005). Comparison of FLDA, MLP and SVM in diagnosis of lung nodule. Lect Notes Comput Sci., 3587, 285-294.

88. Zhang, C., Chen, X., Chen, M., Chen, S.-C., Shyu, M.-L. et al. (2005). A multiple instance learning approach for content based image retrieval using one-class support vector machine. Proc. of the IEEE ICME 2005, 1142-1145.

89. Wu, K. and Yap, K.-H. (2006). Fuzzy SVM for content-based image retrieval a pseudo-label support vector machine framework. IEEE Computational Intelligence Magazine, 1, 2.

90. Chen, Y. and Wang, J.Z. (2002). A region-based fuzzy feature matching approach to content based image retrieval. IEEE Trans. PAMI, 24(9), 1252-1267.

91. Mamatha, Y.N. and Ananth, A.G. (2010). Content based image retrieval of satellite imageries using soft query based color composite techniques. International J. Computer Applications, 7, 5.

92. Masood, A., Shahid, M.A. and Sharif, M. (2018). Content-based image retrieval features: A survey. International J. Advanced Networking and Applications, 10, 3741-3757.

93. Liu, F., Xiong, X. and Chan, K.L. (2000). Natural image retrieval based on features of homogeneous color regions. Proc. 4th IEEE Southwest Symp. Image Analysis and SSIAI '00.

94. Liu, Y., Zhang, D., Lu, G., Ma, W. et al. (2006). A survey of content-based image retrieval with high-level semantics. Pattern Recognition, 40, 262-282.

Blockchain Technology Enabling Better Services in the Healthcare Domain

V.V. Estrela[1] [0000-0002-4465-7691], M.A. de Jesus[1] [0000-0001-6428-9438],
A.C. Intorne[2,3] [0000-0001-8015-6926], Kate K.S. Batista[4] [0000-0002-5861-4633],
A. Deshpande[5] [0000-0002-1500-0981], Fuqian Shi[6] [0000-0003-4245-5727], A.A. Khan[7]
[0000-0003-2838-7641], Luciana P. Oliveira[8] [0000-0002-3375-3346]

[1] Department of Telecommunications, Federal Fluminense University (UFF), RJ, 24220-900, Brazil, vania.estrela.phd@ieee.org, majesus1977br@gmail.com
[2] Laboratory of Physiology and Biochemistry of Microorganisms, Universidade Estadual do Norte Fluminense Darcy Ribeiro, Campos dos Goytacazes, RJ, 28013-602, Brazil
[3] Laboratory of Chemistry and Biology, Instituto Federal de Educação, Ciência e Tecnologia do Rio de Janeiro, Volta Redonda, RJ, 27213-100, Brazil, aline.intorne@ifrj.edu.br
[4] Fundacao Oswaldo Cruz, FIOCRUZ, Rio de Janeiro, RJ, Brazil, katekbatista@gmail.com
[5] Electronics and Communication Engineering, Angadi Institute of Technology and Management, Belagavi, India, deshpande.anandb@gmail.com
[6] Rutgers Cancer Institute of New Jersey, United States, shifuqian@gmail.com
[7] Research Lab of Artificial Intelligence and Information Security, Faculty of Computing Science and Information Technology, Benazir Bhutto Shaheed University, Lyari, Karachi (75660), Sindh, Pakistan, abdullah.khan0076@gmail.com
[8] IFPB Campus Joao Pessoa, Av. Primeiro de Maio, 720, Jaguaribe, Joao Pessoa, PB, Brazil, oliveira.ifpb@gmail.com

1. Introduction

The Ethereum platform now supports blockchain-based healthcare apps and transactions [1-9]. Blockchain Technology (BT) is a potential topic for numerous applications, including public services, reputation systems, the Internet of Medical Things (IoMT), as well as security services (Figure 1). Blockchain applications use Smart Contracts (SCs) to permit anonymous and distributed storage of any valuable record or transaction viz. cash, energy, real estate contracts, oil, gold, in addition to intellectual property rights (IPR). Without intermediaries like agents or brokers, security, data integrity, privacy decentralization, and fast transactions are all possible. Currently, blockchain 3.0 (aka third generation or digital society) handles health, education/literacy, science, art, and governance applications [1], incorporating advancements, such as cyber-physical systems [2, 3].

BTs with Electronic Medical Records (EMR) can control/supervise with interoperability, accessibility, and auditability over large-scale data frameworks using comprehensive logs. Current BT enables sharing and delivering computing resources anytime, anywhere because it is secure, quick, trustworthy, immutable, and affords public and private transparency. BT transactions lessen the need for documents, duplication, third-party intermediation, and mitigation. Despite BT's extensive use, different challenges arise in healthcare [7-9] because this regulated domain involves patient privacy. This chapter addresses BT implementation in healthcare and Consensus Algorithms (CAs) caveats.

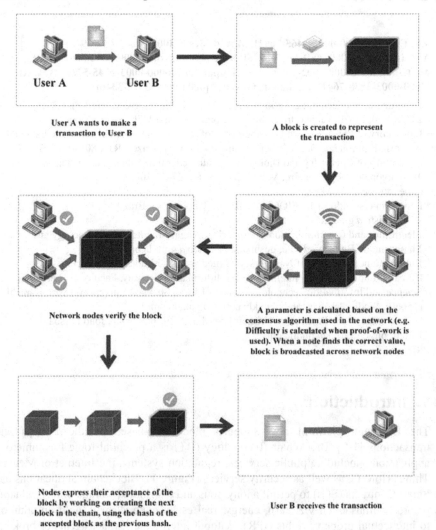

Figure 1. Blockchain process

Section 2 outlines BT and talks over different CAs. Section 3 scrutinizes BT in the healthcare domain. Section 4 considers decentralized consensus platforms for healthcare. Finally, Section 5 lists conclusions about the subject.

2. Blockchain Technology

2.1. Overview

Networks can be (i) centralized, with a single node controlling and coordinating the whole network, or (ii) dispersed, with all nodes interconnected to exclude the need for centralized management. Since, there is no single failure point, the blockchain structure is a P2P distributed network with exceptional processing power and reliability. Because of the high-level security, it protects data integrity [8, 9].

Blockchain employs Distributed Ledger (DL) Technology (DLT), which consists of databases dispersed across several devices (nodes). Each device modernizes itself autonomously by using the identical stored ledger copy. DLs do not utilize a chain of blocks at all times to provide solid and secure distributed consensus. BT divides data into chunks and connects them using encryption for security.

Blockchain consensus entails network nodes (alias miners) adding and endorsing blocks of unchangeable data (e.g., transactions) [10]. Blockchain nodes link Blockchain Network (BN) points by storing ledger information, listening to transactions and recently sealed blocks, authenticating freshly sealed blocks (transaction confirmation), sending valid transactions to the network, and creating/passing new blocks [10]. The DL corroborates the most recent data on the ledger (transactions). Each block is produced once specified, and preset conditions occur. All miners receive transaction information and must verify/validate it. Ethereum entails all nodes to accept and understand data. In Corda, only involved nodes obtain transaction information. Unknown dependability and trustworthiness may be existent when the BN contains malicious users since anonymous peers can exploit or break into the network due to huge requirements, e.g., computing power.

2.1.1. Main Algorithms

Merkle Trees (MTs) or Hash Trees enable fast and safe data verification. Each block is interconnected to the one preceding it. A hash function or the Merkle root hash (MRH) method helps responsible miners to digitally sign. The hash function deciphers each input into a distinctive hash value, which abolishes repeated hashings. Each block includes the preceding block's contents as well as hashes to prevent any modifications or manipulation. When miners endorse data, then occurs a Proof of Work (PoW) in addition to a Proof of Stake (PoS) that generates new blocks [11]. PoW requires computing power for fast block hash calculation and validation. Miners control blocks added to the blockchain and receive rewards. Application and security mechanisms regulate block creation time.

A conventional Public Ledger (PL) storing a complete transaction (Tx) records list on a block sequence (hashed timestamps) emerges in Figure 2. Each block is linked to a parental block. This reference or hash value represents a single unique value corroborating each block. The first or genesis blockchain contains a hash value with straight zeros, i.e., no parent block. In the Ethereum blockchain, an uncle block

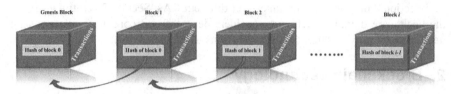

Figure 2. Blockchain architecture

occurs when mining two blocks simultaneously. One block becomes the official block and enters the chain. The other remains a stale block called an uncle block (like Bitcoin's orphan block). Ethereum stores uncle block hashes, unlike Bitcoin, which neglects the whole block.

In Figure 2, block i (i = 0, ..., N) partakes a block version, parent block hash, MT root hash, timestamp, nBits, and nonce. Block versions exemplify the validation rules. A parent hash block denotes the previous 256-bit block hash to form a chain. The unsigned integer nBits indicates the current hashing target. The header is operational if the header hash stays below or equal to it [12]. A nonce is nothing more than a 4-byte random number producing a hash and validating the block. The block hash commences with zeros. The number of zeros increases with time, complicating hash retrieval [13]. As a result, miners continuously compute and guess the nonce, generating the precise hash (and the number of starting zeros). This forces miners to generate outputs meeting changeable pre-requisites when the nonce is plugged into the hashing procedure. Any input data change alters outcomes utterly.

The MT root is the hash of all block transactions (Figures 3 and 4). Transaction pair hashes merge until reaching a single hash for all transactions named Root Hash or Merkle Root. e.g., merging transaction A and B hashes generates a new Hash AB and Idem for transactions C and D. Combining Hashes AB and CD generates the root

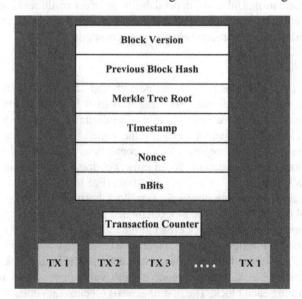

Figure 3. Typical block header organization

Hash ABCD. The block body comprehends transactions and associated counters. Block and transaction sizes define the number of single block transactions [14].

BT validates authentication of transactions with symmetric/asymmetric private key cryptography to sign and encrypt the sender-side data. The public key helps decrypt information on the receiver side(s). Signing transactions produces a two-phase digital signature (signing and verification). User X starting an operation with user Y creates the specified transaction hash value. The encryption process employs user X's (sender) private key. User Y receives the original data and encrypted hash. Anyone can decrypt the hash using X's public key. Thus, Y decrypts the incoming hash and relates it with the received data's derived hash using X's hash function for transaction verification.

The Elliptic Curve Digital Signature Algorithm (ECDSA) [15] is popular with shorter key lengths than other procedures. A color spectrum chain helps store the authentication of the device statuses for IoT access via BT. Cloud Computing (CC) server algorithms acknowledge devices, keeping the authentication state of the recognized blockchain device [16]. Blockchain IoT sensors and multi-platforms utilizing color spectrum chains minimize devices' vulnerability.

Confidentiality, integrity, and availability guarantee security. Blockchain decentralization can ensure global functionality when there are compromised nodes. Confidentiality secures users' private and public keys, preventing identity theft while ensuring integrity and security when exchanging information. Each user's private key is unique, guaranteeing data ownership for someone who signs employing a private key indicating authorship to the entire network. The unalterable public key comes from the private key by means of a particular algorithm and exists across the network.

Integrity prevents data tampering by unauthorized parties. Key management controls and unleashes encryption by (i) verifying receivers' public keys and (ii) checking keys, ensuring invariance over time. Third party trust becomes unnecessary if distributed systems implement blockchain concept.

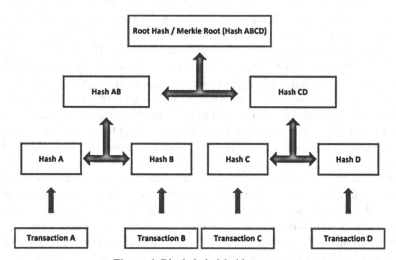

Figure 4. Blockchain Merkle tree root

Security inhibits hacking through distributed consensus, warranting safe management systems in addition to centralized data storage with all transactions verified and validated by miner groups. Moreover, all network nodes monitor a BN. Any malicious node (i.e., suspicious user) cannot embed manipulate blocks into the public ledger for the reason that all nodes maintain a blockchain copy. Blockchain copies from others are reliable backups, and even hacking numerous ledgers will secure the network from malicious activities despite causing some BN problems [17, 18].

Nevertheless, many security challenges, like interoperability, scalability, besides data privacy, happen [1-6]. A double-spending security concern [1-6, 17] arises when a user pays more than once in a P2P network, i.e., broadcasting incomplete payments. The network simultaneously can experience propagation delays or unsubstantiated transactions at multiple intervals. Miners verify transactions by deciphering complex mathematical problems, which are time-consuming and hard to solve. Habitually, only one disbursement passes through correctly with blockchain registration with a digital identity (private key) safeguard for privacy/anonymity. If a key leaks, no third party can recover it, and all the identity information will vanish [1-6].

2.2. Consensus Algorithms (CAs)

Different network CAs for specific domain requirements like low-computational power and faster transactions warrant blockchain security. The BT key function is the CA seeking to reach a total agreement with equality between miners during block verification [19]. CAs give the same weight to all miners, and the majority decides, which suits controlled environments, resulting in Sybil attacks in public blockchains from users holding multiple identities. Only a single user adds a single block in decentralized architectures. Users can be selected randomly or utilize certain prerequisites. Still, random selection is predisposed to attacks.

The CA relies on the Byzantine Generals (BG) enigma that requires generals to decide whether to start an attack with traitor-free communication between them because any agreement difficulty can lead to a confrontation. These challenges pervade BT given it has no dominant node controlling the whole network and fosters decentralized CAs to enforce data consistency and reliability [20, 23, 24].

Proof of Work (PoW) assumes nodes are less likely to suffer network attacks if they work a lot. PoW makes adding a block computationally expensive, complicating Sybil attacks. PoW nodes will work until a solution emerges, e.g. Bitcoin miners compute a random number (aka nonce) to generate the correct block header hash. When a miner elucidates the puzzle, all other nodes verify the answer's correctness. PoW consumes more energy, is inefficient in low-power applications, and is unscalable [33-37].

Proof of Stake (PoS) classifies users by their stake. Each node with some blockchain stake can mine. PoS assumes users with more stakes have a lower network attack probability. Nodes allocate part of their stake in case they become miners to warrant user trustworthiness and the right to mine. PoS consumes less energy than PoW because fewer computations are called for. However, the PoS blockchain mining process targets the wealthiest members since they have high stakes.

Delegated Proof of Stake (DPoS) enhances PoS since some delegates generate and validate blocks, making transactions faster as fewer nodes are involved. Moreover, chosen nodes can alter block sizes besides intervals. Delegated nodes can be replaced easily to treat dishonesty quickly. In Transactions-as-Proof-of-Stake (TaPoS) schemes, all nodes handle security. Accumulated stake age limits PoS even for disconnected nodes. Proof of Activity (PoA) [21] rewards nodes using blockchain activity and ownership [33-37].

Practical Byzantine Fault Tolerance (PBFT) unravels the Byzantine Generals Problem (BFT) in an asynchronous manner [22, 23] if more than 2/3 of the nodes are legitimate and the rest are malicious. Each block generation has a selected leader ordering transactions. At least 2/3 of all nodes must support block validation to add a block. Delegated BFT (DBFT) partakes some nodes validating as well as generating blocks similar to DPoS. Stellar Consensus Protocol (SCP) looks a lot like PBFT, albeit it uses Federated Byzantine Agreement (FBA) [28-30] and avoids node agreement, relying on an essential node subset.

Synchronous trusted node communications address light latency issues by creating a subset to determine consensus and connecting it to a specific server [31-33]. BFTRaft enhances and reformulates the Raft security generating a Byzantine fault-tolerant algorithm [36]. Tendermint CA tolerates up to 33.33% of failures and can accommodate arbitrary application states [34]. Miners create blocks and vote validity. Tendermint considers a two-fold validation containing pre-vote and pre-commit stages to allow block insertion. More than 2/3 of validator votes endorse a block. Bitcoin NG CA improves latency, throughput, and scalability but restricts propagation time and node bandwidths [24-27].

Proof-of-Burn (PoB) requests miners to prove their activities by spending cryptocurrency or data related to a specific address instead of draining (burning) resources [24-27]. The Proof-of-Personhood (PoP) procedure delivers anonymity by establishing correspondence among physical and virtual identities via ring signatures with collective signing [66]. A Hyperledger-Fabric deployment such as the Sieve algorithm [31, 32] relies on BFT duplication in permissioned blockchain meant for non-deterministic SCs. The network replicates non-deterministic SC processes and compares results seeking divergences to filter operations if deviations grow. BT can merge and integrate with applications like the IoMT, healthcare, and food security. Healthcare is a great blockchain application because it is a highly regulated, critical business [37-40] to secure infrastructure and mix private health archives [70]. Blockchain provides secure exchanges among stakeholders and yields clinical reports efficiently.

3. BT in the Healthcare Domain

BT allows partaking in an Electronic Health Record (EHR) securely among all stakeholders with many advantages, such as patient privacy, improved medical care, patient-centric services, and heterogeneous system connections. Blockchain provides patients with complete control over their EMRs. Case-sensitive patient data requires secure, confidential shared storage to avoid malicious attacks (e.g., Mining, Denial of Service (DoS), storage, and dropping attacks). A secure and robust healthcare BT platform uses different mechanisms to prevent failures and attacks [40-43].

The healthcare BT usage does not focus on privacy and security only but addresses other vital issues like interoperability. Executing secured methodologies to share medical data is burdensome because heterogeneous data structures involving diverse, heterogeneous persons and organizations prevent compatibility. Medical data sharing entails both data structure and semantics. However, consistency and security concerns still exist because of cyber-attacks on centralized authorities and data warehouses. In consequence, establishing consistent views of data sharing systems for EHRs is tricky.

Figure 5 categorizes healthcare BT applications into several areas to determine critical requirements, e.g., security, integrity, data interoperability, cost/resources effectiveness, trustworthiness, transparency, and complexity.

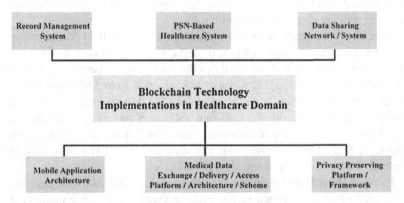

Figure 5. Blockchain implementation for a healthcare application.

3.1. Data Sharing Network/System

Secure and effective data-sharing appears in [44] using an MT-based structure linking each block with the previous one. A transaction does not embrace factual patient info but utilizes Fast Healthcare Interoperability Resources (FHIRs), an emerging standard to share EHRs by providing public accessibility APIs. FHIR resource specification occurs through a definite URL to preserve the operational control of patient data, providing better and safe integrity by hiding sensitive knowledge out of the blockchain. The Proof of Interoperability (POI) works for mining blocks and relies on FHIR protocol conformance. Miners must verify healthcare-related data to guarantee semantic and structural standard interoperability, but it differs from PoW whenever appending blocks to the blockchain. The coordinating miner performs and distributes transactions. Miners will corroborate the block after the managing node assembles all transactions and signs the block throughout the signed block reappearance phase. The block is, at that moment, added and dispersed. This process ensures each block's integrity because all nodes are digitally signing blocks with at least one transaction. Discoverability, searchability, and control means for data access are prerequisites as the genuine record data does not go into the block. A storehouse enclosing a single failure point holds value sets. However, this expedient eliminates the concept of decentralization. Patient identification assigns addresses to data, allowing a single patient to keep multiple Blockchain addresses, which may disturb and overload the system with a high number of users.

A BT Cloud framework addressed the access control challenges for sensitive data [45], taking on built-in autonomy and immutability of the permissioned blockchain (where only certified and trusted customers can access data). Permissioned blockchains keep sensitive data in pools. Efficient access control occurs via secure cryptographic techniques. After attesting identities and cryptographic keys, a shared repository allows handlers to access and share EMRs besides archiving user memberships via identity-based authentication. It also guarantees security through multiple cryptographic keys and utilizes three layers: storage, management, and stakeholders (users). These layers perform specific tasks and afford secure data sharing structures. This lightweight and scalable framework arranges for efficiency, identity management, in addition to remote access but needs algorithms for entities, authentication, and communication protocols.

A BT framework can access, audit, and share private healthcare data [46]. This architecture hinges on properties and SCs to ensure an automated workflow, patient pseudo-anonymity, information integrity, auditability, and accountability. The design utilizes a consortium blockchain, which allows all participating miners to be verified off-chain and has three layers: (i) Web Cloud Platforms (ii) CC middleware and (iii) BN. SCs can be threefold: (i) Registry Contract (RC) is a registry mapping all miners, (ii) Patient Data Contract (PDC) has unique patient indicators linking hashed data to the actual information in the Web Cloud Platform using URL, and (iii) Permissions Contract (PC) manages network permissions associating PDC addresses and data requesting entities.

A BT patient-centered protocol and ineffective communication amid EHR institutions handled cost and interoperability [47], focusing on critical care physicians while accessing prior patient imaging studies, present-day medications, and history. This simplified design supported many existing dataset silos. Patio Tory tokens (PTOYs) control the storage, revenue payment cycles, as well as service quality measurements while minimizing provider breaches.

A user-centric BT can secure information exchange by pairing user-generated policies with SCs [48]. Data owners control records after exchanges with cryptographic keys guaranteeing access, security, and abuse prevention. The arrangement contains users, query managers, processing nodes, SC centers, local storage, besides BN. It starts with registration via stored credentials and set up policies. Customer requests use private and membership keys to query managers. Processing nodes recuperate accompanying policies from storage if the information is authentic, and SCs are generated. Data-attached SCs and the monitoring process begins. Surveillance is vital to ensure computations reasonably, data protection, and user privacy but discards scalability and efficiency. An efficient way to share continuous IoT data via BT appeared in [49] to classify data based on characters (static or dynamic) and acquisition (instant and constant). A Machine-Learning (ML)-based inspection module controls data quality, which is paramount because IoT devices entail massive noisy data. The data quality inspection can filter noise and guarantee data reliability with accurate user activity prediction. This design defines three roles: stakeholders generating the information, key keepers storing privately to decrypt information, and customers providing financial or service compensations in exchange for data. Inspected data shares or performs transactions using the blockchain module. Symmetric-key algorithms perform encryption before uploading data to the Cloud [50, 51]. The symmetric key is distributed to keepers to enhance decryption. Crypto tokens stimulate users to share welfare data commercially and for research. Med Chain data-sharing incorporates blockchains, digests chains, and P2P networks to overcome efficiency resultant from metadata modification when sharing records among different entities [37]. Such operations require checking the integrity of the disclosed medical IoMT data stream with a digest chain structure. Hence, these actions happen in a session-based manner to allow further flexibility during data sharing. Med Chain nodes are twofold: (i) super peers include organization servers with high storage and computing power (i.e., hospitals), and (ii) edge nodes become servers from small groups such as community clinics. This Med Chain arrangement expedites data query and access by means of mutable data while maintaining immutable information authenticity, integrity, and security. Elliptic Curve Cryptography (ECC) [89] generates keys resilient to masquerading and replaying attacks with integrity info, forward secrecy, privacy security, and unauthorized access non-repudiation. Med Chain lessens computation and storage overhead for generating new descriptions and supports metadata updating, storage space recycling, and streaming.

3.2. Record Management Structure

MedRec is a decentralized Electronic Management Records (EMRs) arrangement that leverages BT properties [52-55], addressing significant healthcare issues: data quantity and quality, interoperability, fragmented data, patient insurance info, and slow data access. A set of APIs affords interoperability with the provider database. Ethereum's SCs handle information retrieval commands and viewing permissions by means of a log of medical interactions among patients and suppliers to ensure data correction with a cryptographic hash. Stakeholders control records by acquiescing or rejecting new information. By linking a specific Ethereum address to a single patient's ID, a DNS-like structure sanctions identity. A syncing algorithm handles off-chain exchanges between the provider and patient's database. A database authentication server confirms blockchain permissions and provides easy access to patients, an immutable log, and widespread services across treatment sites and Healthcare Organizations (HOs). MedRec allows data partaking, privacy, authentication, as well as accountability for sensitive material using multiple participants to avoid single-point failure without contract encryption and auditability. Improving obfuscation and scalability are open issues not tested in large-scale deployments. MedRec is not ready for complex data since it only validates the EMRs. Collecting and sharing EMRs as compensation is proscribed in many nations due to privacy and reducing data usage efficiency.

The work in [56] uses SCs as mediators to access EHRs in large-scale Ethereum architectures. SCs are the system core, registering all data accesses, processing, requests, and storing new transactions in the ledger. The patient, not HOs, owns data. A DL implements SCs, maintains transaction records, saves health records, keeps users' public and private cryptographic keys by means of wallets, and works as an information index discovery service to accelerate searches. Transactions are threefold: (i) New Record, (ii) Request Access, and (iii) Notification. A notification, for instance, is a special transaction indicating a public health issue. One of this design's advantages is delegating complete EMR administration to patients (i.e., their private key control). Nonetheless, if a customer is not tech-savvy or loses a private key, then a patient's health record may vanish or get lost. Data is not in a centralized ledger for performance reasons. Hence, retrieving data will be a challenge.

Med Block [57] manages information utilizing an improved hybrid-CA addressing network congestion and significant energy consumption issues since DPoS and PBFT are unsuitable. The CA works as a board vote where one node within a region has voted the supporter to act in the best interests of other nodes. This policy permits effective data upload to evade network congestion due to many centralized procedures, combining symmetric cryptography with custom-made access control with high information security. Bread crumb mechanisms enable stakeholders to encounter encrypted information of their interest efficiently. The Med Block platform delivers able EMR access, retrieval, and processing. It has fewer access times than other methodologies with a consistent data flow in different epochs to aid large-scale system information sharing and data management. Since hospital databases store EMRs, they reduce blockchain decentralization to avoid malicious actors.

The SMEAD [38] healthcare paradigm handles diabetic patients over an end-to-end protected structure with wearable devices to observe the patient status and predict eventually dangerous conditions. A self-served collaborative platform for pharmacy and other healthcare product e-distributions rely on MEDIBOX, to alert and remind patients/caregivers to continuously monitor insulin dosages. These tasks occur with security and access control for trusted parties via SCs. Social networks like Facebook, WhatsApp, and Twitter can be emergency mechanisms for caretakers over the internet and integrate medication administrator, IoMT, wearables, and CC. Public key cryptography protects the data and authenticates users. SCs address privacy concerns by securing transactions.

Med Share [39] is another efficient organizational system to handle EMRs for Cloud repositories managing shared EMRs and data among big medical entities. This platform safeguards auditing, data provenance and security, in addition to stakeholder verification through cryptographic keys. The Med Share data partaking mechanism contains four layers aimed at (i) users (ii) data query (iii) data structuring and provenance, and (iv) existing database infrastructure. When a stakeholder wants database access, a private key is created and digitally signed. Then, the query framework directs the request to the data structuring and provenance layer. An SC then executes data sharing among CC service providers.

BT can manage and share EMR cancer patient data using permissioned blockchain to tackle primary care, aggregate data, and afford better care by connecting different HOs [58]. The multi-node framework has to reach network consensus, handle databases in conjunction with off-chain storage, membership services, and APIs for different stakeholders. The membership service registers patients, caretakers, and health specialists, which defines the functionality of the chain code. Two distinct databases store patient data, namely a local database and a Cloud-based platform.

Each database holds records, employing several data structures and other traits. Consensus nodes control their custom chain code, acting as a Hyperledger validating peers through PBFT, reducing turnaround time and overall price tags while refining decision-making practices [78, 79]. Efficient storage depends on data semantics and sensitivity.

Transparency complicates data protection against malicious traffic while upholding accountability and transaction secrecy. Henceforth, a Machine-to-Machine (M2M) messaging as well as a rule-based platform [59] deals with decision synthesis and the data role in seamless data administration. This Field Programmable Gate Array (FPGA) design has IoT sensors to probe biological information. An IoT gateway broadcasts data wirelessly to the Cloud. A blockchain with a distributed database hardens medical reports from damage. Disparate parties like patients, caregivers, regulators, pharmacies, insurance companies, besides hospitals can manage deployed databases. The overlay network between nodes provides stakeholder confidentiality by selecting random communication paths. Data combination and decision fusions increase the accuracy.

Privacy is crucial to sidestep medical data jeopardies, digitize and popularize well-being services. If an EMR breach happens, caretakers/patients will lose faith and desist from disclosing their situation. It may yield a negative effect on all stakeholders. To avoid such a situation, a blockchain-based data-sharing system results from a Genetic Algorithm (GA) with other metaheuristics [60, 74-76] and Discrete Wavelet Transform (DWT) [61, 77]. A GA optimizes queuing, while DWT enhances security. This structure allows fast verification using a cryptography key generator, besides improving access control and immunity. This design facilitates further accountability. This issue follows the fact that all caretakers/patients are acknowledged, and their actions belong to blockchain records. Collective queuing requests can only be opened after identity and cryptographic keys are confirmed. The system has a private blockchain. Blocks rely on Dual Tree (DT) Complex Wavelet Transform (DT-CWT) working with multiple watermarking measures. Multiple watermarking forms with BT coordinate health records while enhancing confidentiality, transparency, and security. The information from various physicians is embedded one after another. Their extraction happens in reverse order using watermarking.

The investigation from [62] introduces a blockchain-based welfare data ecosystem managing high health data amounts. This approach uses Exonum [63] (peer-to-peer service-oriented architecture) an open-source platform divided into two segments open and closed. The closed segment houses medical data. Meanwhile, the open segment stores each patient's unique identifier. System nodes are twofold. Auditors check blockchain consistency for the reason that they possess a full blockchain ledger replica. Validator nodes handle network viability tasks and are responsible for new block creations using the BFT as CA. In Exonum, the services module acts as SCs in the BN, while the client modules identify customer specific functionalities. The middleware module arranges for transactions with atomicity in addition to ordering, fulfilling the interactions/replications of services with stakeholders, accessing control, and retaining data consistency.

3.3. Medicinal Data Exchange, Delivery and Access

BlocHIE [64] is a healthcare information platform with EMRs, in addition to Personal Healthcare Data (PHD) warehoused with EMR-Chain and PHD-Chain, and loosely-coupled blockchains. The EMR-Chain takes away the dependency on cloud services by merging on-chain verification with off-chain storage to enhance privacy. BlocHIE uses hospital distributed databanks to warrant off-chain storage. Medical record hash values assist in an operation for on-chain verification. FAIR-FIRST and TP& FAIR are two fairness-based transaction packing algorithms recommended to expand fairness and throughput. BlocHIE consensus algorithm is PoW.

A platform constructed over NEM multi-signature blockchain contracts, cryptography, and tokens comes from [65]. Multi-signature contracts control and administrate specific account activity by establishing powers and rights to that account. Multi-signature contracts permit multiple keys to edit health data on the chain. Thus, the entities holding all the keys can edit the records, while others can only read or commence transactions from the ledger. This scheme handles key loss for the reason that trusted parties (i.e., governmental representatives) can get another key pair. The data is not housed on the blockchain, but rather in a data lake repository characterized by scalability and supporting various data varieties. The data lake only stores encrypted data, and patients still hold the right to read and access the data.

This approach's main benefits from a patient's standpoint follow. Firstly, patients/ caretakers can manage and control their EMRs. Next, it permits cross-institutional distribution. Many types of devices share data easily e.g. home devices. Still, some BT implementation challenges are not considered. For example, data access during an emergency or acute treatment.

The decentralized app (DApp) prototype works with FHIRChain [66]. This platform encapsulates the FL7's Fast Healthcare Interoperability Resources (FHIR) standard for sharable medical data with context blockchains, off-chain storage, token-based permission models, exchange reference pointers, and Model-View-Controller (MVC) patterns, affording a comprehensive way out. Public-key cryptography to craft and manage health identities exists in it. The new DApp includes a registry SC to map between FHIRChain and stakeholders, where digital identities are warehoused. DApp can deliver augmented modularity, scalable data integrity, fine access control, and superior trust. Unfortunately, FHIRChain does not support semantic interoperability and is not friendly to legacy systems.

A multiple authority, attribute-based signature structure for EHR guarantees the encapsulated blockchain EHR validity [67]. Patients endorse messages using specific attributes without revealing other facts. The only parameter obligatory to access messages is giving evidence to the verifier. Allocating the patient's public and private keys is done without a central or single authority. Multiple authorities handle this task, conforming to the blockchain distributed data storage mode to avoid escrow problems. Patient information such as consumption patterns, insurance records, and, once treatment ends, a single block encapsulates the EHRs. When patients go to other Hos, the new entities need to identify patients and authenticate their available blockchains.

3.4. Mobile Application Architecture

Healthcare Data Gateways (HDGs) [68] are blockchain-built smartphone applications for patients/caretakers managing their EMRs through purpose-centric access to preserve patient confidentiality. This model organizes data through a unified and unpretentious Indicator Centric Schema (ICS). This application partakes a regular database with a gateway to handle data on the blockchain storage system, assess data requests, and exploit secure further multi-party processing. HDG has three layers: (i) storage (lower layer) (ii) data management and (iii) data usage (upper layer). Cryptography e.g., signatures, hashes, in addition to encryption secure and protect data. Data gateways hybridize database and firewall design. HDG offers anonymization, resourceful communication among HDGs, data backup, and Cloud recovery. Nonetheless, data processing while keeping data private is an issue. The Secure Multi-Party Computation (MPC) technique enables untrusted third parties to process patient records without breaching privacy trust.

A blockchain-based App manages healthcare data in [69]. It securely collects patient data with Cloud synchronization while partaking in information with healthcare and insurance suppliers. However, a user-centric model implements data-sharing solutions. Applications use a blockchain-supported membership service and a channel establishment scheme to boost identity management and privacy protection with permissioned blockchain. Manual input, medical/wearable devices collect patient information, sharing data with Hos by synchronizing them utilizing a Cloud databank. Proof of integrity and validation are perpetually retrievable for well-being data integrity.

DApp for Smart Health (DASH) [70] tolerates patient and caretaker access, edit their EMRs, and submit prescription requests by a web-based portal using the Patient Registry contract to map patient exclusive identifiers and accompanying Patient Account contract addresses. Multiple software pattern designs address challenges with evolvability, scalability, data storage, a proxy for protected/private services, and publish-subscribe intended for scalable information filtering.

3.5. Pervasive Social Network (PSN)-based Healthcare

Blockchain can also rely on Pervasive Social Network (PSN)-based healthcare to contain many medical sensors/actuators and mobile devices with two enhanced protocols. The first improves the IEEE 802.15.6 to address resource-limited device requirements through secure links using Wireless Body Area Networks (WBANs). A blockchain-based protocol is the second protocol for sharing medical data among PSN devices. Health information contributors/stakeholders realize network consensus, where each stakeholder's address is deposited and shared in this blockchain. Other node addresses help access the health records only through authorized PSN nodes. A patient or caretaker can press a sensor device button to create secure smartphone links. Adding data to the blockchain happens automatically via smartphones, storing them and broadcasting transactions to the neighbor PSN nodes (i.e., miners). Engendering a new block comes about through multiple automatic stages. As a final point, someone authorized can view the patient's data to create an accurate treatment plan remotely. The suggested design authenticates messages and network communications, deals with the confidentiality of generated secret keys , forwards the master key confidentially, and maintains integrity of transactions [80, 81]. It reduces the sensor devices' computational burden and data leakage from illegal acts of various parties. It resembles cryptography, besides focusing on computational power, as well as energy needs. The system does not entirely explore the blockchain benefits. It has not been appraised for large-scale environments and addresses only PSN network challenges, deemed unsuitable for other implementations. Furthermore, SCs are one of the core points of employing blockchain in healthcare.

3.6. Privacy Conserving Framework

The patient-centric data management structure called Medibchain [74] is blockchain based. It addresses storage and has flexible control via BT to encrypt well-being data hinging on decentralized storage. Because of pseudonymity, Medibchain allows patients and other stakeholders full control over their medical data. Information stored in the blockchain affords accountability, integrity, and security. Cryptographic functions give immutability and eradicate data security vulnerabilities. Medibchain has two levels:

Level 1 where a Registration Unit executes authentication. A Private Accessible Unit (PAU) intermediates stakeholders and blockchain. Finally, a Graphical User Interface (GUI) allows stakeholders to interact with the system.

Level 2 represents the system backend (for the permissioned blockchain), encompassing the proposed system's low-level elements.

ModelChain [71] consists of a BT framework meant for distributed, privacy-maintaining, predictive medical modeling. It aims to augment network security and robustness using BT. It also employs transaction metadata for model broadcasting while mingling blockchains with ML. Since BT in healthcare accelerates medical research, ModelChain uses blockchain's characteristics to increase the privacy-preserving predictive model's security and robustness among Hos. Since ModelChain propagates predictive models, network transparency is stable. A proof-of-information algorithm determines the blockchain-based, online ML order, increasing efficiency, and accuracy. This algorithm stems from PoW and uses a proof-of-information procedure that respects a concept called Boosting. The site containing the material must possess an upper priority over other sites since a partial model cannot accurately predict it. As a consequence, it must correspond to the subsequent model-updating site. A privacy-preserving framework called Ancile [72] offerring interoperability, efficacious access, and security for EMRs for third parties, suppliers, health staff, caretakers, and patients. This framework focuses on preserving patient privacy and security via cryptography besides allowing access control and data obfuscation by applying Ethereum and SCs. They use six SCs types to optimize patient experience, minimize any dealings among contracts and possible stakeholders, and curb privacy threats. These SCs permit patients to manage and control their EMRs. Query links and cryptographic hashes confirm the integrity of EHR databases.

A privacy-preserving methodology grounded on Personal Health Information (PHI), sharing a BSPP scheme and BT to improve e-health system diagnoses appears in [73]. This design employs private and consortium blockchains. The consortium blockchain tracks Secure PHI indexes while the private blockchain retains the PHI. The public key encrypts all data, together with PHI with keyword exploration, to attain secure search, privacy safeguarding and access control, in addition to data security. System availability requires block generators to arrange for proof of conformance in case new blocks are inserted. System entities or stakeholders are users, caretakers, medical/service suppliers, and system managers, keeping the public key tree and generating system parameters. The framework affords access control, data auditing, secure search, privacy defense, and time-controlled revocation. However, modifying the URL is an issue. Since blockchain only stores records, data location may change; thus, old URLs cannot be modified, and new URLs must be generated. Furthermore, the data-sharing session takes a new block because there is no space reclaim after a sharing.

4. Case Study

To integrate BT with healthcare, a policy should address interoperability, privacy, safety, scalability, as well as regularity while responding to design questions. For example:

- How authenticated parties access and retrieve data from Hos while preserving patient privacy
- How to warrant secure interactions among patients and systems
- How to curb legal/regulatory sanctions and unethical data usage when exchanging information
- How patients access various data types from multiple HOs through a single system.

Some existing work contains non-user-friendly, intricate validation and authentication schemes, adding extra overload. There are three primary considerations to study, namely the BN, CA, and system design. A BN stores all logs of medical records when executing transactions, grouping them into blocks and storing extra information (viz. requests, policies, data states to warrant privacy and regularity). A permissioned blockchain allows unambiguous access control for specifically identifiable participants to enhance network performance/security while reducing node costs and workload from the mining process. These permissioned blockchain processes perform necessary calculations only for a particular application where each transaction stands for a relationship between an organizational entity and a stakeholder (i.e., patient, caretaker, staff). It holds identifiable numbers to be searched by patients using a mobile application. A BN design appears in Figure 6.

Cryptography ensures data legitimacy, confidentiality, and security. ECC encrypts private data with shorter encryption keys, safeguarding high-speed data transfers and using less computing power while supporting Cloud storage by allotting data access pointers whenever an authorized entity asks for them. Yet, ECC limits data searchability. An identification number mitigates this issue. Data encryption must occur before parameter searching for exchanging public keys. Discovering data items in Cloud storage embraces procedures for downloading and decrypting, besides searching. Access control models satisfactorily control external attacks while enforcing cost matters, regulations and accessing times. Still, they need enhanced access models with cryptographic primitives and attribute-based encryption for detecting internal attacks.

The CA choice entails a procedure involving the utmost critical parameters for blockchain-based systems with optimal performance and regularity requirements. Regularity is vital because some implementations offer patient data rewards whenever tallying a block to the blockchain. Still, this serious issue needs thinking about why it is evading the PoW algorithm. Instead, QuorumChain CA helps add the next block via majority-based voting with SCs tracking and identifying eligible node votes to determine the next block. The next block's voting process starts whenever possible. A threshold value helps match the total votes. When the total votes go beyond the specified threshold, then the block enters the blockchain. A threshold value avoids adding blocks that already exist in transactions. Likewise, timeout sessions can elude the creation of identical blocks by innumerable miners. Specific nodes will handle the voting process reducing the BN workload, thus delegating block additions to specific nodes.

Since IoMT devices carry patient information, they require low energy consumption. PBFT authentication generates public and private keys for each node while verifying network agreement message formats with low-latency storage, sufficient throughput, and fast, efficient transaction processing.

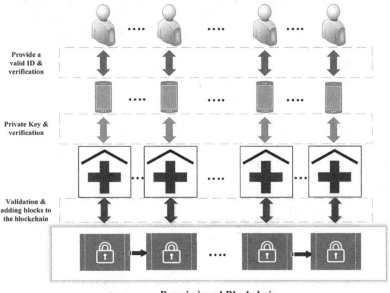

Permissioned Blockchain

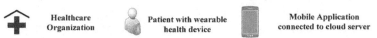

Figure 6. Typical blockchain network infrastructure

Authentication and access layers are used in a multi-layer paradigm to authenticate, verify, validate, and control access. The first layer validates data. Since, the BN is the sole blockchain entity that provides total network security, authenticated and validated data is sent to the second tier via a protected route for data dissemination. Specific parameters regulate network access. SCs manage the information flow and control these parameters. Users have unique identifiers and passwords to guarantee permission. Received data is transformed to a 256-bit hash before transmission to the requester, allowing SCs to compare and verify data dependability.

SCs created Common Device Metadata (CDM) for wearables to link the platform to Apps keeping transaction security and privacy. When wearables acquire data, SCs are also involved in the authentication. After evidence gathering, the system incorporates it by adding a block to the blockchain and keeping it in the Cloud for additional processing. When notifications reach cellphones, users handle data exchange with HFs and other types of providers.

The logical execution flow for a smart wearable handling user data appears in Figure 7. This user interacts with the primary contract process through the authentication layer, comprising software patterns for translating data to sensors. A particular contract in the access layer adds fresh data to the blockchain while also analyzing characteristics. The blockchain incorporates it if it is correct. If an emergency occurs for a certain SC's regulations, smart devices will transmit notifications to ensure patient safety.

A smartphone can communicate with the Cloud server through BT to secure patient data to avoid tampering or counterfeiting efforts. The application runs on the target platform's hyperledger. Interoperability, accessible storage, security, and transaction speed help assess and validate a decentralized, safe platform and application (Figure 8). To approve medical data access, the App requires the user's ID and password. ECC encrypts data being sent, which entails a valid ID and password with the right cryptographic keys. This strategy comes in handy when another entity requests and accesses data, as revealed in Figure 8. A patient

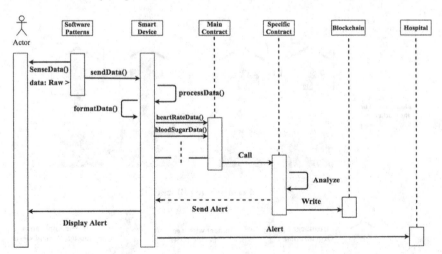

Figure 7. Logical flow for an intelligent wearable

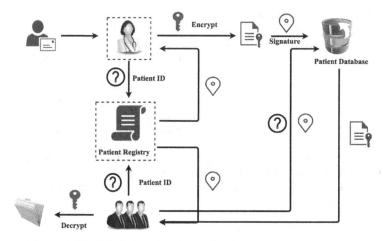

Figure 8. Blockchain-based health application environment workflow.

registration database managed by SCs can keep IDs and passwords. A tree-based scheme affords scalability, performance and takes large data sets uploaded by Apps because of batching and processing.

5. Conclusions

Given today's environmental challenges, Information and Communication Technology (ICT) criticality has augmented. However, the healthcare domain confronts several challenges due to patient-centric methods, connecting heterogeneous systems, inadequate interoperability across systems, and EHR accuracy. Due to its enormous potential, there has recently been an outpouring of awareness in adopting blockchain in the healthcare trade to address difficulties with EMRs while offering privacy, security, validation, authentication, besides interoperability. Blockchain can help to tackle real-world issues, including unreported clinical trials, health data failures, and misleading data mistakes. This chapter overviews various consensus healthcare algorithms while highlighting their basic concepts and challenges. Finally, it addresses research hiatuses from existing work.

References

1. Efanov, D. and Roschin, P. (2018). The all-pervasiveness of the blockchain technology. Procedia Comp. Sci., 123, 116-121.
2. Kanna, K., Estrela, V.V. and Rodrigues, J.J.P.C. (2021). Cyber Security and Digital Forensics. Proc. ICCSDF 2021, Springer Nature, Zurich, Switzerland.
3. Khelassi, A. and Estrela, V.V. (2020). Advances in Multidisciplinary Medical Technologies — Engineering, Modeling and Findings. Proc. International Workshop on Medical Technologies 2019 (ICHSMT 2019), Springer Nature, Zurich, Switzerland.

4. Estrela, V.V., Saotome, O., Loschi, H.J., Hemanth, D.J., Farfan, W.S. et al. (2018). Emergency response cyber-physical framework for landslide avoidance with sustainable electronics. Technologies, 6, 42.

5. Chen, H., Pendleton, M., Njilla, L. and Xu, S. (2020). A survey on Ethereum systems security. ACM Computing Surveys (CSUR), 53, 1-43.

6. Zubaydi, H.D., Chong, Y., Ko, K., Hanshi, S.M., Karuppayah, S. et al. (2019). A review on the role of blockchain technology in the healthcare domain. Electronics, 8, 679.

7. Kuo, T.T., Kim, H.E. and Ohno-Machado, L. (2017). Blockchain distributed ledger technologies for biomedical and health care applications. J. Am. Med. Inf. Assoc., 24, 1211-1220.

8. McGhin, T., Choo, R., Liu, C. and He, D. (2019). Blockchain in healthcare applications: Research challenges and opportunities. J. Netw. Comput. Appl., 135, 62-75.

9. Drescher, D. (2017). Blockchain Basics: A Non-Technical Introduction in 25 Steps. Apress: New York, NY, USA.

10. Holbl, M., Kompara, M. and Kamisali A. (2018). A systematic review of the use of blockchain in healthcare. Symmetry, 10, 470.

11. Merkle, R.C.A. (1988). Digital signature based on a conventional encryption function. *In:* Advances in Cryptology—CRYPTO 1987; LNCS 293; pp. 369-378. Springer: Berlin/Heidelberg, Germany.

12. Chatterjee, J., Son, L.H., Ghatak, S., Kumar, R., Khari, M. et al. (2018). Bitcoin exclusively informational money: A valuable review from 2010 to 2017. Quality & Quantity, 52, 2037-2054.

13. Iavorschi, M. (2013). The Bitcoin project and the free market, CES Working Papers, Centre for European Studies. Alexandru Ioan Cuza University, vol. 5(4), pp. 529-534.

14. Burgess, K. and Colangelo J. (2015). The Promise of Bitcoin and the Blockchain: Consumers' Research. Washington, DC, USA.

15. Johnson, D., Menezes, A. and Vanstone, S. (2001). The elliptic curve digital signature algorithm (ECDSA). Int. J. Inf. Secur., 1, 36-63.

16. Kim, S.K., Kim, U.M. and Huh, J.H. (2019). A study to improvement of blockchain application to overcome vulnerability of IoT multiplatform security. Energies, 12, 402.

17. Xu, J.J. (2016). Are blockchains immune to all malicious attacks? Financ. Innov., 2, 25.

18. Cai, Y. and Zhu, D. (2016). Fraud detections for online businesses: A perspective from blockchain technology. Financ. Innov., 2, 20.

19. Zheng, Z., Xie, S., Dai, H., Chen, X., Wang, H. et al. (2017). An overview of blockchain technology: Architecture, consensus, and future trends. Proc. 2017 IEEE 6th Int'l Cong. Big Data: BigData Congress, pp. 557-564. Honolulu, HI, USA, 25-30 June 2017.

20. Li, X., Jiang, P., Chen, T., Luo, X., Wen, Q. et al. (2017). A survey on the security of blockchain systems. Future Gener. Comput. Syst., 107, 841-853.

21. Bentov, I., Lee, C., Mizrahi, A. and Rosenfeld, M. (2014). Proof of activity: Extending bitcoin's proof of work via proof of stake. *In:* SIGMETRICS Performance Evaluation Reviews; ACM: New York, NY, USA.

22. Vukolic, M. (2016). The quest for scalable blockchain fabric: Proof-of-work vs. BFT replication. Lect. Notes Comput. Sci., 9591, 112-125.

23. Kotla, R., Alvisi, L., Dahlin, M., Clement, A., Wong, E. et al. (2009). Zyzzyva: Speculative byzantine fault tolerance. ACM Trans. Comput. Syst., 27, 1-39.

24. Buchman, E. (2019). Byzantine fault tolerant state machine replication in any programming language. Proc. 2019 ACM Symp. Principles of Distributed Computing.

25. An, A., Diem, P., Lan, L.T., Toi, T.V., Binh, L.D. et al. (2019). Building a Product Origins Tracking System Based on Blockchain and PoA Consensus Protocol. ACOMP.

26. Ali, M., Blankstein, A., Freedman, M., Galabru, L., Gupta, D. et al. (2020). PoX: Proof of Transfer Mining with Bitcoin. Blockstack PBC.

27. Borge, M., Kokoris-Kogias, E., Jovanovic, P., Gasser, L., Gailly, N. et al. (2017). Proof-of-personhood: Redemocratizing permissionless cryptocurrencies. Proc. 2nd IEEE European Symp. Sec. and Privacy, pp. 23-26. Paris, France, 26-28 April 2017.

28. Ghosh, M. and Richardson, M. (2014). A TorPath to TorCoin: Proof-of-bandwidth altcoins for compensating relays. Proc. HotPETs'14: 7th Workshop on Hot Topics in Privacy Enhancing Technologies. Available online: http://dedis.cs.yale.edu/dissent/papers/hotpets14-torpath-abs/ (accessed on 12 March 2021).

29. Intel. (2017). Proof of Elapsed Time (PoET), Available online: http://intelledger.github.io/ (accessed on 28 January 2021).

30. Mazieres, D. (2015). The Stellar Consensus Protocol: A Federated Model for Internet-Level Consensus. Available online: https://www.stellar.org/papers/stellar-consensus-protocol.pdf (accessed on 28 January 2021).

31. Metropolitana, Z., Le, N., California, B., Ju, C., Ta, C.I. et al. (2016). Bitcoin-NG: A scalable blockchain protocol. Proc. 13th USENIX Symp. Networked Systems Design and Implementation, Santa Clara, CA, USA, 16-18 March 2016.

32. Cachin, C., Schubert, S. and Vukolic M. (2016). Non-determinism in byzantine fault-tolerant replication. Proc. Int. Conf. Princ. Distrib. Syst. (OPODIS 2016), pp. 1-20. Madrid, Spain, 13-16 December 2016.

33. Schwartz, D., Youngs, N. and Britto, A. (2014). The Ripple Protocol Consensus Algorithm; Ripple Labs Inc White Paper; 2014. Available online: https://ripple.com/files/ripple_consensus_whitepaper.pdf (accessed on 28 January 2021).

34. Kwon, J. (2014). TenderMint: Consensus without Mining. Available online: https://www.weusecoins.com/ assets/pdf/library/Tendermint%20Consensus%20without%20Mining.pdf (accessed on 28 January 2021).

35. Kim, S.K. and Huh, J.H. (2018). A study on the improvement of smart grid security performance and blockchain smart grid perspective. Energies, 11, 1973.

36. Ongaro, D. and Ousterhout, J. (2014). In search of an understandable consensus algorithm. Proc. 2014 USENIX Annual Technical Conference, volume 37, pp. 1-16. Philadelphia, PA, USA, 19-20 June 2014.

37. Syta, E., Tamas, I., Visher, D., Wolinsky, D.I., Jovanovic, P. et al. (2016). Keeping authorities 'honest or bust' with decentralized witness cosigning. Proc. 37th IEEE Symp. Security and Privacy, San Jose, CA, USA, 23-25 May 2016.

38. Saravanan, M., Shubha, R., Marks, A.M. and Iyer, V. (2017). SMEAD: A secured mobile enabled assisting device for diabetics monitoring. Proc. 11th IEEE Int'l Conf. Adv. Networks and Telecomm. Systems 2017, Odisha, India, pp. 1-6. 17-20 December 2017.

39. Xia, Q., Sifah, E.B., Asamoah, K.O., Gao, J., Du, X. et al. (2017). MeDShare: Trust-less medical data sharing among cloud service providers via blockchain. IEEE Access, 5, 14757-14767.

40. Zhang, J., Xue, N. and Huang, X. (2016). A secure system for pervasive social network-based healthcare. IEEE Access, 4, 9239-9250.

41. Esposito, C., Santis, A.D., Tortora, G., Chang, H., Choo, K.K.R. et al. (2018). Blockchain: A panacea for healthcare cloud-based data security and privacy? IEEE Cloud Comput., 5, 31-37.

42. Omar, A.A., Rahman, M.S. and Kiyomoto, A.B. (2017). MediBchain a blockchain based privacy preserving platform for healthcare data. Proc. International Conf. Security, Privacy and Anonymity in Computation, Communication and Storage, Guangzhou, China, 12-15 December 2017.

43. Dwivedi, A.D., Srivastava, G., Dhar, S. and Singh, R. (2019). A decentralized privacy-preserving healthcare blockchain for IoT. Sensors, 19, 326.

44. Peterson, K., Deeduvanu, R., Kanjamala, P. and Boles, K. (2016). A blockchain-based approach to health information exchange networks. Proc. NIST Workshop Blockchain Healthc., 1, 1-10.

45. Xia, Q., Sifah, E.B., Smahi, A., Amofa, S., Zhang, X. et al. (2017). BBDS: Blockchain-based data sharing for electronic medical records in cloud environments. Information, 8, 44.

46. Theodouli, A., Arakliotis, S., Moschou, K. and Votis, K. (2018). On the design of a blockchain-based system to facilitate healthcare data sharing. Proc. 12th IEEE Int'l Conf. Big Data Science and Eng. (TrustCom/BigDataSE), New York, NY, USA, 1-3 August 2018.

47. Mcfarlane, C., Beer, M., Brown, J. and Prendergast, N. (2017). Patientory: A healthcare peer-to-peer EMR storage network v1.0, Entrust Inc.: Addison, TX, USA.

48. Amofa, S., Sifah, E.B., Kwame, O.B., Abla, S., Xia, Q. et al. (2018). A Blockchain-based architecture framework for secure sharing of personal health data. Proc. 2018 IEEE 20th Int'l Conf. e-Health Networking, Applications and Services (Healthcom), Ostrava, Czech Republic, 17-20 September 2018.

49. Zheng, X., Mukkamala, R.R., Vatrapu, R. and Ordieres-Mere, J. (2018). Blockchain-based personal health data sharing system using cloud storage. Proc. IEEE 20th Int'l Conf. e-Health Networking, Applications and Services (Healthcom), Ostrava, Czech Republic, 17-20 September 2018.

50. Daemen, J. and Rijmen, V. (2013). The design of Rijndael: AES – The Advanced Encryption Standard, Springer Science and Business Media: Berlin/Heidelberg, Germany.

51. Desmedt, Y. (1992). Threshold cryptosystems. Proc. International Conf. Theory and Application of Cryptology and Information Security 1992, pp. 1-14. 88. QLD, Australia, 13-16 December 1992.

52. Shen, B., Guo, J. and Yang, Y. (2019). MedChain: Efficient healthcare data sharing via blockchain. Appl. Sci., 9, 1207.

53. Koblitz, N. (1987). Elliptic curve cryptosystems. Math. Comput., 48, 203-209.

54. Azaria, A., Ekblaw, A., Vieira, T. and Lippman, A. (2016). MedRec: Using blockchain for medical data access and permission management. Proc. 2nd Int'l Conf. Open Big Data, OBD 2016, pp. 25-30. Vienna, Austria, 22-24 August 2016.

55. Ekblaw, A., Azaria, A., Halamka, J.D. and Lippman, A. (2016). A case study for blockchain in healthcare: 'MedRec' prototype for electronic health records and medical research data. Proc. IEEE BigData 2016: IEEE Int'l Conf. Big Data, Washington, DC, USA, 5-8 December 2016.

56. Conceiçao, A.F., da Silva, F.S.C., Rocha, V., Locoro, A., Barguil, J.M. et al. (2018). Electronic health records using blockchain technology. arXiv 2018, arXiv:1804.10078.

57. Fan, K., Wang, S., Ren, Y., Li, H., Yang, Y. et al. (2018). MedBlock: Efficient and Secure Medical Data Sharing Via Blockchain. J. Med. Syst., 42, 1-11.

58. Dubovitskaya, A., Xu, Z., Ryu, S., Schumacher, M., Wang, F. et al. (2017). Secure and trustable electronic medical records sharing using blockchain. Am. Med. Inf. Assoc. 2018, 2017, 650-659..

59. Salahuddin, M.A., Al-Fuqaha, A., Guizani, M., Shuaib, K., Sallabi, F. et al. (2017). Softwarization of internet of things infrastructure for secure and smart healthcare. IEEE Comput. Mag., 50, 74-79.

60. Holland, J.H. (1992). Adaptation in Natural and Artificial Systems: An Introductory Analysis with Applications to Biology, Control, and Artificial Intelligence. MIT Press: Cambridge, MA, USA, 1992.

61. Shensa, M.J. (1992). The discrete wavelet transform: Wedding the a trous and Mallat algorithms. IEEE Trans. Signal Process., 40, 2464-2482.

62. Kotsiuba, I., Velvkzhanin, A., Yanovich, Y., Bandurova, I.S., Dyachenko, Y. et al. (2018). Decentralized e-Health architecture for boosting healthcare analytics. Proc. 2018 2nd World Conf. Smart Trends in Systems, Security and Sustainability (WorldS4), pp. 113-118. London, UK, 30-31 October 2018.

63. What Is Exonum? Available online: https://exonum.com/doc/getstarted/what-is-exonum/ (accessed on 29 January 2021).

64. Jiang, S., Cao, J., Wu, H., Yang, Y., Ma, M. et al. (2018). Blochie: A blockchain-based platform for healthcare information exchange. Proc. SMARTCOMP 2018: The 4th IEEE Int'l Conf. Smart Computing, pp. 49-56. Sicily, Italy, 18-20 June 2018.

65. Cichosz, S.L., Stausholm, M.N., Kronborg, T., Vestergaard, P., Hejlesen, O. et al. (2018). How to use blockchain for diabetes health care data and access management: An operational concept. J. Diabetes Sci. Technol., 13, 248-253.

66. Zhang, P., White, J., Schmidt, D.C., Lenz, G., Rosenbloom, S.T. et al. (2018). FHIRChain: Applying Blockchain to Securely and Scalably Share Clinical Data. Comput. Struct. Biotechnol. J., 16, 267-278.

67. Guo, R., Shi, H., Zhao, Q. and Zheng, D. (2018). Secure attribute-based signature scheme with multiple authorities for blockchain in electronic health records systems. IEEE Access, 6, 11676-11686.

68. Yue, X., Wang, H., Jin, D., Li, M., Jiang, W. et al. (2016). Healthcare data gateways: Found healthcare intelligence on blockchain with novel privacy risk control. J. Med. Syst., 40, 218.

69. Liang, X., Zhao, J., Shetty, S., Liu, J., Li, D. et al. (2017). Integrating blockchain for data sharing and collaboration in mobile healthcare applications. Proc. PIMRC 2017: 28th Annual IEEE Int'l Symp. Personal, Indoor and Mobile Radio Communications, Montreal, QC, Canada, 8-13 October 2017.

70. Zhang, P., White, J., Schmidt, D.C. and Lenz, G. (2015). Design of blockchain-based apps using familiar software patterns to address interoperability challenges in healthcare. Available online: https://www.dre. vanderbilt.edu/~schmidt/PDF/PLoP-2017-blockchain.pdf (accessed on 20 September 2021).

71. Kuo, T. and Ohno-Nachado, L. (2018). ModelChain: Decentralized privacy-preserving healthcare predictive modeling framework on private blockchain networks. arXiv 2018, arXiv:1802.01746.

72. Dagher, G.G., Mohler, J., Milojkovic, M. and Marella, P.B. (2018). Ancile: Privacy-preserving framework for access control and interoperability of electronic health records using blockchain technology. Sustain. Cities Soc., 39, 283-297.

73. Zhang, A. and Lin, X. (2018). Towards secure and privacy-preserving data sharing in e-health systems via consortium blockchain. J. Med. Syst., 42, 140.

74. Monteiro, A.C.B., França, R.P., Estrela, V.V., Razmjooy, N., Iano, Y. et al. (2021). Metaheuristics applied to blood image analysis. *In:* Razmjooy, N. et al. (eds). Metaheuristics and Optimization in Computer and Electrical Engineering. Lecture Notes in Electrical Engineering, vol. 696. Springer, Cham.

75. Deshpande, A., Razmjooy, N. and Estrela, V.V. (2021). Introduction to computational intelligence and super-resolution. *In:* Deshpande, A. et al. (eds). Computational Intelligence Methods for Super-Resolution in Image Processing Applications. Springer, Cham, Switzerland.

76. Chaabane, L., Khelassi, A., Terziev, A., Andreopoulos, N., Jesus, M.A. et al. (2021). Particle swarm optimization with tabu search algorithm (PSO-TS) applied to multiple sequence alignment problem. *In:* Khelassi, A., Estrela, V.V. (eds), Advances in Multidisciplinary Medical Technologies — Engineering, Modeling and Findings. Springer, Cham, Switzerland.

77. Kalantari, S., Ramezani, M., Madadi, A. and Estrela, V.V. (2021). Reduction AWGN from digital images using a new local optimal low-rank approximation method. *In:* Iano, Y. et al. (eds). Proc. 5th Brazilian Technology Symposium (BTSym 2019). Smart Innovation, Systems and Technologies, vol. 201. Springer, Cham.

78. Razmjooy, N. and Estrela, V.V. (2019). Applications of Image Processing and Soft Computing Systems in Agriculture. 1-300, 2019, IGI Global, Hershey, PA, USA.

79. Hemanth, J. and Estrela, V.V. (2017). Deep Learning for Image Processing Applications. Advances in Parallel Computing, Vol. 31, IOS Press, Amsterdam, Netherlands.

80. Loschi, H.J., Estrela, V.V., Hemanth, D.J., Fernandes, S.R., Iano, Y. et al. (2020). Communications requirements, video streaming, communications links and networked UAVs. *In:* Estrela V.V. et al. (eds). Imaging and Sensing for Unmanned Aircraft Systems, 2(6), 113-132, IET, London, UK.

81. Padilha, R., Iano, Y., Monteiro, A.C., Arthur, R., Estrela, V.V. et al. (2019). Betterment proposal to multipath fading channels potential to MIMO systems. *In:* Iano, Y. et al. (eds). Proc. 4th BTSym, Springer, Cham, Switzerland.

6G in Healthcare – Anticipating Needs and Requirements

Vania V. Estrela[1] [0000-0002-4465-7691], Anand Deshpande[2] [0000-0002-1500-0981],
Dalmo Stutz[3] [0000-0003-1408-1756], Joaquim T. de Assis[3] [0000-0002-2802-1298],
Asif A. Laghari[4] [0000-0001-5831- 5943], Hugo H.P. da Silva[5] [0000-0001-6764-8432],
Fuqian Shi[6] [0000-0003-4245-5727], Yu-Da Lin[7] [0000-0001-5100-6072],
J.M.R.S. Tavares[8] [0000-0001-7603-6526]

[1] Telecommunications Department, Fluminense Federal University (UFF), RJ, Brazil,
vania.estrela.phd@ieee.org
[2] Electronics and Communication Engineering, Angadi Institute of Technology and
Management, Belagavi, India, deshpande.anandb@gmail.com
[3] Instituto Politecnico do Rio de Janeiro, Nova Friburgo, RJ, Brazil,
stutz@iprj.uerj.br, joaquim@iprj.br
[4] Faculty of Computer Science, Sindh Madressatul Islam University, Karachi (74000),
Sindh, Pakistan, asif.laghari@smiu.edu.pk
[5] Instituto de Telecomunicacoes, Instituto Superior Tecnico, Torre Norte - Piso 10,
Av. Rovisco Pais, 1, 1049-001, Lisboa, Lisboa, Portugal, hsilva@lx.it.pt
[6] Rutgers Cancer Institute of New Jersey, United States, shifuqian@gmail.com
[7] National Penghu University of Science and Technology, Magong, TW,
yudalinemail@gmail.com
[8] Departamento de Engenharia Mecanica (DEMec), Faculdade de Engenharia da
Universidade do Porto (FEUP)/Instituto de Engenharia Mecanica e Gestao Industrial
(INEGI), Porto, Portugal, tavares@fe.up.pt

1. Introduction

Recent advancements in wireless communications and smart devices have extended the Internet of Medical Things (IoMT) encompassing ubiquitous sensing with high processing capabilities. Because of its enormous potential to deliver customer services, the IoMT receives much attention from academia and industry [1]. IoMT permits seamless communications and automatic administration among heterogeneous devices and Cyber-Physical Systems (CPSs) [19] without human intercession, with significant societal benefits through expert, automated remote management systems.

Notably, inherent 5G traits like enhanced mobile broadband (eMBB), energy-efficient service, massive Machine-Type Communication (mMTC), massive UltraReliable Low-Latency Communication (mURLLC) require high throughput [2]. However, the enormous proliferation of smart devices and IoMT networks will intensify technical criteria, such as self-governing, ultra-large-scale, vastly dynamic, and intelligent services. 6G wireless networks with accompanying technological trends necessitate much attention because their features (viz. ultra-low-latency communications, tremendously elevated throughput, satellite-centered customer services, huge autonomous networks) outwit previous generations [3, 4]. This infrastructure type augments Quality of Service (QoS) as well as Quality of Experience (QoE) in IoMT [5, 6]. These ground-breaking advancements will hasten 6G-IoMT applications and deployments in IoMT data sensing, wireless communications, device connectivity, and 6G network management (Figure 1).

6G Technologies (6GTs) enable mobile AI answers for optimized 6G network projects. Holistic convergence studies of 6G and IoMT (6G- IoMT) try to circumvent limitations. Edge intelligence (EI), Reconfigurable Intelligent Surfaces (RISs), space-air-ground-underwater (SAGU) communications, THz communications, mURLL communications, and blockchain are the most fundamental 6GTs for IoMT networks that we identify and discuss. Previous works [7-10] only discussed essential technologies such as wireless communications and networks but 6GTs directly impact IoMT and need

(1) 6G- IoMT convergence and technical integration requirements;
(2) EI, RISs, SAGU communications, THz communications, mURLLC, and blockchain infrastructures;
(3) Provision for Internet of Medical Things (IoMT), Unmanned Aerial Vehicles (UAVs), besides Vehicular Internet of Medical Things (VIoMT).
(4) Discussions about 6G- IoMT implementation potentials.

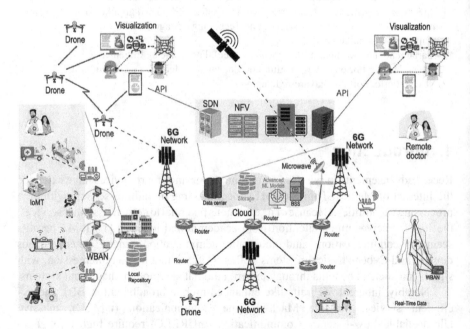

Figure 1. 6G Medical Cyber-Physical System (MCPS)

Section 2 discusses 6G-IoMT advancements, besides integration requirements. Section 3 examines fundamental technologies enabling 6G-IoMT. Section 4 investigates 6G IoMT applications, such as IoMT, UAVs, VIoMT, and Autonomous Driving (AD) [7-10]. Section 5 identifies 6G-IoMT vital challenges, e.g., security, privacy, energy efficiency, hardware, standard specifications, and research directions. To conclude, Section 6 finishes the text.

2. 6G-IoT Rationale and Requirements

2.1. 6G-IoT

Rapidly developing wireless technologies are fundamental for future services and applications, owing to the unparalleled manufacturing of mobile devices and exponential global traffic growth. 5G improved QoS but fully meet emerging IoMT services requirements was difficult [7, 8]. The rich video usage amended screen resolution, mobile edge services, machine-to-machine (M2M) communications, and extra factors driving this exponential growth. The growth of mobile devices and data services increases traffic demands for Mobile Broadband (MBB), e.g., new technologies for video services entail high, growing video data traffic [7-10]. Furthermore, the rapid prototyping of data-centric intelligent structures reveals new 5G latency constraints.

Compared to 5G, 6G will provide disruptive technologies and networking infrastructures for many new IoMT applications by holistically meeting strict network demands [3, 9, 10]. EI, THz, and large-scale satellite constellations require 6GTs for more powerful IoMT ecosystems. While 5G has some critical limitations concerning mobile traffic capability, device density, and network latency, 6G-IoMT networks can bring new outstanding qualities such as:

- High data rate to address large-scale IoMT connectivity where seamless mobility, spectrum availability, and mobile traffic coexist.
- Super high throughput and device density for increasing mobile traffic;
- Extremely high device connectivity density for massively dense networks;
- Ultra-low network latencies for haptic applications like e-health and AD.

2.1.1. Internet of Things (IoT)

IoMT data from ubiquitous devices (viz. sensors, actuators, mobiles, and radiofrequency identifications (RFIDs)) [11, 99] serve end-users. The Internet of Nano-Things (IoNT) also affects future IoMT ecosystems [12]. IoNT's nano-devices and things can probe, transmit, process, in addition to store data using nano units to support customer services like healthcare monitoring. Interconnecting nano-networks seamlessly demands new architectures and communication paradigms with full-dimensional wireless coverage and functionalities, including sensing, actuating, speed, computing, intelligence, fully autonomous control, scalability, superior connectivity, and service delivery.

2.1.2. 6G-IoT Requirements

6G-IoMT will require more stringent requirements to fully implement intelligence, colossal device connectivity and coverage, autonomous frameworks, and data-driven services as below.

1. **Broad IoMT Connectivity:** The explosion of smart devices and fast wireless communication development have increased mobile connectivity dramatically [8, 9]. The global mobile traffic volume is expected to increase exponentially. Broadband access platforms and satellite networks employing Low Earth Orbit (LEO) satellites [13] will impact smart device large-scale communications. UAVs' flying platforms will support seamless connectivity over large-scale IoMT networks since fixed Base Stations (BSs) cannot ensure stable, reliable device and ad hoc network (AHN) communications. For example, UAV swarms in 6G networks can provide wireless connectivity for terrestrial IoMT users over a distributed motion algorithm supporting each drone to autonomously attain the optimal location in a continuous IoMT space [14-19, 109-111].

2. **mURLL IoMT Communications:** 5G-IoMT introduced mURLLC [20] requiring further support for emerging 6G-IoMT applications like fully autonomous flying systems. mURLLCs will be critical for video feeds going from cameras to vehicles in self-controlled real-time coordinated, timely vehicle signaling safely. Information delivery timeliness will assist the future intelligent, interconnected societies. The tactile internet will provide haptic communications for mission-critical services with real-time touch and actuation.

3. **Better 6G-IoMT Communication Protocols:** Future IoMT applications in intelligent networks necessitate significant architectural changes to support multiple rigorous requirements like e-healthcare. As a result of integrating other computing services such as edge (EC)/cloud computing (CC) and wireless technologies, network communication standards and protocols become critical in large-scale 6G-IoMT ecosystems. The IEEE 802.11 working group has recently initiated conversations on releasing the IEEE 802.11 being an extremely High Throughput Wi-Fi standard [21] to reach the 6G-IoMT peak throughput requirements. These standards will assist service suppliers to set up intelligent IoMT services at the network edge.

4. **Extended IoMT Network Coverage:** Large-dimensional SAGU networks, EI, and UAVs can achieve full coverage beyond terrestrial networks [5]. UAVs deliver autonomous and intelligent network edge solutions. The latter supports flying BSs in extending current mobile network coverage from 2D terrestrial networks to 3D systems. High-altitude UAVs, for example, can serve as agile aerial platforms for on-demand maritime coverage [22], with the promise of establishing shore-based stations.

5. **Next-generation Smart IoMT Devices:** 6G-IoMT networks will rely on smart devices that have total EI and computing power. Since, smart devices will not only engender or exploit information but will also actively participate in network management and operation processes, a device-centric network possesses new necessities and challenges to the wireless communication designs and operations. Device-centric wireless solutions include device-to-device communications and multi-hop cellular networks, both on the 3GPP

roadmap [23]. Without a centralized controller, each IoMT smart device can behave as an end-user terminal, providing connectivity and services (e.g., caching, intelligent control, and network signaling) to other network edge devices [24]. This can extend demand-driven opportunistic networking tailored to different users, services, or network demands viz. energy cost minimization or maximization of spectrum efficiency for end-user devices [25, 59]. Furthermore, various wearables and implants proliferate, with functionalities gradually replacing smartphone-centric 4G/5G networks. These devices will power the evolving human-centric 6G services.

3. 6GT-IoMT Fundamentals

EI, Reconfigurable Intelligent Surfaces (RISs), SAGU communications, THz communications, mURLLC, and blockchains illustrate technologies that will support 6G-IoMT.

3.1. Edge Intelligence (EI)

AI will reach the network edge due to edge node computational capabilities [26], producing the EI paradigm [27], which merges AI, communications, and EC. The EI potential in 6G-IoMT and 6G-AHNs comprise self-learning solutions to recognize and classify emerging unidentified services from crude crowdsourcing data across a wide geographical area [28]. A latency-sensitive vehicular system linked to edge servers where each vehicle has a Generative Adversarial Network (GAN) for high EI efficiency will generate synthetic data, reducing the uploading volume and total network traffic [13]. However, this architecture must consider how user mobility affects training latency in distributed vehicles, 6G-IoMT, and self-driving cars.

EI enables dynamic spectrum access at the edge through fast, dependable, intelligent data processing supporting collaborative robots (cobots), and large-scale EI services besides big data analytics [29, 30]. Data analytics must sustain high data volumes, velocities, and varieties for IoMT users to significantly improve large-scale transmission and computation rates. Edge computing (EC) and fog computing (FC) relieve cloud server loads via computation besides storage at fog nodes near IoMT devices to improve QoS [3, 31]. Fog nodes manage idle and resourcs of spare devices to improve network efficiency, especially where CC cannot handle all user computation demands. FC combined with AI leads to fog intelligence.

Federated Learning (FL) has emerged as a distributed collaborative AI tactic in recent times to transform edge/fog intelligence designs. FL is a distributed AI methodology for training high-quality models by averaging local updates gathered from manifold learning edge clients lacking direct access to local data [3, 31]. Intelligent, distributed IoMT can collaborate with a data aggregator (e.g., an edge server) to train where devices only exchange parameters and raw data sharing is not required. FL working concepts offers unique IoMT features. A paramount data privacy feature is distributed model training without exposing raw data to external servers. Stringent, critical data privacy legislation viz. the General Data Protection Regulation (GDPR), guards user information in 6G-IoMT systems. FL also enables low-latency communications by avoiding large data offloads to remote servers during training and reducing network spectrum resources for iterative data training.

The huge IoMT device collaborations entail large-scale datasets and processing resources in the FL system to improve the overall training process's convergence rate, learning performances, accuracy rates, and 6G-IoMT services [32]. The Air-Ground Integrated Federated Learning (AGIFL) approach can assess the impact on privacy awareness of various hovering UAVs. Multiple terrestrial nodes (mobile users) participate in collaborative training with UAV deployed servers where each user has a dataset that performs local training and sends updated parameters to the UAV. A drone aggregates all updates to create a global model before distributing info to all users during location deployment for the next training round. Compared to 6G non-federated schemes, AGIFL methods perform promising classification accuracy on image classification tasks via convolutional neural networks (CNNs). The UAV's local computation security should help federated training by incorporating attack detection methods (e.g., data authentication and access control).

AI on embedded hardware, mobiles, and edge servers will leverage EI for 6G-IoMT to meet the rapid growth of smart devices. Compared to cloud training, Deep Learning (DL) can provide on-device low-latency inference. E.g., Binary Neural Networks (BNNs) can run on Graphic Processing Units (GPUs) for devices based on Android and optimize software /hardware for AI on resource-constrained devices [33]. The BNN computation capability can work on mobiles with decoupled parallel optimizations using OpenCL for real-time and reliable Android deployments. A MobileNet app trains an on-device CNN for IoMT localization applications. It feeds smartphone images to the CNN for object centroid determination (e.g., a hand) for human motion detection and people counting [44].

EI is primarily dependent on edge devices performing essential learning functions, such as classification or regression. However, adversaries can steal data and change parameters during data transmission and training. Untrusted edge devices exploiting private information from exchanges in collaborative training pose high data risks. Thus, 6G-IoMT solutions for safe and reliable EI ecosystems are necessary. Decentralized data learning can help blockchain ledgers verify EI model processes by allowing edge blockchain peers to authorize accurate models without revealing dataset labels. Data flow within intelligent models can benefit from blockchain cryptography to prevent data modifications.

3.2. Reconfigurable Intelligent Surfaces (RISs)

RISs partake in arrays of passive scattering components with artificial planar structures, each reflecting electromagnetic waves in a software-defined way [35, 36]. By facilitating signal broadcast, channel modeling, and acquisition, RISs can boost wireless system designs and optimization, enabling smart radio environments. Indeed, RIS together with 6G-IoMT empower many applications like multi-cell networks, simultaneously enhancing signals from serving BSs to lessen inter-cell interference between enormous networks of IoMT devices [37]. Another use for RIS is the ability to improve IoMT data offloading rates. The data volume unloaded to edge servers, especially, is heavily influenced by the channel gain of offloading links. RISs can establish gains for virtual arrays and reflection-based beamforming to compute offloading links. They allow offloading more data to edge servers for ultra-fast processing. Current studies integrate RISs into 6G-IoMT applications as is the case with smart buildings [38]. Indeed, RISs can interface with indoor and outdoor entities to facilitate access to households in smart buildings. RISs promise cooperative entity layers to avoid interference and ameliorate spectral efficiencies in device communications indoors and outdoors as part of the wireless communication benefits. A study integrated VIoMT-based vehicle-to-vehicle (V2V) networks of RIS access points for transmission and RIS relays installed on a building for vehicular communication coordination [39].

Radio-frequency (RF) sensing RISs can correct human posture in IoMT and remote health surveillance [40] where the optimal propagation links result from periodically programming RIS configurations. Hence, the system creates multiple independent paths containing helpful human posture information to estimate better arrangements than random configurations and non-configurable environments. UAVs can realize UAV-to all communications to support various data transmission alternatives in IoMT data sensing, emergency search, risk checking, and video streaming in 6G scenarios [41].

3.3. Communications in Terahertz (THz)

The unique traits of the THz band (0.1-10 THz) will drive 6G-IoMT and could meet future 6G-IoMT application requirements, such as picosecond-level symbol duration, ultra-high bandwidth, an amalgamation of thousands of submillimeter-long antennas with weak interference but lacking full legacy regulation [42]. A primary THz spectrum advantage is addressing spectrum scarcity issues in wireless communications while significantly increasing wireless capacities in 6G-IoMT. THz communications allow ultra-broadband applications like Virtual Reality (VR) as well as wireless personal area networks. THz communication technologies have recently helped in user localization by manipulating the ultra-wide bandwidths vacant at THz frequencies [43]. This enables receivers to tackle spaced multipath constituents and effectively appraise the transmitter's signal to estimate the user's location correctly.

THz bands also aid UAV communications [43] in analyzing the coverage probability of UAV networks to THz BS density and signal strength. They work in [44] model THz communication channels in VIoMT networks and hybrid beamforming subarray configurations by accounting for transmitting power consumption in various scenarios, including fully-connected, sub-connected and overlapped subarray structures. The scrutiny of antenna array arrangements can happen using a cellular infrastructure-to-everything application that embraces cellular and vehicular communications with perhaps thousands of channels, multiple pedestrians, several bed-ridden folks, and high-mobility vehicles. Simulation results show that the widespread fully-connected configurations in VIoMT communications with THz massive Multiple-Input Multiple-Output (MIMO) [36, 44, 45, 91] have a balanced performance trade-off concerning spectral efficiency, energy efficiency, and hardware costs. This trend will continue in channel modeling and spectrum allocation in THz band 6G-IoMT. Future considerations should include time-varying THz communication matters caused by vehicle mobility, which predictable AI could address with approaches such as dynamic Deep Reinforcement Learning (DRL).

3.4. Massively Scalable, Ultra-Reliable (UR), Low-Latency Communications (mURLLC)

6G-URLLC will support IoMT services via low-latency, timely, highly reliable connectivity [46] of massive health data for remote healthcare while also reducing regional health staff imbalances. mURLLC can automate mission-critical processes, e.g., automatic manufacturing and remote control. Compared to traditional wired connections, mURLLC technology optimizes operational costs with really low latency and ultra-high reliability. mURLLC also supports transportation with timely data sharing among means of transportation, infrastructures, and pedestrians with elevated reliabilities, which improves road safety and traffic efficiency in AHNs. Integrating mURLLC into the smart grid is an active application replacing cable/ fiber for real-time protection and control of distributed grid lines as well as stations. Consequently, mURLLC helps an eclectic range of mission-critical services viz. accurate positioning, speedy fault diagnosis, trustworthy fault isolation, system restoration, and remote decoupling protections.

Furthermore, AI is ideal for analyzing latency and reliability and enabling mURLLC in 6G-IoMT, with outstanding solutions like exact traffic and mobility prediction via DL and fast DRL network control [47]. AI becomes more important with unavailable network information or highly dynamic environments. For example, the work in [48] hinges on DL to an mURLLC-based virtual robotic arm framework. Deep neural networks (DNNs) accurately predict and control robotic arm locations. Deep Transfer Learning (DTL) can fine-tune pre-trained DNNs in nonstationary networks to improve learning efficiency. DRL optimizes the distributed cooperative sub-channel allotment and transmission power control offering strict URLLC services reliability and latency requirements. Each IoMT device can intelligently access its spectrum using DRL with instantaneous observations to optimize its sub-channel allocation and transmission power regulation. Then, a suitable QoS-aware reward function manages the energy efficiency and QoS requirements of all IoMT users. Compared to other conventional random approaches, the implementation results confirm that DRL saves significantly more energy. DRL without URLLC latency requirements for training latency analysis has limitations.

IoMT applications and services must fulfill numerous critical requirements to accomplish the latency and reliability required by mURLLC. User scheduling, channel access, and resource allocation overheads should be minimum. Latest AI advances open up new avenues for optimal IoMT user choice/ scheduling via DRL and low-latency resource endowment in smart transportation via FL with distributed training techniques. Additionally, minimizing packet error probability may lower traditional methods latency like hybrid automatic repeat request (HARQ) but are ineffective [49]. Still, energy-efficient IoMT devices should deal with the issue of constantly checking pending network packets, incurring high latency. URLLC-based IoMT requires energy-saving measures with solutions for high-frequency data checks.

3.5. Blockchain

6G-IoMT high security and privacy levels are a practical challenge because

6G distributed systems face sophisticated attacks/threats and need data privacy in multi-layer open sharing systems such as AHN data sharing. Blockchain can augment privacy and safety challenges in 6G-IoMT networks [50, 92, 93] due to decentralized, immutable, transparent databases without authorities to manage data because of peer-to-peer network topology. Hence, each entity has an identical right to control and authorize blockchain-stored data. Generally, blockchains can be public (permission-less, i.e., anyone who conducts transactions and participates in the consensus process) or private (permissioned).

Bitcoin and Ethereum are the most well-known public blockchain applications. Alternatively, private blockchains are invitation-only networks regulated by a central entity. A validation mechanism must first approve joining the blockchain network following many desirable characteristics: decentralization, traceability, trustworthiness, and immutability. 6G-IoMT ecosystem security and privacy provisions match these features. Blockchain's decentralized immutability characteristics create a secure, dependable resource access regulation and user privacy preservation. e.g., a Q-learning approach to learning resource usage patterns to perceive abnormal data accesses model virtualized resource states. A combined low-latency and memory saving method preserves privacy, improves response success ratios, and reduces false positives of connected users. The high true positives, accurate access denial, besides the success ratio attest to this solution's benefits. However, mining latencies caused by block verification need consideration, along with the estimation of data leakage probability.

Blockchain applications in 6G-IoMT automation [51] target domains such as UAVs and smart grids. Indeed, blockchain can create secure drone autonomous systems acting as blockchain clients communicating with ground BSs in missions viz. emergency search and environmental monitoring via a peer-to-peer ledger. Drones, terrestrial users besides network operators can rely on the data saved on the ledger employing blockchain with common control and tracing rights delivered over the distributed environment. The well-being data authentication in 6G-IoMT systems can be realized via blockchain and its in-built smart contract technology [52], eliminating third parties while keeping a high trust level. Blockchain in 6G-IoMT networks may incur latency and energy consumption costs. Mining causes significant network delays and consumes energy. Ethereum blockchain miners must run Proof-of-Work (PoW), which is computationally intensive and time-consuming. The repeated information interchange among multiple miners during PoW block verification involves large bandwidths. Hence, operational costs are critical when implementing blockchain in 6G-IoMT networks.

4. 6G-IoMT Applications

4.1. 6G-IoMT

The potential of 6GTs and IoMT via mURLLC and THz communications support extremely low-latency data transmission, hastening network connections among wearables and remote health staff like in [53, 91, 92, 94]. Remote health monitoring necessitates low-latency communications for near-real-time health care with fast and reliable remote diagnoses. 6G robotics can perform remote surgeries, allowing doctors to operate with high reliability. Telesurgery can use UAVs and blockchain due to existing mobile surgery networks. Each robot is a data node that securely stores surgical information in the database ledger without the necessity of a centralized authority. Smart contracts can automatically authenticate health data requests and control data sharing during surgery [13]. UAVs act as relays to address slow healthcare response rates. They transport lightweight healthcare items between hospitals in emergencies, avoiding traffic congestion and thus reducing data exchange latency. mURLLC technology utilizing 6G-IoMT THz bands is ideal for future ultra-high data rates in medical data communications. Consequently, nano-devices, implants, and on-body sensors can communicate in real-time to edge devices or cloud centers for short- as well as long-term healthcare analysis with extremely high reliability and availability.

Particularly, mURLLC matters in telemedicine, where doctors can remotely monitor, manage devices, and operate using real-time streaming from 6G networks. Furthermore, 6G-URLLC has facilitated connected ambulance care by consenting to real-time video streaming along with a high color resolution from the hospital to clinicians and paramedics at high speeds [54]. After performing an electroencephalogram on-board, doctors can provide urgent, real-time indications to ambulance paramedics via URLLC although ambulances need a brief survival time,a must in this scenario.

AI can perform data learning and analytics to realize intelligent 6G-IoMT. Machine learning (ML) techniques like logistic regression, Bayesian classifier, and decision tree can examine past health records of out-patients gathered by means of wearable sensors in 6G heterogeneous networks [55]. An uplink radio resource expedites care with an allocation optimization solution, with assigned resources proportional to patient stroke likelihoods. According to [56], a 6G ML-based solution with EC/CC provides low-latency data analytics for medical services such as diagnosis, illness prediction, and decision-making tasks for physical medicine and rehabilitation. ML can optimize mobility organization processes in 6G-IoMT by considering data rates, traffic, data processing delays, and allocation of resource bandwidth. The implementation results display a good trade-off concerning time and energy efficiency via ML practices while effectively handling and monitoring IoMT device mobility in 6G healthcare services. Wireless technologies such as URLLC, EI, and CC have combated the COVID-19 pandemic [57]. For example, high-speed mURLLC live video conferencing allows healthcare professionals to contact patients with low latencies and reliability for timely outbreak analysis. COVID-19 data can use data-driven EI techniques combining EC and AI for accurate, rapid disease diagnosis [58, 59, 61, 99].

Each local hospital edge server has a local GAN, entailing a discriminator and a generator put up with CNNs, to infer the COVID-19 data distribution from its local image dataset. The learned model parameters are then synchronized and exchanged by the local GANs for aggregation at a CC server, which yields a different version of the global model to all organizations for the subsequent training round. This process repeats until achieving the desired accuracy to produce realistic images for COVID-19 detection, where EI handles analytics advantageously using privacy protection and large-scale processing capabilities.

4.2. 6G for the VIoMT

6GT advancements have transformed VIoMT networks, revolutionizing intelligent transportation systems (ITSs). 6G-VIoMT networks use mMTCs for vehicle-to-everything (V2X) connectivity and transmit short vehicular information payloads by many vehicles without human interaction [87]. To accomplish this, the peculiarities of V2X achieve a trade-off between reliability, scalability, and latency by means of a vehicle discovery methodology in which a detection entity at the BS collects information about the vehicle's proximity. So, signature properties like time slots in addition to hash functions are regulated to optimize discovery schemes and minimize the false-positive probability when scheduling radio resources for V2X data communications within the available spectrum budget. Data rate prediction in 6G-VIoMT is problematic due to the complex interdependence of mobility, channels, and networking factors. ML can be an efficient approach for mimicking the likely behavior of network-supported throughput prediction in 6G-AHNs [60]. Roadside units (RUSs) comprise EI for estimating traffic volume and weather forecasts based on aggregating local vehicle observations [61] to realize the full AI potential in VIoMT. A distributed estimation approach improves the 6G vehicular system's scalability by allowing local estimates at distributed vehicles via wireless data exchange with neighboring means of transportation within the communication range.

DL improves 6G-VIoMT intelligence [62] by augmenting its high-dimensional generalization capability to model vehicular communication channels and support networking administration, e.g., optimal resource provision via DRL algorithms [63]. Building confidence for data learning in addition to reasoning is critical because data training is typically a black-box process with only the input and output known. So, for 6G-VIoMT networks, a trust broker entity provides discernment for learning activities at the DL controller, such as the BS. As a result, the learning process can interpret that business stakeholders comprehend the data training process, such as which data features cause decisions. DL techniques schedule data transmission autonomously using three tactics [64, 95]: (i) supervised learning for data rate assessment, (ii) unsupervised learning for distinguishing geospatially-dependent estimation model uncertainties, and (iii) reinforcement learning (RL) for independently coordinating data transmissions based on expected resource efficiency. From resource apportionment to data rate maximization, this VIoMT scheme employs multi-objective optimization. Because 6G-VIoMT networks will be highly scalable and distributed in the future, developing cooperative DL methodologies like FL will be beneficial. In addition to network administration, DL assists a vehicular data controller in providing useful security solutions in 6G-VIoMT networks [65]. In vehicular communications, a new weighted ensemble DL approach can identify intrusion and attack risks. The support vector machine (SVM) first maps data to a high-dimensional space using a kernel function. Then it finds classification hyperplanes to mine the sample classes.

K-neighborhood can classify extracted samples using a decision tree. Numerical outcomes show that DL performs well concerning high attack recognition accuracy, which improves the reliability as well as security of 6G vehicle networks.

Vehicle networks and AD will significantly improve road safety, transportation quality, and vehicle energy efficiency. 6GTs will facilitate rigorous service requirements of AD applications regarding reliability besides high-speed communications [66, 96, 97]. For the reason that each vehicle is held as an entity with complete control and recognition in the networked vehicular system, it is critical to investigate V2V network performances to realize 6G AD fully. As a result, cooperative driving is enabled by information sharing and vehicle coordination, with DL serving as a natural solution for fast prediction of V2V communication performance restrictions for smart control of inter-vehicle spaces. EI is also critical for smart functions at the network edge, such as RSUs used to control AD systems [67]. AD controllers, for example, can be at edge servers within DL processors to train AD vehicular data for decision making and high-definition course-plotting. FL can also perform federated vehicular communications among vehicles and edge servers while protecting user privacy and reducing network overheads caused by crude data sharing [68].

4.3. 6G for UAVs

Many research efforts investigated applications of 6G-UAV networks. The work in [69] studies a cell-free drone network for wide-area 6G-IoMT focusing on UAV flight optimization by expressing a data diffusion efficiency maximization problem handling large-scale channel state evidence, on-board energy, and interference temperature restrictions. This method can also identify cell-free coverage patterns, which will allow for massive access to wide-area 6G-IoMT devices. A UAV-supported clustered nonorthogonal multiple access (C-NOMA) arrangement [71] for wireless powered communications in 6G-IoMT networks is as in [70]. Given the popularity of cluster IoMT terminals, a terminal clustering strategy with intracluster NOMA communications allows UAVs to send radio signals to IoMT terminals. By dividing the downlink energy transfer sub-slot and the uplink information transmission sub-slot, a synergetic optimal answer for route planning and sub-slot provision is derived. This aims to maximize the feasible sum rates of all IoMT terminals, as validated by numerical simulations. The UAV-to-ground channels involve arbitrary 3D trajectories for UAV-based 6G networks [72, 73].

A 3D nonstationary, geometric stochastic model accomplishes this using MIMO channel configuration with AD altitude distinctions and spatial consistency, in addition to 3D arbitrary trajectories. A collaborative multi-UAV resource scheduling and path optimization framework in a 6G-IoMT network appears in [72, 73]. Multiple UAVs serve as flying BSs to transfer energy to numerous terrestrial IoMT users. The design focuses on the relationship between UAVs and users, with a user association solution used to select the most suitable user to upload data to a particular UAV. The last objective is to optimize the average achievable rate across all VIoMT users in trajectory, sub-slot duration, and user transmission power. A joint algorithm established on relaxation and successive convex optimization methods solves the problem, demonstrating a higher rate than existing schemes. Similarly, [74] focuses on optimizing UAV transmission rates, with UAVs acting as mobile relays in NOMA-centered cognitive 6G-IoMT networks. A flexible approach allows optimal relay selection with higher transmission rates under fixed power.

Artificial Intelligence (AI) schemes can improve 6G-UAV networks with wireless communication, EC, and edge caching services [75]. AI techniques can predict future user and service area demands based on historical datasets of dislocations and user requests to control UAV mobility while keeping mission scheduling for trajectory planning. This optimizes UAV trajectories to save transmission power and improves QoE. Furthermore, data caching with DRL [76] helps create proactive edge data caching in UAV-IoMT networks based on data training and prediction competencies through learning along with feedback processes. FL can provide privacy-preserving intelligence for UAV-6G networks [77]. Each UAV runs a DL model and trades learned parameters with a MEC server for aggregation. A resource allocation problem accommodates federated data training in the UAV network with restricted batteries and bandwidth spectrum via a DRL algorithm. To facilitate UAV operations in 6G-IoMT networks, regulations guiding UAV deployment in IoMT systems, ensuring safety and privacy, should be put in place [78]. Furthermore, local licensing rules are important, especially when countries still define UAV manufacturers' spectrum access rights. Regulatory authorities must address critical issues in UAV integration into existing IoMT networks.

5. Future Directions

6GTs will revolutionize IoMT networks and services with network features like high reliability, ultra-low latency, and massive wireless coverage. However, incorporating 6G-IoMT networks may be susceptible to wireless interface attacks (e.g., unauthorized data access at computing units/servers), dangers to access network infrastructure integrity and denial of service (DoS) to both software and data centers [79]. For illustration, the diversity of IoMT devices and access mechanisms and massive device connectivity in large-scale IoMT access networks introduces new security challenges because handovers concerning different access technologies upsurge the attack risk. Eavesdropping, hijacking, spoofing, and DoS attacks may befall in data communications and management centers as the number of connections among devices and computing nodes at the network edge grows. Furthermore, intelligent 6GT-IoMT entails AI functions employing distributed edge nodes with data training in a spectrum access system that can be manipulated by introducing fake signals or modified parameters. Consequently, a malicious outbreak can illegitimately use a large portion of the spectrum by denying it to other users. Invaders can also exploit the distributed nature of data training and the reliance on EC to launch attacks such as malicious data embedding, data poisoning, or spoofing, which harm the training outputs that feed AI functions in 6G-IoMT structures. EI may also face security weaknesses due to the distributed AI functions at the network edge that cause data breaches or modifications.

In contrast, a function like remotely controlling and managing a 6G core network is limited [80]. Furthermore, deploying SAGU communications over untrustworthy environments can be hampered by data privacy leakage caused by third parties and adversaries during data exchange.

Risk mitigation must ensure high levels of security besides privacy for 6G-IoMT. e.g., via composition theorems with intricate mathematical solutions, perturbation methods viz. differential privacy or dummy help protect training datasets against information breaches in EI 6G-IoMT networks. Differential privacy can insert artificial noise into NN layer gradients to protect training data and hidden personal information from external threats while ensuring convergence [3, 81, 82]. A novel privacy-preserving data aggregation solution integrated into FC can satisfy differential privacy, so aggregation results are close to the actual outcomes. Hence, adversaries cannot extract the ground truth from exchanged gradients [98, 99]. Differential privacy can protect data under various budgets but can reduce training quality. Future research requires accuracy-aware differential privacy designs to balance training quality and privacy protection.

Blockchain is an auspicious solution for launching trust and secure decentralized communications employing VIoMT networks [82, 83, 98]. Each UAV can behave as a blockchain node partaking in decentralized data and communications. Lightweight mining mechanisms should deliver low-latency data consensus, given UAVs' resource constraints. This technique becomes more important for 6G because of large-scale decentralization, which suits blockchain.

5.1. Energy Efficiency

Achieving high energy efficiency in 6GT-IoMT is a significant concern. To ensure network operations, data communications, and service delivery services, such as vehicular data sharing in AD and packet delivery with UAV communications necessitate significant energy resources. Still, BS consumption implies that the deployment of huge 6G-IoMT networks results in colossal energy consumption, increasing carbon emissions. Green 6G-IoMT networks need energy-efficient communication protocols through optimization. QoS and energy consumption are optimized in 6G smart automation systems by implementing a 6G multimedia data structure model of QoS parameters like packet loss ratio and average transfer delay during energy-efficient multimedia transmission [83].

Energy harvesting by exploiting renewable energy resources would help develop green 6G-IoMT systems. For example, in [84], a solar energy harvesting solution for IoMT networks is considered, where implantable sensors can harvest solar power from sunlight to serve sensory data transmissions via a Bluetooth low-energy module in a transparent silicon housing for IoMT monitoring. Experiments using a wireless implantable sensor prototype with a solar panel and access point operating over a 10-minute cycle demonstrate stable energy harvesting while significantly increasing the IoMT system lifetime. Researchers should look into energy efficiency issues in higher-altitude 6G-IoMT networks, such as satellite networks with energy harvesting UAVs and BSs depending on device trajectories and environments [59-69].

5.2. IoMT Hardware Constraints

IoMT devices pose potential challenges in communications and computations in 6G-IoMT networks. Wearable sensors/ actuators and mobile devices should simultaneously use AI to achieve EI and implement data broadcasts with URLLC in intelligent 6G healthcare [85-89, 98]. Specific IoMT sensors/actuators cannot tackle computational requirements due to hardware, memory, and power resource constraints [112]. Data exchange among IoMT sensors, actuators, and the network server generates communication overheads, which grow in proportion to the task size and require new hardware designs for future smart IoMT devices. A software-based DL accelerator supporting data training on mobile sensor equipment appears in [86].

The key is to use a collection of heterogeneous processors (e.g., GPUs), with each computing unit utilizing distinct computational resources for different DL inference phases. This optimizes hardware utilization for data training while maintaining accuracy performance, which is made possible by two algorithms: runtime layer compression with a deep architecture decomposition. Compared to cloud offloading-based approaches, simulation results show that this approach has a better execution time and well-adjusted energy consumption in AI hardware executing with mobile inference for EI, allowing for on-device IoMT implementation. Furthermore, [87] considers a Tiny-transfer learning (TinyTL) scheme for memory-efficient on-device sensor learning. To make up for the capacity loss, a memory-efficient bias module known as the lite residual module is integrated, which improves model capacity by refining the feature extractor's intermediate feature maps with minimal memory overhead. Using image classification datasets, numerical simulations show that the anticipated on-device learning tactic can achieve competitive accuracy compared to traditional training solutions. More research is required to provide hardware-based AI training solutions on nano IoMT and embedded wearable devices in intelligent 6G-IoMT networks e.g. in ambient living assistance services [102, 103].

5.3. 6G-IoMT Specifications

Developing 6G-IoMT systems requires the collaboration of diverse stakeholders [88]. Lack of system standards may obstruct 6GTs implementations. Furthermore, introducing vertical 6G-IoMT use cases in intelligent networks necessitates major architectural changes to support diverse ranges of severe healthcare requirements.

Relying on vital services such as 6G servers with IoMT device communication protocols and network standards is essential in large-scale 6G-IoMT ecosystems [99-101]. The popular MODBUS [89] protocol connects computer servers, sensors, and actuators in IoMT environments allowing Remote Terminal Unit (RTU), TCP/IP, besides UDP. MODBUS employs mesh networking architectures for industrial communications and supervisory control over industrial radio bands. The European Telecommunications Standards Institute's Industry Specification Group released the ETSI Multi-access EC [90] to seamlessly leverage and integrate EC and edge-based IoMT applications from several providers [102, 103]. This scheme simplifies IoMT services like augmented/virtual reality, video analytics, data caching, and content delivery. Interested stakeholders should develop new standard specifications for new SAGU communications, such as further satellite communications critical for deploying new commercial IoMT applications [104, 105].

6. Conclusions

Because of its appealing traits compared to prior generations, 6G has lately sparked a lot of interest in both business and academia. This chapter examines 6G technologies opportunities to support IoMT networks through a comprehensive survey based on emerging research activities in the field. The lack of 6G-IoMT usage information motivates this work. This chapter first introduced recent advances in FL and IoMT recent and then identified and analyzed critical 6G-IoMT requirements enabling EI, RISs, space-air-ground-underwater communications, THz communications, blockchain, IoMT V IoMT, AD, and Medical FANETs (medical UAV comprising a networked swarm) [105-108]. Key technical characteristics and emerging 6G-IoMT cases have also been analyzed with potential challenges alongwith advising future research directions. 6G-IoMT research is still in its early stages, but 6G will transform current IoMT network infrastructures and introduce new service quality together with user experience expedients in future applications.

References

1. Al-Fuqaha, A., Guizani, M., Mohammadi, M., Aledhari, M., Ayyash, M. et al. (2015). Internet of Things: A survey on enabling technologies, protocols, and applications. IEEE Communications Surveys & Tutorials, 17(4), 2347-2376.
2. Chettri L. and Bera, R.A. (2020). Comprehensive Survey on Internet of Things (IoT) Toward 5G Wireless Systems. IEEE Internet of Things Journal (ITJ), 7(1), 16-32.
3. Nguyen, D.C., Ding, M., Pathirana, P.N., Seneviratne, A., Li, J. et al. (2021). 6G Internet of Things: A comprehensive survey. IEEE Access, 8, 133 995–134 030, 2020.
4. Bariah, L., Mohjazi, L.S., Muhaidat, S.H., Sofotasios, P.C., Kurt, G.K. et al. (2020). A prospective look: Key enabling technologies, applications and open research topics in 6G networks. IEEE Access, 8, 174792-174820.
5. Laghari, A.A., Khan, A., He, H., Estrela, V.V., Razmjooy, N., et al. (2020). Quality of experience (QoE) and quality of service (QoS) in UAV systems. *In:* Estrela, V.V. et al. (eds). Imaging and Sensing for Unmanned Aircraft Systems, 2(10), 213-242, IET, London, UK.
6. Estrela, V.V., Andreopoulos, N., Sroufer, R., Jesus, M.A., Mamani, W.D. et al. (2021). Transmedia Ecosystems, Quality of Experience and Quality of Service in Fog Computing for Comfortable Learning. Proc. 2021 IEEE EDUCON, 1003-1009.
7. Letaief, K.B., Chen, W., Shi, Y., Zhang, J., Zhang, Y.-J.A. et al. (2019). The roadmap to 6G: AI empowered wireless networks. IEEE Communications Magazine, 57(8), 84-90, Aug.
8. Chowdhury, M.Z., Shahjalal, M., Ahmed, S. and Jang, Y.M. (2020). 6G wireless communication systems: Applications, requirements, technologies, challenges, and research directions. IEEE Open Journal of the Communications Society, 1, 957-975.
9. Khan, L.U., Yaqoob, I., Imran, M., Han, Z., Hong, C.S. et al. (2020). 6G wireless

systems: A vision, architectural elements, and future directions. IEEE Access, 8, 147 029–147 044.

10. Jiang, W., Han, B., Habibi, M.A. and Schotten, H.D. (2021). The road towards 6G: A comprehensive survey. IEEE Open Journal of the Communications Society, 1-1.
11. Al-Jarrah, M.A., Yaseen, M.A., Al-Dweik, A., Dobre, O.A., Alsusa, E. et al. (2020). Decision fusion for IoT-based wireless sensor networks. IEEE ITJ, 7(2), 1313-1326.
12. Balghusoon, A.O. and Mahfoudh, S. (2020). Routing protocols for wireless nanosensor networks and Internet of nano things: A comprehensive survey. IEEE Access, 8, 200724-200748.
13. Soret, B., Leyva-Mayorga, I. and Popovski, P. (2019). Inter-plane satellite matching in dense LEO constellations. Proc. 2019 IEEE GLOBECOM, Waikoloa, HI, USA, Dec. 2019, 1-6.
14. Estrela, V.V., Hemanth, J., Saotome, O., Nikolakopoulos, G., Sabatini, R. et al. (2020). Introduction to advances in UAV avionics for imaging and sensing. *In:* Estrela, V.V. et al. (eds). Imaging and Sensing for Unmanned Aircraft Systems, 1(1), 1-22, IET, London, UK.
15. Wang, H., Zhao, H., Wu, W., Xiong, J., Ma, D., Wei, J. et al. (2019). Deployment algorithms of flying base stations: 5G and beyond with UAVs. IEEE ITJ, 6(6), 10009-10027.
16. Bertoli, G.C., Saotome, O. and Estrela, V.V. (2020). Computer vision in UAV using ROS. *In:* Estrela, V.V. et al. (eds). Imaging and Sensing for Unmanned Aircraft Systems, 1(9), 217-260, IET, London, UK.
17. Farfan, W.S., Saotome, O., Estrela, V.V. and Razmjooy, N. (2020). Integrated optical flow for situation awareness, detection and avoidance systems in UAV systems. *In:* Estrela, V.V. et al. (eds). Imaging and Sensing for Unmanned Aircraft Systems, 1(3), 4774, IET, London, UK.
18. Razmjooy, N., Estrela, V.V. and Sabatini, R. (2020). Vision in micro-aerial vehicles. *In:* Estrela, V.V. et al. (eds). Imaging and Sensing for Unmanned Aircraft Systems, Vol. 1(8), 173-216, IET, London, UK.
19. Estrela, V.V., Saotome, O., Loschi, H.J., Hemanth, D.J., Farfan, W.S. et al. (2018). Emergency response cyber-physical framework for landslide avoidance with sustainable electronics. Technologies, 6, 42.
20. Nasrallah, A. (2019). Ultra-low latency (ULL) networks: The IEEE TSN IETF DetNet standards and related 5G ULL research. IEEE Communications Surveys & Tutorials, 21(1), 88-145.
21. Lopez-Perez, D., Garcia-Rodriguez, A., Galati-Giordano, L., Kasslin, M., Doppler, K. et al. (2019). IEEE 802.11be extremely high throughput: The next generation of Wi-Fi technology beyond 802.11ax. IEEE Communications Magazine, 57(9), 113-119.
22. Li, Feng W., Wang, J., Chen, Y., Ge, N., Wang, C.-X. et al. (2020). Enabling 5G on the ocean: A hybrid satellite-UAV-terrestrial network solution. IEEE Wireless Communications, 27(6), 116-121.
23. Coll-Perales, B., Gozalvez, J. and Maestre, J.L. (2019). 5G and Beyond: Smart devices as part of the network fabric. IEEE Network, 33(4), 170-177.
24. Mohammadkarimi, M., Raza, M.A. and Dobre, O.A. (2018). Signature-based nonorthogonal massive multiple access for future wireless networks: uplink massive connectivity for machine-type communications. IEEE Vehicular Technology Magazine, 13(4), 40-50.
25. Shafique, K., Khawaja, B.A., Sabir, F., Qazi, S., Mustaqim, M. et al. (2020). Internet of Things (IoT) for next-generation smart systems: A review of current challenges, future trends and prospects for emerging 5GIoT scenarios. IEEE Access, 8, 23 022–23 040.

26. Han, S., Xie, T., Chai, L., Liu, Z., Yuan, Y. et al. (Oct. 2020). Artificial intelligence-enabled air interface for 6G: Solutions, challenges, and standardization impacts. IEEE Communications Magazine, 58(10), 73-79.

27. Deng, S., Zhao, H., Fang, W., Yin, J., Dustdar, S. et al. (2020). Edge intelligence: The confluence of edge computing and artificial intelligence. IEEE ITJ, 7(8), 7457-7469.

28. Xiao, Y., Shi, G., Li, Y., Saad, W. and Poor, H.V. (2020). Toward self-learning edge intelligence in 6G. IEEE Communications Magazine, 58(12), 34-40.

29. Nguyen, D.C., Pathirana, P.N., Ding, M. and Seneviratne, A. (2020). Blockchain and edge computing for decentralized EMRs Sharing in federated healthcare. Proc. 2020 IEEE Global Communications Conference, Taipei, Taiwan, Dec. 2020, 1-6.

30. Lv, Z., Lou, R., Li, J., Singh, A.K., Song et al. (Apr. 2021). Big data analytics for 6G-enabled massive Internet of Things. IEEE ITJ, 8(7), 5350-5359.

31. Yang, Z., Chen, M., Wong, K.-K., Poor, H.V., Cui, S. et al. (2021). Federated learning for 6G: Applications, challenges, and opportunities. arXiv: 2101.01338.

32. Qu, Y., Dong, C., Zheng, J., Wu, Q., Shen, Y. et al. (2020). Empowering the edge intelligence by air-ground integrated federated learning in 6G Networks. arXiv: 2007.13054.

33. Chen, G., He, S., Meng, H. and Huang, K. (2020). PhoneBit: Efficient GPU accelerated binary neural network inference engine for mobile phones. Proc. 2020 Design, Automation & Test in Europe Conf. & Exhibition (DATE), Grenoble, France, Mar., 786-791.

34. Gouidis, F., Panteleris, P., Oikonomidis, I. and Argyros, A. (May 2019). Accurate hand keypoint localization on mobile devices. Proc. 16th International Conference on Machine Vision Applications (MVA), Tokyo, Japan. 1-6.

35. Di Renzo, M., Zappone, A., Debbah, M., Alouini, M., Yuen, C. et al. (2020). Smart radio environments empowered by reconfigurable intelligent surfaces: How it works, state of research, and the road ahead. IEEE J. Sel. Areas in Comm. (JSAC), 38(11), 2450-2525.

36. Huang, C., Hu, S., Alexandropoulos, G.C., Zappone, A., Yuen, C. et al. (2020). Holographic MIMO surfaces for 6G wireless networks: Opportunities, challenges, and trends, IEEE Wir. Comm., 27(5), 118-125.

37. Zeng, S., Zhang, H., Di, B., Tan, Y., Han, Z. et al. (2021). Reconfigurable intelligent surfaces in 6G: Reflective, transmissive, or both? IEEE Comm. Lett., 25(6), 2063-2067.

38. Kisseleff, S., Martins, W.A., Al-Hraishawi, H., Chatzinotas, S., Ottersten, B. et al. (2020). Reconfigurable intelligent surfaces for smart cities: Research challenges and opportunities. IEEE Open Journal of the Communications Society, 1, 1781-1797.

39. Makarfi, A.U., Rabie, K.M., Kaiwartya, O., Li, X., Kharel, R. et al. (May 2020). Physical layer security in vehicular networks with reconfigurable intelligent surfaces. Proc. IEEE 91st Vehicular Technology Conference (VTC2020-Spring), Antwerp, Belgium, 1-6.

40. Hu, J., Zhang, H., Di, B., Li, L., Bian, K. et al. (2020). Reconfigurable intelligent surface based RF sensing: Design, optimization, and implementation. IEEE JSAC, 38(11), 2700-2716.

41. Zhang, S., Zhang, H. and Song, L. (2020). Beyond D2D: Full dimension UAV-to-everything communications in 6G. IEEE Trans. on Veh. Techn., 69(6), 6592-6602.

42. Han, C., Wu, Y., Chen, Z. and Wang, X. (Dec. 2019). Terahertz Communications (TeraCom): Challenges and impact on 6G wireless systems. arXiv: 1912.06040.

43. Rappaport, T.S., Xing, Y., Kanhere, O., Ju, S., Madanayake, A. et al. (2019). Wireless communications and applications above 100 GHz: Opportunities and challenges for 6G and beyond. IEEE Access, 7, 78 729–78 757.

44. Busari, S.A., Huq, K.M., Mumtaz, S., Rodriguez, J., Fang, Y. et al. (2019). Generalized hybrid beamforming for vehicular connectivity using THz massive MIMO. IEEE Trans. Veh. Techn., 68(9), 8372- 8383.
45. Loschi, H.J., Estrela, V.V., Hemanth, D.J., Fernandes, S.R., Iano, Y. et al. (2020). Communications requirements, video streaming, communications links and networked UAVs. *In:* Estrela, V.V. et al. (eds). Imaging and Sensing for Unmanned Aircraft Systems, Vol. 2(6), 113-132, IET, London, UK.
46. Lien, S.-Y., Hung, S.-C., Deng, D.-J. and Wang, Y.J. (Dec. 2017). Efficient ultra reliable and low latency communications and massive machinetype communications in 5G new radio. 2017 IEEE Global Communications Conference, Singapore, 1-7.
47. Nguyen, D.C., Cheng, P., Ding, M., Lopez-Perez, D., Pathirana, P.N. et al. (2021). Enabling AI in future wireless networks: A data life cycle perspective. IEEE Comm. Surv. & Tut., 23(1), 553-595.
48. She, C., Dong, R., Gu, Z., Hou, Z., Li, Y. et al. (2020). Deep learning for ultra-reliable and low latency communications in 6G networks. IEEE Networks, 34(5), 219-225.
49. Li, Z., Uusitalo, M.A., Shariatmadari, H. and Singh, B. (Aug. 2018). 5G URLLC: Design challenges and system concepts. Proc. 15th International Symposium on Wireless Communication Systems (ISWCS), Lisbon, 1-6.
50. Nguyen, D.C., Pathirana, P.N., Ding, M. and Seneviratne, A. (2020). Blockchain for 5G and beyond networks: A state of the art survey. J. Network and Computer Applications, 166, 102693.
51. Sekaran, R., Patan, R., Raveendran, A., Al-Turjman, F., Ramachandran, M. et al. (2020). Survival study on blockchain based 6G-enabled mobile edge computation for IoT automation. IEEE Access, 8, 143453-143463.
52. Nguyen, D.C., Pathirana, P.N., Ding, M. and Seneviratne, A. (2019). Blockchain for secure EHRs sharing of mobile cloud based E-health systems. IEEE Access, 7, 66 792– 66 806.
53. Nayak, S. and Patgiri, R. (2021) 6G communication technology: A vision on intelligent healthcare. *In:* Patgiri, R., Biswas, A., Roy, P. (eds). Health informatics: A computational perspective in healthcare. Studies in Computational Intelligence, 932, 1-18, Springer, Singapore.
54. Cisotto, G., Casarin, E. and Tomasin, S. (2020). Requirements and enablers of advanced healthcare services over future cellular systems. IEEE Communications Magazine, 58(3), 76-81.
55. Hadi, M.S., Lawey, A.Q., El-Gorashi, T.H.E. and Elmirghani, J.M.H. (2020). Patient-centric HetNets powered by machine learning and big data analytics for 6G networks. IEEE Access, 8, 85639-85655.
56. Sodhro, A.H., Zahid, N., Wang, L., Pirbhulal, S., Ouzrout, Y. et al. (2021). Toward ML-based energy-efficient mechanism for 6G enabled industrial network in box systems. IEEE Trans. Industrial Informatics, 17, 7185-7192.
57. Siriwardhana, Y., Gür, G., Ylianttila, M. and Liyanage, M. (2020). The role of 5G for digital healthcare against COVID-19 pandemic: Opportunities and challenges. ICT Express, 7, 244-252.
58. Nguyen, D., Ding, M., Pathirana, P.N. and Seneviratne, A. (2020). Blockchain and AI-based Solutions to Combat Coronavirus (COVID-19)-like Epidemics: A Survey.
59. Kalalas, C. and Alonso-Zarate, J. (2020). Massive connectivity in 5G and beyond: Technical enablers for the energy and automotive verticals. Proc. 2nd 6G Wireless Summit (6G SUMMIT), Levi, Finland, 1-5.
60. Sliwa, B., Falkenberg, R. and Wietfeld, C. (2020). Towards cooperative data rate prediction for future mobile and vehicular 6G networks. Proc. 2nd 6G Wireless Summit (6G SUMMIT), Levi, Finland, 1-5.

61. Yuan, W., Li, S., Xiang, L. and Ng, D.W.K. (2020). Distributed estimation framework for beyond 5G intelligent vehicular networks. IEEE Open Journal of Vehicular Technology, 1, 190-214.

62. Li, C., Guo, W., Sun, S.C., Al-Rubaye, S. and Tsourdos, A. (2020). Trustworthy deep learning in 6G-enabled mass autonomy: From concept to quality-of-trust key performance indicators. IEEE Vehicular Technology Magazine, 15(4), 112-121.

63. Nguyen, D.C., Pathirana, P.N., Ding, M. and Seneviratne, A. (Dec. 2020). Privacy preserved task offloading in mobile blockchain with deep reinforcement learning, IEEE Trans. Network and Service Management, 17(4), 2536-2549.

64. Sliwa, B., Adam, R. and Wietfeld, C. (2021). Client-based intelligence for resource efficient vehicular big data transfer in future 6G networks. IEEE Transactions on Vehicular Technology, 1-1.

65. Zhang, Z., Cao, Y., Cui, Z., Zhang, W., Chen, J. et al. (2021). A many-objective optimization based intelligent intrusion detection algorithm for enhancing security of vehicular networks in 6G. IEEE Trans. Vehicular Technology, 70, 5234-5243.

66. Chen, X., Leng, S., He, J. and Zhou, L. (2020). Deep learning based intelligent inter-vehicle distance control for 6G-enabled cooperative autonomous driving, IEEE ITJ, 1-1.

67. He, J., Yang, K. and Chen, H.-H. (2020). 6G cellular networks and connected autonomous vehicles. IEEE Networks, 1-7.

68. Niknam, S., Dhillon, H.S. and Reed, J.H. (Jun. 2020). Federated learning for wireless communications: Motivation, opportunities, and challenges. IEEE Communications Magazine, 58(6), 46-51.

69. Liu, C., Feng, W., Chen, Y., Wang, C., Ge, N. et al. (2021). Cell-free satellite-UAV networks for 6G wide-area Internet of Things. IEEE JSAC, 39, 1116-1131.

70. Na, Z., Liu, Y., Shi, J., Liu, C., Gao, Z. et al. (2020). UAV-supported clustered NOMA for 6G-enabled Internet of Things: Trajectory planning and resource allocation, IEEE ITJ, 1-1.

71. Islam, S.M.R., Avazov, N., Dobre, O.A. and Kwak, K.-S. (2017). PowerDomain non-orthogonal multiple access (NOMA) in 5G systems: Potentials and challenges. IEEE Communications Surveys & Tutorials, 19(2), 721-742.

72. Chang, H., Wang, C., Liu, Y., Huang, J., Sun, J. et al. (2021). A novel nonstationary 6G UAV-to-ground wireless channel model with 3-D arbitrary trajectory changes. IEEE Internet of Things Journal, 8, 9865-9877.

73. Wang, J., Na, Z. and Liu, X. (2021). Collaborative design of multi-UAV trajectory and resource scheduling for 6G-enabled Internet of Things. IEEE Internet of Things Journal, 8, 15096-15106.

74. Huang, H., Hu, S., Yang, T. and Yuan, C. (2021). Full-duplex nonorthogonal multiple access with layers-based optimized mobile relays subsets algorithm in B5G/6G ubiquitous networks. IEEE Internet of Things Journal, 8, 15081-15095.

75. Dong, C., Shen, Y., Qu, Y., Wu, Q., Wu, F. et al. (2021). UAVs as an intelligent service: Boosting edge intelligence for air-ground integrated networks. IEEE Network, 35, 167-175.

76. Dai, Y., Xu, D., Zhang, K., Maharjan, S., Zhang, Y. et al. (Apr. 2020). Deep reinforcement learning and permissioned blockchain for content caching in vehicular edge computing and networks. IEEE Transactions on Vehicular Technology, 69(4), 4312-4324.

77. Tang, S., Zhou, W., Chen, L., Lai, L., Xia, J., Fan, L. et al. (2021). Battery constrained Federated Edge Learning in UAV-enabled IoT for B5G/6G networks. Physical Communication, p. 101381.

78. Ullah, Z., Al-Turjman, F. and Mostarda, L. (Sep. 2020). Cognition in UAV-aided 5G and beyond communications: A survey. IEEE Transactions on Cognitive Communications and Networking, 6(3), 872-891.
79. Porambage, P., Gur, G., Osorio, D.P., Liyanage, M., Gurtov, A.V. et al. (2021). The roadmap to 6G security and privacy. IEEE Open Journal of the Communications Society, 2, 1094-1122.
80. Wang, M., Zhu, T., Zhang, T., Zhang, J., Yu, S. et al. (Aug. 2020). Security and privacy in 6G networks: New areas and new challenges. Digital Communications and Networks, 6(3), 281-291.
81. Yang, M., Zhu, T., Liu, B., Xiang, Y., Zhou, W. et al. (2018). Machine learning differential privacy with multifunctional aggregation in a fog computing architecture. IEEE Access, 6, 17119–17129.
82. Al-Turjman, F.M., Imran, M. and Bakhsh, S.T. (2017). Energy efficiency perspectives of femtocells in Internet of Things: Recent advances and challenges. IEEE Access, 5, 26 808–26 818.
83. Sodhro, A.H., Pirbhulal, S., Zongwei, L., Muhammad, K., Zahid, N. et al. (2020). Towards 6G architecture for energy efficient communication in IoT-enabled smart automation systems. IEEE ITJ, 1-1.
84. Wu, T., Redoute, J.-M. and Yuce, M.R. (2018). A wireless implantable sensor design with subcutaneous energy harvesting for long-term IoT healthcare applications. IEEE Access, 6, 35 801–35 808.
85. Yang, X., Matthaiou, M., Yang, J., Wen, C.-K., Gao, F. et al. (Jan. 2019). Hardware-constrained millimeter-wave systems for 5G: Challenges, opportunities, and solutions. IEEE Communications Magazine, 57(1), 44-50.
86. Lane, N.D., Bhattacharya, S., Georgiev, P., Forlivesi, C., Jiao, L. et al. (2016). DeepX: A software accelerator for low power deep learning inference on mobile devices. Proc. 15th ACM/IEEE International Conf. Information Processing in Sensor Networks (IPSN), Vienna, Austria, Apr. 2016, 1-12.
87. Cai, H., Gan, C., Zhu, L., Han, S., Tiny, T.L. (2020). Reduce memory, not parameters for efficient on-device learning. Adv. in Neural Inf. Processing Systems, 33.
88. Yeo, J., Kim, T., Oh, J., Park, S., Kim, Y. et al. (Sep. 2019). Advanced data transmission framework for 5G wireless communications in the 3GPP new radio standard. IEEE Communications Standards Magazine, 3(3), 38-43.
89. Yuanyuan, Y. and Meng, C. (Dec. 2020). An improved algorithm for adaptive communication frame length based on modbus protocol. Proc. IEEE 6th International Conference on Computer and Communications (ICCC), Chengdu, China, 132-135.
90. Rayani, M., Glitho, R.H. and Elbiaze, H. (Dec. 2020). ETSI multi-access edge computing for dynamic adaptive streaming in information centric networks. Proc. 2020 IEEE Global Communications Conference, 1-6.
91. Arshaghi, A., Razmjooy, N., Estrela, V.V., Burdziakowski, P., Nascimento, D.A. et al. (2020). Image transmission in UAV MIMO UWB-OSTBC system over Rayleigh channel using multiple description coding (MDC). *In:* Estrela, V.V. et al. (eds). Imaging and Sensing for Unmanned Aircraft Systems, 2(4), 67-90, IET, London, UK, doi: 10.1049/PBCE120G_ch4.
92. Ayub Khan, Abdullah, Laghari, A.A., Shaikh, A., Dootio, M. et al. (2021). A blockchain security module for brain-computer interface (BCI) with multimedia life cycle framework (MLCF). Neuroscience Informatics. 100030. 10.1016/j.neuri.2021.100030.
93. Baloch, J.A., Jumani, A.K., Laghari, A.A., Estrela, V.V., Lopes, R.T. et al. (2021). A preliminary study on quality of experience assessment of compressed audio file format. Proc. 2021 IEEE URUCON, 161-165, doi: 10.1109/URUCON53396.2021.9647114.

94. Deshpande, A., Patavardhan, P. and Estrela, V.V. (2020). Super resolution and recognition of unconstrained ear image. International Journal of Biometrics, Inderscience, 12(4), 396-410. doi: 10.1504/IJBM.2020.110813

95. Deshpande, A., Patavardhan, P., Estrela, V.V. and Razmjooy, N. (2020). Deep learning as an alternative to super-resolution imaging in UAV systems. *In:* Estrela, V.V. et al. (eds). Imaging and Sensing for Unmanned Aircraft Systems, 2(9), 177-212, IET, London, UK.

96. Monteiro, A.C.B., Franca, R.P., Estrela, V.V., Fernandes, S.R., Khelassi, A. et al. (2020). UAV-CPSs as a test bed for new technologies and a primer to Industry 5.0. *In:* Estrela, V.V. et al. (eds). Imaging and Sensing for Unmanned Aircraft Systems, 2(1), 1-22, IET, London, UK.

97. Aroma, R.J., Raimond, K., Razmjooy, N., Estrela, V.V., Hemanth, J. et al. (2020). Multispectral vs. hyperspectral imaging for unmanned aerial vehicles: Current and prospective state of affairs. *In:* Estrela, V.V. et al. (eds). Imaging and Sensing for Unmanned Aircraft Systems, 2(7), 133-156, IET, London, UK.

98. Razmjooy, N., Deshpande, A., Khalilpour, M., Estrela V.V., Padilha R. et al. (2021). Optimal bidding strategy for power market based on improved world cup optimization algorithm. *In:* Razmjooy, N., Ashourian, M., Foroozandeh, Z. (eds). Metaheuristics and Optimization in Computer and Electrical Engineering. Lecture Notes in Electrical Engineering, 696. Springer, Cham.

99. Gupta, R., Sampath, V., Nadeau, K.C. and Maecker, H.T. (2020). Large scale, complex biobanking of biofluids for immunology research and testing. Authorea. doi: 10.22541/au.159551291.16418253

100. Martinez, D.A., Loening, U.E., Graham, M.C. and Gathorne-Hardy, A. (2021). When the medicine feeds the problem: Do nitrogen fertilisers and pesticides enhance the nutritional quality of crops for their pests and pathogens? Front. Sust. Food Syst. doi: 10.3389/fsufs.2021.701310

101. Costa, T.L., Mazzochini, G.G., Oliveira-Filho, A.T., Ganade, G., Carvalho, A.R. et al. (2021). Priority areas for restoring ecosystem services to enhance human well-being in a dry forest. Restoration Ecology, 29.

102. Kaushik, A.K., Khan, R., Solanki, P.R., Gandhi, S., Gohel, H. et al. (2021). From nanosystems to a biosensing prototype for an efficient diagnostic: Special issue honoring Prof. Bansi D. Malhotra. Biosensors, 11.

103. Manga, J.E. and Sonti, V.J. (2022). Internet of Things-empowered next-generation healthcare systems. *In:* Integrating AI in IoT Analytics on the Cloud for Healthcare Applications. pp. 18. DOI: 10.4018/978-1-7998-9132-1

104. Jia, Z., Sheng, M., Li, J., Niyato, D.T., Han, Z. et al. (2021). LEO-satellite-assisted UAV: Joint trajectory and data collection for Internet of remote things in 6G aerial access networks. IEEE Internet of Things Journal, 8, 9814-9826.

105. Li, M., Lei, J., Wang, Z., Dong, J., Chen, Q. et al. (2021). Deformation monitoring in the central route of south-to-north water diversion project using multiple space-air-ground technologies. Proc. 3rd International Academic Exchange Conference on Science and Technology Innovation (IAECST), 2051-2060.

106. Mao, B., Tang, F., Kawamoto, Y. and Kato, N. (2021). Optimizing computation offloading in Satellite-UAV-Served 6G IoT: A deep learning approach. IEEE Network, 35, 102-108.

107. Middleton, W.T., Miller, G.A. and Pollman, A.G. (2019). Architecture Models for Coordination of Unmanned Air and Ground Vehicles Conducting Humanitarian Assistance and Disaster Relief. *In:* Adams, S., Beling, P., Lambert, J., Scherer, W., Fleming, C. (eds). Systems Engineering in Context. Springer, Cham.

108. Sarim, M., Radmanesh, M., Dechering, M., Kumar, M., Pragada, R.V. et al. (2019). Distributed detect-and-avoid for multiple unmanned aerial vehicles in national air space. J. Dyn. Syst., Meas., and Cont. 141(7): 071014.

109. Estrela, V.V. and Galatsanos, N.P. (2000). Spatially adaptive regularized pel-recursive motion estimation based on the EM algorithm. Proc. SPIE 3974, Image and Video Communications and Processing 2000. doi: 10.1117/12.382969

110. Estrela, V.V., de Jesus, M.A., Aroma, J., Raimond, K., Fernandes, S.R. et al. (2021). Motion estimation role in the context of 3D video. Int'l J. Multimedia Data Eng. and Management (IJMDEM), 12(3), 16-38. doi: 10.4018/IJMDEM.291556

111. Estrela, V.V. and Galatsanos, N.P. (1998). Spatially-adaptive regularized pel-recursive motion estimation based on cross-validation. Proc. IEEE ICIP 98, Chicago, IL, USA, IEEE.

112. Wang, K., Xu, P., Chen, C., Kumari, S., Shojafar, M. et al. (2021). Neural architecture search for robust networks in 6G-enabled massive IoT domain. IEEE Internet of Things Journal, 8, 5332-5339.

Part II
Infrastructural Medical Applications

Remote Sensing Applications in Disease Mapping and Public Health Analysis

Vania V. Estrela[1] [0000-0002-4465-7691], Jenice Aroma[2] [0000-0003-4022-1898], Robert Sroufer[3] [0000-0002-7903-9180], Kumudha Raimond[2] [0000-0001-8680-8390], Aline C. Intorne[4,5] [0000-0001-8015-6926], Anand Deshpande[6] [0000-0002-1500-0981], Asif A. Laghari[7] [0000-0001-5831- 5943], Luciana P. Oliveira[8] [0000-0002-3375-3346]

[1] Department of Telecommunications, Federal Fluminense University (UFF), RJ, 24220-900, Brazil, vania.estrela.phd@ieee.org

[2] Department of Computer Science & Engineering, Karunya Institute of Technology & Sciences, India, jenicearoma@gmail.com, kraimond@karunya.edu

[3] Operations Management, Palumbo Donahue School of Business Management, 820 Rockwell Hall, PA, USA, sroufer@duq.edu

[4] Laboratory of Physiology and Biochemistry of Microorganisms, Universidade Estadual do Norte Fluminense Darcy Ribeiro, Campos dos Goytacazes, RJ, 28013-602, Brazil

[5] Laboratory of Chemistry and Biology, Instituto Federal de Educação, Ciência e Tecnologia do Rio de Janeiro, Volta Redonda, RJ, 27213-100, Brazil, aline.intorne@ifrj.edu.br

[6] Electronics and Communication Engineering, Angadi Institute of Technology and Management, Belagavi, India, deshpande.anandb@gmail.com

[7] Faculty of Computer Science, Sindh Madressatul Islam University, Karachi (74000), Sindh, Pakistan, asif.laghari@smiu.edu.pk

[8] IFPB Campus Joao Pessoa, Av. Primeiro de Maio, 720, Jaguaribe, Joao Pessoa, PB, Brazil, oliveira.ifpb@gmail.com

1. Introduction

Remote Sensing (RS) scans the Earth's surface with sensors mounted on a satellite or drone, in order to collect data for monitoring the changes in land use and cover [1-3]. The perceived land cover utilization and alterations are mostly evolutionary environmental interactions. The orbiting satellites could view the Earth in a variety of geographic sizes and intervals or return periods, which are altogether denoted by various spatial and temporal resolutions. Over time, significant innovations in spatial and temporal resolution have been made, accompanied by an upsurge in the visibility and readiness of collected pictures, followed by the increase in an augmented number of spectral bands from sensors, contributing to the creation of aesthetically pleasing images to human eyes [4, 5]. Research and Development efforts must gain much more attention towards these enhanced RS technologies. The introduction of Geospatial maps/cartography maps which are RS-derived data marks the beginning of an era of digital infrastructure in numerous dependent applications. The neighborhood maps developed are utilized for Disease spread mapping to many E-commerce applications. An effective way to mitigate healthcare problems is to visualize the outbreak by building thematic maps. This requires appropriate handling of all sorts of feature-level imagery fusion approaches and changing detection methodologies for tracking the extent of transformation within a region over a chosen period. Suitable Image Quality Assessment (IQA) metrics have been adopted to offer a quantitative image assessment that can provide better epidemiology diagnoses. The outcomes reached by superimposing various images, wavelets, and other reduced feature descriptors can greatly render the real change visualization of a chosen terrain. Thus, even nonexpert remote sensing RS users were attracted to remote sensing by the stunning images and accessibility of some of the final products. As a result, the application of RS Data Products (RSDPs) by different disciplines and research fields was inflated. In PH, RS data products were widely accepted and employed in DME, with illness maps being described as abstract representations of complex geographic data, that offers a panoramic perspective of disease spread in a specific geographic region [6-8].

By contrast, epidemiology examines the incidence, distribution, and tactics for illness prevention and mitigation, as well as other aspects of human and animal health, i.e., the root of a disease outbreak that often changes in frequency and geography. As investigators tried to explicate ecological and climatic variables, this regional variance created a RS niche in PH. In view of that, RS assesses the Earth's surface in panoramic views, which has been used in disease mapping for quick risk assessment and monitoring activities. As a result, RSPs have been widely distributed and utilized in DME for a stretched period. RSDPs involve a variety of environmental and vegetation index elements obtained from satellite imagery and used to decipher changes in land use and cover, as well as estimate climatic and biological conditions on the Earth's surface. Vegetation indices are mathematically combined spectral bands that are used to numerically split or stretch the pixel values of various picture elements to trace the health or changes of underlying vegetation [9]. RS vegetation indices have functioned in a manner comparable to environmental and weather proxies in an infinite number of DME research mechanisms to date, in conjunction with a variety of modeling techniques [16]. RDSPs have handled a variety of DME researches, including risk mapping for soil-passed on helminths [10, 11], malaria [12], schistosomiases, and the prediction of leishmaniasis high-risk zones in Brazil. Previous works have been included combining RS data into PH studies in addition to spatial targeting [13] through the development of a national risk map and habitat suitability mapping for tsetse fly [14]. Additionally, for a given disease like cholera, ecological causes of threats were identified through satellite-derived RSDPs [15].

A city's population density can be determined well using a GeoEye satellite picture with a resolution of 50 meters. The quantity of dwellings and the average amount of occupants per house results in the computation of the populations of cities. The primary benefits of RSPs for DME include near real-time evaluation and prediction of disease dissemination in high-risk areas, particularly in remote places that, likewise, may lack baseline information [17]. The increased deployment of high-resolution satellite sensors and advancements in data processing actions have facilitated the widespread usage of RSDPs [18]. In underprivileged whereabouts with sparse, land-based, networked climatological stations. RS data was frequently favored and employed as environmental and climatic proxies in DME risk assessments and prediction [19].

Primary ecological analyses proved the RSDPs' disease mapping potential [19-22], and similar DME research keeps on proliferating. Geostatistics distinguishes geographic heterogeneities in disease distributions, patterns, and trends, besides conjecturing the purpose of preparing epidemic preparation [23, 24]. Geostatistics examines geographical and temporal quantities [23]. It is frequently included in spatial modeling via coordinates associated with the examined data in biostatistics, which deals with biological data. Thus, these models are deemed as space-time models, owing to the fact that they slot in observation dates in the mapped data. The rationale for including RS data into DME was based on field notes connecting environmental variables with certain disease-causing vectors [24-26], markedly the spatial distinctions. As a case in point, several studies have made known a link between satellite-measured radiation reflectance and certain land cover categories utilized as environmental and climatic proxies for disease and vector detections [27].

By incorporating RSDPs into aerial spatial modeling, photos captured aboard drones and airplanes used to deploy high-resolution imaging sensors may be analyzed. RSDPs have remained at the frontline of scientific studies into the changes in the Earth's Land usage and Land cover (LULC). The RSDP usage, principally in DME, has been widespread throughout the years, for example, in mapping Vector-Borne Diseases (VBDs). Many RS-derived products have been widely used in models as environmental proxies to study a variety of spatial phenomena patterns. Additionally, environmental proxies were used as variables in statistical models to map, analyze, and forecast spatial DME phenomena.

Disease analysis in RS statistical models relied on altering models using geographical variables. It was regressed on whichever outcome of interest utilizing data variables was acquired from RSDPs. As a result, RS environmental factors in addition to proxies in disease spread mapping statistical analysis models, e.g., dengue fever, chikungunya fever, zika virus, malaria, and leishmaniasis, have been augmented dramatically [28]. RSDPs were frequently used as environmental proxies in studies mapping the regional distribution of such VBDs, mimicking either environmental circumstances or land usage/variables. Occasionally, spatial variables are denoted as predictors or risk aspects because of the illness brutality correlations, as proven in some early ecological revisions, demonstrating RSDPs disease mapping potentials. For instance, malaria has been referred to multiple times as an environmental illness. Research on malaria risk mapping has been driven by identifying ecological risk factors connected with the disease [29].

Early usage of RSDPs was limited by the slow first-generation computer processing capacities and the absence of convenient storage for huge dimensional raw RS data sets. Later on, the introduction of fast processing supercomputers enabled the inclusion of RS data in mapping studies. Additionally, storage capabilities of geographic data sets have also been increased. Further, the open access for RSDPs, especially those intended for civilian use, piqued the scientific community's attention and promoted the RS DME adoption and implementation for research purposes. Hence, RSDPs turn into one of the most significant adoption reasons for representing disease risk dispersal in locations with a scarcity of ground-based ecological data gathering stations. Those isolated places encompassed harsh terrain, armed conflicts, and insufficient resources for research, when ground-based weather stations were employed, were frequently constrained by data inconsistencies due to human interference/error, equipment jamming, or even power failure. This recurrently missing data in RS records due to failure in gathering observations on days of bad meteorological conditions have led to the failure of land station observations. Oftentimes, missing data values require complex data duplication procedures during data processing and analysis. As a result, RSDPs provide more dependability and availability in near real-time than other data sources, which have the need for manual surveys and are, hence, prohibitively expensive to replicate. Section 2 overviews how RS can aid local and global medicine. Discussion and future work appear in Section 3. Finally, conclusions appear in Section 4.

2. Mapping Environmental Diseases

The majority of DME studies [21-27] identified environmental VBD components based on recognized scientific data associated with the condition of concern. Currently, an increasing number of DME research works are utilizing environmental and meteorological data to map and forecast disease dispersion in specific geographic regions. These studies can aid in guiding and targeting PH intervention deployment in regions identified as having a high prevalence of the mapped illness. Drones have recently increased the accessibility of photogrammetry for PH activities [30-33]. The motivation for this technology is illustrated in Figure 1, i.e., to photograph the land and create a mosaic that transforms tiny photos into a lengthy panoramically improved landscape portrayal by utilizing the visible and/or infrared (IR) sections of the electromagnetic spectrum.

As the resolutions of RS sensors (both spatial and temporal) improved since the technology's inception, interest and confidence in their data outputs increased among professionals. While computer power and storage are concerns, sensors with insufficient spectral bands impair realistic trait detection. With sensors, the spectral bands record the electromagnetic spectrum's wavelengths. Sensor spectral bands have recently increased in resolution and assisted in the presentation of multicolor images during feature analysis and identification. These advancements in image processing, visualization, and rendering have bolstered mapping efforts and discoveries by providing additional information and a more appealing appearance.

Prospecting efforts in sensors and actuators herald a revolutionary change in which things may be accomplished simply and effectively through good communication. On the other hand, the internet of things (IoT), as well as the Internet of Medical Things (IoMT), have exploded in popularity due to their massive potential and ubiquity. Numerous algorithms and a sophisticated data treatment

Figure 1. Photogrammetry in remote sensing

methodology have been utilized to implement the sensing system's data acquisition and transmission to the receiving end. Technically, it is referred to as telediagnosis and remote digital monitoring, a medical and artificial intelligence (AI) revolution. An important concept is theragnostics, which combines diagnostic tests with therapy and, in future, it will also work and be aided by remote sensing setups. A proof of concept (PoC) was constructed using an algorithm for telediagnosis of degenerative illnesses like Parkinson's disease. Incorporating data collected by an enhanced array of linked electrode monitoring surfaces can assist in achieving high sensitivity. The linear regression value of coefficients were used to determine the limitations and plusses of detection. Additional validation was done and attested to the coordination using the defined algorithm and data processing with the aid of IoT, IoMT, and RS communications. This well-established presumption may be employed optimally with all sensing strategies to afford instantaneous telemedicine via end-to-end communications.

These RS and sensor technology advancements in disease mapping enabled the spatial heterogeneity possibility even at small or local scales. These seminal discoveries in disease mapping enabled epidemiologists to identify critical disease risk factors and hence lead to control strategies more effectively and on the basis of evidence. The prices of RSDPs had been dramatically decreased by the addition of sensors, stabilization of data needs, and dependence on a small number of RS agents. Satellites have been launched into orbit by a rising number of nations and commercial enterprises. The resulting RSPs are freely available to the research community [34], allowing spatial analysts to conduct time series breakdowns, data mining, and other approaches. Additionally, RSPs may generate and include vegetation indices in maps and models, allowing for interpretation by researchers who are not RS specialists. The Normalized Difference Vegetation Index (NDVI), temperature, and rainfall are frequently offered or stored, providing easy and direct access from hosting organizations and websites to include them in interoperable DME models. Advances in mapping software (SW), notably in GIS, sparked interest among disease researchers and epidemiologists. While previous initiatives were primarily targeted at RS professionals, the advent of tailored mapping platforms for spatial DME SW may provide non-RS experts an opportunity. PH studies can be used to help in the creation and modification of SW (e.g., Health Mapper, Epi-Info, and ESRI ArcGIS) to aid with DME initiatives. Again, when more open-source software became accessible, the high prices associated with some commercial software were decreased. For example, open-source GIS software such as QGIS might be downloaded for free access. Additionally, real color visualization web-based SW such as Google Earth kindled the interest in spatial mapping even for novices because of its simplicity. These upgrades of RS technology have raised the excitement around disease mapping, quick risk assessment, and prediction among epidemiologists. In this manner, clinical researchers and professionals may directly address problems concerning disease epidemiology, such as clustering, severity fluctuation, and illness occurrence. Extended mapping and environmental/climatic data analysis can be performed using statistical software packages (e.g., STATA, WINBUGS, and R). Geostatistics is a branch of statistics that integrates geography and statistics with spatial analysis in order to handle and evaluate RS climate data. Statistical software was often utilized in disease risk mapping with respect to space and time analysis. They were frequently utilized in the prediction of DME risks, with mathematical models attempting to describe the causative processes and quantities involved in disease risk modeling. Geostatistics has given crucial advantages in the application and implementation of RSDPs into DME at present while entailing the development of algorithms capable of forecasting disease jeopardies in space and time. This means that control programs could be notified about disease risks in advance, making them better equipped to deal with outbreaks. In comparison to past calculation attempts on comparable data, Markov Chain Monte Carlo (MCMC) and the Integrated Laplace Approximation (INLA) can broadly simulate data to estimate the posterior distribution of RS data in space and time within all-encompassing time frames. MCMC techniques take samples from a probability distribution and utilize simulation to determine a posterior distribution from which to take samples. Rather than that, INLA expends analytical combinations to approximate and combine very precise deterministic estimations of desired posterior values [35, 36]. These advancements significantly boosted the output of environmental and climatic data of disease mapping models.

Recent advancements in big data (BD), machine learning (ML), and other intelligent methods for managing massive data sets have increased public awareness of spatial data and software packages. BD is a term that refers to handling extraordinarily large data collections that may be processed computationally to uncover patterns, trends, and relationships related to human activity. ML may learn underlying data patterns and utilize it as experience in prediction models [37]. These large-scale analyses are frequently carried out on supercomputers. They evaluate and uncover patterns, trends, and relationships in the data using RSDPs such as satellite imaging. DME techniques are critical for determining the risk of disease transmission caused by human behavior and environmental interactions. As a result, the majority of recent practical or theoretical DME initiatives incorporate RSDPs into spatial analytic models. Frequently, the resulting modeling outputs are shown in a mapping environment. Though this work highlights the importance of threat maps for VBDs, still other disease transmission modes can also be checked with similar threat maps. The first pandemic began in early 500 AD, the Justinian Plague which continued for many decades amidst persistent waves of this disease outbreak, [51]. The long duration of recovery from any widespread disease is a real challenge and it can no longer be possible without tracking the source of the transmission and the preventive measures. John Snow is a physician who is honored as the Father of Modern Epidemiology for his intellectual and intelligent forefront in resolving the cholera outbreak in 1854 in London. While the PH community those days believed this outbreak to be air-borne, it was John Snow who mapped the communal spread and traced the commonality/root for the outbreak to be the infectious water fetched from Broad Street Pumps [52]. This finding marked the beginning of modern epidemiology. The disease outbreak may be due to direct or indirect transmission, but it can be checked only by tracing the source of infection. In the case of the Covid-19 pandemic outbreak, though there was an absence of evidence for the mode of transmission to be either droplet or air-borne, it is now widely accepted to be air-borne [53]. Numerous DME tools have been deployed and PH trials are carried out to control this pandemic globally. Many real-time health monitoring applications and crow-sourcing applications have been developed for tracking one's individual health and communal spread alert respectively. A real-world dataset of Covid-19 in the city of Toronto (Open data portal), [54], has been applied with GeoPandas in a Python environment using Jupyter notebook to retrieve the disease threat maps: symbol and chloropleth maps [55], are as shown in Figure 2. The shapefile, map layers, and disease spread counts are accessed from the open data portal of Toronto. A symbol map depicts the disease spread in varied symbol sizes whereas the chloropleth map details the outbreak in different shades of color. In the symbol map: the red color indicates higher counts and the blue color indicates relatively less counts. In a chloropleth map, the darker shade represents a higher disease spread level and vice-versa.

2.1. RS for Vector-Borne Disease Surveillance

Around 1950, aerial photography and cartography were used to map the VBDs. Earlier research converged towards eliminating malaria, dengue fever, in addition to yellow fever, with climatic conditions indicating the most vulnerable places with a higher transmission threat. The Malaria Atlas Project, started in 2006, succeeded in mapping and disseminating accurate malaria endemicity data by utilizing geographic characteristics. Categorizing and mapping vector territories through observation and control deeds are conducted by climate suitability. Different methods, like high-altitude color-IR photography and high-resolution photos, created comprehensive maps with enhanced visualization [22, 24, 26]. Vegetation mappings for vector breeding habitats began in 1973 to monitor vector oviposition habitats by means of tone/texture-based observing and understanding approaches. They were used to detect environments related to tick-borne illnesses using landscape epidemiology

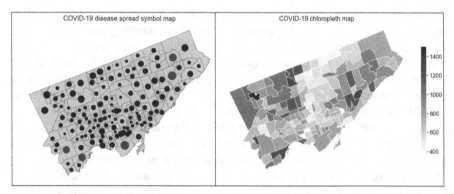

Figure 2. Disease spread maps for Covid 19 in the City of Toronto – June 2020

in some places. MSI emerged as a way of monitoring and mapping ecological circumstances to breed sickness vectors in the 1970s using RS data gathered from satellites and airplanes. Computer algorithms can categorize multispectral (MSI) and hyperspectral (HSI) data [39-42] in order to map and identify plants related to disease-transmitting mosquitoes. Around 1984, RS aided in the management of geographic schistosomiasis characteristics [26-28, 42]. RS-gathered temperatures and precipitations assist in estimating the probability of disease incidence in unsampled sites, identifying and mapping mosquito larval habitats, besides other space and time environmental factors. The majority of research concentrated on RS identification and mapping of probable vector inhabited and breeding territories aligned with vegetation, aquatic, and soil conditions which are inadequate to conduct a thorough survey and management without identifying and mapping all impacted regions. As a result, the majority of studies have used predictive tools to monitor and regulate activities. Thus, exploration must transcend just recognizing habitats and soon-to-be breeding locations to forecast vector spatial and temporal distributions, frequently throughout an entire geographic region of interest. This commonly implicates identifying and representing regions with the uppermost potential for vector generation and illness transmission danger within specified time and geographical constraints [39].

2.2. Disease Prediction Modeling using RSDP

In DME, RS data is very important because predictor variables are used to make RS environmental and climatic proxies from statistical regression models. These proxies can be used to predict spatial and temporal hazards. In certain places, these analyses forecast distributions of maladies , populations of vectors, and transmission risks within impacted populations. Frequently used climatic variables combine RS observations viz precipitation, temperature along with vegetation to determine when and where disease propagation conditions are favorable. RS has also been utilized to forecast temporal/spatial patterns of habitat expansion, vector populations, and disease diffusion risk [36-42]. RS can identify forests, water bodies, meadows, and housing developments in order to connect landscapes and certain VBDs near housings in order to quantify human disease exposure. The greatest benefit of characterizing the mixture of forest and residences is that it brings diseases, vectors, and persons into interaction. Spatial RS simulations can be trained to chart the spread of diseases and forecast transmission risks. GIS may aid in collecting coordinates acquired from the ground-truth or Global Positioning System (GPS) points in order to determine the accuracy of prediction models. RS examined the proximity of particular landscape elements and densely vegetated dwellings as a possible proxy for human-vector interaction, using regression models to determine connections between landscapes and transmission hazards. RS provides the composition as well as structure of the public health landscape, allowing for the evaluation of illnesses, vectors, and human connections. RS models have helped study the dynamics of specific disease vector populations. Satellite images and GIS modeling combine RS ground data linked to vector populations with statistics or GIS to catalog regions with extraordinary, medium, or low VBDs. Accuracy evaluation of the RS prediction models can be aided by ground-truth-based measurements stemming from data discernible through GPS.

2.3. RS Epidemiology Applications

Currently, RSDPs are used to undertake a variety of spatial analyses to characterize the makeup of the landscape (land cover), which helps explain disease dispersion. Spatial models based on various pieces of software like GIS, Earth data science tools, Python, R among others have been constructed and verified using observable data in order to forecast spatial singularities and PH problems. Additionally, the development of methods for processing, analyzing, and fitting data into models are always ongoing. With each exploratory research, new tool extensions and functions arise to capture deterministic and stochastic data components. COVID-19 asks for dynamic models to deal with highly contagious illnesses that may be expanded by including probabilistic-based components that account for uncertainty and rely on climate data for accurate modeling. Nonetheless, satellite imagery might be used to study socioeconomic changes caused by COVID-19 in order to determine the environmental effect of actions such as lockdowns. RS data provides a great deal of potential for monitoring and combating PH. COVID-19 interventions are determined by the resolution, frequency, and relevance of the RSDPs and can greatly benefit from artificial intelligence and metaheuristics to better handle the inherent high dimensionality of RSDPs [41, 43-50]. The major focus has been on remote sensing applications to quantify various disease-causing variables, and predicting the possibility of VBDs will being in greater numbers in certain environments, as well as to isolate transmission, survival, and reproduction factors.

2.4. Theragnostics via Remote Sensing

Mobile devices and wireless communication systems empower a broad range of applications viz. food safety and environmental monitoring, personalized medicine, and healthcare management. Particularly, hybrid smartphones (i.e., with coupled accessories or software to operate towards sensing and actuation). Such emerging technologies can work with microfluidic, implantable, ingestible, on-body, and injectable devices offering an integrated solution for the origination of fresh mobile sensing applications. Mobile sensing and disease regulation based on these devices (broadly defined) and smartphones offer an itinerant laboratory for accomplishing an eclectic range of biochemical recognition and investigational functions, e.g., food/water quality analysis, recurring health tests, in addition to disease identification. This kind of framework partakes significant gains over traditional platforms regarding low cost, test speed, precise control, mobility, ease of operation besides data supervision. These enhancements are auspicious in interdisciplinary, translational basic, and applied studies in particular, by facilitating applications to perform remote infield testing, home-based care, and implementing health procedures in areas with depleted means or even inadequate resources. The well-projected and thoughtful arrangement of smartphones and the previously mentioned remote devices afford powerful off-chip and on-chip operating platforms to assist various biochemical, biophysical, and general well-being tests. Furthermore, remote sensing, data analysis, and management can assist in providing proper service in an effective manner. The repercussions of such integration go beyond medicine, telecommunication, and device-related research and technological expansion [56-58].

3. Discussion and Future Work

Healthcare 4.0 has grown from the Industry 4.0 standard (I4S), which can be perceived as a clear-cut administrative commitment to nurturing a set of knowledge tools while laying the cultural and legal foundations to attain full potential ICT ameliorations along with profits in healthcare. In addition to the technologies encompassed, expansion plans exist, comprising enterprise management and labor organization, regulatory frameworks, dissemination, and training. Healthcare 4.0 or Health 4.0 (H4.0) hinges predominantly on the so-called Medical Cyber-Physical Systems (MCPSs) paradigm, which is the integration of processing capacity, communication, and control [59, 60]. MCPSs rely profoundly on this technological archetype triad:

(i) **Internet of Medical Things (IoMT):** It has the ubiquitous presence of a multiplicity of characteristically addressable items working together, as is the case with mobile paraphernalia, sensors, and actuators;

(ii) **Cloud Computing (CC)/Fog Computing (FC):** They make available virtually unlimited computing, data warehousing, and communication means as conveniences, i.e., according to on-demand as well as pay-per-use demands; and

(iii) **Big Data (BD) Analytics:** It symbolizes all tools, processes, and resources involved in extracting value from perplexing amounts of data.

The healthcare sector undergoes the I4.0 effect, progressing towards H4.0. Awesome healthcare designs and deployments talk about taking on and embedding ICT in healthcare solutions, albeit the H4.0 prototype has its peculiarities. H4.0 employs three main paradigms: the IoT, BD, and CC. The H4.0 multidisciplinary (i.e., translational) nature inhibits operators and stakeholders in this field from following technological progress. This chapter introduces the technical I4S elements fitting healthcare prerequisites to improve H4.0's acceptance and comprehension while framing the cross-disciplinary dealings underneath it. The H4.0 influences fivefold [61-68] arenas: (i) introduction of the paramount properties of I4S pillars;

(ii) assessment of up-to-the-minute applications; (iii) to foster debates leading to benefits and defying issues; and (iv) to draw lessons absorbed.

Deep learning sets of rules have been equivalent to, and even superior to, human performance in an assortment of image recognition assignments, including applications to interpret human diseases (e.g., for the renowned ImageNet challenge [69, 70], several tasks linked to breast cancer histological imageries [71], and inspection of skin cancer imaginings [72]), object uncovering [73, 74], and semantic breakdown [18, 75, 78, 79]. In other words, CNNs make the most of feature depictions learned from crude image pixels besides requiring little in the way of prior knowledge or pre-defined statistical features [71, 76]. Convolutional neural networks (CNNs) absorb key features facilely from the training imageries by optimizing the classification loss function in addition to interleaving convolutional and pooling layers (i.e., spatial reduction of the feature maps in a layer-by-layer manner [77, 79, 88, 89]. On satellite images and several research pieces have effectively utilized deep learning designs and Convolutional Neural Networks (CNNs) for several items for the sake of flora segmentation plus classification tasks. They have achieved excellent accuracy [80, 81].

For imagery segmentation, a Fully Convolutional Network (FCN) remains a characteristic deep learning network that engages convolutional layers [82, 86, 87]. A FCN creates a multilayer convolutional framework and de-convolutional layers to provide pixel-by-pixel segmentation by making use of the benefits of convolutional computing in feature grouping and extraction [78, 83, 84]. FCNs, for illustration, are decent segmentation models for the reason that the multilayer arrangement of these models is well-suited to dealing with the fine details found in pictures.

When it comes to picture segmentation, the U-net is a specific form of FCN. The U-Net has gotten a lot of watchfulness for its aptitude to segment biological imageries using a little dataset [85, 86], albeit it has also proved to be extremely effective for pixel-wise classification of satellite images [81, 90]. E.g., the U-Net design entails two paths: a contracting way for capturing context and another symmetric growing path for pinpointing exact location information. An altered copy of the U-Net algorithm for semantic segmentation of water vegetation employing multispectral satellite scenes consistent with the orthodox U-Net policy [85] was utilized in the deployment of a model aiming at the analysis and mitigation of hazards. The net refinement resulted in a CNN encoder-decoder that was a state-of-the-art design.

4. Conclusion

Prolific studies validating the latent opportunities in RS and DME statistics have been undertaken mostly to analyze and measure prospective associations between environmental and human diseases. Prior results had guided the PH community in intervention planning and decision-making to demonstrate the RS potential within DME and withstand surveillance and control struggles. They have clarified the RS diversity in disease reconnaissance and control agendas [91-94]. However, fruitful RS usage depends on health nonexperts/end-users gaining access, retrieving, and scrutinizing satellite data. Preprocessing steps can be appended as covariates into models to determine nonexpert uptakes and usage [95-100]. The growth and deployment of near real-time watching spatial models can assist in timely predicting spatial/temporal patterns of VBDs and transmission risks motivating RS data use in DME. VBDs dynamics at any place are influenced by processes operating on various landscapes and geographic scales. The previous judgments have exemplified how epidemiologists can benefit from RS to manage environmental drivers of VBDs . Researchers have studied multiple factors impelling VBD patterns and distributions at numerous landscapes and geographic scales. The exploration of opportunities presented by RS to DME is still unfolding along with novel views and eventually will be related to personalized medicine as satellite resolutions decrease and network capillarity increases [101-103].

References

1. Campbell, J.B. and Wynne, R.H. (2011). Introduction to Remote Sensing. 5th ed. New York, NY: Guilford Press.
2. Aroma, J. and Raimond, K. (2015). A review on availability of remote sensing data. Proc. IEEE IEEE Techn. Innovation in ICT for Agriculture and Rural Development (TIAR), 150-155.
3. Aroma, J. and Raimond, K. (2020). Investigation on spectral indices and soft classifiers-based water body segmentation approaches for satellite image analysis. J. Indian Soc. Rem. Sens., 49, 341-356.
4. Breder, R.L., Estrela, V.V. and de Assis, J.T. (2009). Sub-pixel accuracy edge fitting by means of B-spline. Proc. of the IEEE Int'l Workshop on Multimedia Signal Processing.
5. Laghari, A.A., Khan, A., He. H., Estrela, V.V., Razmjooy, N., Hemanth, J. et al. (2020). Quality of experience (QoE) and quality of service (QoS) in UAV systems. *In:* Estrela, V.V. et al. (eds). Imaging and Sensing for Unmanned Aircraft Systems, IET, 2(10), 213-242, London, UK.
6. Jagalingam, P. and Hegde, A.V. (2015). A review of quality metrics for fused image. Aquatic Procedia, 4, 133-142.
7. Abdulaziz, A., Krishna, K., Vijayakumar, S., George, G., Menon, N. et al. (2021). Dynamics of vibrio cholerae in a typical tropical lake and estuarine system: Potential of remote sensing for risk mapping. Remote Sens., 13, 1034.
8. Hanifati, A.A., Permata, A., Mustofa, D., Wulandari, D., Ratnasari, I. et al. (2018). Application of remote sensing and GIS for malaria disease susceptibility area mapping in Padang Cermin sub-district, District of Pesawaran, Lampung Province. Proc. IOP Conf. Series: Earth and Env. Sc.
9. Viña, A., Gitelson, A.A., NguyRobertson, A.L. and Peng, Y. (2011). Comparison of different vegetation indices for the remote assessment of green leaf area index of crops. Rem. Sens. Env., 115(12), 3468-3478.
10. Karagiannis-Voules, D.A., Biedermann, P., Ekpo, U.F., Garba, A., Langer, E. et al. (2015). Spatial and temporal distribution of soil transmitted helminth infection in sub-Saharan Africa: A systematic review and geostatistical meta-analysis. The Lancet Inf. Dis., 15(1), 74-84.
11. Karagiannis-Voules, D.A., Odermatt, P., Biedermann, P., Khieu, V., Schar, F. et al. (2015). Geostatistical modelling of soil transmitted helminth infection in Cambodia: Do socioeconomic factors improve predictions? Acta Tropica, 141(Pt B), 204-212.
12. Noor, A.M., Kinyoki, D.K., Mundia, C.W., Kabaria, C.W., Mutua, J.W. et al. (2014).

The changing risk of Plasmodium falciparum malaria infection in Africa: 2000-10: A spatial and temporal analysis of transmission intensity. Lancet, 383, 9930, 1739-1747.

13. Clements, A.C.A., Kur, L.W., Gatpan, G., Ngondi, J., Emerson, P.M. et al. (2014). Targeting trachoma control through risk mapping: The example of southern Sudan. PLoS Neglected Tropical Diseases, 4(8), e799.

14. Robinson, T., Rogers, D. and Williams, B. (1997). Mapping tsetse habitat suitability in the common fly belt of Southern Africa using multivariate analysis of climate and remotely sensed vegetation data. Medical and Veterinary Entomology, 11(3), 235-245.

15. Xu, M., Cao, C., Wang, D. and Kan, B. (2014). Identifying environmental risk factors of cholera in a coastal area with geospatial technologies. Int'l J. Env. Res. and Pub. Health, 12(1), 354-370.

16. Karume, K., Schmidt, C., Kundert, K., Bagula, M., Safina, B.F. et al. (2017). Use of remote sensing for population number determination. The Open Access J. Science and Technology [Internet], 5, 03, 9.

17. Yang, G.-J., Vounatsou, P., Xiao-Nong, Z., Utzinger, J., Tanner, M. et al. (2005). A review of geographic information system and remote sensing with applications to the epidemiology and control of schistosomiasis in China. Acta Tropica, 96(2), 117-129.

18. Kaptein, A., Janoth, J., Lang, O. and Bernede, N. (2014). Trends in commercial radar remote sensing industry [industrial profiles]. IEEE G. Rem. Sens. Mag., 2(1), 42-46.

19. Correia, V.R.M., Carvalho, M.S., Sabroza, P.C. and Vasconcelos, C.H. (2004). Remote sensing as a tool to survey endemic diseases in Brazil. Cadernos de Saúde Pública, 20(4), 891-904.

20. Thomson, M.C., Connor, S.J., Milligan, P. and Flasse, S.P. (1997). Mapping malaria risk in Africa: What can satellite data contribute? Parasitology Today, 13(8), 313-318.

21. Beck, L.R., Rodriguez, M.H., Dister, S.W., Rodriguez, A.D., Rejmankova, E. et al. (1994). Remote sensing as a landscape epidemiologic tool to identify villages at high risk for malaria transmission. The Am. J. Trop. Med. and Hyg., 51(3), 271-280.

22. Hay, S.I., Packer, M.J. and Rogers, D.J. (1997). The impact of remote sensing on the study and control of invertebrate intermediate hosts and vectors for disease. Int'l J. Rem. Sens., 18(14), 2899-2930.

23. Chilès, J.P. and Delfiner, P. (2009). Geostatistics: Modeling Spatial Uncertainty. Hoboken, New Jersey: John Wiley & Sons, Inc., p. 718.

24. Tran, A., Ippoliti, C., Balenghien, T., Conte, A., Gely, M. et al. (2013). A geographical information system-based multicriteria evaluation to map areas at risk for Rift Valley fever vector-borne transmission in Italy. Transb. and Em. Dis., 60(2), 14-23.

25. Hassan, A.N., Beck, L.R. and Dister, S. (1998). Prediction of villages at risk for filariasis transmission in the Nile Delta using remote sensing and geographic information system technologies. Journal of the Egyptian Society of Parasitology, 28(1), 75-87.

26. Dlamini, S.N., Franke, J. and Vounatsou, P. (2015). Assessing the relationship between environmental factors and malaria vector breeding sites in Swaziland using multi-scale remotely sensed data. Geospatial Health, 10(1), 302.

27. Tran, A., Kassie, D. and Herbreteau, V. (2016). Applications of remote sensing to the epidemiology of infectious diseases: Some examples. *In:* Baghdadi, N. and Zribi, M. (eds). Land Surface Remote Sensing, Elsevier, 295-315.

28. Sadeghieh, T., Waddell, L.A., Ng, V., Hall, A. and Sargeant, J. (2020). A scoping review of importation and predictive models related to vector-borne diseases, pathogens, reservoirs, or vectors (1999-2016). PLoS One, 15(1), e0227678.

29. Leonardo, L.R., Rivera, P.T., Crisostomo, B., Sarol, J.J., Bantayan, N.C. et al. (2005). A study of the environmental determinants of malaria and schistosomiasis in the Philippines using remote sensing and geographic information systems. Parassitologia, 47(1), 105-114.

30. Deshpande, A., Patavardhan, P., Estrela, V.V. and Razmjooy, N. (2020). Deep learning as an alternative to super-resolution imaging in UAV systems. *In:* Estrela, V.V. et al. (eds). Imaging and Sensing for Unmanned Aircraft Systems, IET, 2(9), 177-212. London, UK.

31. Estrela, V.V., Razmjooy, N., Monteiro, A.C., França, R.P., Jesus, M.D. et al. (2020). A computational intelligence perspective on multimodal image registration for unmanned aerial vehicles (UAVs), IET.

32. Lwowski, J., Majumdar, A., Benavidez, P., Prevost, J.J., Jamshidi, M.M. et al. (2019). Bird flocking inspired formation control for unmanned aerial vehicles using stereo camera. IEEE Systems J., 13, 3580-3589.

33. Kim, D., Barraza, J.P., Arthur, R.A., Hara, A.T., Lewis, K.J. et al. (2020). Spatial mapping of polymicrobial communities reveals a precise biogeography associated with human dental caries. Proc. Nat. Acad. Sc. of the United States of Am., 117, 12375-12386.

34. Dlamini, S.N., Beloconi, A., Mabaso, S., Vounatsou, P., Impouma, B. et al. (2019). Review of remotely sensed data products for disease mapping and epidemiology. Rem. Sens. App.: Soc. and Env., 4, 108-118.

35. Geyer, C.J. (1992). Practical Markov Chain Monte Carlo. Statistical Science, 7(4), 473-483.

36. Illian, J.B., Sørbye, S.H. and Rue, H. (2012). A toolbox for fitting complex spatial point process models using integrated nested Laplace approximation (INLA). The Ann. Appl. Statistics, 6(4), 1499-1530.

37. Beam, A.L. (2018). Kohane IS. Big data and machine learning in health care. JAMA, 319, 13, 1317-1318.

38. Wagner, V.E., Hill-Rowley, R., Narlock, S.A. and Newson, H.D. (1979). Remote sensing: A rapid and accurate method of data acquisition for a newly formed mosquito control district. Mosquito News, 39(2), 283-287.

39. Sinka, M.E. (2013). Global Distribution of the dominant vector species of malaria, anopheles mosquitoes – New insights into malaria vectors. Sylvie Manguin, IntechOpen, Croatia, InTech, 109-143.

40. Aroma, J., Raimond, K., Razmjooy, N., Estrela, V.V., Hemanth, J. et al. (2020). Multispectral vs hyperspectral imaging for unmanned aerial vehicles: Current and prospective state of affairs. *In:* Estrela, V.V. et al. (eds). Imaging and Sensing for Unmanned Aircraft Systems, IET, 7, 133-156.

41. Conte, C., de Alteriis, G., de Pandi, F., Caputo, E., Lo Moriello, R.S. et al. (2021). Performance analysis for human crowd monitoring to control Covid-19 disease by drone surveillance. Proc. 8th Int'l Work. Metr. for Aer. (MetroAeroSpace), IEEE, 31-36.

42. Pope, K.O., Sheffner, E.J., Linthicum, K.J., Bailey, C.L., Logan, T.M. et al. (1992). Identification of central Kenyan Rift Valley fever virus vector habitats with Landsat TM and evaluation of their flooding status with airborne imaging radar. Rem. Sens. Env., 40(3), 185-196.

43. Aroma, J. and Raimond, K. (2018). Intelligent land cover detection in multi-sensor satellite images. Proc. 18th Online World Conf. Soft Comp. in Ind. Applications (WSC18).

44. Kumar, A., Sharma, K., Singh, H., Naugriya, S.G., Gill, S.S. et al. (2020). A drone-based networked system and methods for combating coronavirus disease (COVID-19) pandemic. Future Generations Computer Systems, 115, 1-19.

45. Masmoudi, N., Jaafar, W., Cherif, S., Abderrazak, J.B., Yanikomeroglu, H. et al. (2020). UAV-based crowd surveillance in post COVID-19 Era. IEEE Access, 9, 162276-162290.

46. Deshpande, A., Razmjooy, N. and Estrela, V.V. (2021). Introduction to computational intelligence and super-resolution. *In:* Deshpande, A. et al. (eds). Computational Intelligence Methods for Super-Resolution in Image Processing Applications. Springer, Cham, 1(1), 3-23.

47. Munawar, H.S., Inam, H., Ullah, F., Qayyum, S., Kouzani, A.Z. et al. (2021). Towards smart healthcare: UAV-based optimized path planning for delivering COVID-19 self-testing kits using cutting edge technologies. MDPI, Sustainability. 13(18), 10426.

48. Kirkpatrick, A.W., Mckee, J.L. and Conly, J.M. (2021). Longitudinal remotely mentored self-performed lung ultrasound surveillance of paucisymptomatic Covid-19 patients at risk of disease progression. The Ultrasound J., 13.

49. Khelassi, A. and Estrela, V.V. (2021). Advances in multidisciplinary medical technologies –Engineering, modeling and findings. Proc. International Workshop on Medical Technologies 2019 (ICHSMT 2019), Springer Nature, Zurich, Switzerland.

50. Hartono, A.P., Luhur, C.R., Indriyani, C.A., Wijaya, C.R., Qomariyah, N.N. et al. (2021). Evaluating deep learning for CT scan COVID-19 automatic detection. Proc. Int'l Conf. ICT for Smart Soc. (ICISS), 1-7.

51. Justinian Plague – [online – accessed on 29-01-22]: https://en.wikipedia.org/wiki/Plague_of_Justinian

52. Cholera outbreak – [online – accessed on 29-01-22]: https://blogs.cdc.gov/publichealthmatters/2017/03/a-legacy-of-disease-detectives/

53. Covid 19 transmission – [online – a ccessed on 30-01-22]: https://scitechdaily.com/covid-gets-airborne-expert-explains-how-viruses-travel-through-the-air/

54. Toronto open data portal – [online – accessed on 29-01-22]: https://www.toronto.ca/home/covid-19/covid-19-pandemic-data/

55. Covid 19 mapping Tutorial – [online – accessed on 28-01-22]: https://medium.com/analytics-vidhya/mapping-covid-19-infections-in-toronto-with-python-an-introduction-to-plotting-with-geopandas-9e7a3b721c39

56. Gopinath, S.C., Ismail, Z.H., Razak, M.I. and Yasin, M.N. (2021). Advancement in biosensor: 'Telediagnosis' and 'Remote Digital Imaging'. Biotechnology and Applied Biochemistry. 69, 1199-1208.

57. Loschi, H.J., Estrela, V.V., Hemanth, D.J., Fernandes, S.R., Iano, Y. et al. (2020) Communications requirements, video streaming, communications links and networked UAVs. *In:* Estrela, V.V., Hemanth, J., Saotome, O., Nikolakopoulos, G., Sabatini, R. (eds). Imaging and Sensing for Unmanned Aircraft Systems, 2(6), 113-132. IET, London, UK, doi: 10.1049/PBCE120G_ch6

58. Estrela, V.V., Saotome, O., Loschi, H.J., Hemanth, D.J., Farfan, W.S. et al. (2018) Emergency response cyber-physical framework for landslide avoidance with sustainable electronics. Technologies, 6, 42.

59. Laghari, A.A., Estrela, V.V. and Yin, S. (2022). Special Issue: From nanoscale to hyperspectral imaging – How to gather and understand medical images harvested in extremely difficult situations. Curr. Med. Imaging, Bentham Science.

60. Zhou, K., Liu, T. and Zhou, L. (2015). Industry 4.0: Towards future industrial opportunities and challenges. Proc. 2015 12th Int'l Conf. Fuzzy Syst. and Knowledge Disc. (FSKD). IEEE.

61. Aceto, G., Persico, V. and Pescapé, A. (2019). A survey on information and communication technologies for industry 4.0: State of the art, taxonomies, perspectives, and challenges. IEEE Communications Surveys & Tutorials.

62. Islam, S.M.R., Kwak, D., Kabir, M.H., Hossain, M., Kwak, K.S. et al. (2015). The Internet of things for health care: A comprehensive survey, IEEE Access, 3.

63. Hemanth, D.J., Estrela, V.V., Tavares, J.M.R.S., Wang, L. and Shi, F. (2018). Special Issue: Soft computing techniques for image analysis in the medical industry – Current trends, challenges and solutions. Editorial, IEEE Access, IEEE.

64. Kanna, K., Estrela, V.V. and Rodrigues, J.J.P.C. (2021). Cyber security and digital forensics. Proc. ICCSDF 2021, Springer Nature, Zurich, Switzerland. doi: 10.1007/978-981-16-3961-6

65. Ahuja, S.P., Mani, S. and Zambrano, J. A survey of the state of cloud computing in healthcare. Network and Communication Technologies, 1(2), 2012.

66. Ermakova, T. and Huenges, J. (2013). Cloud computing in healthcare – A literature review on current state of research. AMCIS 2013 Proceedings. 17.

67. Archenaa, J. and Anita, E.M. (2015). A survey of big data analytics in healthcare and government. Procedia Comp. Sc., 50.

68. Zou, Q. and Li, X.-B. (2013). Survey of map reduce frame operation in bioinformatics. Briefings in Bioinformatics, 15, 4.

69. Liu, Z.Y.-C., Chamberlin, A.J., Tallam, K., Jones, I.J., Lamore, L.L. et al. (2022). Deep learning segmentation of satellite imagery identifies aquatic vegetation associated with snail intermediate hosts of schistosomiasis in Senegal, Africa. Remote Sensing, 14(6), 1345. https://doi.org/10.3390/rs14061345

70. Russakovsky, O., Deng, J., Su, H., Krause, J., Satheesh, S. et al. (2015). Imagenet large scale visual recognition challenge. Int. J. Comput. Vis., 115, 211-252.

71. Araújo, T., Aresta, G., Castro, E., Rouco, J., Aguiar, P. et al. (2017). Classification of breast cancer histology images using convolutional neural networks. PLoS ONE, 12, e0177544.

72. Esteva, A., Kuprel, B., Novoa, R.A. and Ko, J. (2017). Dermatologist-level classification of skin cancer with deep neural networks. Nature, 542, 115-118.

73. Girshick, R., Donahue, J., Darrell, T. and Malik, J. (2015). Region-based convolutional networks for accurate object detection and segmentation. IEEE Trans. Pattern Anal. Mach. Intell., 38, 142-158.

74. Estrela, V.V., de Jesus, M.A., Aroma, J., Raimond, K., Fernandes, S.R. et al. (2021). Motion estimation role in the context of 3D video. Int'l Journal of Multimedia Data Engineering and Management (IJMDEM), 12(3), 16-38.

75. Noh, H., Hong, S. and Han, B. (2015). Learning deconvolution network for semantic segmentation. Proceedings of the IEEE International Conference on Computer Vision, Boston, MA, USA, 6-12 June 2015, 1520-1528.

76. Spanhol, F.A., Oliveira, L.S., Petitjean, C. and Heutte, L. (2015). Breast cancer histopathological image classification using convolutional neural networks. Proceedings of the International Joint Conference on Neural Networks (IJCNN). Vancouver, BC, Canada, 24-29 July 2016, 2560-2567.

77. LeCun, Y., Bengio, Y. and Hinton, G. (2015). Deep learning. Nature, 521, 436.

78. Long, J., Shelhamer, E. and Darrell, T. (2015). Fully convolutional networks for semantic segmentation. Proceedings of the IEEE Conference on Computer Vision and Pattern Recognition, Boston, MA, USA, 6-12 June 2015, 3431-3440.

79. LeCun, Y. and Bengio, Y. (1995). Convolutional networks for images, speech, and time series. Handb. Brain Theory Neural Netw., 3361.

80. Langford, Z.L., Kumar, J. and Hoffman, F.M. (2017). Convolutional neural network approach for mapping arctic vegetation using multi-sensor remote sensing fusion. Proceedings of the IEEE International Conference on Data Mining Workshops (ICDMW), New Orleans, LA, USA, 18-21 November 2017, 322-331.

81. Rakhlin, A., Davydow, A. and Nikolenko, S.I. (2018). Land cover classification from satellite imagery with U-Net and Lovasz-softmax loss. Proceedings of the 2018 CVPR Workshops, Salt Lake City, UT, USA, 18-22 June 2018, 262-266.

82. Chen, L.C., Papandreou, G., Kokkinos, I., Murphy, K., Yuille, A.L. et al. (2014). Semantic image segmentation with deep convolutional nets and fully connected CRFs. arXiv 2014, arXiv:1412.7062.

83. Dolz, J., Desrosiers, C. and Ayed, I.B. (2018). 3D fully convolutional networks for subcortical segmentation in MRI: A large-scale study. NeuroImage, 170, 456-470.
84. Iglovikov, V., Mushinskiy, S. and Osin, V. (2017). Satellite imagery feature detection using deep convolutional neural network: A Kaggle competition. arXiv 2017, arXiv:1706.06169.
85. Ronneberger, O., Fischer, P. and Brox, T. (2015). U-net: Convolutional networks for biomedical image segmentation. International Conference on Medical Image Computing and Computer-Assisted Intervention; Springer: Cham, Switzerland, 234-241.
86. Zhou, X.Y. and Yang, G.Z. (2009). Normalization in training U-Net for 2-D biomedical semantic segmentation. IEEE Robot. Autom. Lett., 4, 1792-1799.
87. Abadi, M., Barham, P., Chen, J., Chen, Z., Davis, A. et al. (2016). Tensorflow: A system for large-scale machine learning. Proceedings of the 12th USENIX Symposium on Operating Systems Design and Implementation (OSDI 16), Savannah, GA, USA, 2-4 November 2016, 265-283.
88. Van der Walt, S., Schönberger, J.L., Nunez-Iglesias, J., Boulogne, F., Warner, J.D. et al. (2014). Scikit-image: Image processing in Python, Peer J, 2, e453.
89. Coelho, A.M., Estrela, V.V., do Carmo, F.P. and Fernandes, S.R. (2012). Error concealment by means of motion refinement and regularized Bregman divergence. *In:* Yin, H. et al. (eds). Proc. IDEAL 2012. LNCS 2012, vol. 7435. Springer, Berlin, Heidelberg.
90. Yang, W., Zhang, X., Tian, Y., Wang, W., Xue, J.H. et al. (2019). Deep learning for single image super-resolution: A brief review. IEEE Trans. Multimed., 21, 3106-3121.
91. Chen, Y., Qin, R., Zhang, G. and Albanwan, H. (2021). Spatial temporal analysis of traffic patterns during the COVID-19 epidemic by vehicle detection using planet remote-sensing satellite images. Remote. Sens., 13, 208.
92. Gagliardi, V., Benedetto, A., Bianchini Ciampoli, L., D'Amico, F. et al. (2020). Health monitoring approach for transport infrastructure and bridges by satellite remote sensing Persistent Scatterer Interferometry (PSI), Proc. SPIE Rem. Sens. Vol. 11534, Earth Resources and Environmental Remote Sensing/GIS Applications XI, 115340K.
93. Clim, A., Zota, R.D. and Tinică, G. (2018). Big Data in home healthcare: A new frontier in personalized medicine. Medical emergency services and prediction of hypertension risks. International Journal of Healthcare Management, 12, 241-249.
94. Balakrishnan, A., Kadiyala, R., Dhiman, G., Ashok, G., Kautish, S. et al. (2021). A personalized eccentric cyber-physical system architecture for smart healthcare. Security and Communication Networks. Vol. 2021, Article ID 1747077
95. Marinho, C.E.V., Estrela, V.V., Loschi, H.J., Razmjooy, N., Herrmann, A.E. et al. (2019) A model for medical staff idleness minimization. *In:* Iano Y. et al. (eds), Proceedings of the 4th Brazilian Technology Symposium (BTSym'18). BTSym 2018. Smart Innovation, Systems and Technologies, vol. 140. Springer, Cham.
96. Deshpande, A., Estrela, V.V. and Patavardhan, P. (2021). The DCT-CNN-ResNet50 architecture to classify brain tumours with super-resolution, convolutional neural network, and the ResNet50. Neuroscience Informatics, 1(4), 100013, ISSN 2772-5286.
97. Coelho, A.M., de Assis, J.T. and Estrela, V.V. (2009). Error concealment by means of clustered blockwise PCA. Proc. IEEE 2009 Picture Coding Symposium (PCS 2009), doi: 10.1109/PCS.2009.5167442
98. Fadeev, N.B., Skrypitsyna, T.N., Kurkov, V.M. and Sidelnikov, N.I. (2019). Use of remote sensing data and GIS technologies for monitoring stocks of medicinal plants: Problems and prospects. Springer Proceedings in Earth and Environmental Sciences.
99. Barnes, R.Z. (2021). Artificial intelligence-enabled wearable medical devices, clinical and diagnostic decision support systems, and Internet of things-based healthcare

applications in COVID-19 prevention, screening, and treatment. American Journal of Medical Research, 8(2): 9-22.

100. Sogno, P., Traidl-Hoffmann, C. and Kuenzer, C. (2020). Earth observation data supporting non-communicable disease research: A review. Remote. Sens., 12, 2541.

101. Foresti, R., Macaluso, C., Rossi, S., Selleri, S., Perini, P. et al. (2020). 3D reconstruction cutting and smart devices for personalized medicine. 2020 Italian Conference on Optics and Photonics (ICOP), 1-3.

102. Yan, S., Jing, L. and Wang, H. (2021). A new individual tree species recognition method based on a convolutional neural network and high-spatial resolution remote sensing imagery. Remote. Sens., 13, 479.

103. Wang, Y., Gu, L., Li, X. and Ren, R. (2021). Building extraction in multitemporal high-resolution remote sensing imagery using a multifeature LSTM Network. IEEE Geoscience and Remote Sensing Letters, 18, 1645-1649.

On DICOM, HEVC and 3D Medical Image Compression for Volumetric Theragnostics

Vania V. Estrela[1] [0000-0002-4465-7691], Anand Deshpande[2] [0000-0002-1500-0981], Ricardo T. Lopes[3] [0000-0001-7250-824X], Hugo H.P. da Silva[4] [0000-0001-6764-8432], Shoulin Yin[5] [0000-0002-5367-1372], Nikolaos Andreopoulos[6] [0000-0001-9975-7043], Andrey Terziev[7] [0000-0002-7069-367X], A.A. Laghari[8] [0000-0001-5831- 5943], J.J.P.C. Rodrigues[9] [0000-0001-8657-3800]

[1] Telecommunications Department, Fluminense Federal University (UFF), RJ, Brazil, vania.estrela.phd@ieee.org
[2] Electronics and Communication Engineering, Angadi Institute of Technology and Management, Belagavi, India, deshpande.anandb@gmail.com
[3] University Federal of Rio de Janeiro (COPPE/UFRJ), Rio de Janeiro, RJ, Brazil, rlopes@coppe.ufrj.br
[4] Instituto de Telecomunicacoes, Instituto Superior Tecnico, Torre Norte - Piso 10, Av. Rovisco Pais, 1, 1049-001, Lisboa, Lisboa, Portugal, hsilva@lx.it.pt
[5] Harbin Institute of Technology, China, yslin@hit.edu.cn
[6] Computer Science Department, Technological Institute of Iceland, Iceland, nikolaosandreopoulos@yahoo.com
[7] TerziA, Sofia, Bulgaria, andreyterziev@yahoo.com
[8] Faculty of Computer Science, Sindh Madressatul Islam University, Karachi (74000), Sindh, Pakistan, asif.laghari@smiu.edu.pk
[9] Federal University of Piaui (UFPI), Electrical Engineering, Fortaleza, CE, Brazil, joeljr@ieee.org

1. Introduction

Unbroken, balanced imaging encoding and compression reduce broadcast costs, Error Concealment (EC) efforts to repair images without discarding the visual parts received, and the price tag for storing received 3D images [1-3]. Medical images (MIs) pose great restrictions upon storage and real-time handling that impact cost savings directly. For illustration, six sequences of Computed Tomography (CT) of patient MIs under analyses may require six GB of storage. Broadcasting different MI files along with other metadata may simply affect demands on heterogeneous communication systems, thus requiring a cost drop with upgraded access to smartphones anywhere [4]. Figure 1 shows the relationship between slices and a 3D image [1, 2, 63, 64].

The High-Efficiency Video Coding (HEVC) (alias H.265) standard has been introduced by the ITU-T Encoding Expert Group (VCEG) and the ISO/IEC MPEG (Group of Experts in Moving Image) (JCT-VC). HEVC can accommodate H.264, MPEG-4 section 10 of H.265, MPEG-7, and MPEG-H section 2, as well as some legacy codecs while offering a similar video quality level of or an enhanced video version in terms of quality without overloading Cyber-Physical Systems (CPSs) [5-7]. Social welfare benefits of employing the cloud arranges for some rewards, such as information storage/acquisition from healthcare images and electronic medical dealings with time.

The Digital Imaging and Medical Communication (DICOM) healthcare standard supports image reconstruction. Currently, it helps share pictures that can be restored on the end-user side and between health applications/services. Using EC strategies, DICOM can back up JPEG and JPEG 2000 (J2K) for conceivably recoverable and even somewhat irreversible/tarnished image restorations. Reference imageries can be bundled in DICOM as single trustworthy visual representations without any man-made redundancy processing resulting in image adaptations.

Nonetheless, J2K is ill-suited to encoding specific visual groupings and rendering high-quality 3D reproduction. This article examines the HEVC scheme for 3D MI compressions, such as MRI, CT, and angiography, which are presently based on blocks of pixels. To render 3D forms, final users may retrieve voxels from

Figure 1. Transmitted slices (upper part), 3D reconstruction (bottom left), and a new view (bottom right).

previously encoded sliced imageries. The High-Efficiency Coding Standard (HEVC) delivers colossal accomplishments contrasting with H.264/AVC in addition to JPEG/ J2K [8] and can give a more rational use of assets to get an end-result whose quality is still worth application.

A vital reason prompting this work is how to handle possible communication constraints and inherent problems hindering 3D image retrieval when employing HEVC Intra- and Intercoding modes in wellbeing. This investigation considers it paramount to neutralize/lessen the codec performance, particularly in the prediction stages of HEVC-Intra and HEVC-Inter modes with J2K. This work examines inner and outer "frame" experimentation and the utilization of better-organized 3D knowledge. This paper also scrutinizes the exploitation of more imagery modalities and Regions of Interest (ROIs) to delimit body parts, and clever usage of lossy frameworks to obtain improved and less distorted 3D picture renditions by handling sufficient info sets like in Intra HEVC coding of weights [9].

This chapter partakes the following sectors. The second section displays a diagram depicting some video/image coding reference points that frequently appear in conjunction with the traits and phenomena listed in sections 3 and 4, showing some lossy challenges resulting from HEVC strategies. Final points, insights and conclusions appear in sections 5 to 6, correspondingly.

2. Video Coding Standards Overview

DICOM often rebuilds MIs without pre-processing them. This worldwide standard helps trade MI/data in general over networks. It continues to evolve to ensure the compatibility of new devices and medical modalities [11-16]. The rising data volume generated by MI modalities, viz Digital Radiography (DR), CT scans, Magnetic Resonance Imaging (MRI), Nuclear Medicine (NM), besides Ultrasound (US), especially regarding the need for storage. Persistent and continuous MI storage robustify studies, allowing identification of alterations over space and time to aid theragnostics.

3D MIs can consist of a sequence of 2D slices or a collection of voxels [11-19]. Innovative approaches and ideas may expose further data and knowledge concerning Medical Volumes of Interest (MVOI) [20-22]. The budget is still a concern, but its ongoing reduction is expected. Some bottlenecks are high-resolution storage needs, increasing data production, operation/updating/compliance expenses, high-complexity medical CPSs (MCPSs) and data retention/handling legislation [16-18].

Numerous advanced MI compression solutions exist now to cater to the growing demand for MI. With high-quality streaming, one may opt between lossless and lossy (irreversible) compression. At the reception, degradation may be minimized slightly via Super-Resolution (SR) procedures, which produce high-resolution renditions with an augmented resolution by superimposing many low-resolution frames [13, 16-18]. Despite its inefficiency with video sequences and 3D MIs, J2K is a prominent compression standard in DICOM [27-34]. It is, therefore, crucial to conduct research into boosting HEVC compression for J2K. Often, MIs demand high resolutions, which HEVC can provide at modest bit rate savings while still ensuring an acceptable performance with decreased Intra coding complexity together with a little rise in file length .

HEVC expands H.264/MPEG-4 AVC rationales. Both look at modified video ROIs or MVOIs, particularly close to video boundaries, to perceive changes. Then, each of these subdivisions receives a compact representation to characterize it. Nowadays, transmitting a 3D image as a set of slices is more common because handling voxels over networks is still cumbersome. Each slice has a map for color and another for its depth. Figures 2 and 3 depict the 3D-HEVC rationale.

Fundamental variations in 3D-HEVCs include optimization of coding points and correlation intervals with blocks of dimensions16×16 to 64×64 pixels, adjustable dimensionalities, enhanced internal mechanisms for predictions within a similar image/patch, better reception, the combination of motions from blocks, ROIs, screens, cameras, and other advanced partitions. Proper usage of these elements and their upgrades require a meaningfully greater processing load to handle 3D MI compilation flags, but the necessary decompression calculation becomes lighter. Intraframe forecast mode lessens any temporary surplus.

Pixels or blocks of pixels or voxels of already encoded images help render frames/slices and other estimations. The residual edge-coded indicator amounts to the difference concerning the received image part and the estimated block.

The Discrete Wavelet Transform (DWT) can help implement irreversible or reversible image changes for coding an object frame or slice. DWT supports tracking changes in the mosaic fragment at various stages of modification, a subgroup with a coefficient that displays spatial repetition attribute titles for the first mosaic segment. Treated tiles are processed and quantified as scalars, which results in accuracy loss. Quantification generally uses entropy coding that contains losses [7, 8].

The H.265 basic structure resembles H.264 because of entropy coding of transformations, space and time predictions, and quantizations. HEVC sturdily takes advantage of Coding Units (CUs) besides bolstering a wide variety of CUs, e.g., from 4×4 to 64×64 pixels and Transform Unit (TU) from 4×4 to 32×32 pixels. There exist 33 intranet values for planar and DC coefficients besides Intraframe enhancements. The HEVC processing involves transformation, quantization, and dehazing for compressing without data loss. HEVC exploits quite a few prediction types to craft sequential, numeric, and consecutive loss of sequences or groups of MI slices [1, 17, 22].

3. HEVC Coding and Features

The DICOM standard handles the transmission, storing, recovery, printing, handling, and MI data interactive displays (with multiple views) for integrated DICOM printers, workstations, PACS, image capture devices, and so on. DICOM is actively developed and maintained per technology, and MI need. The DICOM MI file typically contains information on MI and metadata data, including information entities (IEs) that provide information such as patient, study, series, and image. This study uses publicly available DICOM that contains many frames to be processed in a one-by-one manner, using an inter- or, intra-picture prediction. It permits irreversible (lossy)

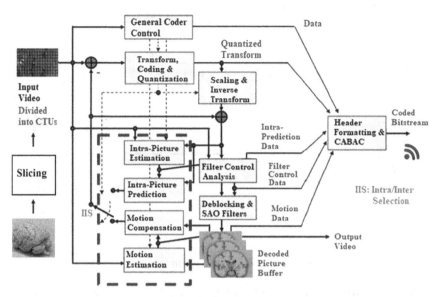

Figure 2. HEVC coder.

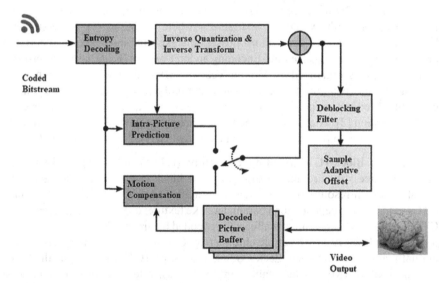

Figure 3. HEVC decoder.

MI compressions for J2K with HEVC and its performance can be evaluated by 2D and 3D similarity metrics [1, 26-34].

It is vital to pack the inter- and intra-slice displacements (here referred to as MVs) while striving as much as possible to keep the 3D object as close as possible to the original. The 3D compression actually involves slice-to-volume (S2V) image registration (IR) where a set of MI slices can be interpolated to render the sought-after volume. The HEVC must meet different goals: several coding possibilities, a

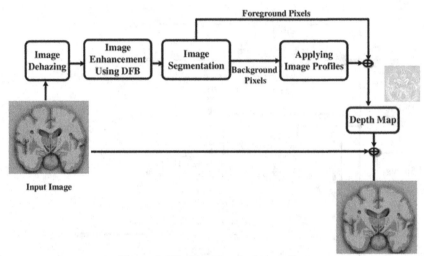

Figure 4. 2D video plus depth encoding.

suitable transport arrangement, information that can help EC, and implementations to manage structures parallelly. Next, the fundamental HEVC segments appear:

The HEVC 3D MI encoding layer conciliates the interpolation projection and 2D video plus depth (V+D), as in Figure 4 where no initial pre-processing has been assumed. Sequence encryptions possess the expected inter-picture material to predict and utilize intra-slice info. Encoding an inter-picture (Exit) has an assortment of displacements organized as Motion Vectors (MVs) data with a reference MI associated with each part projection. The coder and decoder handle displacements expending Motion Compensation (MC), where MVs and mode data are conveyed as side information [2]. Then, change coefficients are pre-processed, quantized, entropy coded, and sent with predicting data. Some relevant HEVC traits are depicted below.

Coding Tree Block (CTB)/Coding Tree Units (CTUs): HEVC splits the picture into a quadtree structure and supports variable block sizes. Larger blocks can be valuable in high-resolution. The efficiency with this variety of block sizes requires CTUs to have sizes dependent on parameters like texture: 64×64, 32×32, or 16×16. A CTU is a logical coding unit that affects the encoded bitstream. There are L×L sample luma (Y) and two L/2×L/2 sample chroma (Cb, Cr) components where bigger sizes normally affect performance. Each Coding Tree Block (CTB) is L×L) as the CTU. The macroblock (MB) is the main point in the past reference slice, containing a 16×16 Luma test block, in typical 4: 2: 0, and two compared chrominance 8×8 test blocks, though they are identical. HEVC relies on CTUs, having encoder picked sizes greater than a typical MB. The CTU contains a CTL (i.e., table lookup codes), a CTB, and etymological structure segments. CTBs can be dissected into lesser blocks through a tree structure and other expedients [8].

Coding Blocks (CBs)/CUs: Each CTB can be divided repeatedly as a quadtree, from the CTB size up to as small as 8×8. The resultant partitions are the CBs and affect inter or intra prediction decision-making. The CU codes are the prediction types with other parameters, being the elementary unit estimates from previously coded data and having CBs with Y, Cb, and Cr samples.

Prediction Blocks (PBs)/Prediction Units (PUs): If CBs are too large to store MVs in inter-picture (temporal) or intra-picture (spatial) prediction modes, PBs can be used. Each CB can be driven into other PBs differently, counting on chronological and/or spatial likelihood. The information on intra-prediction also specifies the CU partitioning on PUs. Each PU designates a group of pixels performing a single prediction mode on a slice for Y, Cb, and Cr samples separately. There are many PB types from 64×64 to 4×4 samples.

Transform Blocks (TBs)/Transform Units (TUs): The remaining expectations are encoded using square changes. The tree structure has its underlying foundations at the level of CU. The end of the BC front cannot be distinguished from the rest of the change (TBs) or can be divided into small TB fronts. The total number of wherewithals, like Discrete Cosine Transforms (DCTs), employs 4×4, 8×8, 16×16, and 32×32 neighborhoods. It is possible to modify the Discrete Sinusoid Transformation (DST) result to alter the 4×4 residuals from previous image projections.

MV Signaling: Advanced MV prediction (AMVP) predicts a current MV by employing a strategy hinging on competition among members of a candidate set, including both spatial and temporal MVs, chosen in terms of information from nearby Bypass (BP) modes and reference MIs. The MV coding consolidation mode can also help migrate moving entities from the PB or PB traffic in the vicinity. Unlike H.264, the alteration was ignored, and the coordinated motion was also determined.

Motion Compensation (MC): The quadrilateral test accuracy for MVs with seven or eight channels assists H.264 split quality positions, employing some reference MIs as in MPEG-4 AVC. Two transmitter vectors can be sent exclusively for each prediction block or non-hazardous or bivalent encryption.

Quantization Control: HEVC supports MPEG-4/H.264 AVC via URQ and contains evaluation grids for various pieces of different sizes.

Coding Scheme: Context-Adaptive Binary Arithmetic Coding (CABAC) helps entropy encoding plus a few upgrades to enhance streams and compression performance chiefly for parallelizations while minimizing contextual memory.

De-blocking Filter: An unlocking filter like the one utilized in H.264/MPEG-4 appeared inside the loop for inter-picture prediction. Yet, design is less complicated in basic leadership and sifting forms and seems more fun and easy to work with for parallel processing.

Sample Adaptive Offset (SAO) Filter (SAOF): This non-linear amplitude mapping filter handles deblocked pixels for each CTU threefold: (a) No SAO filtering, (b) Band Offset (BO), and (c) Edge Offset (EO). BO and EO add an offset quantity to a sample. The BO offset results from a lookup table obtained as per the sample magnitude. In contrast, the EO offset value comes from a received lookup table according to an edge direction and gradient.

4. Discussion

Slice-to-volume (S2V) Image Registration (IR) is still important in 3D MI compression. Intra and HEVC compression ratios are shown on the various DICOM video processors. An algorithm and estimations that analyze each frame are produced. Numerous factors govern research, including the matching criteria, transformation model, optimization technique, number of slices, application, and validation approach.

PACSs are a concern for small to medium medical imaging facilities, research environments, and healthcare organizations in poor nations. Financial restrictions and the uniqueness of these settings lead to low PACS adoption rates. Also, with ubiquitous computing and new initiatives like IHE and XDS-i to improve healthcare information technology and data exchange, a PACS must adapt swiftly. This article introduces Dicoogle, a software framework that allows developers and researchers to easily prototype and deploy new features using integrated DICOM services. Its plugin-based design and out-of-the-box capability enable the study of huge DICOM files and accompanying information. These features make the proposed solution ideal for prototyping, testing, and integrating with deployed applications. It allows for sophisticated data discovery and retrieval via DICOM object indexing, as well as the identification of data and process irregularities. This method has helped several use cases such as radiation dose monitoring, Content-Based Image Retrieval (CBIR), and classes addressing software engineering for therapeutic settings [42-47].

Current work scrutinies indicate that most procedures concentrate on rigid IR, utilizing iconic matching measures and continuous optimization strategies. It is, consequently, advantageous to wonder why this trend is so obvious and marked when dealing with S2V IR. Most works estimate that rigid transformations may stem from two main grounds. The first one has to do with straightforward prerequisites from the application standpoint. Such a rudimentary transformation model must be sufficiently expressive to explain simple S2V mappings since it can deal with in-plane and out-of-plane transformations, e.g., translations, rotations, and contractions/ expansions. This type of model may be adequate in clinical settings that do not inherit image distortion-like basic cases of inter-slice motion correction. In more complex cases like image-guided surgeries, intra-operative images are deformed concerning the pre-operative volume due to tissue modifications, collapse, and breathing/heart motion throughout the procedure.

Moreover, in intra-operative cases and during non-interventional imaging, many body organs (e.g., lung, cardiac, or tongue) have naturalistic elastic movement. Even so, rigid models still monopolize literature. This is related to the second reason: the physicians' widespread skepticism of the non-rigid transformations. It is occasionally preferable to furnish dependable despite inaccurate cues than unrealistic resolutions from a healthcare mindset. Non-rigid and elastic models might yield answers from a geometrical viewpoint but are anatomically negligible.

Further exploration of convincing deformation models will eventually reflect somatic tissue properties, ameliorate the estimations' accuracy, and widen trust in procedures tailored to the health community.

Image-based matching criteria (aka similarity metrics) assist in describing the quality of the retrieved solutions when restoring slice integrity [22-25] or further processing them to render the 3D MI [22-25, 65]. This is somehow unforeseen if bearing in mind the support deficit and adequate real-time computational resources naturally associated with S2V registration. Speaking in realistic terms, the image noise often emerges in real-time, intra-operative, and reduced-quality modalities that, on average, appear corresponding to the input 2D MI, making it challenging to determine in detail image similarities solely established on intensity plus depth information. Two strategies can help curb caveats as follows:

(i) When possible, one can utilize multiple slices as an alternative to a single one to boost the matching quality by amplifying the image support information while keeping lower computational complexity compared to other IR methods, which produces more precise renderings.

(ii) By merging similarity imaging evaluations and description criteria with schemes hinging on geometry or sensor-based traits to display more robustness to image alterations and discontinuities.

Both categories can work in tandem with other sensor-based devices like image-guided interventions, where different imaging devices or surgery tools can create Multispectral or Hyperspectral images (MSIs or HSIs). A HSI tool can pack much more volumetric information about a 3D MI, thus demanding more sophisticated multidimensional similarity metrics valuable enough to refine and allow detail-rich initial estimations with more precise results [48-54].

The last decades witnessed the adoption of discrete optimization strategies by biomedical imaging groups massively. Yet, as far as S2V IR goes the same did not materialize for the most part, with most of the implementations still embracing continuous gradient- and non-gradient-based optimizers. Of late, just a few workings formulated S2V IR from a discrete viewpoint. Recognizable continuous ways and means have shown enough goodness to treat basic S2V registration cases.

Nevertheless, fallouts from other MI analyses can be modeled through discrete techniques, which suggest a great potential to be exploited for S2V registration in cases where the amount of 3D parameters (feature vector entries) to be estimated is too high, as is the case with deformable IR where colossally compact characteristic fields are assumed. Such instances can correspond to transformation models partaking non-convex energy functions as below:

(1) Multimodal IR,
(2) Extraordinarily wide, high-dimensional (HD) searching spaces stemming from weak initializations, and
(3) Discrete alternative procedures that may create different density representations.

Research communities have endured major struggles towards cultivating more accurate S2V IR strategies. Nonetheless, the massive MI data production, together with the up-to-the-minute progresses in Artificial Intelligence (AI) and, in particular, Deep Learning (DL) applied as Convolutional Neural Networks (CNNs), open the prospect to regard S2V IR within an utterly different concept [35-41]. DL architectures can be trained to benefit from gigantic medical data amounts to eventually outperform ongoing state-of-the-art stratagems in other fundamental MI tasks resembling segmentation in addition to object recognition. Recent IR and HD vector flow estimation strategies somehow involve CNNs. These DL structures treat similarity metrics and the de facto IR process that can be learned from examples, suggesting and shedding light on these problems. The S2V IR formulation under the DL paradigm has just commenced being journeyed and persists essentially unexplored. Hence, the auspicious outcomes already attained point out towards shifting gears to a learning-based S2V IR paradigm. By doing so, the research cooperative efforts may accomplish more rapid, precise predictions, unlocking new 3D/4D/5D and HD doors in biomedical explorations.

5. Conclusion

The DICOM medical imaging (MI) standard enables the exchange of images across healthcare applications. JPEG 2000 enhances JPEG for therapeutic imaging utilizing wavelets and a discrete transformation. Still, JPEG 2000 is ill-suited to encoding certain visual groupings and rendering high-quality 3D reconstruction [66-71]. This article scrutinizes HEVC for 3D MI compressions, such as MRI, CT, and angiography, which are presently reliant on blocks of pixels. Voxels may be obtained at the end-user level from already-encoded sliced pictures forge 3D forms, i.e., slice-to-volume (S2V) image registration. HEVC yields high-quality video improvement with a tolerable ratedistortion function. HEVC codecs encode/ decode besides compressing/decompressing pictures. The encoder/compressor deals with 3D objects and partakes a series of frames/slices into a stream that can be safely disseminated. The decoder gathers and decompresses the bitstream to render decoded frames. Several metrics may compare 3D medical dataset studies and byproducts. HEVC reduces computational and data transport burdens for DICOM 3D MI. Savings depend on MI sequence size and characteristics per pixel/voxel. HEVC's complexity increases coding time. HEVC compression limits necessitate objective and subjective assessments to target abnormalities in HD medical structures. MI via artificial intelligence (AI) is growing. Most of this research is done in solitude with small datasets, leading to oversimplified models that are accurate only in specific instances. Smaller hospitals lack the technical skills, computational resources, and data quantities essential for AI to deliver better treatment for their local population. Even with good AI algorithms, integration and scalability issues delay acceptance [55-61].

References

1. de Jesus, M.A., Estrela, V.V., Aroma, R.J., Raimond, K., Fernandes, S.R. et al. (2022). Motion estimation role in the context of 3D video. Int. J. Multim. Data Eng. Manag. (IJMDEM), 12, 16-38, IGI Global, Hershey, PA, USA.
2. Coelho, A.M., Estrela, V.V., do Carmo, F.P. and Fernandes, S.R. (2012). Error concealment by means of motion refinement and regularized Bregman divergence. Yin,

H. et al. (eds). Proc. IDEAL 2012. Lecture Notes in Computer Science, 2012, vol. 7435. Springer, Berlin, Heidelberg.

3. Rahmat, R.F., Andreas, T.S.M., Fahmi, F., Pasha, M.F., Alzahrani, M.Y. et al. (2019). Analysis of DICOM image compression alternative using Huffman coding. J. Healthcare Eng., vol. 2019.

4. Osechinskiy, S. and Kruggel, F. (2011). Slice-to-volume nonrigid registration of histological sections to MR images of the human brain. Anatomy Research International, 287860.

5. Estrela, V.V., Saotome, O., Loschi, H.J., Hemanth, D.J., Farfan, W.S. et al. (2018). Emergency response cyber-physical framework for landslide avoidance with sustainable electronics. Technologies, 6(2), 42.

6. Pole, A. and Shriram, R. (2018). 3-D medical image compression by using HEVC. Proc. Fourth Int'l Conf. Computing Communication Control and Automation (ICCUBEA), 1-5. IEEE.

7. Estrela, V.V., Hemanth, J., Saotome, O., Nikolakopoulos, G. and Sabatini, R. (2020). Imaging and Sensing for Unmanned Aircraft Systems: Control and Performance, Vol. 1, ISBN 978-1-78561-642-6 (Hardback).

8. Sullivan, G.J., Ohm, J.R., Han, W.J. and Wiegand, T. (2012). Overview of the High-Efficiency Video Coding (HEVC) standard. IEEE Trans. Circ. Syst. for Video Tech., 22(12), 1649-1668.

9. Parikh, S., Kalva, H. and Adzic, V. (2016). Evaluation of HEVC compression for high bit depth medical images. Proc. 2016 IEEE Int'l Conf. on Consumer Electronics (ICCE), 311-314. Las Vegas, NV, USA.

10. Ndong, B., Diop, O., Bathily, E.A., Mbodj, M., Gassama, S.S. et al. (2015). JPEG2000 compression for scintigraphic images of metastasis of the prostatic cancer. Proc. 2nd World Symp. Web Appl. and Netw., WSWAN 2015.

11. Dash, S., Shakyawar, S.K., Sharma, M. and Kaushik, S. (2019). Big data in healthcare: Management, analysis and future prospects. J. Big Data, 6, 1-25.

12. De Macedo, D.D.J., Von Wangenheim, A. and Dantas, M.A.R. (2015). A data storage approach for large-scale distributed medical systems. Proc. 9th Int'l Conf. Complex, Int., and Soft. Intensive Systems, CISIS 2015.

13. Deshpande, A., Estrela, V.V. and Razmjooy, N. (2021). Computational intelligence methods for super-resolution in image processing applications. Springer.

14. Patel, D., Lad, T.C. and Shah, D.J. (2015). Review on intra-prediction in High Efficiency Video Coding (HEVC) standard. Int'l Journal of Computer Applications, 132, 26-29.

15. Wang, W., Gang, G.J., Siewerdsen, J.H. and Stayman, J.W. (2019). Volume-of-interest imaging using multiple aperture devices. Proc. SPIE 10948, Medical Imaging 2019: Physics of Medical Imaging, 1094823.

16. Tech, G., Chen, Y., Müller, K., Ohm, J.R., Vetro, A. et al. (2015). Overview of the multiview and 3D extensions of High Efficiency Video Coding. IEEE Trans. Circ. Syst. for Vid. Tech., 26(1), 35-49.

17. Cai, Q., Song, L., Li, G. and Ling, N. (2012). Lossy and lossless intra coding performance evaluation: HEVC, H.264/AVC, JPEG 2000 and JPEG-LS, Proc. 2012 Asia Pac. Sig. and Inf. Proc. Assoc. Annual Summit and Conf., Hollywood, CA, 1-9.

18. Information Technology: JPEG 2000 Image coding System, Part 1: Core Coding System document 15444-1, ISO/IEC, 2000.

19. Roček, A., Javorník, M., Slávicek, K. and Dostál, O. (2017). Reversible watermarking in medical imaging with zero distortion in ROI. Proc. 24th IEEE Int'l Conf. Electronics, Circ. and Syst. (ICECS), 356-359.

20. Wang, W., Gang, G.J., Mao, A., Sisniega, A., Siewerdsen, J.H. et al. (2018). Volume-of-interest CT imaging with dynamic beam filtering using multiple aperture devices. Proc. Int'l Conf. Image Formation in X-Ray Computed Tomography, 213-217.

21. Demircioğlu, A., Grueneisen, J.S., Ingenwerth, M., Hoffmann, O., Pinker-Domenig, K. et al. (2020). A rapid volume of interest-based approach of radiomics analysis of breast MRI for tumor decoding and phenotyping of breast cancer. PLoS ONE, 15.

22. Parikh, S., Kalva, H. and Adzic, V. (2016). Evaluation of HEVC compression for high bit depth medical images. Proc. 2016 IEEE Int'l Conf. on Consumer Electronics (ICCE), 311-314. Las Vegas, NV, USA.

23. Bhardwaj, C., Sharma, U., Jain, S. and Sood, M. (2019). Implementation and performance assessment of biomedical image compression and reconstruction algorithms for telemedicine applications: Compressive sensing for biomedical images. *In:* B. Singh et al. (ed.). Medical Data Security for Bioengineers, IGI, 52-80.

24. Mojica, M., Pop, M. and Ebrahimi, M. (2021). Medical image alignment based on landmark- and approximate contour-matching. Journal of Medical Imaging, 8, 064003-064003.

25. Liu, X., Lu, X.R. and Ma, L. (2020). An improved synthetic aperture radar image denoising method based on block-matching and 3D filtering. ISPRS – Int'l Archives of the Photogrammetry, Remote Sensing and Spatial Information Sciences, 319-323.

26. Argyriou, V., Rincón, J.M., Villarini, B. and Roche, A. (2015). Image, Video and 3D Data Registration: Medical, Satellite and Video Processing Applications with Quality Metrics. Wiley.

27. Karim, S., Zhang, Y., Yin, S., Laghari, A.A., Brohi, A.A. et al. (2019). Impact of compressed and down-scaled training images on vehicle detection in remote sensing imagery. Mult, Tools and App., 78, 32565-32583.

28. Laghari, A.A., He, H. and Channa, M.I. (2018). Measuring effect of packet reordering on quality of experience (QoE) in video streaming. 3D Research, 9(1-11).

29. Trupti, N., Baraskar, T.N. and Mankar, V.R. (2019). The DICOM image compression and patient data integration using run length and Huffman Encoder. *In:* Radhakrishnan S. and Sarfraz M. (eds). Coding Theory, IntechOpen.

30. Parikh, S.S., Ruiz, D., Kalva, H., Fernandez-Escribano, G., Adzic, V. et al. (2018). High bit-depth medical image compression with HEVC. IEEE Journal of Biomedical and Health Informatics.

31. Karim, Sajida, Hui He, Asif Ali Laghari, Arif Hussain Magsi et al. (2021). Quality of service (QoS): Measurements of image formats in social cloud computing. Multimedia Tools and Applications, 80(3), 4507-4532.

32. Karim, Sajida, Hui, He, Asif Ali Laghari, and Hina Madiha et al. (2020). Quality of service (QoS): Measurements of video streaming. arXiv preprint arXiv:2008.12017.

33. Madiha, Hina, Hui, Lei, Asif Ali Laghari and Sajida Karim et al. (2020). Quality of experience and quality of service of gaming services in fog computing. Proceedings of the 2020 4th international Conference on Management Engineering, Software Engineering and Service Sciences, pp. 225-228.

34. Clunie, D.A. (2020). DICOM format and protocol standardization—A core requirement for digital pathology success. Toxicologic Pathology, 49, 738-749.

35. Hu, S., Wang, S., Weng, W., Wang, J., Wang, X. et al. (2020). Weakly supervised context encoder using DICOM metadata in ultrasound imaging. arXiv, abs/2003.09070.

36. Hemanth, J. and Estrela, V.V. (2017). Deep Learning for Image Processing Applications. IOS Press.

37. Deshpande, A., Estrela, V.V. and Razmjooy, N. (2021). Computational Intelligence Methods for Super-Resolution in Image Processing Applications. Springer Nature, Zurich, Switzerland. doi: 10.1007/978-3-030-67921-7

38. Hemant, D.J., Estrela, V.V., Tavares, J.M.R.S., Wang, L. and Shi, F. (2018). Special Issue: Soft computing techniques for image analysis in the medical industry – Current trends, challenges and solutions. Editorial, IEEE Access, IEEE.

39. Ciompi, F., Chung, K., Riel, S.J., Setio, A.A., Gerke, P.K. et al. (2017). Towards automatic pulmonary nodule management in lung cancer screening with deep learning. Scientific Reports, vol. 7.

40. Cheng, J., Ni, D., Chou, Y., Qin, J., Tiu, C. et al. (2016). Computer-aided diagnosis with deep learning architecture: Applications to breast lesions in US images and pulmonary nodules in CT scans. Scientific Reports, vol. 6.

41. Kumar, D., Wong, A. and Clausi, D.A. (2015). Lung nodule classification using deep features in CT images. Proc. International Conference on Computer and Robot Vision.

42. Lin, C.-H., Chen, R.T. and Chan, Y.-K. (2009). A smart content-based image retrieval system based on color and texture feature. Image and Vision Computing, 658-665.

43. Wang, J., Zhang, Z. and Zha, H. (2005). Adaptive manifold learning. Advances in Neural Information Processing Systems, 17, 1473-1480, Cambridge, MA, USA. The MIT Press.

44. Wang, C., Zhang, L. and Zhang, H.J. (2008). Learning to reduce the semantic gap in web image retrieval and annotation. Proc. SIGIR'08.

45. Wang, X.Y., Yu, Y.-J. and Yang, H.-Y. (2011). An effective image retrieval scheme using color, texture and shape features. Computer Standards & Interfaces, Special Issue: Secure Semantic Web, 33(1), 59-68. Elsevier.

46. Fu, X., Li, Y., Harrison, R. and Belkasim, S. (2006). Content-based image retrieval using Gabor-Zernike features. Proc. 18th Int'l Conf. on Pattern Recognition (ICPR 2006), vol. 2, pp. 417-420.

47. Tr, A. and Varghese, A. (2017). CBIR of brain MR images using histogram of fuzzy oriented gradients and fuzzy local binary patterns. IAES International Journal of Artificial Intelligence, 6, 8-17.

48. Li Y., Liu, J., Li, J. Ye, W.D. and Wu, Z. (2003). The fuzzy similarity measures for content based image retrieval. Proc. IEEE 2003 Int'l Conf. on Machine Learning and Cybernetics, vol. 5, pp. 3224-3228.

49. Saha, S.K., Das, A.K. and Chanda B. (2004). CBIR using perception based texture and colour measure. Proc. ICPR 2004, pp. 985-988.

50. Wangming, X., Jin, W., Xinhai, L., Lei, Z., Gang, S. et al. (2008). Application of image SIFT features to the context of CBIR. Proc. IEEE 2008 Int'l Conf. on Computer Science and Software Eng., 4, 552-555.

51. Murthy, V.S., Vamsidhar, E., Rao, P.S., Samuel, G., Raju, V. et al. (2010). Application of hierarchical and K-means techniques in content based image retrieval. IJEST, 2(5), 749-755.

52. Zhuo, L., Cheng, B. and Zhang, J. (2014). A comparative study of dimensionality reduction methods for large-scale image retrieval. Neurocomputing, 141, 202-210.

53. Paredes, R. (2013). Interactive image retrieval based on relevance feedback. *In:* Multimodal Interaction in Image and Video Applications. Intelligent Systems Reference Library, vol 48. Springer, Berlin, Heidelberg.

54. Burges, C.J.C. (2005). Geometric methods for feature selection and dimensional reduction: A guided tour. Data Mining and Knowledge Discovery Handbook: A Complete Guide for Practitioners and Researchers. Kluwer Academic Publishers.

55. Chen, X., Zhang, C., Chen, S.-C. and Chen, M. (2005). A latent semantic indexing based method for solving multiple instance learning problem in region-based image retrieval. Proc. Seventh IEEE Int'l Symposium on Multimedia, pp. 37-45.

56. Cheng, B., Zhuo, L. and Zhang, J. (2013). Comparative study on dimensionality reduction in large-scale image retrieval. Proc. 15th IEEE International Symp. Multimedia – ISM 2013, pp. 445-450. Anaheim, CA, United States.

57. Guo, C. and Wilson, C. (2008). Use of self-organizing maps for texture feature selection in content-based image retrieval. Proc. 2008 IEEE World Cong. Computational Intelligence. pp. 766-771.

58. Verbeek, J. (2006). Learning nonlinear image manifolds by global alignment of local linear models. IEEE Trans. PAMI, 28(8), 1236-1250.
59. Pirolla, F.R., Felipe, J.C., Santos, M.T.P. and Ribeiro, M.X. (2012). Dimensionality reduction to improve content-based image retrieval: A clustering approach. Proc. 2012 IEEE Int'l Conf. Bioinformatics and Biomed. Workshops (BIBMW), pp. 752-753.
60. Lee, J.A. and Verleysen, M. (2005). Nonlinear dimensionality reduction of data manifolds with essential loops. Neurocomputing, 67, 29-53.
61. Veltkamp, R., Burkhardt, H. and Kriegel, H.P. (2008). State-of-the-art in Content-based Image and Video Retrieval. Kluwer Academic Publishers, New York.
62. Venkatarajan, M.S. and Braun, W. (2004). New quantitative descriptors of amino acids based on multidimensional scaling of a large number of physical chemical properties. J. Molecular Modeling, 7(12), 445-453.
63. Coelho, A.M., Estrela, V.V., Carmo, F.P. and Fernandes, S.R. (2012). Error concealment by means of motion refinement and regularized Bregman divergence. Proc. IDEAL, vol. 7435. Springer.
64. Estrela, V.V., Rivera, L.A., Beggio, P.C. and Lopes, R.T. (2003). Regularized pel-recursive motion estimation using generalized cross-validation and spatial adaptation. 16th Brazilian Symposium on Computer Graphics and Image Processing (SIBGRAPI 2003), 331-338.
65. Laghari, A.A., Estrela, V.V. and Yin, S. (2022). Special Issue: From nanoscale to hyperspectral imaging - How to gather and understand medical images harvested in extremely difficult situations. Curr. Med. Imaging, Bentham Science.
66. Devi, V.U. and Suvitha, M. (2017). An efficient re-rank and fuzzy based color & edge feature extraction for CBIR. International Journal of Computer Trends and Technology, 49, 44-50.
67. Hadi, F., Aliouat, Z. and Hammoudi, S. (2020). Efficient Platform as a Service (PaaS) Model on Public Cloud for CBIR System. Ingénierie des Systèmes d Inf., 25, 215-225.
68. Valente, F., Bastião, L., Godinho, T.M. and Costa, C. (2015). Anatomy of an extensible open source PACS. Journal of Digital Imaging, 29, 284-296.
69. Murugan, S., Sumithra, M.G. and Murugappan, M. (2021). Efficient clustering of unlabeled brain DICOM images based on similarity. Journal of Physics: Conference Series, 1916.
70. Deshpande, A., Patavardhan, P. and Estrela, V.V. (2020). Super resolution and recognition of unconstrained ear image. International Journal of Biometrics, Inderscience, vol. 12(4), pp. 396-410. doi: 10.1504/IJBM.2020.110813
71. Popescu, D., Marinescu, R., Lăptoiu, D., Deac, G.C., Cotet, C.E. et al. (2021). DICOM 3D viewers, virtual reality or 3D printing – A pilot usability study for assessing the preference of orthopedic surgeons. Proceedings of the Institution of Mechanical Engineers, Part H: Journal of Engineering in Medicine, 235, 1014-1024.

Deep Learning as a Driving Force for Better Drug Development

Vania V. Estrela[1] [0000-0002-4465-7691], Khuda Bukhsh[2,3], M. Malook Rind[2],
Sarmad Shaikh[2], Abdullah Ayub Khan[2,3] [0000-0003-2838-7641], Asif Ali Laghari[2,3]
[0000-0001-5831-5943], A. Deshpande[4] [0000-0002-1500-0981], Nikolaos
Andreopoulos[5] [0000-0001-9975-7043], Andrey Terziev[6] [0000-0002-7069-367X]

[1] Department of Telecommunications, Federal Fluminense University (UFF), RJ, Brazil,
vania.estrela.phd@ieee.org

[2] Faculty of Computer Science, Sindh Madressatul Islam University, Karachi (74000),
Sindh, Pakistan, khudabukhsh1992@gmail.com, malook.rindh@smiu.com,
sarmad@smiu.edu.pk, asif.laghari@smiu.edu.pk

[3] Research Lab of Artificial Intelligence and Information Security, Faculty of Computing
Science and Information Technology, Benazir Bhutto Shaheed University Lyari, Karachi
(75660), Sindh, Pakistan, abdullah.khan00763@gmail.com

[4] Electronics and Communication Engineering, Angadi Institute of Technology and
Management, Belagavi, India, deshpande.anandb@gmail.com

[5] Computer Science Department, Technological Institute of Iceland, Iceland,
nikolaosandreopoulos@yahoo.com

[6] TerziA, Sofia, Bulgaria, andreyterziev@yahoo.com

1. Introduction

The increasing development of urban populations internationally brings significant difficulties to daily lives of residents, such as environmental pollution, public security, traffic congestion, and so on. By creating smarter cities, new technologies have been handling this fast expansion. Mingling the Internet of Medical Things (IoMT) into health stakeholders' lives allows for developing new intelligent services and apps that serve sectors throughout the city, such as healthcare, surveillance, agriculture, and so on. IoMT devices, actuators, and sensors create massive volumes of data, which may be examined to acquire necessary information and insights. Residents' Quality of Life (QoL) can also grow as a consequence. Deep Learning (DL), a new Artificial Intelligence (AI) branch, has lately shown promise in improving the efficiency and performance of IoMT big data analytics. This chapter overviews the literature on IoMT and DL to build smart cities. To begin with, it defines the IoMT and identifies the features of IoMT-generated big data. Then, this chapter goes through the various computing infrastructures utilized for IoMT big data analytics, for illustration, cloud, fog, besides edge computing. Following that, it explores standard DL models and examines new research that uses IoMT and DL to build smart apps and services for smart cities. Finally, this text discusses the existing problems and concerns encountered when developing smart city services [1-5].

Several DL as well as metaheuristic reviews targeting medicine, computational chemistry, and biological sciences have been published recently [13-20]. This noteworthy quantity augmentation of open chemical activity and biological data [6, 7] is genuine in healthcare, propelled by the advent of novel experimental tactics like high-throughput screening (HTS), parallel synthesis, and others [7, 8]. How to efficiently mine large-scale chemical data has emerged as a critical issue for drug development. Larger data quantities, along with improved automation, have driven the AI expansion. Approaches corresponding to matrix factorization [12] and DL have begun to be employed in addition to known strategies viz. Support Vector Machines (SVM) [9], Neural Networks (NN) [10], in addition to Random Forest (RF) [11]. These tactics have facilitated QSAR model constructions for a long time. DL has benefited from growing data volumes and the continual rise in available computing power. The NN architecture flexibility in DL distinguishes it from most other AI approaches. This text talks about Convolutional Neural Networks (CNNs), Recurrent Neural Networks (RNNs), and fully-linked, feed-forward networks. QSAR modeling has exploited Single-layer NNs for an extensive time [10], and as data quantity and computing capacity have increased, it has become natural to use multilayer feedforward networks for bioactivity predictions. RNN usage in de novo designs was a rather unexpected development that could not have been predicted a few years ago.

CNNs have accomplished great success in computer vision owing to the insertion of high-throughput imaging equipment, and they are a natural option for biological and biochemical image-related processing. Utilizing DL in drug development is constantly evolving, with new studies being published nearly every week. This chapter concentrates on DL drug development, notably in the biological and chemoinformatics image studies, highlighting DL designs that have been employed thus far in drug discovery.

Section 2 talks about deep learning. Section 3 lists several ways DL can be used in drug discovery. A discussion about future work appears in Section 4. Conclusions emerge in Section 5.

2. Deep Learning Building Blocks

DL extends Artificial Neural Networks (ANNs) with numerous layers of nonlinear processing units [2]. Figure 1 portrays the essential ANN structure motivated by the human brain, containing three layers: input, hidden, and output. The nodes, also known as neurons, in surrounding layers are either fully or partly linked depending on ANN. Input nodes accept input variables, and the variables are changed by hidden nodes before being computed at output nodes. Figure 1 depicts the connection among the input and hidden unit output values. The node i's output value Y_i is computed as indicated in (1).

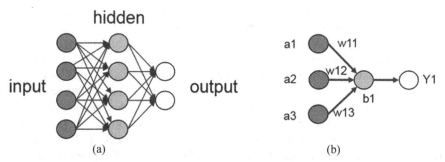

Figure 1. The NN rationale: (a) input, hidden in addition to output layers, and (b) output values of a hidden unit are computed from input values through an activation function

$$Y_i = g(\sum_j W_{ij} * a_j),\tag{1}$$

where a_j represents the input variables. The weight of input node j on node i is W_{ij}. The symbol "g" stands for the habitually nonlinear activation function (viz. sigmoid or Gaussian), which maps the linear combination of the input signals from input nodes to estimate an output value. An ANN is iteratively trained by adjusting weights in the network to minimize the errors between projected and true values, generally using back-propagation methods. Declining gradients, overfitting, and other matters disturb ANNs, which were predominantly superseded by newer algorithms such as SVM [9] and RF [11]. The current DL advancement has stemmed a rebirth of ANNs. NN scales and complexity are the primary differences between DL and conventional ANNs. DL employs more hidden layers, whereas standard ANNs can only treat one or two hidden layers. Hardware limitations in the early days caused this behavior. DL may use copious numbers of nodes in each layer because of the introduction of increasingly powerful CPU and GPU technology. There have also been many algorithmic advances in DL, such as the use of the dropout [21] besides DropConnect [22] tactics to address overfitting. The Rectified Linear Unit (ReLU) [23] bypasses vanishing gradients by employing convolutional and pooling layers for large numbers of input variables. The majority of DL software products are open-source: (i) Caffe [24], (ii) TensorFlow [25], (iii) Keras [26], (iv) PyTorch [27], in addition to (v) Theano [28] which are popular DL tools. This section will quickly describe various prominent NN architectures used in DL (Figure 2). The first is the fully-connected Deep Neural Network (DNN) that partakes many hidden layers with hundreds of nonlinear units in each layer (Figure 2). DNNs can process a colossal quantity of input features, and neurons in countless DNN layers may extract information by design at different hierarchical levels [29].

CNN is another well-known NN that emerges extensively in image recognition (Figure 2a). It often has lots of convolution and subsampling layers. A convolutional layer encompasses a filter (kernel) collection with a constrained receptive field besides learnable parameters. Each filter gets convolved widthwise and height-wise with the input volume throughout the forward pass, figuring out the dot product among the filter's entries with its receptive field inside the input volume, in addition to crafting a 2D feature map for that filter. The subsampling layer compresses feature maps. Finally, the feature maps can be concatenated into fully-connected layers where neurons in surrounding layers are all linked to provide a final output value, exactly like in a standard ANN. Since, each filter utilizes the same parameters, a CNN dramatically cuts the total of free parameters learned, decreasing consumed memory and boosting learning speed. In picture recognition, it outperforms other forms of AI systems [30]. RNN is a further ANN variation (Figure 2c). Unlike feed-forward NNs, it permits neurons in the same hidden layer to link to form a directed cycle. RNNs may accept sequential data as input characteristics, making them ideal for time-dependent applications corresponding to language modeling [31]. RNNs can mitigate the fading gradient problem by applying a Long Short Term Memory (LSTM) [32] architecture. Figure 2b depicts a fully connected Deep Neural Network (DNN).

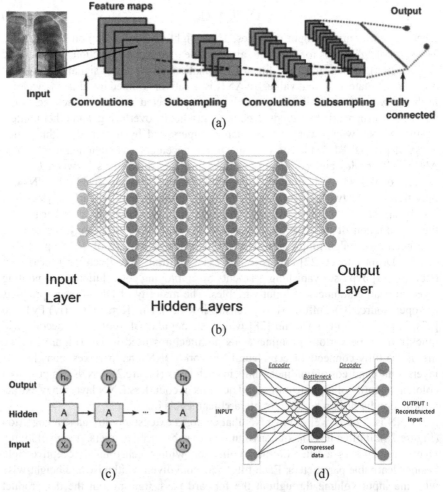

Figure 2. Several popular NN architectures: (a) Convolutional Neural Network (CNN), (b) fully connected Deep Neural Network (DNN), (c) Recurrent Neural Network (RNN), and (d) Autoencoder (AE)

The fourth ANN design seen in Figure 2 is the autoencoder (AE) [33] that is a kind of NN for unsupervised learning. It holds an encoder module, which is a NN that transforms the material obtained from the input layer. This output feeds a bounded quantity of hidden units. Subsequently, a decoder NN with an identical quantity of nodes as shown by the input layer, reestablishes inputs instead of estimating the labels of input occurrences, from a smaller amount of hidden units, which is its goal. The purpose of AE is often to shrink nonlinear dimensionality. The AE approach has recently attained popularity for generative models' data learning [34]. The illustrations below show different DL technologies for drug discovery research.

3. DL in Component Property and Action Prediction

3.1. Foundations and History

For a long time, AI practices such as ANN predicted chemical activity. Naturally, DL techniques first solved the problem of activity prediction. When the same amount of molecular descriptors represent compounds, the most straightforward way is to create models via fully-connected DNNs. A DNN processed the Merck Kaggle competition dataset with an elevated number of 2D topological descriptors [35]. DNNs did somewhat better than traditional RFs in most of the targets. Some key findings are: (i) DNNs can manipulate thousands of descriptors evading feature selection; (ii) dropout can evade the overfitting problem encountered by traditional ANNs; (iii) hyper-parameters (viz. number of layers, amount of nodes per layer, nature of activation functions, and so forth) optimization can lead to maximizing DNN performance; and (iv) multitask DNN models outperform single-task models. Multitask DNN models won the Tox21 challenge whose chemical datasets contained high throughput toxicity experiments [36]. The DNN employed dropout, and ReLU activation functions, similar to [35, 37], and model training happened parallelly on GPU computers. A vast feature set containing static descriptors (e.g., 3D, 2D, and preset toxicophores, among others) along with dynamically created fingerprint descriptors (like ECFP, DFS, RAD2D) let DNNs make self-feature deductions during training. A statistical association breakdown occurred with only DNN models incorporating ECFP, and substructures extensively linked with well-known toxicophores in every hidden layer. These benchmark fallouts show that the multitask DNN outperforms a single-task DNN and traditional AI approaches. Other benchmark revisions have been released supporting outcomes as in [38]. The previous one conducted a comprehensive examination to develop multitask DNNs to compare their performance to single-task DNN models. Their findings demonstrate that multitask models consistently outperform single-task and RF models. Seven datasets from ChEMBL [39, 40], compared a DNN against many frequently used AI approaches such as SVM, RF, and others. DNNs outdid other AI methodologies. Another benchmark research comparing DNN to traditional AI methods such as RF, SVM, naive Bayes, and logic regression methods that consider protein descriptors (the proteochemometric (PCM) investigation [41]). They examined the performance of several classification algorithms on a dataset targeting compound interactions.

The DNN model was shown to be the best model, while multitasking and PCM implementations were proven to outperform single-task DNNs.

Aside from the benchmark DNN research, a DNN relies on 2D topological descriptors to craft an estimate-reliant BACE activity model [42] with a good classification accuracy and a low standard error on the validation set. The study in [43] used LINCS transcriptome data [44] as well as route facts to construct DNNs for forecasting pharmacological drug features and prescription repurposing. DNN models have been demonstrated to predict pharmacological indications with high accuracy using pathway and gene-level knowledge, suggesting that they might be beneficial for medication repurposing. Attempts have also employed representation learning (i.e., okaying NNs to learn straightforwardly from the molecular structure as a replacement to predefined molecular descriptors) [45]. Two other distinct approaches to the problem are

(i)   The UGRNN scheme which is a RNN version that first transforms molecular structures into molecular representation vectors and then utilizes them to link a NN layer fully to create models [46]. The dataset learns the bit values within the vectors. The UGRNN technique could construct predictive solubility models with an accuracy equivalent to building models with molecular descriptors.

(ii) A similar approach is to mimic drug-induced liver damage (DILI) from [47]. The DL models were created using 475 medications and verified using an additional dataset of 198 medicines. The finest model attained very high AUC, greater than the accuracy of previously published DILI models.

To begin with, the 2D molecular structure is scanned to generate a state matrix with atom and bond information (based on each atom's bonds connected to the atom). The state matrix is then convolved using a single-layer NN to produce a fixed-length vector functioning as the molecular representation. The convolution process may occur at several levels by considering the influences of nearby atoms equal to the circular fingerprints at various neighboring levels. The vectors from different convolutions are the first softmax-transformations. Then, they are summed to yield the compound's final vector, a neural fingerprint containing molecule-level information. To yield the final output, the neural fingerprints go through an additional fully-connected NN layer. The neural fingerprint's bit values learning happens in the course of training and is discernible. Significant substructures in the graphical convolution models can elucidate the phenomena. The graph convolution model obtains rewards from automatically generating descriptors during training and does not require any predetermined chemical descriptors. Such a descriptor is not a generic descriptor but rather task-specific and completely differentiable, and therefore can ameliorate prediction. The works from [50-53] informed different molecular graph convolution methods. Google [54] recently recast many existing graph convolution techniques [49, 50, 53, 55, 56] into a mutual arrangement deemed as a Message-Passing Neural Network (MPNN), which were exploited in the MPNNs to predict quantum chemical characteristics.

In addition to graph-based representation learning approaches, DL methods based on various forms of molecular representation were investigated. LSTM RNNs using a SMILES string serve as the input to create predictive models without the requirement for chemical descriptions [57]. It was also discovered that expanding the dataset by utilizing several SMILES strings to epitomize the same chemical produced better aftermaths than canonical SMILES. A CNN worked on 2D molecule drawings and obtained results that were unexpectedly close to DNN prototypes trained on ECFP [58]. Furthermore, the model performance was enhanced even further when the pictures were supplemented with some uncomplicated chemical information [59]. The ability to learn representations from structures directly without utilizing any predetermined structure descriptor is a crucial characteristic that distinguishes DL from other AI approaches, and it effectively eliminates traditional feature selection as well as reduction procedures.

Graph convolution models are another sort of technique. The fundamental concept is comparable to the UGRNN technique, which uses NNs to automatically produce a chemical description vector, using vector values learned by training NNs. Inspired by the circular fingerprint technique [48, 49] the neural fingerprint method was developed as one of the first attempts to create a graph convolution model. Figure 3 depicts the process of this approach [75-78]. To generate a vector of fixed length, a molecular graph first undergoes a convolution operation via a single layer NN. The convolution process can be performed at several neighboring levels. The vectors created by the various convolution procedures are then softmax transformed and summed to yield the compound's neural fingerprints. To craft the final output, the neural fingerprint is sent via another fully connected NN layer. The neural fingerprint's bit values are learned during training and are distinguishable.

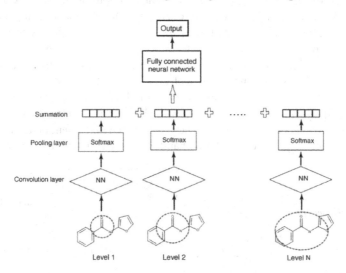

Figure 3. Graphical illustration of CNNs

3.2. DL via *De Novo* Design

Another captivating DL chemoinformatic use of NNs relies on generating novel chemical structures. A unique tactic for engendering chemical structures by means of variational autoencoders (VAE) (Figure 4) can be found in [60]. The NN transforms

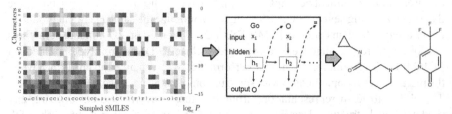

Figure 4. Variational autoencoder (VAE) illustration

a discrete molecule into a Gaussian distribution deterministically. A new point undergoes sampling and is fed into the decoder NN after reparametrizing the latent variables against the Gaussian distribution with the assumed mean and variance. In the generation mode, just the decoder creates a new molecule coming from the sampled latent point. The initial stage is to utilize VAE to start up unsupervised learning on chemical structures (SMILES strings) in the ZINC database to map them into latent space. Once trained, the latent vector in latent space turns out to be a continuous molecular structure representation and may be reversibly converted to a SMILES string using the learned VAE. Creating a new structure with desirable attributes may be accomplished by searching for optimum latent solutions belonging to the continuous latent space using any optimization approach (viz. Bayesian optimization) and decoding the found latent solutions into SMILES. Following in the footsteps of [61], VAE handled a molecular descriptor generator in conjunction with a Generative Adversarial Network (GAN) [62] to yield novel compounds with potential specialized anti-cancer properties. A VAE created new structures with anticipated dopamine receptor type activity [63]. RNNs have prospered in natural language processing [31] and they can produce new chemical structures [64, 65]. After training the RNN employing many SMILES strings, the RNN approach performed remarkably well in creating new valid SMILES strings, not in the training set (Figure 5). The top graphic depicts how the RNN model thinks when it generates the structure on the bottommost right. The y axis displays all potential tokens possibly selected at each step. Given the beforehand elected characters, the color indicates

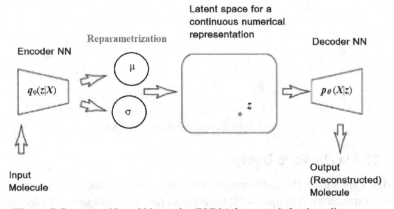

Figure 5. Recurrent Neural Networks (RNNs) framework for drug discovery

the conditional probability of choosing from the current step. The x-axis displays the character sampled in this case. The RNN operates in structure-generation mode as depicted in the bottom left of the above figure. At each phase, a character was sampled employing the RNN model's conditional probability distribution. The generated character was then utilized as the input character to create the following character.

The RNN generates structurally correct SMILES by learning the underlying character probability distribution in a SMILES string; in this situation, the RNN may be considered a molecular generative model. RNNs brought in target-specific libraries by first training a broad-spectrum prior model. At that point, a fine-tuned, dedicated transfer learning model hinging on a limited selection of target-specific active compounds [64] was utilized. In a backward-looking study for testing on two antibioactive objectives, Deep Q-learning, a reinforcement learning method, in juxtaposition with RNN crafts SMILES with the hoped-for chemical characteristics such as cLogP [66, 67] and QED drug-likeness [68]. However, this modus operandi required a reward function that encompassed handwritten rules to punish undesired structures, otherwise leading to rewarding exploitation, which would lead to unrealistically simple molecules. This limitation is addressed and developed by means of a policy-based RL for tuning pre-trained RNNs to produce molecules with specified user-defined properties [69]. In one trial case, for tuning the model in order to engender active compounds against the type-2 receptor, the model created structures with an extremely high percentage of active components, containing experimentally checked actives that were not in the generative model or the activity prediction mode.

The methodologies mentioned above have shown promise as de novo design alternatives to standard rule-based approaches. GANs and reinforcement learning, on the other hand, are known to be vulnerable to mode collapse (i.e., models only engender a single solution or a minor group of similar solutions). This was noted in a recent assessment [70] on the creation of de novo structures utilizing DL techniques. A significant amount of work [71, 72] has been expended to solve this issue.

3.3. DL Application

AI in predicting reactions together with retrosynthetic analysis/ synthesis estimates partakes a long history [73]. Recently, some encouraging findings in response prediction utilizing DL techniques were published. Although no unequivocal comparison with other AI strategies was made, the fallouts suggested that DL can attain performances comparable to, if not superior to, rule-based systems. AI, including DL in response informatics, may solve two sorts of issues schematically. The first kind is forward reaction prediction. The products are anticipated given a set of reactants and the other type results from retrosynthetic prediction. The reaction pathways that generate the product are anticipated given a final product. The work in [74] used NN to score potential outcomes for a group of reactions relying on a training set of docking programs, and numerous scoring functions were built based on force fields or information from known protein-ligand complex structures [79]. Following the accomplishment of CNNs in computer vision investigations, numerous works have recently used them to assess protein-ligand interaction as in [80]. The protein-ligand structures were discretized onto a 0.5-resolution grid. The grid consisted of 24 squares on each side, centered on the binding location. Each atom received a function ,besides atom densities were created throughout the grid to form the input matrix. The Caffe DL structure demarcated and trained multilayer CNN/DNN prototypes [81-85]. Although some promising results came from using convolutional networks, it is unclear if they will continuously outperform present scoring functions.

3.4. Chemoinformatics Benchmark Datasets

The fast imagery recognition gains may have endorsed innovative methods and the availability of canonical and big datasets. The standardized dataset would facilitate the community to benchmark or assess AI deployments. Many significant CNN designs have emerged from initiatives resembling the yearly ImageNet Large Scale Visual Recognition Competition (ILSVRC) [86, 90].

Despite the readiness of numerous open-source chemoinformatic datasets [87, 88], they hamper AI development due to the small extent of those datasets, the lack of diversified forms of splitting training besides test sets, and, most notably, the shortage of a regular appraisal platform for anticipated new algorithms. Inspired by the WordNet, ImageNet, and MoleculeNet datasets [87-91]. Various curating collections emerged, including quantum mechanical, biophysical, and physicochemical, in addition to physiological datasets. Software suites implementing many well-known molecule representations and AI sets of rules have also been developed. MoleculeNet hinges on the open-source software DeepChem [92] and gives simple access to various prominent DeepChem DL algorithms. This will significantly ease future comparison and development of innovative AI procedures.

3.5. Deep Learning Aiding Biological Image Analysis

Biological and biochemical image analyses frequently aid the drug development process, from preclinical research through clinical trials. Scientists can use imaging to see the phenotypes and host (human or animal) behaviors, organs, tissues, and cells, in addition to subcellular parts. The underlying biological, pathological, and pharmacological mechanisms of action are exposed by digital picture analysis. Fluorescently categorized or unlabeled imageries obtained with (1) microscopes, (2) Computed Tomography (CT), (3) tissue pathology visual scrutiny, (4) Magnetic Resonance Imaging (MRI), (5) Positron Emission Tomography (PET), and (6) Mass-Spectrometry Imaging are examples of imaging modalities (MSI). DL has also succeed in biological-imaging analysis, with quite a few study pieces reporting higher performance than traditional classifiers.

CNNs have helped segment and identify subtyping single fluorescently marked cells in microscopic pictures [93, 94] besides unlabeled phase contrast microscopic imageries [95, 96]. Other typically time-consuming preclinical activities, like cell tracking [96] besides colony counting [97], might potentially be automated with DL. Tissue pathology pictures are generally more complicated than fluorescently tagged images due to the rich tissue morphology. Even so, cell segmentation and classification occurred in both breast and colon tissues. The samples were stained with Hematoxylin and Eosin (H&E) at the molecular level [98, 99]. DL identified tumor locations in H&E-stained breast tissue [100], as well as further categories of leukocytes and adipose material [101] at the tissue level. DL has already been utilized for histological diagnosis with H&E and immunohistochemistry stained tissue, in addition to basic image segmentation [102, 103]. The DL also helped analyze CT, MRI, and PET imaging. Aside from the well-known image segmentation and classification applications [104-108], DL has also outperformed the famous ISOMAP and Elastic Net when it comes to finding structures within a Content-Based Image Retrieval (CBIR) [109] setting.

Tumor subtyping can utilize matrix-assisted, high-resolution, laser desorption/ ionization (MALDI) MSI, analogous to the usage of DL in pathology [110]. MSI may already be recognized because MSI can see a tissue's metabolic information and tumor sub-regions with metabolic heterogeneity using desorption electrospray ionization (DESI) [111]. Finally, in a novel imaging field, flow cytometry, DL enabled real-time cell categorization for high-throughput applications have been deployed [112]. DNN training for imaging is time-consuming and necessitates specialized GPU processing. Furthermore, good-quality training sets are scarce in the context of high-throughput imaging screening. As a result, the image features learned on natural sceneries and other datasets assisted in conducting biological image segmentation and classifications, with promising results [101, 113].

4. Future DL Development in Drug Discovery

AI techniques, and particularly DL, require huge datasets for training; nevertheless, the human brain is capable of learning from an insignificant amount of instances. One of the trendiest AI issues is thus how to learn with a limited quantity of accessible data. Matching networks [114], presented as a variation of one-shot learning, exemplify DL with auxiliary data to enhance a model containing merely a few data points. When the supplementary datasets were incorporated, the results improved. One-shot learning schemes are worthwhile in drug development because medicinal chemists often toil on novel targets employing minimal data. Using the LSTM on chemoinformatic datasets to form models with a relatively short training set led to good results [115]. Memory augmented NNs are a novel sort of architecture that has lately been employed in DL (where the first account was the neural Turing machine). A Differentiable Neural Computer (DNC) ameliorated this design meaningfully. DNCs have explained diverse issues, encompassing question-answering systems and outlining the shortest path in graphs. These more sophisticated designs, however, have not yet been used in drug development. AI may be utilized in drug discovery and has shown to be valuable in this field. DL is a recent addition to the AI toolkit. Compared to other techniques, DL offers a considerably more flexible architecture, allowing for creating a NN architecture tailored to a given issue. In general, one DL downside is that it necessitates extensive training sets. A critical subject that must be investigated is if and when DL is superior to other AI approaches. Granting it is too early for sure conclusions, the findings thus far show that for specific tasks such as well-being image analysis is vastly beneficial for innovative molecular designs and reaction predictions and DL outwits other strategies. DL seems to outperform other techniques when utilizing structured input descriptors. Bioactivity prediction is the most critical illustration, where DL gives the impression of producing superior overall performance via multitask learning. Other AI methodologies, on the other hand, are advancing. The XGBoost [116] technique, for example, has dominated Kaggle contests for structured input data [117] since its inception.

Thus, in reality, the procedure employed in bioactivity prediction may be determined by the modeler's familiarity with the method. If multiple AI methodologies achieve approximately the same accuracy, the maximum an AI model can do may be determined by experimental data and dataset size uncertainty rather than the individual algorithm employed.

Drug-Induced Liver Injury (DILI) is a critical cause of discontinuation of efforts in drug development, and safety assessment and management technology at the initial design stage is highly needed. Currently, toxicity prognosis by in silico examination is expected, and machine learning investigation utilizing omics data has drawn awareness [118-120]. Nevertheless, the scarcity of explanations for machine learning is a concern. In order to assemble an appropriate safety assessment, it is essential to elucidate the mechanism of the toxicity (i.e., toxic course). Hence, there is a need for toxic course studies and ontological models of liver toxicity. These two lines of attack can systematize toxicity knowledge established on a consistent perspective. perspective. One may recommend an AI system prototype to sustain toxicity agent understanding that may probe flexibly according to the user's purpose by employing semantic technologies founded on the ontology. The system must have a graph visualization set of functions where nodes represent ideas and arrows corresponding to interactions among concepts. A visualization framework can afford a toxic course map that displays causal associations present in the toxic process. Blockchain technology can also help keep drug development, warehousing, and distribution safe [121-123].

5. Conclusion

Deep learning (DL) has thrived significantly in countless fields of artificial intelligence (AI) research during the previous decade, particularly in machine learning (ML). As a result of prior research into artificial neural networks, this practice has outperformed standard ML procedures in many realms, including image and audio recognition, natural language processing, and others. Recently, the pharmaceutical research community witnessed the birth of the first wave of DL applications trying to unravel a wide range of bioactivity prediction and drug improvement challenges. Bioactivity estimates, de novo chemical manufacture, synthesis prediction, as well as biological-image analyses were all seen in this chapter. AI helps develop drugs with fewer side effects as different models for toxicity effects on the human body emerge along with tools for simulations and visualization of results.

References

1. Chen, H., Engkvist, O., Wang, Y., Olivecrona, M., Blaschke, T. et al. (2018). The rise of deep learning in drug discovery. Drug Discovery Today, 23(6), 1241-1250. doi: 10.1016/j.drudis.2018.01.039

2. Deshpande, A., Patavardhan, P., Estrela, V.V., Razmjooy, N., Hemanth, J.D. et al. (2020). Deep Learning as an Alternative to Super-resolution Imaging in UAV Systems. doi: 10.1049/pbce120g_ch9

3. Fernandes, S.R., de Assis, J.T., Estrela, V.V., Razmjooy, N., Deshpande, A. et al. (2020). Nondestructive Diagnosis and Analysis of Computed Microtomography Images via Texture Descriptors. doi: 10.1007/978-3-030-57552-6_16

4. Chaabane, L., Khelassi, A., Terziev, A., Andreopoulos, N., Jesus, M.A. et al. (2020). Particle Swarm Optimization with Tabu Search Algorithm (PSO-TS) Applied to Multiple Sequence Alignment Problem. doi: 10.1007/978-3-030-57552-6_8

5. Monteiro, A.C., França, R.P., Estrela, V.V., Fernandes, S.R., Khelassi, A. et al. (2020). UAV-CPSs as a Test Bed for New Technologies and a Primer to Industry 5.0. doi: 10.1049/pbce120g_ch1

6. Papadatos, G., Gaulton, A., Hersey, A. and Overington, J.P. (2015). Activity, assay and target data curation and quality in the ChEMBL database. J. Comput. Aided Mol. Des., 29, 885-896.

7. Kim, S., Thiessen, P.A., Bolton, E.E., Chen, J., Fu, G. et al. (2016). PubChem substance and compound databases. Nucleic Acids Res., 44, D1202-1213.

8. Gilson, M.K., Liu, T., Baitaluk, M., Nicola, G., Hwang, L. and Chong, J. (2016). BindingDB in 2015: A public database for medicinal chemistry, computational chemistry and systems pharmacology. Nucleic Acids Res., 44, D1045-1053.

9. Razmjooy, N., Ashourian, M., Karimifard, M., Estrela, V.V., Loschi, H.J. et al. (2020). Computer-aided diagnosis of skin cancer: A review. Cur. Med. Im., 16(7), 781-793.

10. Laghari, A.A., Estrela, V.V. and Yin, S. (2022). Special Issue: From nanoscale to hyperspectral imaging - How to gather and understand medical images harvested in extremely difficult situations. Curr. Med. Imaging, Bentham Science.

11. Ho, T.K. (1998). The random subspace method for constructing decision forests. IEEE Trans. Pattern Anal. Mach. Intell., 20, 832-844.

12. Ammad-ud-din, M., Khan, S.A., Malani, D., Murumägi, A., Kallioniemi, O. et al. (2016). Drug response prediction by inferring pathway-response associations with kernelized Bayesian matrix factorization. Bioinformatics, 32(17), i455-i463.

13. Ching, T., Himmelstein, D.S., Beaulieu-Jones, B.K., Kalinin, A.A., Do, B.T. et al. (2018). Opportunities and obstacles for deep learning in biology and medicine. J. Royal Soc. Interf., 15.

14. Khelassi, A. and Estrela, V.V. (2020). Advances in Multidisciplinary Medical Technologies — Engineering, Modeling and Findings. Proc. ICHSMT 2019, Springer Nature, Zurich, Switzerland.

15. Razmjooy, N., Estrela, V.V. and Loschi, H.J. (2019). A study on metaheuristic-based neural networks for image segmentation purposes. *In:* Memon, Q.A., Khoja, S.A. (eds). Data Science: Theory, Analysis and Applications. CRC Press.

16. Monteiro, A.C.B., França, R.P., Estrela, V.V., Razmjooy, N., Iano, Y. et al. (2021). Metaheuristics applied to blood image analysis. *In:* Razmjooy, N. et al. (eds). Metaheuristics and Optimization in Computer and Electrical Engineering. LNEE, vol. 696. Springer, Cham.

17. Razmjooy, N., Razmjooy, S., Vahedi, Z., Estrela, V.V., de Oliveira, G.G. et al. (2021). Skin color segmentation based on artificial neural network improved by a modified grasshopper optimization algorithm. *In:* Razmjooy, N. et al. (eds). Metaheuristics and Optimization in Computer and Electrical Engineering. LNEE, vol. 696. Springer, Cham.

18. Deshpande, A., Patavardhan, P. and Estrela, V.V. (2020). Super resolution and recognition of unconstrained ear image. Int'l J. Biom., Inderscience, 12(4), 396-410.

19. Hemanth, J., Estrela, V.V., Tavares, J.M.R.S., Wang, L. and Fuqian, S. (2018). Special Issue: Soft Computing Techniques for Image Analysis in the Medical Industry – Current Trends, Challenges and Solutions. Editorial, IEEE Access, IEEE.

20. Marinho, C.E.V., Estrela, V.V., Loschi, H.J., Razmjooy, N., Herrmann, A.E. et al. (2019). A model for medical staff idleness minimization. Proc. 4th Braz, Techn. Symp. (BTSym'18). Smart Innovation, Systems and Technologies, vol. 140. Springer, Cham.

21. Srivastava, N., Hinton, G.E., Krizhevsky, A., Sutskever, I., Salakhutdinov, R. et al. (2014). Dropout: A simple way to prevent neural networks from overfitting. J. Mach. Learn. Res., 15, 1929-1958.

22. Wan, L., Zeiler, M.D., Zhang, S., LeCun, Y. and Fergus, R. (2013). Regularization of neural networks using DropConnect. *In:* Sanjoy, D. and David, M. (eds). Proc. 30th Int'l Conf. on Machine Learning, Vol. 28, pp. 1058-1066. PMLR.

23. Nair, V. and Hinton, G.E. (2010). Rectified linear units improve restricted Boltzmann machines. Proc. 27th Int'l Conf. on International Learning, pp. 807-814, Omnipress.

24. Lee, J.H. and Kim, K.G. (2018). Applying deep learning in medical images: The case of bone age estimation. Healthcare Informatics Research, 24, 86-92.

25. Jospin, L.V., Buntine, W.L., Boussaid, F., Laga, H. and Bennamoun (2022). Handson Bayesian neural networks - A tutorial for deep learning users. IEEE C. Int. Mag., 17, 29-48.

26. Tiwari, T.P., Bharti, V., Srishti and Vishwakarma, S.K. (2021). Facial expression recognition using Keras in machine learning. Proc. 3rd Int'l Conf. on Adv. in Comp., Comm. Control and Networking (ICAC3N), 466-471.

27. Mudigere, D., Naumov, M., Spisak, J., Chauhan, G., Kokhlikyan, N. et al. (2020). Building Recommender Systems with PyTorch. Proc. 26th ACM SIGKDD.

28. Al-Rfou, R., Alain, G., Almahairi, A., Angermuller, C., Bahdanau, D. et al. (2016). Theano: A Python framework for fast computation of mathematical expressions. arXiv, abs/1605.02688.

29. Lee, H., Grosse, R.B., Ranganath, R. and Ng, A. (2011). Unsupervised learning of hierarchical representations with convolutional deep belief networks. Comm. ACM, 54, 95-103.

30. Szegedy, C., Liu, W., Jia, Y., Sermanet, P., Reed, S.E. et al. (2015). Going deeper with convolutions. Proc. 2015 CVPR, pp. 1-9, IEEE Computer Society.

31. Fernandez, S., Graves, A. and Schmidhuber, J. (2007). An application of recurrent neural networks to discriminative keyword spotting. Proc.17th Int'l Conf. Art. Neural Networks, pp. 220-229, Springer-Verlag.

32. Hochreiter, S. and Schmidhuber, J. (1997). Long short-term memory. Neural Comput., 9, 1735- 1780.

33. Bengio, Y. (2009). Learning deep architectures for AI. Found. Tr. M. Learn., 2, 1-127.

34. Kingma, D.P. and Welling, M. (2013). Auto-encoding variational Bayes. arXiv doi: 1312.6114

35. Ma, J., Sheridan, R.P., Liaw, A., Dahl, G.E. and Svetnik, V. (2015). Deep neural nets as a method for quantitative structure–activity relationships. J. Chem. Inf. Model., 55, 263-274.

36. Mayr, A., Klambauer, G., Unterthiner, T. and Hochreiter, S. (2016). DeepTox: Toxicity prediction using deep learning. Front. Environ. Sci. doi:10.3389/fenvs.2015.00080

37. Dahl, G.E., Jaitly, N. and Salakhutdinov, R. (2014). Multi-task neural networks for QSAR predictions. arXiv doi: arXiv:1406.1231

38. Ramsundar, B., Liu, B., Wu, Z., Verras, A., Tudor, M., et al. (2017). Is multitask deep learning practical for pharma? J. Chem. Inf. Model. 57, 2068-2076.

39. Koutsoukas, A., Monaghan, K.J., Li, X. and Huan, J. (2017). Deep-learning:

Investigating deep neural networks hyperparameters and comparison of performance to shallow methods for modeling bioactivity data. J. Cheminformatics, 9, 42.

40. Gaulton, A., Bellis, L.J., Bento, A.P., Chambers, J., Davies, M. et al. (2012). ChEMBL: A large-scale bioactivity database for drug discovery. Nucleic Acids Res., 40, D1100-1107.

41. Lenselink, E.B., Dijke, N., Bongers, B.J., Papadatos, G., van Vlijmen, H.W. et al. (2017). Beyond the hype: Deep neural networks outperform established methods using a ChEMBL bioactivity benchmark set. J. Cheminformatics, 9, 45.

42. Subramanian, G., Ramsundar, B., Pande, V.S. and Denny, R.A. (2016). Computational modeling of beta-secretase 1 (BACE-1) inhibitors using ligand-based approaches. J. Chem. Inf. Model., 56, 1936-1949.

43. Aliper, A., Plis, S., Artemov, A.V., Ulloa, A.E., Mamoshina, P. et al. (2016). Deep learning applications for predicting pharmacological properties of drugs and drug repurposing using transcriptomic data. Molecular Pharmaceutics, 13(7), 2524-2530.

44. Koleti, A., Terryn, R., Stathias, V., Chung, C., Cooper, D.J. et al. (2018). Data Portal for the Library of Integrated Network-based Cellular Signatures (LINCS) program: Integrated access to diverse large-scale cellular perturbation response data. Nucleic Acids Research, 46, D558-D566.

45. Merkwirth, C. and Lengauer, T. (2005). Automatic generation of complementary descriptors with molecular graph networks. J. Chem. Inf. Model., 45, 1159-1168.

46. Lusci, A., Pollastri, G. and Baldi, P. (2013). Deep architectures and deep learning in chemoinformatics: The prediction of aqueous solubility for drug-like molecules. J. Chem. Inf. Model., 53, 1563-1575.

47. Xu, Y., Dai, Z., Chen, F., Gao, S., Pei, J. et al. (2015). Deep learning for drug-induced liver injury. J. Chem. Inf. Model., 55, 2085-2093.

48. Morgan, H.L. (1965). The generation of a unique machine description for chemical structures – A technique developed at Chemical Abstracts Service. J. Chem. Doc., 5, 107-113.

49. Duvenaud, D., Maclaurin, D., Aguilera-Iparraguirre, J., Gomez-Bombarelli, R., Hirzel, T.D. et al. (2015). Convolutional networks on graphs for learning molecular fingerprints. Proc. 28th Int'l Conf. Neural Inf. Proc. Systems, pp. 2224-2232, MIT Press.

50. Kearnes, S., McCloskey, K., Berndl, M., Pande, V.S. and Riley, P.F. (2016). Molecular graph convolutions: Moving beyond fingerprints. J. Comp. Aided Mol. Des., 30, 595-608.

51. Xu, Y., Pei, J. and Lai, L. (2017). Deep learning based regression and multiclass models for acute oral toxicity prediction with automatic chemical feature extraction. J. Chem. Inf. Model., 57, 2672-2685.

52. Jiang, D., Wu, Z., Hsieh, C., Chen, G., Liao, B. et al. (2021). Could graph neural networks learn better molecular representation for drug discovery? A comparison study of descriptor-based and graph-based models. Journal of Cheminformatics, 13.

53. Coley, C.W., Barzilay, R., Green, W.H., Jaakkola, T. and Jensen, K.F. (2017). Convolutional embedding of attributed molecular graphs for physical property prediction. J. Chem. Inf. Model., 57, 1757-1772.

54. Gilmer, J., Schoenholz, S.S., Riley, P.F., Vinyals, O. and Dahl, G.E. (2017). Neural message passing for quantum chemistry. arXiv doi: arXiv:1704.01212

55. Li, Y., Tarlow, D., Brockschmidt, M. and Zemel, R.S. (2016). Gated Graph Sequence Neural Networks. CoRR, abs/1511.05493.

56. Kipf, T.N. and Welling, M. (2016). Semi-supervised classification with graph convolutional networks. arXiv doi: arXiv:1609.02907

57. Bjerrum, E.J. (2017). SMILES enumeration as data augmentation for neural network modeling of molecules. arXiv doi: arXiv:1703.07076

58. Goh, G.B., Siegel, C.M., Vishnu, A., Hodas, N.O. and Baker, N. (2017). Chemception: A deep neural network with minimal chemistry knowledge matches the performance of expert-developed QSAR/QSPR models. arXiv doi: arXiv:1706.06689

59. Goh, G.B., Siegel, C.M., Vishnu, A., Hodas, N.O., Baker, N. et al. (2018). How much chemistry does a deep neural network need to know to make accurate predictions? Proc. 2018 IEEE WACV, 1340-1349.

60. Gómez-Bombarelli, R., Duvenaud, D.K., Hernandez-Lobato, J., Aguilera- Iparraguirre, J., Hirzel, T.D. et al. (2016). Automatic chemical design using a data-driven continuous representation of molecules. arXiv doi: arXiv:1610.02415

61. Kadurin, A. Nikolenko, S.I., Khrabrov, K., Aliper, A. and Zhavoronkov, A. (2017). druGAN: An advanced generative adversarial autoencoder model for de novo generation of new molecules with desired molecular properties in silico. Mol. Pharm., 14, 3098-3104.

62. Goodfellow, I.J., Pouget-Abadie, J., Mirza, M., Xu, B., Warde-Farley, D. et al. (2014). Generative adversarial networks. arXiv doi: arXiv:1406.2661

63. Blaschke, T., Olivecrona, M., Engkvist, O., Bajorath, J. and Chen, H. (2017). Application of generative autoencoder in de novo molecular design. arXiv doi:arXiv:1711.07839

64. Segler, M.H.S., Kogej, T., Tyrchan, C. and Waller, M.P. (2017). Generating focussed molecule libraries for drug discovery with recurrent neural networks. arXiv doi:arXiv:1701.01329

65. Yuan, W., Jiang, D., Nambiar, D.K., Liew, L.P., Hay, M.P. et al. (2017). Chemical space mimicry for drug discovery. J. Chem. Inf. Model., 57, 875-882.

66. Jaques, N., Gu, S.S., Bahdanau, D., Hernandez-Lobato, J., Turner, R.E. et al. (2016). Sequence tutor: Conservative fine-tuning of sequence generation models with KL-control. arXiv doi: arXiv:1611.02796

67. Leo, A., Hansch, C. and Elkins, D. (1971). Partition coefficients and their uses. Chem. Rev., 71, 525-616.

68. Bickerton, G.R., Paolini, G.V., Besnard, J., Muresan, S. and Hopkins, A.L. (2012). Quantifying the chemical beauty of drugs. Nat. Chem., 4, 90-98.

69. Olivecrona, M., Blaschke, T., Engkvist, O. and Chen, H. (2017). Molecular de-novo design through deep reinforcement learning. J. Cheminformatics, 9, 48.

70. Benhenda, M. (2017). ChemGAN challenge for drug discovery: Can AI reproduce natural chemical diversity? arXiv doi: arXiv:1708.08227

71. Metz, L., Poole, B., Pfau, D. and Sohl-Dickstein, J.N. (2016). Unrolled generative adversarial networks. arXiv doi: arXiv:1611.02163

72. Unterthiner, T., Nessler, B., Klambauer, G., Heusel, M., Ramsauer, H. et al. (2017). Coulomb GANs: Provably optimal Nash equilibria via potential fields. arXiv doi: arXiv:1708.08819

73. Corey, E.J. and Wipke, W.T. (1969). Computer-assisted design of complex organic syntheses. Science, 166, 178-192.

74. Coley, C.W., Barzilay, R., Jaakkola, T., Green, W.H. and Jensen, K.F. (2017). Prediction of organic reaction outcomes using machine learning. ACS Cent. Sci., 3, 434-443.

75. Jin, W., Coley, C.W., Barzilay, R. and Jaakkola, T. (2017). Predicting organic reaction outcomes with Weisfeiler–Lehman network. arXiv doi: arXiv:1709.04555

76. Segler, M.H.S. and Waller, M.P. (2017). Neural-symbolic machine learning for retrosynthesis and reaction prediction. Chemistry, 23, 5966-5971.

77. Segler, M.H.S., Preuss, M. and Waller, M.P. (2017). Learning to plan chemical syntheses. arXiv doi: arXiv:1708.04202

78. Liu, B., Ramsundar, B., Kawthekar, P., Shi, J., Gomes, J. et al. (2017). Retrosynthetic reaction prediction using neural sequence-to-sequence models. ACS Central Science, 3, 1103-1113.

79. Pagadala, N.S., Syed, K. and Tuszynski, J.A. (2017). Software for molecular docking: A review. Biophys. Rev., 9, 91-102.
80. Ragoza, M., Hochuli, J., Idrobo, E., Sunseri, J. and Koes, D.R. (2017). Protein–ligand scoring with convolutional neural networks. J. Chem. Inf. Model., 57, 942-957.
81. Trott, O. and Olson, A.J. (2010). AutoDock Vina: Improving the speed and accuracy of docking with a new scoring function, efficient optimization, and multithreading. J. Comput. Chem., 31, 455-461.
82. Dunbar, J.B., Smith, R., Yang, C., Ung, P.M., Lexa, K.W. et al. (2011). CSAR benchmark exercise of 2010: Selection of the protein–ligand complexes. J. Chem. Inf. Model., 51, 2036-2046.
83. Gomes, J., Ramsundar, B., Feinberg, E.N. and Pande, V.S. (2017). Atomic convolutional networks for predicting protein–ligand binding affinity. arXiv doi: arXiv:1703.10603
84. Wallach, I., Dzamba, M. and Heifets, A. (2015). AtomNet: A deep convolutional neural network for bioactivity prediction in structure-based drug discovery. arXiv doi: arXiv:1510.02855
85. Pereira, J.C., Caffarena, E.R. and Santos, C.N. (2016). Boosting docking-based virtual screening with deep learning. J. Chem. Inf. Model., 56, 2495-2506.
86. Russakovsky, O., Deng, J., Su, H., Krause, J., Satheesh, S. et al. (2015). ImageNet large scale visual recognition challenge. In. J. Comput. Vis., 115, 211-252.
87. Mysinger, M.M., Carchia, M., Irwin, J.J. and Shoichet, B.K. (2012). Directory of Useful Decoys, Enhanced (DUD-E): Better ligands and decoys for better benchmarking. J. Med. Chem., 55, 6582-6594.
88. Sun, J., Jeliazkova, N., Chupakhin, V.I., Dzib, J.F., Engkvist, O. et al. (2017). ExCAPE-DB: An integrated large scale dataset facilitating Big Data analysis in chemogenomics. J. Cheminformatics, 9, 17.
89. Miller, G.A. (1995). WordNet: A lexical database for English. Comm. ACM, 38, 39-41.
90. Li, F.-F., Deng, J. and Li, K. (2009). ImageNet: Constructing a large-scale image database. J. Vision, 9, 1037.
91. Wu, Z., Ramsundar, B., Feinberg, E.N., Gomes, J., Geniesse, C. et al. (2017). MoleculeNet: A benchmark for molecular machine learning. arXiv doi: arXiv:1703.00564
92. Zhan, K., Lu, Z. and Zhang Y. (2020). Performance optimization for feature extraction section of DeepChem. *In:* Qiu, M. (eds). Algorithms and Architectures for Parallel Processing. Proc. ICA3PP 2020. LNCS, vol. 12452. Springer, Cham.
93. Deshpande, A., Estrela, V.V. and Razmjooy, N. (2021). Computational Intelligence Methods for Super-Resolution in Image Processing Applications. Springer Nature, Zurich, Switzerland. doi: 10.1007/978-3-030-67921-7
94. Kraus, O.Z., Ramsundar, B., Feinberg, E.N., Gomes, J., Geniesse, C. et al. (2015). Classifying and segmenting microscopy images using convolutional multiple instance learning. arXiv doi: arXiv:1511.05286
95. Ronneberger, O., Fischer, P. and Brox, T. (2015). U-net: Convolutional networks for biomedical image segmentation. Proc. Int'l Conf. Med. Im. Comp. and Computer-Assist. Interv. (MICCAI), pp. 234-241, Springer.
96. Ning, F., Delhomme, D., LeCun, Y., Piano, F., Bottou, L. et al. (2005). Toward automatic phenotyping of developing embryos from videos. IEEE Trans. Im. Proc., 14, 1360-1371.
97. Ferrari, A., Lombardi, S. and Signoroni, A. (2015). Bacterial colony counting by convolutional neural networks. Proc. 37th EMBC, pp. 7458-7461. IEEE.
98. Cireşan, D.C., Giusti, A., Gambardella, L.M. and Schmidhuber, J. (2013). Mitosis detection in breast cancer histology images with deep neural networks. Proc. MICCAI, pp. 411-418, Springer.

99. Sirinukunwattana, K., Raza, S., Tsang, Y., Snead, D.R., Cree, I.A. et al. (2016). Locality sensitive deep learning for detection and classification of nuclei in routine colon cancer histology images. IEEE Transactions on Medical Imaging, 35, 1196-1206.

100. Hemanth J. and Estrela V.V. (2017). Deep learning for image processing applications. Advances in Parallel Computing, Vol. 31. IOS Press, Amsterdam, Netherlands.

101. Turkki, R., Linder, N., Kovanen, P.E., Pellinen, T. and Lundin, J. (2016). Antibody-supervised deep learning for quantification of tumor-infiltrating immune cells in hematoxylin and eosin stained breast cancer samples. J. Path. Inf., 7, 38.

102. Vandenberghe, M.E., Scott, M.L., Scorer, P.W., Soderberg, M., Balcerzak, D. et al. (2017). Relevance of deep learning to facilitate the diagnosis of HER2 status in breast cancer. Sci. Rep. doi: 10.1038/srep45938

103. Litjens, G., Sanchez, C.I., Timofeeva, N., Hermsen, M., Nagtegaal, I.D. et al. (2016). Deep learning as a tool for increased accuracy and efficiency of histopathological diagnosis. Sci. Rep., 6, 26286.

104. Bar, Y., Diamant, I., Wolf, L. and Greenspan, H. (2015). Deep learning with non-medical training used for chest pathology identification. Proc. SPIE, Vol. 9414, pp. 94140V.

105. Cheng, J.-Z., Ni, D., Chou, Y., Qin, J., Tiu, C. et al. (2016). Computer-aided diagnosis with deep learning architecture: Applications to breast lesions in US images and pulmonary nodules in CT scans. Sci. Rep., 6, 24454.

106. Cha, K.H., Hadjiiski, L.M., Samala, R.K., Chan, H., Caoili, E.M. et al. (2016). Urinary bladder segmentation in CT urography using deep-learning convolutional neural network and level sets. Med. Phys., 43, 1882-1896.

107. Avendi, M., Kheradvar, A. and Jafarkhani, H. (2016). A combined deep-learning and deformable-model approach to fully automatic segmentation of the left ventricle in cardiac MRI. Medical Image Analysis, 30, 108-119.

108. Li, R., Zhang, W., Suk, H., Wang, L., Li, J. et al. (2014). Deep learning based imaging data completion for improved brain disease diagnosis. Proc. MICCAI, pp. 305-312, Springer.

109. Liu, S., Liu, S., Cai, W., Che, H., Pujol, S. et al. (2014). High-level feature based PET image retrieval with deep learning architecture. J. Nucl. Med., 55(suppl. 1), 2028.

110. Behrmann, J., Etmann, C., Boskamp, T., Casadonte, R., Kriegsmann, J. et al. (2018). Deep learning for tumor classification in imaging mass spectrometry. Bioinformat., 34, 1215-1223.

111. Inglese, P., McKenzie, J.S., Mroz, A., Kinross, J.M., Veselkov, K.A. et al. (2017). Deep learning and 3D-DESI imaging reveal the hidden metabolic heterogeneity of cancer. Chem. Sci., 8, 3500-3511.

112. Chen, C.L., Mahjoubfar, A., Tai, L., Blaby, I.K., Huang, A. et al. (2016). Deep learning in label-free cell classification. Sci. Rep., 6, 21471.

113. Zhang, W., Li, R., Zeng, T., Sun, Q., Kumar, S. et al. (2016). Deep model based transfer and multi-task learning for biological image analysis. IEEE Transactions on Big Data. doi: 10.1109/TBDATA.2016.2573280

114. Vinyals, O., Blundell, C., Lillicrap, T.P., Kavukcuoglu, K. and Wierstra, D. (2016). Matching networks for one shot learning. arXiv doi: arXiv:1606.04080

115. Altae-Tran, H., Ramsundar, B., Pappu, A.S. and Pande, V.S. (2017). Low data drug discovery with one-shot learning. ACS Cent. Sci., 3, 283-293.

116. Jiang, J., Cui, B., Zhang, C. and Fu, F. (2018). DimBoost: Boosting gradient boosting decision tree to higher dimensions. Proc. of the 2018 Int'l Conf. Manag. Data.

117. Shyam, R., Ayachit, S.S., Patil, V. and Singh, A.K. (2020). Competitive analysis of the top gradient boosting machine learning algorithms. Proc. 2nd ICACCCN, 191-196.

118. Yamagata, Y., Igarashi, Y., Nakatsu, N., Horimoto, K., Fukui, K. et al. (2019). Development of liver toxicity ontology for drug safety evaluation and its application. Trans. of the Jap. Soc. for Art. Intelligence, 34, 2, D-I81_1-18.

119. Liang, G., Fan, W., Luo, H. and Zhu, X. (2020). The emerging roles of artificial intelligence in cancer drug development and precision therapy. Biomed. & Pharmacoth. 128, 110255.

120. Farghali, H., Kutinová Canová, N. and Arora, M. (2021). The potential applications of artificial intelligence in drug discovery and development. Phys. Res., 70(Supp 14), S715-S722.

121. Kaur, I., Kumar, Y. and Sandhu, A.K. (2021). A comprehensive survey of AI, blockchain technology and big data applications in medical field and global health. Proc. Int'l Conf. Technological Advancements and Innovations (ICTAI), 593-598.

122. Ayub Khan, Abdullah, Laghari, A.A, Shaikh, A., Dootio, M., Estrela, V.V. et al. (2021). A Blockchain Security Module for Brain-Computer Interface (BCI) with Multimedia Life Cycle Framework (MLCF). Neurosc. Inform. 100030. 10.1016/j.neuri.2021.100030.

123. Meyliana, M., Fernando, E. and Surjandy, Cassandra, C. (2021). Architecture blockchain technology with IoT for monitoring drug warehouse. Proc. 2021 ICIMTech., 1, 77-81.

In-Body Devices and Sensors Communication – How Implantables, Ingestibles, and Injectables Interact with the Internet

Vania V. Estrela[1] [0000-0002-4465-7691], Edwiges G.H. Grata[1] [0000-0002-7962-9420], Anand Deshpande[2] [0000-0002-1500-0981], Robert Sroufer[3] [0000-0002-7903-9180], Ricardo T. Lopes[4] [0000-0001-7250-824X], Fuqian Shi[5] [0000-0003-4245-5727], Khuda Bukhsh[6], M. Malook Rind[6], Sarmad Shaikh[6]

[1] Department of Telecommunications, Federal Fluminense University (UFF), RJ, Brazil, vania.estrela.phd@ieee.org, edwigesghgrata@gmail.com
[2] Electronics and Communication Engineering, Angadi Institute of Technology and Management, Belagavi, India, deshpande.anandb@gmail.com
[3] Management Department, Duquesne University, Pittsburg, PA, USA, sroufer@duq.edu
[4] Federal University of Rio de Janeiro (COPPE/UFRJ), Nuclear Engineering Laboratory (LIN), Rio de Janeiro, RJ, Brazil, ricardo@lin.ufrj.br
[5] Rutgers Cancer Institute of New Jersey, United States, shifuqian@gmail.com
[6] Faculty of Computer Science, Sindh Madressatul Islam University, Karachi (74000), Sindh, Pakistan, khudabukhsh1992@gmail.com, malook.rindh@smiu.com, sarmad@smiu.edu.pk

1. Introduction

Personal medical care is becoming more accessible as a result of miniaturization and new technology. Devices grow more powerful and less intrusive as technology advances. These new resources will rapidly outweigh any worries about their invasive nature, improving medical prevention, prognosis, and therapy.

Wireless medical devices (WMDs) can detect physiological signals or stimulate the nervous system. Wearables are becoming gradually more popular for tracking heart rate, steps taken, speed, calories burned, oxygenation, and distance [1]. Nonetheless, wearables monitor just a subset of physiological indicators easily accessible from outside the human body. Along these lines, in-body WMDs inside the human body promise a whole new set of uses [2-14]. The mechanism of introduction of in-body WMDs into the human body (Figure 1) differs, with implantables, ingestibles, and injectables being the most common. In-body Wireless Devices (IBs) wirelessly

Implantable

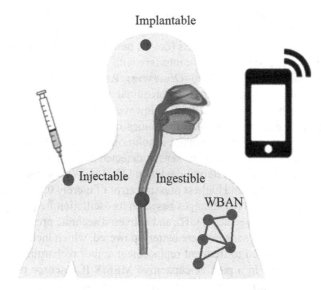

Figure 1. Wireless ingestible, implantable, and injectable devices with
Wireless Body Network (WBAN)

connect with exterior monitoring/control devices (e.g., a smartphone) without wires
piercing tissues.

Medical systems on-body, in-body, and remote access comprise a medical cyber-
physical system (MCPS) [5-7, 39-41].

Implantables: Devices surgically implanted from standard IBs [8] to tiny deep brain
implants [9, 29, 42-47].

Ingestibles: These capsule-shaped gadgets, such as the wireless endoscope, are
ingested like ordinary tablets. Wireless ingestibles with sophisticated capacities may
now even monitor drug responses [10, 11].

Injectables: Needles can inject micro-devices into the human body for medication
administration, sensing, and neuro-stimulation purposes [12, 18].

IBs entail communication, powering, and biocompatibility design problems.
Their applications spread beyond implantables and ingestibles. Section 2 will cover
wireless IB design aspects. Section 3 will address the current state of research,
commercial uses of in-body devices, and future directions. Future directions and
conclusions follow next.

2. Types of In-Body Devices

2.1. Implantables

In general, implantables are surgically placed in the human body for detecting,
actuating (e.g., drug delivery), and stimulating activities. Some applications for
wireless implantables appear below.

1. *Pacemakers:* Many miniature implantables are embedded in the chest or abdomen to adjust cardiac arrhythmias [8, 14, 16, 52]. Some may additionally broadcast critical patient and IBs (device health statuses) information to outer units. Other pacemakers cannot interfere with full-body MRI scans.

2. *Intra-Cranial Pressure (ICP) Observers:* Raised up ICP can result from cerebral edema, head injury, cerebrospinal fluid disorder, and/or confined intracranial mass lesions [42-47]. However, high ICPs pose severe brain damage risk and may provoke disabilities or even pass away. With these in mind, many unobtrusive implantable solutions measured Intraocular Pressure (IOP), e.g., a MEMS pressure sensor detected ICP changes and wirelessly transmitted them to an external device in [13, 14]. With a system's 2.45-GHz operation frequency and highest pressure error of merely 0.8 mmHg. In [15], a RF oscillator detects ICP changes based on its oscillation frequency variations. This device functioned at 2.4 GHz and delivered accurate pressures in the 1070 mmHg range. Both sensors were battery-powered, which increased the overall implant size and led to frequent replacement and/or recharging. The works in [16, 17] brought in a passive-capacitive MEMS ICP sensor powered via an inductive RF coupling to evade batteries. The sensor amounted to a LC tank with a coil on the skull. The tank's resonance frequency was an ICP variation function. An external reader device eventually detected the latter. In-vitro measurement fallouts demonstrated these sensors' ability to perceive ample ICP variations.

3. *Cardiac Pressure Monitors (CVPMs):* CVPMs are paramount for continual assessment of cardiovascular conditions (e.g., hypertension, restenosis, heart failure), besides tracking the progress of surgical interventions (e.g., checking repaired aneurysms) [17]. Still, conventional gold standards, viz. blood pressure cuffs or intra-arterial catheters, exhibit several shortcomings. Examples comprise lack of patient wellbeing, sporadic measurements, possible blood flow occlusion, and long-term difficulties (such as trauma and infection). Intrinsically, totally implantable devices have been popularized for permanent blood pressure monitoring [42-47]. The latter permit continuous observation without obstructing the person's quotidian activities and without associated infection risks, typically for catheters or wires. Fast microfabrication progress has produced low-cost, highly accurate, safe sensors implantable for chronic pressure checking. Implantable blood pressure monitors could use MEMS capacitive sensors [17, 18], Surface Acoustic Wave (SAW) resonators [19], and Pulse Transit Time (PTT) assessed through an accelerometer [20]. The work in [21] depicts a pressure sensor to measure aneurysm sac pressures after endovascular aneurysm reparation (EVAR). The first FDA-approved blood pressure IB to detect pulmonary artery heart failure shows up in [22]. An IB with potential for arterial motion energy harvesting while performing cardiovascular monitoring appears in [23].

4. *Neurosensors:* Deep head neurosensors have enticed noteworthy attention in applications [42-47], comprising epilepsy, dependences, Parkinson's, Alzheimer's to mention a few. RFID-motivated neural tags can assist wireless brain-machine interfaces [18] avoid batteries with power storage via RF energy

harvesting methods. A wireless neurosensor documented neural signals from monkey cortexes in reference [72] with a head-mounted device interconnected to the implant combined with a battery. Presently, wireless fully-passive embedded neurosensorial devices have emerged [12, 18, 24-27] working without internal power supplies with a highly simplified implant structure. Correspondingly, no intra-cranial wires or cables have been utilized. A fully-passive brain neurosensor occupies a 10 mm×8.7 mm footprint and can capture emulated neuropotentials up to 20 μVpp [27], which improves sensitivity 25 times compared to earlier fully-passive configurations [25].

5. *Neurostimulators:* They stimulate the nervous system allowing one to recover from dystonia, brain-computer interfaces (BCIs) [29], artificial limbs, stroke, Parkinson's, depression, sleep apnea, spasticity, Alzheimer's, chronic pain, obesity, epilepsy, incontinence, hypertension, heart problems, cochlear implants and visual impairments (e.g., retinal implants), and more [28-33, 96].

New implantable devices will employ developments in science and technology like stents that wirelessly transmit an artery status, implants that can detect and regulate drugs, IBs to watch and adjust blood sugar levels, and implants to detect cancers [95, 97].

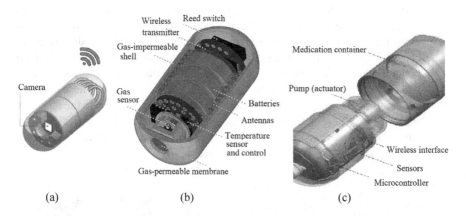

Figure 2. Some ingestibles [10, 11, 34-38]: (a) gastrointestinal imaging capsules, (b) medication adherence checking ingestible capsules, and (c) drug delivery ingestible capsules

2.2. Ingestibles

Ingestibles are tiny capsule-like gadgets taken as regular pills [4, 8, 10, 11, 34-38]. Ingestibles collect images while wandering through the gastrointestinal tract and system, transmit real-time videos, sense physiological signs, deliver drugs and more. Broadcasted data goes to close monitoring/control devices for further analysis. Examples follow:

1. *Imaging Capsules:* Intelligent gastrointestinal tract/system endoscopy capsules remain well-known ingestibles. Fluorescence-based ingestible capsules also help [34] obtain more precise images. These systems characteristically

comprise three submodules: optical imaging, electronics control, image gathering, information processing, and data transmission.

2. *Ingestible Sensors:* Often sense the body's physiological parameters to diagnose numerous conditions. The FDA has sanctioned a sensor from Proteus Digital Health for heart failure [35]. A sensor perceives the pharmaceutical tablet or capsule ingestion [11]. Clinical trials confirmed 99.1% accuracy and no false positives with direct correlations between medication ingestion, health behaviors (e.g., physical activity), and indispensable physiological response metrics (e.g., sleep patterns, heart rate and blood pressure). Custom-made ingestible capsules could measure concentrations of different gases throughout gut digestion [36]. Changes in the formation of certain abdominal gases may lead to gastrointestinal ailments, such as painful constipation and irritable bowel syndrome, in addition to colon cancer.

3. *Drug Delivery Pills:* This class alludes to electronic pills to accurately deliver a drug alongside the gastrointestinal tract. One micropositioning mechanism could easily be embedded in a capsule and convey targeted medication [37]. This allowed placing a needle within a cylindrical capsule , extensible to 1.5 mm and beyond . Another example is a smart pill releasing powdered medicine before arriving at the ileocecal valve (i.e., the meeting place of the small and large intestines) [95, 96]. Once triggered through magnetic proximity, the capsule releases its powdered payload. Plentiful future applications for ingestibles are on the horizon. Examples include (i) personalized drug delivery capsules for digestive diseases, (ii) higher-bandwidth data transmission for better diagnosis, (iii) ingestible sensors taken as pills with the correct dosage, and (iv) electronic capsules that monitor reactions to the dose. These capsules activate and sense specific gastrointestinal tract parts in addition to the digestive system. E.g., these devices can sense gastrointestinal tract electrical activity while measuring transit times and smart capsules releasing specialized drugs at target locations or if they identify an event.

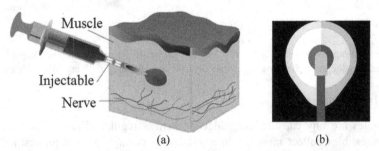

(a)   (b)

Figure 3. Examples of injectable devices: (a) injectable micro-stimulator [12] and (b) electrode formed via sequential material injections [39-41]

2.3. Injectables

Many folks consider injectables as the next IB generation since they come about as minimally intrusive and smart. Examples appear below:

1. *Needle-injected Micro-sensors:* Profusa has created an injectable Oxygen sensor that can check oxygen levels in nearby tissues [39]. The hydrogel permeated sensor has a fluorescent dye responsive to oxygen, the thickness of human hair, and as prolonged as single long-grain rice [93]. Light irradiates the skin, and an optical sensor picks up emissions to read the device. Notably, the fluorescent brightness lessens as oxygen binds to dye receptors. Envisioned applications embrace, albeit are not restricted to, peripheral artery disease checking and tracking of the muscle performance of athletes .

2. *Needle-injected Micro-stimulators:* Injectable stimulators are less invasive and discreet than the previous stimulators [12], covering electrodes, antennas, power harvesting, and electronics to control the stimulation. Preliminary assays for post-stroke shoulder subluxation as well as knee osteoarthritis treatments demonstrated promising results [40].

3. *Sequentially Injected 3D IBs:* They can treat tissues using injections of biocompatible materials, liquid metal inks, and flexible, miniaturized electronics. As a proof-of-concept, assorted Electrocardiogram (ECG) as well as stimulator electrodes have been built at the target tissues and corroborated both in-vitro and in-vivo assays [41].

The most significant challenges of injectables are powering and fabrication of tiny injectable antennas/electronics. Once they are overcome, there will be better treatments for hand contraction, ulcers, hemicranias, seizures, urinary incontinence, sleep apnea, and collecting physiological data from very young individuals like babies [18, 40-45]. These pediatric patients need unobtrusive forms to observe calories burned, breathing rate, heart rate, physical activity, nutritional status, sleep intervals and organ functions to mention a few.

3. Designing In-Body Devices

IB projects commonly utilize human analytical models and sophisticated electromagnetics (EM) simulation software. Experiment validation occurs in-vitro with phantoms that mimic electrical features of biological tissues. The works in [10-15] overview numerical simulations and experimental validation methods used to simulate real-life IB situations correctly. This chapter addresses the problems that IBs confront, such as operating frequency selection, wireless designs, powering, and biocompatibility. All IB forms (comprising ingestibles, implantables, and injectables) must be considered.

3.1. Operation Frequencies

IBs rely on many frequency bands, most notably the (i) Medical Device Radio Communication Service (MedRadio, 403.5 MHz) as well as (ii) Industrial, Scientific, and Medical (ISM) bands (ISM, 2.4 GHz). There are trade-offs to determine operation frequencies. Low frequencies, specifically, are more appealing because they damage biological tissues less. High frequencies (3-5 GHz), for example, indicate attenuation of up to 20-30 dB per 2 cm of tissue [36-48]. Contrariwise, low frequencies limit communication by necessitating big antennas and circuit components, increasing the

IB size. High-frequency connections are standard in ingestibles to achieve high data speeds, higher imaging quality, and downsizing.

3.2. Biocompatibility

The IB's surroundings react to the substance or bacteria on its surface. Blood and tissue fluid proteins first adhere to or infiltrate materials. The body is then protected from the external samples by immunological inflammatory cells like leukocytes, monocytes, and platelets. If the abiotic substance does not fit tissues and cells, then it will not stay in place for long and may be hazardous.

Biocompatibility refers to IBs that do not harm biological tissues [49-51, 53-59]. Examples of biocompatible materials are thin polymer coverings, superstrates coatings of exposed metallic components. It is only temporary since the body encapsulates the IB attempting to eject it. For example, a 24-hour durable coverage enables inexpensive silicon sensors within the body. IBs must typically be enclosed in a steel jacket (e.g., existing pacemakers) to withstand biological conditions.

Microorganisms on material surfaces should be sanitized before implantation, just like implanted medical devices. Formaldehyde, dry heat, ethylene oxide (EtO), peracetic acid, pressurized vapor, gas plasma (H2O2), gamma radiation, and E-beam are IB sterilization methodologies [49-59]. FDA class III medical equipment allows gamma radiation, EtO, and E-beam sterilization. Biocompatible materials completely seal devices such as implantable cardioverter defibrillators (ICDs), pacemakers, and cochlear implants. When choosing a biocompatible material, packing feasibility is essential [50-58]. More suitable biocompatible materials are titanium alloys, noble metals, and many other materials [49-59, 96].

3.3. Packaging and Hermeticity

Implantables require a barrier to protect them from in-body components like cells, platelets, proteins, and chemical vapors. Moreover, packaging should insulate internal electrical/mechanical components from the body environment completely. A hermetically sealed package is airtight. The hermeticity testing technique details are in MIL-STD-883, method 1014.10. The most popular hermeticity measurement method is the helium leak detector, a mass spectrometer that examines helium gas.

The packaging of implantables contains various materials, including quartz, fused silica, polymers, metals, besides ceramics [13-15]. The packaging encloses the electrical or mechanical system by polymer encapsulation and metal, glass, and ceramic welding or bonding. Epoxies, silicon-polyimides, silicones, silicon-carbons, polyurethanes, benzocyclobutenes, parylenes, polycyclic-olefins, and liquid crystal polymers can work as encapsulating packages. Silicone rubber can serve as an encapsulation for arterial line pressure sensors. Epoxies can cover feed through ICD connections. Polyurethanes can conceal platinum wires in pacemakers. Glasses made of quartz, fused silica, and borosilicate are typically finished by melting the glasses with local laser-focused heating. Neuromuscular stimulators, endoscopic tablets, radio-frequency (RF) identification chips, and implanted blood pressure monitors all use glass packings. The most popular hermetic packaging technology is the metallic package, which is created by laser welding of metals.

The metallic packaging comprises, part loop recorders, ICDs, pacemakers, and cochlear implants [96]. IB development begins with information from the patient, healthcare personnel, and engineers. Patients utilizing a device temporarily or permanently are often uneasy with the alien item. They desire rapid medical treatments that are painless, as well as recovery that is smooth. Insertion has become imperceptible due to less invasive techniques and improved device downsizing, and restoration can occur unintentionally. Lithium-carbon monofluoride, lithium-iodine polyvinylpyridine, or lithium-polycarbon fluoride high-power-density batteries extend device-replacement intervals. After implantation, the device functions start automatically. Consumers want testable gadgets performing correctly without additional activities, e.g. magnetic resonance imaging (MRI), computed tomography (CT), or X-rays. A higher quality of life (QoL) results from simple operation techniques, less invasive implantation, enhanced performance, a longer replacement schedule, and easier status access.

Physicians must understand how, why, where and when to implant. The patient's input often supports healthcare staff and engineers with the design proposal. The IB's size and form are essential factors in implantation. Assuming that the region is too small for the entire device the device can have many parts, such as in a cochlear implant, or discrete linked elements e.g. the pressure sensor in addition to the battery in a blood pressure sensor. The device's size and the project also impact its distribution mechanism. If the device is too big for insertion instruments such as a catheter, insertion requires incision surgery. Delivery via minimally invasive surgery should be established or designed for stent-sized systems, which are smaller than a human organ. E.g., one can inject the device through a needle.

Following insertion, the human body attacks the IB material. In this scenario, neointimal material or fibrocellular shields help keep the device apart from tissues. If the gadget is packed or encased in a biocompatible material, the immune response causes severe electrical and chemical material interactions. As a result, the biocompatibility of packed materials needs validation tests and excellent production standards.

The human body is an exceptional environment for the engineer constantly changing due to electrical and chemical interactions, and susceptible to minute changes in a body element. As a result, ethical, rational, and scientifically sound techniques can help this domain. Medical devices can reestablish body functions, sense signals, or sustain an organ mechanically or electrically. Consequently, specialists must investigate the body's environment, functionality, structure, biological responses, electronic circuits, biocompatibility, micro-electro-mechanical structures, hermeticity/packaging, communications, security, batteries, and insertion tools.

Next, a gadget needs validation via modeling and realistic testing. The constructed system benchtop test happens before being implanted into live creatures. Engineers have problems in the following areas: biocompatibility, hermeticity, structural design, delivery system, power management, detection, and wireless communication.

Charge transfer (ChT) is a serious issue to advance biosensors and biofuel cells [71-82]. Nanomaterials can aid chT in these bioelectronics-based devices. This chapter overviews some ChT processes and/or routes among redox enzymes and electrodes. In unison, it discusses indirect ChT with nanomaterials (commonly used in electrochemical enzymatic biosensors besides biofuel cells) and more advanced but still scarce direct charge transfer (DCT), aka direct electron transfer (DET), or DCT/DET. Conducting polymers (CPs) can immobilize enzymes and aid in creating. CP synthesis and applications receive a lot of attention. Some DCT/DET practices in CP take up ChT through electrons and holes as vital in making bioelectronic devices.

Many studies [72-82] investigated the biocompatibility of CPs with proteins, DNA, stem cells, and microbes. However, just a handful of them looked at how polymers impact the immune systems of mammals. Particular biofuel cells in addition to amperometric biosensors have been transplanted into patients' organs or connected to various body components [61-70]. These biocompatibility concerns are the most severe (e.g., eyes, skin, mucosa) [61-70, 74-81]. If IB biocompatibility is insufficient, inflammation and different types of allergies develop. Choosing an immobilization approach that is adequate for retaining the activity of immobilized biomaterial is essential for the creation of biofuel and biosensors cells. As a result, several studies investigated the CP biocompatibility with proteins and the impact of polypyrrole on more sophisticated biological systems. Polypyrrole, for example, partakes in no immune system influence on mouse cells since these hematological characteristics, which indicate the immune system status, stay constant. However, a dose-dependent outcome of polypyrrole-based nanoparticles on stem cells from bone marrow occurred at a somewhat elevated concentration of nanoparticles. The toxic cell effects to human T lymphocyte Jurkat, mouse hepatoma (MH-22A), as well as primary mouse embryonic fibroblast (MEF) were not observed when applying a small polypyrrole nanoparticle concentration. The above assessments demonstrated polypyrrole biocompatibility with tested cell lines in addition to mammalian immune systems. Characteristics of the conducting polymer polyaniline's biocompatibility were also investigated and determined. Furthermore, certain scientific works showed that an electric field stimulation promoted nerve cell differentiation when placed on a composite structure comprising polypyrrole/polyethylene glycol (2-methoxy-5 aniline sulfonic acid). The biocompatibility of CP-modified electrodes may improve biocompatible polymers (e.g., chitosan) and/or developing hydrogels containing a large quantity of water [83-94]. These conducting polymer-based gels can integrate certain tissue-forming cells as scaffolds. Then, these biosystems can serve as engineered tissue for transplantation and other biomedicine uses. Because of the biocompatibility of polypyrrole along with other conducting polymers, they can form enzymatic biofuel cells to power implantable/attachable biomedical equipment. However, the number of genuine biocompatibility-based evaluations is still relatively low; hence, substantial emphasis may go into this study area.

3.4. Design of Implantables and Delivery Systems

The body is a complicated system powered by dint of mechanical, chemical, and electrical systems in various organs, tissues, and cells. In addition, the method includes varied forms, sizes, locations, functioning, and reactions based on age, gender, and race. As a result, designing an entire medical gadget at once is challenging. Design necessitates extensive study, mathematical models and tabletop testing using a human body phantom, animal studies, and actual implants. Designers come across biological, scientific, and health roadblocks throughout the development stage. Suppose an electronic gadget is suitable for managing data, albeit the chip is overly huge to be a human body implant. In that case, one needs to locate a replacement electronic chip or completely redesign the concept.

At large, actively operating implanted devices, such as implants to monitor blood pressure require an energy source (e.g., battery) for data processing in addition to wireless transmission [61-70]. A battery with the appropriate capacity must be integrated with electronics to ensure the power demand for the length of the operation. However, finding a suitable commercial battery is difficult. Until recently, battery issues have been a hurdle in developing arterial blood pressure monitoring systems. Frounhofer's blood pressure measuring device, for example, employs an inner-arterial pressure sensor with an outer-arterial battery.

Device delivery techniques are twofold: incision and instruments. Literature measures implanted blood pressure as inner-artery or outer-artery blood pressure. Both techniques employ direct arterial blood pressure measurements. However, the measurement site differs [18-20, 97].

3.5. Wireless Interface

Wireless interfaces and IB integration provide unobtrusive and ubiquitous wireless connections with external monitoring/control devices such as a smartphone, wristwatch, or other wearables that may send data to distant physicians, caretakers, family members, and so on.

The early implants had inductive coupling (IC) at frequencies up to 20 MHz, inductors inside the implant, and external devices nearby for wireless communication. However, IC drawbacks include poor data rates as well as high sensitivity to misalignment of inductors and wireless antenna communication has lately begun to replace them. In-body antennas alleviate IC constraints and are becoming more prevalent. IB antenna (IBA) design presents several problems, most of which are linked to downsizing while dealing with large operating bandwidth. Antenna designs for IBs can be

(a) Miniaturized Planar Inverted-F Antennas (PIFAs) with many degrees of freedom,
(b) Helical antennas for ingestibles with constant bandwidth, circular polarization, an omnidirectional radiation pattern, and transmission through a broad spectrum of tissues around the IB, and
(c) Injectable loop or dipole antennas.

The Internet of Things (IoT) expands information technology (IT), automating operations and sending data via a wireless network without human involvement [106-111, 114, 116, 117]. The Internet of Medical Things (IoMT) denotes high-tech equipment with wireless connections, greater efficiency, and excellent real-time diagnostics via a sophisticated health-tech ecosystem.

Several healthcare suppliers have invested significantly to capitalize on the IoMT potential and build environments with intelligent services for imaging, sensing, real-time actuation, and diagnostics. Smartphone camera resolutions may help successfull flow cytometry, optical microscopy, and other imaging tools for better-quality real-time discoveries [18, 33, 97, 99-102, 104, 107, 108]. Points of care (PoCs) with Bluetooth Low Energy (BLE) technology can exchange data up to a few feet, which is enough for non-invasive salivary glucose biosensors and fitness trackers, to constantly monitor a patient's physical activity and vital signs [98-105]. The development of smart textiles has resulted in improved sensing of heart rate, blood pressure, ECG, and body temperature. There are several internet-connected gadgets available, including medical booths, fitness tracking gadgets (bracelets, smartwatches, clothes, and so on), clinical wearables, remote patient observing devices, smart medications, and many more. Sweat, saliva, feces, tears, and breath are examples of non-invasive samples in eHealth diagnostic devices (e-Diagnostics) to detect major illness (cancer, viral infections, and HIV) biomarkers. These gadgets, however, are still in development. Surprisingly, smartphone adoption is widespread among low- and middle-income persons, increasing the use of PoC technologies without additional expenditures. It will also afford more services in remote localities and rural communities at a lower cost [106-113, 116, 117].

Improved PoC social networking, communications, and information resources are chief motivators driving the fast adoption of smartphone-based computing in the health system. A web browser provides an interface for delivering and receiving health information in real-time. Additionally, IoMT systems have other gains like global-positioning systems (GPSs), handy message services, e-mails, and interactive voice communications. These features can advance the automation of PoC diagnostics with data collection and continuous transmission to a central database via satellite networks [106-111, 115]. Warehousing patients' well-being information builds a vast array of databases to aid researchers in studying complicated diseases, e.g., asthma, cancer, coronary artery problems, diabetes, and Parkinson's.

The envisioned smartphone-based PoCs can perform either endpoint or real-time testing based on a specific detection mechanisms such as reflections, fluorescenct emissions, currents, colorimetry or turbidity. Smart PoCs, for example, may detect the development of color change in an ELISA-based test, and recorded pictures can be evaluated with custom-made apps to quantify the pathogens. In contrast, a range of optical attachments can accomplish sensitive smartphone fluorescence detection. Likewise, IoMT-based proof-of-concept tools with simple platforms can identify several infectious illnesses through molecular assays, e.g., PCR, loop-mediated isothermal nucleic acid amplification (LAMP), and lateral flow to detect new pathogens. Furthermore, electrochemical IoMT encompasses integrated circuits that gather clinical data and identify pathogens in real-time.

In recent years, the integration of proof-of-concept systems with machine learning (ML) i.e., artificial intelligence (AI), has given rise to significant paradigm shifts toward data-analytics-centered decision making [108-115]. AI gives medical practitioners an extra option to provide personalized therapy to people and monitor their outcomes. These AI systems help healthcare providers analyze the risks of various diseases like cancer, heart attack, and patient traumas. AI sensors initiate the multistep portable analyzer test, which then automatically digitizes the biomarker concentrations. To determine treatment options, the spectrum of illnesses may be anticipated using many algorithms, such as classification, cluster, pattern, and disease characteristics. The M-Health WHO global observatory utilizes wireless devices to present findings to patients. Thus, health analytics give patients tailored therapy for active disease management and prevention. The combination of real-time PoC diagnostics with AI transformed the healthcare industry. An AI ecosystem for automated prescribing can accelerate the growth of the IoMT industry [106-111, 116, 117].

3.6. Energy Harvesting

Most IBs are battery-powered [18]. Nonetheless, this demands greater IB size, patient safety, and biocompatibility issues, in addition to the need for periodic replacement and/or recharging. Batteries still take up the majority of IB space nowadays. Batteryless IBs can rely on power collecting techniques or operate entirely passively, as seen below:

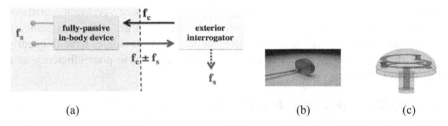

(a)   (b)   (c)

Figure 4. Concept of an entirely passive operation to realize batteryless IBs: (a) diagram (b) sample device, and (c) internal antenna

(i) Power harvesting methods derive energy from the IB environment or bodily sources, such as electromagnetic energy (RF), ultrasound, and so on), tissue motion and heartbeat, temperature gradients in the body, human motion [120, 121, 122], and glucose oxidization [18, 33, 119].

(ii) Completely Passive Operation IBs reduce the need for power storage [12, 18, 54] since they function similarly to a RFID near an exterior interrogator (EI) outside the patient's body, such as a cap or bracelet. The interrogator wirelessly transmits a carrier signal f_c to the IB (Figure 4). In turn, the IB combines the carrier with the detected physiological signal f_s and immediately sends a signal with frequency ($f_c \pm f_s$) to the EI for further demodulation (to retrieve f_s) and decision-making/recommendation/mitigation.

Owing to their small size and high capacity requirements, electric power additions to IBs complicate their design. Implantable batteries can be both disposable and rechargeable [17-22, 28]. One-time-usage batteries power pacemakers, ICDs, and deeply implanted stimulators. Continuously charged batteries help cochlear, cardiac replacement, and retinal implantations. When the electrical power is insufficient to run the gadget effectively, the single-use battery should change by operation. Wireless inductive telemetry [23-25, 52] repeatedly measures the residual power capacity in a non-rechargeable battery. First-generation pacemakers relied on wireless telemetry in medical equipment. However, real-time power transmission to devices proved inefficient, and the patients felt uncomfortable with an external power-transferring coil. An inner-body receiving coil with an extracorporeal power delivering system work wirelessly. When an energy-containing frequency communicates with an external coil, the latter creates magnetic fields over a certain distance. Suppose the inner inductor coil stands approximately perpendicular to the exterior coil and within range. In that case, the magnetic flux causes current to flow over the inner coil, resulting in constant voltage via rectification and regulation. The voltage then recharges the rechargeable battery. Still, if the distance among the inner and outer coils is excessive for acceptable inductive connection, there is a feeble induced current or no current.

Much recent investigations have concentrated on energy generation utilizing inner body mechanical, chemical, physical, and electrical phenomena to address the energy issue of implanted devices [60-71], aka energy harvesting or scavenging. Examples of energy harvesting are a self-winding timepiece, a shake-driven lamp, a bicycle dynamo, the latest phone charger, a self-winding watch mechanism to power pacemakers, and ultrasonic energy transfer. These energy-generating methods still need a battery to store the generated electrical charge, such as a standard rechargeable battery [33]. However, energy collecting technologies have frequently caused deficient energy output levels with restrictions due to poor efficiency as a direct energy source.

3.7. Big Data, Security, and Privacy

3.7.1. High-Dimensionality, Scalability, and Sub-Networks' Hierarchical/Distributed Organization

Eventually, healthcare data accumulated over time will allow for individualized therapy and, as a result, far more efficient and cost-effective treatments. This big-data strategy intends to facilitate the transition from reactive and symptom-based treatment to a proactive healthcare paradigm. There are various applications, ranging from geriatric monitoring to monitoring people in developing nations to military, space, and sports arenas [95-106].

Big Data (BD) and the aptitude to amass medical measurements, including genetic biobanks, enable the assessment of features, their analysis, and the identification of clinical symptoms. Their investigation uncovered three underlying transdiagnostic factors: anxiety/depression, compulsion, intrusive thinking, and social anxiety. A further experiment found that compulsion and invasive thinking affected task performance. The same transdiagnostic component could boost confidence but lessen self-evaluation ability. Anxiety/depression decreased confidence but with good self-evaluation ability. AMT has also been utilized to characterize the landscape of emotional experience, with a component analysis of emotion labels and ratings generated by 2,185 films. Notably, after one week, depressed symptoms show good test-retest reliability ($r = 0.87$), indicating that online data might be adequately trustworthy. Attempts to use online data gathering and testing for therapeutic purposes are more directly relevant to mental health. A cognitive-behavioral therapy (CBT) mobile trial for insomnia patients, for example, efficaciously lessened insomnia while also facilitating paranoia and hallucinations diminutions.

Online tests facilitate quick novel paradigm prototyping in diverse samples of persons with a wide variety of clinically relevant symptoms. Depression and anxiety amount to the most expensive mental illnesses, and they are both as frequent in online samples as they are in the general population. Hence, online data collecting may enable more rapid, inexpensive data gathering, allowing for sufficient data acquisition to facilitate more complex analysis albeit with a few drawbacks. Online community employees might be prejudiced as well, further complicating issues. Individuals require incentives to share their knowledge accurately. Some people, however, may be more ready to give intimate information anonymously than in front of a researcher. Auspicious innovations from undisclosed researchers should be reproduced in more controlled laboratory experiments besides less controlled smartphone studies.

Smartphones passively gather a plethora of data streams for a better understanding. Through various sensors, elements such as acceleration, movement, location, voice, keyboard use habits, and social interactions may eventually become part of an individual's digital phenotyping.

3.7.2. Theory- and Data-driven Methodologies

Data-driven analyses disregard the data type/structure, which makes algorithms vulnerable. Generating knowledge of processes may be utilized to construct what are known as adequate statistics, statistically optimum summaries that capture non-random variance in the data. General-purpose ML algorithms may not recover enough statistics, albeit theory-driven models ideally do so. As a result, theory-driven models may quickly summarize intricate data given what is known about a generative process. These summaries can become ML inputs. Combining theory-driven with data-driven techniques has the potential to outperform data-driven approaches alone [6, 18]. Reinforcement-learning procedures are widely employed and extensively explored in neuroscience. Likewise, generative processes are becoming more understood at the neurobiological level.

Big data (BD) and ML can enhance results. IBs will create substantial data sets that professionals will need to parse, and these records will contain the illness complexity. This necessitates collaboration between academics and industry. Machine-learning approaches can better realize their promise for finding more expressive functions in data, such as non-linearities or higher-order interaction effects, with sufficiently big data sets.

Second, clinical research must monitor therapies or risk failing to fulfill the primary psychiatry goal, which is to lessen the disease burden. Interventions are more involved and hazardous than cross-sectional research, raising significant ethical problems and necessitating time-consuming longitudinal designs for all parties. It is unsafe for inexperienced scientists since failures are costly yet common. Nonetheless, some restrictions are: (i) recovering imprecise diagnostic labels, besides (ii) cognitive and neurological process comparisons in healthy and sick groups. Standard techniques are unlikely to result in therapy breakthroughs. However, AI and semantic procedures can improve this scenario.

These challenges embrace a wide gamut of topics in the development of innovative prediction techniques. A roadmap influenced by the drug development pipeline is in [37, 54, 116]. This distinguishes between the early stages (producing relevant probes) and the middle stages (linking probes and clinical concerns, especially in therapy). Later phases (comparable to phase III or phase IV medical assays) assess probe usage in clinical improvement. Adopting such a paradigm might assist in organizing the research and highlight the relevance of investigating the link between probes and clinical outcomes.

3.8. Security and Privacy

Although IBs are beneficial to a patient's well-being and quality of life, the availability of IB-related goods, their rising complexity, and communication advancements do not have correspondingly smooth cybersecurity [5, 6, 117, 118, 125]. Recent IB can be incorporated into IoT, making it vulnerable to assaults affecting privacy and, more importantly, device the health and life of device users. Security procedures rely on present protocols and models in the early stages of IB development. Functional capabilities focus on development issues. Recent efforts have addressed security with innovative IB cybersecurity contributions, representing new design paradigms for next-generation devices. This encourages technological growth, and attackers' growing access to resources for exploiting numerous flaws can significantly influence the IB in the patient's body after many years. It also necessitates new and robust protocols to provide security while working with limited computational resources and meager energy needs. Finally, addressing security and privacy matters throughout the design process and policies should shift from damage mitigation to prevention.

With its vast array of applications, the Internet of medical things (IoMT) has attracted wide-reaching companies and academics, facilitating operations through pervasive Internet access to devices with computer capability. With the wireless infrastructure advancement, the emphasis went from simple IoMT to smart, connected devices/platforms, allowing low-complexity, inexpensive, and efficient computing via machines, sensors, actuators, and even crowdsourcing. All these devices may be clubbed together under the umbrella of IoMT. Security, privacy, and trust remain critical problems despite benefiting enormously from health applications. Poor enforcement of these standards poses non-negligible risks to IoMT devices and platforms. As a result, it is critical to comprehend the multiple options for delivering safe, privacy-compliant, and trustworthy IoMT mechanisms. Smart IoMT requires more research about security, physical-layer safety, confidentiality, trust, secure protocols, and handover safeguards as these requirements will provide cutting-edge solutions.

4. Future Directions

IBs evolve fast, requiring tiny power sources [61, 64-67, 71-73]. Biofuel cells for implantable bioelectronics, especially biosensors, are in increasing demand. Power management is key. Pacemakers require a dependable, always-on power supply for life-critical tasks. Whether such gadgets use a primary or rechargeable battery affects battery life. IBs must be transferred. Multi-module implants for new applications need critical considerations, definitions, and power management optimization [119].

However, this research direction faces numerous challenges, e.g., innumerable biocompatibility facets of implanted biosensors or biofuel cell structures. Proteins or other biomolecules from body fluids can foul implants or irritate the patient's immune system. Regardless, biofuel cells are emerging for implantation into many plants and animals, and despite widespread disagreement, the human body will soon use them. Developing optimal energy control/harvesting and communication schemes for IBs to reach many structures via WBANs is somewhat complex. Optimization and AI aid in maximizing data transmission rates for WBANs with RF energy garnering without subsystems' interference. This optimization problem handles plenty of constraints and can be non-convex, transforming it into solvable convex subproblems. Simulations are valuable to analyze, model, and solve such problems [123, 124].

5. Conclusion

This chapter discussed in-body wireless devices (IBs), such as implantables, ingestibles, and injectables, including existing technology and future potential. IB design is complicated by frequency, antenna, power, and biocompatibility considerations. Efforts focus on innovative sensing techniques, materials, and medicinal uses. IBs are vital for medical prevention, diagnosis, and treatment, outweighing any concerns about their invasiveness. Unobtrusive IBs sometimes capture physiological data from all life phases. Healthy newborns, children, teens, and adults use remote or concealed sensors to monitor heart rate, breathing rate, nutrition, physical activity, calories burnt, organ function, and sleep patterns. Data acquired over time would allow targeted, cost-effective medical intervention. Big data moves from reactive/symptom-centered to proactive well-being. Uses include elderly surveillance in underdeveloped nations, space, and sports venues.

References

1. Cunningham, M. (2021). Special Issue. IEEE Trans. Techn. and Soc. 2, 2.
2. Harary, M., Dolmans, R.G.F. and Gormley, W.B. (2018). Intracranial Pressure Monitoring – Review and Avenues for Development. Sensors, 18, 465.
3. Burleson, W. and Carrara, S. (2014). Security and Privacy for Implantable Medical Devices, Springer.
4. Yuce, M. and Dissanayake, T. (2012). Easy-to-swallow wireless telemetry. IEEE Microw. Mag., 13, 90-101.
5. Kanna, K., Estrela, V.V. and Rodrigues, J.J.P.C. (2021). Cyber security and digital forensics. Proc. ICCSDF 2021, Springer Nature, Zurich, Switzerland.
6. Khelassi, A. and Estrela, V.V. (2020). Advances in multidisciplinary medical technologies – Engineering, modeling and findings. Proc. ICHSMT 2019, Springer Nature, Zurich, Switzerland.
7. Estrela, V.V., Saotome, O., Loschi, H.J., Hemanth, D.J., Farfan, W.S. et al. (2018). Emergency response cyber-physical framework for landslide avoidance with sustainable electronics. Technologies, 6, 42.

8. Khanna, V.K. (2016). Implantable Medical Electronics, Springer Cham.
9. Kiourti, A., Cedric, C.W.L., Chae, J. and Volakis, J.L. (2016). A wireless fully-passive neural recording device for unobtrusive neuropotential monitoring. IEEE Trans. Biomed. Eng., 63, 131-137.
10. Goenka, M.K., Majumder, S. and Goenka, U. (2014). Capsule endoscopy: Present status and future expectation. World J. Gastroenterol., 20, 10024-10037.
11. Kalpouzos, I., Giokas, K. and Koutsouris, D.D. (2015). A survey on an ingestible sensor for evaluating medication adherence in elderly people. Proc. 8th ACM PETRA.
12. Li, X., Serdijn, W.A., Zheng, W., Tian, Y., Zhang, B. et al. (2015). The injectable neurostimulator: An emerging therapeutic device. Tr. Biotech, 33, 388-394.
13. Alhawari, M., Mohammad, B., Saleh, H. and Ismail, M. (2018). Energy Harvesting for Self-Powered Wearable Devices, Springer, Cham.
14. Meng, X., Browne, K.D., Huang, S., Cullen, D.K., Tofighi, M. et al. (2012). Dynamic study of wireless intracranial pressure monitoring of rotational head injury in swine model. Electron. Lett., 48, 363-364.
15. Khan, M.W.A., Bjorninen, T., Sydanh Eimo, L., Ukkonen, L. et al. (2016). Remotely powered piezoresistive pressure sensor: Toward wireless monitoring of intracranial pressure. IEEE Microw. Wireless Compon. Lett., 26, 549-551.
16. Behfar, M.H., Bjorninen, T., Moradi, E., Sydanheimo, L. and Ukkonen, L. (2015). Biotelemetric wireless intracranial pressure monitoring: An in vitro study. Int. J. Antennas Propag. ID 918698, doi: 10.1155/2015/918698.
17. Yu, L., Kim, B.J. and Meng, E. (2014). Chronically implanted pressure sensors: Challenges and state of the field. Sensors, 14, 20620-20644.
18. Kiourti, A. and Nikita, K.S. (2017). A review of in-body biotelemetry devices and sensors: Implantables, ingestibles, and injectables. IEEE Tr. Bio. Eng., 64, 1422-1430.
19. Murphy, O.H., Bahmanyar, M.R., Borghi, A., McLeod, C., Navaratnarajah, M. et al. (2013). Continuous in vivo blood pressure measurements using a fully implantable wireless SAW sensor. Biom. Microdev., 15, 737-749.
20. Theodor, M., Ruh, D., Fiala, J., Forster, K., Heilmann, C. et al. (2013). Subcutaneous blood pressure monitoring with an implantable optical sensor. Biomed. Microdev., 15, 811-820.
21. Ellozy, S.H., Carroccio, A., Lookstein, R.A., Minor, M.E., Sheahan, C.M. et al. (2004). First experience in human beings with a permanently implantable intrasac pressure transducer for monitoring endovascular repair of abdominal aortic aneurysms. J. Vasc. Surg., 40, 405412.
22. Adamson, P.B., Abraham, W.T., Aaron, M.F., Aranda, J.M., Bourge, R.C. et al. (2011). Champion trial rationale and design: The long term safety and clinical efficacy of a wireless pulmonary artery pressure measurement system. J. Card. Fail., 17, 3-10.
23. Karageorgos, G., Manopoulos, C., Tsangaris, S. and Nikita, K.S. (2016). Self-powered impantable electromagnetic device for cardiovascular system monitoring through arterial wall deformation. Proc. 6th Int. Conf. Wireless Mob. Commun. Healthc.
24. Yin, M., Borton, D.A., Komar, J., Agha, N., Lu, Y. et al. (2014). Wireless neurosensor for full-spectrum electrophysiology recordings during free behavior. Neuron., 84, 1-13.
25. Schwerdt, H.N., Xu, W., Shekhar, S., Abbaspour-Tamijani, A., Towe, B.C. et al. (2011). A fully passive wireless microsystem for recording of neuropotentials using RF backscattering methods. J. Microelectromech. Syst., 20, 1119-1130.
26. Lee, C.W., Kiourti, A., Chae, J. and Volakis, J.L. (2015). A high-sensitivity fullypassive wireless neurosensing system for unobtrusive brain signal monitoring. Proc. 2015 IEEE MTT-S Int'l Microw. Symp., 1-4.
27. Lee, C., Kiourti, A. and Volakis, J.L. (2016). Miniaturized fully -assive brain implant for wireless acquisition of very low-level neural signals, IEEE A. Wir. Prop. L., 1-4.

28. Shire, D.B., Kelly, S.K., Chen, J., Doyle, P.S., Gingerich, M.D. et al. (2009). Development and implantation of a minimally invasive wireless subretinal neurostimulator. IEEE Trans. Biomed. Eng., 56, 2502-2511.

29. Weiss, J.N. (2022). Visual Prosthesis: A Concise Guide 1st ed., Springer Cham.

30. Watson, L.M., Archbold, S.M. and Nikolopoulos, T.P. (2013). Children's communication mode five years after cochlear implantation: Changes over time according to age at implant. Cochl. Impl. Int., 7, 77-91.

31. Tarsy, D. (2009). Does subthalamotomy have a place in the treatment of Parkinson's disease. Journal of Neurology, Neurosurg. Psychiatry, 80, 939-940.

32. Khan, A.A., Laghari, A., Shaikh, A.A., Dootio, M.A., Estrela, V.V. et al. (2021). A blockchain security module for brain-computer interface (BCI) with multimedia life cycle framework (MLCF). Neuroscience Informatics. 100030.

33. Chiu, H.-W., Lin, M., Lin, C., Ho, I., Lin, W. et al. (2010). Pain control on demand based on pulsed RadioFrequency stimulation of the dorsal root ganglion using a batteryless implantable CMOS SoC. IEEE Trans. Biomed. Circ. Syst., 4, 350-359.

34. Kfouri, M., Marinov, O., Quevedo, P.A., Faramarzpour, N., Shirani, S. et al. (2008). Towards a miniaturised wireless fluorescence-based diagnostic imaging system. IEEE J. Select. Topics Quantum Electron., 14, 226-234.

35. Shabaz, M., Sharma, A., AlAjrawi, S. and Estrela, V.V. (2022). Multimedia-based emerging technologies and data analytics for Neuroscience as a Service (NaaS). Neuroscience Informatics, 2(3), 100067.

36. Kalantar-Zadeh, K., Yao, C.K., Berean, K.J., Ha, N., Ou, J. et al. (2016). Intestinal gas capsules: A proof-of-concept demonstration. Gastroent., 150, p. 27.

37. Woods, S.P. and Constandinou, T.G. (2013). Wireless capsule endoscope for targeted drug delivery: Mechanics and design considerations. IEEE Trans. Biomed. Eng., 60, 945-953.

38. Yu, W., Rahimi, R., Ochoa, M., Pinal, R. and Ziaie, B. (2015). A smart capsule with GI-tract-location-specific payload release. IEEE Trans. Biom. Eng., 62, 2289-2295.

39. http://profusa.com/lumee/ Accessed on January 31, 2022.

40. Dupont, A.C., Bagg, S.D., Creasy, J.L., Romano, C.L., Romano, D. et al. (2004). First clinical experience with BION implants for therapeutic electrical stimulation. Neuromod., 7, 38-47.

41. Jin, C., Zhang, J., Li, X., Yang, X., Li, J. et al. (2013). Injectable 3-D fabrication of medical electronics at the target biological tissues. Scientif. Rep., 3.

42. Baker, L.L., Eberly, V.D., Rakoski, D., Waters, R.L., Palmer, E. et al. (2006). Preliminary experience with implanted microstimulators for management of post-stroke impairments. J. Neurol. Phys. Ther., 30, 209-222.

43. Kane, M.J., Breen, P.P., Quondamatteo, F. and OLaighin, G. (2011). BION microstimulators: A case study in the engineering of an electronic implantable medical device. Med. Eng. Phys., 33, 7-16.

44. Burns, B., Watkins, L. and Goadsby, P.J. (2008). Treatment of hemicranias continua by occipitalnerve stimulation with a bion device: Long-term follow-up of a crossover study. Lancet Neurol., 7, 1001-1012.

45. Groen, J., Amiel, C. and Bosch, J.R. (2005). Chronic pudendal nerve neuromodulation in women with idiopathic refractory detrusor overactivity incontinence: Results of a pilot study with a novel minimally invasive implantable ministimulator. Neurol. Urodyn., 24, 226-230.

46. Towe, B.C., Larson, P.J. and Gulick, D.W. (2012). A microwave powered injectable neural stimulator. Proc. Eng. Med. Biol. Soc., 5006-5009.

47. Onuki, Y., Bhardwaj, U., Papadimitrakopoulos, F. and Burgess, D.J. (2008). A review

of the biocompatibility of implantable devices: Current challenges to overcome foreign body response. J Diabetes Sci Technol., 2, 1003-1015.

48. Williams, D.F. (2008). On the mechanisms of biocompatibility. Biomat. 29, 2941-2953.

49. Shabalovskaya, S.A. (2002). Surface, corrosion and biocompatibility aspects of Nitinol as an implant material. Biomed. Mat. Eng., 12, 69-109.

50. Soontornpipit, P., Furse, C.M. and Chung, Y.C. (2005). Miniaturized biocompatible microstrip antenna using genetic algorithm. IEEE T. Ant. Prop., 53, 1939-1945.

51. Ramesh, A., Ren, F., Berger, P.R., Casal, P.V., Theiss, A. et al. (2013). Towards in vivo biosensors for low-cost protein sensing. Electron. Lett., 49, 450-451.

52. Plummer, C.J., Henderson, S.M., Gardener, L. and Mccomb, J.M. (2001). The use of permanent pacemakers in the detection of cardiac arrhythmias. Europace, 3, 229-232.

53. Silindir, M. and Ozer, A.Y. (2009). Sterilization methods and the comparison of E-Beam sterilization with gamma radiation sterilization. FABAD J. Pharm. Sci., 34, 43-53.

54. Lambert, B.J. and Mendelson, T.A. (2011). Craven MD. Radiation and ethylene oxide terminal sterilization experiences with drug eluting stent products. AAPS Pharm. Sci. Tech., 12, 1116-1126.

55. Schuettler, M., Schatz, A., Ordonez, J.S. and Stieglitz, T. (2011). Ensuring minimal humidity levels in hermetic implant housings. Conf. Proc. IEEE Eng Med. Biol. Soc., 2296-2299.

56. Antunes, R.A. and de Oliveira, M.C. (2012). Corrosion fatigue of biomedical metallic alloys: Mechanisms and mitigation. Acta Biomater., 8, 937-962.

57. Witte, F. (2010). The history of biodegradable magnesium implants: A review. Acta Biomater., 6, 1680-1692.

58. Jiang, G., Mishler, D., Davis, R., Mobley, J.P., Schulman, J.H. et al. (2005). Zirconia to Ti-6Al-4V braze joint for implantable biomedical device. J. Biomed. Mater Res. B Appl. Biomater., 72, 316-321.

59. Mailley, S., Hyland, M., Mailley, P., McLaughlin, J.A., McAdams, E.T. et al. (2004). Thin film platinum cuff electrodes for neurostimulation: In vitro approach of safe neurostimulation parameters. Bioelectrochemistry, 63, 359-364.

60. Joung, Y.H. (2013). Development of implantable medical devices: From an engineering perspective. Int. Neurourol J., 17(3), 98-106.

61. Zebda, A., Alcaraz, J., Vadgama, P., Shleev, S., Minteer, S.D. et al. (2018). Challenges for successful implantation of biofuel cells. Bioelectrochemistry, 124, 57-72.

62. Novak, M.T., Yuan, F. and Reichert, W.M. (2010). Modeling the relative impact of capsular tissue effects on implanted glucose sensor time lag and signal attenuation. Anal. Bioanal. Chem., 398, 1695-1705.

63. Sheikh, Z., Brooks, P.J., Barzilay, O., Fine, N., Glogauer, M. et al. (2015). Macrophages, foreign body giant cells and their response to implantable biomaterials. Materials, 8, 5671-5701.

64. MacVittie, K., Conlon, T. and Katz, E. (2015). A wireless transmission system powered by an enzyme biofuel cell implanted in an orange. Bioelectrochemistry, 106, 28-33.

65. Miyake, T., Haneda, K., Nagai, N., Yatagawa, Y., Onami, H. et al. (2011). Enzymatic biofuel cells designed for direct power generation from biofluids in living organisms. Energy Environ. Sci., 4, 5008-5012.

66. Katz, E. and MacVittie, K. (2013). Implanted biofuel cells operating in vivo—Methods, applications and perspectives. Energy Environ. Sci., 6, 2791-2803.

67. Cosnier, S., Le Goff, A. and Holzinger, M. (2014). Towards glucose biofuel cells implanted in human body for powering artificial organs: Review. Electrochem. Commun., 38, 19-23.

68. Chlebowski, A.L., Chow, E.Y., Ellison, C. and Irazoqui, P.P. (2012). Integrated LTCC packaging for use in biomedical devices. Biomed Mater Eng., 22, 361-372.

69. Chen, G.Q. (2011). Biofunctionalization of polymers and their applications. Adv. Biochem. Eng. Biotechnol., 125, 29-45.
70. Guenther, T., Dodds, C.W., Lovell, N.H. and Suaning, G.J. (2011). Chip-scale hermetic feedthroughs for implantable bionics. Proc. IEEE C. Eng. Med. Biol. Soc., 6717-6720.
71. Ramanavicius, S. and Ramanavicius, A. (2021). Charge transfer and biocompatibility aspects in conducting polymer-based enzymatic biosensors and biofuel cells. Nanomaterials (Basel), 11(2), 371.
72. MacVittie, K., Halamek, J., Halamkova, L., Southcott, M., Jemison, W.D. et al. (2013). From "cyborg" lobsters to a pacemaker powered by implantable biofuel cells. Energy Environ. Sci., 6, 81-86.
73. Ramanavicius, S. and Ramanavicius A. (2021). Conducting polymers in the design of biosensors and biofuel cells. Polymers., 13, 49.
74. Falk, M., Psotta, C., Cirovic, S. and Shleev, S. (2020). Non-invasive electrochemical biosensors operating in human physiological fluids. Sensors, 20, 6352.
75. Andriukonis, E., Celiesiute-Germaniene, R., Ramanavicius, S., Viter, R., Ramanavicius, A. et al. (2021). From microorganism-based amperometric biosensors towards microbial fuel cells. Sensors, 21(7), 2442.
76. Lee, Y.S., Ruff, A., Cai, R., Lim, K., Schuhmann, W. et al. (2020). Electroenzymatic nitrogen fixation using a MoFe protein system immobilized in an organic redox polymer. Angew. Chem. Int. Ed., 59, 16511-16516.
77. Białek, R., Thakur, K., Ruff, A., Jones, M., Schuhmann, W. et al. (2020). Insight into electron transfer from a redox polymer to a photoactive protein. J. Phys. Chem. B., 124, 11123-11132.
78. Lakard, B. (2020). Electrochemical biosensors based on conducting polymers: A review. Appl. Sci., 10, 6614.
79. Sangiorgi, N., Sangiorgi, A., Tarterini, F. and Sanson, A. (2019). Molecularly imprinted polypyrrole counter electrode for gel-state dye-sensitized solar cells. Electrochim. Acta, 305, 322-328.
80. Felix, F.S. and Angnes, L. (2018). Electrochemical immunosensors—A powerful tool for analytical applications. Biosens. Bioelectron., 102, 470-478.
81. Milton, R.D., Lim, K., Hickey, D.P. and Minteer, S.D. (2015). Employing FAD-dependent glucose dehydrogenase within a glucose/oxygen enzymatic fuel cell operating in human serum. Bioelectrochemistry, 106, 56-63.
82. German, N., Popov, A., Ramanaviciene, A. and Ramanavicius A. (2019). Enzymatic formation of polyaniline, polypyrrole, and polythiophene nanoparticles with embedded glucose oxidase. Nanomaterials, 9, 806.
83. Bornscheuer, U.T. (2003). Immobilizing enzymes: How to create more suitable biocatalysts. Angew. Chem. Int. Ed., 42, 3336-3337.
84. Sheldon, R.A. and van Pelt, S. (2013). Enzyme immobilisation in biocatalysis: Why, what and how. Chem. Soc. Rev., 42, 6223-6235.
85. Genys, P., Aksun, E.T., Tereshchenko, A., Valiuniene, A., Ramanaviciene, A. et al. (2019). Electrochemical deposition and investigation of poly-9,10-phenanthrenequinone layer. Nanomaterials, 9, 702.
86. German, N., Ramanaviciene, A. and Ramanavicius A. (2019). Formation of polyaniline and polypyrrole nanocomposites with embedded glucose oxidase and gold nanoparticles. Polymer, 11, 377.
87. Apetrei, R.-M., Cârâc, G., Bahrim, G. and Camurlu, P. (2018). Sensitivity enhancement for microbial biosensors through cell self-coating with polypyrrole. Int. J. Polym. Mater., 68, 1058-1067.
88. Sherman, H.G., Hicks, J.M., Jain, A., Titman, J.J., Alexander, C. et al. (2019). Mammalian-cell-driven polymerisation of pyrrole. ChemBioChem., 20, 1008-1013.

89. Le, T.-H., Kim, Y. and Yoon, H. (2017). Electrical and electrochemical properties of conducting polymers. Polymer, 9, 150.
90. Kumar, R., Singh, S. and Yadav, B.C. (2015). Conducting polymers: Synthesis, properties and applications. Int. Adv. Res. J. Sci. Eng. Technol., 2, 110-124.
91. Ratautaite, V., Topkaya, S.N., Mikoliunaite, L., Ozsoz, M., Oztekin, Y. et al. (2013). Molecularly imprinted polypyrrole for DNA determination. Electroanalysis, 25, 1169-1177.
92. Ramanavicius, A., Ryskevic, N., Kausaite-Minkstimiene, A., Bubniene, U., Baleviciute, I. et al. (2012). Fluorescence study of glucose oxidase self-encapsulated within polypyrrole. Sens. Actuators B Chem., 171, 753-759.
93. Li, L., Shi, Y., Pan, L., Shi, Y. and Yu, G. (2015). Additional Article Notification: Rational design and applications of conducting polymer hydrogels as electrochemical biosensors. J. Mater. Chem. B., 3, 5111-5121.
94. Chen, G.Q. (2011). Biofunctionalization of polymers and their applications. Adv. Biochem. Eng. Biotec., 125, 29-45.
95. Guenther, T., Dodds, C.W., Lovell, N.H. and Suaning, G.J. (2011). Chip-scale hermetic feedthroughs for implantable bionics. Proc. IEEE Eng. Med. Biol. Soc., 6717-6720.
96. Zeng, F.G., Rebscher, S., Harrison, W., Sun, X., Feng, H. et al. (2008). Cochlear implants: System design, integration, and evaluation. IEEE Biom. Eng., 1, 115-142.
97. Cong, P., Young, D.J., Hoit, B. and Ko, W.H. (2006). Novel long-term implantable blood pressure monitoring system with reduced baseline drift. Proc. IEEE Conf. Eng. Med. Biol. Soc., 1, 1854-1857.
98. Christodouleas, D.C., Kaur, B. and Chorti, P. (2018). From point-of-care testing to eHealth diagnostic devices (eDiagnostics). ACS Cent. Sci., 4, 1600-1616.
99. Ding, X., Mauk, M.G., Yin, K., Kadimisetty, K., Liu, C. et al. (2019). Interfacing pathogen detection with smartphones for point-of-care applications. Anal. Chem., 91, 1, 655-672.
100. Kaushik, A.K, Dhau, J.S., Gohel, H., Mishra, Y.K., Kateb, B. et al. (2020). Electrochemical SARS-CoV-2 sensing at point-of-care and artificial intelligence for intelligent COVID-19 management. ACS Appl. Bio. Mater., 3, 11, 7306-7325.
101. McRae, M.P., Simmons, G., Wong, J. and McDevitt, J.T. (2016). Programmable bio-nanochip platform: A point-of-care biosensor system with the capacity to learn. Acc. Chem. Res., 49, 1359-1368.
102. Nayak, S., Blumenfeld, N.R., Laksanasopin, T. and Sia, S.K. (2017). Point-of-Care diagnostics: Recent developments in a connected age. Anal. Chem. Rev., 89(1), 102-123.
103. Shrivastava, S., Trung, T.Q. and Lee, N.E. (2020). Recent progress, challenges, and prospects of fully integrated mobile and wearable point-of-care testing systems for self-testing. Chem. Soc., 49, 1812-1866.
104. Gupta, R., Kumar, A., Kumar, S., Pinnaka, A.K., Singhal, N.K et al. (2021). Naked eye colorimetric detection of Escherichia coli using aptamer conjugated graphene oxide enclosed Gold nanoparticles. Sensor. Actuator. B Chem., 329.
105. Wang, L.J., Chang, Y.C., Sun, R. and Li, L. (2017). A multichannel smartphone optical biosensor for high-throughput point-of-care diagnostics. Biosens. Bioelectron, 87, 686-692.
106. Joyia, G.J., Liaqat, R.M., Farooq, A. and Rehman, S. (2017). Internet of medical things (IoMT): applications, benefits and future challenges in healthcare domain. J. Comm., 12, 240-247.
107. Mujawar, M.A., Gohel, H., Bhardwaj, S.K., Srinivasan, S., Hickman, N. et al. (2020).

Aspects of nano-enabling biosensing systems for intelligent healthcare: Towards COVID-19 management. Mater. Today Chem., 1003.

108. Monteiro, A.C., Iano, Y., França, R.P., Arthur, R., Estrela, V.V. et al. (2018). A Comparative Study Between Methodologies Based on the Hough Transform and Watershed Transform on the Blood Cell Count. Springer, Cham.

109. Monteiro, A.C.B., Franca, R.P., Estrela, V.V., Razmjooy, N., Iano, Y. et al. (2021). Metaheuristics applied to blood image analysis. *In:* Razmjooy, N. et al. (eds). Metaheuristics and Optimization in Computer and Electrical Engineering. Lecture Notes in Electrical Engineering, LNEE, vol. 696.

110. Deshpande, A., Razmjooy N. and Estrela, V.V. (2021). Introduction to computational intelligence and super-resolution. *In:* Deshpande, A. et al. (eds). Computational Intelligence Methods for Super-Resolution in Image Processing Applications. Springer, Cham, Switzerland.

111. Chaabane, L., Khelassi, A., Terziev, A., Andreopoulos, N., Jesus, M.A. et al. (2021). Particle swarm optimization with tabu search algorithm (PSO-TS) applied to multiple sequence alignment problem. *In:* Khelassi, A., Estrela, V.V. (eds). Advances in Multidisciplinary Medical Technologies – Engineering, Modeling and Findings. Springer, Cham, Switzerland.

112. Razmjooy, N. and Estrela, V.V. (2019). Applications of Image Processing and Soft Computing Systems in Agriculture. 1-300, IGI Global, Hershey, PA, USA.

113. Hemanth, J. and Estrela, V.V. (2017). Deep Learning for Image Processing Applications. Advances in Parallel Computing, Vol. 31, IOS Press, Amsterdam, Netherlands.

114. Razmjooy, N., Razmjooy, S., Vahedi, Z., Estrela, V.V., de Oliveira, G.G. et al. (2021). Skin color segmentation based on artificial neural network improved by a modified grasshopper optimization algorithm. *In:* Razmjooy, N. et al. (eds). Metaheuristics and Optimization in Computer and Electrical Engineering. LNEE, vol. 696. Springer, Cham.

115. Estrela, V.V., Razmjooy, N., Monteiro, A.C., Franca, R.P., Jesus, M.D. et al. (2021). A computational intelligence perspective on multimodal image registration for unmanned aerial vehicles (UAVs). *In:* Razmjooy, N. et al. (eds). Metaheuristics and Optimization in Computer and Electrical Engineering. LNEE, vol. 696. Springer, Cham.

116. Finelli, L.A. and Narasimhan, V. (2020). Leading a digital transformation in the pharmaceutical industry: Reimagining the way we work in global drug development. Clinical Pharmacology and Therapeutics, 108, 756-761.

117. Brito, C., Pinto, L., Marinho, V., Paiva, S. and Pinto, P. (2021). A review on recent advances in implanted medical devices security. Proc. 16th Iberian Conf. on Inf. Syst. and Techn. (CISTI), 1-6.

118. Sharma, V., You, I., Andersson, K., Palmieri, F., Rehmani, M.H. et al. (2020). Security, privacy and trust for smart mobile-internet of things (M-IoT): A survey. IEEE Access, 8, 167123-167163.

119. Haci, D., Liu, Y., Ghoreishizadeh, S.S. and Constandinou, T.G. (2020). Key considerations for power management in active implantable medical devices. Proc. IEEE 11th LASCAS, 1-4.

120. Coelho, A.M. and Estrela, V.V. (2012). EM-based mixture models applied to video event detection. *In:* Sanguansat, P. (ed.). Principal Component Analysis – Engineering Applications. IntechOpen, London, UK, 101-124.

121. França, R.P., Monteiro, A.C.B., Estrela, V.V. and Razmjooy, N. (2021). Using metaheuristics in discrete-event simulation. *In:* Razmjooy, N. et al. (eds). Metaheuristics and Optimization in Computer and Electrical Engineering. LNEE, vol. 696. Springer, Cham.

122. Archasantisuk, S. and Aoyagi, T. (2019). Transmission power control using human motion classification for reliable and energy-efficient communication in WBAN. IEICE Trans. Commun., 102-B, 1104-1112.

123. Marinho, C.E.V., Estrela, V.V., Loschi, H.J., Razmjooy, N., Herrmann, A.E. et al. (2019). A model for medical staff idleness minimization. *In:* Iano, Y. et al. (eds). Proc. 4th Brazilian Technology Symposium (BTSym'18). Smart Innovation, Systems and Technologies, vol. 140. Springer, Cham, Switzerland, Zurich.

124. Zhang, R. and Li, X. (2020). Joint power control and time allocation for WBANs with RF energy harvesting. 2020 IEEE/CIC Int'l Conf. on Comm. in China (ICCC), 342-347.

125. Loschi, H.J., Estrela, V.V., Hemanth, D.J., Fernandes, S.R., Iano, Y. et al. (2020). Communications requirements, video streaming, communications links and networked UAVs. *In:* Estrela, V.V. et al. (eds). Imaging and Sensing for Unmanned Aircraft Systems, vol. 2(6), 113-132. IET, London, UK, doi: 10.1049/PBCE120G_ch6

Nanotechnology, Internet of Nanothings and Nanorobotics in Healthcare – Nano for All

Vania V. Estrela[1] [0000-0002-4465-7691], Aline C. Intorne[2,3] [0000-0001-8015-6926],
Kate K.S. Batista[4] [0000-0002-5861-4633], Anand Deshpande[5] [0000-0002-1500-0981],
Robert Sroufer[6] [0000-0002-7903-9180], Ricardo T. Lopes[7] [0000-0001-7250-824X],
Fuqian Shi[8] [0000-0003-4245-5727], Shoulin Yin[9] [0000-0002-5367-1372], Yu-Da Lin[10]
[0000-0001-5100-6072]

[1] Department of Telecommunications, Federal Fluminense University (UFF), RJ, 24220-900,
Brazil, vania.estrela.phd@ieee.org
[2] Laboratory of Physiology and Biochemistry of Microorganisms, Universidade Estadual do
Norte Fluminense Darcy Ribeiro, Campos dos Goytacazes, RJ, 28013-602, Brazil
[3] Laboratory of Chemistry and Biology, Instituto Federal de Educação, Ciência e Tecnologia
do Rio de Janeiro, Volta Redonda, RJ, 27213-100, Brazil, aline.intorne@ifrj.edu.br
[4] Fundacao Oswaldo Cruz, FIOCRUZ, RJ, Brazil, katekbatista@gmail.com
[5] Electronics and Communication Engineering, Angadi Institute of Technology and
Management, Belagavi, India, deshpande.anandb@gmail.com
[6] Management Department, Duquesne University, Pittsburg, PA, USA, sroufer@duq.edu
[7] Federal University of Rio de Janeiro (COPPE/UFRJ), Nuclear Engineering Laboratory
(LIN), Rio de Janeiro, RJ, Brazil, ricardo@lin.ufrj.br
[8] Rutgers Cancer Institute of New Jersey, United States, shifuqian@gmail.com
[9] Harbin Institute of Technology, China, yslin@hit.edu.cn
[10] National Penghu University of Science and Technology, Magong, TW,
yudalinemail@gmail.com

1. Introduction

Nanoparticles, nanomaterials, nanoscale electronics, and sensing devices have all been developed as an end result of nanotechnology albeit still, call for protocols from agencies resembling the Food and Drug Administration (FDA). High-tech advancements have facilitated the production of nanodevices along with nanocomponents to accomplish unpretentious functions like sensing and actuation while also connecting to the Internet via smooth communications and information handling. This technical breakthrough has resulted in a concept, known as the Internet of Nano things (IoNT) [1] which, when paired with advances in nanotechnology, will alter virtually every aspect of human existence.

Nanotechnology and IoNT by this time have noteworthy roles in several applications through diverse sectors like food, agriculture, environment, defense, electronics, energy, and biomedicine. Its extensive healthcare deployment can bring in the most significant benefits to society, generating a new generation of medication known as nanomedicine, which means applying nanotechnology to biological and medical applications as in [2]. A more meticulous explanation states that nanomedicine is an interdisciplinary, scientific field involving biology, medicine, physics, chemistry, and engineering for illness diagnostics and treatments employing nanotechnology [2-4]. Endowing nanomedicine with the IoNT will modernize alterations in illness avoidance, diagnosis, besides treatment. In other words, detecting and making diagnoses in the early disease periods will allow for effective and careful treatment, cures of life-threatening diseases , saving a significant number of lives, and extending the average lifespan. These benefits justify the global consideration given to research and development [5].

In the coming years, nanotechnology and the IoNT will brunt all aspects of life. They gather mounting attention worldwide. New, enhanced functionalities and properties stem from the novel nanomaterials and nanodevices manufactured. Hence, new arrangements to synthesize nanoparticles, shape nanomaterials [6-20], appraise the prospective toxicity of nanoparticles and nanomaterials [12, 20-30], nanodevices/nano sensors/nano communications developments [13, 18, 20, 31-35], implementation of green practices and IoNT advances [11, 24, 36-41] will emerge. The specific nanotechnology awareness and the IoNT have unlocked a whole new potential for remarkable improvements in wellbeing.

Furthermore, the worldwide nanotechnology market will expand vastly after the pandemic. In contrast, the nanomedicine and IoNT markets will rise with an even higher CAGR [26, 42]. Thus, these particulars will lead to possibly gigantic revenue from commercializing nanotechnology and the IoNT.

All the factors described above support the mounting interest in utilizing nanotechnology and the IoNT in healthcare. Consequently, this chapter struggles to get as much knowledge and insight into this topic as possible. A comprehensive search of pertinent literature was done on these online databases: Scopus, EBSCO, Science Direct, Google Scholar and ResearchGate to examine the nanotechnology and IoNT roles in healthcare transformation. However, the literature in this study is by no means complete, and it has been used to illustrate, as much as conceivable, the current status of nanotechnology and IoNT use in healthcare. Since, the review's goal is to examine the roles and plusses of nanotechnology developments, a mixture of quantitative and qualitative investigation practices was used. The analysis of publications on nanotechnology, nanomedicine, and IoNT, as well as their connections, has demonstrated the importance of novel nanotechnology techniques in medicine and healthcare. Despite the shortcomings and risks (often related to the potential nanomaterials toxicity, as well as privacy and security concerns with the IoNT), the listed benefits (e.g., patient-personalized, exact, on-time, accessible, and reasonably priced healthcare) justify the need for further development and innovation in nanomedicine. There exist also various prospects for nanotechnology and the IoNT, driven by healthcare, which will definitely result in further advantages and revolutionize healthcare. As an end result, the remainder of this chapter goes as follows.

Section 2 focuses on nanotechnology applications in medicine, whereas Section 3 is dedicated to the implementation of the IoNT paradigm for healthcare objectives. Section 4 discusses nanotechnology and the IoNT gains, as well as obstacles, dangers, and issues associated with their adoption in medicine and healthcare. This section also scrutinizes nanotechnology and IoNT in healthcare change. Finally, the final portion concludes with some final thoughts and probable future possibilities in the next generation of medical innovations.

2. Nanomedicine and the Future

2.1. Bio and Medical Cyber-Physical Systems

A Cyber-Physical System (CPS) is a heterogeneous structure made up of and reliant on the seamless amalgamation of computer and physical components. CPSs permit going beyond the capabilities of today's embedded systems. While CPSs have the potential to assist a wide range of societal areas, comprising healthcare signs of progress in actuators, sensors, and wearables can potentially improve aspects of medicinal care, ranging from prevention to emergency response. Synthetic biology and robotics can possibly regenerate while maintaining the human body in drastic new ways, albeit little is known about in what manner CPS advances can assimilate these technologies to augment health outcomes [46-48, 55-58].

The CPS reasoning helps develop systems that combine the capabilities of nanoscale robots with specifically developed synthetic creatures (aka Bio CPSs or BCPSs). This hybrid BCPS will be capable of hitherto unthinkable capabilities going from microscopic assembly to the cell sensing of organisms. BCPSs associate synthetic biology encompassing micron-scale robotic entities to observe looked-for behaviors in groups of bacterial and mammalian cells that may affect a wide diversity of applications, stretching from tissue engineering to medication development.

A BCPS relies on prior research in different fields by each team member, as well as early proof-of-concept designs of BCPS, and is also motivated by recent breakthroughs in the growing area of synthetic biology, particularly the capacity to swiftly add new capabilities to basic cells. So far, investigators could not firmly regulate and coordinate synthetic cell activities in isolation, however, micro-robots can be transformational in focusing on minuscule bio-CPSs that can perceive, transport, and collaborate in this new project. A concept example , is their intention to create teams of synthetic cells and micro-robot hybrids that build complex fabric-like surfaces.

Wearables and implantable tools are already in use to monitor health, ameliorate the quality of life, deliver cost-effective cures, and maybe expedite sickness detection and prevention. Innovative virtual design techniques for implanted medical devices will accelerate device development while also producing safer, more resourceful devices and novel therapies than are presently achievable.

MCPSs use a patient-specific computational model of cardiac dynamics and apply advanced mathematical approaches to analyze how these models cooperate with medical tools. The analytical approaches can be used to discover possible faults in device behavior early in the device-design course, preceding the start of safe animal and human testing. They can also help a clinical environment to improve equipment settings in a patient-by-patient manner prior to implanting devices.

Coordination of multidisciplinary techniques that balance theoretical, experimental, and practical considerations will provide transformative advances in medical device design and the foundations of CPS verification. They will foster the construction of virtual device models that can function together with virtual organ models developed to create a complete virtual platform that can be exposed to computational analyses and simulations.

Nanomedicine engages nanodevices and nanostructures operational at the molecular level to observe, repair, or control human biological systems. The subsequent subsection debates concocted nanodevices and nanostructures applied in medicine together with a diversity of nanomaterials and nanodevices planned to work precisely in biological milieus with nanoscale accuracy, e.g., quantum dots, nanoparticles, nanochips, nanorobots, nanovalves, and so on [2]. The major nanomedicine research and development topics are biopharmaceutics, antimicrobial characteristics, implantable materials/devices, and diagnostic tools.

2.2. Nanorobotics

Nanorobotics is a new technological sector that develops equipment or robots with modules that are at or near the nanometer scale. Nanorobotics (contrasting with micro-robotics) develops and manufactures nanorobots with devices varying in size from 0.1 to 10 micrometers and organized with nanoscale or molecular modules. The words nanite, nanomachine, nanobot, nanoid, and nanomite have also characterized similar devices that are now under development [59-65].

Although most nanomachines are still in the developmental stage, plentiful rudimentary molecular machines, as well as nanomotors, have been examined [66-77]. E.g., consider a sensor with a 1.5-nanometer-wide switch that can count particular molecules in chemical samples. Nanomachines may find their first useful uses in nanomedicine. Biological machines, for example, might be employed to identify and destroy cancerous cells. Another possible use is the identification of hazardous substances in the environment and the surveillance of their quantities. Rice University has exhibited a chemically created single-molecule vehicle with wheels made of "Buckminsterfullerenes" (buckyballs). It works by adjusting the temperature of the surroundings and placing a scanning tunneling microscope tip. It is a robot that can interact with nanoscale things precisely or manipulate with nanoscale resolution. Instead of being described as molecular machines, such devices are more closely connected to microscopy (or scanning probe microscopy). When equipped to conduct nanomanipulation, even big equipment such as an Atomic Force Microscope (AFM) might be regarded as a nanorobotic instrument under the microscopy definition. According to this perspective, nanorobots are minuscule robots capable of moving with nanoscale exactitude. Nanorobotics might be used in medicine for early cancer detection and targeted biomedical equipment, medication distribution, surgery, pharmacokinetics, diabetes monitoring, and health care [46, 66-77].

Future medical nanotechnology will utilize nanorobots inoculated into patients to do cellular level tasks in such designs. Such nanorobots designed for medical application should not be self-replicating, since this would intensify device complexity, impair dependability, and hamper the medical goal.

Nanotechnology offers a plethora of new technologies for designing tailored methods to enhance pharmaceutical medication delivery. Today, severe side effects of therapies such as chemotherapy are frequently the consequence of drug delivery systems that fail to precisely address their intended target cells. Researchers, on the other hand, were able to connect unique RNA strands spanning almost 10-nm nanoparticle diameters loaded with a chemotherapeutic medication. Cancer cells are drawn to these RNA strands. When the nanoparticle encounters a cancer cell, it glues to it and releases the medicine. This targeted medication delivery technique offers enormous prospects for treating cancer while minimizing harmful side effects (often associated with inappropriate drug delivery). One possible predecessor of nanorobots are MRI-guided nano capsules.

Another interesting application of nanorobots is to aid in the healing of tissue cells in conjunction with white blood cells. The first reaction of tissues to damage is a call for inflammatory cells or white blood cells (embracing lymphocytes, monocytes, neutrophil granulocytes, and mast cells). The small nanorobot sizes may allow attaching them to recruited white cell surfaces and squeezing their way through the walls of blood arteries to the damaged site, where they could aid in tissue repair. Certain drugs may be utilized to hasten the healing process.

This mechanism's science is extremely complicated. Transmigration, or the passage of cells through the blood endothelium, is a mechanism that involves cell surface receptors that adhere to molecules, wherein, active vessel walls force application and dilatation, and physical deformation of migrating cells physical . By attaching themselves to displacing inflammatory cells, robots may go through the blood arteries, eliminating the requirement for their own complicated transmigration process.

Nanocomposite particles that can be manipulated remotely by an electromagnetic field and utilized to interact with biological cells have also been created. Scientists believe that this technique might be used to cure cancer. With a single Wi-Fi access point, an indoor localization estimation structure for micro aerial vehicles (MAVs) may communicate with a large number of micro- and nanodevices [55, 77-84]. Conventional computer vision techniques are constrained by lighting and texture in the surroundings. This solution is visually limited and quickly deployable, operating on current Wi-Fi infrastructure with no implementation costs. This system contains two interconnected components. To begin, one presents an angle-of-arrival (AoA) estimation technique for estimating MAV attitudes and disentangling the AoA for positioning. Second, we develop a Wi-Fi-inertial sensor fusion model that combines AoA and inertial sensor odometry to improve MAV poses. Assumed the practicality of MAVs, real-time and initialization-free systems can meet the demand for agile flying in unfamiliar settings. Indoor studies indicate that our system achieves posture estimate accuracy [83-87].

2.3. Intelligent Drug Delivery

The usage of nanoparticles as a medication delivery method has already proven to be quite effective. Medication delivery is a major nanomedicine topic since nano-enhanced drug delivery systems are currently a commercial reality. The tiny particles/molecules (with unique medicinal effects due to their structure) which encapsulate the medication, carry it to the target locations, and release it in regulated ways to heal injured cells are included in the evolution of nano-based drug dispensing systems. Drug delivery systems are most utilized to treat neurological illnesses (such as Alzheimer's and Parkinson's disease), HIV/AIDS, and cancer. Biological, polymersome, lipid-based medicine distribution systems, micelles, and other nanoparticles occur in nanomedicine for drug delivery systems in variable forms and sizes. Nanovalves, which are small valves that are embedded in nanostructure pores, are also utilized for medication administration. Materials that encapsulate medicines to safeguard them during transit inside the body include nanoscale silica in addition to calcium phosphates [2]. Dendrimers, liposomes (and virosomes), polymeric nanoparticles, carbon nanotubes, inorganic nanoparticles, fullerenes, nanosuspensions, and nanoshells typify nanoscale particles/molecules to increase therapeutic bioavailability and pharmacokinetics. Engineered nanoparticles responsive to particular pH levels have shown to be the most effective medication delivery method while avoiding intrusive procedures. When pH-responsive nanoparticles contact the proper pH environment, they release the medication, making them ideal for drug delivery to certain cells, tissues, or organs [10]. The gold nanoparticles with or without antibiotics can enhance antibiotic delivery (targeting and dose). The authors of [15, 16] emphasize the use of nano silver particles in medicine, while the research piece in [17] describes the production and use of gold nanoparticles in detail. It is worth perceiving that gold nanoparticles coupled with conventional medicines can reduce drug adverse effects [14]. Similarly, silver nanoparticles have improved wound healing in a range of settings (e.g., chronic ulcers, toxic epidermal necrolysis, burns, and pemphigus), resulting in considerably shorter wound healing times [16]. Copper oxide nanoparticles are also antimicrobial, implying they might clean surfaces and medical equipment in addition to antimicrobial wound dressings, coatings, and fabrics [13]. Silver nanoparticles can function in eye care to coat contact lenses for the delivery of therapeutic medicines [15]. Gold nanoparticles in biomedicine can also target the delivery of peptides or DNA, as well as the detection and photo thermolysis of harmful bacteria and cancer cells [17].

Cancer is the world's leading mortality cause, yet it is also the major field in which nano-enabled technology treatments have made substantial advances. Silver nanoparticles are utilized in cancer unearthing and therapy. Similarly, gold nanoparticles working with certain biomolecules to exterminate cancer cells or germs can be successful [14]. In other terms, gold nanoshells can combat cancer by absorbing energy and heating up appropriately to eradicate cancer cells while causing minimal harm to surrounding healthy cells after penetrating tumor cells and receiving radiation therapy. Other variables can also be used to fight cancer, such as magnetic nanoparticles capable of attaching themselves to cancer cells in the circulation, allowing the elimination of cancer cells before they form new tumors. The research in [10] emphasizes the significance of magnetic nanoparticles in magnetic field hyperthermia, a promising and more successful cancer therapy method. The work in [9] created and presented thermosensitive yolk-shell nanoparticles as a novel remote-controlled targeted drug delivery technology for multimodal imaging and combination cancer treatment. The authors of [18] debate the usage of platinum nanoparticles to treat several cancer kinds. Paclitaxel, Vincristine, Camptothecin, Doxorubicin, and Etoposide are presented and evaluated as naturally occurring anti-cancer medicines in [43]. The authors of [44] offer albumin-based nano-enabled methods for cancer discovery and treatment. The study in [45] depicts shell-stacked nanoparticles with ameliorated tumor infiltration besides cell uptake in deep tumors. The antimicrobial, magnetic, as well as optical Fe3O4AuxAgy nanoparticle activities, justify their use in anti-cancer drug delivery because they allow one to observe what happens to cancerous cells without harming healthy cells [19]. Based on the outcomes obtained in fighting cancer, the primary use of nanoparticles may be in cancer treatment. The reason for this is that nanodevices are more sensitive and quicker than standard medication delivery methods. They can deliver powerful controlled release medicines directly to a specific location within the body while producing no adverse effects. As a result, the advantages of targeted medicine include considerably reduced medication consumption, improved patient care, less intrusive drug administration, and cost-effective therapies [46]. However, creating ways for regulating sensitive medicines (targeting and triggering), nanochips for nanoparticle discharges, virus-like system development for intracellular systems, and so on brings in significant technological hurdles [8].

Recent breakthroughs in controlled drug release have had a significant influence on medicine, bioscience, and tissue engineering. As a result, a comprehensive range of improved drug delivery vehicles have either already hit the market or are nearing completion. The progressive rise of the drug delivery business has necessitated serious consideration of economically feasible, up-scalable, and long-term technologies for large-scale manufacture of drug delivery carriers. Three appealing natural drug carriers are aluminosilicate clays, calcium carbonate minerals, and cellulose. Vaterite crystals, halloysite nanotubes, and nanocellulose are three drug carriers produced from these natural materials. These carriers can be manufactured utilizing "green" methods from some of the most plentiful materials on the planet, and they have a very high potential to satisfy all requirements used in the production of current delivery vehicles. This chapter presents an up-to-date overview of these drug transport vehicles in preparation for their usage in bioapplications, specifically medication delivery and tissue engineering. The subsequent research topics are addressed: (i) the obtainability, sources, and policies used to manufacture these drug delivery vehicles, (ii) medicine loading of delivery vehicles and discharge mechanisms, (iii) in vitro, in vivo, and clinical investigations related to these vehicles, and (iv) use of these vehicles for tissue engineering. To conclude, the possibilities for further vehicle development and industrialization are evaluated critically, highlighting the most promising future research paths such as the invention of third-generation active biomaterials.

2.4. Implants and Nanosurgery

Nanomaterials and nanocomponents are being exploited more and more as implantable materials and devices. These technologies allow the development of nanoparticles and coatings to improve implant adhesion, durability, and life in tissue reparation and replacement. Nanostructures are also utilized to construct and enhance tissue regeneration scaffolds. Soft tissue implants, along with nanotechnology can advance bone replacement constituents, hard tissue implants, and dental restoratives. Nanomaterials utilized as structural implant materials include bone healing materials (e.g., calcium phosphate apatite, hydroxyapatite) as well as bioresorbable and smart materials (that react to environment changes) [2]. As a consequence, nanoparticles are more biocompatible and stimulate new bone formation [1]. Because of their anti-thrombogenic and antibacterial characteristics, silver nanoparticles have proved as suitable coatings for stents and cardio valves. Furthermore, their use as catheter coatings greatly reduces bacterial development. Owing to their bacterial resistance, silver nanoparticles can also be used to coat contact lenses. The aptitude of Silver nanoparticles to preserve or upgrade shear bond strength, makes them appropriate for use in dental tools and dressings, as well as orthopedic/orthodontic implantations and fixations [16].

Carbon nanotubes can also extend the lifespan of orthopedic implants [10]. Nonetheless, the use of implanted nanosensors allows for more efficient detection of a certain chemical or physical characteristic. An external user (or a healthcare expert) can manage nanomedical devices or nanomachines embedded inside the human body to answer commands or remotely regulate them from a macro scale via the Internet [1]. Nanotechnology also permits surgical equipment and robot designs that allow for precise and accurate microsurgery. Nano cameras can better surgery visualization, and help operate nano-sized surgical tools. This allows surgery to be conducted at the tissue, genetic, as well as cellular levels with a markedly lower error risk. Although research into nanosurgery is in its early stages, it represents a possible future use of nanoscience. Nanoneedles, nano tweezers, and precision lasers that are now commercially available will help to realize the nanosurgery goal [47]. The research piece in [20] describes full nanomaterial-based medicinal devices. Medicinal nanomachines for extinguishing kidney stones, nanorobots for cleansing arteries, lungs, and teeth, or to support skin, organs (viz. gastrointestinal and abdominal tissue repairs), or bones (reparation of bone deficiencies and fractures) are closer to reality than ever before [2, 4].

2.5. Diagnostic Tools

Nanodiagnostics denote nanotechnology for health diagnostic reasons. There exist various nanoparticles that can detect pre-cancerous cells, viral fragments, particular proteins, antibodies, and other disease markers and indications [48]. Quantum dots or tiny semiconductor particles can expand the sensitivity and accuracy of disease detection systems [2]. The use of new sensors and lab-on-a-chip ideas based on cantilevers, nanotubes, Atomic Force Microscopy (AFM), or nanowires, for diagnostics, improves sensitivity and allows for faster and more accurate diagnoses while lowering costs. Gold nanoparticles and carbon nanotubes existing in sensors, for example, facilitate the detection of oral cancer indicators. Nanoflaring nanoparticles can detect bloodstream cancerous cells. Silver partake has the potential to isolate viruses, bacteria, and other microscopic components of blood samples , among other things. Additionally, in vivo imaging can be accomplished utilizing nanoparticle contrast ants, mostly for MRI and ultrasound, or small imaging equipment, such as a pill carrying a miniature camera system that captures photos throughout the digestive system. Because of their unique dimensions and half-life, iron oxide nanoparticles have proven to be a sufficient contrast agent for enhanced detailing in MRIs, notably for a more accurate diagnosis of circulatory system abnormalities [10]. Perfluorocarbon emulsion nanoparticles (PFC) aid in increasing the contrast of ultrasound images, therefore enhancing their worth. This is of particular relevance in medicine since ultrasonography is less costly than other noninvasive schemes and can aid in the diagnosis, especially when imaging malignancies [10]. The use of luminous platinum nanoclusters as novel biocompatible bioimaging probes for diagnostic reasons has been proposed in [18]. Platinum nanoparticles have also been employed to develop molecular types of machinery and movement-based detecting techniques. The work in [20] examines nanoparticle-centered diagnostic and therapeutic strategies more thoroughly. As an end result, nanoparticles and nanomaterials in imaging and visualization have the potential for faster, more sensitive and cost-effective diagnostic processes [4].

3. Internet of Nano-Things (IoNT) in Medicine and Healthcare

The Internet of Things (IoT) embraces a network of smart things/devices coupled to the Internet. The IoT can make its component members intermingle with devices and humans, bringing significant benefits to modern civilization. Further device size reductions to the nanoscale and their connectivity to the Internet have prompted the paradigm emergence, namely the Internet of Nano things (IoNT). The IoNT is intended for nanomachines, which are small components capable of sensing, actuating, processing, and controlling tasks and assist in creating nano clocks, nano memories and nano processors, along with nanobots. The top-down analysis (comprising molecular modules self-assembly) is a bottom-up methodology to synthesize nano materials from atoms or molecules. Bio-hybrid tactics are an option to build nano machines whose design is established on molecular signaling exchanges [42]. Nano nodes are also nano machines enclosing a control module, storage unit, communication structures, power units, and numerous actuators and sensors. Interconnected nano nodes (e.g., devices capable of sensing, collecting, processing, and storing data) inside, on, or external to the human body can directly communicate with external devices employing nano-routers, nano-micro interface gadgets, and forming nano networks. Along with data aggregation from nano nodes, nano routers and also nano node controls by swapping very plain control commands (such as sleep, on/off, read value, and so on) gateway devices (Figure 1) help operate nanodevices remotely from side to side of the Internet [1, 49-51]. In terms of communication, the 1-10 MHz range radio-frequency messaging is one method of sending a message into the body, although most cell communication involves chemical signals [2]. The nanodevices and nanonetwork uniqueness calls for novel methods for interacting with the outer world and nanodevices. It is critical to note that molecular communication implies nano-electromagnetic fields, and that connecting nanodevices entails THz radio-frequency waves [42, 50].

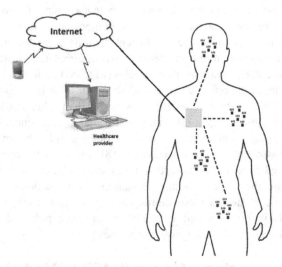

Figure 1. IoNT architecture for healthcare

In medicine, nanonetworks may be found in nanoscale surgery, intelligent medication delivery, and the detection/treatment of infectious diseases [50]. The nanonetwork paradigm enables physicians and healthcare providers obtain insights into the patient's current health state as well as remotely watching and regulating any unexpected bodily alterations related to nanomachines within the patient's body using nanosensors or nanorobots. Monitoring blood glucose levels, administering medication in the event of a necessity, and monitoring cancer biomarkers are a few examples [51]. Employing nanodevices in addition to the IoNT allows access to previously inaccessible areas and critical information at new levels (molecular data) [1]. In this way, it is feasible to detect illnesses, make correct diagnoses early, and respond faster than ever before, greatly increasing the odds of effective therapy and overcoming problems.

4. Nanotechnology and IoNT Utilization

The nanotechnology and IoNT benefits are numerous. The next generation of healthcare will realize nanotechnology and IoNT frameworks earlier, facilitating speedier, more precise, and refined disease diagnoses, more effective treatments, enhanced patient health status monitoring, and illness prevention. Nanoparticles, nanosensors, nanoactuators (e.g., nanorobots), and other nanodevices linked in nanonetworks deliver a whole new healthcare milieu.

Despite the obvious advantages, there is legitimate concern about the possible negative consequences. Nanoparticles may be mass-produced with almost any material and have any form or structure using various processing techniques. The function and uses of nanoparticles are mostly determined by their size [2]. After targeted nanoparticle treatment, smaller nanoparticles are simpler to remove from the circulation. Nonetheless, it is critical to think that the smaller a particle is, the greater is its toxicity. Furthermore, certain nanomaterials may induce harmful responses in patients. As a result, nanotoxicology as a study subject is becoming increasingly essential to comprehend the dangers of nanomaterials and the cost vs. benefit issues of consequential harm [22, 23, 36].

Nanoparticles and nanomaterials, whether inadvertently or purposefully introduced into the human body (that is, through dermal nodes, respiratory system, ingestion, or implanting), can produce a variety of health-related issues, as seen in Figure 2. As a result, numerous research studies are being conducted to examine the various healthcare nanoparticle toxicologies [6-8], including quantum dots, silver, gold, platinum, silica/titanium/manganese/inorganic nanoparticles, copper oxide, zinc oxide, fullerene, nanospheres, carbon nanotubes, nanoshells, and nanocapsules [18, 20, 24, 28, 29, 52]. The authors from [21] investigated the ecological impact and health risks of 2D nanomaterials, primarily relying on transition metal dichalcogenides, graphene, and black phosphorus, which are common in the fabrication of electrodes, electronic, photovoltaic, and assorted sensing/actuation devices. Because of the fast advancement of nanotechnology and its healthcare usage, there is a pronounced demand for toxicological investigations on nanoparticles, nanomaterials, and nanosystems. As a result, both in-vitro and in-vivo investigations of biological impacts of nanoparticles are required. Some of the current schemes for assessing nanotoxicity are in [27].

As a result of the deliberate nanoparticles and nanomaterials usage in healthcare, it is critical to strike a balance between nanoparticle safety and therapeutic efficacy. When nanoparticles and nanomaterials are utilized for health diagnoses and treatments, several toxicity issues must be accounted for. As a result, the primary issue for nanotoxicology is to pinpoint nanoparticle characteristics that may produce substantial adverse health consequences when administered to patients during diagnostic or therapeutic operations [30].

Numerous organizations [24], are addressing nanotechnology toxicity. However, other than those that apply to comparable materials in bulk, there are no specific rules for nanoparticles. This is the primary problem and impediment to the advancement of nanotechnology. The absence of legislation and standards governing this scientific and research sector is mostly due to the intricacy of nanoparticles, nanomaterials, and nanotechnology. Despite the lack of a particular regulatory framework for nanotechnology-based goods, the text in [26] offers a regulatory plan for nanotechnology-based devices. To become more alert to the potentially detrimental impacts of nanotechnology, all-inclusive investigations on nanomaterial interactions with biological arrangements, as well as worldwide collaborative research, are necessary. Furthermore, considerable effort in defining nanotechnology-specific laws for manufacturing and labeling nanoproducts is required [53]. Yet, some standard-setting organizations continue to work on nanotechnology norms.

Up-to-date research emphasizes Green Nanotechnology (GN) in order to mitigate the negative nanotechnology facets. GN depends on green chemistry

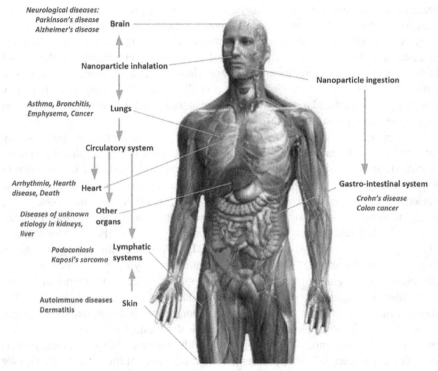

Figure 2. Potential harmful effects of nanoparticles

concepts involved in nanoscale goods design, nanomaterial manufacturing processes, and the exploitation of nanomaterials. Notwithstanding the fact that most potential GN solutions are still in the lab/startup phase [36], GN will bring numerous gains across diverse healthcare sectors, primarily by dropping the negative nanotechnology influences on individuals, and their environments. The use of green chemistry synthesis methods to yield nanoparticles must be ecologically benign, non-toxic, as well as economical. Plants, algae, bacteria, yeast, fungus, and human cells can all synthesize nanoparticles [37, 40, 54]. The authors of [39] describe a range of green techniques for iron nanoparticles production hinging on plant extracts, fungus, bacteria, amino acids, and other natural resources. There are also several examples of utilizing a variety of plants to create nanoparticles, notably silver and gold nanoparticles. Leaf extracts, lemongrass, and aloe vera, for example, can be utilized to create silver and gold nanoparticles [37]. Furthermore, the work in [11] demonstrates gold nanoparticles utilizing a natural biomaterial, eggshell membranes, sodium dehydrates, high-power ultrasound, and solar irradiation techniques or exposing edible mushrooms to sunlight. The studies from [38, 54] impart a more thorough examination of green nanoparticle production, properties, and applications. That green technique was primarily concerned with the metallic/bimetallic creation of nanoparticles. GN may have anti-cancer, antibacterial, and imaging characteristics, making them ideal for diagnostic applications, drug administration, and anti-cancer activities [38, 54]. Furthermore, green nanoparticle synthesis is less harmful and based on the use of natural chemical-free ingredients; hence, the poisonousness of the nanoparticles is lowered when compared to those manufactured traditionally. Low energy consumption and environmental impact, as well as considerably fewer side effects, are green nanoparticle production returns.

Nonetheless, GN particles hold colossal prospects for handling an ample range of illnesses. Concurrently, the IoNT, which can change health more than before, introduces dangers and problems that must be addressed. The IoNT enables one to obtain greater insights into health problems, remotely monitor and manage, and respond to unforeseen human body alterations rapidly and accurately. Nonetheless, the main worries are safety and privacy. Health-related data is extremely sensitive, and it must be appropriately safeguarded. A robust network defense infrastructure for all frequency ranges of communications (i.e., encompassing nanodevices, routers, gateways, and the Cloud) is required to curb malicious attacks (e.g., interruption of harmful or lethal applications that can affect drug distribution and radio communication [31]). For the motive that nanodevices in nanonetworks operate in the THz gamut, security lines of attack are ineffective and somewhat inapplicable. Because existing security solutions are inadequate for securing the IoNT, new and suitable security and privacy frameworks and procedures, as outlined in numerous research publications [31-34, 51], are required. Some of the suggested solutions comprise checksum algorithms to ensure the information integrity, encryption to code material before transmitting it among nanodevices, special data hiding procedures, and multi-layer authentication authenticated stakeholders only within nanonetworks [51].

5. Discussion

This section summarizes the strengths, flaws, opportunities, and dangers. There are manifold concerns concerning nanotechnology and IoNT, besides engineering, which are also social, financial, and ethical, as per the lists below.

Strengths:
  i. Earlier, quicker, and more precise diagnostic processes;
  ii. Ground-breaking, adequate therapies and painless cures;
  iii. Less adverse drug effects and better, precise surgical techniques;
  iv. Novel drugs and drug delivery frameworks;
  v. Faster, reduced, highly-sensitive investigative and treatment tools (e.g., nanocameras, nanorobots, nanoneedles, nanotweezers and more.);
  vi. Smart nanodevices using the IoNTs;
  vii. Real-time and remote observing of disease and treatments through the IoNT; and
  viii. Significant decrease in medical and healthcare costs.

Problems:
  i. Regulation of nanotechnology for healthcare;
  ii. Nonexistence of proper knowledge on the subject of reactions inside the human body;

   iii. Possible toxicity of nanoparticles and nanomaterials;
   iv. Health data privacy and safety matters;
    v. Lack of standards and regulations;
   vi. Novel methodologies should not harm the general public; and
  vii. Immature public consciousness and understanding of ethical concerns and trust issues.

Vulnerabilities:

    i. Security and privacy issues about nanonetworks are not abundantly addressed;
   ii. Concerns about medical nanotechnologies control;
  iii. The lack of suitable mechanisms exposes a potential for harm or kill;
  iv. Toxicological behavior of Nanoparticles and nanomaterials; and
   v. Assuring the nanomedicine evolution and provision of nano-based welfare quality to all.

Prospects:

    i. Decreasing the gap between individuals and robots/computers;
   ii. Optimal standards and regulatory issues;
  iii. Significant progress in fighting numerous unsolved medical problems and diseases, such as cancer;
  iv. Reduction of mortality and morbidity rates, the extension of patient lives;
   v. Moving towards green nanotechnology and green IoNT holds the potential to create smarter, safer, and more sustainable medical practices;
  vi. Development of computational models that will predict the toxicity and other potential side effects of nanomaterials used in medical and healthcare purposes based on nanoparticle structures; and
  vii. Maximization of the return on investments in research and development.

DNA nanotechnology has experienced immense growth in recent years, allowing for the robust creation of multifaceted nanostructures besides hybrid materials. Coupling DNA nanotechnology with precise optical detection to produce practical single-molecule devices opens up new avenues of research in single-molecule biosensing and super-resolution imaging. Super-resolution increases the resolving capability of microscopes and the smartphone camera sensitivities using super-resolution nanorulers with intensity reference samples. Optical antennas for metal-enriched fluorescence employing DNA origami can boost the nanotechnologies' sensitivity. They possess the unique ability to put molecular assays exactly in the plasmonic hotspot utilized to detect Zika-virus nucleic acids. The corresponding fluorescence intensification is then used to provide ultra-sensitive recognition on low-priced devices viz. a modified smartphone, democratizing single-molecule detection [84-88].

Medicine has long attempted to overcome key impediments to improving treatment results. These include, among other things, increasing the capacity to target illness locations, reducing medication toxicity, and boosting treatment effectiveness. The introduction of nanotechnology-based medication delivery has made significant strides toward significantly improving patient treatment results, both during drug development and clinical validation. This has eventually resulted in FDA-approved treatments that have leveraged the deployment of clinical nanomedicine. As the science of nanomedicine progresses toward in-human research and more FDA clearances, other developing techniques, such as Artificial Intelligence (AI), will conquer an emergent role in improving nanotechnology-based medication delivery. This is because cornerstone regimens for treatment methods ranging from cancer to infectious illnesses rely on combination therapy. Traditional techniques for creating combination treatment begin with medication selection and then go on to dosage determination. While nanoparticle-based medicine delivery is being broadly investigated for drug delivery from a distinct particle or multiagent distribution via different particle classes, and nanomedicine-established combination therapy is being studied for prospective advancement, new tactics to sufficiently plan both the drug and its dose spaces are required to truly optimize designs. This chapter looks at current advancements in nanomedicine-based drug delivery as well as potent clinically verified AI methods that might successfully connect nanotechnology with globally tailored combo treatments [89-96].

6. Conclusions

Nanotechnology has the apparently limitless potential to change all aspects of human life and has already demonstrated various advantages and astonishing unique medicinal benefits. Nanotechnology-enhanced illness detection and therapy have the potential to usher in a completely new age of healthcare. Realizing IoT notions on the nanoscale empowers more effective and accurate well-being surveillance situations, resulting in acceptable and timely interventions. Despite the numerous benefits of nanomedicine and the IoNT, several concerns require careful attention. The primary problems and roadblocks to completing nanotechnology and IoNT implementation in healthcare are privacy, security, and nanotoxicity issues. Nanotechnology and IoNT will efficaciously supplant traditional healthcare practices and techniques if they move toward a greener future, raise awareness about nanotechnology usage, effectively deal with nanotoxicity, and develop security and privacy solutions hinging on IoNT ideas. A future with fully integrated green (nano) knowledge and key beliefs in green chemistry would dramatically change healthcare, introducing more strict, on-time, reachable, and affordable possibilities than ever before. Better and longer lives are the primary goals of the next generation of medical breakthroughs powered by nanotechnology and IoNT, which will undoubtedly play a critical part in achieving this goal.

References

1. Omanović-Mikličanin, E., Maksimović, M. and Vujović, V. (2015). The future of healthcare: Nanomedicine and internet of nano things. Folia Medica Fac. Med. Univ. Saraeviensis, 50(1), 23-28.
2. Letfullin, R.R. and George, T.F. (2016). Introduction to nanomedicine. *In:* Computational Nanomedicine and Nanotechnology, pp. 1-61. Cham: Springer International Publishing.

3. Howard, K.A., Vorup-Jensen, T. and Peer, D. (2016). Nanomedicine. New York, NY: Springer New York.
4. Ge, Y., Li, S., Wang, S. and Moore, R. (2014). Nanomedicine: Principles and perspectives. New York, NY: Springer New York.
5. Maksimovic, M. (2017). The roles of nanotechnology and internet of nano things in healthcare transformation. Tecno Lógicas, 20, 139-153.
6. Rajput, N. (2015). Methods of preparation of nanoparticles – A review. Int. J. Adv. Eng. Technol., 7(4), 1806-1811.
7. Pal, S.L., Jana, U., Manna, P.K., Mohanta, G.P. and Manavalan, R. (2011). Nanoparticles – An overview of preparation and characterization. J. Appl. Pharm. Sci., 1(6), 228-234.
8. Shen, S., Ding, B., Zhang, S., Qi, X., Wang, K. et al. (2017). Nearinfrared light-responsive nanoparticles with thermosensitive yolk-shell structure for multimodal imaging and chemo-photothermal therapy of tumor. Nanomedicine Nanotechnology, Biol. Med., 13(5), 1607-1616.
9. Jones, D.E., Ghandehari, H. and Facelli, J.C. (2016). A review of the applications of data mining and machine learning for the prediction of biomedical properties of nanoparticles. Computer Methods and Programs in Biomedicine, 132, 93-103.
10. Khan, A., Rashid, R., Murtaza, G. and Zahra, A. (2014). Gold nanoparticles: Synthesis and applications in drug delivery. Trop. J. Pharm. Res., 13(7), 1169.
11. Marijnissen, J. and Gradoń, L. (2010). Nanoparticles in medicine and environment: Inhalation and health effects. J. Aerosol Med. Pulm. Drug Deliv., 23(5), 339-341.
12. Grigore, M., Biscu, E., Holban, A., Gestal, M., Grumezescu, A. et al. (2016). Methods of synthesis, properties and biomedical applications of CuO nanoparticles. Pharmaceuticals, 9(4), 75.
13. Alaqad, K. and Saleh, T.A. (2016). Gold and silver nanoparticles: Synthesis methods, characterization routes and applications towards drugs. J. Environ. Anal. Toxicol., 6(4), 525-2161.
14. Xing, M., Ge, L., Wang, M., Li, Q., Li, X. et al. (2014). Nanosilver particles in medical applications: Synthesis, performance, and toxicity. Int. J. Nanomedicine, 9, 2399.
15. Murphy, M., Ting, K., Zhang, X., Soo, C., Zheng, Z. et al. (2015). Current development of silver nanoparticle preparation, investigation, and application in the field of medicine. J. Nanomater., 2015, 1-12.
16. Shah, M., Badwaik, V., Kherde, Y., Waghwani, H.K., Modi, T. et al. (2014). Gold nanoparticles: Various methods of synthesis and antibacterial applications. Front. Biosci. (Landmark Ed.), 19, 1320-1344.
17. Pedone, D., Moglianetti, M., De Luca, E., Bardi, G., Pompa, P.P. et al. (2017). Platinum nanoparticles in nanobiomedicine. Chem. Soc. Rev., 46(16), 4951-4975.
18. Fodjo, E.K., Gabriel, K.M., Serge, B.Y., Li, D., Kong, C. et al. (2017). Selective synthesis of $Fe_3O_4Au_xAg_y$ nanomaterials and their potential applications in catalysis and nanomedicine. Chem. Cent. J., 11(1), 58.
19. Devasena, T. (2017). Diagnostic and Therapeutic Nanomaterials. Springer, 1-13.
20. Fojtů, M., Teo, W.Z. and Pumera, M. (2017). Environmental impact and potential health risks of 2D nanomaterials. Environ. Sci. Nano, 4(8), 1617-1633.
21. Goyal, P. and Basniwal, R.K. (2017). Toxicity of nanoparticles and their impact on environment. *In:* Ghorbanpour, M., Manika, K., Varma, A. (eds). Nanoscience and Plant–Soil Systems. Soil Biology, vol. 48. Springer, Cham.
22. Wolfram, J., Zhu, M., Yang, Y., Shen, J., Gentile, E. et al. (2015). Safety of nanoparticles in medicine. Current Drug Targets, 16(14), 1671-1681.
23. Viswanath, B. and Kim, S. (2016). Influence of nanotoxicity on human health and environment: The alternative strategies. *In:* Reviews of Environmental Contamination and Toxicology, vol. 242, 61-104. Springer.

24. Pérez-Hérnandez, H., Fernández-Luqueño, F., Huerta-Lwanga, E., Mendoza-Vega, J., Álvarez-Solís José, D. et al. (2020). Effect of engineered nanoparticles on soil biota: Do they improve the soil quality and crop production or jeopardize them? Land Degradation & Development, 31, 2213-2230.
25. Limaye, V., Fortwengel, G. and Limaye, D. (2014). Regulatory roadmap for nanotechnology based medicines. Int. J. Drug Regul. Aff., 2(4), 33-41.
26. Takhar, P. and Mahant, S. (2011). In vitro methods for nanotoxicity assessment: Advantages and applications. Arch. Appl. Sci. Res., 3(2), 389-403.
27. Umair, M., Javed, I., Rehman, M., Madni, A., Javeed, A. et al. (2016). Nanotoxicity of inert materials: The case of gold, silver and iron. J. Pharm. Pharm. Sci., 19(2), 161-180.
28. Ankamwar, B. and Yadwade, R. (2021). A review: Non-antibacterial, non-antifungal and non-anticancer properties of nanoparticles the forgotten paradigm. Nano Express, 2.
29. Anderson, D.S., Sydor, M.J., Fletcher, P. and Holian, A. (2016). Nanotechnology: The risks and benefits for medical diagnosis and treatment. J. Nanomed. Nanotechnol., 7(4), e143.
30. Dressler, F. and Kargl, F. (2012). Security in nano communication: Challenges and open research issues. Proc. 2012 IEEE International Conference on Communications (ICC), 6183-6187.
31. Dressler, F. and Kargl, F. (2012). Towards security in nano-communication: Challenges and opportunities. Nano Commun. Netw., 3(3), 151-160.
32. Atlam, H.F., Walters, R.J. and Wills, G.B. (2018). Internet of Nano Things: Security Issues and Applications. Proc. ICCBDC'18.
33. Galal, A. and Hesselbach, X. (2018). Nano-networks communication architecture: Modeling and functions. Nano Commun. Networks, 17, 45-62.
34. Mohammad, F. and Al-Lohedan, H.A. (2017). Chitosan-mediated layer-by-layer assembling approach for the fabrication of biomedical probes and advancement of nanomedicine. *In:* Nanocellulose and Nanohydrogel Matrices. Weinheim, Germany: Wiley-VCH Verlag GmbH & Co. KGaA, 91-124.
35. Maksimović, M. and Omanović-Mikličanin, E. (2017). Towards green nanotechnology: Maximizing benefits and minimizing harm. CMBEBIH 2017, Springer, 164-170.
36. Parveen, K., Banse, V. and Ledwani, L. (2016). Green synthesis of nanoparticles: Their advantages and disadvantages. 2016 AIP Conference Proceedings, 1724(1), 20048.
37. Kumar, S., Lather, V. and Pandita, D. (2015). Green synthesis of therapeutic nanoparticles: An expanding horizon. Nanomedicine, 10(15), 2451-2471.
38. Saif, S., Tahir, A. and Chen, Y. (2016). Green synthesis of iron nanoparticles and their environmental applications and implications. Nanomaterials, 6(11), 209.
39. Velusamy, P., Kumar, G.V., Jeyanthi, V., Das, J., Pachaiappan, R. et al. (2016). Bio-inspired green nanoparticles: Synthesis, mechanism, and antibacterial application. Toxicol. Res., 32(2), 95-102.
40. Nikolić, G.S., Cakić, M.D., Glišić, S., Cvetković, D.J., Mitić, Z.J. et al. (2017). Study of green nanoparticles and biocomplexes based on exopolysaccharide by modern fourier transform spectroscopy. *In:* Fourier Transforms – High-tech Application and Current Trends. InTechopen.
41. Nayyar, A., Puri, V. and Le, D.N. (2017). Internet of Nano Things (IoNT): Next evolutionary step in nanotechnology. Nanosci. Nanotechnol., 7(1), 4-8.
42. Ni, S. (2017). Nanoparticles carrying natural product for drug delivery. J. Drug Deliv. Ther., 7(3), 73-75.
43. Bhushan, B., Khanadeev, V., Khlebtsov, B., Khlebtsov, N., Gopinath, P. et al. (2017). Impact of albumin based approaches in nanomedicine: Imaging, targeting and drug delivery. Adv. Colloid Interface Sci., 246, 13-39.

44. Chen, J., Ding, J., Wang, Y., Cheng, J., Ji, S. et al. (2017). Sequentially responsive shell-stacked nanoparticles for deep penetration into solid tumors. Adv. Mater., 29(32), 1701170.

45. Nikalje, A.P. (2015). Nanotechnology and its applications in medicine. Med. Chem. (Los. Angeles), 5(2), 81-89.

46. Wong, K.K. and Liu, X. (2012). Nanomedicine: A primer for surgeons. Pediatric Surgery International, 28, 943-951.

47. Alharbi, K.K. and Al-sheikh, Y.A. (2014). Role and implications of nanodiagnostics in the changing trends of clinical diagnosis. Saudi J. Biol. Sci., 21(2), 109-117.

48. Balghusoon, A.O. and Mahfoudh, S. (2020). Routing protocols for wireless nanosensor networks and Internet of nano things: A comprehensive survey. IEEE Access, 8, 200724-200748.

49. Bhatt, Y. and Bhatt, C. (2017). Internet of things in healthcare. *In:* Internet of Things and Big Data Technologies for Next Generation Healthcare. Springer, 13-33.

50. El-Din, H.E. and Manjaiah, D.H. (2017). Internet of nano things and industrial Internet of things. *In:* Internet of Things: Novel Advances and Envisioned Applications, 25, D.P. Acharjya and M.K. Geetha (eds). Springer Cham, 109-123.

51. Chang, Y.N., Zhang, M., Xia, L., Zhang, J., Xing, G. et al. (2012). The toxic effects and mechanisms of CuO and ZnO nanoparticles. Materials (Basel), 5(12), 2850-2871.

52. Nelson, B.C., Minelli, C., Doak, S.H. and Roesslein, M. (2020). Emerging standards and analytical science for nanoenabled medical products. Annual Review of Analytical Chemistry, Ann. Reviews, 13, 431-452.

53. García-Quintero, A. and Palencia, M. (2021). A critical analysis of environmental sustainability metrics applied to green synthesis of nanomaterials and the assessment of environmental risks associated with the nanotechnology. The Science of the Total Environment, 793, 148524.

54. Estrela, V.V., Saotome, O., Loschi, H.J., Hemanth, D.J., Farfan, W.S. et al. (2018). Emergency response cyber-physical framework for landslide avoidance with sustainable electronics. Technologies, 6, 42.

55. Vaseashta, A. (2019). Cyber-physical systems—Nanomaterial sensors based unmanned aerial platforms for real-time monitoring and analysis. Proc. 4th Int'l Conf. Nanotechn. and Biom. Eng. ICNBME 2019. IFMBE, vol. 77. Springer, Cham.

56. Estrela, V.V., Saotome, O., Hemanth, J. and Cabral RJR (2017). Emergency response cyber-physical system for disaster prevention with sustainable electronics. Proc. of the ACM PETRA 2017, Rhodes, Greece.

57. Monteiro, A.C.B., Franca, R.P., Estrela, V.V., Fernandes, S.R., Khelassi, A. et al. (2020). UAV-CPSs as a test bed for new technologies and a primer to Industry 5.0. *In:* Estrela V.V. et al. (eds). Imaging and Sensing for Unmanned Aircraft Systems, 2(1), 1-22, IET, London, UK.

58. Vaughn, J.R. (2006). Over the Horizon: Potential Impact of Emerging Trends in Information and Communication Technology on Disability Policy and Practice. National Council on Disability, Washington DC: 1-55.

59. Ghosh, A. and Fischer, P. (2009). Controlled propulsion of artificial magnetic nanostructured propellers. Nano Letters, 9(6), 2243-2245.

60. Tarakanov, A.O., Goncharova, L.B. and Tarakanov, Y.A. (2009). Carbon nanotubes towards medicinal biochips. Wiley Interdisciplinary Reviews: Nanomedicine and Nanobiotechnology, 2(1), 1-10.

61. Ignatyev, M. B. (2010). Necessary and sufficient conditions of nanorobot synthesis. Doklady Mathematics. 82(1), 671-675.

62. Cerofolini, G., Amato, P., Asserini, M. and Mauri, G. (2010). A surveillance system

for early-stage diagnosis of endogenous diseases by swarms of nanobots. Advanced Science Letters, 3(4), 345-352.

63. Yarin, A.L. (2010). Nanofibers, nanofluidics, nanoparticles and nanobots for drug and protein delivery systems. Scientia Pharm. Central Eur. Symp. on Pharm. Techn., 78(3), 542.

64. Wang, J. (2009). Can man-made nanomachines compete with nature biomotors?. ACS Nano. 3(1), 4-9.

65. Amrute-Nayak, M., Diensthuber, R.P., Steffen, W., Kathmann, D., Hartmann, F.K. et al. (2010). Targeted optimization of a protein nanomachine for operation in biohybrid devices. Angewandte Chemie, 49(2), 312-316.

66. Neves, M. and Martín-Yerga, D. (2018). Advanced nanoscale approaches to single-(bio)entity sensing and imaging. Biosensors, 8.

67. Pajorová, E., Hluchý, L., Kostic, I., Pajorova, J., Bačáková, M. et al. (2018). A virtual reality visualization tool for three-dimensional biomedical nanostructures. J. Phys. Conf. Series, 1098, 012001.

68. Priya, R.K., Anns, T.R., Kadhirunnisa, S. and Ananth, C. (2017). Nanorobots control activation for stenosed coronary occlusion. Int' J. Adv. Res. in Man., Architecture, Technology and Eng. (IJARMATE), 2(13), 60-76.

69. Lavan, D.A., McGuire, T. and Langer, R. (2003). Small-scale systems for in vivo drug delivery. Nature Biotechnology, 21(10): 1184-1191.

70. Leary, S.P., Liu, C.Y. and Apuzzo, M.L.J. (2006). Toward the emergence of nanoneurosurgery: Part III – Nanomedicine: Targeted nanotherapy, nanosurgery, and progress toward the realization of nanoneurosurgery. Neurosurgery, 58(6), 1009-1026.

71. Couvreur, P. and Vauthier, C. (2006). Nanotechnology: Intelligent design to treat complex disease. Pharmaceutical Research, 23(7), 1417-1450.

72. Hu, M., Ai, X., Wang, Z., Zhang, Z., Cheong, H. et al. (2018). Nanoformulation of metal complexes: Intelligent stimuli-responsive platforms for precision therapeutics. Nano Research, 11, 5474-5498.

73. Kaviarasi, S., Yuba, E., Harada, A. and Krishnan, U.M. (2019). Emerging paradigms in nanotechnology for imaging and treatment of cerebral ischemia. J. Cont. Release, 300, 22-45.

74. Wong, P.C., Wong, K.K. and Foote, H. (2003). Organic data memory using the DNA approach. Communications of the ACM, 46, 95-98.

75. Rifat, T., Hossain, S., Alam, M. and Rouf, A.S. (2019). A review on applications of nanobots in combating complex diseases. Bangladesh Pharmaceutical J., 22, 99-108.

76. Melki, B. (January 31, 2007). Nanorobotics for Diabetes. nanovip.com

77. Li, J., Ávila, B.E., Gao, W., Zhang, L. and Wang, J. (2017). Micro/nanorobots for biomedicine: Delivery, surgery, sensing, and detoxification. Science Robotics, 2.

78. Razmjooy, N., Estrela, V.V. and Sabatini, R. (2020). Vision in micro-aerial vehicles. *In:* Estrela, V.V. et al. (eds). Imaging and Sensing for Unmanned Aircraft Systems, 1(8), 173-216. IET.

79. Bertoli, G.C., Saotome, O. and Estrela, V.V. (2020). Computer vision in UAV using ROS. *In:* Estrela, V.V. et al. (eds). Imaging and Sensing for Unmanned Aircraft Systems, 1(9), 217-260. IET.

80. Monteiro, A.C.B., Franca, R.P., Estrela, V.V., Fernandes, S.R., Khelassi, A. et al. (2020). UAV-CPSs as a test bed for new technologies and a primer to Industry 5.0. *In:* Estrela, V.V. et al. (eds). Imaging and Sensing for Unmanned Aircraft Systems, 2(1), 1-22. IET.

81. Burdziakowski, P., Razmjooy, N., Estrela, V.V. and Hemanth, J. (2020). Open source software (OSS) and hardware (OSH) in UAVs. *In:* Estrela, V.V. et al. (eds). Imaging and Sensing for Unmanned Aircraft Systems, 2(3), 49-66. IET.

82. Khelassi, A. and Estrela, V.V. (2020). Advances in multidisciplinary medical technologies – Engineering, modeling and findings. Proc. International Workshop on Medical Technologies 2019 (ICHSMT 2019), Springer Nature, Zurich, Switzerland.

83. Loschi, H.J., Estrela, V.V., Hemanth, D.J., Fernandes, S.R., Iano, Y. et al. (2020). Communications requirements, video streaming, communications links and networked UAVs. *In:* Estrela, V.V. et al. (eds). Imaging and Sensing for Unmanned Aircraft Systems, 2(6), 113-132. IET.

84. Padilha, R., Iano, Y., Monteiro, A.C., Arthur, R., Estrela, V.V. et al. (2019). Betterment proposal to multipath fading channels potential to MIMO systems. *In:* Iano, Y. et al. (eds). Proc. 4th BTSym, Springer, Cham, Switzerland.

85. Tinnefeld, P., Acuna, G.P., Wei, Q., Ozcan, A., Vietz, C. et al. (2019). DNA origami nanotools for single-molecule biosensing and superresolution microscopy. Proc. Bioph. Congress: Optics in the Life Sciences Congress 2019 (BODA, BRAIN, NTM, OMA, OMP), paper AW5E.5, https://doi.org/10.1364/OMA.2019.AW5E.5

86. Deshpande, A., Razmjooy, N. and Estrela, V.V. (2021). Introduction to Computational Intelligence and Super-Resolution. Springer, Cham.

87. Dagdas, Y.S., Aslan, M.N., Tekinay, A.B., Guler, M.O. and Dana, A. (2011). Nanomechanical characterization by double-pass force–distance mapping. Nanotechnology, 22, 295704.

88. Kluczyk-Korch, K., Palazzo, D., Waag, A., Diéguez, Á., Prades, J.D. et al. (2020). Optical design of InGaN/GaN nanoLED arrays on a chip: Toward: highly resolved illumination. Nanotechnology, 32(10), 105203. Doi:10.1088/1361-6528/abcd60

89. Ogut, E., Yanik, C., Kaya, I.I., Ow-Yang, C.W., Şendur, K. et al. (2018). Focusing short-wavelength surface plasmons by a plasmonic mirror. Optics Letters, 43(9), 2208-2211.

90. Adir, O., Poley, M., Chen, G., Froim, S., Krinsky, N. et al. (2019). Integrating Artificial Intelligence and Nanotechnology for Precision Cancer Medicine. Advanced Materials, e1901989.

91. Singla, V.K., Aggarwal, V., Priyanka and Gupta, S. (2021). Artificial Intelligence and Nanotechnology. Artificial Intelligence, CRC Press, Doi:10.1201/9781003095910-1

92. Razmjooy, N., Ashourian, M., Karimifard, M., Estrela, V.V., Loschi, H.J. et al. (2020). Computer-Aided Diagnosis of Skin Cancer: A Review. Current Medical Imaging, 16(7), 781-793.

93. Razmjooy, N., Estrela, V.V. and Loschi, H.J. (2020). Entropy-based breast cancer detection in digital mammograms using world cup optimization algorithm. Int. J. Swarm Intell. Res., 11, 1-18.

94. Deshpande, A., Patavardhan, P., Estrela, V.V., Razmjooy, N., Hemanth, J.D. et al. (2020). Deep learning as an alternative to super-resolution imaging in UAV systems. doi: 10.1049/pbce120g_ch9

95. Silva, G.A. (2018). A new frontier: The convergence of nanotechnology. Brain Machine Interfaces, and Artificial Intelligence. Frontiers in Neuroscience, 12.

96. Tajunisa, M., Sadath, L. and Nair, R.S. (2021). Nanotechnology and Artificial Intelligence for Precision Medicine in Oncology. Artificial Intelligence. CRC Press, eBook ISBN: 9781003095910

Digital Twin Framework for Intelligent Healthcare Facilities through ISO/IEEE 11073

Vania V. Estrela[1] [0000-0002-4465-7691], Anand Deshpande[2] [0000-0002-1500-0981], Robert Sroufer[3] [0000-0002-7903-9180], Ricardo T. Lopes[4] [0000-0001-7250-824X], Edwiges G.H. Grata[1] [0000-0002-7962-9420], Nikolaos Andreopoulos[5] [0000-0001-9975-7043], Andrey Terziev[6] [0000-0002-7069-367X], Asif Ali Laghari[7] [0000-0001-5831- 5943]

[1] Telecommunications Department, Federal Fluminense University (UFF), RJ, Brazil vania.estrela.phd@ieee.org, edwigesghgrata@gmail.com
[2] Angadi Institute of Technology and Management, ECE Department, Savagaon Road, 591108 Belagavi, India, deshpande.anandb@gmail.com
[3] Management Department, Duquesne University, Pittsburg, PA, USA, sroufer@duq.edu
[4] Universidade Federal do Rio de Janeiro (UFRJ), LIN, COPPE, RJ, Brazil, ricardo@lin.ufrj.br
[5] Computer Science Department, Technological Institute of Iceland, Iceland nikolaosandreopoulos@yahoo.com
[6] TerziA, Sofia, Bulgaria andreyterziev@yahoo.com
[7] Faculty of Computer Science, Sindh Madressatul Islam University, Karachi (74000), Sindh, Pakistan, asif.laghari@smiu.edu.pk

1. Introduction

A Digital Twin (DT) performs a Virtual Description (VD) of a real thing that is either digital (hardware and software) or alive [1, 2]. Information is exchanged seamlessly among the Physical Worlds (PWs) and Virtual Worlds (VWs), permitting the virtual entity to cohabit alongside the actual entity. A DT enables the monitoring, comprehension, and optimization of a PW entity's functioning besides also sending continuous feedback to ameliorate one's Quality of Life (QoL) and welfare.

Data visualization integrates Artificial Intelligence (AI), data analytics, haptics (brainwave-based schemes), the Internet of Medical Things (IoMT), data rendering methodologies, cybersecurity, and communication networks. This chapter uses the terminology Personal Health Devices (PHDs) as a simplification for the set of healthcare gadgets comprising on-body and in-body devices, i.e., wearables, injectables, implantables, ingestibles, and other non-mainstream possibilities.

The DT, as defined in [2] possesses a number of unique qualities. Apart from its unique identity, the DT utilizes sensors and actuators to continuously collect data, enabling it to be an accurate real-twin replica at any given instant and to offer feedback to the real twin. These sensors and actuators may be found in PHDs, which have exploded in popularity lately. Wearables are growing in popularity, and the massive amount of PHDs data enfolds critical health information [3] that is mostly unexplored. This data will be gathered over time through the use of the DT and the physical twin concept. It will arrange for critical information about individual wellness problems in smart societies, as clever healthcare is critical [4]. As noted in [5], DT technology may provide solutions to a variety of smart welfare challenges in smart towns. The authors emphasize the importance of tailored overall healthcare efficiency, good data analytics, and data interoperability. Indeed, this approach collects data as per the X73-S, facilitating interoperability. Then, it goes to data analytics. The resulting feedback is tailored for each citizen's collected data, on a personalized basis.

One plus of this technology is that a particular product has structured cloud storage for all digital information duplicates that can be edited similarly and the physical product would be manipulated but at a lower cost. According to one of the survey findings [6], the DT serves a multitude of roles.

Another industry study of DTs [7] identifies this technology as tremendously auspicious as smart manufacturing progresses. Along with cost and production inefficiencies in technology it looks at additional DT domain components [8]. The findings advocate for the implementation of a DT that represents a synchronized copy of manufacturing components and processes and is focused on gathering and evaluating historical and current tracking data for future decision-making. In reference [9], a DT architectural reference model for medical cyber-physical systems (MCPSs) is shown, in which each physical object connects to a cyber-thing via actuators and sensors. An additional study focuses on 3D printing [10]. It demonstrates how a digital replica of 3D printing equipment may help reduce printing expenses by lowering the number of trials and errors and hasten the process.

While interest in DT is increasing in industry and academia [7], there is less concern for wellness. The investigation in [2] discusses the potential applications of DT to people and defines DT as a replica of any living or nonliving item that helps people. Additionally, this concept can have a beneficial effect on the fields of health, athletics, and well-being. Rather than human health, publications such as [11-14] emphasize prognostics and control of industrial process constituents or equipment.

Certain publications are not about individual human DTs but rather about the DT of an emergency unit, as in [15], the hospital twin, as in [16], or the chain supervision twin of healthcare aiding equipment, as in [17]. Another research examines the ethical implications of DT in healthcare [18]. It raises concerns about potential societal benefits and potential unavailability, i.e., the chance that the technology may not be within the reach of everyone. Several papers in the health field [19, 20] advocate the use of human DTs, (a) describing a DT for the human head that may determine the magnitude of carotid stenosis together with (b) developing a monitoring framework for older adults and aiding with potential sickness diagnosis or emergency measures that are mandated when the DT is used. These systems are medical in nature, the DT literature promotes individual well-being, and there is a lack of support.

This chapter addresses a DT in its most extensive definition, assuming it to be a duplicate of any living or nonliving creature [2] equipped with sensors similar to how humans use their five senses. The DT uses these sensors to acquire as much information as attainable about the real twin's health and environment. The obtained data is then stored in the cloud, which acts as the memory for the digital twin. Data processing by means of AI algorithms and data analytics serves as the mapping for the DT of human intelligence. This technique enables decision-making and feedback from the virtual twin to the real twin. Feedback can take the form of actuation, e.g., haptic actuation or alarms, or it can take the form of modifying the actual twin's living environment in order to stimulate health.

2. ISO/IEEE 11073 Standards in Health Systems

The PHD technology escalation and the general populace's easy access to these gadgets can soon make medical care noticeably more efficient. These innovations compel interoperability, allowing increasingly efficient well-being services with reduced technical complications by slotting in the ISO/IEEE 11073 standards.

2.1. ISO/IEEE 11073 Standards

The ISO/IEEE 11073 standards, otherwise known as X73 Standards or X73-Ss, were developed as a consequence of a partnership encompassing the International Organization for Standardization (ISO) as well as the IEEE. These standards were developed when the demand for such a health sector standard has never been larger.

The ISO/IEEE 11073 PHD standards make it easier to communicate among PHDs and administrators, such as computer systems, cellphones, and so on. They seek to encourage the interchange of health data while also facilitating plug-and-play instantaneous interoperability. The X73-S communication model is the minimal requirement for PHDs and managers to be X73-S-compliant. As a result, the X73-Ss ensure that a PHD and compliance management may effectively complete the data transmission. The X73-Ss include no mention of security or other associated issues, such as user privacy. Given the relevance of these difficulties, some research works suggest remedies [21].

The X73-Ss deliver ways out for standardizing PHD systems employed by the scientific community and industry. The use of standardized X73-S techniques in research is growing. A study, for example, offers health-related practices utilizing the X73-S to service people at home , and mimicking the system in [22], displaying a personal linked health system. Other mobile technologies, such as fall detection, remotely monitor people's health parameters [23].

2.2. X73-S and PHDs

There exist manifold X73-S-compliant devices available, such as a pulse oximeter with an Android-based framework. An in-home blood pressure monitor observes certain older people who are prone to illness. Other X73-S devices comprise the weighing scale, blood glucose meter, body temperature sensor, electrocardiogram (EKG or ECG), thermometer, electronic ankle bracelet, and shoe insole [24-31].

2.3. Medical X73-Ss

Some medical systems that employ X73-S compliant personal devices deliver medical-care material to mobile phones [24]. This information differs contingent on the patient's profile and medical conditions. Some studies apply the X73-S to cardiovascular diseases like [32], which investigates mobile checking of cardiovascular activity as well as identifies faults while preserving patient mobility. Another research, [33], focuses on patient mobility and utilizes X73-S ECG equipment with an Android system permitting patients to monitor their heart condition without being admitted to the hospital. An EKG simulator provides ECG data for testing and demonstrating the system's ability to render the ECG signal in real-time visually.

A system for detecting acute myocardial infarction diseases to supply patients with the necessary early intervention appears in [34] with a non-X73-S compatible wearable device. Consequently, a specification for this type that follows the X73-S has been anticipated in research. The data from this gadget goes to a server for diagnosing and handling acute myocardial infarctions.

The work in [28] demonstrates the possibility of X73-S-compliant devices for medical diseases other than cardiovascular problems by employing corporal temperature sensors for patients requiring hypothermic therapy. When caregivers have access to registration data, this research recommends using technology as part of local first-aid monitoring of a patient's temperature until patient arrival at the HF or hospital emergency department, for instance, in sports, where body temperatures of athletes are sometimes lower due to their attire. These systems target patients who have a specific condition that doctors must monitor. Nonetheless, the primary objective is to support individuals in reaching and maintaining a healthy state while also making medical specialists ready as required.

2.4. X73-S Adoption

There are PHDs too for subject monitoring to enrich their wellbeing. The work in [35] remotely observes the user's behavior via instructions provided by a monitoring server. Users wear an activity monitor managed by the server as needed. This type of setting is not unique to any health condition. It has no limitations in terms of improving an individual's wellness and healthy persons.

The X73-S potential emulates a manager acting together with specific agents while covering issues like transitioning from fixed to mobile systems and developing the X73-S from the Point of Care (PoC) for Healthcare Facilities (HFs) operation in conjunction with personal health devices for any user [36]. According to [36], the progression from point-of-care to PHDs has stemmed end-to-end platform optimization with ubiquitous benefits in addition to plug-and-play resolutions. There is an option of exchanging data obtained from PHDs that adhere to the X73-S format across various managers in different places as in [37]. A middleware for mobile well-being services collects data from PHDs and sends it to a log data node [38]. It puts the suggested middleware to test with the help of a pulse oximeter that connects with an Android platform.

These systems are adequate steps toward utilizing technology advancements to give individuals more effective alternatives for personal health systems. These solutions assure standard adoption while concentrating on spending on a single health device besides gathering and transferring health data to a server. On the other hand, this study offers individuals and caregivers an end-to-end framework for data gathering and transferring, as well as their analysis and the derivation of essential information to provide user feedback. Once a specification adheres to the X73-S, it is critical to support any PHD while maintaining interoperability. The adoption of X73-Ss in PHDs is a vital piece ensuring the interoperability of data collected on people's health when it comes to sports and theragnostics. As a result, it assures this data's usability for caregivers by removing proprietary record formatting that patients and caregivers should handle if they want to access personal health data from the cloud.

3. Digital Twin Requirements

Based on studies from [2, 39], and the conditions that a DT system must meet to offer value to the actual twin initially, the actual twin must be continually watched to verify if the data acquisition is correct. The vast majority of self-reported information is incorrect. As an assumption one considers a typical example of physical exercise. In such a scenario, one learns that most individuals are unaware of how long they sit throughout the day and just how little they physically move. However, with a growing number of individuals wearing various kinds of health surveillance devices, their data can be used to their advantage. The proliferation of wearables occurred at precisely the correct time to allow the DT creation.

PHDs generate colossal data amounts. A significant quantity of data is lost because data usefulness is regulated and constrained by trademarked data formats from an expanding number of manufacturers, demonstrating the importance of standardization to simplify interoperability [2]. As a result, data may be sent to a coach to assist in following up with the exact time spent working out in addition to the stated time.

Given the large quantity of data gathered in the DT system, data visualization is critical. The more remarkable the accumulated data quantity throughout time, the more difficult it is to discern any patterns from numbers. Yet, by converting these statistics into useful graphs, caregivers will see trends that might otherwise go undiscovered. This phase affords a virtual feedback source for monitoring the real twin's health and/or athletic ambitions.

The DT also provides physical input to the actual twin through actuators, reminding the user of their workout time and incentive constantly. To give accurate feedback while being observed, gathered data must be processed, allowing tailored actuations for physical activity suggestions and reminders to be created and delivered properly. There is a noteworthy demand for data analytics and/or AI. Reminders sent by devices such as cellphones with loaded fitness applications, for example, are frequently ignored by users. This is for the reason that they are often triggered somewhat randomly at a desired user reminder time. They do not contemplate the individual's health characteristics, which personal health devices may record over time. However, utilizing PHDs to gather data and their analytics to evaluate results may entail a far more customized approach.

DTs entail cybersecurity and privacy to send acquired data to the cloud safely. This chapter addresses critical system aspects. Notably, all data transmissions take place through a secure connection. In addition, all sensitive data in a database is encrypted. To summarize, the previously mentioned criteria are as follows:

1. Information gathering through sensory devices;
2. Data communication standardization;
3. Information analytics to identify patterns; and
4. Providing real twins and caregivers with feedback by hard and soft actuators.

Figure 1 depicts a DT ecosystem with a high-level view of several DT modules and their interactions [39]. The information sources, AI-inference engines, and multimodal interactions among real entities and DTs are among these modules. The ecosystem also demonstrates the need to handle vastly efficient networks, security, and privacy in all parts of the DT. This ecosystem serves as the framework for the subsequent discussion.

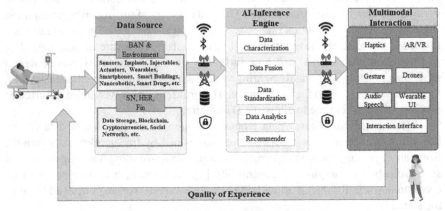

Figure 1. Possible digital twin ecosystem

4. Cloud-based X73 Standard Digital Twin System

This section talks about the X73-S-based DT architecture's uses, and benefits as regards designing and building systems via digitizing, processing, and analyzing health data with today's computing power.

4.1. DT Data Sensing

4.1.1. Well-Being Data Collection

The system's input comes from the gathered health data via sensors that after processing and analyses may trigger actuator actions like an insulin bomb. Self-reported statistics proved inaccurate by investigators [40, 41]. Manual data entry into a system via a user interface is time-consuming. Instead, automatic data gathering simplifies and improves the job, aided by the PHDs' proliferation and other equipment. Given the rapid PHD technology growth in recent years, instituting a standard to guarantee interoperability has become critical. Disappointingly, the data acquired by PHDs, comprising vital signs of users, are rubbish without standards. The ISO/IEEE 11073 (X73-S) PHD standards try to meet the serious interoperability demand.

Figure 2 shows PHD types with some data transfer standardization efforts among PHDs and servers. X73-S-compatible gadgets can interact directly with other X73-S communication units. Non-compliant gadgets comprise a category to be addressed.

4.1.2. DT Standardization

The objective is to create a system that caregivers or coaches may utilize to convey tailored services to athletes. This concept eradicates the necessity for a PHD's proprietary communication protocols or data formats. Stakeholders benefiting from this service will employ X73-S-compliant PHDs. A more austere matter for healthcare service suppliers is interoperability for their subjects to customize services. A recommended X73-S communication system module can resolve this problem.

Only some PHD companies in the market stick to the IEEE standard at present. Most stay non-compliant owing partly to the X73-S's recent developments, albeit [21] reveals the interest in X73-S compatible systems. While the standardization of PHDs slowly impacts them, an alternative solution can be implemented quickly to incorporate current ones. As a result, a DT framework encompasses both standardized and non-standardized PHDs.

4.1.3. PHD Categories

The X73-S supports several PHDs. ISO/IEEE defines a standard document called device specialization for each of these device types. Each device specialization document includes a set of specifications on the communication protocol required to conform to the X73-S. PHDs, such as the DT data sensing components in Figure 2, can be twofold based on equipment compliance with the current X73-S device specializations:

The X73-S communication server adheres to the standard, utilizes device specifications prepared by the ISO/IEEE workgroup, and stays in the server's database. These standards offer the information to be transmitted in the X73-S communication stages for each device type.

Non-X73-S PHDs: This second group covers all other non-standardized well-being devices. These devices adhere to some manufacturer-specific standards. There are two subcategories.

i. Non-compliant PHDs: This first subcategory embraces devices that have a specialization listed in the standard albeit were not followed by the maker. An X73-S wrapper module behaves as a gateway between the server and non-standardized devices.

ii. No X73-S device specialty: This subcategory accommodates current non-standardized PHDs on the market besides lacking a specified standard

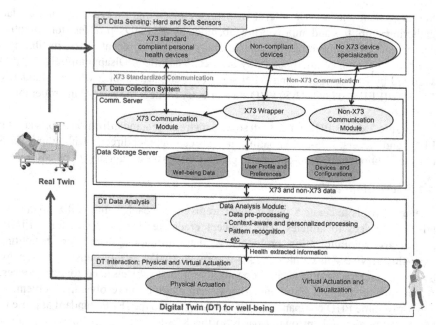

Figure 2. Digital twin (DT) architecture using X73-S

specialization. The DT paradigm must contemplate and try to take in all device kinds while standard acceptance continues.

4.1.4. X73 Mobile App

In Figure 2, a generic mobile application connects with compliant devices to gather health data and deliver it to the X73-S communication system model via an app for the X73-S devices category. The first subcategory is PHDs that are X73-S-compatible. An agent is a node in the X73-S that collects and transmits health data to X73-S management. A manager, alternatively, is a node that gets health data from agents. As a result, a personal health device that implements this standard can join the X73-S communication module over Wi-Fi and send data as an X73-S agent. However, most private health gadgets use Bluetooth and will not communicate directly with the X73 communication module. As a result, developing an X73-S-conforming mobile app is critical, as it will act as a data-gathering point and preserve the data acquired by the personal device. In its connection with a conforming device agent, this mobile app works as an X73-S manager. This data will go to the server later via the X73-S mobile app. The mobile app will communicate with the X73-S communication module, which serves as the manager, and an X73-S agent. That is, the mobile app supports both the X73-S agent and management protocols.

The exceptional feature of this app is customization for usage with any compliant device by simply updating its local database to reflect the X73-S configuration that is device-specific. The mobile app's customizable design lets stakeholders utilize a single or many X73-S devices. The app may operate with one or more devices depending on the user's preferences.

This smartphone app gathers and retains data from the X73-S personal health gadget. The software uploads data to the server at the stakeholder's request (menu choice) or at a time determined by the user every day. When the app transmits data to the server, data from the previous seven days is saved locally for offline stakeholder access. Data submitted to the server is marked to avoid duplicate transmission. Due to limited mobile phone storage, one can change the default value to 7 days to permit more data to be retained on a smartphone as determined by the user. Once the transfer is complete, the leftover data is erased.

4.2. DT Data Collection

The DT data acquisition system comprises two modules for communication and data storage. The communication server has three modules, as in Figure 2.

1. **X73-S Communication Module:** It is compliant with the X73-S communication modules serving as supervisors. The manager gets requests from PHDs known as agents. To begin, the X73-S manager or administrator gets an association request and parses it to decide the type of device. This device type allows the administrator to access the database to reply to the device's association response. The administrator also examines the agent identifier and states whether it recognizes it and has information about this specific agent configuration in the database in the association response. If the administrator does not recognize the identification, the agent must transmit its full configuration, including device configuration information. The configuration is saved in the database by the manager, who then provides the acceptable configuration response. The operational process is the following stage in the protocol, and it is during this step, the healthcare data is transferred twice. The agent waits for the manager to request the Medical Device System (MDS) characteristics in the first step, which follows the configuration stage. Depending on the device, the agent answers with a set of features. Data transmission is the subsequent stage of the operational method. During this step, the agent sends data measures to the manager, who saves the data on the cloud. When the data transmission is complete, the agent and management exchange a disassociation request/ response, closing the current connection. The exchange of communication messages happens with the X73-S agent serving as the personal wellness device, which is one conceivable case scenario. As previously stated, the communication module may accept communication from a private appliance using the X73-S application as an agent. The communication module may also accept connections from the X73-S wrapper.

2. **X73-S Wrapper Module:** The module that connects non-compliant personal health equipment to the standardized communication module. The module's primary function is to convert data from a proprietary format to a X73-S format. It implies that it accommodates non-compliant devices by getting personal health data from them using the proprietary data format. The module then connects with the X73-S communication part as an X73-S agent and sends the gathered data to the DT cloud database. It's worth noting that the X73-S wrapper is a standalone module that may run on a different server when

needed and sends data to the X73-S system. This architecture is understandable for a caregiver who hosts the standardized system and does not worry about any proprietary device connection. The wrapper module is then hosted and conserved by a third party that arranges for this service and allows data from as many devices as possible to benefit the people who use these PHDs. If a device specialization exists, the wrapper module can transmit data from a proprietary device. The ISO/IEEE PHD standard presently has 15 active dedicated devices. On the other hand, many different gadgets do not have a clear specialty, despite being widely used. Some research articles suggest specializations for specific devices, such as smartphone cameras and WII Balance Boards.

3. **X73 DT System Configurability:** The X73-S communication module must be configured by adhering to (a) the primary standard document for X73-S PHDs (11073-20601), containing all device specializations, and (b) specifications retrieved from each device specialization (which are changeable) in the system database. The communication module reads these specs from the database while removing any device-specific settings from the code. Following that, all specifications from accessible specializations are added to a server database. Because each of these specializations is required, any X73-S compliant device can connect with the system using this architecture. As a result, the gadget may send data without requiring any human involvement. This method avoids the requirement for specific device kinds. Any more device classes would need design/code modifications or the development of additional modules to handle them. Configurability is critical since any new device developed as per the ISO/IEEE working group may be seamlessly integrated without the need for further implementation. The new device requirements will be uploaded to the database, and the system will automatically recognize PHDs that obey these criteria. Because the standards are relatively new, this configurability is even more essential owing to the ongoing development and modifications introduced by the ISO/IEEE working group to the device specializations. Changes may be added to the database without modifying the code, which is continuously handy for caretakers.

4.3. Data Analytics

The DT goal is to comprehend the actual twin's health and wellbeing, which may be accomplished by data collection, storage, and analysis, as well as taking into consideration the past and current levels of wellness to discover trends. This technique uses algorithms, AI and considers as much of the genuine twin's external surroundings as feasible. Performing data analytics on the cloud enables AI algorithms to operate on vast volumes of data collected from many users and kept for more extended periods. This expedites extracting patterns from a large number of user data histories. Following that, feedback is supplied to all users individually, based on their unique circumstance. However, given the rising capacity of today's PHDs, certain data analytics may be conducted on the edge, such as on the user's smartphone.

This has the benefit of providing immediate and ongoing user input. The DT purpose is to offer context-aware feedback and orientations through real and virtual actuators based on the customized objectives of the real twin and the real twin scenario. This notion has an eclectic range of possible applications, and it can improve people's well-being. The proliferation of PHDs and the vast range of health characteristics that they can measure and make available for data analysis, the rising processing capacity of today's technologies, and developments in AI support this result. As a result, the DT system's capabilities are broad and accessible to researcher imaginations and caretaker aspirations.

4.4. DT Physical and Virtual Actuators

1. Actuators for Customer Feedback

Based on DTs' inspection to gather data throughout time, physical and virtual actuation offer feedback to the actual twins. The objective is to elevate awareness of the health status of genuine twins, favorably impacting their behavior, and inspiring them to improve their health. Different motivators, such as exploiting people's proclivity for social good, might motivate individuals to exercise while providing green energy to the needy. With technological advancements, multiple physical actuators now exist and can positively influence the actual twin's life if utilized creatively. For example, as indicated in [42], haptic feedback can help with sports training while augmenting physical and mental wellbeing. Virtual feedback, such as persuasive alerts, is another example that can improve social welfare [43].

2. Information Visualization

Data visualization is part of the virtual feedback sent to the actual twin and/or caretakers. Nevertheless, it is not always done in real-time. Data visualization is crucial because it allows caregivers to examine data and discover trends that would otherwise get missed out in the data. Graphs that demonstrate how the real twin has improved through time, for example, in terms of physical exercise, are examples. Another example is heat map visualization, which displays foot pressure and allows a health care practitioner or sports physiologist to identify abnormalities in an athlete's posture.

5. Case Study

5.1. Methodology

The DT architecture applies to an extensive range of welfare cases like an end-to-end multimodal collaboration with the real twin, from continued data gathering and analysis to personalized feedback.

The DT system assists the real twin to become physically active, involving the previous system requirements. The first prerequisite is data collection through sensors. A personal health device to track the real twin's physical activity helped track and recognize physical activity and have multiple healthcare applications, e.g., Ambient Assisted Living (AAL), rehabilitation and elderly care. If a smart insole and an electronic ankle bracelet are PHDs [44-46], they gather valuable, promising data for the healthcare domain.

This device for motivating physical exercise can work in two steps. First, activity acknowledgment lets the DT know whether the real twin performs physical activities, such as walking or running, or sitting for extensive periods. This recognition will provide DTs with the vital information to track the real twin. Next, once the individual is walking and running, the DT encourages the real twin besides providing goals when the person is not moving enough.

To meet the second criterion, i.e., data transfer standardization, an X73-S smart insole [31] allowed caregivers the use of gathered data in future applications. This smart insole captures data about physical activity and sends it to the X73-S mobile application, which then transmits it to the server. Following data gathering, the next stage in the DT system was to evaluate and extract meaningful information from them, as per the third criterion, to offer constructive feedback to the actual twin. This phase is carried out by the data analysis module, which is part of the intelligent DT.

5.2. User Study

Participants can wear smart insoles and follow instructions for walking, running, and sitting with their legs moving. Bluetooth can gather mobile app data and categorize it based on the performed activities. Each physical activity was preceded by selecting the corresponding activity category on the mobile phone before acquiring data to guarantee appropriate data labeling. Data pre-processing may diminish the initial noise at the start of a participant's walk and during deceleration at the finish of a run. Data segmentation guarantees that every sample has at least two steps while walking and the same sample duration for running (with more phases) and sitting. After collecting and pre-processing the pressure data, it was split into training and test data.

First, data can be divided such that 80 percent is for training and 20 percent is for testing, with participant data becoming part of both the training and testing sets. The model would be trained on a subset of each participant's data. In a subsequent step, all data from all participants became entirely included in the training set. In contrast, instead of the conventional random split, which might result in an uneven distribution of data instances, data from two participants are utilized just for testing without training. Cross-validation assisted in mitigating issues by making full use of the data gathered from participants. The testing data gave the model's performance assessment.

One theory is that the first example produces superior results since the model was trained on a subset of all user data. Nonetheless, this theory indicates that any new system user would need instruction.

The following phase can employ deep learning to categorize various activities via a convolutional neural network (CNN) trained with the teaching dataset. TensorFlow can assist in developing code to execute the model on the smartphone to offer mobile tracking and feedback to the actual twin. The CNN model was trained on the server before running on the mobile phone once it had been optimized. The CNN model was optimized by doing several tests with various model topologies. Using three convolution layers, a pair of pooling layers, two dropout layers, and three output neurons yield the most remarkable results (Softmax).

Executing a CNN relying on a smartphone is important because it allows stakeholders to receive feedback and encouragement when the application detects walking, more vigorous reinforcement when it perceives running, and a persuasion message for physical activity when the activity matches sitting. The fourth need for the DT system is to communicate feedback to users, which uses hard and soft actuation to send input to the actual twin and/or caretakers. The system then continues to gather data to provide longer-term data analysis and feedback. This system's objective is long-term data gathering paired with the usage of numerous PHDs to give complete insight into individual wellbeing and more helpful feedback.

5.3. Additional Research Topics

Sensor data, experimental data, and knowledge-based data are widely used in data-driven models for energy reduction. Making data-driven models assures the quality of health-related data and requires too much academic focus [47-55]. Furthermore, the main difficulty of Health 4.0 is with data transmission and infrastructure issues rather than creating modeling approaches [56]. Current methodologies and data infrastructures for energy conservation must be thoroughly evaluated to demonstrate the possibility for a more accurate as well as effective DT architecture. The healthcare sector will shift to a DT-based strategy with a few more advancements in supporting technologies like 5G/6G advances, IoMT standards, AI, and blockchain use. Global government activities and legislation are already geared toward maximizing energy efficiency and savings in healthcare institutions.

This bodes well for forthcoming developments in DT-based energy-saving systems for the welfare sector. In terms of possible obstacles, the need for collaboration between academics and healthcare stakeholders in transitioning from traditional industrial to DT-based energy-saving measures cannot be overstated. DT energy savings apply to cutting-edge technology. Health 4.0 will standardize and modularize medical data infrastructure to save energy. For academics and other stakeholders wishing to deploy refined energy-saving technologies, succinct recommendations must be appraised on a regular basis.

MCPSs are sophisticated engineering systems with a large number of interconnected elements and their interactions. The complexity of MCPSs increases by unplanned events and interruptions that might occur in real-world situations. The welfare industry is quickly evolving in Health 4.0 as new technologies emerge. However, in many cases, the effectiveness and dependability of these systems are still in doubt. Observation frameworks based on AI methods can create predictive and reactive maintenance plans for MCPSs [57-63] to solve this issue.

These tools can upsurge dependability and assist maintenance managers in making maintenance choices. Healthcare systems are now experiencing a digital revolution, which has been primarily fueled by new technology and digital representations of patients and ecosystems. The growing virtualization of care is one of the outcomes of this change. Regardless of the treatment setting, trust among caregivers and patients is critical for attaining positive health results. Given the plentiful information security and patient safety breaches, today's health data portfolios are insufficient for building and sustaining confidence in virtual care settings. For better theoretical foundations for a complex healthcare system intervention, a cryptographically protected infrastructure must create and maintain confidence in virtualized care settings. Proofs of concept must meet the standards based on this theoretical foundation. Stakeholder input and expert engagement are required for the design and assessment of complex interventions in healthcare. Critical functional and nonfunctional criteria and principles must exist within a virtualized healthcare system to improve trust between providers and patients. A cornerstone is a blockchain-based decentralized system that provides an innovative governance framework for a unique trust model. A service for creating trust in a virtualized environment assembled on a public blockchain is well suited to sustaining security and privacy in Healthcare 4.0 [64-74].

6. Conclusion

This chapter provided a DT architecture for health and wellness that allows for the integration of personal health devices (PHDs) as well as the collection of as much data on actual twins as possible to improve their quality of life [75-79]. As evidence of the concept's potential, there is also a physical wellness application of the DT system to demonstrate how the DT may enhance the health and welfare of the actual twin through data collection, storage, analysis, and user input. A potential design, its implementation, and some conclusions have been reached. A system like this offers individuals and caregivers information on their health and wellbeing. Using this method as part of an intelligent facility or plant can mimic stakeholder needs and alert them of corrective action. The effectiveness of this activity is assessed once again by ongoing health data collection, analysis, and feedback. In the future, research will be conducted to determine the long-term impact of this system on the real twin, which will necessitate a longer-term experiment and a larger-scale study to employ DT technology to support smart healthcare services effectively [80-85].

References

1. Grieves, M. and Vickers J. (2017). Digital twin: Mitigating unpredictable, undesirable emergent behavior in complex systems. *In:* Transdisciplinary Perspectives on Complex Systems. Cham, Switzerland: Springer. 85-113.
2. Saddik, A.E. (2018). Digital twins: The convergence of multimedia technologies. IEEE Multimedia Mag., 25(2), 87-92.
3. Badawi, H.F. and Saddik, A.E. (2020). Biofeedback in healthcare: State of the art and meta-review. *In:* Connected Health Smart Cities. Cham, Switzerland: Springer. 113-142.
4. Lytras, M. and Visvizi, A. (2018). Who uses smart city services and what to make of it: Toward interdisciplinary smart cities research. Sustainability, 10(6), p. 1998.
5. Lytras, M.D., Papadopoulou, P. and Sarirete, A. (2020). Smart healthcare: Emerging technologies, best practices, and sustainable policies. *In:* M. Lytras and A. Sarirete (eds). Innovation in Health Informatics. Amsterdam, The Netherlands: Elsevier. 3-38.
6. Sturm, C., Steck, M., Bremer, F., Revfi, S., Nelius, T. et al. (2021). Creation of digital

twins – Key characteristics of physical to virtual twinning in mechatronic product development. Proceedings of the Design Society.

7. Tao, F., Zhang, H., Liu, A. and Nee, A.Y.C. (2019). Digital twin in industry: State-of-the-art. IEEE Trans. Ind. Informat., 15(4), 2405-2415.

8. Park, K.T., Nam, Y.W., Lee, H.S., Im, S.J., Noh, S.D. et al. (2019). Design and implementation of a digital twin application for a connected micro smart factory. Int. J. Comput. Integr. Manuf., 32(6), 596-614.

9. Alam, K.M. and Saddik, A.E. (2017). C2PS: A digital twin architecture reference model for the cloud-based cyber-physical systems. IEEE Access, 5, 2050-2062.

10. Mukherjee, T. and DebRoy, T. (2019). A digital twin for rapid qualification of 3D printed metallic components. Appl. Mater. Today, 14, 59-65.

11. Li, C., Mahadevan, S., Ling, Y., Choze, S. and Wang, L. (2017). Dynamic Bayesian network for aircraft wing health monitoring digital twin. AIAA J., 55(3), 930-941.

12. Tygesen, U.T., Jepsen, M.S., Vestermark, J., Dollerup, N., Pedersen, A. et al. (2018). The true digital twin concept for fatigue re-assessment of marine structures. Proc. 37th Int. Conf. Ocean, Offshore Arctic Eng., vol. 1, Art. no. V001T01A021.

13. Sivalingam, K., Sepulveda, M., Spring, M. and Davies, P. (2018). A review and methodology development for remaining useful life prediction of offshore fixed and floating wind turbine power converter with digital twin technology perspective. Proc. 2nd Int. Conf. Green Energy Appl. (ICGEA), Mar. 2018, 197-204.

14. Mavris, D.N., Balchanos, M.G., Pinon-Fischer, O.J. and Sung, W.J. (2018). Towards a digital thread-enabled framework for the analysis and design of intelligent systems. Proc. AIAA Inf. Systems-AIAA Infotech. Aerosp., Jan. 2018, p. 1367.

15. Augusto, V., Murgier, M. and Viallon, A. (2018). A modelling and simulation framework for intelligent control of emergency units in the case of major crisis. Proc. Winter Simul. Conf. (WSC), Dec. 2018, 2495-2506.

16. Karakra, A., Fontanili, F., Lamine, E., Lamothe, J., Taweel, A. et al. (2018). Pervasive computing integrated discrete event simulation for a hospital digital twin. Proc. IEEE/ACS 15th Int. Conf. Comput. Syst. Appl. (AICCSA), Oct. 2018, 1-6.

17. Landolfi, G., Menato, S., Sorlini, M., Valdata, A., Rovere, D. et al. (2018). Intelligent value chain management framework for customized assistive healthcare devices. Procedia 2018 CIRP, 67, 583-588.

18. Bruynseels, K., Santoni, De Sio F. and van den Hoven, J. (2018). Digital twins in health care: Ethical implications of an emerging engineering paradigm. Frontiers Genet., 9, 31.

19. Chakshu, N.K., Carson, J., Sazonov, I. and Nithiarasu, P. (2019). A semi-active human digital twin model for detecting severity of carotid stenoses from head vibration—A coupled computational mechanics and computer vision method. Int. J. Numer. Biomed. Eng., 35(5), e3180.

20. Liu, Y., Zhang, L., Yang, Y., Zhou, L., Ren, L. et al. (2019). A novel cloud-based framework for the elderly healthcare services using digital twin. IEEE Access, 7, 49088-49101.

21. Badawi, H.F., Laamarti, F. and Saddik, A.E. (2019). ISO/IEEE 11073 personal health device (X73-PHD) standards compliant systems: A systematic literature review. IEEE Access, 7, 3062-3073.

22. Santos, D.F.S., Almeida, H.O. and Perkusich, A. (2015). A personal connected health system for the Internet of Things based on the constrained application protocol. Comput. Electr. Eng., 44, 122-136.

23. Talaminos, A., Naranjo, D., Barbarov, G., Roa, L.M., Reina-Tosina, J. et al. (2017). Design and implementation of a standardised framework for the management of a

wireless body network in a mobile health environment. Healthcare Technol. Lett., 4(3), 88-92.

24. Ji, Z., Ganchev, I., O'Droma, M., Zhang, X. and Zhang, X. (2014). A cloud-based X73 ubiquitous mobile healthcare system: Design and implementation. Sci. World J., 1-14.

25. Lim, J.-H., Park, C. and Park, S.-J. (2010). Home healthcare settop-box for senior chronic care using ISO/IEEE 11073 PHD standard. Proc. Annu. Int. Conf. IEEE Eng. Med. Biol., 216-219.

26. Chen, X., Bao, X., Fang, Z. and Xia, S. (2016). Design and development of a ubiquitous healthcare monitoring system based on Android platform and ISO/IEEE 11073 standards. Proc. 2016 IEEE Int. Conf. Inf. Autom. (ICIA), 1165-1168.

27. Nam, J.-C., Seo, W.-K., Bae, J.-S. and Cho, Y.-Z. (2011). Design and development of a u-Health system based on the ISO/IEEE 11073 PHD standards. Proc. 17th Asia Pacific Conf. Commun., 789-793.

28. Frohner, M., Urbauer, P., Bauer, M., Gerbovics, F., Mense, A. et al. (2009). Design and realisation of a framework for device end communication according to the IEEE 11073-20601 standard. Proc. 2009 Tagungsband der eHealth, Vienna, Austria, 135-139.

29. Yao, J. and Warren, S. (2005). Applying the ISO/IEEE 11073 standards to wearable home health monitoring systems. J. Clin. Monitor. Comput., 19(6), 427-436.

30. Carot-Nemesio, S. and Santos, J.A. (2010). OpenHealth – The OpenHealth FLOSS implementation of the ISO/IEEE 11073-20601 standard. Proc. 3rd Int. Conf. Health Informat., 505-511.

31. Badawi, H.F., Laamarti, F., Arafsha, F. and Saddik, A.E. (2019). Standardizing a shoe insole based on ISO/IEEE 11073 personal health device (X73-PHD) standards. Proc. 2019 ICITS, 764-778.

32. Gangwar, D.S. (2013). Biomedical sensor network for cardiovascular fitness and activity monitoring. Proc. IEEE Point-of-Care Healthcare Technol. (PHT), Jan. 2013, 279-282.

33. Xiong, Z.Q., Fan, H.H., Wang, W.Z., Xie, G.S., Hwang, B.Y. et al. (2014). Design and development of a 3-lead ECG system based on the ISO/IEEE 11073-10406 standards. *In:* Y. Zhang, G. Yao, J. He, L. Wang, N.R. Smalheiser and X. Yin (eds). Health Information Science (Lecture Notes in Computer Science), vol. 8423. Cham, Switzerland: Springer.

34. Jung, J., Lee, J., Lee, J. and Ki, Y.T. (2013). Development of service network for wearable type acutel myocardial infarction diagnosis system. Proc. IEEE 2013 SENSORS, Nov. 2013, 1-4.

35. Park, K. and Lim, S. (2015). A multipurpose smart activity monitoring system for personalized health services. Inf. Sci., 314, 240-254.

36. Martinez, I., Escayola, J., de Bobadilla, I.F., Martinez-Espronceda, M., Serrano, L. et al. (2008). Optimization proposal of a standard-based patient monitoring platform for ubiquitous environments. Proc. 30th Annu. Int. Conf. IEEE Eng. Med. Biol. Soc., Aug. 2008, 1813-1816.

37. Santos, D.F.S., Perkusich, A. and Almeida, H.O. (2014). Standard-based and distributed health information sharing for mHealth IoT systems. Proc. IEEE 16th Int. Conf. e-Health Netw., Appl. Services (Healthcom), Oct. 2014, 94-98.

38. Ji, Z., Zhang, X., Ganchev, I. and O'Droma, M. (2012). A personalized middleware for ubiquitous mHealth services. Proc. IEEE 14th Int. Conf. e-Health Netw., Appl. Services (Healthcom), Oct. 2012, 474-476.

39. Saddik, A.E., Badawi, H., Velazquez, R.A.M., Laamarti, F., Diaz, R.G. et al. (2019). Dtwins: A digital twins ecosystem for health and wellbeing. Proc. IEEE COMSOC MMTC Commun. Frontiers, 2019, 39-43.

40. Adams, A.S., Soumerai, S.B., Lomas, J. and Ross-Degnan, D. (1999). Evidence of self-report bias in assessing adherence to guidelines. International Journal for Quality in Health Care: J. International Society for Quality in Health Care, 11(3), 187-192.

41. de Reuver, M. and Bouwman, H. (2015). Dealing with self-report bias in mobile Internet acceptance and usage studies. Inf. Manage., 52(3), 287-294.

42. Laamarti, F., Arafsha, F., Hafidh, B. and Saddik, A.E. (2019). Automated athlete haptic training system for soccer sprinting. Proc. IEEE Conf. Multimedia Inf. Process. Retr. (MIPR), Mar. 2019, 303-309.

43. Laamarti, F. and El Saddik, A.E. (2018). Multimedia for social good: Green energy donation for healthier societies. IEEE Access, 6, 43252-43261.

44. Arafsha, F., Hanna, C., Aboualmagd, A., Fraser, S., Saddik, A.E. et al. (2018). Instrumented wireless Smart Insole system for mobile gait analysis: A validation pilot study with tekscan strideway. J. Sensor Actuator Netw., 7(3), 36.

45. Flores-Cuadras, J.R., Medina-Monroy, J., Chávez-Pérez, R. and Lobato-Morales, H. (2018). Flexible thin antenna solution for wearable ankle bracelet applications with GNSS and BLE connectivity. Microwave and Optical Technology Letters, 60, 1239-1245.

46. Fatima, T., Miyan, Z., Naeem, N., Riaz, M., Basit, A. et al. (2020). Foot practices in patients with type 2 diabetes: Where do we stand? Journal of Diabetology, 11, 8-12.

47. Laamarti, F., Badawi, H.F., Ding, Y., Arafsha, F., Hafidh, B. et al. (2020). An ISO/IEEE 11073 standardized digital twin framework for health and well-being in smart cities. IEEE Access, 8, 105950-105961.

48. Bagaria, N., Laamarti, F., Badawi, H.F., Albraikan, A., Velazquez, R.A. et al. (2020). Health 4.0: Digital twins for health and well-being. *In:* El Saddik, A., Hossain, M., Kantarci, B. (eds). Connected Health in Smart Cities. Springer, Cham.

49. Teng, S.Y., Touš, M., Leong, W.D., How, B.S., Lam, H.L. et al. (2021). Recent advances on industrial data-driven energy savings: Digital twins and infrastructures. Renewable & Sustainable Energy Reviews, 135, 110208.

50. Shabalov, M.Y., Zhukovskiy, Y.L., Buldysko, A., Gil, B., Starshaia, V.V. et al. (2021). The influence of technological changes in energy efficiency on the infrastructure deterioration in the energy sector. Energy Reports, 7, 2664-2680.

51. Monteiro, A.C.B., Padilha, R.F., Estrela, V.V., Fernandes, S.R., Khelassi, A. et al. (2020). UAV-CPSs as a test bed for new technologies and a primer to Industry 5.0. *In:* Imaging and Sensing for Unmanned Aircraft Systems, 2(1), 1-22. IET, London, UK.

52. Estrela, V.V., Saotome, O., Loschi, H.J., Hemanth, D.J., Farfan, W.S. et al. (2018). Emergency response cyber-physical framework for landslide avoidance with sustainable electronics. Technologies, MDPI, 6(2), 42.

53. Laghari, A., Khan, A., He, H., Estrela, V.V., Razmjooy, N. et al. (2020). Quality of experience (QoE) and quality of service (QoS) in UAV systems. doi: 10.1049/pbce120g_ch10

54. Marinho, C.E., Estrela, V.V., Loschi, H.J., Razmjooy, N., Herrmann, A.E. et al. (2019). A model for medical staff idleness minimization. *In:* Iano, Y. et al. (eds). Proceedings of the 4th Brazilian Technology Symposium (BTSym'18). BTSym 2018. Smart Innovation, Systems and Technologies, vol. 140.

55. Khelassi, A. and Estrela, V.V. (2020). Advances in multidisciplinary medical technologies – Engineering, modeling and findings. Proc. International Workshop on Medical Technologies 2019 (ICHSMT 2019), Springer Nature, Zurich, Switzerland.

56. Lutze, R. (2020). Digital twin based software design in ehealth – A new development approach for health/medical software products. 2020 IEEE Int'l Conf. on Eng., Technology and Innovation (ICE/ITMC), 1-9.

57. Abdoune, F., Nouiri, M., Castagna, P. and Cardin, O. (2020). Toward digital twin for cyber physical production systems maintenance: Observation framework based on artificial intelligence techniques. Service Oriented, Holonic and Multi-Agent Manufacturing Systems for Industry of the Future, 952, 123-134.

58. Monteiro, A.C.B., França, R.P., Estrela, V.V., Razmjooy, N., Iano, Y. et al. (2021). Metaheuristics applied to blood image analysis. *In:* Razmjooy, N. et al. (eds). Metaheuristics and Optimization in Computer and Electrical Engineering. Lecture Notes in Electrical Engineering, vol. 696. Springer, Cham.

59. Deshpande, A., Razmjooy, N. and Estrela, V.V. (2021). Introduction to computational intelligence and super-resolution. *In:* Deshpande, A. et al. (eds). Computational Intelligence Methods for Super-Resolution in Image Processing Applications. Springer, Cham, Switzerland.

60. Chaabane, L., Khelassi, A., Terziev, A., Andreopoulos, N., Jesus, M.A. et al. (2021). Particle swarm optimization with tabu search algorithm (PSO-TS) applied to multiple sequence alignment problem. *In:* Khelassi, A. and Estrela, V.V. (eds). Advances in Multidisciplinary Medical Technologies – Engineering, Modeling and Findings. Springer, Springer, Cham, Switzerland.

61. Kalantari, S., Ramezani, M., Madadi, A. and Estrela, V.V. (2021). Reduction AWGN from digital images using a new local optimal low-rank approximation method. *In:* Iano, Y. et al. (eds). Proc. 5th Brazilian Technology Symposium (BTSym 2019). Smart Innovation, Systems and Technologies, vol. 201. Springer, Cham.

62. Deshpande, A., Estrela, V.V. and Patavardhan, P. (2021). The DCT-CNN-ResNet50 architecture to classify brain tumours with super-resolution, convolutional neural network, and the ResNet50. Neuroscience Informatics, 1(4), 100013, ISSN 2772-5286.

63. Hemanth, J. and Estrela, V.V. (2017). Deep learning for image processing applications. Advances in Parallel Computing, vol. 31, IOS Press, Amsterdam, Netherlands.

64. Hasselgren, A., Hanssen Rensaa, J., Kralevska, K., Gligoroski, D., Faxvaag, A. et al. (2021). Blockchain for increased trust in virtual health care: Proof-of-concept study. Journal of Medical Internet Research, 23.

65. Kanna, K., Estrela, V.V. and Rodrigues, J.J.P.C. (2021). Cyber Security and Digital Forensics. Proc. ICCSDF 2021, Springer Nature, Zurich, Switzerland.

66. Zhang, P., Walker, M.A., White, J., Schmidt, D.C., Lenz, G. et al. (2017). Metrics for assessing blockchain-based healthcare decentralized apps. Proc. 2017 IEEE 19th International Conference on e-Health Networking, Applications and Services (Healthcom), 1-4.

67. Rensaa, J.H., Gligoroski, D., Kralevska, K., Hasselgren, A., Faxvaag, A. et al. (2020). VerifyMed – A blockchain platform for transparent trust in virtualized healthcare: Proof-of-concept. Proceedings of the 2020 2nd International Electronics Communication Conference.

68. Hasselgren, A., Kralevska, K., Gligoroski, D., Pedersen, S.A., Faxvaag, A. et al. (2020). Blockchain in healthcare and health sciences – A scoping review. International J. Medical Informatics, 134, 104040.

69. Kuo, T., Rojas, H.Z. and Ohno-Machado, L. (2019). Comparison of blockchain platforms: A systematic review and healthcare examples. Journal of the American Medical Informatics Association: JAMIA, 26, 462-478.

70. Raikwar, M., Gligoroski, D. and Kralevska, K. (2019). SoK of used cryptography in Blockchain. IEEE Access, 7, 148550-148575.

71. Sakallaris, B.R., Miller, W.L., Saper, R.B., Kreitzer, M.J., Jonas, W.B et al. (2016). Meeting the challenge of a more person-centered future for US healthcare. Global Advances in Health and Medicine, 5, 51-60.

72. Bahri, L. and Girdzijauskas, S. (2018). When Trust Saves Energy: A Reference Framework for Proof of Trust (PoT) Blockchains. Companion Proceedings of The Web Conference 2018.

73. Guo, S., Guo, X., Zhang, X. and Vogel, D.R. (2018). Doctor-patient relationship strength's impact in an online healthcare community. Information Technology for Development, 24, 279-300.

74. Chang, Y., Hsu, P., Wang, Y. and Chang, P. (2019). Integration of online and offline health services: The role of doctor-patient online interaction. Patient Education and Counseling, 102(10), 1905-1910.

75. Ricci, A., Croatti, A., Mariani, S., Montagna, S., Picone, M. et al. (2022). Web of digital twins. ACM Trans. on Internet Techn. (TOIT), Feb., https://doi.org/10.1145/3507909

76. Herrgårdh, T., Hunter, E., Tunedal, K., Örman, H., Amann, J. et al. (2022). Digital twins and hybrid modelling for simulation of physiological variables and stroke risk. bioRxiv.

77. Silfvergren, O., Simonsson, C., Ekstedt, M., Lundberg, P., Gennemark, P. et al. (2021). Digital twin predicting diet response before and after long-term fasting. bioRxiv.

78. Herrgårdh, T., Madai, V.I., Kelleher, J.D., Magnusson, R., Gustafsson, M. et al. (2021). Hybrid modelling for stroke care: Review and suggestions of new approaches for risk assessment and simulation of scenarios. NeuroImage: Clinical, 31.

79. Herrgårdh, T., Li, H., Nyman, E. and Cedersund, G. (2021). An updated organ-based multi-level model for glucose homeostasis: Organ distributions, timing, and impact of blood flow. Frontiers in Physiology, 12.

80. Ha, J. and Sherman, A.S. (2020). Type 2 Diabetes: One disease, many pathways. Am. J. of Physiology, Endocrin, and Metabolism, 319(2), E410-E426.

81. Huang, Y., Li, W., Macheret, F., Gabriel, R.A., Ohno-Machado, L. et al. (2020). A tutorial on calibration measurements and calibration models for clinical prediction models. Journal of the American Medical Informatics Association: JAMIA, 27, 621-633.

82. Yuan, B., Shen, C., Luna, A., Korkut, A., Marks, D.S. et al. (2020). CellBox: Interpretable machine learning for perturbation biology with application to the design of cancer combination therapy. Cell Systems, 12(2), P128-140.E4.

83. Shabaz, M., Sharma, A., Ajrawi, S.A. and Estrela, V.V. (2022). Multimedia-based emerging technologies and data analytics for Neuroscience as a Service (NaaS). Neuroscience Informatics, 2(3), 100067. Elsevier.

84. Sujith, A., Sajja, G.S., Mahalakshmi, V., Nuhmani, S., Balaji, P. et al. (2021). Systematic review of smart health monitoring using deep learning and artificial intelligence. Neuroscience Informatics, 2(3), 100028. Elsevier.

85. Akundi, A., Euresti, D., Luna, S., Ankobiah, W., Lopes, A. et al. (2022). State of Industry 5.0 – Analysis and Identification of Current Research Trends. Applied Syst. Innov., 5(1), 27, https://doi.org/10.3390/asi5010027

Part III
Advanced Applications Using AI

Medical Visual Theragnostic Systems Using Artificial Intelligence (AI) – Principles and Perspectives

V.V. Estrela[1] [0000-0002-4465-7691], M.A. de Jesus[1] [0000-0001-6428-9438], Aline C. Intorne[2,3] [0000-0001-8015-6926], Kate K.S. Batista[4] [0000-0002-5861-4633], Anand Deshpande[5] [0000-0002-1500-0981], Fuqian Shi[6] [0000-0003-4245-5727], Asif Ali Laghari[7] [0000-0001-5831-5943], Abdullah A. Khan[7] [0000-0003-2838-7641], L.P. Oliveira[8] [0000-0002-3375-3346]

[1] Department of Telecommunications, Federal Fluminense University (UFF), RJ, 24220-900, Brazil, vania.estrela.phd@ieee.org, majesus1977br@gmail.com

[2] Laboratory of Physiology and Biochemistry of Microorganisms, Universidade Estadual do Norte Fluminense Darcy Ribeiro, Campos dos Goytacazes, RJ, 28013-602, Brazil

[3] Laboratory of Chemistry and Biology, Instituto Federal de Educação, Ciência e Tecnologia do Rio de Janeiro, Volta Redonda, RJ, 27213-100, Brazil, aline.intorne@ifrj.edu.br

[4] Fundacao Oswaldo Cruz, FIOCRUZ, Rio de Janeiro, RJ, Brazil, katekbatista@gmail.com

[5] Electronics and Communication Engineering, Angadi Institute of Technology and Management, Belagavi, India, deshpande.anandb@gmail.com

[6] Rutgers Cancer Institute of New Jersey, United States, shifuqian@gmail.com

[7] Faculty of Computer Science, Sindh Madressatul Islam University, Karachi (74000), Sindh, Pakistan, asif.laghari@smiu.edu.pk, abdullah.khan0076@gmail.com

[8] IFPB Campus Joao Pessoa, Av. Primeiro de Maio, 720, Jaguaribe, Joao Pessoa, PB, Brazil, oliveira.ifpb@gmail.com

1. Introduction

Disease theragnostics (DT) of imageries plays a vital role, involving any physical or mental cause or circumstance leading to distress, illness, dysfunction, or, ultimately, a human being's passing. Theragnostics comprise tactics combining therapeutics with diagnostics. Diagnosis spots a disease from its symptoms to settling on its pathology (Figure 1). Medical data (MD) from an individual's physical examination and history constitutes the facts required for DT. Often, at least one diagnostic practice like medical tests occurs during this procedure.

A physician will perform several steps to collect as much material as possible to develop a honest diagnosis. DT is a challenging, tiresome, and intricate procedure that impacts medical professionals before implementing actions. To minimize DT

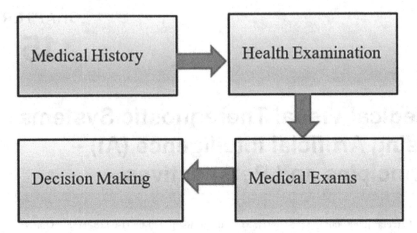

Figure 1. Block diagram of the diagnosis process

uncertainty, experts gather empirical data to discover a patient's disease. Still, the correct treatment may be postponed or missed with grave health concerns due to an incorrect diagnosis. Unfortunately, no doctor knows all medical domains. Several Artificial Intelligence (AI) practices have aided in diagnosing illnesses accurately. They entail three concepts:

(i) Machine Learning (ML): This algorithm category can enrich outputs automatically leaning on experience and data usage. e.g., the simple k-nearest neighbors (KNN) procedure is a supervised algorithm for classification and regression, easily implemented and understood, whose major caveat is that it evolves considerably slower as data size augments.

(ii) Metaheuristics: Sophisticated problem-independent sets of rules that implement heuristic optimization procedures. Some metaheuristic schemes find, spawn, or choose a heuristic (aka, partial exploration procedure) that yields a satisfactorily good solution according to some metrics to an optimization problem, principally with incomplete or imperfect datasets or limited computation power. They sample a solution subset that is otherwise excessively large to permit exhaustive searches, exploiting relatively few problem assumptions. Genetic algorithms (Gas) exemplify this class.

(iii) Deep Learning (DL): These strategies comprise an extensive ML family relying on Artificial Neural Networks (ANNs) to learn in an unsupervised, supervised, or semi-supervised fashion. DL architectures include Convolutional Neural Networks (CNNs), Autoencoders (AEs), Deep Belief Networks (DBNs), Deep Reinforcement Learning (DRL), Deep Neural Networks (DNNs), in addition to Recurrent Neural Networks (RNNs). They deliver results akin to and sometimes outdoing human professional performance. Data treatment in addition to distributed communication nodes emerges in biological structures and inspired ANNs, which have a tendency to be static and symbolic, unlike natural brain neurons that are dynamic (plastic), analog living entities.

Hence, automatic DT can enhance human knowledge and accuracy [1, 2]. A properly designed Decision Support System (DSS) attains accurate results from the analysis process inexpensively. Disease classification depends upon various parameters, and it is complex for human professionals, albeit AI would help perceive and handle such cases [3-5] for automatic training and learning. Realizing possibilities and forecasts about health issues is tiresome for medics. In some cases, ANN delivers healthcare decisions fast enough to collect data, understand them, and detect pieces playing crucial prediction roles [6, 7]. DL assists specialists in examining any illness with better health decisions. DL benefits occur in different fields viz. medical imaging, drug discovery, and genomics [8]. This text primarily focuses on metaheuristics, ML, and DL. A major DL healthcare trend is breast cancer (BC) detection, where the accuracy of automatic systems at least rivals that of a radiologist. Likewise, AI trains a framework continuously, creating more accurate outcomes than before.

The Internet of Medical Things (IoMT) can benefit from AI, which enables gathering MD using IoT-connected medical devices. AI-based software can detect a disease before its manifestation by detecting its symptoms as in Figure 1. NNs can be trained to discover lung cancer, BC, and stroke faster than a trained specialist. Various AI algorithms help doctors scrutinize images from Magnetic Resonance Images (MRIs), X-rays, and Computed Tomography (CT) scans to spot specific diseases by analyzing visual signs. DT is a complicated and multifaceted process since some conditions have similar symptoms. Medical expert systems can aid physicians in diagnosing patients more accurately and specifying the most appropriate treatment. AI tools not only help detect illnesses but can also label them as fatal diseases or not. Present-day AI helps health specialists with disease management and surgical robots that accomplish highly intricate operations. This chapter's main contributions are

1. How the present element descriptions affect disease detection (DD) outbreaks
2. AI techniques for DT
3. A thorough analysis of DT systems.

Sections 2, 3, and 4 present DT systems using ML, metaheuristics, and DL algorithms, respectively. AI instance studies come into view in section 5. Section 6 reviews some important points, research findings, discussion, as well as future research, while Section 7 completes this review.

2. DT via Machine Learning

An ML procedure learns and completes tasks by means of supervised learning (SL), which involves professional human guidance with an initial awareness about both inputs and fallouts. SL contrasts with unsupervised learning (UL), necessitating very little human intercession or domain expert's service without knowing the effects. After training, a machine learns a model, i.e., creating pattern models to distinguish two or more objects. ML assists the experts in handling large and complicated MD and probing the results for further research. Therefore, applying ML in healthcare increases patient trust in healthcare to predict disease. ML algorithms can detect the early disease stages before occurring or coming to be dangerous to someone.

The popularity of ML algorithms in different areas produced more correct outcomes than usual ways with little raw data processing. ML algorithms, for illustration, KNN, Decision trees, Support Vector Machines (SVMs), Multilayer perceptrons (MPs), Bayes' classifiers, ensemble classifiers, among others, help determine various ailments with rapid disease prediction and high accuracy. The learning process initiates with observations, samples, direct experience, or knowledge. Next, algorithms look for MD patterns to make better decisions to permit the architecture to learn without human interference and regulate responses accordingly [8-11]. AI can support a medical expert and even give a more accurate diagnosis. The disease forecast plays a vital role in ML. Next, examples of how ML predicts various disease types appear. An automated survey for healthcare-associated infections in [8-11] describes

(i) In what way do automatic ML surveillance systems augment performance and reliability in contrast to a manual investigation,
(ii) How regression models can increase the surveillance program's efficiency and sensitivity, and
(iii) Some difficulties regarding post-discharge monitoring, therapy adjustment, and device utilization quantification, among other factors.

Bronchiolitis (lung infection type) is commonly seen in younger kids and infants. The review provided some predictive modeling insights and reported how ML could overcome the predictive modeling restrictions.

Sepsis happens due to one's body's response to infection, which triggers inflammation that simultaneously results in multiple organ failures. A systematic review can be found in [11], showing current sepsis detection trends in healthcare facilities, various scores for sepsis detection/screening tools, and their pros and cons. Lastly, Electronic Health Records (EHRs) and biomarkers helped predict sepsis considerably. The study from [12] reported some drawbacks in

(i) Routine blood culture testing,
(ii) Suitable automatic methods for seven molecular technologies utilizing blood samples,
(iii) Discussing the various present/future trends, and
(iv) Evaluating the impact of combining ML with EHRs before concluding that merging multiple technologies can ameliorate detection and minimize the wrong antibiotic prescription risk.

A DSS to detect kidney disease appears in [13], relating the performance of the SVM and KNN classifiers based on accuracy, precision, and execution time for both algorithms, with the KNN working better than the SVM. The study in [14] classified outcomes by performing a comparative breakdown employing KNN, Logistic Regression (LR), SVM, and Decision Tree classifiers to diagnose kidney disease. Their performances have been compared with each other to pick the best deployment (the SVM method excelled over the others).

Recently, ML has detected BC efficiently. The structure from [15] concentrated on developing a model for BC diagnosis based on the mined tumor features. The K-means algorithm identified the hidden designs of non-threatening and malignant tumors to remove valuable data and make diagnoses. Afterward, SVM classified the incoming tumors. Using the BC dataset, a comparative performance-based analysis of methods viz. SVM, KNNs, and Decision Tree appear in [16] to appraise the data classifying data accuracy corresponding to each algorithm for exactness, precision, and sensitivity. Outcomes from those procedures exposed the SVM as possessing the highest accuracy.

Arthritis reduces people's quality of life and its premature detection is necessary. A system and a dataset to categorize patients with arthritis employing features such as identity, treatment, gender, and age via a CART algorithm are in [17]. Orange and WEKA tools comprise a Parkinson's system for experimentation analysis, classification, and evaluation [18] using Random Forest Classification, SVM, and Naïve Bayes. A supervised ML process distinguished Parkinson's disease and Progressive Supranuclear Palsy in patients (PSP) [19], setting the pathologies apart.

Concerning cancer in liver cells, the model for lung images from [20, 21] distinguishes normal or dangerous categories with high accuracy results. Through EHR records, ML can predict innumerable diseases. ML has granted computational systems new-fangled abilities via these stages [22] (Figure 4):

1. MD Collection: This is a critical step. Quality and quantity affect the overall system performance.
2. MD Preparation or Image Preprocessing (IPP) or Cleaning: This stage treats crude data to simplify decision-making.
3. Model Choice: A model is assigned to preprocessed data, i.e., one decides on an apt algorithm for the task.
4. Model Training: Supervised learning with ML trains a model increasing the accuracy of decision-making or predictions.
5. Model Evaluation: Metrics help appraise the model along with defined objectives.
6. Parameter Tuning: It includes training steps, performance evaluation, outcome analyses, learning rate, initialization values, probability distributions, and so on.
7. Predictions: It is paramount to predict some outcomes using the test data set to adequately develop a model for the real world. If the result matches domain expert opinions, the model makes useful predictions.

The basic steps for DT using ML are in [23-25]

1. Gather test data with patient minutiae.
2. The feature extraction module picks traits useful for DT prediction;
3. Next, select attributes, then choose and process the dataset;
4. Various classification algorithms can preprocess datasets to evaluate DT accuracy; and
5. One may compare different classifier performances to select the highest accuracy classifier.

ML extracts features with specialist assistance to minimize data complications and develop easily distinctive ML algorithm patterns. However, DL can mine features without human intervention, providing accurate testing data while eliminating human experts for feature extraction.

3. DT by Metaheuristics

Nature-inspired algorithms are a popular subclass of metaheuristic algorithms that are frequently employed to solve high-dimensional and difficult optimization issues. They are general-purpose, quick, assumption-free, effective, and simple to implement for solving a wide variety of difficult optimization problems involving an extraordinarily large collection of variables. Numerous codes are publicly available on plentiful websites.

Particle Swarm Optimization (PSO), Differential Evolution (DE), Gray Wolf (GW), and Cuckoo Search [25-29] are just a few notable nature-inspired examples. Each algorithm is motivated differently by Mother Nature and operates differently. Each algorithm is typically composed of a few tuning parameters and a limited number of random components. Each process updates its trajectory by employing a couple of equations that mimic natural phenomena or an animal's behavior [30-33].

PSO creates the illusion of a bird swarm flying and seeking food. Each bird has its own perception of where food is located (local optimum), but they communicate with one another and within a group to determine where food is located (global optimum). Each bird flies toward it without totally abandoning its preconceived notion of where food is located (local optimum) [26]. These algorithms frequently lack rigorous convergence proofs and theoretical characteristics. They remain popular, however, since they frequently can find an optimal or nearly optimal resolution to a wide variety of optimization problems.

Medical scientists have increasingly relied on and continue to rely on metaheuristics to solve a variety of optimization-related medical challenges. A fairly prevalent issue is classifying individuals into distinct groups of illness progression based on their baseline data. Assume one wishes to determine if a patient's ailment will remain stable over some months or whether the patient's condition will improve or deteriorate. Such difficulties are difficult to address since the dataset is huge and a large number of alternative explanatory factors may be plausible for properly forecasting outcomes. The task, therefore, becomes one of selecting a limited subset of characteristics that offers the best-desired outcome estimate across the whole dataset (Figure 2) [34-36].

Hybridized algorithms aiming at getting better performance are trendy and becoming gradually more prevalent [37-39]. Hybrid algorithms associate techniques to increase search capability by using the unique qualities of the two algorithms, with the goal of the hybridized version outperforming the individual algorithms. There may be two or more practices involved, and they may employ a combination of metaheuristic and deterministic methods.

Metaheuristic-based optimization issues are no magic potion. Optimizing parameters for rapid convergence and assuring algorithm convergence to the theoretical global optimum are prominent problems. Both issues remain important areas of healthcare study, and significant advancements have been made [40, 41].

4. DT by Deep Learning

While ML approaches break down a problem into smaller discrete components and

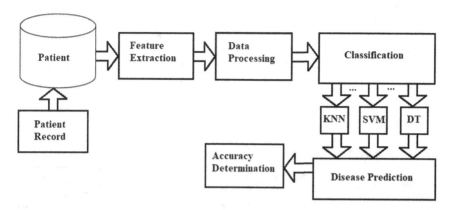

Figure 2. AI system for theragnostics

then combine the results, DL solves the problem in its entirety. In healthcare, DL outperforms standard ML models [42].

DL hinges on Deep Neural Network (DNN) models, whose primary component is the neuron, i.e., a human brain simulation. A neuron accepts several input signals, weights them, and generates an output [43]. AANs and DLs may be distinguished by the quantity of hidden layers, and in what way they interrelate, and their aptitude to get meaningful output from the inputs. By and large, ANNs are composed of three distinct layers and extract well-structured data to realize a specific task. Otherwise, in DL, the patient's evaluation is determined by the disease type. While DT employs a variety of instruments and approaches, a degree of inaccuracy and ambiguity continues throughout the diagnostic process.

Additionally, machine learning has limitations in that it evaluates just qualities when determining illnesses. The typical method of picking features for illness prediction produces incorrect findings. In contrast to ML, DL can extract the most influential properties from a database, allowing precise illness prediction [44, 45].

Skin illnesses may offer crucial indications about interior ailments. Early skin disease identification is vital to prevent future dermatological disorders. The work in [46] identified various skin conditions using Deep CNNs (DCNNs). Using photos from the Dermnet and OLE datasets, this system can train the CNN and appraise fallouts with top accuracy. In [47], skin cancer detection relied on an SVM model recognizing the affected skin portion and CNN extracting characteristics. The CNN trains the model to categorize skin images as MD with substantial enhancement and accuracy compared to earlier ones. When chronic disorders viz BC are identified with DL, they acquire greater accuracy than other strategies. A CAD strategy for BC diagnosis occurs in [48]. A DBN, where a BP supervised phase utilizing the Levenberg–Marquardt (LM) algorithm with weights set through the deep network path follows the unsupervised phase. Another BC CNN diagnosis [49] has been tested through mammographies. Their results indicated the efficiency of DL for BC diagnosis in mammographies [47].

A deeper multilayer perceptron augmented a DNN to identify heart disease operated as a model that categorized data gotten from the training set [50]. This

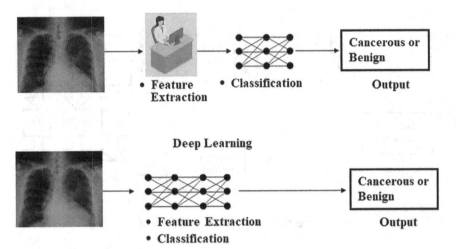

Figure 3. Machine learning (human performed feature extraction) and deep learning (with automatic feature extraction) differences

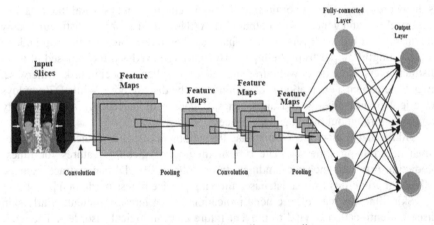

Figure 4. Deep processing to diagnose a disease

study employed test data from a patient with coronary disease. Three DL algorithms using CNN, DBNs, and SDAE to detect lung cancer evaluated their performance in the lungs dataset [51].

COVID-19 infection causes fever, coughing, and breathing difficulties. With more instances and fewer test kits, detecting COVID-19 gets more challenging. Alternatives like X-rays are required here. COVID-19 detection using AI X-rays [52, 53]. DL was part of a framework containing data augmentation, preprocessing, with stage-I/stage-II deep network models. The model was applied to 1215 X-ray pictures. The model distinguishes between induced pneumonia, bacterial pneumonia, and normal/healthy persons. Then, pictures with viral pneumonia move to step 2 for COVID-19 identification, which has obtained high accuracy. Overall, this model's findings were accurate, trustworthy, and speedy [80]. The COVID-19 illness is frequently misdiagnosed as a lung infection. Consequently, it is paramount to diagnose rapidly using different deep models when employing chest X-ray pictures [54]. For this investigation, a trained DNN analyzed upper body CT scans to spot COVID 19.

When a brain hemorrhage occurs, oxygen cannot permeate the brain cells, and they end up dying [55]. Likewise, a novel CNN based on ResNet identifies and forecasts brain bleeding [56] with excellent accuracy. As previously stated, the classic automated diagnostic methodology would include a ML system in which clinical personnel manually retrieve features from diagnosis reports. Yet, pulling out features from colossal data volumes data might be challenging at times [10, 57, 58]. As a byproduct, those developments were deficient in terms of precision and efficiency.

The lack of critical information significantly impairs deep learning models. Presently, there is no prediction methodology to assess EHRs, limiting computerized diagnostic accuracy. If the system does not collect reliable data, the model will be unable to detect an illness, making accurate prediction difficult . This issue was addressed by an effective DL model for the valid, early identification of many disorders [42, 59]. Typically, when a Deep CNN model detects illnesses, each layer inside the CNN filters the raw visual data to produce a certain pattern. The early layers capture important elements as diagonal lines, while successive layers improve detail by grouping them into useful features. The last layer functions similarly to a conventional NN, and the network remains fully linked [43, 44]. Then, it combines specific characteristics of the disease, including distinct symptoms, and conducts disease prediction. The efforts in [59] and [60] corrected it by addressing the issue of incomplete data or values. Following that, a DL model trained on the processed data and exhibited efficiency.

5. Case Study: Fuzzy Logic

Fuzzy Logic (FL) is a metaheuristic that can uncover potentially fatal illnesses such as cancer and provides dynamic solutions to complex topics. FL is a dependable tool for decision-support systems such as expert or pattern categorization systems [9, 61-63]. FL is critical in the medical evaluation process by providing complete examination reports. These frameworks give a quick and simple technique for clinical evaluation and are particularly useful when an expert or clinical specialist is unavailable. The outcomes are contingent upon the knowledge bases. Numerous clinical diagnostic methods are dependent on the used fuzzy set model [67]. Occasionally, one encounters a situation in which one is unsure if the state is valid or invalid; FL gives reasoning for such cases, as seen in Figure 2. It is a method based on rules. In healthcare, the Fuzzy Rule-Based System (FRBS) is a regularly used technology derived from Fuzzy Inference Systems (FIS). FRBS portrays information using IF-THEN rules [65]. FIS and FDSS are identified as the most often used medical procedures [66]. FL's primary characteristic is that it mitigates the influence of errors and uncertainties. Although there is no reasoning for the absolute valid and invalid values, a FL system contains an intermediate value that is partially true and partially false.

FL has steadily gained popularity in diagnostics based on several factors, e.g., coronary disease destroys or restricts veins in the heart, resulting in less oxygen to the organs. Cardiologic illnesses such as heart failure, arterial blockage, heart attack, and stroke are common. FL is always evolving to differentiate patients worldwide with fresh AI approaches (Figure 5).

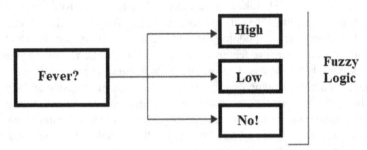

Figure 5. Process of fuzzy logic

Coronary disease detection can reach a level similar to a doctor's opinion for high/low cardiac risk with a neuron-fuzzy system [67]. A cardiovascular arrhythmia framework which relies on fuzzy classifiers to distinguish the precise electroencephalogram (EEG) point by applying fuzzy network rules appears in [68]. Their system reduced the total ECG signal processing time by a sequence of samples without any indispensable loss. ECG signals are cleaned by the framework and clustered by the Gustafson–Kassel fuzzy algorithm for subsequent classification and correlation. This study suggested easy detection of common cardio diseases similar to myocardial infarct, coronary arterial complications, and angina with better diagnosis (DD) for Pulse Pressure Variation than other systems.

Ebola fuzzy clinical informatics schemes helped analyze the Ebola Virus Disease (EVD) exploiting FL as an inference engine relying on Root Sum Square and a collection of rules, building a knowledge base with a great performance [69].

Brain diseases make a person lose reasoning/memory, alter personality and minor seizures, and convulsing are common symptoms, e.g., stroke, Brain Tumors (BTs), Alzheimer's disease that can cause vision loss, weakness, paralysis, and more. [70]. e.g., early BT detection is essential to start the treatment using MRI images combined with Fuzzy C means clustering with Genetic Algorithms (GAs) and Particle Swarm Optimization (PSO) [71] to fragment suspicious structures. Another representation treats a brain problem detection system employing fuzzy KNN (FKNN) or a Support Vector Machine (SVM) for Parkinson's disease [72]. A comparative experimental analysis between SVM and FKNN disclosed that the FKNN outdid the SVM classifier. Different diseases like diabetes, heart maladies, neurological diseases, cancer, thyroid disorders, and asthma were diagnosed by various ANNs. The Neuro-Fuzzy (NF) model from [73] diagnoses adult asthma properly. The dataset samples came from multiple hospitals using 3 AI algorithms: (1) ANN using Self Organizing Maps (SOM), (2) ANN with Learning Vector Quantization (LVQ), along with (3) ANN with Backpropagation (BP) along with a NF to get accurate results. Fuzzy inference classifies MD for DD.

The Fuzzy Omega algorithm automatically detects BC lesions [74] by examining elements like the outline, size, as well as density, with Bi-Rads classification for nodules and calcifications. The work in [75] is for early diagnosis with an information-based BC architecture (that can be used as a DSS) employing Expectation-Maximization (EM) for MD clustering. At the same time, classification relies on Fuzzy rules and Regression Trees. Hepatic sicknesses can partially stop the liver with the majority of liver ailment factors due to alcohol or heredity. The most eminent is the fatty liver. An expert system with FL diagnoses liver disease by recognizing risk factors, predicting cirrhosis, and avoiding liver biopsy [76].

Dental diseases can be investigated and mapped with FL. In [77], periodontal disease used 164 fuzzy rules with the prime goal to anticipate early dental disease recognition. The Dental Diagnosis System (DDS) finds dental problems depending on hybrid fragmentation, classification, and decision-making [78]. FL can handle semantic data and outcomes utilizing probabilities of medical findings [79] in diagnosis processes. Human thinking and decision-making helped develop a proof-based theory to ameliorate diagnosis [80]. Since fuzzy procedures are feasible in healthcare to display uncertainty, they have various applications as per the illness and targets [81]. The healthcare framework has two significant parts: symptoms (inputs) and the disorder as output. Commonly, the FL DD process is four-fold (Figure 3):

(i) **Fuzzifier:** Fuzzification changes (maps) a crisp observed input value to the fuzzy set.

(ii) **Inference engine:** It receives and processes the fuzzy value by mimicking the knowledge base rules.

(iii) **Knowledge base:** This is the central FL system component. The overall fuzzy system hinges on the knowledge base. It consists of rules besides structured and unstructured data from a database.

(iv) **Defuzzifier:** It converts the inference engine output into crisp logic. A fuzzy value feeds the defuzzification that maps a fuzzy value into a crisp value.

FL portrays intelligent behavior by forming fuzzy categories of some parameters whose rules and criteria are comprehensible by humans (Figure 6). A domain expert

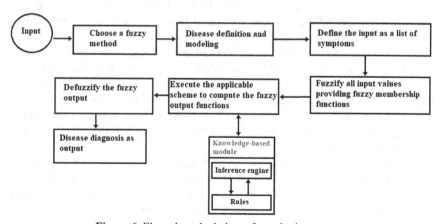

Figure 6. Flow chart depicting a fuzzy logic process

defines these fuzzy rules and classes mostly. Hence, FL entails a great deal of human intercession. The data processing can use FL with statistical models to yield good performance results.

6. Discussions and Future Research

AI algorithms can contribute significantly to diagnostic systems. Nonetheless, the maximum AI potential for mining comes from novel insights about associated MD. AI-built diagnostics must allude to some major concerns as follows.

6.1. Preprocessing and Data Augmentation

Resizing, orienting, and color adjustments are examples of image preprocessing (IPP) activities to alter images to create new versions of the same material. Thus, a model may be trained by randomly rotating, brightening, or resizing imagery to assess how an image topic looks under diverse contexts [82-85]. DA manipulations are IPP forms, yet DA only works with training data, unlike IPP steps. A Data Augmentation (DA) change may sometimes function as an IPP step. If a dataset has only low contrast images, then it may need a specific amount of contrast modification for each to improve performance. This IPP phase is for training and testing images. Presume, however, that the training data does not portray all the phenomena data, then a continuous contrast tuning is less certain to work in the situation. Instead, altering visual contrast randomly during training may boost generalization. One must first understand the current circumstances to make knowledgeable IPP and DA judgments. IPP cleans visual data for model input. For connected CNN layers, all images must have the same sized arrays. IPP may also accelerate model training and inference. Reducing input image size increases model training time without compromising model performance.

A ML model may generate masks and execute part of it to return the full image. DA generates new training data from old. It is difficult to capture every possible real-world scenario. To learn from a greater variety of possibilities, generalize current training data. A DL model will overfit the test data. Changing the input photographs provides more useful training examples. The best IPP and DA techniques must be chosen to comprehend the problem, data collection, and the environment, which is not the case at all times to enable informed choices.

While image resizing may seem straightforward, there are several factors to ponder. Few technologies record square images completely, just like many model architectures need. To render a square picture, either expand its dimensions or maintain its aspect ratio constant while providing additional pixels to the image. Also, input images may be differently sized, with some smaller than planned. Keeping scale is often unnecessary, and down sampling huge imagery to smaller ones is frequently safer.

A captured image has information that informs machines how to display it relative to its storage. Inconsistent EXIF data processing has long troubled developers everywhere. This also applies to models, like when creating bounding boxes for an image and the model captures it in another direction. So, one has trained the model wrong.

Color alterations exemplify image transformations influencing all images (during training and testing) or in DA. Gray scaling is a color alteration that affects all images. While some like stronger intensity variations, others prefer to see the model's color. However, grayscale representations may perform faster. Color photos are kept as RGB values, but grayscale images are stored in a black-to-white range. For CNNs, a model needs just one matrix per picture, not three. Grayscale is simple but unsuitable when the condition demands color (like outlining a read line on veins using a white or green color).

A model must know that an item is not always read from left to right or up to down when it is randomly mirrored. In order-dependent circumstances, flipping is nonsensical. Flipping most real-world objects improves performance.

When a model is working on a mobile application, gyrating an image is vital. Rotating pictures can cause dead edge pixels and requires trigonometry to depict bounding boxes. In contrast to snapshots, where the image content is constantly fixed, rotation is useful when an item has several orientations relative to the acquired photos.

If a model performs in varied lighting conditions, adjusting the image intensity is critical looking at the maximum and minimum intensities. Fortunately, intensity is also intuitive. The model can assess this need and change the brightness accordingly.

Making imageries noisier is simple. Salt-and-Pepper (S&P) noise is a typical technique in which picture pixels are randomly blacked out. An overfitting model may assist reduce training performance by intentionally adding noise. S&P noise can significantly minimize model overfitting on imaging artifacts.

6.2. Explainable Diagnosis

AI simulations are frequently criticized for their internal ambiguous decision-making mechanisms. In addition, there is a concern with incorporating unambiguousness into the actions of statistical black-box AI methods, most notably DL. Apart from answering pattern recognition questions, AI systems should craft causal environmental models that aid in explanation and comprehension. This is especially true when considering AI uses in medical diagnosis. Researchers think it is critical to consider AI that is not explicable [87]. Causality will finally result in a diagnosable condition that encompasses all measures.

6.3. Quality of Training

The performances of ML and DL algorithms fundamentally depend on the readiness of first-rate training models to attain the sought-after diagnostic capability. Moreover, data scarcity can impact them. There exist a number of initiatives to create supplementary annotated information by alternative methods, such as DA and image synthesis. Nonetheless, it is unclear whether they suit AI-based DT [88, 89].

6.4. Clinical Translation

The AI research development for DT is indeed rapid, and feasible, viz. the detection of several cancer metastases [90], brain recognition [91], and identifying retinal diseases. Nevertheless, AI-based system adoption in clinical sites will endure various transformations besides phases with many approaches still to arise [88]. Present investigations focus mainly on optimizing intricate ML model performances while disregarding their explicability. So, health specialists struggle to understand these models and have problems trusting them. Hence, reliable communications between health professionals and AI model experts are also paramount to transforming the AI diagnostic potential into medical practice.

6.5. Medial Data Characteristics

Since mining knowledge requires MD for DT, the information should possess high quality. Besides, the MD volume is usually very high, from several sources, and often comes from real-time sensors. Thus, preserving data quality is challenging. More and more mobile MD sources, and complex applications requiring remote access make the Cloud more viable [92]. Even if various designs have tried to solve Cloud storage issues, none of them can grasp all MD aspects and traits precisely owing to the additional prerequisite to comply with health security policies.

6.6. Standardization and Interoperability

There are countless ways that suppliers can manufacture DT products while combining AI procedures chosen from many potential algorithms. Still, they may not obey standard regulations for friendly interfaces and related protocols across assorted computing platforms, thus prompting interoperability matters. Immediate standardization efforts are required [93] to address system diversity in AI-based medicine and diagnosis.

6.7. Secure Diagnosis

AI tactics, and DL schemes, in particular, are vastly application-specific, where a model trained for diagnosing one ailment might not work fine for another. Algorithms frequently require retraining with respective MD for other conditions; otherwise, the incorrect diagnosis will be inescapable. Also, improper hyperparameters' selections can invoke a large change in the model's performance ensuing in a wrong diagnosis. For example, while supervised learning is deemed stable due to fixed data sets, reinforcement learning is unstable [94-100]. More awareness is required for AI algorithms optimization for particular diagnoses. Another critical secure diagnosis trait is protection from attackers exploiting features from AI procedures to disturb the system. For illustration, an enemy can transmute the training parameters and deceive the DT system to learn the contrary of what it should do. And so, it is vital to investigate the AI algorithms profoundly, reexamine their diagnostic roles, and address the corresponding challenges.

7. Conclusion

AI practices lead to rewarding applications in healthcare. It has turned out to be a hot discussion topic whether AI will in the long run replace human specialists. Still, AI expert systems can assist human doctors in reaching better assessments or even replace human judgment sometimes. Different AI techniques can find relevant evidence from a large MD amount. Also, AI methods are self-learning, error-correcting, and give highly accurate results. This text assesses the impact of AI methods and their reliability to minimize misdiagnoses.

AI in healthcare ameliorates the diagnoses and helps discover illnesses in the early stages. Examples of widely used AI tactics in healthcare are metaheuristics, ML, and DL. Major medical areas reviewed were cancer, cardiology, kidney disease, neurology, and dental disease, using AI diagnostic criteria. AI is not restricted to a specific condition. Still, it can detect any disease or improve the diagnosis process for all diseases, with more than 90% of AI methods reporting a positive impact on DD. The efficiency of detecting disease by AI cannot be overlooked. Another significant finding is that most researchers used MATLAB, Java, Python, R, and C# to design AI architectures. Moreover, AI roles for using sensors-based computing frameworks need investigation [101, 102].

References

1. Kaur, S., Singla, J., Nkenyereye, L., Jha, S., Prashar, D. et al. (2020). Medical diagnostic systems using artificial intelligence (AI) algorithms: Principles and perspectives. IEEE Access, 8, 228049-228069.
2. Choi, E., Bahadori, M.T., Schuetz, A., Stewart, W.F., Sun, J. et al. (2016). Doctor AI: Predicting clinical events via recurrent neural networks. Machine Learning for Healthcare Conference, 301-318.
3. Lee, C.-C. (1990). Fuzzy logic in control systems: Fuzzy logic controller. IEEE Transactions on Systems, Man, and Cybernetics, 20(2), 404-418.
4. Yen, J. and Langari, R. (1999). Fuzzy Logic: Intelligence, Control, and Information, vol. 1. Prentice-Hall, Upper Saddle River, NJ.
5. Beale, H.D., Demuth, H.B. and Hagan, M. (1996). Neural Network Design. PWS, Boston.
6. Weng, C.-H., Huang, T.C.-K. and Han, R.-P. (2016). Disease prediction with different types of neural network classifiers. Telematics and Informatics, 33(2), 277-292.
7. Chen, M., Hao, Y., Hwang, K., Wang, L. and Wang, L. (2017). Disease prediction by machine learning over big data from healthcare communities. IEEE Access, 5, 8869-8879.
8. Betancur, J., Commandeur, F., Motlagh, M., Sharir, T., Einstein, A.J. et al. (2018). Deep learning for prediction of obstructive disease from fast myocardial perfusion SPECT: A multicenter study. JACC: Cardiovascular Imaging, 11(11), 1654-1663.
9. Aras, M.S.M., Ali, F.A., Azis, F.A., Hamid, S.M.S.S.A., Basar, M.F.H.M. et al. (2011). Performances evaluation and comparison of two algorithms for fuzzy logic rice cooking system (MATLAB fuzzy logic toolbox and fuzzytech). Proc. 2011 IEEE Conf. Open Syst., IEEE, 400-405.
10. Zhang, G. (2009). A modified SVM classifier based on RS in medical disease prediction. Proc. 2009 2nd Int'l Symp. Comp. Intell. and Design, vol. 1. IEEE, 144-147.
11. Bhattacharjee, P., Edelson, D.P. and Churpek, M.M. (2017). Identifying patients with sepsis on the hospital wards. Chest, 151(4), 898-907.
12. Sinha, M., Jupe, J., Mack, H., Coleman, T.P., Lawrence, S.M. et al. (2018). Emerging technologies for molecular diagnosis of sepsis. Clinical Microbiology Reviews, 31(2).

13. Sinha, P. and Sinha, P. (2015). Comparative study of chronic kidney disease prediction using KNN and SVM. Int'l J. Eng. Research and Technology, 4(12), 608-612.

14. Charleonnan, A., Fufaung, T., Niyomwong, T., Chokchueypattanakit, W., Suwannawach, S. et al. (2016). Predictive analytics for chronic kidney disease using machine learning techniques. Proc. 2016 Manag. and Inn. Techn. Int'l Conf. (MITicon). IEEE, MIT–80.

15. Zheng, B., Yoon, S.W. and Lam, S.S. (2014). Breast cancer diagnosis based on feature extraction using a hybrid of k-means and support vector machine algorithms. Expert Systems with Applications, 41(4), 1476-1482.

16. Asri, H., Mousannif, H., Al Moatassime, H. and Noel, T. (2016). Using machine learning algorithms for breast cancer risk prediction and diagnosis. Procedia Computer Science, 83, 1064-1069.

17. Bhargava, N., Purohit, R., Sharma, S. and Kumar, A. (2017). Prediction of arthritis using classification and regression tree algorithm. Proc. 2017 2nd Int'l Conf. Comm. and Electronics Systems (ICCES), IEEE, 606-610.

18. Sriram, T.V., Rao, M.V., Narayana, G.S., Kaladhar, D. and Vital, T.P.R. (2013). Intelligent Parkinson disease prediction using machine learning algorithms. Int'l J. Eng. and Innovative Techn. (IJEIT), 3(3), 1568-1572.

19. Salvatore, C., Cerasa, A., Castiglioni, I., Gallivanone, F., Augimeri, A. et al. (2014). Machine learning on brain MRI data for differential diagnosis of Parkinson's disease and progressive supranuclear palsy. J. Neurosc. Meth., 222, 230-237.

20. Pineda, A.L., Ye, Y., Visweswaran, S., Cooper, G.F., Wagner, M.M. et al. (2015). Comparison of machine learning classifiers for influenza detection from emergency department free-text reports. J. Biomed. Inform., 58, 60-69.

21. Dwivedi, S.A., Borse, R. and Yametkar, A.M. (2014). Lung cancer detection and classification by using machine learning and multinomial Bayesian. IOSR J. Electronics and Communication Engineering (IOSR-JECE), 9(1), 69-75.

22. Kononenko, I., Bratko, I. and Kukar, M. (1997). Application of machine learning to medical diagnosis. Machine Learning and Data Mining: Methods and Applications, 389, p. 408.

23. Suzuki, K. (2017). Overview of deep learning in medical imaging. Radiological Physics and Technology, 10(3), 257-273.

24. Marsland, S. (2015). Machine learning: An Algorithmic Perspective. CRC Press.

25. Estrela, V.V. and Hemanth, J. (2015). Special Issue Preface. International Journal of Information and Communication Technology, Tamil Nadu.

26. de Jesus, M.A., Estrela, V.V., Saotome, O. and Stutz, D. (2018). Optimization variants. *In:* Hemanth, J., Balas, V. (eds), Biologically Rationalized Computing Techniques for Image Processing Applications. Lecture Notes in Computational Vision and Biomechanics, vol. 25, 317-337. Springer, Cham, Switzerland.

27. Zhu, H., Zhao, Y., Wang, X. and Xu, Y. (2021). Research on data analysis of traditional Chinese Medicine with improved differential evolution clustering algorithm. J. Healthcare Eng., 23(9).

28. Mohammdian-Khoshnoud, M., Soltanian, A.R., Dehghan, A. and Farhadian, M. (2021). Optimization of fuzzy c-means (FCM) clustering in cytology image segmentation using the Gray Wolf Algorithm. BMC Mol. and Cell Biol., 23(9).

29. Zhang, Z. (2021). An improved BM25 algorithm for clinical decision support in Precision Medicine based on co-word analysis and Cuckoo Search. BMC Medical Informatics and Decision Making, 21.

30. Razmjooy N., Deshpande, A., Khalilpour, M., Estrela, V.V., Padilha, R. et al. (2021). Optimal bidding strategy for power market based on improved world cup optimization algorithm. *In:* Razmjooy, N., Ashourian, M., Foroozandeh, Z. (eds). Metaheuristics

and Optimization in Computer and Electrical Engineering. Lecture Notes in Electrical Engineering, vol. 696. Springer, Cham.

31. Razmjooy, N., Vahedi, Z., Estrela, V.V., Padilha, R., Monteiro, A.C.B. et al. (2021). Speed control of a DC motor using PID controller based on improved whale optimization algorithm. *In:* Razmjooy, N. et al. (eds). Metaheuristics and Optimization in Computer and Electrical Engineering. Lecture Notes in Electrical Engineering, vol. 696. Springer, Cham.

32. Razmjooy, N., Razmjooy, S., Vahedi, Z., Estrela, V.V., de Oliveira, G.G. et al. (2021). Skin color segmentation based on artificial neural network improved by a modified grasshopper optimization algorithm. *In:* Razmjooy, N., Ashourian, M., Foroozandeh, Z. (eds). Metaheuristics and Optimization in Computer and Electrical Engineering. Lecture Notes in Electrical Engineering, vol. 696. Springer, Cham.

33. Razmjooy, N., Razmjooy, S., Vahedi, Z., Estrela, V.V., de Oliveira, G.G. et al. (2021). A new design for robust control of power system stabilizer based on moth search algorithm. *In:* Razmjooy, N., Ashourian, M., Foroozandeh, Z. (eds). Metaheuristics and Optimization in Computer and Electrical Engineering. Lecture Notes in Electrical Engineering, vol. 696. Springer, Cham.

34. Estrela, V.V., Razmjooy, N., Monteiro, A.C.B., França, R.P., de Jesus, M.A. et al. (2021). A computational intelligence perspective on multimodal image registration for unmanned aerial vehicles (UAVs). *In:* Razmjooy, N., Ashourian, M., Foroozandeh, Z. (eds). Metaheuristics and Optimization in Computer and Electrical Engineering. Lecture Notes in Electrical Engineering, vol. 696. Springer, Cham. https://doi.org/10.1007/978-3-030-56689-0_13

35. Thangaraj, R., Pant, M., Abraham, A. and Bouvry, P. (2011). Particle swarm optimization: Hybridization perspectives and experimental illustrations. Appl. Math. Comput., 217, 5208-5226.

36. de Jesus, M.A., Estrela, V.V., Saotome, O. and Stutz, D. (2018). Super-resolution via particle swarm optimization variants. *In:* Hemanth, J., Balas, V. (eds). Biologically Rationalized Computing Techniques for Image Processing Applications. Lecture Notes in Computational Vision and Biomechanics, vol. 25. Springer, Cham. https://doi.org/10.1007/978-3-319-61316-1_14

37. El-Hasnony, I.M., Barakat, S.I. and Mostafa, R.R. (2020). Optimized ANFIS model using hybrid metaheuristic algorithms for Parkinson's disease prediction in IoT environment. IEEE Access, 8, 119252-119270.

38. Panahi, M., Gayen, A., Pourghasemi, H.R., Rezaie, F., Lee, S. et al. (2020). Spatial prediction of landslide susceptibility using hybrid support vector regression (SVR) and the adaptive neuro-fuzzy inference system (ANFIS) with various metaheuristic algorithms. The Science of the Total Environment, 741, 139937.

39. Ting, T.O., Yang, X., Cheng, S. and Huang, K. (2015). Hybrid metaheuristic algorithms: Past, present, and future. Recent Advances in Swarm Intelligence and Evolutionary Computation. vol 585. Springer, Cham. https://doi.org/10.1007/978-3-319-13826-8_4

40. Nayak, J., Naik, B., Dinesh, P., Vakula, K., Dash, P.B. et al. (2020). Firefly algorithm in biomedical and health care: Advances, issues and challenges. SN Computer Science, 1(6), 311. https://doi.org/10.1007/s42979-020-00320-x

41. Boveiri, H.R. and Khayami, R. (2020). On the performance of metaheuristics: A different perspective. ArXiv, abs/2001.08928.

42. LeCun, Y., Bengio, Y. and Hinton, G. (2015). Deep learning. Nature, 521(7553), 436-444.

43. Suzuki, H., Ohsaki, H. and Sawai, H. (2010). A network-based computational model with learning. Proc. Int'l Conf. Unconventional Computation. Springer, 193-193.

44. Miotto, R., Wang, F., Wang, S., Jiang, X. and Dudley, J.T. et al. (2018). Deep learning for healthcare: Review, opportunities and challenges. Briefings in Bioinf., 19(6), 1236-1246.

45. Anderson, R., Biong, A. and Gómez-Gualdrón, D.A. (2020). Adsorption isotherm predictions for multiple molecules in MOFs using the same deep learning model. J. Chem. Th. and Comp., 2020.

46. Liao, H. (2016). A deep learning approach to universal skin disease classification. University of Rochester Department of Computer Science, CSC. [MY PAPER]

47. Shoieb, D.A., Youssef, S.M. and Aly, W.M. (2016). Computer-aided model for skin diagnosis using deep learning. Journal of Image and Graphics, 4(2), 122-129.

48. Abdel-Zaher, A.M. and Eldeib, A.M. (2016). Breast cancer classification using deep belief networks. Expert Systems with Applications, 46, 139-144.

49. Charan, S., Khan, M.J. and Khurshid, K. (2018). Breast cancer detection in mammograms using convolutional neural network, Proc. Int'l Conf. Computing, Math. and Eng. Technologies (iCoMET). IEEE, 1-5.

50. Miao, K.H. and Miao, J.H. (2018). Coronary heart disease diagnosis using deep neural networks. Int. J. Adv. Comput. Sci. Appl., 9(10), 1-8.

51. Sun, W., Zheng, B. and Qian, W. (2016). Computer aided lung cancer diagnosis with deep learning algorithms. *In:* Medical Imaging 2016: Computer-Aided Diagnosis, vol. 9785. International Society for Optics and Photonics, 97850Z.

52. Jain, G., Mittal, D., Thakur, D. and Mittal, M.K. (2020). A deep learning approach to detect Covid-19 coronavirus with x-ray images. Biocybernetics and Biomedical Engineering, 40(4), 1391-1405.

53. El-Rashidy, N., El-Sappagh, S., Islam, S., El-Bakry, H.M. and Abdelrazek, S. et al. (2020). End-to-end deep learning framework for coronavirus (Covid-19) detection and monitoring. Electronics, 9(9), 1439.

54. Jaiswal, A., Gianchandani, N., Singh, D., Kumar, V., Kaur, M. et al. (2020). Classification of the Covid-19 infected patients using densenet201 based deep transfer learning. J. Biomolecular Structure and Dynamics, 1-8.

55. Ginat, D.T. (2020). Analysis of head CT scans flagged by deep learning software for acute intracranial hemorrhage. Neuroradiology, 62(3), 335-340.

56. Lewick, T., Kumar, M., Hong, R. and Wu, W. (2020). Intracranial hemorrhage detection in CT scans using deep learning. Proc. 2020 IEEE 6th Int'l Conf. Big Data Computing Service and Applications (BigDataService). IEEE, 169-172.

57. Niculescu, V. (2020). On the impact of high performance computing in big data analytics for medicine. Applied Medical Informatics, 42, 9-18.

58. Cho, W.K. and Liu, Y. (2019). Parallel hybrid metaheuristics with distributed intensification and diversification for large-scale optimization in big data statistical analysis. 2019 IEEE International Conference on Big Data (Big Data), 3312-3320.

59. Suzuki, K. (2017). Overview of deep learning in medical imaging. Radiological Physics and Technology, 10(3), 257-273.

60. Chen, F.-C. and Jahanshahi, M.R. (2017). NB-CNN: Deep learning-based crack detection using convolutional neural network and naïve Bayes data fusion. IEEE Trans. Ind. Electronics, 65(5), 4392-4400.

61. Uzoka, F.-M.E., Osuji, J., Aladi, F.O. and Obot, O.U. (2011). A framework for cell phone based diagnosis and management of priority tropical diseases. Proc. 2011 IST-Africa Conf. IEEE, 1-13.

62. Nesteruk, P., Nesteruk, L. and Kotenko, I. (2014). Creation of a fuzzy knowledge base for adaptive security systems. Proc. 2014 22nd Euromicro Int'l Conf. Parallel, Distributed, and Network-Based Processing. IEEE, 574-577.

63. Licata, G. (2010). Employing fuzzy logic in the diagnosis of a clinical case. Health, 2(03), 211-224.
64. Rana, M. and Sedamkar, R. (2013). Design of expert system for medical diagnosis using fuzzy logic. International Journal of Scientific & Engineering Research, 4(6), 2914-2921.
65. Zadeh, L.A. (1965). Fuzzy sets. Information and Control, 8(3), 338-353.
66. Phuong, N.H. and Kreinovich, V. (2001). Fuzzy logic and its applications in medicine. International J. Medical Informatics, 62(2-3), 165-173.
67. Ansari, A. and Gupta, N.K. (2011). Automated diagnosis of coronary heart disease using neuro-fuzzy integrated system. Proc. 2011 World Congress on Information and Communication Technologies. IEEE, 1379-1384.
68. de Carvalho Junior, H.H., Moreno, R.L., Pimenta, T.C., Crepaldi, P.C., Cintra, E. et al. (2013). A heart disease recognition embedded system with fuzzy cluster algorithm. Computer Methods and Programs in Biomedicine, 110(3), 447-454.
69. Oluwagbemi, O., Oluwagbemi, F. and Abimbola, O. (2016). Ebinformatics: Ebola fuzzy informatics systems on the diagnosis, prediction and recommendation of appropriate treatments for ebola virus disease (EVD). Inf. Medicine Unlocked, 2, 12-37.
70. Insel, T.R. and Cuthbert, B.N. (2015). Brain disorders? precisely. Science, 348(6234), 499-500.
71. Gopal, N.N. and Karnan, M. (2010). Diagnose brain tumor through MRI using image processing clustering algorithms such as fuzzy c-means along with intelligent optimization techniques. Proc. 2010 IEEE Int'l Conf. Comp. Intell. and Computing Research IEEE, 1-4.
72. Chen, H.-L., Huang, C.-C., Yu, X.-G., Xu, X., Sun, X. et al. (2013). An efficient diagnosis system for detection of Parkinson's disease using fuzzy k-nearest neighbor approach. Expert Systems with Applications, 40(1), 263-271.
73. Patra, S. and Thakur, G. (2013). A proposed neuro-fuzzy model for adult asthma disease diagnosis. Comput. Sci. Informa. Technol., 3, 191-205.
74. Miranda, G.H.B. and Felipe, J.C. (2015). Computer-aided diagnosis system based on fuzzy logic for breast cancer categorization. Comp. Biology and Med., 64, 334-346.
75. Nilashi, M., Ibrahim, O., Ahmadi, H. and Shahmoradi, L. (2017). A knowledge-based system for breast cancer classification using fuzzy logic method. Telematics and Informatics, 34(4), 133-144.
76. Satarkar, S. and Ali, M. (2015). Fuzzy expert system for the diagnosis of common liver disease. Int'l Engineering J. Research & Development, 1(1), 2-7.
77. Allahverdi, N. and Akcan, T. (2011). A fuzzy expert system design for diagnosis of periodontal dental disease. Proc. 2011 5th Int'l Conf. App. of Inf. and Comm. Technologies (AICT). IEEE, 1-5.
78. Tuan, T.M., Fujita, H., Dey, N., Ashour, A.S. et al. (2018). Dental diagnosis from X-ray images: An expert system based on fuzzy computing. Biom. Signal Proc. Control, 39, 64-73.
79. Godil, S.S., Shamim, M.S., Enam, S.A. and Qidwai, U. (2011). Fuzzy logic: "A simple" solution for complexities in neurosciences. Surgical Neurology International, 2.
80. Brust-Renck, P.G., Reyna, V.F., Wilhelms, E.A. and Lazar, A.N. (2016). A fuzzy-trace theory of judgment and decision-making in health care: Explanation, prediction, and application. Handbook of Health Decision Science. Springer, 71-86.
81. Roveri, M.I., Manoel, E.J., Onodera, A.N., Ortega, N.R.S., Tessutti, V.D. et al. (2017). Assessing experience in the deliberate practice of running using a fuzzy decision-support system. PloS One, 12(8).
82. Boucheham, A., Batouche, M.C. and Meshoul, S. (2015). An ensemble of cooperative parallel metaheuristics for gene selection in cancer classification. Proc. IWBBIO.

83. Liu, L., Zhan, X., Wu, R., Guan, X., Wang, Z. et al. (2021). Boost AI power: Data augmentation strategies with unlabeled data and conformal prediction, a case in alternative herbal medicine discrimination with electronic nose. IEEE Sensors Journal, 21, 22995-23005.

84. Lin, S., Song, X., Xu, Z., Zhang, X., Lin, Y. et al. (2021). Moment invariants with data augmentation for tongue image segmentation. Proc. 2021 IEEE BIBM, 988-993.

85. Rostom, Y.A., Abd-El-Moneim, S., Labib, N.M., Gharib, S., Shaker, M.R. et al. (2021). Python-based preprocessing for applying machine learning in breast cancer metastasis prediction. Journal of Clinical Oncology, 39.

86. Elasnaoui, K. and Chawki, Y. (2020). Using X-ray images and deep learning for automated detection of coronavirus disease. J. Biomol. Struct. and Dynamics, no. just-accepted, 1-22.

87. Holzinger, A., Langs, G., Denk, H., Zatloukal, K., Müller, H. et al. (2019). Causability and explainability of artificial intelligence in medicine. Wiley Interdisciplinary Reviews: Data Mining and Knowledge Discovery, 9(4), e1312.

88. Elazab, N., Soliman, H., El-Sappagh, S., Islam, S., Elmogy, M. et al. (2020). Objective diagnosis for histopathological images based on machine learning techniques: Classical approaches and new trends. Mathematics, 8(11), 1863.

89. Tellez, D., Litjens, G.J.S., Bandi, P., Bulten, W., Bokhorst, J.M. et al. (2019). Quantifying the effects of data augmentation and stain color normalization in convolutional neural networks for computational pathology. Med. Image Analysis, 58, 101544.

90. Saha, S.K., Islam, S.R., Kwak, K.-S., Rahman, M.S., Cho, S.-G. et al. (2020). Prom1 and prom2 expression differentially modulates clinical prognosis of cancer: A multiomics analysis. Cancer Gene Therapy, 27(3), 147-167.

91. El-Sappagh, S., Abuhmed, T., Islam, S.R. and Kwak, K.S. (2020). Multimodal multitask deep learning model for Alzheimer's disease progression detection based on time series data. Neurocomputing, 412, 197-215.

92. Yaya, X. and Bi-Geng, Z. (2020). Research on medical image storage and retrieval system based on Hadoop. Journal of Physics: Conf. Series, 1544(1). IOP Publishing, 012119.

93. Zielke, T. (2020). Is artificial intelligence ready for standardization? Proc. European Conference on Software Process Improvement. Springer, 259-274.

94. Hussain, F., Hussain, R., Hassan, S.A. and Hossain, E. (2020). Machine learning in IoT security: Current solutions and future challenges. IEEE Communications Surveys & Tutorials.

95. Khelassi, A. and Estrela, V.V. (2021). Advances in multidisciplinary medical technologies – Engineering, modeling and findings. Proceedings of the International Workshop on Medical Technologies 2019 (ICHSMT 2019), Springer Nature, Zurich, Switzerland.

96. Deshpande, A., Patavardhan, P. and Estrela, V.V. (2020). Super resolution and recognition of unconstrained ear image. International Journal of Biometrics, Inderscience, 12(4), 396-410. doi: 10.1504/IJBM.2020.110813

97. Razmjooy, N., Estrela, V.V. and Loschi, H.J. (2020). Entropy-based breast cancer detection in digital mammograms using World Cup Optimization algorithm. International Journal of Swarm Intelligence Research (IJSIR), 11(3), 1-18.

98. Deshpande, A., Estrela, V.V. and Patavardhan, P. (2021). The DCT-CNN-ResNet50 architecture to classify brain tumours with super-resolution, convolutional neural network, and the ResNet50. Neuroscience Informatics, 1(4), 100013, ISSN 2772-5286.

99. Ayub Khan, Abdullah, Laghari, A.A, Shaikh, A., Dootio, M., Estrela, V.V. et al. (2021). A Blockchain Security Module for Brain-Computer Interface (BCI) with Multimedia

Life Cycle Framework (MLCF). Neuroscience Informatics. 100030. 10.1016/j. neuri.2021.100030.

100. Chlioui, I., Idri, A. and Abnane, I. (2020). Data preprocessing in knowledge discovery in breast cancer: Systematic mapping study. Computer Methods in Biomechanics and Biomedical Engineering: Imaging & Visualization, 8, 547-561.

101. Deshpande, A., Estrela, V.V. and Razmjooy, N. (2021). Computational Intelligence Methods for Super-Resolution in Image Processing Applications. Springer Nature, Zurich, Switzerland. doi: 10.1007/978-3-030-67921-7

102. Razmjooy, N., Deshpande, A., Khalilpour, M., Estrela, V.V., Padilha, R. et al. (2021). Optimal bidding strategy for power market based on improved world cup optimization algorithm. *In:* Razmjooy, N., Ashourian, M., Foroozandeh, Z. (eds). Metaheuristics and Optimization in Computer and Electrical Engineering. Lecture Notes in Electrical Engineering, vol. 696. Springer, Cham. https://doi.org/10.1007/978-3-030-56689-0_7

Metaheuristics Applied to Pathology Image Analysis

Vania V. Estrela[1] [0000-0002-4465-7691], Aline C. Intorne[2,3] [0000-0001-8015-6926],
Kate K.S. Batista[4] [0000-0002-5861-4633], Anand Deshpande[5] [0000-0002-1500-0981],
Jenice Aroma[6] [0000-0003-4022-1898], Kumudha Raimond[6] [0000-0001-8680-8390],
Fuqian Shi[7] [0000-0003-4245-5727], Asif Ali Laghari[8] [0000-0001-5831-5943],
Yu-Da Lin[9] [0000-0001-5100-6072]

[1] Department of Telecommunications, Federal Fluminense University (UFF), RJ,
24220-900, Brazil, vania.estrela.phd@ieee.org
[2] Laboratory of Physiology and Biochemistry of Microorganisms, Universidade Estadual do
Norte Fluminense Darcy Ribeiro, Campos dos Goytacazes, RJ, 28013-602, Brazil
[3] Laboratory of Chemistry and Biology, Instituto Federal de Educação, Ciência e Tecnologia
do Rio de Janeiro, Volta Redonda, RJ, 27213-100, Brazil, aline.intorne@ifrj.edu.br
[4] Fundacao Oswaldo Cruz, FIOCRUZ, RJ, Brazil, katekbatista@gmail.com
[5] Electronics and Communication Engineering, Angadi Institute of Technology and
Management, Belagavi, India, deshpande.anandb@gmail.com
[6] Department of Computer Science & Engineering, Karunya Institute of Technology &
Sciences, India jenicearoma@gmail.com, kraimond@karunya.edu
[7] Rutgers Cancer Institute of New Jersey, United States, shifuqian@gmail.com
[8] Faculty of Computer Science, Sindh Madressatul Islam University, Karachi (74000),
Sindh, Pakistan, asif.laghari@smiu.edu.pk
[9] National Penghu University of Science and Technology, Magong, TW,
yudalinemail@gmail.com

1. Introduction

Clinical analysis laboratories partake in various methods and exams that help physicians diagnose diseases of all types. Very commonly, blood tests serve as the beginning point for patients to receive exact information about any condition that affects them and their current state of well-being. The blood count remains the most frequent and most common test for the preliminary screening of some illnesses. This type of test permits knowledge of the patient's physiology from his/her blood. Blood cell formation (i.e., Red Blood Cells (RBCs) or erythrocytes, leukocytes otherwise known as White Blood Cells (WBCs), besides platelets) befall in the bone marrow. The primary function of RBCs is the transportation of oxygen and nutrients. Leukocytes are the organism's defense, and the platelets take care of the blood coagulation [1].

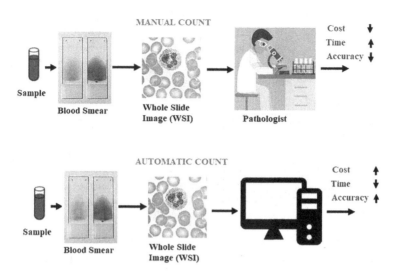

Figure 1. Blood count systems

The blood count offers a means to explore the three most crucial blood constituents (i.e., erythrocytes, leukocytes, in addition to platelets). Figure 1 illustrates the blood analysis rationale and forms of analytical procedures to identify RBSs, WBCs, hemoglobin, hematocrits, platelet (which modulate coagulation) count, and (global and local) leukocyte (which are accountable for working on the immune system) indexes [1-5]. Consequently, the test appraises the amount and quality of blood cells [2].

It is a dominant investigative and control test for both hematological and systemic ailments. Blood exams can point out besides routinely gauging infectious/ inflammatory reactions, anemia, hematological distortions, drug therapy follow-ups, and appraisal of platelet disorders. Altogether, it identifies ailments that mess up the blood composition, such as leukemia, bacterial, or viral infections. It also helps detect allergies and bleeding. The different blood counts help discern viral, bacterial, and parasitic infections (Figure 1). These counts also relate to intoxication, neoplasms, inflammation, and infections throughout global/differential leukocyte tallies and morphological assessments. The blood count is also utilized to guarantee that one can go through surgery and check the body's reaction to distinctive treatments [3].

For these test findings to assess the patient's clinical state properly, a meticulous procedure is essential in clinical analysis laboratories for collecting raw data, storing data, transferring acquired samples whenever needed, task executions, examining several sample aspects, information typing, and publicizing outcomes. To guarantee the accuracy and precision of findings, it is also critical to have perfect uniformity in all laboratory process segments. All this must be accompanied by adequate facilities, calibrated equipment, and knowledgeable staff. As a result, this procedure is enlightening and entails a great deal of human labor. Even taking the expensive equipment cost into account , which, in addition to requiring annual maintenance, is non-existent in many developing country scenarios [4]. Figure 2 portrays an archetypal pathology laboratory and a complete blood analysis process. Because

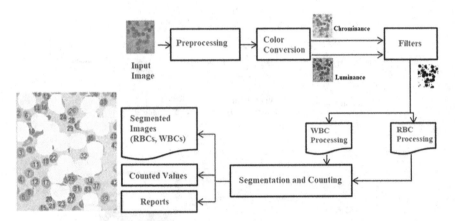

Figure 2. Case study of histopathological analysis: Blood-processing pipeline

components of this laboratory may be spread worldwide, it can be linked to a Medical Cyber-Physical System (MCPS) [87].

Of late, there has been an ample technical change in how these tests are completed. Automated systems delivering better precision in the discoveries within smaller time frames have replaced several human-performed procedures. These enhancements have transformed test center routines, ameliorating their efficiency and speediness while also refining the quality of outcomes. Since, the automation of these exam procedures has been beneficial, assuring the reliability of all hematological test phases, and standardization ensures more efficient fallouts [2-4].

Blood count findings are now more reliable thanks to technological advancements. New techniques can be created with more remarkable technical assistance to provide the physician with additional options for the accurate interpretation of these tests. In this circumstance, metaheuristics offer outstanding stability and accuracy while circumventing mistakes. These characteristics make room for a far-reaching efficiency gamut attained through Artificial Intelligence (AI) training [1-6, 58, 59]. In this respect, and given the health sector's reliance on innovations, it is clear that new technology-based methods must be developed that are less expensive and have an eclectic range of applications, viz. the use of digital blood cell visualization and image segmentation procedures, meeting the effectiveness and reliability criteria for satisfactory blood cell detection along with counting [7].

Metaheuristic approaches, which are high-level processes meant to seek, develop, or choose a heuristic that gives a sufficiently correct answer for a given issue, have just gotten attention and significance, where they have been utilized to aid in the optimization problem-solving. To develop a process that can evade local minima and execute a robust solution for space exploration, a metaheuristic must connect local search processes with higher-level strategies. In a nutshell, a meta-heuristic is a method that combines the probing and exploitation of ideas, in a quest to refine an auspicious response throughout vast sections of the search space [8-10].

Metaheuristics are used to solve issues with little knowledge, albeit if a solution emerges, candidates can be evaluated. They do not, however, ensure that they are optimum. Even while metaheuristic techniques have no defined domains and may be utilized for any issue, they are generally enthused by some biological phenomena or natural behavior, consisting of basic local searches and fancy learning. These are, in a nutshell, techniques that direct the search process in the direction of near-optimal answers [9].

Metaheuristics have arisen as promising algorithms for handling intricate optimization problems, demanding alternative solutions to traditional approaches. In this setting, there exist several types, e.g., Genetic Algorithms (GAs) [23, 24], Fuzzy Logic (FL), Particle Swarm Optimization (PSO) [29], DL [57], Ant Colony Optimization (ACO) [51, 52], and Differential Evolution (DE) [61], all viewed as highly auspicious procedures for optimization and unraveling countless problems in real-time. Yet, in image processing, one often bumps into irregular silhouettes that are challenging when it comes to detecting and categorizing, whether due to overlap or the actual outline of a biological item of concern within an image. All these issues are resolved by engaging global, stochastic, optimization metaheuristics envisioned to handle complicated optimization problems, while also including machine learning as a powerful ally. As a result, using metaheuristics in picture segmentation is effective [11].

As a result, this chapter's goal is to explicate metaheuristics in discrete-event simulation, as well as catalog and synthesize the possibilities of these technologies. As a result, Section 2 describes how to analyze blood using image processing. Section 3 delves into blood image analysis metaheuristics. The fourth section contains various case studies. Finally, Section 5 discusses future technological developments. Finally, Section 6 brings the chapter to a close.

2. Blood Analysis through Image Processing

Computer vision aims to aid in the solution of tough issues by emulating human cognition and judgments grounded on visual input. Medicinal image investigation combines visual goings-over and information in this field. The previously mentioned traits permit segmentation plus identification of regions and other items in an image and extraction of geometrical characteristics of interest [12].

Digital image processing embodies a collection of computer-assisted techniques for collecting, representing, and altering pictures. These approaches allow for extracting and identifying information from pictures besides upgrading the visual excellence of specific biomedical structures, empowering human perception and machine interpretation [13]. It is widely employed in biological imaging to check the contour discovered so that the cells were accurately categorized, even in small places, as in blood pictures. The goal of picture analysis or interpretation is to provide a representation that comprehends enough information to consistently discriminate between distinct objects of interest with little human intervention [14].

Discrete imagery is equivalent to a $N \times M$ matrix made up of positive integer pel $p(x, y)$ values, indicating the tone at each image location (x, y). The form, texture, gray intensities, or object colors are commonly used in image analysis. Image analysis is inherently complex due to its translational nature, which has the need for the knowledge of numerous domains to solve the problem satisfactorily, including science, psychophysics, computational geometry, statistics, visualization, information theory, and countless others [15, 16].

This indicates that the digital image partakes in an integer value consistent with a shade of gray, an entry numeral in a color table, or three integers matching the R (red), G (green), and B (blue) bands for each sampled pel. With the advancement of digital technology and new algorithms, the number of pathological applications has increased [15, 16].

The use of digital imaging may assist medical diagnostics, and it is acknowledged by several health specialties by this time. In particular, oncology has profited from better-quality diagnostics. Analysis of imageries and interpretation, for example, make it simpler to identify cancerous lesions or areas, allowing clinicians to make more precise and opportune diagnoses with better-planned treatments and procedures [17].

A sequence of steps is generally included in a digital image processing system to produce a result from the issue domain. A knowledge base can warehouse information about a specific issue area in an image processing system. This database hinges on existing solutions and adequate query mechanisms. The associated data size and complexity might vary considerably but this data can be distributed/exchanged among computational units to complete this task [18].

A digital picture is often the product of the capture process, which may have flaws or degradations due to lighting or device features. A preprocessing stage improves picture quality by employing noise reduction, contrast or brightness adjustment, and smoothing specific image features [19].

The segmentation phase discovers discontinuities (boundaries) or similarities (regions), isolates, and identifies Regions of Interest (ROIs) included in the image. As a result, recognition or classification denotes the process of handing over the identification or label to picture objects based on their descriptor properties [18, 19, 81-85].

Blood tests are the most commonly used clinical analytic techniques for the vast range of abnormalities they may identify. Blood cell counts are still manually performed by a human operator who relies on microscopic analyses of treated or colored samples. By means of automatically counting cells in a blood sample, the blood cell outlines, for example, may aid in diagnosing anemia. Because of the technical content [1-3], as stated above, this work is outstandingly more efficient and can attain elevated levels of accuracy.

As a result, most image processing approaches are established on mathematical tactics for the quantitative portrayal of images from innumerable sources. Imagery may be expressed by listing all characteristics that have, e.g., a two-dimensional or topological feature, independent of what it depicts. In a nutshell, each item described in this 2-D space contains surface dimensions, lengths, thicknesses, outer limits, and location, among other properties that may be recorded digitally and then derived as statistical numbers in a digitally automated manner (Figure 3) [18, 20].

Whole Slide Imaging (WSI) yields a material that may be kept in hematology databases through PACS [76-80, 89, 90]. Images from a wide assortment of modalities, multidimensional imageries, and asemantic data may all be found in these histological archives. Evidence-based analysis, health teaching, and research are all

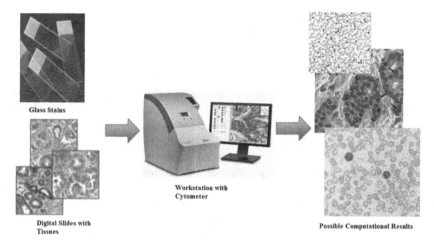

Figure 3. Whole Slide Imaging (WSI)

possible with these resources. Hematological evidence retrieval demands appropriate techniques to examine groups of pictures that have the potential to handle features that are similar to the important case(s). Content-based Image Retrieval (CBIR) uses visual characteristics viz. color, texture, and silhouette as exploration criteria to supplement text-based queries to pictures [78, 88]. When it comes to extremely multidimensional and multimodality well-being data, medical CBIR is still in its embryonic stage. To enhance the blood element retrieval from various research group datasets, contemporary biomedical CBIR techniques include 2D, 3D, or higher-dimensional image retrieval, and semantic (non-image facts). As a framework for locating different diseases, blood smear pictures may be classified into numerous categories, targeting the features and modalities gained through laboratory exams, medicinal image retrieval, and related metadata.

3. Metaheuristics for Blood Image Analysis

In brief, metaheuristics can find helpful or even optimum solutions to a problem by iteratively employing a subordinate heuristic (for local search) and can have the means to escape from dangerous situations (valleys). Metaheuristics based on population search with multiple solutions retain a set of decent solutions and merge them to generate even better solutions, and do not typically undertake refinement processes, i.e., local search, and therefore must uphold a set of current solutions [21].

3.1. Genetic Algorithms

Genetic Algorithms (GA) optimize and search for solutions contingent on evolutionary means of live organisms. They are algorithms based on naturalist Charles Darwin's idea that individuals that are more suited to their environment possess a better chance of surviving and reproducing children. These GAs are probabilistic algorithms, but because they mix supervised and stochastic searches, they are not utterly random exploration techniques [22].

These algorithms use language derived from natural selection theory and genetics, with an operation logic based on the fact that each person in a populace is characterized by a single chromosome, which has the candidate coding, genotype, and phenotype to resolve the problem. A chromosome is generally represented as a vector with a list of characteristics, with each component being referred to as a gene. As a result, GAs frequently aim at solving intricate optimization problems, such as those involving multiple constraints (or conditions) that cannot be denoted mathematically, features that must be integrated to discern the best resolution, or problems encompassing multiple parameters, or large search spaces [23].

They were able to answer complicated issues in a clear manner, and their methodology was centered on a collection of bit strings, 0's and 1's, known as individuals. Thus, even without knowing the features of the issue to be handled, the system progresses until the optimal chromosome meets a given challenge. Likewise, this solution is learned in an unsupervised, automated manner, with the only input provided to the algorithm being chromosomal changes. Several studies in digital image processing cope with the identification and categorization of areas, which, although necessary, is a difficult task. As a result, GA models for picture classification established on the genetic evolution of association rules from a training sample set color and texture characteristics which may be utilized [24].

A standard GA has been exploited in combination with a Support Vector Machine (SVM) to discriminate blood cells from an aspirated bone sample picture. The main GA purpose in this study was to make a choice of SVM features for enhanced recognition and final classification. This has demonstrated that using GA to select diagnostic features was effective for refining the overall system accuracy. There exist numerous bone marrow cell lines, albeit the most significant are the granulocytic series, lymphocytic series, WBCs, and erythrocytes (or RBCs). Counting and evaluating patient blood cells in the bone marrow is very revealing in clinical practice.

The difference between lines perpendicular to the central axis in addition to the cell border is still considered when examining geometric characteristics defining different parts of cell geometry and utilizing descriptive parameters for perimeter, area, radius, and symmetry. As a result, the use of GA for feature selection and to recognize adjacent blood cells had the benefit of improving blood cell identification accuracy [25].

It was achievable, and the practicality of using GAs in picture categorization is obvious, based on the preceding facts. GA region identification and categorization by means of color or hyperspectral imageries offers a broad variety of prospects in a large variety of knowledge arenas [22-24, 71].

3.2. Fuzzy Logic (FL)

Fuzzy Logic (FL) captures vague information by applying logic to cope with states containing a certain uncertainty degree and often accomplishes better outcomes than classical logic. FL fills a gap concerning human communication and computational structures. The FL building element is the concept of fuzzy set, which is more suited to dealing with information defects than probability theory [26].

Some systems function utilizing classical logic, where the associated facts/ events are either completely true (1) or totally false (0), and without a middle ground.

FL allows additional prospects since there exist values in the middle of false (0) and true (1) that may be used. Nonetheless, FL relies on the premise of the degree of truth, which fluctuates within the interval [0, 1] making it possible to have a partially true or partially incorrect circumstance. Membership functions, which might be triangular, trapezoidal, or sigmoidal, are used to create these associations [27].

The work in [28] has automated the identification of blood components by employing a watershed moment. Hematological image segmentation has permitted the blood components to be divided into groups and processed independently. This broad computer-based tactic segmented and categorized blood components from microscopic pictures termed Whole Slide Imaging (WSI) for automatic analysis. Microscopic blood smear samples were analyzed, and fuzzy sets were automatically created based on histogram peaks corresponding to the green channel of the RGB versions of WSIs. Next, the Euclidean distances amid leukocyte nucleus centroids and the residual pixels have been evaluated.

The outcomes have been compared to other techniques in terms of accuracy rates as well as to previously labeled results obtained by expert manual segmentation. The FL procedure correlates the degree of pertinence of each pixel's gray level in particular areas of the histogram with the closeness of the leukocyte nucleus centroid closest to a given pixel during processing with the segmentation of leukocytes, which includes the nucleus, cytoplasm, erythrocytes, and blood plasma. Postprocessing helps reduce false positives. The WSI is also subjected to fuzzy criteria, resulting in four categorization areas: leukocyte cytoplasm, leukocyte nuclei, erythrocytes, and blood plasma, respectively [28].

3.3. Particle Swarm Optimization (PSO)

PSO is a group of population metaheuristics for optimizing functions that rely upon techniques for mimicking animal social behavior, such as flocks of birds. It makes use of a particle set traveling throughout the solution space as a metaphor for the method of impact on human thought and behavior. Each particle in this structure determines its route by comparing its earlier experiences to neighbors and other particles communicating with it [29, 55].

PSO is a stable, adaptable, simple, and widely distributable approach with minimal memory needs, low computing power, and quick convergence to the best solution. One of its downsides is the fast loss of variety and early convergence of solutions to extrema [30].

In brief, PSO attempts to replicate the swarm comportment seen in nature in some animal species, where one or more pack leaders constantly urge the movement of others while migrating from one location to another. PSO is thus seen as an evolutionary computing approach, although one that employs a distinct paradigm for species evolution [29, 30, 55].

In 2005, a pictorial resource extraction established on PSO for hyperspectral imageries [71] was developed with the goal of extracting the resources that produce the best depiction of a blood-covered region (blood smear). A binary PSO version helped select wavelengths in the near-infrared gamut. Optical blood absorption physiognomies allow some visual information to be extracted in this process. A linear image transformation, which uses two transformation equations to collect three to four bands, aids feature selection. Four distinct criteria helped gauge the adjusted imagery: Euclidean distance, entropy, contrast, and correlation. The four-band transformation produced improved visualization, as well as enhanced photos of extracted characteristics, revealing excellent views behind the layer of spilled blood, according to experimental results [31].

3.4. Watershed Transform (WT)

The Watershed Transform (WT) subdivides an image inspired by the split of surfaces in watersheds, with many definitions and methods to choose from. WT presents a metaheuristic for image segmentation that interprets images as surfaces, with each pixel corresponding to a location and gray levels determining elevations. This idea necessitates the identification of watersheds, which are characterized by regional minima and their domain areas. The WT, on the surface, seeks to locate the locations where a droplet of water can go to two distinct regional minima [32].

Trustworthiness, practicality, and agility requirements have impacted the deployment of new health instruments, with the blood cell count as an essential test for diagnosing various disorders. The WT can extract and compute the amounts of Red Blood Cells (RBC) in addition to White Blood Cells (WBC) via MATLAB software. The results revealed pronounced performances in execution time, along with a computational performance [33].

Blood tests utilizing erythrocyte and leukocyte counts have proved to be directly helpful in identifying many sorts of illnesses in 2018, e.g., leukemia, anemia, viral, and parasitic infections which may all be diagnosed using red blood cell and leukocyte analysis. It is plausible to segment health pictures in this setting, given the relevance and application of WT and Morphological Operations (MOs).

As an effect, the molded WT-MO procedure can recognize, segment, and count these blood cells while aiming at efficiency and reliability requirements. The WT-MO algorithm hinges on the Watershed Transform (WT) with extremely high accuracy and was performed on a variety of hardware platforms with an average processing time of fewer than 3seconds per sample. As a result, the WT-MO algorithm was shown to be accurate and trustworthy, and it may be used as a third approach for speeding up medical diagnosis [1].

Engineering approaches were increasingly used in health-related fields in 2019, with the goal of addressing basic issues or perhaps developing new diagnostic procedures. The Hough Transform (HT) has been exploited to segment blood smear pictures for tallying blood cells. However, the WT was more efficient. This knowledge has helped develop a hybrid, HT-based technique created for pinpointing and counting both erythrocytes and leukocytes , with a comparison to a Watershed Transform-based methodology termed WT-MO [2-4].

3.5. Deep Learning

Deep Learning (DL) trains models to accomplish human tasks, comprising speech identification, image recognition, and change detection among other duties. Before shaping the processed data with standard equations, DL sets the fundamental values of data and trains them or employs pattern recognition methodologies to take various processing steps. This emerging theme belongs to the Artificial Intelligence (AI) category, related to Neural Networks (NNs) to improve things, which is turning into a vastly explored and coveted field [35].

DL has boosted the aptitude of computational structures to sort, recognize, identify, describe, and, understand massive data. It is used to train a computer model so that it can understand natural language. This approach uses relationships between keywords and words to extract semantic features from massive data [36]. Because of the repetitive facets of DL processes, their complexity escalates as the number of layers upsurges, and huge data quantities are required to train networks.

Therefore, solving deep learning caveats entails a lot of computing power. Given their capacity to continuously improve and react to deviations in the underlying patterns, DL approaches deliver an ideal opportunity to inspect more dynamic behaviors [37].

It is feasible to identify WBC pictures using deep learning algorithms with the understanding that the density of leukocytes in one's circulation gives a peek at any potential threat to the body as well as the immune system status. A significant change in cell count, for example, is typically an indication that the body is being impacted by an antigen, much as a change in a certain kind of leukocyte is usually associated with a specific antigen type [38].

To conduct this type of job using this approach, one will need a data collection (or several databases) encompassing leukocyte pictures It is worth stating that the grander the total imageries, the superior will accuracies be as datasets will aid training. To ameliorate training accuracies, datasets should undergo the previous categorization by experts. As an end outcome, training takes place by first appraising standardized datasets [36, 37].

Deep learning, for the most part, Convolutional Neural Networks (CNNs), brought noteworthy medicinal improvements, where a huge number of pictures may be processed and evaluated. A CNN framework for automatic cataloging of blood cell pictures into cell subtypes was created for this method, which intended to categorize blood cells, one of the most difficult issues in blood diagnostics. A collection of 13,000 blood cell pictures with subtypes was employed, with excellent classification results [4]. Many metaheuristics work with DL algorithms [105].

4. Case Studies

Metaheuristics arrange for feasible solutions of tolerable quality albeit without excellence assurance. They are created utilizing the structural aspects and characteristics of the corresponding problems, with a lower level of complexity than standard precise algorithms [40, 41]. In a nutshell, metaheuristics are employed when closed, well-defined mathematical or logical modeling remains difficult. Combining fundamental metaheuristics at a higher structural level is what computational intelligence is all about. These optimization tools may elucidate complex or huge issues on every occasion one has too many variables together with constraints to use accurate procedures. The mixture of random selections and historical medical information directs the assessment of the target search space to appropriate neighborhoods, avoiding premature stops in suboptimal local optimum places. Hybrid approaches typically use a strategy that directs or alters a metaheuristic to come up with answers superior to those found in the real world [42-45].

An evaluation of metaheuristic papers connected with discrete-event technology has explored the topic's history, focusing on publishing and indexing in well-known databases. In 2014, investigators tried the use of biological procedures and software/ hardware frameworks, merging mathematical with metaheuristic algorithms to unravel medical segmentation problems via metaheuristics. Medical imagery segmentation is crucial in welfare computer-aided diagnosis and classification [46].

In 2015, a hybrid method of medical picture segmentation [47] was investigated, which integrated area and border-based information with previous knowledge provided via deformable registration, logic, and metaheuristic algorithms. The qualitative cataloging of milled rice grains was studied in 2016 with a machine vision system in addition to some metaheuristic classifiers. The obtained results have assisted in *developing* an efficient system for fully automated classification [48].

There exist manifold tracking methods with different manners of handling changes when an object appears in a scene. Examples of changes relate to illumination, occlusions, scale, rotations, and pose variation. A non-occlusion tracking method can be extremely simplified by means of an adaptive metaheuristic-looking model with satisfactory results. In 2018, researchers looked at how contemporary fast developments in medicinal data acquisition and automated image breakdowns may enhance one's knowledge of natural life, disease processes, as well as the capacity to offer high-quality healthcare along with a variety of processing possibilities. Nature-centered or bio-inspired metaheuristics can discover an almost perfect global solution faster than other conventional and artificial [50] strategies.

Since, the logic for a heuristic method is short of far-reaching solid mathematical knowledge apropos its behavior, i.e., it can be put into operation in terms of time consumption in general. The idea is to yield an almost optimum, satisfactory solution in a reasonable duration [42-45].

Metaheuristic byproducts denote a higher level of heuristics possessing several generic adaptable heuristics. These techniques led to broad-spectrum problem optimizations and may enclose different algorithm combinations in their structure. They explore the space for feasible solutions effectively when one has particular knowledge of the problem [43, 44].

5. Discussion and Future Trends

Metaheuristics are probabilistic and population-based algorithms that humans employ, as is the case with the Ant Colony Optimization (ACO) strategy that emulates how actual ants discern the shortest path in their colony to a food source. Ant colonies are responsible for management without a central management unit. ACO is a metaheuristic for approximating solutions to challenging optimization problems. Artificial ants behave as if elucidating combinatorial optimization issues by passing through a fully-connected graph.

Conceiving an intelligent search system from the cooperative and self-adaptive behavior of these artificial ants partakes a unique challenge. The fictitious ants absorb the indispensable information about the problem's structure, make stochastic judgments, and generate a collection of solutions. Each management step may ask for (i) a given pheromone concentration, (ii) problem-specific information, and (iii) heuristic function values [51].

Since each pel is related to one of its edges or corners, ACO may be utilized for edge detection. Hence, an artificial "ant" may only migrate to an adjacent pixel if it is linked to the pixel where the ant is now positioned. When fake ants are dispersed throughout the imagery to craft a final pheromone matrix, replicating edge evidence, each element in the pheromone matrix correlates directly to a pixel and defines whether the pixel is a border or not [52].

More precisely, image processing continues to use DL architectures, viz. Multilayer Perceptron Network (MPN) is a straightforward binary classification method. The MPN predicts whether an item matches a certain group of concerns, for example, whether a given structure is a melanoma or not. As a linear classifier, the MPN is an algorithm that uses a straight line to categorize data into two sets. Typically, the input vector x is multiplied by weights w plus a bias b [53].

CNNs (or ConvNets) are advanced artificial neural networks (NNs) capable of discriminating between faces, persons, street signs, plants, and microbes, among other visual input items. They can classify images, sort them according to their similarity (image search and retrieval), and recognize objects within scenes. They include visual feature processing via semantic information, utilizing computational and cognitive methods to represent these visual and semantic attributes using a neural network, similar to how object recognition has been investigated recently [54, 57, 91].

In terms of computing burden, blob categorization and clustering are highly demanding jobs. With dimensionality reduction, metaheuristics can also enhance AI deployments [72-75]. Every day, several new soft computing approaches emerge that can aid in processing blood smear pictures. Here are several examples [76-90, 97-104]:

- World Cup Optimization (WCO) [56];
- Grey Wolf Optimization (GWO) [62];
- Cuckoo search [63];
- Artificial Immune Systems (AISs) [64];
- Artificial life (also refered to as digital organisms) [65];
- Synergistic Fibroblast Optimization (SFO) [66];
- Self-Organizing Maps (SOMs) [67];
- Bee algorithms [68];
- Whale Algorithm (WA) [69];
- Firefly Algorithm (FA) [70]; and
- Harmony Search (HS) [60], among others.

Peripheral blood smear studies are critical for hematologists to deliberate about the human immune system's conditions. This exam class is one of the preliminary clinical studies taking advantage of automatic computer-aided analysis. Modifications in the white blood cells (WBC) ratio assist in spotting blood diseases, and consequently, exact classification guarantees dependable therapy. Deep convolutional networks (DNNs) on hyperspectral imageries from microscopy can advance WBC classification. A 3D CNN can enable spectral and spatial features learning, making it possible to tackle 3D Hyperspectral imaging (HSI) data for WBC classification fully. Appending a 3D attention module to the last model block may emphasize essential features while efficiently improving the model's representative power [90-93].

Safe surgical navigation is paramount in spinal surgery, for effective intervention, comprising the placement of minuscule elements without injuring nerves, blood vessels, and other types of tissues. Available systems normally depend on reference images (ground truth) that can be displaced or hidden throughout surgery, occasioning navigation losses. HSI obtains a larger amount of spectral bands across the electromagnetic spectrum, offering image information undetected by human specialists. When devices HSI detect safely and non-invasively in-vivo, in-body images, then internal tissues of patients will be much more reliable and may avoid surgeries. HSI may espouse locally handcrafted feature detection schemes and deeply learned feature detection approaches, contingent on manifold system constraints. In general, deep-learned characteristics are perceived and localized more precisely as per literature [94-96], outdoing handcrafted traits with regard to the ground truth relying on markers.

6. Conclusions

As can be grasped throughout this chapter, metaheuristic practices have been applied for a variety of purposes, containing digital medical image computational resources and byproducts, and have made revelations in conjunction with other hybrid processing schemes. These usages brought in positive characteristics such as ease of implementation and efficiency. Developing approaches based on digital image processing offers much promise for tackling numerous difficulties and challenges in the medical profession, whether they are connected to new diagnostic procedures or lowering the cost of existing ones. As shown in this study, Fuzzy Logic, GAs, PSO, Watershed Transform, Deep Learning, and Ant Colony Optimization, among other trends, have a lot of potential for categorizing and totaling blood cells. They can be comprehended as steps toward reducing the complexity of medical examinations and generating social and economic benefits through technology.

References

1. Monteiro, A.C., Iano, Y., França, R.P., Arthur, R., Estrela, V.V. et al. (2019). A comparative study between methodologies based on the Hough transform and watershed transform on the blood cell count. Proceedings of the 4th Brazilian Technology Symposium (BTSym'18).
2. Razmjooy, N., Estrela, V.V. and Loschi, H.J. (2019). A study on metaheuristic-based neural networks for image segmentation purposes. *In:* Data Science: Theory, Analysis, and Applications, 1st ed., CRC Press, pp. 25-49.

3. Dese, K., Raj, H., Ayana, G., Yemane, T., Adissu, W. et al. (2021). Accurate machine-learning-based classification of leukemia from blood smear images. Clinical Lymphoma, Myeloma & Leukemia, 21(11), e903-e914.

4. Razmjooy, N., Ashourian, M., Karimifard, M., Estrela, V.V., Loschi, H.J. et al. (2020). Computer-aided diagnosis of skin cancer: A review. Current Medical Imaging Reviews, 16(7), 781-793.

5. Monteiro, A.C., Iano, Y., França, R.P., Arthur, R., Estrela, V.V. et al. (2019). Development of digital image processing methodology WT-MO: An algorithm of high accuracy in detection and counting of Erythrocytes, Leucocytes, Blasts. *In:* Anais do IV Int'l Symp. on Immunobiological e VII Sem. Anual Cient. e Tecnológico de Bio-Manguinhos.

6. Sahastrabuddhe, A.P. and Ajij, S.D. (2016). Blood group detection and RBC, WBC counting: An image processing approach. IJECS, 5, 10.

7. Estrela, V.V., Saotome, O., Loschi, H.J., Hemanth, D.J., Farfan, W.S. et al. (2018). Emergency response cyber-physical framework for landslide avoidance with sustainable electronics. Technologies, 6, 42.

8. Blum, C. and Roli, A. (2003). Metaheuristics in combinatorial optimization: Overview and conceptual comparison. ACM Computing Surveys (CSUR), 35(3), 268-308.

9. Nesmachnow, S. (2014). An overview of metaheuristics: Accurate and efficient methods for optimization. International Journal of Metaheuristics, 3(4), 320-347.

10. Gendreau, M. and Jean-Yves, P. (2010). Handbook of Metaheuristics. Vol. 2. New York: Springer.

11. Sörensen, K., Sevaux, M. and Glover, F. (2018). A history of metaheuristics. Handbook of Heuristics, 1-18.

12. Dubois, G. (2018). Modeling and Simulation: Challenges and Best Practices for Industry. CRC Press.

13. Birkfellner, W. (2016). Applied Medical Image Processing: A Basic Course. CRC Press.

14. Robertson, S., Azizpour, H., Smith, K. and Hartman, J. (2018). Digital image analysis in breast pathology – From image processing techniques to artificial intelligence. Transl. Res., 194, 19-35.

15. Stearns, S.D. and Donald, R.H. (2016). Digital Signal Processing with Examples in MATLAB. CRC Press.

16. Nixon, M. and Aguado, A. (2019). Feature Extraction and Image Processing for Computer Vision. Academic Press.

17. de Azevedo-Marques, P.M., Mencattini A., Salmeri M. and Rangayyan R.M. (2017). Medical Image Analysis and Informatics: Computer-Aided Diagnosis and Therapy. CRC Press.

18. Sebesta, R.W. (2016). Concepts of Programming Languages. 12th ed. Pearson.

19. McAndrew, A. (2015). A Computational Introduction to Digital Image Processing. Chapman and Hall/CRC.

20. Tan, L. and Jean, J. (2018). Digital Signal Processing: Fundamentals and Applications. Academic Press.

21. Rabadi, G. (ed.) (2016). Heuristics, Metaheuristics and Approximate Methods in Planning and Scheduling, Vol. 236. Springer.

22. Kurniasih, J., Utami, E. and Raharjo, S. (2019). Heuristics and metaheuristics approach for query optimization using genetics and memetics algorithm. Proc. 2019 1st Int'l Conf. on Cybernetics and Intelligent System (ICORIS), vol. 1, pp. 168-172. IEEE.

23. Kramer, O. (2017). Genetic Algorithm Essentials, Vol. 679. Springer.

24. Mirjalili, S. (2019). Genetic algorithm. *In:* Evolutionary Algorithms and Neural Networks, pp. 43-55. Springer, Cham.

25. Costin, H.N. and Thomas, M.D. (2018). Computational intelligence re-meets medical image processing. Methods of Information in Medicine, 57, 05/06, 270-271.
26. De Silva, C.W. (2018). Intelligent Control: Fuzzy Logic Applications. CRC Press.
27. De Barros, L.C., Rodney, C.B. and Weldon, A.L. (2017). A first course in fuzzy logic, fuzzy dynamical systems, and biomathematics: Theory and applications. Springer.
28. Osowski, S., Siroic, R., Markiewicz, T. and Siwek, K. (2008). Application of support vector machine and genetic algorithm for improved blood cell recognition. IEEE Trans. Instrum. and Measurement, 58(7), 2159-2168.
29. Du, Ke-Lin and Swamy, M.N.S. (2016). Particle swarm optimization. Search and Optimization by Metaheuristics. Birkhäuser, Cham, 153-173.
30. Marini, F. and Beata, W. (2015). Particle swarm optimization (PSO). A tutorial. Chemometrics and Intelligent Laboratory Systems, 149, 153-165.
31. Vale, A.M.P.G., Guerreiro, A.M.G., Doria-Neto, A.D., Cavalvanti-Junior, G.B., Leitao, et al. (2014). Automatic segmentation and classification of blood components in microscopic images using a fuzzy approach. R. Bras. Eng. Biom., 30(4), 341-354.
32. Romero-Zaliz, R. and Reinoso-Gordo, J.F. (2018). An updated review on watershed algorithms. Soft Computing for Sustainability Science. Springer, Cham, 235-258.
33. Monteiro, S.T., Uto, K., Kosugi, Y., Kobayashi, N., Watanabe, E. and Kameyama, K. (2005). Feature extraction of hyperspectral data for under spilled blood visualization using particle swarm optimization. International Journal of Bioelectromagnetism 7(1), 232-235.
34. Khelassi, A. and Estrela, V.V. (2021). Advances in multidisciplinary medical technologies – Engineering, modeling and findings. Proc. ICHSMT 2019. Springer Nature, Zurich, Switzerland.
35. Jordan, M.I. and Mitchell, T.M. (2015). Machine learning: Trends, perspectives, and prospects. Science, 349(6245), 255-260.
36. Goodfellow, I., Yoshua, B. and Aaron, C. (2016). Deep learning. MIT Press.
37. LeCun, Y., Yoshua, B. and Geoffrey, H. (2015). Deep learning. Nature, 521.7553, 436-444.
38. Tiwari, P., Qian, J., Li, Q., Wang, B., Gupta, D. et al. (2018). Detection of subtype blood cells using deep learning. Cognitive Systems Research, 52, 1036-1044.
39. Maier, H.R., Razavi, S., Kapelan, Z., Matott, L.S., Kasprzyk, J. and Tolson, B.A. (2018). Introductory overview: Optimization using evolutionary algorithms and other metaheuristics. Env. Modelling & Software, 114, 195-213.
40. Glover, F. and Cotta, C. (2019). An overview of meta-analytics: The promise of unifying metaheuristics and analytics. Business and Consumer Analytics: New Ideas. Springer, Cham. 693-702
41. Datta, S., Sandipan, R. and Davim, J.P. (2019). Optimization techniques: An Overview. Optimization in Industry. Springer, Cham. 1-11.
42. Cuevas, E., Espejo, E.B. and Enríquez, A.C. (2019). Introduction to metaheuristics methods. Metaheuristics Algorithms in Power Systems. Springer, Cham. 1-8.
43. Bhattacharyya, S. (ed.) (2018). Hybrid Metaheuristics for Image Analysis. Springer.
44. Hussain, K., Salleh, M.N.M., Cheng, S. and Shi, Y. (2018). Metaheuristic research: A comprehensive survey. Art. Int. Review, 52, 2191-2233.
45. Fernandez, S.A., Angel A., Juan, A.A., Adrian, J.A., Silva, D.G. and Terren, D.R. (2018). Metaheuristics in telecommunication systems: Network design, routing, and allocation problems. IEEE Systems Journal, 12.4, 3948-3957.
46. Sahoo, A. and Satish, C. (2014). Metaheuristic approaches for active contour model based medical image segmentation. Int'l J. Adv. Soft Comp. and Its App., 6.2.
47. Mesejo, P., Valsecchi, A., Marrakchi-Kacem, L., Cagnonia, S. and Damas, S. (2015).

Biomedical image segmentation using geometric deformable models and metaheuristics. Computerized Medical Imaging and Graphics, 43, 167-178.

48. Zareiforoush, H., Minaei, S., Alizadeh, M.R. and Banakar, A. (2016). Qualitative classification of milled rice grains using computer vision and metaheuristic techniques. J. Food Sc. and Techn, 53.1, 118-131.

49. Sardari, F. and Moghaddam, M.E. (2017). A hybrid occlusion free object tracking method using particle filter and modified galaxy based search metaheuristic algorithm. Applied Soft Computing, 50, 280-299.

50. Costin, H.N. and Deserno, T.M. (2018). Computational Intelligence Re-meets Medical Image Processing. Methods of Information in Medicine 57.05/06, 270-271.

51. López-Ibáñez, M., Stützle, T. and Dorigo, M. (2016). Ant colony optimization: A component-wise overview. Handbook of Heuristics. 1-37.

52. Dorigo, M. and Stützle, T. (2019). Ant colony optimization: Overview and recent advances. Handbook of Metaheuristics. Springer, Cham. 311-351.

53. da Silva, I.N., Spatti, D.H., Flauzino, R.A., Liboni, L.H.B. and Alves, S.F.R. (2017). Multilayer perceptron networks. Artificial Neural Networks. Springer, Cham. 55-115.

54. Vedaldi, A. and Karel, L. (2015). Matconvnet: Convolutional neural networks for MATLAB. Proceedings of the 23rd ACM International Conference on Multimedia. ACM, 2015.

55. de Jesus, M.A., Estrela, V.V., Saotome, O. and Stutz D. (2018). Super-resolution via particle swarm optimization variants. *In:* Hemanth, J., Balas, V. (eds). Biologically Rationalized Computing Techniques for Image Processing Applications. Lecture Notes in Computational Vision and Biomechanics, vol 25. Springer.

56. Razmjooy, N., Ramezani, M. and Estrela, V.V. (2019). A solution for Dubins path problem with uncertainties using world cup optimization and Chebyshev polynomials. *In:* Iano, Y., Arthur, R., Saotome, O., Vieira Estrela, V., Loschi, H. (eds). Proc. 4th Brazilian Technology Symp. (BTSym'18). Smart Innovation, Systems and Technologies, vol. 140. Springer.

57. Hemanth, D.J. and Estrela, V.V. (2017). Deep learning for image processing applications. Advances in Parallel Computing Series, vol. 31, IOS Press, ISBN 978-1-61499-821-1 (print), ISBN 978-1-61499-822-8 (online)

58. Shabaz, M., Sharma, A., Ajrawi, S.A. and Estrela, V.V. (eds) (2022). Multimedia-based emerging technologies and data analytics for Neuroscience as a Service (NaaS). Special Issue, Neuroscience Informatics, Elsevier.

59. de Jesus, M.A., Estrela, V.V., Khelassi, A., Aroma, R.J., Raimond, K. et al. (2021). Motion estimation role in the context of 3D video. Int'l Journal of Multimedia Data Engineering and Management (IJMDEM), 12, 16-38. IGI Global. Hershey, PA, USA.

60. Mahdavi, M., Fesanghary, M. and Damangir, E. (2007). An improved harmony search algorithm for solving optimization problems. Applied Mathematics and Computation, 188, 1567-1579.

61. Li, Y., Zhan, Z., Gong, Y., Chen, W., Zhang, J. et al. (2015). Differential evolution with an evolution path: A DEEP evolutionary algorithm. IEEE Transactions on Cybernetics, 45, 1798-1810.

62. Heidari, A.A. and Pahlavani, P. (2017). An efficient modified grey wolf optimizer with Lévy flight for optimization tasks. Appl. Soft Comput., 60, 115-134.

63. Rajabioun, R. (2011). Cuckoo Optimization Algorithm. Appl. Soft Comput., 11, 5508-5518.

64. Coello, C.A. and Cortés, N.C. (2005). Solving multiobjective optimization problems using an artificial immune system. Genetic Programming and Evolvable Machines, 6, 163-190.

65. Kanakubo, M. and Hagiwara, M. (2007). Speed-up technique for association rule mining based on an artificial life algorithm. 2007 IEEE International Conference on Granular Computing (GRC 2007), 318-318.

66. Dhivyaprabha, T.T. and Subashini, P. (2017). Performance analysis of synergistic fibroblast optimization (SFO) algorithm. 2017 IEEE Int'l Conference on Current Trends in Advanced Computing (ICCTAC), 1-7.

67. Majumder, A., Behera, L. and Venkatesh, K.S. (2014). Emotion recognition from geometric facial features using self-organizing map. Pattern Recognition, 47, 1282-1293.

68. Karaboga, D. and Basturk, B. (2007). A powerful and efficient algorithm for numerical function optimization: Artificial bee colony (ABC) algorithm. Journal of Global Optimization, 39, 459-471.

69. Mirjalili, S.M. and Lewis, A. (2016). The whale optimization algorithm. Advances in Engineering Software, 95, 51-67.

70. Tilahun, S.L. and Ong, H.C. (2012). Modified firefly algorithm. J. Applied Mathematics, 467631:1-467631:12.

71. Aroma, J., Raimond, K., Razmjooy, N., Estrela, V.V., Hemanth, J.D. et al. (2020). Multispectral vs hyperspectral imaging for unmanned aerial vehicles: Current and prospective state of affairs. *In:* Estrela V.V., Hemanth J., Saotome O., Nikolakopoulos G., Sabatini R. (eds). Imaging and Sensing for Unmanned Aircraft Systems, 2(7), 133-156, IET, London, UK.

72. Coelho, A.M., Assis, J.T. and Estrela, V.V. (2009). Error concealment by means of clustered blockwise PCA. 2009 Picture Coding Symposium, 1-4, IEEE.

73. Coelho, A.M. and Estrela, V.V. (2012). EM-based mixture models applied to video event detection Principal Component Analysis – Engineering Applications. IntechOpen.

74. Ravi, V., Naveen, N. and Pandey, M. (2013). Hybrid classification and regression models via particle swarm optimization auto associative neural network-based nonlinear PCA. Int. J. Hybrid Intell. Syst., 10, 137-149.

75. Miranda, V., Martins, J.D. and Palma, V. (2014). Optimizing large scale problems with metaheuristics in a reduced space mapped by autoencoders – Application to the wind-hydro coordination. IEEE Transactions on Power Systems, 29, 3078-3085.

76. Kriegel, H., Kröger, P. and Zimek, A. (2009). Clustering high-dimensional data: A survey on subspace clustering, pattern-based clustering, and correlation clustering. TKDD, 3, 1:1-1:58.

77. Dragan, D. and Ivetic, D. (2009). Architectures of DICOM based PACS for JPEG2000 medical image streaming. Comput. Sci. Inf. Syst., 6, 186-203.

78. Estrela, V.V. and Herrmann, A.E. (2016). Content-Based Image Retrieval (CBIR) in remote clinical diagnosis and healthcare. *In:* M. Cruz-Cunha, I. Miranda, R. Martinho, R. Rijo (eds). Encyclopedia of E-Health and Telemedicine. Hershey, PA: IGI Global, 495-520.

79. Caya, M.V., Arturo, E.D. and Bautista, C.Q. (2021). Dog identification system using nose print biometrics. 2021 IEEE 13th Int'l Conf. Humanoid, Nanotechnology, Information Technology, Communication and Control, Environment, and Management (HNICEM), 1-6.

80. Chen, L., Papandreou, G., Kokkinos, I., Murphy, K. and Yuille, A.L. (2016). DeepLab: Semantic image segmentation with deep convolutional nets, atrous convolution, and fully connected CRFs. IEEE Trans. Pattern Analysis and Machine Intelligence, 40, 834-848.

81. Kothari, S., Phan, J.H., Stokes, T.H. and Wang, M.D. (2013). Pathology imaging informatics for quantitative analysis of whole-slide images. JAMIA (2013).

82. Fernandes, S.R., Estrela, V.V. and Saotome, O. (2014). On improving sub-pixel accuracy by means of B-Spline. Proc. 2014 IEEE International Conference on Imaging Systems and Techniques (IST). https://doi.org/10.1109/IST.2014.6958448

83. Ghaznavi, F., Evans, A., Madabhushi, A. and Feldman, M. (2013). Digital imaging in pathology: Whole-slide imaging and beyond. Annual Review of Pathology, 8, 331-359.

84. Goacher, E., Randell, R., Williams, B.J. and Treanor, D. (2017). The diagnostic concordance of whole slide imaging and light microscopy: A systematic review. Archives of Pathology & Laboratory Medicine, 141(1), 151-161.

85. Kaur, S. and Kaur, P. (2016). An edge detection technique with image segmentation using ant colony optimization: A review. Proc. 2016 Online International Conference on Green Engineering and Technologies (IC-GET), 1-5.

86. Stack, G. (2021). Post-transfusion detection of RBC alloimmunization: Timing is everything. Transfusion, 61.

87. Das, D., Samal, C., Ukey, D., Chowdhary, G., Mohanty, S.P. et al. (2022). CoviLearn: A machine learning integrated smart X-Ray device in healthcare cyber-physical system for automatic initial screening of COVID-19. Sn Computer Science, 3.

88. Gupta, S., Girshick, R.B., Arbeláez, P.A. and Malik, J. (2014). Learning rich features from RGB-D images for object detection and segmentation. Proc. 2014 ECCV.

89. Sucaet, Y. and Waelput, W. (2014). Digital Pathology. Springer.

90. Ferrer-Roca, O., Marcan, F., Vidal, M., Ruckhaus, E., Fernández-Baíllo, R. et al. (2011). Grid technology in telepatology and personalised treatment. *In:* E. Kldiashvili (ed.). Grid Technologies for E-Health: Applications for Telemedicine Services and Delivery, pp. 117-128. Hershey, PA: IGI Global.

91. Razmjooy, N., Razmjooy, S., Vahedi, Z., Estrela, V.V., Oliveira, G.G. et al. (2020). Skin color segmentation based on artificial neural network improved by a modified grasshopper optimization algorithm. *In:* Razmjooy, N., Ashourian, M., Foroozandeh, Z. (eds). Metaheuristics and Optimization in Computer and Electrical Engineering. Lecture Notes in Electrical Engineering, vol. 696. Springer, Cham.

92. van Manen, L., Birkhoff, W.A., Eggermont, J., Hoveling, R.J., Nicklin, P.J. et al. (2021). Detection of cutaneous oxygen saturation using a novel snapshot hyperspectral camera: A feasibility study. Quantitative Imaging in Medicine and Surgery, 11(9), 3966-3977.

93. Yellin, F., Haeffele, B.D. and Vidal, R. (2017). Blood cell detection and counting in holographic lens-free imaging by convolutional sparse dictionary learning and coding. 2017 IEEE 14th International Symposium on Biomedical Imaging (ISBI 2017), 650-653.

94. Wang, Q., Li, Q., Zhou, M., Sun, Z., Liu, H. et al. (2017). A hyperspectral vessel image registration method for blood oxygenation mapping. PLoS ONE, 12.

95. Manni, F., van der Sommen, F., Zinger, S., Shan, C., Holthuizen, R. et al. (2020). Hyperspectral imaging for skin feature detection: Advances in markerless tracking for spine surgery. Applied Sciences, 10, 4078.

96. Cuevas, E., Díaz, P. and Camarena, O. (2020). Detection of White Blood Cells with Metaheuristic Computation. Intelligent Systems Reference Library.

97. Sharma, P., Sharma, M., Gupta, D. and Mittal, N. (2021). Detection of white blood cells using optimized qGWO. Intell. Decis. Technol., 15, 141-149.

98. Anita Davamani, K., Rene Robin, C.R., Doreen Robin, D. and Jani Anbarasi, L. (2022). Adaptive blood cell segmentation and hybrid Learning-based blood cell classification: A metaheuristic-based model. Biomedical Sig. Processing and Control. 75, 103570.

99. Alizamir, A., Gholami, A., Bahrami, N. and Ostadhassan, M. (2022). Refractive index of hemoglobin analysis: A comparison of alternating conditional expectations and Computational Intelligence Models. ACS Omega, 7, 33769-33782.

100. Sadiq, S., Khalid, M.U., Mui-Zzud-Din, Ullah, S., Aslam, W. et al. (2021). Classification of β-Thalassemia carriers from red blood cell indices using ensemble classifier. IEEE Access, 9, 45528-45538.

101. El-aziz, M.E., Neggaz, N., Moghdani, R., Ewees, A.A., Jiménez, E.V. et al. (2021). Multilevel thresholding image segmentation based on improved volleyball premier league algorithm using whale optimization algorithm. Multimedia Tools and Applications, 80, 12435-12468.

102. Rai, R., Das, A. and Dhal, K.G. (2022). Nature-inspired optimization algorithms and their significance in multi-thresholding image segmentation: An inclusive review. Evolving Systems, 1-57. Springer Cham, Zurich, Switzerland.

103. Zhao, D., Liu, L., Yu, F., Heidari, A.A., Wang, M. et al. (2021c). Ant colony optimization with horizontal and vertical crossover search: fundamental visions for multi-threshold image segmentation. Expert Syst Appl., 167, 114122.

104. Saeidifar, M., Yazdi, M. and Zolghadrasli, A.A. (2021). Performance improvement in brain tumor detection in MRI images using a combination of evolutionary algorithms and active contour method. Journal of Digital Imaging, 34, 1209-1224.

105. Sahlol, A.T., Kollmannsberger, P. and Ewees, A.A. (2020). Efficient classification of white blood cell leukemia with improved swarm optimization of deep features. Scientific Reports, 10.

Super-resolution Image Processing for Hemoglobin Quantification: A Case Study

A.A. Khurshid[1], Soni Chaturvedi[2], Boudjelal Meftah[3] [0000-0001-5772-1878]

[1] Shri Ramdeobaba College of Engineering and Management, Nagpur, India
khurshidaa@rknec.edu
[2] PIET, Nagpur, India, soni2569@gmail.com
[3] University of Mascara, Algeria, boudjelal.meftah@univ-mascara.dz

1. Introduction

Blood is an essential liquid that helps humans accomplish crucial activities. Many illnesses, including anemia, leukemia, and malaria, are diagnosed via peripheral blood smear analysis. Red blood cells (RBCs), white blood cells (WBCs), and platelets make up the blood.

Red blood cells (RBCs), white blood cells (WBCs), plasma, and platelets are the major components of human blood. RBCs, on the other hand, take up the most space in blood. RBCs may be both healthy and harmful. An unhealthy or abnormal red blood cell count suggests a blood disease. RBCs can be distinguished by differences in size, shape, and color. RBCs can be assessed by standard microscopy, which leads to misreported results and a heavy burden for specialists. Many technologies aid health technicians, hematologists, and pathologists in recognizing RBCs and measuring various RBC characteristics such as area, perimeter, diameter, shape geometric factor (SGF), and detecting the center pallor and target flag.

WBCs play a vital function in monitoring a person's health. WBCs are classified into five types: lymphocytes, monocytes, neutrophils, eosinophils, and basophils. Hematological diseases are indicated by changes in the number and/or appearance of these cells. Manual microscopic examination of white blood cells is carried out with the gold standard approach. Nonetheless, the outcome is dependent on the hematologist's ability and experience. An increase or decrease in the number of WBCs in the peripheral blood suggests a problem. Morphological differences, such as form, size, and color, also aid in diagnosis. Thus, WBC detection and categorization are critical in peripheral blood smear studies [23-26]. Total WBC count, differential WBC count, and morphological analysis are all part of the manual examination of WBCs. Manual WBC evaluation is time-consuming and prone to inter-observer variance. Computer-assisted WBC analysis is gaining popularity as a way to minimize' the workload of hematologists. Automated blood cell analysis allows for rapid and accurate findings. It can also efficiently process large amounts of data.

Pre-processing, segmentation, feature extraction, classifier, and disease detection are steps of the microscopic blood cell analysis framework. Pre-processing entails enhancing the obtained image quality and removing noise. Grayscale conversion, thresholding, filtering, histogram stretching, and morphological procedures are all included. The pre-processed picture is portioned to get the region of interest for further processing. WBCs, RBCs, and platelets are isolated here. Edge detection, watershed transformation, mathematical morphology, Zack algorithm, K-means clustering, SDM, HSV thresholding, and Otsu's method are computer vision techniques used for segmentation. When staining a blood smear, there are overlapping cells. Expulsion of these overlapping cells during segmentation is an arduous task. The Hough transform removes some overlapping; nevertheless, it slows down the framework.

Support Vector Machines (SVMs) and various variations of the Hough transform are used to classify segmented pictures. Quite a few datasets are available for research and analysis of microscopic blood cells, including the BCCD (Kaggle) Database, ALL-IDB1, ALL-IDB2, Atlas of Hematology by Nivaldo Meridos, Leukocyte pictures for division and characterization (LISC), Ash image library, and C-NMC dataset.

There are several application fields where microscopic blood cell inspection plays an important role. Complex image processing and computer vision techniques might be used to conduct RBC, WBC count, blood group identification, leukemia detection, sickle cell detection, the partition of distinct WBC sub-classes, and malaria parasite detection.

There are two approaches for achieving automatic classification: conventional image processing and deep learning. Segmentation, feature extraction, and classification are all interrelated processes in the traditional image processing technique. Due to the presence of a dark nucleus, segmenting WBCs using an image processing technique is not a demanding operation; nevertheless, precise identification of WBC borders and separation of overlapping cells are demanding problems in automated detection and classification of WBCs.

Many approaches for classifying WBCs using neural networks have been developed. It is a supervised machine learning method with three layers: input, hidden, and output. As a result, the prediction is dependent on the provided features in a technique.

Several works [23-24, 27-35, 57] used computational intelligence, such as metaheuristics, to tackle this problem. The automated categorization of WBCs using standard image processing methods has received attention in recent decades. These approaches employed either grayscale representations of the source pictures or any color components. Jaroonrut et al. [40] utilized an effective Naive Bayes (NB) classifier to detect WBC kinds.

Mathur et al. [41] combined a Naive Bayesian classifier with an incremental learning classifier to classify WBCs and reported an overall accuracy of about

92 percent. WBC classification was also accomplished using neural network classifiers [42, 43]. Sedat et al. [42] compared neural network results with and without the Principal Component Analysis (PCA) technique [44, 45], achieving an overall accuracy of about 95% with PCA and 65% without PCA.

Seyed et al. [43] compared the effectiveness of Support Vector Machines (SVMs) and Neural Network (NN) classifiers for categorizing WBCs into five categories and found that SVMs had a classification accuracy of 90 to 96 percent. In addition, Neelam et al. [46] compared the results of SVMs and NN for WBC classification, revealing an average accuracy of about 97 percent for NN and 94 percent for SVMs. Qingli et al. [47] investigated morphological characteristics for WBC categorization and obtained a classification accuracy of 94%.

Omid et al. [48] presented a technique for detecting and classifying normal WBCs that resulted in a 93 percent accurate classification rate. Siroic and Moradi et al. [49, 50] utilized SVM to detect lymphoblast WBCs with an average accuracy of 96% [49, 50]. Rawat et al. [51] utilized a genetic algorithm and an SVM classifier to detect acute leukemia in peripheral blood smear pictures. Using PBS pictures, Mohapatra et al. [52] presented a technique for detecting ALL.

Multiple classifiers were tested for ALL detection, including NB, KNN, MLP, SVM, and an ensemble of classifiers. Using an ensemble of classifiers, they achieved an average classifier sensitivity of about 90%. WBC analysis using standard image processing methods is difficult because of its complicated biological appearance, staining method employed, and changes in obtained illumination.

A Convolutional Neural Network (CNN) is widely used for image categorization [4-6, 55, 56]. It may classify medical images in three ways: full-training CNN, transfer learning, and CNN as a feature generator. In the case of complete training, the network is built from the ground up. This necessitates a significant amount of labeled data, which is difficult to get in the medical sector. In contrast, the network is pre-trained with huge non-medical data in the transfer learning technique, which can then be fine-tuned for a given application.

The third technique extracts characteristics from specific levels of the pre-trained network. These characteristics can then be utilized to train external classifiers. Deep learning algorithms work directly on raw pixels and discover features on their own. As a result, deep learning techniques such as stacked autoencoders and CNN have been developed for medical image processing that is resistant to noise and changes in illumination.

Stacked autoencoders have been used in several investigational works for medical picture segmentation and classification [36-39]. Auto-encoder is a type of deep learning machine learning algorithm that works similarly to a neural network. It is a learning approach that converts inputs to outputs with the least amount of feasible error. A feature set or pictures can be used as input to the autoencoder. Encoders, decoders, and a loss function are all part of it. An encoder is a neural network that generates output y based on the size of the given hidden layer input x. A decoder is a neural network that generates output x from a given input y. The output of an encoder is sent into a decoder. For classification, it employs output functions such as sigmoid, softmax, and others.

Anemia is a disorder in which the body's red blood cells cannot transport oxygen to various tissues and organs. This condition is more common in women, especially during pregnancy. Fatigue, weakness, and pale skin with eye yellowing are all symptoms that can be easily diagnosed by looking at the conjunctiva or thumb (palm) pallor [53, 54]. The gold standard is the direct cyanmethemoglobin technique. Other approaches, such as indirect cyanmethemoglobin and hemocue, necessitate well-equipped clinical laboratories and competent technicians, both of which are sometimes unavailable in rural primary health care centers. Kuenster [16] proposed a noninvasive hemoglobin (Hb) estimate methodology based on optical imaging. George Zonios et al. [17] proposed estimating melanin and Hb in the skin using diffuse reflectance spectroscopy. Although these approaches are noninvasive, they still require particular sensors that detect specific wavelengths, which is another disadvantage in rural regions. The accuracy and reliability of pallor for anemia identification were investigated [18]. They discovered that the presence of pallor could help diagnose severe anemia but not mild anemia.

Rebecca et al. [12] published a study evaluating the utility of clinical pallor in detecting severe anemia, indicating that clinical pallor is closely linked with hemoglobin concentration and that conjunctiva pallor had the best sensitivity and specificity among the several pallor sites. Despite the fact that numerous researchers have found a link between clinical pallor and Hb values, the accuracy is not comparable to the gold standard. Srinivasan et al. [19] proposed a noninvasive method of detecting anemia using color information from a photograph of a fingertip (usually the thumb) taken under standard settings and with blood flow to the fingertip occluded in the same standard conditions. Though the approach is straightforward, the setup and method for occluding the blood are unclear. Jay et al. [20] developed a noninvasive approach of determining Hb concentration by taking a digital image of a target area, such as the palpebral conjunctiva, nail beds, palm, and so on, and comparing it to a reference color card. Vitoantonio Bevilacqua et al. [21] proposed constructing a simple wearable gadget that patients can use at home to determine their demand for blood transfusion on their own using images of the conjunctiva.

During the literature review, it was discovered that traditional Hb detection methods are invasive. At the same time, noninvasive approaches presented by various researchers help detect severe anemia but not for detecting moderate anemia. As a result, research efforts can be focused on developing a simple, noninvasive technology. Such efforts may also provide clinical support to physicians for the accurate detection of moderate anemia caused by a drop in Hb levels by assessing the color of the conjunctival membrane. Thus, with little resources and competent labor, digital image processing techniques can be employed to investigate primitive diagnostics methods for anemia diagnosis at an early stage. By quantifying conjunctival/ fingertip pallor, an image captured with a digital consumer camera or smartphone can be used to detect anemia. It is based on a subjective assessment of the color of the conjunctival membrane, with pallor indicating anemia. Despite developments in collection technology and the performance of optimized reconstruction algorithms over the last two decades, imaging conditions, as well as factors such as Noise and Blur, make it difficult to capture an image at the desired resolution. The quality of an image is often restricted by hardware equipment such as the imaging system and the bandwidth during the image transmission process. A low-resolution (LR) image with missing details is eventually presented. The promising solution to this problem is employing Super-Resolution (SR) techniques which can be applied in image processing where multiple frames of the same scene are captured.

The following sections describe deep learning super-resolution approaches for improving picture details for efficient color information-based detection to quantify anemia from pallor locations. The sensitivity and specificity of anemia detection are also studied to determine the diagnostic value of conjunctival examination. Such implementations can pave the way for creating a noninvasive screening .test for anemia under low-resource settings specifically for rural areas and can be useful in the early treatment of anemia. The chapter is organized into different sections. Section 2 presents the need and methods to improve image resolution for enhanced color-based feature extraction. Section 3 details the approach used for hemoglobin quantification. Section 4 offers the conducted experiment details while Sections 5 and 6 cover discussions and conclusions drawn.

2. Image Super-Resolution Method

A lower resolution image can be caused by a decreased spatial resolution (i.e., size) or deterioration (blurring). Thus the High-Resolution (HR) and Low-Resolution (LR) images can be related. If the exact degradation function is known, the HR picture can be reconstructed by applying its inverse on the LR image. The goal of super-resolution (SR) is to produce a HR output from one of its LR variants. A high-resolution image has a high pixel density, which means it contains more information about the original image. The high-resolution requirements are important in medical imaging for diagnosis since they allow for improved image analysis.

2.1. Basic Super-Resolution Algorithm

The increase in the number of pixels per unit area in the original sample causes image super-resolution. It is based on reconstruction or learning in the case of a single input image. The single-image super-resolution approaches are primarily classified according to whether they use reconstruction or learning [7]. The goal of image super-resolution methods based on reconstruction is to restore image details by interpolating a low resolution (LR) input sample while keeping the sharpness of the picture's edges. However, the performance is dependent on prior information and requires post-processing. Learning-based methods provide a training model for determining the correspondences between low and high-resolution images from a database. The "trained" model created is then used to rebuild HR images from the LR input sample. The method utilized is either pixel or frame-based. The quality and amount of the training sample determine the success of such approaches. Pyramid of features [8] and sparse representation [9] are two other ways.

In recent years, example-based super-resolution algorithms for reconstructing a high-resolution image from a single low-resolution image have been presented. This method uses a library of existing low- and high-resolution image pairings to learn the correlation between and related high-resolution images. This knowledge is then applied to a fresh low-resolution image to obtain the image's most likely high-resolution counterpart. Deep learning algorithms have been successful in handling the challenge of image super-resolution when only a single low-resolution image is available. Deep learning algorithms based on artificial neural networks (ANNs) undergo complete learning of informative hierarchical representations automatically and then leverage them to achieve the final purpose, in contrast to traditional learning algorithms that select useful hand-derived features with expert domain knowledge [4]. ANNs have made significant progress, yet they still have some flaws that limit their evolution. With the resuscitation of the modern ANN, highlighted by Hinton's proposal of the restricted Boltzmann machine (RBM) in 2006 [5], the deep neural network (DNN) was born. Models based on the DNN have gained amazing performance due to the availability of massive computational power and the development of new methods, with generative adversarial networks (GAN) [6] garnering interest due to their capacity to solve tough unlabeled data problems.

Generative Adversarial Networks (GANs) are commonly employed for picture Super-Resolution due to their high capacity for deriving effective high-level abstractions that connect the LR and HR space. Enhanced Generative Adversarial Networks (EGANs) are often used to improve visual quality further. This section explains how to use the EGANs. Figure 1 shows the procedure for obtaining super-resolution images. Low-resolution images are supplied into the generator. The SR images are then distinguished from the ground truth using HR images to ensure that the SR picture is generated as close to the ground truth as possible. The loss is determined using the SR feature maps that have been processed through the discriminator, and the HR picture is extracted using the VGG model's feature maps. The loss is updated such that the SR images are adjusted to match the HR. The

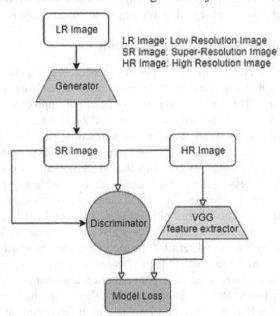

Figure 1. Process for obtaining super-resolution images

discriminator's and generator's losses are then back-propagated to update the process until the discriminator can no longer distinguish the generated images further.

2.2. Enhanced Super-Resolution Generative Adversarial Network (ESRGAN)

This is a perceptual-driven technique to single-image super-resolution that can improve quantitative processing and analysis of image data. A Generative Adversarial Network (GAN) is an image texture recovery technique that tries to restore structure information locally and globally. The generative model is lined against a discriminative model in adversarial networks, distinguishing whether a sample comes from the model distribution or the data distribution. The generative model aims to create a fake sample that can be used without being detected, whereas the discriminative model aims to detect the fake sample. Both sides compete to enhance their procedures until the false sample is indistinguishable from the real one. The GAN's top-level architecture consists of the generator and discriminator networks. The generator network seeks to generate fake data, while the discriminator network tells the difference between genuine and fake data, assisting the generator in producing more realistic data. Residual Dense Block (RRDB) is a feature of ESRGAN that combines a multi-level residual network with a dense connection without Batch Normalization [1]. This study improves the discriminator by employing the Relativistic average GAN (RaGAN), which allows the discriminator to predict relative realness rather than absolute value. Network architecture, adversarial loss, and eternal loss are the three fundamental components of Super-resolution GAN. The discriminator uses a relativistic GAN to forecast relative realness rather than absolute value. The basic architecture is depicted in Fig. 2, with residual blocks reflecting a mix of context, perceptual, and adversarial losses. For image upscaling, context and perceptual losses are applied. In contrast, adversarial loss drives the neural network to the natural image manifold using a discriminator network trained to distinguish between super-resolved and original images. Perceptual quality is improved by the network rather than objective quality, which is a measure of quality that is considerably closer to human vision. The model is built in the TensorFlow framework. The results of studies utilizing a deeper network with RRDB show that

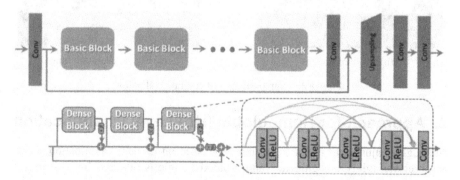

Figure 2. Basic architecture with residual in residual blocks

artifacts are removed and that the model can capture more semantic information with sharper edges and richer textures.

Since, the PSNR measure fundamentally contradicts the subjective judgment of human observers [2], PSNR-based techniques are prone to over-smoothed outputs with insufficient high-frequency details and are not suitable for the described application where texture-based characteristics are retrieved. The super-resolution image reconstruction (ESRGAN) technique is used to improve the spatial resolution of conjunctival pallor images obtained with a camera, resulting in superior feature extraction based on color and texture, which is required for hemoglobin measurement. Figure 3 (a, b) shows examples of original and high-resolution conjunctival pallor photographs. Dr. Ching-chao Fan of the Saint Mary's Hospital in Luodog provided the experimentation data [3]. The data comprises of a rectangular patch sliced from a digital camera image of the palpebral conjunctiva and the actual Hb concentration of the individuals. There are 103 photos in all, each with its own Hb concentration value.

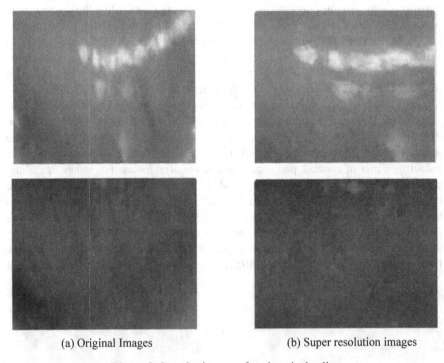

(a) Original Images   (b) Super resolution images

Figure 3. Samples images of conjunctival pallor

3. Approach for Hemoglobin (Hb) Level Quantification

Although conjunctival pallor is related to anemia on clinical examination, inter-observer variability is significant, and a blood sample is required for a definitive diagnosis of anemia. Anemia point-of-care testing methods are widely available. They entail the analysis of blood by a finger-prick sample and the use of liquid reagents, which expose healthcare personnel to the risk of blood-borne infections. The following work attempts to detect and measure anemia under difficult working conditions, as anemia continues to be a global health concern.

This section outlines the processes for noninvasive anemia identification in settings with limited resources, such as rural clinics and hospitals, by quantifying conjunctival pallor using digital images taken with a consumer camera, allowing for faster anemia screening. The hemoglobin (Hb) level is calculated from the captured images using color and texture data effectively. Rotation, translation, size alterations, and deformations do not affect the color characteristics. When machine learning techniques are employed for hemoglobin quantification, feature extraction translates image information into numerical features, identifying the most discriminating properties in images that may be treated to provide better results. The color-based features are useful for picture level categorization for anemia since paleness or pallor is a symptom of anemia, suggesting low hemoglobin concentrations in the blood. As a result, each color image is subjected to plane color changes. The collected pictures of palpebral conjunctiva subjected to denoising, segmentation, and super-resolution are further processed as indicated in Fig. 4 to determine the Hb concentration present in human blood.

The first stage gets a high-resolution image of the subject's palpebral conjunctiva captured with a camera whose Hb concentration is determined. The image is then processed by extracting the essential features in the next stage. The extraction of invariant features is processed using an intelligent machine-learning algorithm to obtain helpful information for estimating the value of Hb concentration existing in the human subject's blood.

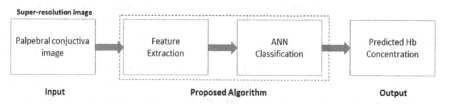

Figure 4. Steps involved in hemoglobin quantification

3.1. Feature Extraction

Because the color distribution of the palpebral conjunctiva is the conventional approach for anemia diagnosis, the original images of the palpebral conjunctiva are treated to an appropriate feature extraction approach. Super-resolution digital images capture a significant quantity of color information near what the human eye sees and are used to interpret color changes between images using color and texture-based characteristics.

Color is generally divided into device-dependent color spaces like RGB color and perception-oriented color spaces like CIELAB color space [10]. A color space is a crucial tool for analyzing an image's color capabilities, and device-independent spaces express color in absolute terms. Therefore CIE 1976 L*a*b* is used to extract color features that are important for quantifying Hb values, resulting in more precise computations. Furthermore, it creates a more perceptually linear color space than other color spaces. The features that were extracted are the image's mean RGB value, brightness, and Erythema index (EI = log(Sred) – log(Sgreen)) are extracted from the CIE 1976 L*a*b* color scale, with Sred and Sgreen representing the image's red and green channel brightness, respectively. The a* value is extracted from the CIE 1976 L*a*b* color scale, with positive a* values indicating the presence of the red component in the image. To characterize the texture of the image, the other two parameters, High Hue Ratio (HHR) and Entropy, are also retrieved. Texture, a significant element of natural photographs, offers information about the spatial arrangement of colors in an image, and Hue enables simpler interpretation of color characteristics. The color and texture data combination provides a robust feature set for Hb value prediction because entropy is a measure of information content. The image is first converted to the HSV color scale, after which the image's mean hue is computed. If the hue of a pixel is greater than the image's mean hue value, it is regarded as a high hue pixel, which is beneficial in scenarios when the lighting level changes. The image is histogram equalized after conversion to grayscale, and the entropy (Ent) is calculated using a statistical methodology.

3.2. Hb Value Prediction

The images of the palpebral conjunctiva are pre-processed, then features are extracted, and these features are used as input for the machine-learning methods that can be used to quantify Hb values. In general, supervised, semi supervised, unsupervised, and reinforcement learning are used in machine learning algorithms. The size, quality, and diversity of the data and the expected output from the data all influence which machine learning technique to choose. Accuracy, training duration, parameters, and data points must all be taken into account. To process information, an artificial neural network (ANN) based reinforcement learning system is utilized here, which consists of 'units' organized in a succession of layers, each of which connects to layers on either side, working in unison to solve specific problems. It is preferable to quantify Hb values because this is a common learning strategy capable of handling huge learning issues. The convergent neural network consists of a single hidden layer in the input layer with eight nodes and a single node in the output layer. The network with a single hidden layer can handle the most demanding functions. The final converged minimum network is trained with the Levenberg-Marquardt backpropagation algorithm with the best learning rate to determine, outperforming straightforward gradient descent and other conjugate gradient methods. The mean squared error is the evaluation metric, and it is reduced by modifying the network parameters. The Levenberg-Marquardt algorithm is derived from Newton's method for minimizing functions that are sums of squares of nonlinear functions [11]. While backpropagation is the steepest descent algorithm, the Levenberg-Marquardt algorithm is derived from Newton's method for minimizing functions that are sums of squares of nonlinear functions.

The experimentation data consists of 103 samples, of which 70 samples were utilized for training the network, and 33 samples were used to test the network. After extensive simulation based on input data distribution, the deduction reached is that on employing the hyperbolic tangent sigmoid function, the network converges with fewer computational nodes and fewer network defects. The inclusion of the hyperbolic tangent sigmoid activation function in the hidden units also ensures that no hidden layer unit freezes, ensuring that the desired constraints are enforced on the output.

4. Experiment Results

The Hb value determined in a laboratory test is compared to the results obtained after evaluating 33 samples for the suggested approach. Subjects with hemoglobin levels ranging from 8 to 13.7 g/dL were included in the 33 test samples. A confusion matrix is shown to evaluate the performance and appropriateness of the suggested algorithm for identifying anemia, as given in Table 1. Because the data does not indicate gender, age, or sex, the results for those with Hb concentrations less than 11 are identified as anemic; otherwise, the patient is not anemic.

Table 1. Experimental results for Hb cutoff 11 gm/dL

	Actual Anemia	Actual non-anemia
Predicted anemia	11 (TP)	1 (FP)
Predicted non-anemia	2 (FN)	19 (TN)

Table 2 shows the sensitivity, specificity, and accuracy of the above-mentioned algorithm, determined using the equations given in [12]. According to the manual for health workers for anemia detection methods in low-resource settings, the coefficient of variance for a test to be acceptable for diagnosis should be less than 5% [12]. The test can be considered acceptable because the obtained coefficient of variance for the suggested algorithm is less than 5%. A higher priority is placed on high sensitivity when evaluating the performance as such tests necessitate a high level of sensitivity. Second, SR can be utilized as the first stage to improve the detection rate, while machine learning is the second step to reduce false positives. Differences in color saturation due to differences in imaging parameters caused slight differences with the potential for inaccurate quantification of Hb values and was avoided by performing image SR.

Table 2. Performance of the proposed algorithm

Performance Parameter	Value in percentage
Sensitivity	84.61
Specificity	95
Accuracy	90.90

Hemoglobin concentration ranges are used to classify anemia severity. Mild and moderate anemia types are defined by hemoglobin values between 7.0 and 11 g/dl [12]. According to the experiment, all samples examined in the above-mentioned range were accurately identified with an accuracy of 86.18 percent. As a result, compared to other ' published work [13-15] of researchers, the proposed method with image super-resolution and derived characteristics is suitable for identifying mild and moderate anemia with enhanced accuracy. Detection of rare hemoglobin H (HbH) inclusions in red cells in the peripheral blood has been proposed in [22] using a convolutional neural network on digital images of HbH-positive and HbH-negative blood smears (invasive method). Table 3 compares the suggested algorithm's performance to that of earlier research by other researchers, demonstrating its applicability.

Table 3. Performance comparison of proposed method

Parameter	[13]*	[14]**	[15]***	****[21]	***Proposed method	Non-invasive method based on Clinical Signs as given by WHO [12]
Sensitivity	0.74	0.78	0.71	91	84.61	0.64
Specificity	0.83	0.83	0.89	0.99	0.95	0.70-1.00

*43 testing samples with no cross-validation, **100 testing samples with 10-fold cross-validation [63-65], ***33 testing samples with no cross-validation, ****100 samples of blood smears for detection of rare hemoglobin H (HbH) inclusions in red cells

5. Discussion

There is always a need to get proper and trusted diagnoses in the medical science field. Machine learning (ML) and computer vision (CV) can prove the system of suggestive diagnosis to achieve better accuracy than existing approaches. Where the morphology is concerned with microscopic imaging, pathologists' experience and skillset always matter in a significant case. There is a need to have software frameworks utilizing machine learning and artificial intelligence to conquer this problem. Also, there is a problem with the explainability of AI algorithms towards particular diagnostic decisions. To take care of this, AI explainable frameworks could be utilized in the future [58-62]. For the treatment of different diseases, AI can also play its role in a very trusted manner.

The findings of the experiments show that the suggested minimum artificial neural network system can be used to aid medical practitioners in noninvasive Hb detection in clinics with limited resources. The proposed technique is appropriate for detecting mild and moderate anemia. The use of super-resolution to improve deep feature extraction increases the accuracy of noninvasive Hb detection and quantification in low-resource situations, which is a strength of this study. The palpebral conjunctiva's pale appearance can detect anemia. Although different studies presented noninvasive approaches for anemia detection that are useful for detecting severe anemia, they did not work well for detecting mild anemia. As a result, this work represents a step in the right direction. Invasive blood sampling is still the gold standard, but it cannot be utilized for continuous monitoring in cases of intensive care and premature infants who are at higher risk of infection and blood loss. There is an evident need for noninvasive Hb testing in this susceptible patient group. Super-resolution can provide high-resolution images, revealing additional details about the original image, and it could be a valuable tool for diagnostic and therapeutic recommendations. As a widely available computing platform, the smartphone provides a noninvasive alternative to traditional blood Hb readings. In addition to conjunctival pallor, we recommend the fingertip as a data collecting site for the ideal creation of an accurate Hb prediction model since it is easier to access, and these two data collection methods can provide improved reliability and accuracy. To measure the Hb level, an external mobile phone-based device that is cost-effective, readily attachable, correctly fits with the finger, and user-friendly can be constructed in the future. Future clinical investigations comparing AI-assisted diagnoses" sensitivity, specificity, and relative efficiency to the standard approach will build on our findings [66-74]. The disclosed development methodology could be used for various types of image-based rare cell detection in the future.

6. Conclusion

Anemia is a potentially fatal disease that affects individuals all over the world. Conjunctival/fingertip pallor may be quantified using digital pictures acquired with a camera or a simple smartphone, which can be used to identify anemia. Super-resolution image reconstruction can improve the spatial resolution of recorded pictures, allowing for rich feature extraction based on color and texture, which is required for hemoglobin measurement. According to WHO standards, an artificial neural network classifier is employed to correlate the hemoglobin level to be assessed with the values of the amount measured by the conventional technique. The sensitivity and specificity of anemia detection, which is important for reliable anemia diagnosis, define the diagnostic value of conjunctival analysis in the clinic and low-resource settings.

The results of the studies demonstrate that the proposed minimal artificial neural network system can assist medical practitioners in noninvasive Hb detection in clinics with limited resources. The suggested method is suitable for identifying mild to moderate anemia. The use of super-resolution to improve deep feature extraction increases the accuracy of noninvasive Hb detection and quantification in low-resource conditions, which is a study's strength. The pale appearance of the palpebral conjunctiva indicates anemia.

References

1. Wang, X., Yu, K., Wu, S., Gu, J., Liu, Y. et al. (2018). ESRGAN: Enhanced super-resolution generative adversarial networks. Proc. ECCV Workshops.

2. Ledig, C., Theis, L., Huszár, F., Caballero, J., Aitken, A.P. et al. (2017). Photo-realistic single image super-resolution using a generative adversarial network. 2017 IEEE Conference on Computer Vision and Pattern Recognition (CVPR), 105-114.

3. Collings, S., Thompson, O., Hirst, E., Goossens, L., George, A. et al. (2016). Noninvasive detection of anaemia using digital photographs of the conjunctiva. PLoS ONE, doi:10.1371/journal.pone.0153286, April 12, 2016.

4. Song, H.A. and Lee, S.-Y. (2013). Hierarchical representation using NMF. Proceedings of the International Conference on Neural Information Processing, pp. 466-473.

5. Hinton, G.E. (2007). Learning multiple layers of representation. Trends in Cognitive Sciences, 11(10), 428-434.

6. Goodfellow, I.J., Pouget-Abadie, J., Mirza, M., Xu, B., Warde-Farley, D. et al. (2014). Generative adversarial nets. Proceedings of the Advances in Neural Information Processing Systems (NIPS), pp. 2672-2680.

7. Nasrollahi, K. and Moeslund, T.B. (2014). Super-resolution: A comprehensive survey. Machine Vision and Applications, 25(6), 1423-1468.

8. Datsenko, D. and Elad, M. (2007). Example-based single document image super-resolution: A global map approach with outlier rejection. Journal of Multidimensional Systems and Signal Processing, 18(2-3), 103-121.

9. Zeyde, R., Elad, M. and Protter, M. (2010). On single image scale-up using sparse representations. pp. 711-730. Springer.

10. Forsyth, D.A. and Ponce, J. (2003). Computer Vision: A Modern Approach. Upper Saddle River: Pearson Education.

11. Bishop, C.M. (2006). Pattern Recognition and Machine Learning. Springer.

12. Anemia detection in low resource settings: A manual for health workers. Avalilable: http://www.path.org Accessed August 21, 2021.

13. Fan, C.C. (2013). Application of artificial classification techniques to assess the anemia conditions via palpebral conjunctiva color component. Master thesis. National Ilan University, Taiwan.

14. Chen, Y.-M., Miaou, S.-G. and Bian, H. (2016). Examining palpebral conjunctiva for anemia assessment with image processing methods. Journal of Computer Methods and Programs in Biomedicine, 125-135, Elsevier.

15. Das, M. and Khurshid, A. (2020). Image processing to quantitate hemoglobin level for diagnostic support. Helix, 10, 01.

16. Kuenster, J.T. (1997). Method for noninvasive (in-vivo) total hemoglobin, oxyhemoglobin, deoxy hemoglobin, carbooxy hemoglobin and methemoglobin concentration determination. United State Patent, US patent 5,692,503, issued, Dec. 2,1997

17. Zonios, G., Bykowski, J. and Kollias, N. (2001). Skin melanin, hemoglobin, and light scattering properties can be quantitatively assessed in vivo using diffuse reflectance spectroscopy. Journal of Investigative Dermatology. Elsevier.

18. Kalantri, A., Karambelkar, M., Joshi, R., Kalantri, S., Jajoo, U. et al. (2010). Accuracy and reliability of pallor for detecting anemia: A hospital-based diagnostic accuracy study. PLoS ONE, 5(1), January.

19. Srinivasan, K.S., Lakshmi, D., Ranganathan, H. and Gunasekaran N. (2006). Noninvasive estimation of hemoglobin in blood using color analysis. Proc 1st International Conference on Industrial and Information Systems, ICIIS 2006, 8-11 August 2006, Sri Lanka.

20. Mehta, D.S. and Srivastava, V. (2012). Quantitative phase imaging of human red blood cells using phase-shifting white light interference microscopy with colour fringe analysis. Applied Physics Letters, 101, 203701.

21. Bevilacqua, V., Dimauro, G., Marino, F., Brunetti, A., Cassano, F. et al. (2016). A novel approach to evaluate blood parameters using computer vision techniques. Proc. IEEE Symp. Medical Measurements and Applications, May.

22. Lee, S.Y., Chen, C.M.E., Lim, E.Y.P., Shen, L., Sathe, A. et al. (2021). Image analysis using machine learning for automated detection of hemoglobin H inclusions in blood smears – a method for morphologic detection of rare cells. Technical Note, Journal of Pathology Informatics, 12, 12-18.

23. Monteiro, A.C.B., Iano, Y., França, R.P., Arthur, R., Vieira Estrela, V. et al. (2019). A comparative study between methodologies based on the Hough transform and Watershed transform on the blood cell count. Iano, Y. et al. (eds). Proc. of the 4th Brazilian Technology Symposium (BTSym'18). BTSym 2018. Smart Innovation, Systems and Technologies, vol. 140. Springer, Cham.

24. Monteiro, A.C.B., França R.P., Estrela, V.V., Razmjooy, N., Iano, Y. et al. (2021). Metaheuristics applied to blood image analysis. *In:* Razmjooy, N., Ashourian, M., Foroozandeh, Z. (eds). Metaheuristics and Optimization in Computer and Electrical Engineering. Lecture Notes in Electrical Engineering, vol. 696. Springer, Cham, Zurich, Switzerland.

25. Hegde, R.B., Prasad, K., Hebbar, H. and Singh, B.M. (2019). Comparison of traditional image processing and deep learning approaches for classification of white blood cells in peripheral blood smear images. Biocybernetics and Biomedical Engineering, 39, 382-392.

26. Monteiro, A.C.B., França, R.P., Arthur, R., Estrela, V.V., Rodriguez, A.A.D. et al. (2019). Development of digital image processing methodology WT-MO: An algorithm of high accuracy in detection and counting of Erythrocytes, Leucocytes, Blasts, January, Proc. IV International Symposium on Immunobiologicals and VII Seminário Anual Científico e Tecnológico, (7), 160-160, Rio de Janeiro, RJ, Brazil.

27. Cabrera, R.J., Legaspi, C.A., Papa, E.J., Samonte, R.D., Acula, D.D. et al. (2017). HeMatic: An automated leukemia detector with separation of overlapping blood cells through Image Processing and Genetic Algorithm. 2017 International Conference on Applied System Innovation (ICASI), 985-987.

28. Sharma, A. and Buksh, B. (2019). Processing and Neural Network Toolbox within MATLAB Software. incom

29. Abedy, H., Ahmed, F., Bhuiyan, M.N., Islam, M., Ali, M. et al. (2018). Leukemia prediction from microscopic images of human blood cell using HOG feature descriptor and logistic regression. 2018 16th International Conference on ICT and Knowledge Engineering (ICT&KE), 1-6.

30. Sahlol, A., Abdeldaim, A.M. and Hassanien, A. (2019). Automatic acute lymphoblastic leukemia classification model using social spider optimization algorithm. Soft Computing, 23, 6345-6360.

31. Tarek, S., Ebied, H.M., Hassanien, A. and Tolba, M. (2021). White blood cells segmentation and classification using swarm optimization algorithms and multilayer perceptron. Int. J. Sociotechnology Knowl. Dev., 13, 16-30.

32. Viswanathan, P. (2015). Fuzzy c means detection of leukemia based on morphological contour segmentation. Procedia Computer Science, 58, 84-90.

33. Tan, T.Y., Zhang, L., Lim, C., Fielding, B., Yu, Y. et al. (2019). Evolving ensemble models for image segmentation using enhanced particle swarm optimization. IEEE Access, 7, 34004-34019.

34. Jothi, G., Inbarani, H., Azar, A., Koubaa, A., Kamal, N.A. et al. (2020). Improved dominance soft set based decision rules with pruning for leukemia image classification. Electronics, 9, 794.

35. Bhattacharjee, R. and Saini, L. (2015). Detection of Acute Lymphoblastic Leukemia using watershed transformation technique. 2015 International Conference on Signal Processing, Computing and Control (ISPCC), 383-386.

36. Shin, H.C., Orton, M.R., Collins, D.J., Oran, S.J. and Leach, M.O. (2013). Stacked autoencoders for unsupervised feature learning and multiple organ detection in a pilot study using 4D patient data. IEEE Trans Pattern Anal Mach Intell, 35(8), 1930-1943.

37. Andrew, J., Ajay, B. and Anant, M. (2017). Stain normalization using sparse autoencoders (StaNoSA): Application to digital pathology. Comput. Med. Imaging Graph, 57, 50.

38. Dolz, J., Betrouni, N., Quidet, M., Kharroubi, D., Leroy, H.A. et al. (2016). Stacking de-noising autoencoders in deep network to segment the brainstem on MRI brain cancer patients: A clinical study. Comput. Med. Imaging Graph, 52, 8.

39. Bejoy, A. and Madhu, S.N. (2015). Computer-aided diagnosis of clinically significant prostate cancer from MRI images using sparse autoencoder and random forest classifier. Biocybern. Biomed. Eng., 2018, 38(3), 733.

40. Jaroonrut, P. and Charnchai, P. (2015). Segmentation of white blood cells and comparison of cell morphology by linear and naive Bayes classifiers. Biomed. Eng. Online, 14(63). http://dx.doi.org/10.1186/s12938-015-0037-1

41. Mathur, A., Tripathi, S. and Kuse, M. (2013). Scalable system for classification of white blood cells from Leishman stained blood stain images. J. Pathol. Inform., 4(15), 6.

42. Sedat, N., Deniz, K., Tuncay, E., Murat, S., Husnu, Osman K. et al. (2014). Automatic segmentation, counting, size determination and classification of white blood cells. J. Measure, 55-58.

43. Hamid, Seyed R. and Soltanian Hamid Z. (2011). Automatic recognition of five types of white blood cells in peripheral blood. Comp. Med. Imaging Graph, 35, 333.

44. Coelho, A.M., de Assis, J.T. and Estrela, V.V. (2009). Error concealment by means of clustered blockwise PCA. Proc. IEEE 2009 Picture Coding Symposium (PCS 2009), Chicago, IL, USA. doi: 10.1109/PCS.2009.5167442

45. Carmo, F.P., Estrela, V.V. and de Assis, J.T. (2009). Estimating motion with principal component regression strategies. Proceedings of the 2009 IEEE International Workshop on Multimedia Signal Processing. Rio de Janeiro RJ, Brazil.

46. Neelam, S. and Ramakrishnan, G.A. (2003). Automation of differential blood count. Proc. IEEE Conference on Convergent Technologies for the Asia-Pacific Region, vol. 2, p. 547.

47. Qingli, L., Yiting, W., Hongying, L., Xinofu, H., Dongrong, X. et al. (2014). Leukocytes cells identification and quantitative morphometry based on molecular hyperspectral imaging technology. Comp. Med. Imaging Graph, 38, 171.

48. Omid, S., Hossein, R., Ardeshir, T., Hossein, B. and Yousefi (2014). Selection of the best features for leukocytes classification in blood smear microscopic images. Proc. SPIE – Progress in Biomedical Optics and Imaging, vol. 9041, p. 8

49. Siroic, R., Osowski, S., Markiewicz, T. and Siwek, K. (2009). Application of support vector machine and genetic algorithm for improved blood cell recognition. IEEE Trans. Instr. Measure, 58(7), 2159.

50. Morteza, A., Moradi, Saeed K., Ardeshir, T., Mostafa, O. and Ghelich (2015). Recognition of acute lymphoblastic leukemia cells in microscopic images using k-means clustering and support vector machine classifier. J. Med. Signals Sensors, 5(1), 49.

51. Jyoti, R., Annapurna, S., Bhadauria, H., Jitendra, V. and Singh, J.D. (2017). Computer assisted classification framework for prediction of acute lymphoblastic and acute myeloblastic leukemia. Biocybern. Biomed. Eng., 37(4), 637.

52. Mohapatra, S., Patra, D. and Satpathy, S. (2014). An ensemble classifier system for early diagnosis of acute lymphoblastic leukemia in blood microscopic images. Neural Comput. Appl., 24(7), 1887.

53. Sazuka, S., Koshika, K., Watanabe, Y., Ouchi, T., Serita, R. et al. (2014). Accuracy of continuous and noninvasive hemoglobin monitoring during prolonged surgery: 3AP4-3. European Journal of Anaesthesiology, 31, 39.

54. Kim, S., Choi, J.M., Kim, H.J., Choi, S. and Choi, I. (2014). Continuous noninvasive hemoglobin measurement is useful in patients undergoing double-jaw surgery. Journal of Oral and Maxillofacial Surgery: Official Journal of the American Association of Oral and Maxillofacial Surgeons, 72(9), 1813-1819.

55. Meftah, B., Lézoray, O., Chaturvedi, S., Khurshid, A.A. and Benyettou A. (2013). Image processing with spiking neuron networks. *In:* Yang, X.S. (eds). Artificial Intelligence, Evolutionary Computing and Metaheuristics. Studies in Computational Intelligence, vol. 427. Springer, Berlin, Heidelberg.

56. Hemanth, J. and Estrela, V.V. (2017). Deep Learning for Image Processing Applications. Advances in Parallel Computing, vol. 31, IOS Press, Amsterdam, Netherlands. ISSN: 978-1-61499-822-8.

57. Razmjooy, N., Estrela, V.V. and Loschi, H. (2019). A study on metaheuristic-based neural networks for image segmentation purposes. *In:* Memon, Q.A., Khoja, S.A. (eds). Data Science Theory, Analysis, and Applications. CRC Press, UK, London.

58. Deshpande, A., Patavardhan, P. and Rao, D.H. (2015). Super resolution based low cost vision system. Proc. 2015 IEEE International Conference on Computational Intelligence and Computing Research (ICCIC), 1-6.

59. Deshpande, A. and Patavardhan, P. (2016). Gaussian Process Regression based iris polar image super resolution. Proc. 2nd International Conference on Applied and Theoretical Computing and Communication Technology (iCATccT), pp. 692-696.

60. Deshpande, A. and Patavardhan, P. (2017). Super resolution and recognition of long range captured multi-frame iris images. IET Biom., 6, 360-368.

61. Deshpande, A. and Patavardhan, P. (2017). Multi-frame super-resolution for long range captured iris polar image. IET Biom., 6, 108-116.

62. Deshpande, A., Patavardhan, P. and Rao, D.H. (2015). Iterated back projection based super-resolution for iris feature extraction. Procedia Computer Science, 48, 269-275.

63. Estrela, V.V., Rivera, L.A., Beggio, P.C. and Lopes, R.T. (2003). Regularized pel-recursive motion estimation using generalized cross-validation and spatial adaptation. Proc. 16th Brazilian Symposium on Computer Graphics and Image Processing (SIBGRAPI 2003), pp. 331-338.

64. Han, D., Bashar, S.K., Zieneddin, F., Ding, E.Y., Whitcomb, C. et al. (2020). Digital image processing features of smartwatch photoplethysmography for cardiac arrhythmia detection. Proc. 42nd Annual International Conference of the IEEE Engineering in Medicine & Biology Society (EMBC), pp. 4071-4074.

65. Gokkan, O. and Tozburun, S. (2020). Automatic classification of melanocytic skin tumors based on hyperparameters optimized by cross-validation using support vector machines. BiOS.

66. Jeon, K., Kwon, J., Kim, K., Kim, M., Lee, S. et al. (2020). Deep-learning-based artificial intelligence algorithm for detecting anemia using electrocardiogram. European Heart Journal, 41.

67. An, R., Man, Y., Iram, S., Kucukal, E., Hasan, M.N. et al. (2020). Computer vision and deep learning assisted microchip electrophoresis for integrated anemia and sickle cell disease screening. Blood, 136, 46-47.

68. Hekim, M., Cömert, O. and Adem, K. (2020). A hybrid model based on the convolutional neural network model and artificial bee colony or particle swarm optimization-based iterative thresholding for the detection of bruised apples. Turkish J. Electr. Eng. Comput. Sci., 28, 61-79.

69. An, R., Huang, Y., Man, Y., Valentine, R.W., Kucukal, E. et al. (2021). Emerging point-of-care technologies for anemia detection. Lab on a chip, 10, 1843-1865.

70. Ilyas, S., Simonson, A.E. and Asghar, W. (2019). Emerging point-of-care technologies for sickle cell disease diagnostics. Clinica Chimica Acta, Feb, 501, 85-91.

71. Arishi, W.A., Alhadrami, H.A. and Zourob, M.M. (2021). Techniques for the detection of sickle cell disease: A review. Micromachines, 12.

72. Nair, S.B. (2018). Potential pitfalls in using HPLC and its interpretation in diagnosing HbS. J. Rare Dis. Res. Treat., 3(3), 9-12.

73. Jain, P., Bauskar, S. and Gyanchandani, M. (2020). Neural network based non-invasive method to detect anemia from images of eye conjunctiva. International Journal of Imaging Systems and Technology, 30, 112-125.

74. Sambyal, N., Saini, P., Syal, R. and Gupta, V. (2021). Aggregated residual transformation network for multistage classification in diabetic retinopathy. International Journal of Imaging Systems and Technology, 31, 741-752.

BrATCat: Data Augmentation of MRI Scans via Image-to-Image Translation Using CycleGAN Followed by Pre-Trained Model Categorization

Preet Sanghavi[1] [0000-0001-7046-5901], **Shrey Dedhia**[1]**, Siddharth Salvi**[1]**,**
Kriti Srivastava[2] [0000-0001-9849-8908]

[1] Undergraduates, Department of Computer Engineering, Dwarkadas Jivanlal Sanghvi
College of Engineering, Mumbai, India
sanghavipreet2001@gmail.com, shreydedhia@yahoo.in, siddharthsalvi99@gmail.com
[2] Assistant Professor, Department of Computer Engineering, Dwarkadas Jivanlal Sanghvi
College of Engineering, Mumbai, India, kriti.srivastava@djsce.ac.in

1. Introduction

Artificial intelligence (AI) and machine learning (ML) have gradually advanced prominently in welfare, transportation, banking, retail, education, and e-commerce. The capability of emulating human decision-making, problem-solving skills, precise object recognition, and workability at any given time has made AI and ML key components for the prosperity and sustainability of any business and profession. AI has significantly transmuted patient diagnosis, record generation, prognosis, and treatment procedures [1]. ML and deep learning (DL) medical image diagnoses [55-57] have advanced, e.g., brain tumors (BTs) [2], lung diseases [3, 4], dental conditions [5, 6, 67]. ML models apply to clinics, radiology [7], and dermatology [8]. Electronic health records (EHRs) facilitate retrieving a patient's entire history for a more efficient and scalable treatment. Booming technologies such as cloud computing and big data [9, 65] can use ML and AI to alleviate disease impacts and expedite their treatment and recovery. A tumor is an aberrant mass-created tissue following abnormal cell divisions. Ideally, abnormal cells should. Rapid cell reproduction escalate tumor growth. Tumors can be benign, premalignant, or malignant. BT denotes accelerated cell proliferation around the brain or inside the skull. Its most prominent symptoms are severe headaches, reduced sentience, lack of control on voluntary body functions, impaired vision, appetite loss, unusual drowsiness, memory issues, cognitive difficulties, altered speech, and personality transition. The World Health Organization (WHO) has classified BTs into multiple categories, including

1. Glioma – They (or "intra-axial") 30% of all BTs and the majority of the malignant ones [10]. They grow within the brain, amalgamating with brain tissues. Glioma subtypes are Astrocytoma, Glioblastoma, and Oligodendroglioma. The WHO indexed Gliomas as low (LGGs – Grade 1 and 2) and high (HGGs – Grade 3 and 4) grades.
2. Pituitary tumor – Often benign and gradual regarding growth. Autopsy and radiological encountered Pituitaries in 1 out of every 6 people [11]. 33% of Pituitaries can cause infertility, diabetes, obesity, and behavioral disorders [12].
3. Meningioma – These benign tumors represent about 13-26% of "intracranial tumors" [13], twice more likely in women [14] and occurring in arachnoid cap cells [15].

Around 700,000 people are currently diagnosed with BTs in the United States. Projections for 2021 expect more than 24,530 adults with the deadly tumor. BTs are the 10th cause of human deaths in USA. The UK's National Health Service has stated that only 15 people out of every 100 diagnosed with BTs survive more than ten years post diagnosis. In 2018, BTs were the 10th most common disease in India. These statistics call for accurate early, precise, detailed, and swift BT diagnosis systems to ensure timely treatment and significantly ameliorate patient survival chances.

Magnetic Resonance Imaging (MRI) is a radiology procedure employing magnetism to generate images of the body structure. The MRI scanning technique applies the machine's magnetic field to a particular body part and causes the hydrogen ions from water molecules to spin identically. The spin direction can vary by changing the magnetic field strength and the orientation, thus building detailed layers . Switching off the magnetic field returns the ions to their original positions, gradually releasing energy. Different tissues release different amounts of energy, thus helping visualization. The Dataset comprises 3 BT image types, Glioma, Meningioma, and Pituitary along Axial, Sagittal, and Coronal orientations. T1-weighted and T2-weighted scans are the two MRI pulse sequences or modalities used where T1-weighted scans rely upon the longitudinal relaxation of a tissue's net magnetization vector. According to [16, 62, 66], the brain scalp and tissues are brighter than the cerebrospinal fluid (CSF), skull, and the background. Concisely, T1-weighted scans demonstrate tissues with high-fat content to appear bright where sections filled with water appear dark, demonstrating the brain's anatomy. The Dataset used consisted of T1-weighted scans. Modality switching between different BTs helps data augmentation via CycleGAN, e.g. as the base modality, Meningioma allows generating augmented Glioma and Pituitary images.

2. Literature Review

The meteoric rise in medical imaging like MRIs, computed tomography (CTs), and X-rays has ameliorated the efficacy of computer vision models and scalability for image segmentation/classification and domain adaptation. MRIs employ radio waves and magnets to view internal body structures comprehensively. BT segmentation and classification have appreciably improved over the last few years using these images thanks to past image segmentation progress [17-20, 68]. An eclectic BT image range helped classify them appropriately in the mentioned works. This approach was extremely time-consuming and expensive due to the need for domain experts to perform feature extraction manually. [21] classified BT images by DL neural networks (DLNNs), with some autoencoders and a single softmax layer used for classification. The segmentation and feature extraction occurred before feeding the images into the DLNN layers. Pathak et al. [22] employed convolutional neural networks (CNNs) to detect BTs in MRI images. The architecture has two convolution layers, two max-pooling layers, a flattening layer, an ultimate dense layer, 240 training images, and a 98% training accuracy, but their model failed BT classification. Pereira et al. [23] explored CNNs with diminutive 3×3 kernels to prevent overfitting and building a deeper architecture with training/testing utilizing the BraTS dataset and the Dice similarity coefficient as metrics. The elementary approach from Abiwinanda et al. [24] classified BTs as Glioma, Pituitary, and Meningioma. The architecture comprises three layers: convolution, maxpooling, and flattening. The training occurred on the Figshare dataset. The training and validation accuracies achieved were 98.51% and 84.19% without image augmentation, which would aid in training and allayed the impact of limited datasets. The U-Net architecture for "Multimodal BT Image Segmentation" and segmenting Gliomas on the BraTS dataset appeared in [25, 26]. [27] achieved 96.1% training Accuracy for BT segmentation utilizing U-Net and VGG-16 architectures. However, the U-Nets have limited scope in efficiently learning image representation features due to a small memory capacity [28]. Domain adaptation was used in many approaches. Transfer learning (TL) provided numerous benefits, including saving training time, computational resources, and achieving decent classification accuracy despite low data availability. Grampurohit et al. [29] did BT segmentation into either tumorous or non-tumorous sections with CNNs and VGG-16. The VGG16 pre-trained model performed better, with 97.16% training accuracy but used much computational time and resources. VGG-16 demands substantial computational time and resources. Ref. [30] utilized both AlexNet and GoogLeNet for Glioma grading. GoogLeNet outperformed AlexNet with a validation accuracy of 86.7%. Lu et al. [31] used AlexNet, VGG-16, and VGG-19 pre-trained models for BT classification. VGG19 gave the best results with an accuracy of 94.82%. Kaur and Gandhi [32] tested and applied many pre-trained models, namely – Alexnet, VGG-16, VGG19, GoogLeNet, Inceptionv3, InceptionResNetV2, Resnet50, Resnet101. Multiple testing datasets, i.e., Figshare, Harvard, and clinical repository, achieved 95.92%, 100%, and 94% accuracy, respectively. Deepak and Ameer [33] employed TL with the GooLeNet pre-trained model. K-nearest neighbor (KNNs), and (SVMs) classifiers. Meningioma misclassification and persistent overfitting due to insufficient dataset sizes were major drawbacks. [34] considered the InceptionV3 model for glioma, meningioma, and pituitary classification on the Figshare dataset. Razzak et al. [35] employed the AlexNet, VGG16, and GoogLeNet applied to the Figshare dataset with image augmentation through flipping and rotation, but fine-tuned VGG-16 gave the best accuracy of 98.69%. Arbane et al. [36] tried out MobileNetV2, Xception, and

ResNet models. MobileNetV2 outperformed the other two with 98.24% Accuracy and a 98.42% F1-score. Dataset augmentation occurs before feeding the pretrained model. Rotations, height-width alterations, and brightness changes occured. Once again, the classification only indicated whether a tumor was detected or not. Most of the mentioned approaches enlarged images geometrically via rotation, flipping, cropping, translation, and color space transformation [37].

Generative adversarial networks (GANs) with data augmentation [38] can discern minute details and spawn similar-looking data. GANs learn data representations and their intricate details and recognize distributions, aiding ML and DL problems. GANs for data augmentation of liver lesions from CT images appear in [39]. [40] synthesized retinal color images using GANs. Deep Convolutional GANs (DCGANs) synthesized chest X-ray images in [41]. Gupta et al. [42] augmented data for bone lesion X-ray images. Han et al. [43] synthesized T1-weighted brain MRI images using Progressive Growing of GANs (PGGANs).

Han et al. [44] performed data augmentation on the BraTS dataset using DCGAN and Wasserstein GAN (WGAN). The latter demonstrated a better performance in terms of the value function. Qi et al. [45] proposed a Semi-Supervised Attention-Guided GAN (SAG-GAN) to augment BT MRI images. The classification categories were only tumorous and non-tumorous. Ge et al. [46] attempted to enhance Gliomas classification by pairwise GANs.

3. Data Augmentation using CycleGAN

Using image-to-image translations, new image generation creates a fake version of a given image [47], e.g., converting a winter landscape to summer or autumn. However, this approach may need a significantly large dataset part. Moreover, this dataset's images should be paired with each other. This task can be cumbersome and sometimes impossible where required pairings may not be available anymore (unpaired image-to-image generation). GANs can overcome such problems by learning data augmentation tasks in two modules: generator and discriminator systems. The generator synthesizes images from a particular domain as input by selecting a point from space. The discriminator detects whether the image is a part of a dataset or newly generated. Architecture training deceives the discriminator using the generator, and the discriminator is trained better for efficient detection. The CycleGAN is an add-on to GANs to parallel train generator and discriminator models to create a fake image version without learning from any paired dataset. This makes it an unsupervised learner considering only the original and the phony domain images that may or may not be connected. In GAN, one of the two generators takes input from one field to synthesize images for the subsequent domain.

In contrast, the second synthesizer takes information from another field to generate images for the first field. These images feed their corresponding discriminator systems to determine the relevance of these images and simultaneously update the learnings of the model. However, this methodology may not be enough to generate translated input field images. The CycleGAN utilizes cycle consistency, which works because the newly synthesized image created in the initial generator feeds the next synthesizer. The synthesized image should be similar to the real image to make a cycle by creating a pairing system for both generators. The same is true for input images for the first generator that is synthesized in the second one. This crucial method provides seemingly good output images on various situations, most significantly augmenting photographs of apples to oranges and vice versa.

3.1. Working of CycleGAN

1. Generator – Used to generate synthesized images from the required distribution. The generator encompasses three more parts.
   (a) Encoder: The input can go through the encoder, where features come from the image. The image may be scaled down. Convolutions involved in this phase help lower the original image by a fourth. E.g., a 3-channel (256, 256, 3) image downgrades to (256/4, 256/4, 256), or (64, 64, 256) increasing the number of channels.
   (b) Transformer: The encoder output goes to the transformer. The residual blocks are scaled based on the size of the image received from the encoder phase. Then, the final output from the transformer enters the decoder.
   (c) Decoder: This block augments dimensions of visualization compared to the actual image.
2. Discriminator – Used to separate the real images from the actual and fake pictures from the images generated by the generator.

3.2. Cycle Consistency Loss, Cost, and Aim Functions

Normal adversarial network mapping generally involves having an arbitrary set of images to randomly map input images in the output folder, thereby making the final segregation comparatively similar to that of the target distribution. Thus a cycle-consistent network can guarantee the input **x** to output **y**. BrATCat's aim and cost functions appear below.

Cost:

$$L(G, F, D_x, D_y) = L_{advers}(G, D_y, X, Y) + L_{advers}(F, D_x, Y, X) + \lambda L_{cyc}(G, F, X, Y) \quad (1)$$

Aim:

$$\arg\min_{G, F, D_x, D_y} \max L(G, F, D_x, D_y) \quad (2)$$

3.3. Applications of CycleGAN

1. Transformation of styles: The original training is the first proposed model. The authors had trained the model on landscape images from WIKIART. CycleGAN manages to transfer single art pieces and learn to simulate a whole different art compilation. It can create artwork resembling Monet's, Picasso's and Van Gogh's among others.
2. Object Transformation: Objects can also be transferred from one class to another, for example, tigers to leopards and leopards to tigers.
3. Season Transfer: Season images can also be transferred from one season to another, viz from autumn to summer or from summer to autumn.

4. Photo Generation from Painting: CycleGAN can convert images from drawings and drawings from images.
5. Photo Enhancement: Images from smartphone cameras can be converted to DSLR and enhanced to handle low field depth.

3.4. Drawbacks and Limitations

CycleGAN fails to do well whenever one wishes to enforce changes or transformations that are geometric. On the other hand, color or text changes are made very well as per our studies because the architecture learns under an environment to make visual changes in the photograph.

4. Classification using Transfer Learning

ML processes utilize a pre-trained model for training other models or solving tasks in another domain. TL is highly beneficial in the case of data scarcity. The technique generalizes multiple tasks. The pre-trained model utilizes acquired information gained by training on a colossal amount of data (original task) to work on other domain (target) tasks. Pan and Yang [48] mathematically stated TL definitions and constituents:

Domain – "A domain D consists of a feature space X and a marginal probability distribution $P(X)$ over the feature space, where $X = \{x_1, ..., x_n\} \in X$."

Task – "Given a domain, $D = X, P(X)$, a task T consists of a label space Y and a conditional probability distribution $P(Y|X)$ that is typically learned from the training data consisting of pairs $x_i \in X$ and $y_i \in Y$."

Transfer learning – "Given a source domain D_S and learning task T_S, a target domain D_T and learning task T_T, TL aims to help improve the learning of the target predictive function $f_T(.)$ in D_T using the knowledge in D_S and T_S where $D_S 6 = D_T$, or $T_S 6 = T_T$."

TL significantly reduces the time required to train the models for a particular task where a pre-trained model of a similar domain is available. Enormous amounts of hours and heavy computational resources are extricated from the routine of building and training a model from scratch. Domain adaptation is also preferred when one does not have enough data for a relatively new domain. Traditionally, industry professionals and domain experts labeled specialized data, which was heavily expensive and would take a long time. The mentioned approach of domain adaptation also has the potential of saving a massive amount of money. By considering the generalization concept and implementing it through domain adaptation, one can employ a time-efficient, cost-efficient approach of dexterously training and fine-tuning a model for specific tasks.

Various TL settings exist, viz inductive, transductive, and unsupervised [48, 63, 64]. The source (original) and target tasks differ in inductive TL, keeping the domain constant, whereas domains vary in transductive TL. In contrast, both the corresponding tasks hold some similarities. Unsupervised TL is analogous to inductive TL, but the data is unlabeled in both domains.

There are multiple types of transfers relying on instances, features representations, parameters, and relational knowledge. As the name suggests, in an instance-based procedure, parts of data used in the source domain can be directly utilized and applied for the training in the target task along with the new data provided. Feature-based transfer extracts features (representations) appropriate to source and target domains, thereby lowering error rates and curtailing domain divergence. The parameter-based approach presumes the distribution and sharing of some parameters and hyperparameters between the source and target domains. The relation knowledge-based approach does not assume that data for both domains originates from independent and identically distributed sources.

Concerning image classification, [49, 65] lists down a few steps to conduct TL. After choosing the desired pre-trained model suitable to the target task, all the layers except a few terminating ones are frozen. This helps keep the majority of the pre-trained parameter values constant and fixed during the new training process. A set of fresh layers added to the existing model can handle the new training data and adjust according to its parameter types and quantities. The relevant amount and type of channels are appropriately allocated. The current modified model now undergoes training on the target data. The model Accuracy can be additionally enhanced by fine-tuning.

Few of the sought-after and extensively used pre-trained models are:

1. VGG19 – The Visual Geometry Group -19 architecture [50], designed at the University of Oxford, has a depth of 19 layers, which constitutes 16 convolution layers, five max pool layers, three fully connected layers, and one softmax layer. The Rectified Linear Unit (ReLU) activation function was used due to its non-linearity. Depth wise 3×3 convolutional filters decreased parameter tally. The pooling (aggregation of features and statistics [51]) in the max pool layers happens on a 2×2 pixel window. The first couple of fully connected layers had 4096 channels, while the last one comprised 1000 channels.

2. MobileNetV2 – Sandler et al. [52] (Google) proposed the MobileNetV2 CNN architecture. The prime motive of the model was to ameliorate its performance on devices of relatively low computational capability such as mobile phones and reducing the mathematical calculations. MobileNetV2 constitutes approximately 53 convolutional layers, 19 "residual bottleneck" layers, and one average pooling layer. The 32 filters in each convolutional layer are either pointwise (1×1) or depth wise convolutions (3×3). The model was divided into a couple of blocks: the bottleneck residual and the inverted residual block. MobileNet was pre-trained on the popular ImageNet Dataset [53].

3. DenseNet201 – Huang et al. [54] introduced the "Dense Convolutional Network" (DenseNet) model. The model attenuated the complications due to the vanishing gradient and reduced the number of parameters. A vanishing gradient is a scenario when the gradient becomes extremely small, almost zero, due to backpropagation in a very dense neural network. DenseNet employs a "feed-forward fashion" in which every layer is connected to all the subsequent forward layers. Thus, the entire architecture has a total of $\dfrac{n(n+1)}{2}$ connections where n

is the number of layers in the network. DenseNet201 is a CNN with a depth of 201 layers.

5. BrATCat Implementation and Architecture

5.1. Pipeline Proposition and Overview

Figure 1 portrays the BrATCat pipeline structure. The entire architecture aims to counter the lack of data availability by producing more data (images) without compromising the quality of generated imageries. Model training to classify data follows data increase. The entire pipeline functions as follows:

1. Input data (images) – The imageries selected for our training and testing data come from the BT image dataset of Figshare. The dataset has approximately 3064 T-1 BT images of the three types. More than 200 patients contributed to this dataset, compiling up to 3000 slices in the resulting data warehouse. These include 1400 Glioma slices, approximately 900 Pituitary slices, and 700 Meningioma slices. These images contain more or less 760 slices and are distributed into different folders to avoid computational complexity.
2. Image preprocessing – To make the images suitable for feeding the GANs, preprocessing is paramount. Firstly, converting an image from the "mat" to the "png" format occurs. Normalization is essential as it speeds up the convergence during neural network (NN) training and diminishes very high or low-frequency outliers. After normalization, the classification of dataset images into coronal, sagittal, and axial occurs.
3. Image augmentation – After preprocessing dataset images, augmentation takes place. Synthesizing artificial data addresses the lack of datasets for specialized cases and prevents the massive costs incurred by data labeling. Augmentation improved the generalization-making capabilities of the model, lessened overfitting, and solved imbalance concerns of the categories. The study makes use of the generative adversarial network (GAN) based technique, CycleGAN. A significant advantage of CycleGAN is the nonrequirement of paired data during training, which makes collecting data for training a lot easier and quicker. Image-to-image translation occurs because underlying patterns are found, with the input and output images matching each other.
4. Image classification – Several individually trained models classify unseen tumors in three categories (Glioma, Pituitary, and Meningioma). The original dataset was split into the training and testing parts, and augmented images were appended to the training dataset. A simple CNN built from scratch with state-of-

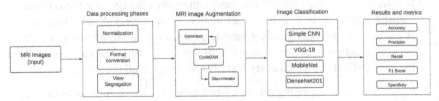

Figure 1. BrATCat pipeline

the-art pre-trained models viz. VGG19, MobileNetV2, and DenseNet201. The metrics employed for result analysis were Accuracy, Precision, Recall, F1-score, and Specificity.

A comprehensive explanation for all the mentioned steps is in the subsequent subsections.

5.2. Data Preprocessing Phases

1. Phase 1: Converting file type format to png.
   The dataset has images for three types of tumors in *.mat* format. Each one of these mat files possesses data fields with a predefined structure for every dataset image. The fields are *Label, PID, Image, tumorBorder* and *tumorMask*. The *label* field stores the tumor type. Here 1 is for meningioma, 2 is for glioma and 3 is for pituitary-based tumor images. The *PID* denotes the unique patient number that is related to the image. The image field stores the image, whereas the *tumorBorder* field stores points residing along the border of the tumor in that image as a vector. *TumorMask* has values 1 that indicate regions impacted by the tumor, whereas 0 represents unaffected regions . To convert, the *image* and the *label* fields are used, and each image change to a png format with *cmap* equal to gray. These images go to the next layer – layer 2 for further preprocessing.
2. Phase 2: Normalizing images.
   This preprocessing layer normalizes input images to create usable images from the Figshare dataset after enforcing the proposition strictly in layer 1. Normalization is critical, usually ensuring that all the data comes together with the dimensions and pixel values as the chief parameters. Some powerful image normalization techniques include pixel normalization, pixel standardization, and pixel centering. Our pipeline uses pixel normalization in which all the values are within 0 and 1. This rescaling of the input images is considered image normalization.
3. Phase 3: View wise image separation after dataset normalization ensures images are further separated into coronal, sagittal, and axial views similar to the stratum of the human body for Glioma, Meningioma, and Pituitaries. This method has been enforced primarily by naked eye image separation. The coronal MRI scans differed from the sagittal and the axial MRI scans by identifying a spinal cord part and the frontal brain lobe, characteristic of the coronal brain MRI scan. On the other hand, the sagittal MRI scan shows the outline of the nose and a part of the nasal cavity. After implementing the third layer successfully, the final preprocessed Dataset feeds the data augmentation part.

5.3. Brain MRI Image Augmentation

Consider the problem of translating images from Glioma to Meningioma images and vice-versa. These image datasets are unrelated (unpaired), meaning they are photos of variable instances at varying epochs.

1. Dataset *a*: Glioma images.
2. Dataset *b*: Meningioma images.

Four modes, i.e., two generators and two discriminators, are trained in the overall system. The initial network will create images of the Meningiomas with input as photos of the Gliomas. The next GAN will create Glioma images from Meningiomas.

1. GAN 1: Translates photos of Glioma (Dataset *a*) to Meningioma (dataset *b*).
2. GAN 2: Translates photos of Meningioma (dataset *b*) to Glioma (Dataset *a*).

Each GAN creates fake images given a particular category input. Moreover, the corresponding discriminator detects how well the newly synthesized images match the original Dataset. If they fit well, then they become valid images; while discarding others. The normal GAN loss function is the normal adversarial loss. The first-stage generator and discriminator are as follows:

1. Generator Model 1:
    (a) Input: Gliomas (Dataset *a*).
    (b) Output: Generates Meningiomas (Dataset *b*).
2. Discriminator Model 1:
    (a) Input: Meningiomas from Dataset *b* and output from Generator Model 1.
    (b) Output: Likelihood of Dataset *b* images.

The working of the generator and discriminator for the second part follows:
1. Generator Model 2:
    (a) Input: Meningiomas (Dataset *b*).
    (b) Output: Gliomas (Dataset *a*).
2. Discriminator Model 2:
    (a) Input: Gliomas from Dataset *a* and output from Generator Model 2.
    (b) Output: Likelihood of image from Dataset *a*.

The newly created images are relevant, but they do not translate the input or the source images. Then, generative networks use a new cycle consistency (forward cycle consistency) loss function to incorporate translations amongst the datasets *a* and *b*. Cycle consistency loss, as seen in equation 1 can evaluate the differences between the input and the synthesized photo using the L1 norm between pixel values. Calculating cycle consistency loss due to changes in the generator architectures for each executing iteration can be twofold. The first GAN (GAN 1) receives Glioma images and generates a Meningioma input to the second GAN (GAN 2) to create the Glioma dataset. The cycle loss evaluates the distance between the image loaded in GAN 1 and the yield of GAN 2, updating the models for better training and decreasing picture changes. Similarly, the reverse or backward cycle consistency loss calculates the loss from GAN 2 to GAN 1, evaluating the difference between the original Meningioma and the fake image.

1. Procedure for Forward Cycle Unity Loss:
    (a) Load a Glioma (Dataset *a*) from GAN 1.
    (b) Get a Meningioma from GAN 1.
    (c) Load a Meningioma from GAN 1 to GAN 2.
    (d) Get a Glioma from GAN 2.
    (e) Calculate the distance of Glioma (Dataset *a*) to the Glioma from GAN 2.

2. Steps for Reverse Cycle Unity Loss:
   (a) Load Meningioma (dataset *b*) in GAN 2.
   (b) Get Glioma from GAN 2.
   (c) Load Glioma from GAN 2 to GAN 1.
   (d) Get Meningioma from GAN 1.
   (e) Calculate the distance of Meningioma (Dataset *b*) to the Meningioma from GAN 1.

Table 1. Brain tumor comparison before and after applying data augmentation techniques

Tumor Type	Original	Augmented
Glioma		
Meningioma		
Pituitary		

5.4. MRI Classification Description

The Dataset possesses 1046 T1-weighted coronal orientation images with 493 Gliomas, 232 Meningiomas, and 321 Pituitary BTs. These images had a shape of (512, 512, 3). The augmented original Dataset using CycleGAN generated 270 images (i.e., 90 Gliomas, 90 Meningiomas, and 90 Pituitary BTs as in Table 1). Table 2 shows images in every class of the original and the augmented datasets.

Table 2. MRI image distribution in each brain tumor category.

	Original Dataset	Augmented Dataset
Glioma	493	583
Meningioma	232	322
Pituitary	321	411
Total	1046	1316

Initially, *imread* from the Python OpenCV library loaded the original and the augmented datasets. Next, the training and the validation sets stemmed from the original 224×224 resized Dataset. The validation set has 25% of the original Dataset (262 images) and the training set has 784 images. The 874 augmented images generated using CycleGAN were appended to the training set, to test augmented images. The same testing set generated from the original Dataset validated original and augmented datasets. Table 3 compares the number of training images used in the original and the augmented Dataset.

Table 3. Comparison of the number of training images in the original and augmented datasets

	Original Dataset	Augmented Dataset
Training	784	874

Implementing TL models (VGG19, MobileNetV2, and DenseNet201) helped build a CNN for the MRI scan multiclass classification. Model training used the original training data and generated results after appending augmented images to the training set. The validation set generated from the original data helped assess their performance .

CNN Implementation: A Keras sequential model implements a CNN for the multiclass BT segmentation. The Keras library *Conv2D* class helped add a convolutional layer to the sequential model with 48 filters for a 3×3 kernel to identify image patterns. It primarily moves the filter over the input image and computes the dot product between the filter and the corresponding input image parts setting the input shape parameter to (224, 224, 3) with a maxpooling layer. The strides parameter set to 2 reduces the size or downsamples the feature map by summarizing particular region features in the feature map. Next, an additional convolutional layer with 48 filters of a 3×3 kernel and the input shape (224, 224, 3) was inserted. Subsequently, a similar 2×2 maxpooling layer was added with two strides. The output shape of the Max Pooling layer was (None, 54, 54, 48). A *Flatten* layer followed this Max-Pooling layer converts the output of the pooling layer to 1D input to the fully connected deep NN (DNN) layers. It reshapes the input to the flattened layer to the number of elements contained in the tensor, which was (54×54×48), that is 139,968. Subsequently, four dense layers were added to the sequential model having 512, 256, 128, and 64 nodes in the hidden layer to robustify the DLNN. The final fully 3-node connected NN (one per class) segments BTs. The last layer activation function was softmax because of multiple classes. Subsequently, the layers added to the sequential model compilation used the *compile* function, optimizer parameter set to' adam,' with loss parameter *sparse categorical cross-entropy*, and initially utilized the original training set. The steps mentioned earlier were for the model's training on the augmented training set, and validating the trained model via Accuracy, Precision, Recall, F1-score, Specificity, and Sensitivity.

VGG19 Implementation: The VGG19 TL model needs to first create a VGG19 object. The input object shape parameter was set to (224, 224, 3), the image shapes for the implementation. The *include top* parameter was set to 'False,' which essentially made the VGG19 model a feature extractor. The model's convolutional layers helped identify the unique features or patterns in the images. The *weights* parameter was set to *imagenet* to load the model with the weights trained on the ImageNet Dataset. The next stage freezes the pre-trained VGG19 model layers to prevent the reinitialization of their weights with the added output comprehending learned VGG19 model features. This implementation sets the value of the *trainable* property of the layers of the VGG19 model to *False*. Subsequently, the *Sequential* model of the Keras library adds layers to the VGG19 model one by one. Dense, fully-connected layers improve the VGG19 model convolutional layers. The 3-node dense layer initially added had a hidden layer with output shape (None, 7, 7, 512). The *Flatten* layer to the Sequential NN layer model helps convert the entire feature map matrix to a single long feature vector. A multidimensional feature vector could not feed a fully connected NN layer. It reshaped the flatten layer input to the number of tensor elements, which was 147. Therefore, the output shape of the flatten layer becomes (None, 147). Subsequently, the sequential model receives a final fully-connected NN layer. The number of nodes is equal to the number of image segmentation classes, 3 in this case. The *softmax* activation function for the NN layer suits multiple classes, and the softmax function returns the confidence score per class with the highest confidence score. After applying the exponential function to the input vector, the values procured are normalized, ensuring that the values obtained are between 0 and 1. The NN layers added to the convolutional layers of the VGG19 model were compiled using the *compile()* method. The optimizer parameter was set to *adam*, which optimized the gradient descent. The *loss* parameter was set to *sparse categorical cross-entropy* for the loss computation. The metric parameter was set to Accuracy to evaluate the Accuracy during each epoch. Subsequently, the model was trained on the original Dataset, with the number of epochs being set to 15, primarily the number of passes through the complete Dataset. The model's training on the original Dataset was followed by validating the validation set and the computation of the confusion matrix. The confusion matrix computes the Accuracy, Recall, Precision, and the original dataset F1-score. Similar steps were followed for the training of the VGG19 model on the augmented training data, with the same number of epochs, followed by testing on the validation set procured from the original Dataset. The training loss and Accuracy comparison for the 15 epochs was plotted and compared.

MobileNetV2 Implementation: The MobileNetV2 model initially created an object of the MobileNetV2 model, with the top parameter set to *False* to have a feature extractor. Other parameters follow: (224, 224, 3) for *input shape* and *imagenet* for weights. This was followed by freezing the MobileNetV2 model layers to make them untrainable and prevent reinitialization of weights. Subsequently, densely connected NN layers were added to the convolutional layers by using the Sequential class of the Keras library. Initially, the framework received a 3-hidden node dense layer. The layer output shape utilized (None, 7,7,3). The output of this layer went to the flatten layer to produce a single-dimensional vector as input to the final fully connected layer. The flatten layer output had a shape of (None, 147). This was followed by a densely connected layer having the number of hidden nodes as the number of classes that the images needed to be segmented into, 3 in this case. The activation function for this layer was set to *softmax* since there are multiple image classes. Then, layers compilation used the *compile* method, where the optimizer parameter was set to *adam*, and the loss parameter to *sparse categorical cross-entropy*. The model was subsequently trained, on initially, the original data and validated on the validation set, repeating the same steps for the augmented training data. Next, the validation set corroborated the trained model. Result assessments for the original and augmented training data sets employ metrics such as Accuracy, Precision, Recall, F1-score, Specificity, and Sensitivity.

DenseNet201 Implementation: Initially, the DenseNet201 model implementation created an object of the model. The *include top* parameter was set to *False*, making the model essentially a feature extractor. The 'input shape' parameter was set to (224, 224, 3), which was the shape of the input images. This was followed by wrapping the model for a Keras layer via the *hub.KerasLayer* function. Subsequently, the model layers were frozen or made untrainable by setting the trainable parameter *False* to prevent reinitialization of model weights. The DLNN layers fed the DenseNet201 convolutional layers using the Sequential model. Initially, the sequential model received a 3-node dense layer. The shape of the output of this layer was (None, 7, 7, 3). This was followed by the flattening of this layer's output generated by the *Flatten* layer. The Flatten layer converted the multidimensional vector output of the previous layer into a single-dimensional vector, appropriate for input to the fully connected DLNN layer, followed by the final 3-node NN layer, the number of segmentation classes. Layer activation functions added to the DenseNet201 model used *softmax* with *compile* method, optimizer parameter selected to *adam* for gradient descent, and the loss parameter set *sparse categorical cross-entropy* for multiple classes. Subsequently, the model was trained on the original training set, with 15 epochs. The trained model validation employed the validation set. The same steps were repeated for model training on the augmented training data, followed by verification with the validation set. Accuracy, Precision, Recall, F1-Score, Sensitivity, and Specificity metrics were computed and compared with those from the model trained on the original training data.

6. Results and Accuracy

The four realized models, namely, CNN Classification Model, VGG19 Model, MobileNetV2 Model, and DenseNet201 Model, were trained on the original training set and validated using the validation set. Similarly, the models described above were also trained on the augmented training set and subsequently validated on the same validation set. The metrics used to relate the original and the augmented training sets were accuracies, Precision, Recall, F1-score, and Specificity. These metrics result from a confusion matrix representing the different numbers and model predictions made from a structured tabular format. Table 4 has the confusion matrix structure with a multiclass image segmentation comprising three categories. The True Positives (TPs) are the number of predictions that the classifier predicted as true and actually true. TPs are the diagonal elements of the confusion matrix. The TP value is '*a*' for the Gliomas, '*b*' for Meningiomas, and '*c*' for Pituitaries. The True Negatives (TNs)

Table 4. Sample confusion matrix for 3-class segmentation

	Glioma (Pred)	Meningioma (Pred)	Pituitary (Pred)
Glioma (True)	a	b	c
Meningioma (True)	d	e	f
Pituitary (True)	g	h	i

amount to the number of predictions that the classifier predicted as false and which were actually false, can be calculated as follows:

TN (Glioma) = (e + i + f + h),

TN (Meningioma) = (a + i + c + g), and TN (Pituitary) = (d + h + g + e),

which is primarily the sum of the elements not belonging to the row or the column of the corresponding class. The False Positives (FP) comprise the number of predictions that the classifier predicted as positive but was negative, as follows:

$$FP \text{ (Glioma)} = (d + g),$$

FP (Meningioma) = (b + h), FP (Pituitary) = (c + f), which is primarily the sum of the values in the column of the corresponding class, excluding the TP value. A False Negative (FN) for each class is the number of predictions that the classifier acknowledged as negative but were positive, according to

$$FN \text{ (Glioma)} = (b + c),$$

FN (Meningioma) = (d + f), FN (Pituitary) = (g + h), which is primarily the sum of the values in the corresponding row class, excluding the TP value. The metrics rely on the TP, TN, FP, FN values obtained from the confusion matrix. The Accuracy amounts to the ratio of the total number of samples correctly categorized to the total number of observations, as follows:

$$\text{Accuracy} = \frac{(TP + FP)}{(TP + FP + TN + FN)}$$

The Precision corresponds to the fraction of the total predictions classified as positive and which were positive, as follows:

$$\text{Precision} = \frac{(TP)}{(TP + FP)}$$

The Recall (aka TP rate or Sensitivity) is the fraction of the positive samples present in the Dataset correctly classified as positive, as follows:

$$\text{Recall} = \frac{(TP)}{(TP + FN)}$$

The F1-score mathematically amounts to the harmonic mean of the Precision and Recall, result from

$$F1 - Score = \frac{(2 * Recall * Precision)}{(Recall + Precision)}$$

The Specificity defines the fraction of all the negative dataset samples correctly classified as negative, which can be calculated as:

$$Specificity = \frac{(TN)}{(TN + FP)}$$

The previous metrics were calculated for each model, for both the original and the augmented training set to compare their respective performances.

VGG19 Results: The Accuracy after training for 15 epochs for the original training set was 83%. When validated on the same validation set as the original training set, the augmented training set was around 89%, with an approximate 6% Accuracy rise for the augmented data. Table 5 shows results from training the VGG19 model on the original training set. Table 6 resulted from the VGG19 model training on the augmented training set. The Precision for the three tumors increased by 0.1 (i.e., the fraction of predictions correctly classified as positive increased). The Recall increased by 0.1 for Gliomas and by 0.04 for Pituitaries, suggesting a more precise identification of Gliomas and Pituitaries in the augmented compared to the original dataset. The Specificity for all tumor types increased significantly for the augmented dataset. For instance, non-Glioma images were more accurately classified. The F1-score also increased by 0.2 for all three tumor forms from the original dataset. Figure 2 compares the training loss for the original and the augmented training sets. Figure 3 associates the training Accuracy for the original and the augmented training sets.

Table 5. VGG19 – Original dataset results

	Glioma	Meningioma	Pituitary
Precision	0.88	0.66	0.93
Recall	0.80	0.81	0.90
F1-score	0.84	0.72	0.91
Specificity	0.919	0.87	0.965

Table 6. VGG19 – Augmented dataset results

	Glioma	Meningioma	Pituitary
Precision	0.92	0.77	0.94
Recall	0.90	0.79	0.94
F1-score	0.91	0.78	0.94
Specificity	0.939	0.925	0.9715

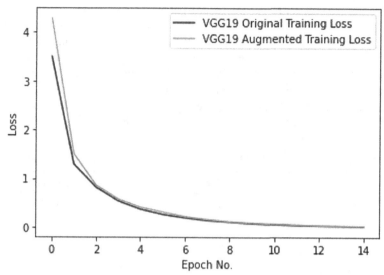

Figure 2. VGG19 training loss comparison for original and augmented datasets

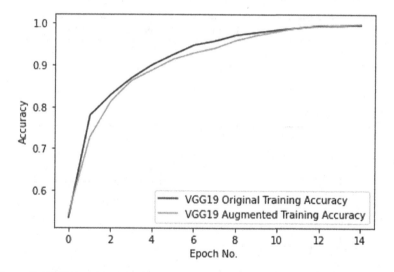

Figure 3. VGG19 training Accuracy comparison for original and augmented datasets

CNN Results: The original training set Accuracy for about 15 epochs was approximately 93.89%. After validation with the same validation set as the original dataset, the augmented training set was about 95.04%. Hence, the Accuracy increased by 1% for the augmented training set. The loss also decreased from 0.4696 to approximately 0.4185. Table 7 displays outcomes for CNN trainings on the original set. Table 8 has results for model training on the augmented training set. The Glioma Precision decreased by about 0.01. Meningioma Precision improved by about 0.06. Hence, the Meningioma classification Accuracy increased compared to the original training set. The Glioma TP rate increased by about 0.06, showing correct and accurate predictions, while that for Meningioma decreased by about 0.02. The TP rate for Pituitary tumors was almost 1.00, which signifies that nearly all images of Pituitaries were correctly classified, with none incorrectly classified as Pituitary images. The Specificity was nearly unchanged for the original and the augmented training sets, although the values were considerably high. Figure 4 relates the training loss for the original and augmented training sets after training for 15 epochs. Figure 5 compares training accuracies for the original and augmented training sets.

Table 7. CNN – Original dataset results

	Glioma	Meningioma	Pituitary
Precision	0.99	0.83	0.97
Recall	0.89	0.94	1.00
F1-score	0.94	0.88	0.98
Specificity	0.993	0.940	0.983

Table 8. CNN – Augmented dataset results

	Glioma	Meningioma	Pituitary
Precision	0.98	0.89	0.96
Recall	0.94	0.92	0.99
F1-score	0.96	0.90	0.97
Specificity	0.986	0.965	0.977

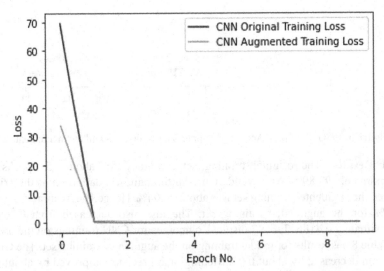

Figure 4. CNN training loss comparison for original and augmented datasets

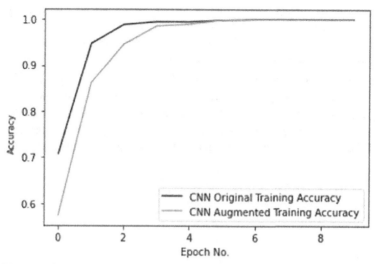

Figure 5. CNN training Accuracy comparison for original and augmented datasets

MobileNetV2 Results: After training for 15 epochs using the original training set, the model Accuracy was about 91%, and for the augmented training set was around 92%. Hence, the Accuracy for the augmented set had a 0.1% increase.

Table 9 has outcomes after training the MobileNetV2 model on the original training set. Table 10 has results attained after model training on the augmented training set. The Glioma Precision decreased by 0.01, while that for Meningiomas increased by 0.06. Hence, the Meningioma images were more precisely classified. The Glioma TP rate increased by 0.04, i.e., Gliomas were classified more precisely and correctly in the augmented training set. The Specificity, however, decreased for Gliomas, increased by 0.03 for Meningiomas, and remained almost the same for

Table 9. MobileNetV2 – Original dataset results

	Glioma	**Meningioma**	**Pituitary**
Precision	0.95	0.81	0.94
Recall	0.89	0.89	0.97
F1-score	0.92	0.85	0.95
Specificity	0.966	0.935	0.972

Table 10. MobileNetV2 – Augmented dataset results

	Glioma	**Meningioma**	**Pituitary**
Precision	0.94	0.87	0.94
Recall	0.93	0.85	0.97
F1-score	0.93	0.86	0.95
Specificity	0.952	0.96	0.972

Pituitaries. Hence, images were more accurately identified as non-Meningiomas for the augmented dataset. The F1-score almost remained the same for all three BT types. Figure 6 compares training losses. Figure 7 compares training accuracies for the original and the augmented training sets for 15 epochs.

DenseNet201 Results: The Accuracy obtained for the original training set after training for around 15 epochs was 91.98%, and that received for the augmented training set was found to be about 93.51%. Hence, there was an increase of around 1.5% for the augmented dataset. The loss also decreased for the augmented set from 0.2416 to 0.2066. Table 11 demonstrates the results obtained after training

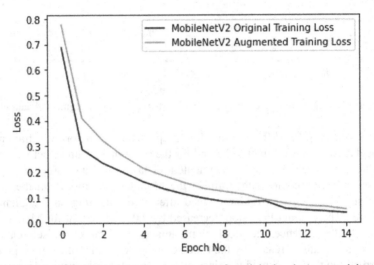

Figure 6. MobileNetV2 training loss comparison for original and augmented datasets

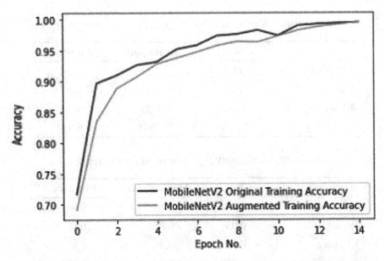

Figure 7. MobileNetV2 training Accuracy comparison for original and augmented datasets

the DenseNet201 model on the original training set. Table 12 shows results after training the model on the augmented training set. The Precision almost remained the same for the Gliomas, increased by 0.03 for the Meningiomas and by 0.03 for Pituitaries meaning more accurate BT classifications. The Recall increased by 0.03 for Gliomas and decreased to 0.05 for Meningiomas, signifying that the number of images is correctly classified as Gliomas or Meningiomas over the total number of images for Glioma or Meningioma increased. The Specificity remained the same for Gliomas and increased by about 0.01 for Meningiomas and Pituitaries. The F1-score increased for Gliomas and Meningiomas but stabilized for the Pituitary class. Figure 8 compares the training loss for the original and the augmented training set after 15 epochs. Figure 9 relates the training Accuracy for the original and the augmented training set for the DenseNet201 model.

Table 11. DenseNet201 – Original dataset results

	Glioma	**Meningioma**	**Pituitary**
Precision	0.94	0.84	0.96
Recall	0.91	0.82	1.00
F1-score	0.92	0.83	0.98
Specificity	0.953	0.950	0.9777

Table 12. DenseNet201 – Augmented dataset results

	Glioma	**Meningioma**	**Pituitary**
Precision	0.94	0.87	0.98
Recall	0.95	0.85	0.98
F1-score	0.94	0.86	0.98
Specificity	0.953	0.960	0.989

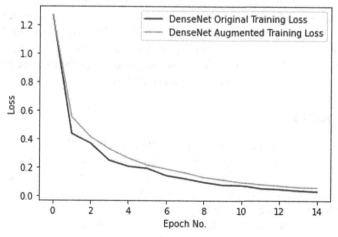

Figure 8. DenseNet201 training loss comparison for original and augmented datasets

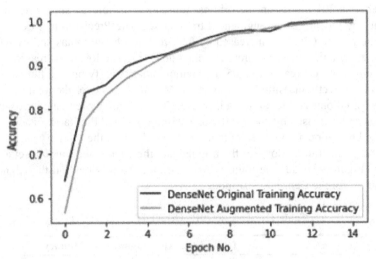

Figure 9. DenseNet201 training Accuracy comparison for original and augmented datasets

7. Future Scope

This chapter has displayed the data augmentation potential using image-to-image translation through GANs in data classification. For training purposes, the image data proliferation produced fruitful outcomes in Accuracy and various other metrics during testing. The prototype presented can be further enhanced by incorporating more training authentic data for augmentation. Different classifiers can further explore the impact of training data increase in image synthesis, e.g., decision trees, gradient boosting, KNN, and random forests. Another vital factor that could impact the performance of the current architecture is collecting and using the image datasets region-wise. Environmental factors, radiation exposure, family history, and lifestyle affect the onset or prevention of tumors. A highly reliable diagnostic system results from carefully analyzing these factors. The scope of employing more extensive preprocessing and further enhancing augmented images for training persists. With the help of experts, the images can be further isolated based on the patient's age since there exists a possibility of dimensional irregularities during GAN training. Although being done manually right now, view-wise separation can be automated by setting up a classifier of its own, thus saving time and human effort.

8. Conclusion

BrATCat augment, classify and separate MRI data efficiently. A timely and correct BT diagnosis can significantly reduce mortality. The BrATCat architecture initially preprocessed the Figshare images. The next stage employed data augmentation to synthesize images of close correspondence to the authentic ones artificially. CycleGAN, a technique utilizing GANs, performed an image-to-image translation. A simple CNN with pre-trained models like VGG19, MobileNetV2, and DenseNet201, trained part of authentic images besides the augmented (synthesized) images. The remaining authentic images assisted testing. The results demonstrated a substantial performance improvement using synthesized images for the training and original ones instead of those only trained on few authentic images. This work accessed performance with Accuracy, Precision, Recall, F1-score, and Specificity. Future research entails realistic data, implementation, more classifier observations, analyzing topographical features, demographic statistics, lifestyle and medical history among other characteristics . Thus, this research showed pragmatic and efficacious results for a possibly similar architecture to assist real-world healthcare systems.

References

1. Collins, A. and Yao, Y. (2018). Machine learning approaches: Data integration for disease prediction and prognosis. *In:* Applied Computational Genomics. Springer, 137-141.
2. Havaei, M., Davy, A., Warde-Farley, D., Biard, A., Courville, A. et al. (2017). Brain tumor segmentation with deep neural networks. Medical Image Analysis, 35, 18-31.
3. Tariq, Z., Shah, S.K. and Lee, Y. (2019). Lung disease classification using deep convolutional neural network. Proc. 2019 IEEE International Conf. Bioinformatics and Biomedicine (BIBM). 732-735.
4. Bharati, S., Podder, P. and Mondal, M.R.H. (2020). Hybrid deep learning for detecting lung diseases from x-ray images. Inf. Medicine Unlocked 20, 100391.
5. Cantu, A.G., Gehrung, S., Krois, J., Chaurasia, A., Rossi, J.G. et al. (2020). Detecting caries lesions of different radiographic extension on bitewings using deep learning. J. Dentistry 100, 103425.
6. Chang, H.J., Lee, S.J., Yong, T.H., Shin, N.Y., Jang, B.G. et al. (2020). Deep learning hybrid method to automatically diagnose periodontal bone loss and stage periodontitis. Scientific Reports 10(1), 1-8.
7. Montagnon, E., Cerny, M., Cadrin-Chênevert, A., Hamilton, V., Derennes, T. et al. (2020). Deep learning workflow in radiology: A primer. Insights into Imaging, 11(1), 22.
8. Young, A.T., Xiong, M., Pfau, J., Keiser, M.J., Wei, M.L. et al. (2020). Artificial intelligence in dermatology: A primer. J. Investigative Dermatology, 140(8), 1504-1512.
9. Latif, S., Asim, M., Usman, M., Qadir, J. and Rana, R. (2018). Automating motion correction in multishot MRI using generative adversarial networks. Proc. 32nd Conf. on Neural Inf. Proc. Systems (NIPS 2018), Montreal, Canada.
10. Goodenberger, M.L. and Jenkins, R.B. (2012). Genetics of adult glioma. Cancer Genetics, Elsevier, 205(12), 613-621.
11. Gittleman, H., Ostrom, Q.T., Farah, P.D., Ondracek, A., Chen, Y. et al. (2014). Descriptive epidemiology of pituitary tumors in the United States, 2004-2009: Clinical article. J. Neurosurgery, 121(3), 527-535.
12. Asa, S.L. and Ezzat, S. (2002). The pathogenesis of pituitary tumours. Nature Reviews Cancer, 2(11), 836-849.
13. Marosi, C., Hassler, M., Roessler, K., Reni, M., Sant, M. et al. (2008). Meningioma. Critical Reviews in Oncology/Hematology, 67(2), 153-171.
14. Wiemels, J., Wrensch, M. and Claus, E.B. (2010). Epidemiology and etiology of meningioma. J. Neurooncology, 99(3), 307-314.

15. Fathi, A.R. and Roelcke, U. (2013). Meningioma. Current Neurology and Neuroscience Reports, 13(4), 337.

16. Somasundaram, K. and Kalaiselvi, T. (2010). Brain extraction method for T1-weighted magnetic resonance scans. Proc. 2010 International Conf. Signal Processing and Communications (SPCOM), 1-5.

17. Kleesiek, J., Biller, A., Urban, G., Kothe, U., Bendszus, M. et al. (2014). Ilastik for multi-modal brain tumor segmentation. Proc. MICCAI BraTS (brain tumor segmentation challenge), 12-17.

18. Meier, R., Bauer, S., Slotboom, J., Wiest, R. and Reyes, M. (2014). Appearance and context sensitive features for brain tumor segmentation. Proc. of MICCAI BRATS Challenge, 020-026.

19. Soltaninejad, M., Ye, X., Yang, G., Allinson, N. and Lambrou, T. (2014). Brain tumour grading in different MRI protocols using SVM on statistical features. Proc. 18th Medical Image Understanding and Analysis, 259-264.

20. Goetz, M., Weber, C., Bloecher, J., Stieltjes, B., Meinzer, H.P. et al. (2014). Extremely randomized trees based brain tumor segmentation. Proc. of BRATS challenge-MICCAI, 006-011.

21. Gawande, S.S. and Mendre, V. (2017). Brain tumor diagnosis using deep neural network (DNN). International J. of Advanced Research in Electrical, Electronics and Instrumentation Engineering, 5(5).

22. Pathak, K., Pavthawala, M., Patel, N., Malek, D., Shah, V. et al. (2019). Classification of brain tumor using convolutional neural network. Proc. 3rd International Conf. on Electronics, Communication and Aerospace Technology (ICECA), 128-132.

23. Pereira, S., Pinto, A., Alves, V. and Silva, C.A. (2016). Brain tumor segmentation using convolutional neural networks in MRI Images. IEEE Trans. on Medical Imaging (TMI), 35(5), 1240-1251.

24. Abiwinanda, N., Hanif, M., Hesaputra, S.T., Handayani, A., Mengko, T.R. et al. (2019). Brain tumor classification using convolutional neural network. Proc. 2018 World Cong. Medical Physics and Biomedical Engineering. Springer Singapore. 183-189.

25. Dong, H., Yang, G., Liu, F., Mo, Y. and Guo, Y. (2017). Automatic brain tumor detection and segmentation using U-net based fully convolutional networks. *In:* Valdes Hernandez, M., Gonzalez-Castro, V. (eds). Medical Image Understanding and Analysis, Springer Cham, 506-517.

26. Beers, A., Chang, K., Brown, J., Sartor, E., Mammen, C. et al. (2017). Sequential 3D U-nets for biologically-informed brain tumor segmentation. arXiv preprint arXiv:1709.02967

27. Pravitasari, A.A., Iriawan, N., Almuhayar, M., Azmi, T., Fithriasari, K. et al. (2020). Unet-VGG16 with transfer learning for MRI-based brain tumor segmentation. Telkomnika, 18(3), 1310-1318.

28. Liu, G., Si, J., Hu, Y. and Li, S. (2018). Photographic image synthesis with improved U-net. Proc. Tenth Int'l Conf. on Advanced Computational Intelligence (ICACI). 402-407.

29. Grampurohit, S., Shalavadi, V., Dhotargavi, V.R., Kudari, M. and Jolad, S. (2020). Brain tumor detection using deep learning models. Proc. 2020 IEEE India Council International Subsections Conference (INDISCON). 129-134.

30. Yang, Y., Yan, L.F., Zhang, X., Han, Y., Nan, H.Y. et al. (2018). Glioma grading on conventional MR images: A deep learning study with transfer learning. Frontiers in Neuroscience, 12, 804.

31. Swati, Z.N.K., Zhao, Q., Kabir, M., Ali, F., Ali, Z. et al. (2019). Brain tumor classification for MR images using transfer learning and fine-tuning. Computerized Medical Imaging and Graphics, 75, 34-46.

32. Kaur, T. and Gandhi, T.K. (2020). Deep convolutional neural networks with transfer learning for automated brain image classification. Machine Vision and Applications, 31(3), 1-16.

33. Deepak, S. and Ameer, P. (2019). Brain tumor classification using deep CNN features via transfer learning. Comp. in Biology and Medicine, 111, 103345.

34. Soumik, M.F.I. and Hossain, M.A. (2020). Brain tumor classification with inception network based deep learning model using transfer learning. Proc. 2020 IEEE Region 10 Symposium (TENSYMP). 1018-1021.

35. Rehman, A., Naz, S., Razzak, M.I., Akram, F. and Imran, M. (2020). A deep learning based framework for automatic brain tumors classification using transfer learning. Circuits, Systems, and Signal Processing, 39(2), 757-775.

36. Arbane, M., Benlamri, R., Brik, Y. and Djerioui, M. (2021). Transfer learning for automatic brain tumor classification using MRI images. Proc. 2nd International Work. on Human-Centric Smart Environments for Health and Well-being (IHSH). 210-214.

37. Shorten, C. and Khoshgoftaar, T.M. (2019). A survey on image data augmentation for deep learning. J. Big Data, 6(1), 1-48.

38. Goodfellow, I.J., Pouget-Abadie, J., Mirza, M., Xu, B., Warde-Farley, D. et al. (2014). Generative adversarial networks. arXiv preprint arXiv:1406.2661

39. Frid-Adar, M., Klang, E., Amitai, M., Goldberger, J. and Greenspan, H. (2018). Synthetic data augmentation using GAN for improved liver lesion classification. Proc. IEEE 15th International Symp. Biomedical Imaging (ISBI 2018). 289-293.

40. Costa, P., Galdran, A., Meyer, M.I., Niemeijer, M., Abramoff, M. et al. (2018). End-to-end adversarial retinal image synthesis. IEEE TMI, 37(3), 781-791.

41. Salehinejad, H., Colak, E., Dowdell, T., Barfett, J. and Valaee, S. (2019). Synthesizing chest X-ray pathology for training deep convolutional neural networks. IEEE TMI, 38(5), 1197-1206.

42. Gupta, A., Venkatesh, S., Chopra, S. and Ledig, C. (2019). Generative image translation for data augmentation of bone lesion pathology. *In:* Cardoso, M.J. et al. (eds). Proc. 2nd International Conf. Medical Imaging with Deep Learning. Vol. 102 of PMLR. (08-10 Jul 2019), 225-235.

43. Han, C., Rundo, L., Araki, R., Furukawa, Y., Mauri, G. et al. (2018). Infinite brain tumor images: Can GAN-based data augmentation improve tumor detection on MR images? Proc. Meeting on Image Recognition and Understanding (MIRU 2018), Sapporo, Japan.

44. Han, C., Hayashi, H., Rundo, L., Araki, R., Shimoda, W. et al. (2018). GAN-based synthetic brain MR image generation. Proc. IEEE 15th ISBI, 734-738.

45. Qi, C., Chen, J., Xu, G., Xu, Z., Lukasiewicz, T. et al. (2020). SAG-GAN: Semisupervised attention-guided GANs for data augmentation on medical images. arXiv preprint arXiv:2011.07534

46. Ge, C., Gu, I.Y.H., Jakola, A.S. and Yang, J. (2020). Enlarged training dataset by pairwise GANs for molecular-based brain tumor classification. IEEE Access 8, 22560-22570.

47. Zhu, J.Y., Park, T., Isola, P. and Efros, A.A. (2017). Unpaired image-to-image translation using cycle-consistent adversarial networks. Proc. 2017 IEEE International Conf. on Computer Vision (ICCV). 2242-2251.

48. Pan, S.J. and Yang, Q. (2010). A survey on transfer learning. IEEE Trans. on Knowledge and Data Engineering, 22(10), 1345-1359.

49. Chollet, F. (2020). Transfer learning & fine-tuning. Accessed June 6, 2021.

50. Simonyan, K. and Zisserman, A. (2014). Very deep convolutional networks for large-scale image recognition. arXiv preprint arXiv:1409.1556

51. Murray, N. and Perronnin, F. (2014). Generalized max pooling. 2014 IEEE Conf. on Computer Vision and Pattern Recognition. 2473-2480.

52. Howard, A., Zhmoginov, A., Chen, L.C., Sandler, M. and Zhu, M. (2018). Inverted residuals and linear bottlenecks: Mobile networks for classification, detection and segmentation. Proc. 2018 IEEE Conf. Computer Vision and Pattern Recognition (CVPR).

53. Deng, J., Dong, W., Socher, R., Li, L.J., Li, K. et al. (2009). Imagenet: A large-scale hierarchical image database. 2009 IEEE CVPR. 248-255.

54. Huang, G., Liu, Z., Van Der Maaten, L. and Weinberger, K.Q. (2017). Densely connected convolutional networks. Proc. 2017 IEEE CVPR. 2261-2269.

55. Hemanth, J. and Estrela, V.V. (2017). Deep Learning for Image Processing Applications. Advances in Parallel Computing, Vol. 31, IOS Press, Amsterdam, Netherlands.

56. Razmjooy, N. and Estrela V.V. (2019). Applications of Image Processing and Soft Computing Systems in Agriculture. 1-300. IGI Global, Hershey, PA, USA.

57. Deshpande, A., Patavardhan, P., Estrela, V.V. and Razmjooy, N. (2020). Deep learning as an alternative to super-resolution imaging in UAV systems. *In:* Estrela, V.V. et al. (eds). Imaging and Sensing for Unmanned Aircraft Systems, vol. 2(9), 177-212. IET, London, UK.

58. França, R.P., Monteiro, A.C.B., Estrela, V.V. and Razmjooy, N. (2021). Using Metaheuristics in Discrete-Event Simulation. *In:* Razmjooy, N. et al. (eds). Metaheuristics and Optimization in Computer and Electrical Engineering, vol. 696. Springer, Cham, Switzerland.

59. Deshpande, A., Razmjooy, N. and Estrela, V.V. (2021). Introduction to Computational Intelligence and Super-Resolution. *In:* Deshpande, A. et al. (eds). Computational Intelligence Methods for Super-Resolution in Image Processing Applications. Springer, Cham, Switzerland.

60. de Jesus, M.A., Estrela, V.V., Saotome, O. and Stutz, D. (2018). Super-resolution via particle swarm optimization variants. *In:* Hemanth, J., Balas, V. (eds). Biologically Rationalized Computing Techniques for Image Processing Applications, vol. 25, 317-337. Springer, Cham, Switzerland, Springer.

61. Laghari, A.A., Khan, A., He, H., Estrela, V.V., Razmjooy, N. et al. (2020). Quality of experience (QoE) and quality of service (QoS) in UAV systems. *In:* Estrela V.V. et al. (eds). Imaging and Sensing for Unmanned Aircraft Systems, vol. 2(10), 213-242. IET, London, UK.

62. Khan, A.A., Laghari, A.A. and Awan, S.A. (2021). Machine Learning in Computer Vision: A Review. EAI Endorsed Trans. Scalable Inf. Syst., 8, e4.

63. Khan, A.A., Shaikh, A.A., Cheikhrouhou, O., Laghari, A.A., Rashid, M. et al. (2021). IMG-forensics: Multimedia-enabled information hiding investigation using convolutional neural network. IET Image Processing, 16, 2854-2862.

64. Khan, A.A., Laghari, A.A., Awan, S. and Jumani, A.K. (2021). Fourth Industrial Revolution Application: Network Forensics Cloud Security Issues. Security Issues and Privacy Concerns in Industry 4.0 Applications, pp. 15-33.

65. Khan, A.A., Uddin, M., Shaikh, A., Laghari, A.A. and Rajput, A. (2021). MF-Ledger: Blockchain hyperledger shawtooth-enabled novel and secure multimedia chain of custody forensic investigation architecture. IEEE Access, 9, 103637-103650.

66. Khan, Abdullah A., Asif A. Laghari, De-Sheng Liu, Aftab A. Shaikh, Dan-An Ma et al. (2021). EPS-Ledger: Blockchain hyperledger sawtooth-enabled distributed power systems chain of operation and control node privacy and security. Electronics, 10(19), 2395. https://doi.org/10.3390/electronics10192395

67. Laghari, A.A., Wu, K., Laghari, R.A., Ali, M. and Khan, A.A. (2021). A review and state of art of Internet of Things (IoT). Archives of Computational Methods in Engineering, pp. 1-19.

68. Jumani, A.K., Laghari, A.A. and Khan, A.A. (2021). Blockchain and big data: Supportive aid for daily life. Security Issues and Privacy Concerns in Industry 4.0 Applications, pp. 141-178.

Conclusion

Vania V. Estrela

Department of Telecommunications, Federal Fluminense University (UFF), RJ, 24220-900, Brazil, vania.estrela.phd@ieee.org

The healthcare sector relies heavily on information, including extensive data, medical epidemiology sets, Internet surfing histories, surveys, and complicated engineering models, all of which are accessible via Cloud. This pursuit of knowledge results in increased data dimensionality, necessitating the development of more complex and efficient information techniques. Health science and biology are very complicated subjects that rely on information technology, but the underlying processes are too detailed to accurately model. Extracting information from raw data is not straightforward, and it is also costly.

The fundamental goal of artificial intelligence (AI) in healthcare (AIH) has been to construct expert systems for diagnostic and decision-making purposes in knowledge acquisition, representation, reasoning, and explanation. Numerous healthcare facilities (HFs) have linked data collection, monitoring, and storage technologies into large-scale information systems. This massive volume of data and databases generated by medical apps obstruct analysis and decision-making. As a result, improved methods for obtaining, storing, and analyzing knowledge are required, as is the effective use of multimodal data. These requirements become critical in the healthcare arena when decision-making requires expertise from several disciplines. This book presents computational approaches for intelligent health data analysis, with applications in medicine, health care, biology, pharmacology, and related fields. Intelligent Data Analysis (IDA) accelerates the analysis and use of healthcare data. IDA analyzes data and deduces the mechanisms generated using specific statistical, pattern recognition, machine learning (ML), data abstraction, and visualization capabilities. Typically, healthcare data consists of many records/variables, nuanced relationships between entities, or a mix of all of the above. Engineering, computer science, and machine learning facilitate data analysis jobs.

The IDA collects knowledge from an excessive amount of data that contains a large number of variables, data that reflects extremely complex, nonlinear, real-world issues. IDA can assist with raw data analysis, prediction jobs without knowledge of the underlying process's theoretical description, novel event categorization tasks, and modeling unknown processes. IDA's pillars are classification, prediction, and modeling. This book discusses AIH methodologies and tools for bridging the gap between data collection and data comprehension. Additionally, an emphasis is placed on problem-solving inside HFs for the purpose of managing patient information, data warehousing, intelligent alarms, and competent monitoring. In medicine, bridging this divide is critical, as medical decision-making requires an understanding of healthcare data regularities and patterns. This book discusses many IDA techniques.

Prospective readers will encounter several elements of intelligence through the lens of artificial intelligence and various smart designs, in addition to monitoring the target subjects' developing nature. This book discusses various alternatives and methods for effectively expanding existing implementations in a variety of domains, including graduate course classrooms, research facilities, healthcare services, non-destructive investigations, ambient intelligence, medical education, and healthcare facility plants. Additionally, this book enables the gathering of an intriguing collection of invited worldwide writers who advance a specific knowledge within their various study disciplines with experimental results.

The eyes frequently seek or are motivated to observe something more than a fuzzy representation of an image. The editor recognizes and accepts the critical nature of and need for improved medical systems, namely human information and machine perception. Visual information should be enhanced and, in certain situations, interpolated for human interpretation. On the other hand, the machine's perception requires an improvised image to make judgments.

Putting the concepts and expertise necessary to produce this book on paper was scary. It is awe-inspiring to discover writers with the possibility of focusing their efforts on such a particular study objective and then pouring their passion into publishing a book.

Contributors from all across the world add to the excitement and anxiety. Aligning information and all participants' opinions to complete this book effectively is an appealing endeavor. The more in-depth study we conduct, the more diversified the detailed outcomes and the more forms of data investigation we can accomplish. The editors think that the study and publication of this book will broaden minds and assist mankind while also harmonizing the interests of other professions.

Index

Printed in the United States
by Baker & Taylor Publisher Services